Collins

COBUILD
English
Grammar

13/3

Published by Collins
An imprint of HarperCollins Publishers
Westerhill Road
Bishopbriggs
Glasgow G64 2QT

Fourth Edition 2017

10 9 8 7 6 5 4 3 2 1

© HarperCollins Publishers 2017

ISBN 978-0-00-813581-2 (PB)
ISBN 978-0-00-821314-5 (EB)

Collins® and COBUILD® are registered
trademarks of HarperCollins Publishers Limited

www.collinsdictionary.com
www.collinselt.com

Typeset by Davidson Publishing Solutions,
Glasgow

Printed in China by RR Donnelley APS

Entered words that we have reason to believe
constitute trademarks have been designated
as such. However, neither the presence nor
absence of such designation should be
regarded as affecting the legal status of
any trademark.

The contents of this publication are believed
correct at the time of printing. Nevertheless
the Publisher can accept no responsibility
for errors or omissions, changes in the detail
given or for any expense or loss thereby
caused.

HarperCollins does not warrant that any
website mentioned in this title will be
provided uninterrupted, that any website will
be error free, that defects will be corrected,
or that the website or the server that makes it
available are free of viruses or bugs. For full
terms and conditions please refer to the site
terms provided on the website.

A catalogue record for this book is available
from the British Library.

If you would like to comment on any aspect
of this book, please contact us at the given
address or online.
E-mail: dictionaries@harpercollins.co.uk
facebook.com/collinselt
@CollinsELT

Acknowledgements
We would like to thank those authors and
publishers who kindly gave permission for
copyright material to be used in the Collins
Corpus. We would also like to thank Times
Newspapers Ltd for providing valuable data.

FOUNDING EDITOR-IN-CHIEF: John Sinclair
FOR THE PUBLISHER: Maree Airlie,
Robin Scrimgeour, Lisa Todd, Celia Wigley
CONTRIBUTORS: Penny Hands, Kate Mohideen,
Julie Moore, Damian Williams

MIX
Paper from
responsible sources
FSC
www.fsc.org   **FSC™ C007454**

About COBUILD

When the first COBUILD dictionary was published in 1987, it revolutionized dictionaries for learners. It was the first of a new generation of language reference materials that were based on actual evidence of how English was used, rather than lexicographer intuition.

Collins and the University of Birmingham, led by the linguist John Sinclair, developed an electronic corpus in the 1980s, called the Collins Birmingham University International Language Database (COBUILD). This corpus, which for several years was known as the Bank of English®, became the largest collection of English data in the world. COBUILD dictionary editors use the corpus to analyse the way that people really use the language.

The Collins Corpus now contains 4.5 billion words taken from websites, newspapers, magazines and books published around the world, and from spoken material from radio, TV and everyday conversations. New data is added to the corpus every month, to help COBUILD editors identify new words, grammatical structures, and meanings from the moment they are first used.

All COBUILD language reference books are based on the information our editors find in the Collins Corpus. Because the corpus is so large, our editors can look at lots of examples of how people really use the language. The data tells us how the language is used; the function of different structures; which words are used together; and how often these words and structures are used.

All of the examples in COBUILD language materials are examples of real English, taken from the corpus. The examples have been carefully chosen to demonstrate typical grammatical patterns, typical vocabulary and typical contexts.

COBUILD English Grammar is no exception: Collins editors and researchers have been able to use this wealth of information to establish a unique and full description of English grammar, and to track the development of certain grammatical structures over time.

The corpus lies at the heart of COBUILD, and you can be confident that COBUILD will show you what you need to know to be able to communicate easily and accurately in English.

If you would like to learn more about COBUILD and the Collins Corpus, go to **www.collinselt.com** and click on 'COBUILD Reference'.

Acknowledgements

The publishers would like to acknowledge the following for their invaluable contribution to the third edition:

Managing Editor
Penny Hands

Editorial Consultant
Roger Berry
Lingnan University, Hong Kong

Project Manager
Lisa Sutherland

Senior Corpus Researcher
Kate Wild

The Grammar of Academic English
University of Glasgow Language Centre
Dr Esther Daborn
Anneli Williams
Louis Harrison

Corpus Researchers
George Davidson
Kate Mohideen
Elspeth Potter
Elspeth Summers
Laura Wedgeworth

The Grammar of Business English
Simon Clarke

American English Consultant
Orin Hargraves

Founding Editor-in-Chief
John Sinclair

We would also like to thank the following people for their contributions to previous editions of the text:

Maree Airlie, Mona Baker, Henri Béjoint, Adriana Bolívar,
Jane Bradbury, David Brazil, Dominic Bree, Nicholas Brownlees, Tony Buckby,
Stephen Bullon, Annette Capel, Michela Clari, Jane Cullen, John Curtin, Richard Fay,
Gwyneth Fox, Richard Francis, Iria Garcia, Gottfried Graustein, John Hall, M.A.K. Halliday,
Patrick Hanks, Ron Hardie, Anthony Harvey, Lorna Heaslip, Michael Hoey, Roger Hunt,
Sue Inkster, Andy Kennedy, Lorna Knight, Ramesh Krishnamurthy, Tim Lane,
Marcel Lemmens, Helen Liebeck, Alison Macaulay, Elizabeth Manning, Agnes Molnar,
Rosamund Moon, Sue Ogden, Charles Owen, Georgina Pearce, Georgina Pert,
Anne Pradeilles, Christopher Pratt, Christina Rammell, Clare Ramsey, Ramiro Restrepo,
Christopher Royal-Dawson, Toñi Sanchez, Katy Shaw, Sue Smith, Mary Snell-Hornby,
Tom Stableford, John Todd, Bob Walker, Laura Wedgeworth, Herman Wekker,
Douglas Williamson, Jane Winn, Deborah Yuill

Contents

Introduction

This grammar is suitable for anyone who is interested in the English language and how it works in everyday current contexts. It has been written mainly for advanced-level students and their teachers, but any serious learner will find it a valuable reference tool.

The information in this book is taken from a long and careful study of present-day English involving the analysis of the Collins Corpus – a corpus of many millions of words of speech and writing.

A functional approach

Most people who study and use a language are interested in how they can *do things* with the language – how they can make meanings, get attention, influence people, and learn about the world. They are interested in the grammatical structure of the language as a way of getting things done.

A grammar that puts together the patterns of the language and the things you can do with them is called a *functional grammar*.

This is a functional grammar; that is to say, it is based on the important relation between structure and function.

Each chapter is built around a major function of language, such as *describing people and things*, and *reporting what someone said*. Each of these functions is regularly expressed in English by particular structures. For example, describing people and things is usually expressed by adjectives, and reporting what people say or think typically involves a reporting verb such as *say*, followed by a clause beginning with *that* or a clause with quotation marks (' ') around it.

This grammar follows up each major statement (often called a *rule* in other grammars) with a detailed description of the uses surrounding it – including any exceptions. The scope of the original function may then be extended. For example, the basic, central function of reporting verbs (chapter 7) is to state what someone has said.

He said he would be back soon.

It can easily be extended to include what someone has written.

His mother wrote that he had finally arrived home.

Then it can be widened to include thoughts and feelings; these do not need to be expressed in words, but the reporting structure is very convenient.

The boys thought he was dead.

From this we can see the reporting clause as a more general way of introducing another clause.

Examples

All the examples in this book are taken from the Collins Corpus.

As ever, the corpus lies at the heart of each grammar point described, helping compilers to make confident and accurate decisions about different structures and usage. Examples themselves remain close to the corpus, with minor changes made so that they are more accessible to the learner. They are carefully chosen so as to illustrate typical patterns and collocations in real-life situations.

Groups of words that behave in the same way

As well as providing a wealth of illustrative examples, this book gives further information about the grammar of a large number of specific words. The actual words and phrases that are regularly used in each structure are given in a series of lists. In this way, the learner can get a good idea of how large or small a grammatical class is, and how many words a certain rule applies to.

Wherever there is good reason to do so, the words and phrases are grouped together in a list in a meaningful arrangement. So, for example, at 1.21, separate groups are set out in a single list, including animals, fish, words ending in -*craft*, and foreign words ending in -*s*. These all share the same feature, i.e. that they can be either singular or plural nouns without any change in form – *moose*, *salmon*, *aircraft*, *corps*. From a purely grammatical point of view, they could all go in a single alphabetical list; however from a teaching and learning point of view, it is helpful to have them further classified according to their meaning.

'Be creative'

Certain areas of English grammar are very flexible and *productive*. Some are well known, such as the fact that almost any noun in English can modify another noun. For example, the noun *steam* can be used in, among others, the following combinations: *steam bath*, *steam room*, *steam engine*, *steam iron*, *steam power*, and *steam train*.

With this in mind, several 'Be creative' features are included to encourage learners to use their imagination, and to be more confident about expressing themselves. In such cases, rather than giving a definite rule, we prefer to give guidance so that the user can make individual choices with no serious risk of error. By describing the language in this way, we give plenty of scope for creativity and innovation.

Accessibility

When using a grammar, it can be difficult to find the information that you want. This is often the biggest single problem for users of grammars, and a good reason why grammars are often unpopular with learners. This grammar makes a special effort to support the user.

We have aimed to use the most up-to-date and commonly used grammatical terminology throughout. Technical terms have been used only where there is no obvious alternative. A glossary of terms is provided and they are also all listed in the index.

There is a contents list at the beginning of the book, and there is an individual contents list at the beginning of each chapter. Using these or the index, the user will be able to find the section or paragraph where a function is associated with a structure.

Throughout the book there are paragraph headings that show the topic of almost every paragraph, and there are frequent additional headings for each section of a chapter. At the top of each page, there is another heading to guide the user.

New developments in language

The continued development of the corpus enables us to keep up with the ever-changing nature of language. At COBUILD, we continually track and research the development of grammatical features, such as:

(i) the use of the progressive with so-called stative verbs (e.g. *I'm loving every minute of it*)

(ii) the use of *much* in affirmative unmodified statements (e.g. *There was much debate*)

(iii) the spread of generic pronouns (e.g. *You get some people who are very difficult*)

(iv) the use of *like* in reporting structures (e.g. *And I was like, 'wow!'*)

(v) the use of all-purpose question tags in some varieties of spoken informal English (e.g. *innit*)

The results are often fascinating and surprising, and enable us to ensure that each new edition of the Grammar gives you a clear portrayal of real English as it is written and spoken today.

The grammar of business and academic English

An extension of our functional approach has been to focus on two main contexts in which English is used as a lingua franca throughout the world – business and academic English.

As a result, two supplementary sections identify the principal areas of grammar that learners need to master if they wish to communicate effectively in business and academic contexts.

The section on the grammar of business English looks at typical structures used in such contexts as sharing information, negotiating, and giving presentations. The academic English section covers such areas as explaining results, reviewing research, and reporting findings. Extensive cross-referencing allows the user to refer back to the main text, where structures are discussed in greater detail.

We hope that you will enjoy learning about English grammar from a functional perspective – from exploring the wealth of real-world examples of current language, to understanding how certain structures work in business and academic contexts. We hope, too, that as a result, you will gain the confidence to use English creatively and effectively in a wide range of everyday situations.

Getting the most out of COBUILD English Grammar

Would you like to discover more about the wealth of information COBUILD English Grammar has to offer, and explore the subject of grammar further? If so, go to **www.collinselt.com/cobuildenglishgrammar**, where you will find a range of blogposts, written by experts in the field, that encourage focused thinking and discussion with your peers on a variety of topics, for example:

- questioning traditionally accepted grammar 'rules'
- establishing the difference between nonstandard usage and errors
- thinking about why some people avoid using the word 'tense' to talk about perfect and progressive forms.

To help you examine each topic in turn in greater detail, each blogpost has a link to a corresponding worksheet. You'll find all these and more on our blog at **www.collinselt.com/cobuildenglishgrammar**.

How to use this Grammar

The COBUILD English Grammar is designed to be used both for quick reference and for in-depth study.

Organization of the main text

The main text of the Grammar is divided into ten chapters. The first two chapters deal with the noun phrase, chapters 3, 4, and 5 with the verb phrase. Chapter 6 deals with adverbs and prepositions, chapter 7 with reporting, chapter 8 with joining words, phrases and clauses, and chapters 9 and 10 with continuous text.

Each chapter consists of a series of main topics and each topic is divided into sections. Paragraphs in the chapter are numbered, so that chapter 1 runs from 1.1 to 1.251, chapter 2 from 2.1 to 2.302 and so on.

This numbering system makes it easy for the user to refer to different but related points. There are cross-references throughout the text, either pointing to the main place where a topic is dealt with or to another paragraph where more information is given.

Most paragraphs also have a heading, saying in a few words what it deals with, especially which grammatical structure is being explained. Some paragraph headings do not show specifically what the paragraph deals with, but indicate information of a different kind. These paragraphs have the headings 'Be careful', 'Be Creative', and 'Usage Note'.

! 'Be Careful' highlights points where people often have problems with a particular grammatical feature of English, for example because it is a feature where English is different from many other languages.

★ 'Be Creative' indicates that the rule that has been mentioned can be applied in English to a very large number of words. For example, it is nearly always possible to make the -ing participle of a verb into an adjective that is used in front of a noun. By taking note of these features, you can use the rules that have been presented in a creative and original way, giving you greater freedom to express yourself in English. 'Be Creative' features are explained in greater detail in the Introduction.

ℹ 'Usage Note' gives information about the use of individual words or small groups of words. This information is important but cannot be generalized into a grammatical rule. The Usage Notes help you to understand points that are important for the understanding of particular words, rather than points that relate to large numbers of words.

≣ The U.S. flag symbol highlights paragraphs containing information about typical American English usage.

💬 The speech bubble symbol identifies paragraphs describing structures that are most commonly found in spoken English.

Most of the grammatical explanations are followed by examples showing how the structure is used. These examples are all taken from the Collins Corpus, and show how the structures are used naturally in speech or writing. The examples therefore give important information about the typical use of a structure, the words it is frequently used with, and the contexts in which it is likely to occur.

Throughout the book, grammatical explanations are followed by lists of the words that typically illustrate that grammatical point. For example, in Chapter 3, the point is made that many verbs can be either transitive or intransitive with the same meaning. This is followed by a list of verbs that are frequently used in this way.

The lists go beyond the actual examples of use that are given, to other words that behave in similar ways. They show whether the point being made can be applied to a small number or a large number of words. If the group is small, all members of it are given. If it is large, then the most frequently used words are given.

These lists can be used to help you increase your vocabulary and to check that you are using newly learned English words correctly.

Additional contents

In addition to the main text, various other sections are included to help you to get the most out of this Grammar. These additional sections are described below.

Glossary of grammatical terms

The Glossary explains the meaning of grammatical terms. It covers the terms that are used in this grammar, and also includes terms that are used in other grammars, with a cross-reference to the term used in this book, where appropriate. For example, this grammar talks about the *present progressive*, whereas some other grammars call it the *present continuous*. Both of these terms are mentioned in the Glossary, with the explanation being given at *present progressive*.

Reference section

This section at the back of the book provides an easy-to-use reference guide that shows how the following groups of words are formed:

- plurals of nouns
- the comparative and superlative of adjectives
- '-ly' adverbs formed from adjectives
- the comparative and superlative of adverbs
- tenses
- other verb forms
- passives
- principal parts of irregular verbs

The Reference section also includes other topics. For example, it starts with a pronunciation guide, to remind you of the sounds of English. There are also lists of numbers, and an explanation of how numbers are expressed aloud.

The grammar of business and academic English

These sections provide key guidance in the principal areas of grammar that learners need to master for effective communication in business and academic contexts.

Index

The Index is a comprehensive list of everything dealt with in the Grammar. It covers:

- the grammatical and functional topics dealt with in the Grammar;
- individual words which are used as examples of a particular grammatical point;
- grammatical terms, both those used in this book and those commonly used in other books.

Glossary of grammatical terms

abstract noun a noun used to describe a quality, idea, or experience rather than something physical or concrete; e.g. *joy, size, language.* Compare with **concrete noun**.

active used for describing verb phrases such as *gives,* and *has made,* where the subject is the person or thing doing the action or responsible for the action. Compare with **passive**.

adjectival clause another name for **relative clause**.

adjective a word used to tell you more about a thing, such as its appearance, colour, size, or other qualities; e.g. *...a pretty blue dress.*

adverb a word that gives more information about when, how, where, or in what circumstances something happens; e.g. *quickly, now.* There are several different kinds of adverb; adverbs of degree, manner, place, time, duration, and frequency. There are also **focusing adverbs**.

adverbial a word or combination of words added to a clause to give more information about time, place, or manner. See also **sentence adverbial** and **sentence connector**.

adverb of degree an adverb indicating the amount or extent of a feeling or quality; e.g. *extremely.*

adverb/adverbial of duration an adverb or adverbial indicating how long something lasts; e.g. *briefly, for a long time.*

adverb/adverbial of frequency an adverb or adverbial indicating how often something happens; e.g. *often, once a week.*

adverb of manner an adverb indicating the way in which something happens or is done; e.g. *carefully.*

adverb of place an adverb that gives more information about position or direction; e.g. *Move closer.*

adverb particle an adverb used as part of a phrasal verb; e.g. *hide out, sit up, turn round.*

affirmative not containing a negative word. Also called **positive**.

agent another name for **performer**.

agreement the relationship between a subject and its verb, or between a number or determiner and its noun; e.g. *I look/she looks... one bell/three bells.* Also called **concord**.

apostrophe s an ending ('s) added to a noun to mark possession; e.g. *...Harriet's daughter... the professor's husband... the Managing Director's secretary.*

article see **definite article, indefinite article**.

aspect the use of verb forms to show whether an action is continuing, repeated, or finished.

attributive used for describing the position of adjectives when they are used in front of a noun. Compare with **predicative**.

auxiliary verb one of the verbs *be, have,* and *do* when they are used with a main verb to make verb forms, negatives, questions, and so on. Also called **auxiliary. Modals** are also auxiliary verbs.

bare infinitive another name for **infinitive without to**.

base form the form of a verb that has no letters added to the end and is not a past form; e.g. *walk, go, have, be.* The base form is the form you look up in a dictionary.

broad negative one of a small group of adverbs including *barely* and *seldom* which are used to make a statement almost negative; e.g. *I barely knew her.*

cardinal number a number used for counting; e.g. *one, seven, nineteen.*

classifying adjective an adjective used to identify something as being of a particular type; e.g. *Indian, wooden, mental.* They do not have comparatives or superlatives. Compare with **qualitative adjective**.

clause a group of words containing a verb. See also **main clause** and **subordinate clause**.

clause of manner a subordinate clause that describes the way in which something is done, usually introduced with *as* or *like*; e.g. *She talks like her mother used to.*

collective noun a noun that refers to a group of people or things; e.g. *committee, team.*

colour adjective an adjective referring to a colour; e.g. *red, blue, scarlet.*

common noun a noun used to refer to a person, thing, or substance; e.g. *sailor, computer, glass.* Compare with **proper noun**.

comparative an adjective or adverb with *-er* on the end or *more* in front of it; e.g. *friendlier, more important, more carefully.*

complement a noun phrase or adjective that comes after a linking verb such as *be*, and gives more information about the subject or object of the clause; e.g. *She is a teacher, She is tired, They made her chairperson.*

complex sentence a sentence consisting of two or more main clauses linked by a subordinating conjunction; e.g. *We went inside when it started to rain.*

compound a combination of two or more words functioning as a unit. For example, *self-centred* and *free-style* are compound adjectives, *bus stop* and *state of affairs* are compound nouns, and *dry-clean* and *roller-skate* are compound verbs.

compound sentence a sentence consisting of two or more main clauses linked by a coordinating conjunction; e.g. *They picked her up and took her into the house.*

concessive clause a subordinate clause, usually introduced by *although* or *while*, that contrasts with a main clause; e.g. *Although I like her, I find her hard to talk to.*

concord another name for **agreement**.

concrete noun a noun that refers to something we can touch or see; e.g. *table, dress, flower.* Compare with **abstract noun**.

conditional clause a subordinate clause usually starting with *if*. The event described in the main clause depends on the condition described in the subordinate clause; e.g. *If it rains, we'll go to the cinema... They would be rich if they had taken my advice.*

conjunction a word linking together two clauses, phrases, or words. There are two types of conjunction – **coordinating conjunctions**, which link parts of a sentence of the same grammatical type (*and, but, or*), and **subordinating conjunctions**, which begin subordinate clauses (*although, when*).

continuous another name for **progressive**.

contraction a shortened form in which an auxiliary verb and *not*, or a subject and an auxiliary verb, are joined together and function as one word; e.g. *aren't, she's.*

coordinate clause a clause that is connected to another clause with a coordinating conjunction such as *and* or *but*; e.g. *He fell and broke his leg.*

coordinating conjunction a word such as *and, but*, or *or* which joins together two clauses, phrases, or words of the same grammatical type.

copula a name sometimes used to refer to the verb *be*. In this grammar, the term **linking verb** is used.

countable noun a noun that can be singular or plural; e.g. *dog/dogs, lemon/lemons, foot/feet.* Also called **count noun**.

declarative a clause in the declarative form has the subject followed by the verb. Most statements are made in the declarative form. Also called **indicative**.

defining non-finite clause a participle clause that is placed after a noun phrase to identify the person or thing you are talking about; e.g. *The girl wearing the red hat*.

defining relative clause a relative clause that identifies the person or thing that is being talked about; e.g. *I wrote down everything that she said*.

definite article the determiner '*the*'.

delexical verb a verb that has very little meaning in itself and is used with an object that carries the main meaning of the structure. *Give, have*, and *take* are commonly used as delexical verbs; e.g. *She gave a small cry... I've had a bath*.

demonstrative one of the words *this, that, these*, and *those* used in front of a noun; e.g. *... this woman... that tree*. They are also used as pronouns; e.g. *That looks nice... **This** is fun*.

dependent clause another name for **subordinate clause**.

definite determiner one of a groups of determiners including *the, that* and *your* which you use when the person you are speaking to understands which person or thing you are talking about; e.g. *the old man, my ideas*.

determiner one of a group of words including *the, a, some*, and *my* which are used at the beginning of a noun phrase.

direct object a noun phrase referring to a person or thing affected by an action, in a sentence with an active verb; e.g. *She wrote her name.... I shut the windows*.

direct speech speech reported in the words actually spoken by someone, without any changes in tense, person, and so on.

ditransitive verb a verb such as *give, take*, or *sell* which can have both an indirect and a direct object; e.g. *She gave me a kiss*.

dynamic verb a verb such as *run, give* or *slice* which describes an action. Compare with **stative verb**.

-ed adjective an adjective that ends in *-ed*, and usually has the same form as the *-ed* participle of a verb, or is formed by adding *-ed* to a noun; e.g. *a worried look... skilled workers*. Adjectives that do not end in *-ed* but have the same forms as irregular *-ed* participles are also called *-ed* adjectives; e.g. a *broken* bone.

-ed participle a verb form such as *walked* or *played*, which is used to make perfect forms and passives, or in some cases an adjective. Irregular participles such as *given* and *broken* are also called *-ed* participles because they behave like regular *-ed* participles. Also called **past participle**.

ellipsis when you leave out words because they are obvious from the context.

emphasizing adjective an adjective such as *complete, utter* or *total* which stresses how strongly you feel about something; e.g. *I feel a complete fool*.

ergative verb a verb that can be either transitive or intransitive in the same meaning. To use the verb intransitively, you use the object of the transitive verb as the subject of the intransitive verb; e.g. *He had boiled a kettle... The kettle had boiled*.

exclamation a word or sentence spoken suddenly and loudly in order to express surprise, anger, and so on; e.g. *Oh gosh!*

finite a finite verb is inflected according to person or tense rather than being an infinitive or a participle.

first person see **person**.

focusing adverb a sentence adverb that indicates the most relevant thing involved; e.g. *only, mainly, especially*.

future the use of *will* or *shall* with the base form of the verb to refer to future events; e.g. *She will come tomorrow*.

future progressive the use of *will be* or *shall be* and an *-ing* participle to refer to future events; e.g. *She will be going soon.* Also called **future continuous**.

future perfect the use of *will have* or *shall have* and an *-ed* participle to refer to future events; e.g. I *shall have finished* tomorrow.

future perfect progressive the use of *will* or *shall* with *have been* and an *-ing* participle to refer to future events; e.g. *I will have been walking* for three hours by then. Also called **future perfect continuous**.

gender a grammatical term referring to the difference between masculine and feminine words such as *he* and *she*.

generic pronoun one of a group of pronouns including *you* and *they* which are used to refer to people in general.

gerund another name for *-ing* **noun**.

gradable a gradable adjective can be used with a word such as *very* to say that the person or thing referred to has more or less of a quality; e.g. *very boring, less helpful.*

idiom a group of two or more words with a meaning that cannot be understood by taking the meaning of each individual word; e.g. *to kick the bucket, to run wild.*

*if-***clause** a **conditional clause**; or a clause used to report a *yes/no*-question.

imperative a clause in the imperative has the base form of the verb without a subject, e.g. *Come here... Take two tablets every four hours... Enjoy yourself.*

impersonal *it* *it* is an impersonal subject when it is used to introduce a fact, or when it is used in a split sentence; e.g. *It's raining... It was you who asked.*

indefinite article the determiners *a* and *an*.

indefinite determiner one of a group of determiners including *a, many* and *several* which you use to refer to someone or something of a particular type, without saying which person or thing you mean; e.g. *an old man, several suggestions.*

indefinite place adverb one of a group of adverbs including *anywhere* and *somewhere* which are used to indicate position or location in a general or vague way.

indefinite pronoun one of a group of pronouns including *someone* and *anything* which are used to refer to a person or thing in a general way.

indicative another name for **declarative**.

indirect object a second object used with a transitive verb to indicate who or what benefits from an action, or gets something as a result of it; e.g. *She gave me a rose.*

indirect question a way of asking a question that makes it sound more polite; e.g. *Can you tell me where the bank is?* instead of *Where is the bank?*

indirect speech another name for **reported speech**.

infinitive the base form of a verb. It is often used with *to* in front of it; e.g. *(to) take, (to) see, (to) bring.*

infinitive without to the infinitive form without *to* in front of it, used with modals and certain other verbs; e.g. *You must go... Let me think.*

inflection the variation in the form of a word to show differences in tense, number, case, and degree.

-ing adjective an adjective that has the same form as the *-ing* participle of a verb; e.g. ... a *smiling* face... a *winning* streak.

-ing participle a verb form ending in *-ing* that is used to make verb forms, and as an adjective. Also called the **present participle**.

-ing noun a noun that has the same form as the *-ing* participle of a verb; e.g. *Swimming* is good for you.

interjection another name for **exclamation**.

interrogative adverb one of the adverbs *how, when, where,* and *why* when they are used to ask questions.

interrogative a clause in the interrogative form has part or all of the verb phrase in front of the subject. Most questions are asked in the interrogative form.

interrogative pronoun one of the pronouns *who, whose, whom, what,* and *which* when they are used to ask questions.

intransitive verb a verb that is used to talk about an action or event that only involves the subject and so does not have an object; e.g. *She arrived... I was yawning.*

inversion changing the word order in a sentence, especially changing the order of the subject and the verb.

irregular not following the normal rules for inflection. An irregular verb has a past form and/or *-ed* participle that is formed in a different way from the regular ending.

lexical verb another name for **main verb**.

linking verb a verb that links the subject and complement of a clause; e.g. *be, become, seem, appear.* Also sometimes called **copula**.

main clause a clause that is not dependent on, or is not part of, another clause.

main verb any verb that is not an auxiliary verb. Also called **lexical verb**.

mass noun (in this grammar) a noun that is usually an uncountable noun, but that can be used as a countable noun when it refers to quantities or types of something; e.g. *... two sugars... cough medicines.*

measurement noun a noun that refers to a unit of size, volume, weight, speed, temperature, etc.; e.g. *mile, litre, degree.*

modal an auxiliary verb that is used with a main verb to indicate a particular attitude, such as possibility, obligation, prediction, or deduction; e.g. *can, could, may, might.* Also called *modal auxiliary* or *modal verb*.

modifier a word or group of words that come in front of a noun; e.g. *...a beautiful sunny day... ...a psychology conference.*

negative used for describing a sentence that uses a word like *not, never,* or *no one* to indicate the absence or opposite of something, or to say that something is not the case; e.g. *I don't know you... I'll never forget.* The opposite is **affirmative**.

negative word a word such as *never* and *not* which expresses a negative meaning.

nominal relative clause a subordinate clause that functions as a noun and often begins with *what* or *whatever*; e.g. *What he said was true.*

nominal *that*-clause a subordinate clause that functions as a noun and begins with *that*; e.g. *He showed that it was true.*

non-defining relative clause a relative clause that gives more information about someone or something, but that is not needed to identify them; e.g. *That's Mary, who was at university with me.* Compare with **defining relative clause**.

non-finite the non-finite forms of a verb are the infinitive and participle forms; e.g. *to take, taking, taken.*

noun a word that refers to people, things, and abstract ideas such as feelings and qualities; e.g. *woman, Harry, guilt.*

noun phrase a group of words that acts as the subject, complement, or object of a clause, or as the object of a preposition.

noun modifier a noun used in front of another noun, as if it were an adjective; e.g. *...a car door... a steel works.*

number the way in which differences between singular and plural are shown; e.g. *flower/ flowers, that/those.* See also **cardinal number** and **ordinal number**.

object a noun phrase that refers to a person or thing, other than the subject, which is involved in or affected by the action of a verb. See also **direct object** and **indirect object**. Prepositions are also followed by objects.

object complement a word that is used to describe the object of a clause and that occurs with verbs such as *make* and *find*; e.g. *It made me* tired... *I found her* asleep.

ordinal number a number that is used to indicate where something comes in an order or sequence; e.g. *first, fifth, tenth, hundredth*.

participle a verb form used for making different tenses. See **-ed participle** and **-ing participle** for more details.

partitive a word that gives information about the amount of a particular thing; e.g. *pint, loaf, portion*.

passive verb forms such as *was given, were taken, had been made*, where the subject is the person or thing that is affected by the action. Compare with **active**.

past form the form of a verb, often ending in *-ed*, that is used for the past simple.

past participle another name for **-ed participle**.

past perfect the use of *had* with an *-ed* participle to refer to past events; e.g. *She* had finished.

past perfect progressive the use of *had been* with an *-ing* participle to refer to past events; e.g. *He* had been waiting *for hours*. Also called **past perfect continuous**.

past progressive the use of *was* or *were* with an *-ing* participle, usually to refer to past events; e.g. *They* were worrying *about it yesterday*. Also called **past continuous**.

past simple the use of the past form of a verb to refer to past events; e.g. *They* waited... *It* fell *over*.

past tense a tense used to describe actions or events that took place in the past. See **tense** for more details.

perfect form a verb form with *have* and an *-ed* participle; e.g. *I* have met *him... We had* won.

performative verb a verb that states explicitly what action the speaker is performing when he or she uses it; e.g. *apologize, resign, christen*.

performer the person or thing that is responsible for the action expressed by the verb; e.g. Mark *phoned ... Our dinner was eaten by* the dog.

person a term used to refer to the three classes of people who are involved in something that is said. They are the first person (the person speaking or writing), the second person (the person being addressed), and the third person (the people or things that are being talked about).

personal pronoun one of a group of pronouns including *I, you*, and *me* which are used to refer back to the people or things you are talking about.

phrasal verb a combination of a verb and an adverb and/or a preposition, which have a single meaning; e.g. *back down, hand over, look after, look forward to*.

phrase a set of words that is smaller than a clause, and that is based around a particular word class: for example, a verb phrase is based around a main verb, and can also contain auxiliary verbs. See also **noun phrase**, **verb phrase** and **prepositional phrase**. **Phrase** is also sometimes used to refer to any group of words.

plural the form used to refer to more than one person or thing; e.g. *dogs, women*.

plural noun a noun that is only used in the plural form; e.g. *trousers, scissors, vermin*.

possessive a structure used to show possession; e.g. *your, Jerry's, mine*.

possessive determiner a determiner such as *my, your*, and *their*. Also called **possessive adjective**.

possessive pronoun one of the words *mine, yours, hers, his, ours*, and *theirs*.

postdeterminer a small group of adjectives used after a determiner and in front of other adjectives; e.g. *certain, remaining*.

predeterminer a word that comes in front of a determiner; e.g. all *the boys...* double *the trouble...* such *a mess*.

predicative used for describing the position of adjectives when they are used after a linking verb such as 'be'. Compare with **attributive**.

preposition a word such as *by, with* or *from*, which is usually followed by a noun phrase or an *-ing* form.

prepositional phrase a structure consisting of a preposition and its object; e.g. *on the table, by the sea*.

present participle another name for *-ing* **participle**.

present progressive the use of the present simple of 'be' with an *-ing* participle to refer to present events; e.g. *Things are improving*. Also called **present continuous**.

present perfect the use of the present simple of *have* with an *-ed* participle to refer to past events that exist in the present; e.g. *She has loved him for ten years*.

present perfect progressive the use of *have been* and *has been* with an *-ing* participle to refer to past events that exist in the present; e.g. *We have been sitting here for hours*. Also called **present perfect continuous**.

present simple the use of the base form or the *s* form of a verb, usually to refer to present events; e.g. *I like bananas... My sister hates them*.

present tense a tense used to describe events taking place in the present, or situations that exist in the present.

progressive a verb form that contains a form of the verb 'be' and an *-ing* participle; e.g. *She was laughing... They had been playing badminton*. Also called **continuous**.

pronoun a word used instead of a noun, when you do not want to name someone or something directly; e.g. *it, you, none*.

proper noun a noun that refers to a particular person, place, or institution; e.g. *Nigel, Edinburgh, Christmas*. Compare with **common noun**.

purpose clause a subordinate clause, usually introduced by *in order to*, or *so that*; e.g. *I came here in order to ask you out to dinner*.

qualifier any word, phrase, or clause that comes after a noun phrase, and gives extra information to expand its meaning; e.g. *...a book with a blue cover...* the shop *on the corner*.

qualitative adjective an adjective that is used to indicate a quality, and is gradable; e.g. *funny, intelligent, small*. Compare with **classifying adjective**.

quantity expression a phrase ending in *of* that allows you to refer to a quantity of something without being precise about the exact amount; e.g. *some of, a lot of, a little bit of*.

question a structure that typically has the verb in front of the subject and that is used to ask someone about something; e.g. *Have you any money?* Also called **interrogative**.

question tag a structure or word that is used at the end of a statement in order to form a question.

reason clause a subordinate clause, usually introduced by *because, since*, or *as*; e.g. *Since you're here, we'll start*.

reciprocal pronoun the pronouns *each other* and *one another*, used to show that two or more people do or feel the same thing; e.g. *They loved each other*.

reciprocal verb a verb that describes an action that involves people affecting each other in the same way with the same action; e.g. *They met in the street... He met her yesterday*.

reflexive pronoun a pronoun ending in *-self*, such as *myself* or *themselves*, which is used as the object of a verb when the person affected by an action is the same as the person doing it.

reflexive verb a verb that is typically used with a reflexive pronoun; e.g. *enjoy yourself; pride yourself on*.

relative clause a subordinate clause that gives more information about someone or something mentioned in the main clause. See also **defining relative clause** and **non-defining relative clause**.

relative pronoun a wh-word such as *who* or *which*, used to introduce a relative clause; e.g. *...the girl who was carrying the bag.*

reported clause the part of a reporting structure that describes what someone has said; e.g. *She said that I couldn't see her.*

reported question a question that is reported using a reporting structure rather than the exact words used by the speaker.

reported speech speech that is reported using a reporting structure rather than the exact words used by the speaker. Also called **indirect speech**.

reporting clause a clause that contains a reporting verb, which is used to introduce what someone has said; e.g. *They asked if I could come.*

reporting verb a verb that describes what people say or think; e.g. *suggest, say, wonder.*

reporting structure a structure that reports what someone has said by using a reported clause rather than repeating their exact words; e.g. *She told me she'd be late.*

result clause a subordinate clause introduced by *so that* which gives the result of something; e.g. *The house was severely damaged, so that it is now uninhabitable.*

rhetorical question a question that you use in order to make a comment rather than to obtain information; e.g. *Oh, isn't it silly?*

second person see **person**.

semi-modal the verbs *dare, need,* and *used to* which behave rather like modals.

sentence a group of words that express a statement, question, or command. A sentence usually has a verb and a subject, and may consist of one clause, or two or more clauses. A sentence in writing has a capital letter at the beginning and a full-stop, question mark, or exclamation mark at the end.

sentence adverbial an adverbial that applies to the whole clause, rather than to part of it; e.g. *We possibly have to wait and see.* See also **sentence connector**.

sentence connector a sentence adverbial used to introduce a comment or reinforce what is said; e.g. *moreover, besides.*

s form the base form of a verb with s on the end, used in the present simple.

simple sentence a sentence that contains only one clause.

singular the form used to refer to or talk about one person or thing; e.g. *dog, woman.* Compare with **plural**.

singular noun a noun typically used in the singular form; e.g. *sun, business.*

split infinitive the placing of a word between *to* and the base form of a verb; e.g. *...to boldly go where no man has gone before.*

split sentence a sentence in which emphasis is given to either the subject or the object by using a structure beginning with *it, what,* or *all*; e.g. *It's a hammer we need...What we need is a hammer.*

stative verb a verb that describes a state; e.g. *be, live, know.* Compare with **dynamic verb**.

subject a noun phrase that usually comes before a verb, and agrees with the verb in person and number. In active sentences, the subject usually refers to the person or thing who does the action expressed by the verb; e.g. *We were going shopping.*

subjunctive a verb form that is used in some languages to express attitudes such as wishing, hoping, and doubting. The subjunctive is not very common in English, and is used mainly in conditional clauses such as *If I were you....*

submodifying adverb an adverb that is used in front of an adjective or another adverb in order to strengthen or weaken its meaning; e.g. *...very interesting... quite quickly.*

subordinate clause a clause that begins with a subordinating conjunction such as *because* or *while* and which must be used with a main clause.

subordinating conjunction a conjunction that begins a subordinate clause.

substitution the special use of pronouns and other words to replace part or all of a clause; e.g. *'Are you going to the party?'– 'I hope so'.*

superlative an adjective or adverb with *-est* on the end or *most* in front of it; e.g. *thinnest, quickest, most wisely.*

tense the verb form that shows whether you are referring to the past or the present.

that-clause a clause starting with '*that*' which is used mainly when reporting what someone has said; e.g. *She said that she'd wash up for me. That* can be omitted when the clause is used after a reporting verb.

third person see **person**.

time adverbial an adverbial that gives more information about when something happens; e.g. *I saw her yesterday.*

time clause a subordinate clause that indicates the time of an event; e.g. *I'll phone you when I get back.*

title a word used before a person's name to show their position or status; e.g. *Mrs, Lord, Queen.*

to-infinitive the base form of a verb preceded by *to*; e.g. *to go, to have, to jump.*

transitive verb a verb used to talk about an action or event that involves more than one person or thing, and so is followed by an object; e.g. *She's wasting her money.*

uncountable noun a noun that refers to a general kind of thing rather than to an individual item, and so has only one form; e.g. *money, furniture, intelligence.* Also called **uncount noun**.

verb a word used with a subject to say what someone or something does, or what happens to them; e.g. *sing, spill, die.*

verb phrase a main verb, or a main verb preceded by one or more auxiliary verbs, which combines with a subject to say what someone or something does, or what happens to them; e.g. *I'll show them... She's been sick.*

vocative a word used when speaking to someone, just as if it were their name; e.g. *darling, madam.*

wh-clause a clause starting with a *wh-* word.

whether-clause a clause used to report a *yes/no*-question; e.g. *I asked her whether she'd seen him.*

wh-question a question that expects an answer giving a particular person, place, thing, amount, and so on, rather than just *yes* or *no.*

wh-word one of a group of words starting with *wh-*, such as *what, when* or *who*, which are used in *wh*-questions. *How* is also called a *wh*-word because it behaves like the other *wh*-words.

yes/no-question a question that can be answered simply with either *yes* or *no*; e.g. *Would you like some more tea?*

Chapter 1

Referring to people and things: nouns, pronouns, and determiners

1 Referring to people and things: nouns, pronouns, and determiners

Introduction to the noun phrase

1.1 At its simplest, language is used to talk about people and things. People do this by using words in a variety of ways, for example to make statements, to ask questions, and to give orders. The words chosen are arranged into groups, either around a noun or around a verb. They are called **noun phrases** and **verb phrases**.

Noun phrases tell us which people or things are being talked about. **Verb phrases** tell us what is being said about them, for example what they are doing.

Chapters 1 and 2 of this grammar deal with noun phrases. For information about verb phrases, see Chapter 3.

position

1.2 A noun phrase can be the **subject** or **object** of a verb, it can follow a **linking verb**, or it can be the object of a **preposition**.

Babies cry when they are hungry.
I couldn't feel anger against him.
They were teachers.
Let us work together in peace.

common nouns and proper nouns

1.3 You use a noun phrase to talk about someone or something by naming them. You do this by using a general name, called a **noun** or **common noun**, or by using a specific name, called a **proper noun**.

Proper nouns are mainly used for people, places, and events.

Mary likes strawberries.
I went to Drexel University and then I went to Pittsburgh to work for a psychiatrist.
We flew to Geneva with British Airways.

See paragraphs 1.52 to 1.58 for more information about **proper nouns**.

determiners with common nouns

1.4 If you use a common noun, you are saying that the person or thing you are talking about can be put in a set with others that are similar in some way.

If you just want to say that the person or thing is in that set, you use an **indefinite determiner** with the common noun.

I met a girl who was a student there.
Have you got any comment to make about that?
There are some diseases that are clearly inherited.

If you want to show which member of a set you are talking about, you use a **definite determiner** with a common noun.

I put my arm round her shoulders.
...the destruction of their city.
She came in to see me this morning.

See paragraphs 1.162 to 1.251 for more information about **determiners**, and paragraphs 1.13 to 1.92 for more information about **nouns**.

personal and demonstrative pronouns

1.5 You may decide not to name the person or thing and to use a **pronoun** rather than a proper noun or common noun.

You usually do this because the person or thing has already been named, so you refer to them by using a **personal pronoun** or a **demonstrative pronoun**.

Max will believe us, won't he?
'Could I speak to Sue, please?'–'I'm sorry, she doesn't work here now.'
Some people have servants to cook for them.
This led to widespread criticism.

See paragraphs 1.95 to 1.106 for more information about **personal pronouns**, and paragraphs 1.124 to 1.127 for more information about **demonstrative pronouns**.

indefinite pronouns

1.6 You may decide not to name the person or thing at all, for example because you do not want to, you think it is not important, you do not know, or you want to be vague or mysterious while telling a story. In such cases you use an **indefinite pronoun**, which does not refer to any particular person or thing.

I had to say something.
In this country nobody trusts anyone.
A moment later, his heart seemed to stop as he sensed the sudden movement of someone behind him.

See paragraphs 1.128 to 1.141 for more information about **indefinite pronouns**.

adding extra information

1.7 If you want to give more information about the person or thing you are talking about, rather than just giving their general or specific name, you can use a **modifier** such as an **adjective**, or you can add extra information in the form of a phrase or a clause, for example.

modifiers

1.8 Most **adjectives** are used as modifiers. Nouns are also often used as modifiers.

...a big city.
...blue ink.
He opened the car door.
...the oil industry.

See paragraphs 2.2 to 2.168 for more information about **adjectives**, and paragraphs 2.169 to 2.174 for more information about **noun modifiers**.

adding information after the noun

1.9   You can add a prepositional phrase, a relative clause, an adverb of place or time, or a *to*-infinitive after the noun.

>...a girl *in a dark grey dress*.
>...the man *who employed me*.
>...the room *upstairs*.
>...the desire *to kill*.

Adjectives and participles are also sometimes used after the noun, usually in combination with other words.

>...the Minister *responsible for national security*.
>...the three cards *lying on the table*.

See paragraphs 2.272 to 2.302 for more details about information that is added after the noun.

1.10   In particular, prepositional phrases beginning with *of* are very common, because they can express many different kinds of relationship between the two noun phrases.

>...strong feelings *of jealousy*.
>...a picture *of a house*.
>...the rebuilding *of the old hospital*.
>...the daughter *of the village cobbler*.
>...problems *of varying complexity*.
>...the arrival *of the police*.

For more information about the use of *of* in the noun phrase see paragraphs 2.277 to 2.283.

linking noun phrases and linking words within them

1.11   If you want to refer separately to more than one person or thing, or you want to describe them in more than one way, you link noun phrases using the **conjunctions** *and*, *or*, or *but*. Sometimes you use a comma instead of *and*, or just put one word next to another.

>...a *table and chair*.
>...his obligations with regard to *Amanda, Robert and Matthew*.
>...some *fruit or cheese* afterwards.
>...her *long black skirt*.

See paragraphs 8.171 to 8.201 for more information about the use of conjunctions to link noun phrases and words within noun phrases.

numbers and quantity expressions

1.12   If you want to say how many things you are talking about, or how much of something there is, you use **numbers** and **quantity expressions**.

>Last year I worked *seven* days a week *fourteen* hours a day.
>She drinks *lots of* coffee.

Numbers are dealt with in paragraphs 2.208 to 2.239, and **quantity expressions** are dealt with in 2.175 to 2.193.

Identifying people and things: nouns

1.13 A noun is used to identify a person or thing. In this chapter six main types of noun are described. They are classified according to whether they have a plural form, whether they need a determiner in front of them, and whether they occur with a singular verb or a plural verb when they are the subject of the verb.

The six types are:

classificaton	example	comments	paragraph
countable nouns	a bird birds	have plural need determiner	1.15 to 1.22
uncountable nouns	happiness equipment	no plural usually no determiner	1.23 to 1.33
singular nouns	the moon a day	no plural need determiner	1.34 to 1.40
plural nouns	clothes scissors	no singular	1.41 to 1.46
collective nouns	the public the staff	either singular or plural verb	1.47 to 1.51
proper nouns	Mary London The United Nations	start with capital letter	1.52 to 1.58

Many nouns have a number of different meanings, and so can be, for example, a countable noun for one meaning, an uncountable noun for another, and a singular noun for another.

There are a few other groups of nouns with special features. These are dealt with in paragraphs 1.59 to 1.92.

capital letters

1.14 Most nouns do not begin with a capital letter, unless they are used to start a sentence. However, the following types of noun are always spelled with a capital letter:

▶ **proper nouns** or names

...my sister Elizabeth.
I love reading Shakespeare.
I'll be in the office on Monday.
I think he's gone to London.

For more information on proper nouns, see paragraphs 1.52 to 1.58. Proper nouns that are time expressions are dealt with in Chapter 4, and those that are place names in Chapter 6.

▶ nouns that identify people of a particular nationality, or languages

Can you think of some typical problems experienced by Germans learning English?

▶ nouns that are the name of a particular product

He drives a Porsche.
Put a bit of Sellotape across it.

Things that can be counted: countable nouns

1.15 Many nouns have two forms, the **singular** form, which is used to refer to one person or thing, and the **plural** form, which is used to refer to more than one person or thing.

These nouns refer to people or things that can be counted. You can put numbers in front of them.

...book...books.
...day...days.
...three brothers.
...ten minutes.

These nouns make up the largest group of nouns in English. They are called **countable nouns**.

noun–verb agreement

1.16 When you use the singular form of a countable noun as the subject of a verb, you use a singular verb. When you use the plural form of a countable noun as the subject, you use a plural verb.

A dog likes to eat far more meat than a human being.
Bigger dogs cost more.

use of determiners

1.17 Countable nouns have a determiner in front of them when they are used in the singular.

He got into the car and started the motor.
They left the house to go for a walk after lunch.

When you use the plural form of a countable noun to talk about something in general, you do not use a determiner.

They all live in big houses.
Most classrooms have computers.

However, if you are specifying a particular instance of something, you need to use a determiner.

The houses in our street are all identical.
Our computers can give you all the relevant details.

list of countable nouns

1.18 Here is a list of some common countable nouns:

accident	article	bed	boy	card
account	artist	bell	bridge	case
actor	baby	bill	brother	castle
address	bag	bird	bus	cat
adult	ball	boat	bush	chair
animal	bank	book	camp	chapter
answer	battle	bottle	captain	chest
apartment	beach	box	car	child

cigarette	face	husband	motor	shop
city	factory	idea	mouth	sister
class	farm	island	nation	smile
club	father	issue	neck	son
coat	field	job	newspaper	spot
college	film	journey	office	star
computer	finger	judge	page	station
corner	foot	key	park	store
country	friend	king	party	stream
crowd	game	kitchen	path	street
cup	garden	lady	picture	student
daughter	gate	lake	plan	table
day	girl	library	plane	task
desk	group	line	plant	teacher
doctor	gun	list	problem	tent
dog	hall	machine	product	thought
door	hand	magazine	programme	tour
dream	handle	man	project	town
dress	hat	meal	ring	valley
driver	head	meeting	river	village
ear	heart	member	road	walk
edge	hill	message	room	wall
effect	horse	method	scheme	week
egg	hospital	minute	school	window
election	hotel	mistake	ship	woman
engine	hour	model	shirt	yard
eye	house	month	shock	year

Note that many of these nouns have some meanings in which they are uncountable nouns, but they are countable nouns in their commonest meanings.

singular and plural forms

1.19 For most countable nouns the plural form has -s at the end, which distinguishes it from the singular form.

...bed... beds.
...car... cars.

Some countable nouns have other differences between the singular and plural forms.

...bus...buses.
...lady... ladies.
...calf...calves.
...man...men.
...mouse...mice.

For full information about the plural forms of countable nouns, see the Reference section.

same form for singular and plural

1.20 Some countable nouns have the same form for both singular and plural.

...a sheep.
...nine sheep.

Many of these nouns refer to animals or fish; others are more varied in meaning:

bison	~	trout	dice	species
deer	cod	whitebait	fruit	~
elk	fish	~	gallows	bourgeois
greenfly	goldfish	aircraft	grapefruit	chassis
grouse	halibut	hovercraft	insignia	corps
moose	mullet	spacecraft	mews	patois
reindeer	salmon	~	offspring	précis
sheep	shellfish	crossroads	series	rendezvous

singular form with plural meaning

1.21 The names of many animals and birds have two forms, one singular and one plural. However, when you are referring to them in the context of hunting or when you are saying that there are large numbers of them, it is quite common to use the form without -s, even though you are referring to several animals or birds.

We went up north to hunt deer.

Note that the plural form of the verb is used when several animals or birds are the subject of the sentence, even if you use the form without -s.

Zebra are a more difficult prey.

Similarly, when you are referring to a large number of trees or plants growing together, you can use the singular form of their name. When you are referring to a small number or to individual trees or plants, you usually use the form with -s.

...the rows of willow and cypress which lined the creek.
...the poplars and willows along the Peshawar Road.

⊗ **BE CREATIVE**

1.22 Although some names of animals, birds, trees, and plants are commonly used in the singular form with plural meaning, in fact all such names can be used in this way.

Things not usually counted: uncountable nouns

1.23 Some nouns refer to general things such as qualities, substances, processes, and topics rather than to individual items or events. These nouns have only one form, are not used with numbers, and are not usually used with the determiners *the*, *a*, or *an*.

...a boy or girl with intelligence.
Make sure everyone has enough food and drink.
...new techniques in industry and agriculture.
I talked with people about religion, death, marriage, money, and happiness.

These nouns are called **uncountable nouns**.

noun–verb agreement

1.24 When you use an uncountable noun as the subject of a verb, you use a singular form of the verb.

Love makes you do strange things.
They believed that poverty was a threat to world peace.
Electricity is potentially dangerous.

list of uncountable nouns

1.25 Here is a list of some common uncountable nouns:

absence	education	help	pleasure	status
access	electricity	history	policy	stuff
age	energy	ice	poverty	teaching
agriculture	environment	independence	power	technology
anger	equipment	industry	pride	time
atmosphere	evil	insurance	protection	trade
beauty	existence	intelligence	purity	training
behaviour	experience	joy	rain	transport
cancer	failure	justice	reality	travel
capacity	faith	labour	relief	trust
childhood	fashion	loneliness	religion	truth
china	fear	love	respect	violence
comfort	finance	luck	rice	waste
concern	fire	magic	safety	water
confidence	flesh	marriage	salt	wealth
courage	food	mercy	sand	weather
death	freedom	music	security	welfare
democracy	fun	nature	silence	wind
depression	ground	paper	sleep	work
design	growth	patience	strength	worth
duty	happiness	peace	snow	youth
earth	health	philosophy	spite	

! BE CAREFUL

1.26 There are some words that are uncountable nouns in English, but that refer to things that are considered countable in other languages.

Here is a list of the most common uncountable nouns of this type:

advice	hair	knowledge	money	research
baggage	homework	luggage	news	spaghetti
furniture	information	machinery	progress	traffic

1.27 Although uncountable nouns refer to things that cannot be counted and are not used with numbers, you often want to talk about an amount of something that is expressed by an uncountable noun.

Sometimes, you can do this by putting an **indefinite determiner** such as *all*, *enough*, *little*, or *some* in front of the noun.

Do you have enough money?
There's some chocolate cake over there.

For more information on indefinite determiners that can be used with uncountable nouns, see paragraph 1.225.

You can also put a **quantity expression** in front of the noun. For example, when you refer to water you can say *drops of water, a cup of water, four gallons of water,* and so on.

The use of quantity expressions with uncountable nouns is explained in paragraphs 2.194 to 2.207.

mass nouns

1.28 When you are sure that your reader or hearer will understand that a quantity of something is being referred to, you do not need to use a quantity expression.

For example, in a restaurant you can ask for *three cups of coffee,* but you can also ask for *three coffees* because the person you are talking to will know that you mean *three cups of coffee.* In this way, the uncountable noun *coffee* has become countable.

Nouns used in this way are called **mass nouns**.

1.29 Mass nouns are often used to refer to quantities of a particular kind of food or drink.

We spent two hours talking over coffee and biscuits in her study.
We stopped for a coffee at a small café.

1.30 Similarly, some uncountable nouns can be mass nouns when they refer to types of something. For example, *cheese* is usually an uncountable noun but you can talk about *a large range of cheeses.*

...plentiful cheap beer.
...profits from low-alcohol beers.
We were not allowed to buy wine or spirits at lunch time.
We sell a wide variety of wines and liqueurs.

Mass nouns referring to different types of a substance are mainly used in technical contexts. For example *steel* is nearly always an uncountable noun, but in contexts where it is important to distinguish between different kinds of steel it can be a mass noun.

...imports of European steel.
...the use of small amounts of nitrogen in making certain steels.

list of mass nouns

1.31 The following is a list of frequently used mass nouns:

adhesive	bread	claret	coffee	cotton
beer	cake	cloth	cognac	curry
brandy	cheese	coal	coke	deodorant

detergent	insecticide	medicine	poison	sugar
disinfectant	iron	metal	preservative	tea
dye	jam	milk	ribbon	vodka
fabric	jelly	oil	salad	whisky
fertilizer	juice	ointment	sauce	wine
fuel	lager	ore	sherry	wood
fur	liqueur	paint	soap	wool
gin	lotion	perfume	soil	yarn
glue	material	pesticide	soup	yoghurt
ink	meat	plastic	steel	

nouns that are uncountable and countable

1.32   There are also some other nouns that can be uncountable nouns when they refer to a thing in general, and countable nouns when they refer to a particular instance of it.

Some nouns are commonly both uncountable nouns and countable nouns. For example, *victory* refers to the idea of winning in general but *a victory* refers to a particular occasion when someone wins.

He worked long and hard and finally led his team to victory.
...his victory in the Australian Grand Prix.
Many parents were alarmed to find themselves in open conflict with the church.
Hundreds of people have died in ethnic conflicts.

Some uncountable nouns are rarely or never countable nouns; that is, they do not occur in a plural form, or with a number.

...a collection of fine furniture.
We found Alan weeping with relief and joy.
He saved money by refusing to have a telephone.

uncountable nouns ending in -s

1.33   Some nouns that end in -s and look as if they are plural are in fact uncountable nouns. This means that when they are the subject of a verb, the verb is in the singular.

These nouns refer mainly to subjects of study, activities, games, and diseases.

Physics is fun.
Politics plays a large part in village life.
Economics is the oldest of the social sciences.
Darts is a very competitive sport.
Measles is in most cases a relatively harmless disease.

Here are three lists of uncountable nouns ending in -s.

These nouns refer to subjects of study and activities:

acoustics	classics	linguistics	physics
aerobics	economics	logistics	politics
aerodynamics	electronics	mathematics	statistics
aeronautics	genetics	mechanics	thermodynamics
athletics	gymnastics	obstetrics	

Note that some of these nouns are occasionally used as plural nouns, especially when you are talking about a particular person's work or activities.

His politics are clearly right-wing.

These nouns refer to games:

billiards	cards	draughts	tiddlywinks
bowls	darts	skittles	

These nouns refer to diseases:

diabetes	mumps	rickets
measles	rabies	shingles

When there is only one of something: singular nouns

1.34 There are certain things in the world that are unique. There are other things that you almost always want to talk about one at a time. This means that there are some nouns, or more often some meanings of nouns, for which only a singular form is used.

When a noun is used with such a meaning, it is called a **singular noun**. Singular nouns are always used with a determiner, because they behave like the singular form of a countable noun.

`noun–verb agreement`

1.35 When you use a singular noun as the subject of a verb, you use a singular form of the verb.

The sun was shining.
The atmosphere is very relaxed.

`things that are unique`

1.36 Some singular nouns refer to one specific thing and therefore are used with *the*. Some of these nouns, in fact, refer to something of which there is only one in the world.

There were huge cracks in the ground.
The moon had not yet reached my window.
Burning tanks threw great spirals of smoke into the air.
He's always thinking about the past and worrying about the future.

`using the context`

1.37 Other singular nouns can be used to refer to one thing only when it is obvious from the context what you are referring to. For example, if you are in Leeds and say *I work at the university*, you will almost certainly mean Leeds University.

However, in the following examples it is not clear exactly who or what the singular noun refers to, because there is not enough context.

In many countries the market is small numerically.
Their company looks good only because the competition looks bad.
You've all missed the point.

Unless it is made clear which goods or products are being talked about, it is not possible for the reader or listener to be sure which group of potential buyers *the market* refers to. Similarly it is not possible to know exactly which company or group of companies *the competition* refers to. In the last example, the speaker is presumably going to state what he or she thinks *the point* is.

used in verb + object idioms

1.38 There are some activities that you do not usually do more than once at a time. The nouns that refer to them are usually the object of a verb, and are used with the determiner *a*.

In this structure the verb has very little meaning and the noun carries most of the meaning of the whole structure. For more information about these verb + object idioms, see paragraphs 3.32 to 3.45.

I went and had a wash.
Bruno gave it a try.

Some singular nouns are used so regularly with a particular verb that they have become fixed phrases and are idiomatic.

I'd like very much for you to have a voice in the decision.
Isn't it time we made a move?

singular noun structures

1.39 There are two special kinds of structure in which a singular noun is used.

A singular noun is sometimes used with the determiner *a* after a linking verb. See paragraphs 3.126 to 3.181 for more information about **linking verbs**.

Decision-making is an art.
The quickest way was by using the car. It was a risk but he decided it had to be taken.
They were beginning to find Griffiths' visits rather a strain.

A singular noun is sometimes used with the determiner *the*, followed by a prepositional phrase beginning with *of*.

Comedy is the art of making people laugh.
Old machines will be replaced by newer ones to reduce the risk of breakdown.
He collapsed under the strain of a heavy workload.

This group includes nouns used metaphorically; see paragraph 1.64 for more details.

Some singular nouns are always used to refer to one particular quality or thing, but are rarely used alone; that is, they need to be specified in some way by the use of supporting material. They can be used with a number of different determiners.

There was a note of satisfaction in his voice.
Bessie covered the last fifty yards at a tremendous pace.
Simon allowed his pace to slacken.
She was simply incapable of behaving in a rational and considered manner.
...their manner of rearing their young.

Nouns that are rarely used alone without supporting material are discussed in detail in paragraphs 1.59 to 1.65.

ℹ️ USAGE NOTE

1.40 Some nouns are used in the singular with a particular meaning only in an idiomatic phrase. They have the appearance of singular nouns, but they are not used as freely as singular nouns.

What happens down there is <u>none of my business</u>.
<u>It's a pity</u> I can't get to him.

Referring to more than one thing: plural nouns

1.41   There are some things that are considered to be plural rather than singular, so some nouns have only a plural form. For example, you buy *goods*, but not *a good*. These nouns are called **plural nouns**.

Other nouns have only a plural form when they are used with a particular meaning. For example, an official meeting between American and Russian leaders is usually referred to as *talks* rather than as *a talk*. In these meanings, these nouns are also called **plural nouns**.

Union leaders met the company for wage <u>talks</u> *on October 9.*
It is inadvisable to sell <u>goods</u> *on a sale or return basis.*
Take care of your <u>clothes</u>.
The weather <u>conditions</u> *were the same.*
All <u>proceeds</u> *are going to charity.*
Employees can have meals on the <u>premises</u>.

Note that some plural nouns do not end in -s: for example *clergy, police, poultry,* and *vermin.*

noun–verb agreement

1.42   When you use a plural noun as the subject of a verb, you use a plural form of the verb.

<u>Expenses</u> *for attending meetings* <u>are</u> *sometimes* <u>claimed</u>.
The <u>foundations were shaking</u>.
<u>Refreshments were</u> *on sale in the café.*
Attempts were made where <u>resources were</u> *available.*

use with modifiers

1.43   You do not usually use numbers in front of plural nouns. You can, however, use some **indefinite determiners** such as *some* or *many*. For more information about the indefinite determiners that can be used with plural nouns, see the section beginning at paragraph 1.223.

Some plural nouns usually have a definite determiner in front of them, because they are specific; some never have a determiner at all, because they are very general; and some are rarely used alone without extra information in the form of a phrase or a clause, for example, because they need supporting material.

The lists in the following two paragraphs contain some common plural nouns that are frequently used in one of these ways. Many of them have other meanings in which they are countable nouns.

with or without determiners

1.44   Some plural nouns are most commonly used with *the.*

Things are much worse when <u>the rains</u> *come.*
<u>The authorities</u> *are concerned that the cocaine may be part of an international drug racket.*
The coach tour of Gran Canaria was a wonderfully relaxing way to see <u>the sights</u>.

Here is a list of plural nouns that are most commonly used with *the:*

authorities	heavens	pictures	sights
foundations	mains	races	waters
fruits	odds	rains	wilds

Some plural nouns are most commonly used with a possessive determiner such as *my* or *his*.

It offended her feelings.
My travels up the Dalmation coast began in Dubrovnik.
This only added to his troubles.

Here is a list of plural nouns that are most commonly used with a possessive determiner:

activities	feelings	movements	terms	troubles
attentions	likes	reactions	travels	wants

Some plural nouns are most commonly used without a determiner.

There were one or two cases where people returned goods.
There is only one applicant, which simplifies matters.
They treated us like vermin.

Here is a list of plural nouns that are most commonly used without a determiner:

airs	expenses	matters	solids
appearances	figures	refreshments	talks
events	goods	riches	vermin

Some plural nouns can be used both with or without determiners.

The house was raided by police.
We called the police.
A luxury hotel was to be used as headquarters.
The city has been his headquarters for five years.
We didn't want it to dampen spirits which were required to remain positive.
The last few miles really lifted our spirits.

Here is a list of plural nouns that can be used with or without a determiner:

arms	grounds	particulars	specifics
basics	handcuffs	people	spirits
brains	headquarters	police	supplies
clergy	interests	poultry	talks
costs	looks	premises	thanks
directions	means	proceeds	tracks
essentials	morals	rates	troops
greens	papers	resources	values

modifiers and other forms of extra information

1.45 Some plural nouns are rarely used alone without a modifier, or some other form of extra information, because they need supporting material.

He doesn't tolerate <u>bad manners</u>.
Our country's <u>coastal defences</u> need improving.
...the hidden <u>pressures of direct government funding</u>.

Here is a list of plural nouns that are rarely used alone without a modifier or some other extra information:

affairs	effects	materials	relations	wastes
conditions	forces	matters	remains	ways
defences	hopes	pressures	sands	words
demands	lines	proportions	services	works
details	manners	quarters	thoughts	writings

typical meanings: clothes and tools

1.46   Two special groups of nouns are usually plural: nouns referring to clothes and some other things that people wear, and nouns referring to tools and some other things that people use.

This is because some clothes and tools, such as *trousers* and *scissors*, are made up of two similar parts.

She wore brown <u>trousers</u> and a green sweater.
He took off his <u>glasses</u>.
...using the <u>pliers</u> from the toolbox.

When you want to refer to these items in general, or to an unspecified number of them, you use the plural form with no determiner.

Never poke <u>scissors</u> into a light bulb socket.
The man was watching the train through <u>binoculars</u>.

Here is a list of some plural nouns that refer to clothes and other things that people wear:

braces	jeans	panties	specs	trunks
briefs	jodhpurs	pants	spectacles	underpants
cords	knickers	pyjamas	sunglasses	
dungarees	leggings	shorts	tights	
glasses	overalls	slacks	trousers	

Here is a list of plural nouns that refer to tools and other things that people use:

binoculars	dividers	pliers	secateurs	tweezers
clippers	nutcrackers	scales	shears	
compasses	pincers	scissors	tongs	

When you want to refer to a single piece of clothing or a single tool, you use *some* or *a pair of* in front of the noun. You refer to more than one item by using a number or a quantity expression with *pairs of*.

I got <u>some scissors</u> out of the kitchen drawer.
I went out to buy <u>a pair of scissors</u>.
He was wearing <u>a pair of</u> old grey <u>trousers</u>.
Liza has <u>three pairs of jeans</u>.

You can also use *a pair of* when you are talking about things such as gloves, shoes, and socks that typically occur in twos.

...a pair of new gloves.

A possessive determiner such as *my* can be used instead of *a*.

...his favourite pair of shoes.

When you use *a pair of* with a noun in the plural form, the verb is singular if it is in the same clause. If the verb is in a following relative clause, it is usually plural.

It is likely that a new pair of shoes brings more happiness to a child than a new car brings to a grown-up.
I always wear a pair of long pants underneath, or a pair of pyjamas is just as good.
He put on a pair of brown shoes, which were waiting there for him.
He wore a pair of earphones, which were plugged into a radio.

You use a plural pronoun after *a pair of*.

She went to the wardrobe, chose a pair of shoes, put them on and leaned back in the chair.
He brought out a pair of dark glasses and handed them to Walker.

Referring to groups: collective nouns

1.47 Some nouns in English refer to a group of people or things. These nouns are called **collective nouns**. They have only one form, but many collective nouns have other meanings in which they are countable nouns with two forms.

singular or plural verb

1.48 When you use a collective noun, you can use either a singular verb or a plural verb after it.

You choose a singular verb if you think of the group as a single unit, and a plural verb if you think of the group as a number of individuals.

Our little group is complete again.
A second group are those parents who feel that we were too harsh.
Our family isn't poor any more.
My family are all perfectly normal.
The enemy was moving slowly to the east.
The enemy were visibly cracking.
His arguments were confined to books which the public was unlikely to read.
The public were deceived by the newspapers.

 In American English, it is more usual to use a singular verb unless the sentence contains an element that clearly refers to more than one person or thing.

The names of many organizations are collective nouns, and can be used with a singular or a plural verb.

The BBC is sending him to Tuscany for the summer.
The BBC are planning to use the new satellite next month.
England was leading 18-0 at half-time.
England are seeking alternatives for their B team.

 American English uses a singular verb for these.

GE reports its second-quarter financial results on July 16.
New England is going to sign him to a long-term contract.

If you want to refer back to a collective noun, you choose a singular pronoun or determiner if the previous verb is singular, and a plural pronoun or determiner if the previous verb is plural.

The government has said it would wish to do this only if there was no alternative.
The government have made up their minds that they're going to win.

ℹ USAGE NOTE

1.49 Note that the words *bacteria*, *data*, and *media* are now often used as collective nouns, that is with either a singular or a plural verb and no change in form. Some careful speakers think they should only be used with a plural verb because they have the rare singular forms *bacterium*, *datum*, and *medium* and are therefore countable nouns.

Medieval Arabic data show that the length of the day has been increasing more slowly than expected.
Our latest data shows more firms are hoping to expand in the near future.

❗ BE CAREFUL

1.50 Although you can use a plural verb after a collective noun, these nouns do not behave like the plural forms of countable nouns. For example, you cannot use numbers in front of them. You cannot say *Three enemy were killed*. You have to say *Three of the enemy were killed*.

list of collective nouns

1.51 Here is a list of common collective nouns:

aristocracy	committee	enemy	herd	panel
army	community	family	jury	press
audience	company	flock	media	proletariat
bacteria	council	gang	navy	public
brood	crew	government	nobility	staff
cast	data	group	opposition	team

Some collective nouns are also **partitives** (nouns that are used to talk about a quantity of something). For example, you talk about *a flock of sheep* and *a herd of cattle*. See paragraph 2.198 for more information about these.

Referring to people and things by name: proper nouns

1.52 When you talk about a particular person, you can use their name. Names are usually called **proper nouns**.

People's names are spelled with a capital letter, and do not have a determiner in front of them.

...Michael Hall.
...Jenny.
...Smith.

Ways of using people's names when you are speaking to them directly are explained in paragraphs 9.95 to 9.99.

1.53 Sometimes a person's name is used to refer to something they create. You can refer to a painting, sculpture, or book by a particular person by using the person's name like a countable noun. You still spell it with a capital letter.

In those days you could buy a Picasso for £300.
I was looking at their Monets and Matisses.
I'm reading an Agatha Christie at the moment.

You can refer to music composed or performed by a particular person by using the person's name like an uncountable noun.

I remembered it while we were listening to the Mozart.
...instead of playing Chopin and Stravinsky all the time.

relationship nouns

1.54 Nouns that refer to relationships between the people in a family, such as *mother*, *dad*, *aunt*, and *grandpa*, can also be used like names to address people or refer to them. They are then spelled with a capital letter.

I'm sure Mum will be pleased.

titles

1.55 Words that show someone's social status or job are called **titles**. They are spelled with a capital letter.

You use a title in front of a person's name, usually their surname or their full name, when you are talking about them in a fairly formal way or are showing respect to them.

...Doctor Barker.
...Lord Curzon.
...Captain Jack Langtry.
...Mrs Ford.

Here is a list of the most common titles that are used before names:

Admiral	Dame	Lord	Private
Archbishop	Doctor	Major	Professor
Baron	Emperor	Miss	Queen
Baroness	Father	Mr	Rabbi
Bishop	General	Mrs	Representative
Brother	Governor	Ms	Saint
Captain	Imam	Nurse	Senator
Cardinal	Inspector	Police Constable	Sergeant
Colonel	Justice	Pope	Sir
Congressman	King	President	Sister
Constable	Lady	Prince	
Corporal	Lieutenant	Princess	

A few titles, such as *King*, *Queen*, *Prince*, *Princess*, *Sir*, and *Lady*, can be followed just by the person's first name.

...Queen Elizabeth.
...Prince Charles' eldest son.

Sir Michael has made it very clear indeed.

Ways of using titles when you are speaking to people directly are explained in paragraphs 9.97 and 9.98.

titles used without names

1.56　Determiners, other modifiers, and phrases with *of* are sometimes used with titles, and the person's name is omitted.

...Her Majesty the Queen and the Duke of Edinburgh.
...the Archbishop of Canterbury.
...the President of the United States.
...the Bishop of Birmingham.

titles used as countable nouns

1.57　Most words that are titles can also be countable nouns, usually without a capital letter.

...lawyers, scholars, poets, <u>presidents</u> and so on.
...a foreign <u>prince</u>.
Maybe he'll be a <u>Prime Minister</u> one day.

other proper nouns

1.58　The names of organizations, institutions, ships, magazines, books, plays, paintings, and other unique things are also proper nouns and are spelled with capital letters.

...British Broadcasting Corporation
...Birmingham University.

They are sometimes used with *the* or another determiner.

...the United Nations ...the Labour Party ...the University of Birmingham ...the Queen Mary ... the Guardian ...the Wall Street Journal ...the British Broadcasting Corporation.

The determiner is not spelled with a capital letter, except in the names of books, plays, and paintings.

...The Grapes of Wrath
...A Midsummer Night's Dream.

Some time expressions are proper nouns, and are dealt with in Chapter 4.

Nouns that are rarely used alone

1.59　There are some nouns that are rarely used alone. They need extra material such as an adjective or a following phrase, because the meaning of the noun would not be clear without it. Some of these nouns have many meanings; others have very little meaning on their own.

For example, you cannot usually refer to someone as *the head* without saying which organization they are head of. Similarly, you cannot say that there was *a note* in someone's voice without describing it as, for example, *a triumphant note* or *a note of triumph*.

These nouns are used on their own only if it is obvious from the context what is meant. For example, if you have just mentioned a mountain and you say *the top*, it is clear that you mean the top of that mountain.

used with modifiers

1.60 A **modifier** is an adjective or a noun that is added to a noun in order to give more information about it.

> *...her wide experience of political affairs.*
> *I detected an apologetic note in the agent's voice.*
> *He did not have British citizenship.*
> *Check the water level.*

For more information on modifiers, see Chapter 2.

extra information after the noun

1.61 Extra information after the noun is usually in the form of a phrase beginning with *of*.

> *...at the top of the hill.*
> *There he saw for himself the extent of the danger.*
> *Ever since the rise of industrialism, education has concentrated on producing workers.*
> *...a high level of interest.*

For more information, see paragraphs 2.272 to 2.302.

always used with modifiers

1.62 Some nouns are always used with a modifier. For example, you would not say that someone is *an eater* because all people eat, but you may want to say that he or she is *a meat eater* or *a messy eater*.

Similarly, if you use *range*, you have to refer to a particular *price range* or *age range*. If you use *wear* to mean *clothing*, you have to say what sort of clothing, for example *sports wear* or *evening wear*.

> *Tim was a slow eater.*
> *...the other end of the age range.*
> *The company has plans to expand its casual wear.*

always used with possessives

1.63 Some nouns are almost always used with a possessive, that is a **possessive determiner**, **'s**, or a prepositional phrase beginning with *of*, because you have to show who or what the thing you are talking about relates to or belongs to.

> *The company has grown rapidly since its formation ten years ago.*
> *Advance warning of the approach of enemies was of the greatest importance.*
> *...the portrait of a man in his prime.*

metaphorical uses

1.64 Nouns that are being used metaphorically (= when one thing is used to describe another thing) often have a modifier or some other form of extra information, often in the form of a phrase beginning with *of*, to show what is really being referred to.

> *...the maze of politics.*
> *He has been prepared to sacrifice this company on the altar of his own political ambitions.*
> *He has worked out a scheme for an economic lifeline by purchasing land.*
> *Lloyd's of London is the heart of the world's insurance industry.*
> *...those on the lower rungs of the professional ladder.*

1.65 Many nouns have some meanings that need a modifier or some other form of extra information, and other meanings that do not.

Here is a list of these nouns:

affair	edge	limit	stage
approach	edition	line	status
area	element	matter	structure
back	end	movement	stuff
band	enterprise	nature	style
base	epidemic	note	system
bottom	experience	period	texture
boundary	extent	point	theory
branch	feeling	position	thought
case	field	power	time
centre	formation	prime	tone
circumstances	fringe	range	top
citizenship	ground	rate	transfer
class	growth	regime	type
condition	head	relic	version
crisis	height	repertoire	view
culture	impression	rise	wave
depth	inception	role	way
development	kind	scale	wear
discovery	length	side	wing
eater	level	sort	world

Adjectives used as nouns: *the poor, the impossible*

1.66 When you want to talk about groups of people who share the same characteristic or quality, you can use *the* + adjective. For example, instead of saying *poor people*, you can say *the poor*.

...the help that's given to the blind.
No effort is made to cater for the needs of the elderly.
...the task of rescuing the injured.
...men and women who would join the sad ranks of the unemployed.
Working with the young is stimulating and full of surprises.
...providing care for the sick, the aged, the workless and the poor.

Note that you never add -s to the adjective, even though it always refers to more than one person.

 BE CREATIVE

1.67 Although some adjectives are commonly used in this way, in fact it is possible to use almost any adjective in this way.

noun–verb agreement

1.68 When the adjective being used as a noun is the subject of a verb, you use a plural form of the verb.

The rich have benefited much more than the poor.

being more specific

1.69 If you want to talk about a more specific group of people, you put a **submodifying adverb** (= an adverb that you put in front of an adjective to give more information about it) or another adjective in front of the headword. For more information about submodifying adverbs, see paragraphs 2.140 to 2.168.

In this anecdote, Ray shows his affection for the very old and the very young.
...the highly educated.
...the urban poor.

If you mention two groups, you sometimes omit *the*.

...a study that compared the diets of rich and poor in several nations.
...to help break down the barriers between young and old.

With a few words such as *unemployed* and *dead*, you can say how many people you are referring to by putting a number in front of them.

We estimate there are about three hundred dead.

qualities

1.70 When you want to refer to the quality of something rather than to the thing itself, you can use the appropriate adjective with *the*.

Don't you think that you're wanting the impossible?
He is still exploring the limits of the possible.
...a mix of the traditional and the modern.

colours

1.71 All colour adjectives can also be used as nouns.

...patches of blue.
...brilliant paintings in reds and greens and blues.

Clothing of a particular colour can be referred to simply by using the colour adjective.

The men wore grey.
...the fat lady in black.

USAGE NOTE

1.72 Nationality adjectives that end in *-ch*, *-sh*, *-se*, or *-ss* can be used in a similar way, unless there is a separate noun for the people. For example, French people are referred to as *the French* but Polish people are referred to as *Poles* or *the Poles*.

For many years the Japanese have dominated the market for Chinese porcelain.
Britons are the biggest consumers of chocolate after the Swiss and the Irish.

Nouns referring to males or females

1.73   English nouns are not masculine, feminine, or neuter in the way that nouns in some other languages are. For example, most names of jobs, such as *teacher*, *doctor*, and *writer*, are used for both men and women.

But some nouns refer only to males and others only to females.

For example, some nouns indicating people's family relationships, such as *father*, *brother*, and *son*, and some nouns indicating people's jobs, such as *waiter* and *policeman*, are used only to refer to males.

In the same way *mother*, *sister*, *daughter*, *waitress*, *actress*, and *sportswoman* are used only to refer to females.

-ess and -woman

1.74   Words that refer to women often end in -*ess*, for example *actress*, *waitress*, and *hostess*. Another ending is -*woman*, as in *policewoman* and *sportswoman*.

> ...his wife Susannah, a former <u>air stewardess</u>.
> A <u>policewoman</u> dragged me out of the crowd.
> Steph Burton was named <u>sportswoman</u> of the year.

-man and -person

1.75   Words ending in -*man* are either used to refer only to men or to both men and women. For example, a *postman* is a man, but a *spokesman* can be a man or a woman.

Some people now use words ending in -*person*, such as *chairperson* and *spokesperson*, instead of words ending in -*man*, in order to avoid appearing to refer specifically to a man.

ⓘ   USAGE NOTE

1.76   Most names of animals are used to refer to both male and female animals, for example *cat*, *elephant*, *horse*, *monkey*, and *sheep*.

In some cases there are different words that refer specifically to male animals or female animals, for example a male horse is a *stallion* and a female horse is a *mare*.

In other cases the general name for the animal is also the specific word for males or females: *dog* also refers more specifically to male dogs, *duck* also refers more specifically to female ducks.

Many of these specific words are rarely used, or used mainly by people who have a special interest in animals, such as farmers or vets.

Here is a list of some common specific words for male and female animals:

stallion	~	vixen	ram	tiger
mare	dog	~	ewe	tigress
~	bitch	gander	~	~
bull	~	goose	buck	boar
cow	drake	~	hind	sow
~	duck	lion	stag	
cock	~	lioness	doe	
hen	fox	~	~	

Referring to activities and processes: -ing nouns

1.77   When you want to talk about an action, activity, or process in a general way, you can use a noun that has the same form as the *-ing* participle of a verb.

These nouns are called different things in different grammars: gerunds, verbal nouns, or *-ing* forms. In this grammar they are referred to as **-ing nouns**.

It is sometimes difficult to distinguish an **-ing noun** from an **-ing participle**, and it is usually not necessary to do so. However, there are times when it is clearly a noun, for example when it is the subject of a verb, the object of a verb, or the object of a preposition.

Swimming is a great sport.
The emphasis was on *teaching* rather than *learning*.
The *closing* of so many mills left thousands unemployed.
Some people have never done any public *speaking*.

The spelling of *-ing* nouns is explained in the Reference section. The use of *-ing* adjectives is explained in paragraphs 2.63 to 2.76.

uncountable nouns

1.78   Because *-ing* nouns refer to activities in a general way, they are usually **uncountable nouns**; that is, they have only one form, cannot be used with numbers, and do not usually have a determiner in front of them.

For more information on uncountable nouns, see paragraphs 1.23 to 1.33.

1.79   You often use an *-ing* noun because it is the only noun form available for certain verbs, such as *eat, hear, go, come,* and *bless*. Other verbs have related nouns that are not *-ing* nouns: for example *see* and *sight, arrive* and *arrival, depart* and *departure*.

Eating is an important part of a cruise holiday.
...loss of *hearing* in one ear.
Only 6 per cent of children receive any further *training* when they leave school.

used with adjectives

1.80   If you want to describe the action expressed by the noun, you use one or more adjectives or nouns in front of it.

He served a jail sentence for *reckless driving*.
The police need *better training* in dealing with the mentally ill.
He called for a national campaign against *under-age drinking*.

1.81   A few *-ing* nouns, mostly words for sporting or leisure activities, are much more common than their related verbs. In some cases there is no verb, although it is always possible to invent one. For example, you are more likely to say *We went caravanning round France* than *We caravanned round France*.

Here is a list of the commonest of these nouns:

angling	hang-gliding	skateboarding	windsurfing
boating	mountaineering	snorkelling	yachting
bowling	paragliding	snowboarding	
canoeing	shoplifting	surfing	
caravanning	shopping	weightlifting	
electioneering	sightseeing	window-shopping	

Although these words are not always associated with a verb, most of them can be used as -ing participles.

I spent the afternoon <u>window-shopping</u> with Grandma.

1.82 Some -ing nouns that are related to verbs are **countable nouns**. They generally refer to the result of an action or process, or to an individual instance of it. Sometimes their meaning is not closely related to that of the verb.

Here is a list of the commonest of these nouns:

beginning	feeling	meeting	setting	turning
being	finding	offering	showing	warning
building	hearing	painting	sitting	
drawing	meaning	saying	suffering	

For more information on countable nouns, see paragraphs 1.15 to 1.22.

Compound nouns: *car park, mother-in-law, breakdown*

1.83 A single noun is often not enough to refer clearly to a person or thing. When this is the case, a **compound noun** can be used. A compound noun is a fixed expression that is made from more than one word, and that behaves as a noun.

Some people write out a new <u>address book</u> every January.
How would one actually choose a small <u>personal computer</u>?
Where did you hide the <u>can opener</u>?
...a private <u>swimming pool</u>.

Once it is clear what you are referring to, it is sometimes possible to use just the second word of a two-word compound noun. For example, after mentioning *a swimming pool*, you can just refer to *the pool*.

Most compound nouns consist of two words, but some consist of three or more words.

...a vase of <u>lily of the valley</u>.

1.84 Some compound nouns are written with hyphens instead of spaces between the words.

I'm looking forward to a <u>lie-in</u> tomorrow.
He's very good at <u>problem-solving</u>.
Judy's <u>brother-in-law</u> lived with his family.

Some compound nouns, especially very frequent ones, are written as one word.

...patterned <u>wallpaper</u>.
They copied questions from the <u>blackboard</u>.

In some cases, you can choose whether to write a compound noun with or without a hyphen, or with or without a space. For example, both *air-conditioner* and *air conditioner* are possible, and both *postbox* and *post box* are possible.

A few compound nouns that consist of more than two words are written partly with hyphens and partly with spaces, for example *back-seat driver* and *bring-and-buy sale*.

...children from <u>one-parent families</u>.
...a <u>Parent-Teacher Association</u>.

1.85 Compound nouns may be countable, uncountable, singular, or plural.
Here is a list of some common countable compound nouns:

address book	drawing pin	package holiday
air conditioner	driving licence	Parent-Teacher Association
air raid	estate agent	
alarm clock	fairytale	parking meter
assembly line	father-in-law	pen-friend
baby-sitter	film star	personal computer
back-seat driver	fire engine	polar bear
bank account	fork-lift truck	police station
bird of prey	frying pan	post office
book token	guided missile	rolling pin
blood donor	health centre	sister-in-law
bride-to-be	heart attack	sleeping bag
bring-and-buy sale	high school	swimming pool
brother-in-law	human being	T-shirt
burglar alarm	letter box	tea bag
bus stop	lily of the valley	telephone number
can opener	mother-in-law	traveller's cheque
car park	musical instrument	washing machine
compact disc	nervous breakdown	X-ray
contact lens	news bulletin	youth hostel
credit card	old hand	zebra crossing
dining room	one-parent family	

1.86 Here is a list of some common uncountable compound nouns:

air conditioning	do-it-yourself	hire purchase
air-traffic control	dry-cleaning	income tax
barbed wire	family planning	junk food
birth control	fancy dress	law and order
blood pressure	fast food	lost property
bubble bath	first aid	mail order
capital punishment	food poisoning	mineral water
central heating	further education	nail varnish
chewing gum	general knowledge	natural history
common sense	hay fever	old age
cotton wool	heart failure	pocket money
data processing	higher education	remote control

science fiction	soda water	unemployment benefit
show business	stainless steel	value added tax
show jumping	table tennis	washing powder
sign language	talcum powder	washing-up liquid
social security	toilet paper	water-skiing
social work	tracing paper	writing paper

1.87 Here is a list of some common singular compound nouns:

age of consent	general public	open air
arms race	generation gap	private sector
brain drain	greenhouse effect	public sector
continental divide	hard core	rank and file
cost of living	human race	solar system
death penalty	labour force	sound barrier
diplomatic corps	labour market	space age
dress circle	long jump	welfare state
fire brigade	mother tongue	women's movement

1.88 Here is a list of some common plural compound nouns:

armed forces	industrial relations	social services
baked beans	inverted commas	social studies
civil rights	licensing laws	swimming trunks
current affairs	luxury goods	vocal cords
French fries	modern languages	winter sports
grass roots	natural resources	yellow pages
high heels	race relations	
human rights	road works	

composition of compound nouns

1.89 Most compound nouns consist of two nouns, or an adjective and a noun.

I listened with anticipation to the radio news bulletin.
...a big dining room.
Old age is a time for reflection and slowing down.

However, some compound nouns are related to **phrasal verbs**. These are sometimes written with a hyphen, and sometimes as one word. They are rarely written as separate words.

The President was directly involved in the Watergate cover-up.
I think there's been a mix-up.
...a breakdown of diplomatic relations.
The singer is making a comeback.

Here is a list of frequent nouns based on phrasal verbs. They are shown in this list in the form in which they are most frequently written, either with a hyphen or as one word.

backup	buyout	drawback	meltdown	set-up
bailout	check-in	feedback	mix-up	show-off
blackout	checkout	follow-up	passer-by	slowdown
breakaway	check-up	giveaway	run-in	takeaway
breakdown	comeback	handout	runner-up	take-off
break-in	countdown	kick-off	run-off	turnover
breakout	cover-up	lead-up	run-up	warm-up
break-up	crackdown	lookout	sell-out	
build-up	cutbacks	make-up	setback	

For more information about phrasal verbs, see paragraphs 3.83 to 3.116.

 **USAGE NOTE**

1.90 In some cases, the meaning of a compound noun is not obvious from the words it consists of.

For example, someone's *mother tongue* is not the tongue of their mother but the language they learn as a child, and an *old hand* is not a hand that is old but a person who is experienced at doing a particular job.

 In other cases, the compound noun consists of words that do not occur on their own, for example *hanky-panky*, *hodge-podge*, and *argy-bargy*. These nouns are usually used in informal conversation rather than formal writing.

Most of what he said was a load of hocus-pocus.
She is usually involved in some sort of jiggery-pokery.

plural forms

1.91 The plural forms of compound nouns vary according to the type of words that they consist of. If the final word of a compound noun is a countable noun, the plural form of the countable noun is used when the compound noun is plural.

Air raids were taking place every night.
...health centres, banks, post offices, and police stations.
Loud voices could be heard through letter boxes.
...the refusal of dockers to use fork-lift trucks.

For full information about the plural forms of countable nouns, see the Reference section.

Compound nouns that are directly related to phrasal verbs usually have a plural form ending in -s.

Nobody seems disturbed about cover-ups when they are essential to the conduct of a war.
Naturally, I think people who drive smarter, faster cars than mine are show-offs.

A few compound nouns are less directly related to phrasal verbs, and consist of a countable noun and an adverb. In these cases, the plural form of the countable noun is used before the adverb when the compound noun is plural.

For example, the plural of *runner-up* is *runners-up*, and the plural of *summing-up* is *summings-up*.

Passers-by helped the victim, who was unconscious.

Compound nouns that consist of two nouns linked by the prepositions *of* or *in*, or a noun followed by *to-be*, have a plural form in which the first noun in the compound is plural.

I like birds of prey and hawks particularly.
She was treated with contempt by her sisters-in-law.
Most mothers-to-be in their forties opt for this test.

Some compound nouns have been borrowed from other languages, mainly French and Latin, and therefore do not have normal English plural forms.

Agents provocateurs were sent to cause trouble.
The nouveaux riches of younger states are building palatial mansions for themselves.

1.92 Compound nouns are fixed expressions. However, nouns can always be used in front of other nouns in order to refer to something in a more specific way. For the use of nouns as **modifiers**, see paragraphs 2.169 to 2.174.

Talking about people and things without naming them: pronouns

1.93 When you use language, both in speech and writing, you constantly refer to things you have already mentioned or are about to mention.

You can do this by repeating the noun phrase, but unless there is a special reason to do so, you are more likely to use a **pronoun** instead.

Pronouns make statements less repetitive.

John took the book and opened it.
Deborah recognized the knife as hers.
Shilton was pleased with himself.
This is a very busy place.

However, if you have mentioned two or more different things, you usually have to repeat the noun phrase to make it clear which thing you are now talking about.

Leaflets and scraps of papers were scattered all over the floor. I started to pick up the leaflets.
I could see a lorry and a car. The lorry stopped.

For other ways of talking about things that have already been mentioned, see paragraphs 10.2 to 10.39.

types of pronoun

1.94 There are several different types of pronoun:

▶ **personal pronouns**. See paragraphs 1.95 to 1.106.
▶ **possessive pronouns**. See paragraphs 1.107 to 1.110.
▶ **reflexive pronouns**. See paragraphs 1.111 to 1.118.
▶ **generic pronouns**. See paragraphs 1.119 to 1.123.
▶ **demonstrative pronouns**. See paragraphs 1.124 to 1.127.
▶ **indefinite pronouns**. See paragraphs 1.128 to 1.141.
▶ **reciprocal pronouns**. See paragraphs 1.142 to 1.145.
▶ **relative pronouns**. See paragraphs 1.146 to 1.150.
▶ **interrogative pronouns**. See paragraphs 1.151 to 1.153.

There are a few other words that can be used as pronouns. For more information about these, see paragraphs 1.154 to 1.161.

Talking about people and things: personal pronouns

1.95 You use **personal pronouns** to refer to yourself, the people you are talking to, or the people or things you are talking about.

There are two sets of personal pronouns: subject pronouns and object pronouns.

subject pronouns

1.96 Subject pronouns refer to the subject of a clause.

Here is a table of subject pronouns:

	singular	plural
1st person	I	we
2nd person	you	
3rd person	he she it	they

1.97 You refer to yourself by using the pronoun *I*. *I* is always written with a capital letter.

I don't know what to do.
I think I made the wrong decision.
May I ask why Stephen's here?

you

1.98 You refer to the person or people you are talking to as *you*. Note that the same word is used for the singular and the plural.

You may have to wait a bit.
Would you come and have a drink?
How did you get on?

You is also used to refer to people in general, rather than to the person you are talking or writing to. For more information on this, see paragraph 1.120.

If you want to make it clear that you are addressing more than one person, you can create a plural form by using *you* followed by a determiner, a number or a noun. Forms like this can also be used in object position.

My granddad wants you both to come round next Saturday.
As you all know, this is a challenge.

Here is a list of the most common plural forms of *you*.

you all	you lot	you three
you guys	you two	you both

You guys and *you lot* are more frequent in informal English. *You lot* is not commonly used in American English.

I love working with you guys.
You guys are great!
So you lot will have to look after yourselves.

Note that people often use *you lot* when they are being very direct with a group of people, as in the last example above.

 Some varieties and dialects of English have developed particular forms of plural *you*. In American English, particularly Southern American English, *y'all* is sometimes used, especially in speech.

What did y'all eat for breakfast?
I want to thank y'all.

In some dialects of British and American English, *yous* and *youse* are used as plural forms: *I know what some of yous might be thinking.*

Another plural form is *you people*. However, this can sound rude, and should only be used if you want to show that you are angry or annoyed with the people you are talking to.

'Why can't you people leave me alone?' he says.
'I can't work with you people,' Zoe said.

Some plural forms of *you* – *you guys*, *you lot*, *you two*, *you three* and *y'all* – can also be used as **vocatives**. For more information on vocatives, see paragraphs 9.95 to 9.99. *You all* and *you both* cannot be used as vocatives.

'Listen, you guys,' she said. 'I'll tell you everything you want.'
Come on, you two. Let's go home.
Bye, y'all!

For more information on *you* as an **object pronoun**, see paragraphs 1.104 to 1.106.

1.99 You refer to a man or a boy as *he*, and to a woman or a girl as *she*.

My father is 78, and he's very healthy and independent.
Billy Knight was a boxer, wasn't he?
Mary came in. She was a good-looking woman.
'Is Sue there?' – 'I'm sorry, she doesn't work here now.'

 it

1.100 You use *it* to refer to anything that is not male or female; for example, an object, a place, an organization, or something abstract.

Have you seen Toy Story? It's a good film for kids.
'Have you been to London?' – 'Yes, it was very crowded.'
How much would the company be worth if it were sold?
It is not an idea that has much public support.

It is often used to refer to an animal when its gender is not known or not considered to be important. Some people also refer to babies in this way.

They punched the crocodile until it let go of her.
If the shark is still around it will not escape.
How Winifred loved the baby! And how Stephanie hated it!

You also use *it* in general statements, for example to refer to a situation, the time, the date, or the weather.

It is very quiet here.
It is half past three.
It is January 19th.
It is rainy and cold.

For more information on the use of *it* in general statements, see paragraphs 9.31 to 9.45.

Note that *it* is also an **object pronoun**. For more information on this, see paragraphs 1.104 to 1.106.

ℹ USAGE NOTE

1.101 Although *it* is used as a pronoun to refer to something that is not male or female, *she* is sometimes used to refer to ships, cars, and countries. Some people do not like this usage.

When the repairs had been done she was a fine and beautiful ship.

---

we

1.102 You use *we* to refer to a group of people that includes yourself. The group can be:

▶ you and the person or people you are talking to

Where shall we meet, Sally?

▶ you and the person or people you are talking to and one or more others not there at the time

We aren't exactly gossips, you and I and Watson.

▶ you and one or more other people, but not including the person or people you are talking to

I do the washing; he does the cooking; we share the washing-up.

▶ any group that you feel yourself to be part of, such as a school, your local community, or even mankind as a whole. For more information on this, see paragraph 1.122.

they

1.103 You use *they* to refer to a group of things, or to a group of people not including yourself or the person or people you are talking to.

All the girls think he's great, don't they?
Newspapers reach me on the day after they are published.
Winters here vary as they do elsewhere.

They is also often used to refer to people in general. For more information on this, see paragraph 1.123.

object pronouns

1.104 Object pronouns refer to the same sets of people or things as the corresponding subject pronouns.

Here is a table of object pronouns:

	singular	plural
1st person	me	us
2nd person	you	
3rd person	him her it	them

position in clause

1.105 Object pronouns are used as the object of a clause.

The nurse washed me with cold water.
He likes you; he said so.
The man went up to the cat and started stroking it.

They can be the indirect object of a clause.

Send us a card so we'll know where you are.
A man gave him a car.
You have to offer them some kind of incentive.

They can also be the object of a preposition.

She must have felt intimidated by me.
Madeleine, I want to talk to you immediately.
We were all sitting in a café with him.

1.106 Object pronouns can also be used after **linking verbs**. For example, you can say *It was me, It's her*. However, in formal or written English, people sometimes use a subject pronoun after a linking verb. For example, *It was I, It is she*.

For more information on linking verbs, see paragraphs 3.126 to 3.181.

Talking about possession: possessive pronouns

1.107 When you are talking about people or things, you often want to say how they are connected with each other. There are several different ways in which you can do this, but you usually do it by using a **possessive pronoun** to show that something belongs to someone or is associated with them.

Here is a table showing possessive pronouns:

	singular	**plural**
1st person	mine	ours
2nd person	yours	
3rd person	his hers	theirs

Note that *its* cannot be used as a possessive pronoun.

typical use

1.108 You use possessive pronouns when you are talking about the same type of thing that has just been mentioned but want to show that it belongs to someone else.

For example, in the sentence *Jane showed them her passport, then Richard showed them his*, *his* refers to a passport and shows that it belongs to Richard.

Possessive pronouns are often used to contrast two things of the same type that belong to or are associated with different people. For example, *Sarah's house is much bigger than ours.*

Her parents were in Malaya, and so were mine.
He smiled at her and laid his hand on hers.
Is that coffee yours or mine?
My marks were higher than his.

Fred put his profits in the bank, while Julia spent <u>hers</u> on a car.
That's the difference between his ideas and <u>ours</u>.
It was his fault, not <u>theirs</u>.

used with *of*

1.109 Possessive pronouns are used with *of* to add information to a noun phrase. This structure suggests that you are talking about one of a group of things.

For example, if you say *a friend of mine* you are talking about one of a number of friends whereas if you say *my friend* you are talking about one friend in particular.

He was an old friend <u>of mine</u>.
A student <u>of yours</u> has just been to see me.
David Lodge? I've just read a novel <u>of his</u>.
It was hinted to him by some friends <u>of hers</u>.
The room was not a favourite <u>of theirs</u>.

1.110 For other ways of showing that something belongs to someone or is connected with them, see paragraphs 1.211 to 1.221.

Referring back to the subject: reflexive pronouns

1.111 When you want to show that the object or the indirect object of a verb is the same person or thing as the subject of the verb, you use a **reflexive pronoun**.

Some verbs are very frequently used with reflexive pronouns. For information about these, see paragraphs 3.26 to 3.31.

Here is a table of reflexive pronouns:

	singular	plural
1st person	myself	ourselves
2nd person	yourself	yourselves
3rd person	himself herself itself	themselves

!   BE CAREFUL

1.112 Unlike personal pronouns and possessive pronouns, there are two forms of the reflexive pronoun used for the second person. You use *yourself* when you are talking to one person. You use *yourselves* when you are talking to more than one person, or referring to a group that includes the person you are talking to.

used as object

1.113 You use a reflexive pronoun to make it clear that the object of a verb is the same person or thing as the subject of the verb, or to emphasize this.

For example, *John killed himself* means that John did the killing, and he was also the person who was killed.

He forced <u>himself</u> to remain absolutely still.
She stretched <u>herself</u> out on the sofa.
I'm sure history repeats <u>itself</u>.

We all shook hands and introduced <u>ourselves</u>.
The boys formed <u>themselves</u> into a line.
Here is the question you have to ask <u>yourselves</u>.

You also use reflexive pronouns to show or emphasize that the indirect object of a verb is the same person or thing as the subject of the verb. For example, in the sentence *Ann poured herself a drink*, Ann did the pouring and she was also the person who the drink was for.

Here's the money, you can go and buy <u>yourself</u> a watch.

❗ BE CAREFUL

1.114 Reflexive pronouns are not usually used with actions that people normally do to themselves, such as washing, dressing, or shaving. So you do not usually say *He shaves himself every morning.*

You can, however, sometimes use reflexive pronouns with these actions for emphasis, or to talk about a surprising event, such as a child doing something that they were not previously able to do.

used as objects of prepositions

1.115 If the subject of a clause and the object of a preposition refer to the same person, and the clause does not have a direct object, you use a reflexive pronoun after the preposition.

I was thoroughly ashamed of <u>myself</u>.
Barbara stared at <u>herself</u> in the mirror.
We think of <u>ourselves</u> as members of the local community.
They can't cook for <u>themselves</u>.

However, if the clause does have a direct object, you usually use a personal pronoun after the preposition.

I will take it home with <u>me</u>.
They put the book between <u>them</u> on the kitchen table.
I shivered and drew the rug around <u>me</u>.
Mrs Bixby went out, slamming the door behind <u>her</u>.

Note that if the clause has a direct object and it is not obvious that the subject of the clause and the object of the preposition refer to the same person, you use a reflexive pronoun. For example, *The Managing Director gave the biggest pay rise to himself.*

used for emphasis or contrast

1.116 Especially in speech, people sometimes use reflexive pronouns rather than personal pronouns as the object of a preposition, in order to emphasize them.

...people like <u>myself</u> who are politically active.
...the following conversation between <u>myself</u> and a fifteen-year-old girl.
The circle spread to include <u>himself</u> and Ferdinand.
People like <u>yourself</u> still find new things to say about Shakespeare.
There is always someone worse off than <u>yourself</u>.
With the exception of a few Algerians and <u>ourselves</u>, everyone spoke Spanish.

1.117 You can use reflexive pronouns in addition to nouns or personal pronouns. You usually do this in order to make it clear or to emphasize who or what you are referring to.

I myself sometimes say things I don't mean.
Sally herself came back.

You also use a reflexive pronoun to compare or contrast one person or thing with another.

His friend looked as miserable as he felt himself.
It is not Des Moines I miss, but Iowa itself.

The reflexive pronoun follows the noun or pronoun that it relates to.

It is hot in London; but I myself can work better when it's hot.
The town itself was so small that it didn't have a priest.
The lane ran right up to the wood itself.

It can also be placed at the end of the clause.

I am not a particularly punctual person myself.
You'll probably understand better when you are a grandparent yourself.
It is rare for Governments to take the initiative themselves.

1.118   You use a reflexive pronoun to emphasize that someone did something without any help or interference from anyone else. In this use, the reflexive pronoun is normally placed at the end of the clause.

She had printed the card herself.
I'll take it down to the police station myself.
Did you make these yourself?

People in general: generic pronouns

1.119   When you want to talk about people in general, you can use a **generic pronoun**.

Here is a list of pronouns that can be used as generic pronouns:

Subject:	you	one	we	they
Object:	you	one	us	them
Possessive:	yours	–	ours	theirs
Reflexive:	yourself	oneself	ourselves	themselves

> **you, yours and yourself**

1.120   *You* is sometimes used to make statements about people in general, or about a person in a situation that you are imagining. *You* is used in this way in both subject and object position. The possessive form *yours* and the reflexive form *yourself* can also be used as generic pronouns.

To be a good doctor you need to have good communication skills.
Champagne can give you a headache.
Once you've bought a physical book, you own it: you can lend it to people, donate it, and, well, it's yours.
When you live alone you have to force yourself to go out more.

In informal English, you can use *you get* or *you have* to make a general statement about something that exists in the world.

You get some old people who are very difficult.
Anytime you have over eight inches of snow, driving becomes problematic.

one and oneself

1.121   In formal writing, *one* is sometimes used instead of *you*. *One* can be used in subject or object position. The reflexive form *oneself* is also used, but there is no possessive pronoun form of *one*.

Going round Italy, one is struck by the number of opera houses there are.
This scene makes one realize how deeply this community has been afflicted.
If one puts oneself up for public office, then it is inappropriate that one should behave badly.

we, us, ours and ourselves

1.122   You can refer to a general group that includes yourself as *we* or, in object position, *us*. This group can be all of mankind, or it can be a smaller group such as a nation or a community. The possessive form *ours* and the reflexive form *ourselves* can also be used in this way.

We all need money.
This survey gives us insight into our attitudes and behaviour as a nation.
No other language has ever advanced as far, as fast, as ours.
We need a change of government; just ridding ourselves of the prime minister isn't enough.

they, them, theirs and themselves

1.123   You can use *they* to refer to people in general.

Isn't that what they call love?

They can also refer to a group of people whose identity does not need to be stated. For example, in the sentence *They've given John another pay rise* it is clear that *they* refers to John's employers.

'Don't worry', I said to Mother, 'they are moving you from this ward soon.'

You can also use *they* in subject position, or *them* in object position, to refer to an individual when you do not know, or do not want to specify, whether the individual is male or female. The possessive form *theirs* and the reflexive form *themselves* can also be used in this way. This use is very common after:

▶ the **indefinite pronouns** *anyone*, *anybody*, *someone* and *somebody*. These are explained in paragraphs 1.128 to 1.141.

▶ singular nouns such as *person*, *parent* and *teacher*, which do not specify whether the person is male or female

If anyone wants to be a childminder, they must attend a course.
If I think someone is having problems, I will spend hours talking to them.
A person's body fat determines how long they can withstand cold water.

Note that the plural form of the verb is always used after *they*, even when it refers to only one person.

You can also use *they*, *them*, *theirs* and *themselves* to refer to:

▶ the **indefinite pronouns** *everyone*, *everybody*, *no one* and *nobody*. These are explained in paragraphs 1.128 to 1.141.

▶ noun phrases with the determiners *each*, *every* and *any*

In these cases, although the pronouns or noun phrases are grammatically singular, they refer to groups of people.

I never avoid my obligations and I expect everyone else to meet theirs.
Each parent was sent an individual letter informing them of the situation.

We want every player to push themselves to get into the team.

Another way is to use *he or she* instead of *they*, *him or her* instead of *them*, *himself or herself* instead of *themselves* and *his or hers* instead of *theirs*. This is often used in formal or written English.

Would a young person be able to get a job in Europe? That would depend on which country he or she wanted to go to.
The student should feel that the essay belongs to him or her.

Some people use *he* and *him* in general statements or after indefinite pronouns, but many people object to this use because it suggests that the person being referred to is male.

Referring to a particular person or thing: *this*, *that*, *these* and *those*

1.124 When *this*, *that*, *these*, and *those* are used as pronouns, they are called **demonstrative pronouns**. They are used as the subject or the object of a clause, or the object of a preposition.

Demonstrative pronouns are rarely used as the indirect object of a clause, because the indirect object is usually a person, and demonstrative pronouns normally refer to things.

this and *that*

1.125 *This* and *that* are usually used as pronouns only when they refer to things. You use them instead of a singular countable noun or an uncountable noun. *This* refers to something that is close to you in place or time, and *that* refers to something that is more distant in place or time.

This is a list of the rules.
This is the most important part of the job.
The biggest problem was the accent. That was difficult for me.
That looks interesting.

1.126 *This* and *that* are used as pronouns to refer to a person when you are identifying someone or asking who they are.

Who's this?
He stopped and looked at a photograph that stood on the dressing table. Is this your wife?
Was that Patrick on the phone?

When you are introducing people, you can say *This is Mary* or *This is Mr and Mrs Baker*. Note that you use *this* even when you are introducing more than one person.

these and *those*

1.127 *These* and *those* can be used as pronouns instead of a plural countable noun. They are most often used to refer to things, although they can be used to refer to people. *These* refers to a number of people and things that are close to you in place or time, and *those* refers to a number of people and things that are more distant in place or time.

'I brought you these.' Adam held out a bag of grapes.
Vitamin tablets usually contain vitamins A, C, and D. These are available from any child health clinic.
These are no ordinary students.
It may be impossible for them to pay essential bills, such as those for heating.
Those are easy questions to answer.

> There are a lot of people who are seeking employment, and a great number of those are married women.

> This, that, these, and those can also be **definite determiners**. For more information, see paragraphs 1.184 to 1.193. See also *Referring back* and *Referring forward* in Chapter 10.

Referring to people and things in a non-specific way: *someone, anyone, everyone,* etc.

1.128 When you want to refer to people or things but you do not know exactly who or what they are, or their identity is not important, you can use an **indefinite pronoun** such as *someone, anyone,* or *everyone*. An indefinite pronoun shows only whether you are talking about people or about things, rather than referring to a specific person or thing.

> I was there for over an hour before *anybody* came.
> Jack was waiting for *something*.

Here is a list of indefinite pronouns:

anybody	everybody	nobody	somebody
anyone	everyone	no one	someone
anything	everything	nothing	something

 Note that all indefinite pronouns are written as one word except *no one*. It is always two words in American English, but in British English it can also be spelled with a hyphen: *no-one*.

used only with singular verbs

1.129 You always use singular verbs with indefinite pronouns.

> Is anyone here?
> Everybody recognizes the importance of education.
> Everything was ready.
> Nothing is certain in this world.

referring to things

1.130 You use the indefinite pronouns ending in -*thing* to talk about objects, ideas, situations, or activities.

> Can I do anything?
> Jane said nothing for a moment.

referring to people

1.131 You use the indefinite pronouns ending in -*one* and -*body* to refer to people.

> It had to be someone like Dan.
> Why does everybody believe in the law of gravity?

Note that indefinite pronouns ending in -*body* are more frequent in informal English.

used with personal pronouns and possessive determiners

1.132 Although you use singular verbs with indefinite pronouns, if you want to refer back to an indefinite pronoun, you use the plural pronouns *they, them,* or *themselves*, or the possessive determiner *their*.

Ask anyone. They'll tell you.
There's no way of telling somebody why they've failed.
No one liked being young then as they do now.
Everybody's enjoying themselves.
Everyone put their pens down.

See paragraph 1.123 for more information about *they* used to refer to one person.

 USAGE NOTE

1.133 In more formal English, some people prefer to use *he, him, his,* or *himself* to refer back to an indefinite pronoun, but many people dislike this use because it suggests that the person being referred to is male.

If someone consistently eats a lot of fatty foods, it is not surprising if he ends up with clogged arteries.
Everybody has his dream.

For other ways of using pronouns when you do not want to specify whether the person you are talking about is male or female, see paragraph 1.123.

's

1.134 You add 's (apostrophe s) to an indefinite pronoun to refer to things that belong to or are associated with people.

She was given a room in someone's studio.
That was nobody's business.
I would defend anyone's rights.
Everything has been arranged to everybody's satisfaction.

! **BE CAREFUL**

1.135 You do not usually add 's to indefinite pronouns referring to things. So, for example, you would be more likely to say *the value of something* than *something's value*.

adding information

1.136 When you want to give more information about the person or thing referred to by an indefinite pronoun, you can use a phrase or a clause after it.

Anyone over the age of 18 can apply.
He would prefer to have somebody who had a background in the humanities.

1.137 You can also use adjectives to add information. Note that adjectives are placed after the indefinite pronoun rather than in front of it, and that you do not use a determiner. You do not say *an important someone*, you say *someone important*.

What was needed was someone practical.
They are doing everything possible to take care of you.
There is nothing wrong with being popular.

used with *else*

1.138 If you have already mentioned a person or thing, and you want to refer to a different person or thing, or an additional one, you use *else* after an indefinite pronoun.

Somebody else will have to go out there.
She couldn't think of anything else.

Everyone knows what everyone else is doing.
He got that job because nobody else wanted it.

Note that if you want to show association or possession with an indefinite pronoun and *else*, you add the *'s* to *else*.

Problems always became someone else's fault.
No one has control over anyone else's career.

structures used with *some-* and *every-*

1.139   Just like nouns, indefinite pronouns are used as the subject, object, or indirect object of clauses. They can also be used as the objects of prepositions. The indefinite pronouns beginning with *some-* and *every-* are most often used in affirmative clauses.

Everything went according to plan.
I remember somebody putting a pillow under my head.
'Now you'll see something,' he said.
I gave everyone a generous helping.
I want to introduce you to someone who is helping me.
Is everything all right?

They are sometimes used as the subject of a negative clause.

He could tell that something wasn't right.

Note that the indefinite pronouns beginning with *some-* cannot be used as the object of a negative clause, unless they are followed by a phrase or a clause.

He wasn't someone I admired as a writer.

structures used with *any-*

1.140   Indefinite pronouns beginning with *any-* can be used as the object or indirect object of a question or a negative clause.

Don't worry – I won't tell anyone.
You still haven't told me anything.
Take a good look and tell me if you see anything different.
I haven't given anyone their presents yet.

They are often used as the subject of both negative and affirmative questions. Note that they are not used as the subject of a negative statement. You do not say, for example, *Anybody can't come in.*

Does anybody agree with me?
Won't anyone help me?
If anything unusual happens, could you call me on this number?

Note that when you are making an affirmative statement, *anyone* and *anybody* are used to refer to people in general and not to only one person.

Anybody who wants to can come in and buy a car from me.

structures used with *no-*

1.141   Indefinite pronouns beginning with *no-* are always used with the affirmative form of a verb, and they make the clause negative. For more information on **negative statements**, see paragraphs 5.49 to 5.93.

Nobody said a word.
There was nothing you could do, nothing at all.
She was to see no one, to speak to nobody, not even her own children.

Note that they are sometimes used in questions. When this is the case, the answer to the question is usually expected to be *no*.

'Is there nothing I can do?' – 'Not a thing'.
'Is there nobody else?' – 'Not that I know of'.

Showing that people do the same thing: *each other* and *one another*

1.142   *Each other* and *one another* are called **reciprocal pronouns**. They are used to say that people do the same thing, feel the same way, or have the same relationship.

For example, if your brother hates your sister and your sister hates your brother, you can say *My brother and sister hate each other* or *They hate one another*.

Reciprocal pronouns are not used as the subject of a clause. You use them as the object or indirect object of a verb.

We help each other a lot.
You and I understand each other.
We support one another through good times and bad.
They sent each other gifts from time to time.

You also use them as the object of a preposition.

Terry and Mark were jealous of each other.
The two lights were moving towards one another.
They didn't dare to look at one another.

Some verbs are very commonly used with reciprocal pronouns. For more information about these, see paragraphs 3.68 to 3.72.

1.143   Note that there is very little difference between *each other* and *one another*. They are both used to talk about two or more people or things, although some people prefer the use of *each other* when there are only two people or things, and *one another* when there are more than two.

each as subject

1.144   In formal written English, you can also use *each* as the subject of a clause and *the other* as the object of a clause or preposition. So, a more formal way of saying *They looked at each other* is *Each looked at the other*. Note that *each* is always followed by a singular verb.

Each accuses the other of lying.
Each is unwilling to learn from the experience of the others.

Each is also a determiner. For more information about this, see paragraph 1.243.

 's

1.145   You add *'s* (apostrophe s) to *each other*, *one another*, and *the other* to form possessives.

I hope that you all enjoy each other's company.
Apes spend a great deal of time grooming one another's fur.
The males fight fiercely, each trying to seize the other's long neck in its beak.

Joining clauses together: relative pronouns

1.146   When a sentence consists of a main clause followed by a **relative clause** introduced by *who*, *whom*, *which*, or *that*, these words are called **relative pronouns**.

Relative pronouns do two things at the same time. Like other pronouns, they refer to someone or something that has already been mentioned. At the same time they join clauses together.

For more information about relative clauses, see paragraphs 8.83 to 8.116.

who and whom

1.147   *Who* and *whom* always refer to people.

Who can be the subject of a relative clause.

…mathematicians <u>who</u> are concerned with very difficult problems.

In the past, *whom* was normally used as the object of a relative clause. Nowadays, *who* is more often used, although some careful speakers of English think that it is more correct to use *whom*.

…a man <u>who</u> I met recently.
He's the man <u>who</u> I saw last night.
…two girls <u>whom</u> I met in Edinburgh.

Who is sometimes used as the object of a preposition when the object is separated from the preposition. Some careful speakers think that it is more correct to use *whom*.

That's the man <u>who</u> I gave it to.
…those <u>whom</u> we cannot talk to.

Whom is almost always used when the object comes immediately after the preposition.

…Lord Scarman, a man <u>for whom</u> I have immense respect.

which

1.148   *Which* always refers to things. It can be used as the subject or object of a relative clause, or as the object of a preposition. *Which* is often used in British English to introduce relative clauses that refer to things.

…a region <u>which</u> was threatened by growing poverty.
…two horses <u>which he owned</u>.
…the house in <u>which</u> I was born.

Note that *which* cannot be used as the indirect object of a clause.

that

1.149   *That* refers to either people or things. It is used as the subject or the object of a relative clause or the object of a preposition. *That* is generally preferred in American English to introduce relative clauses that refer to things or to combinations of people and things.

…the games <u>that</u> politicians play.
He's the boy <u>that</u> sang the solo last night.
It was the first bed <u>that</u> she had ever slept in.

That cannot be used as the indirect object of a clause.

<code>whose</code>

1.150 *Whose* shows who or what something belongs to or is connected with. Note that it cannot be used by itself, but must come in front of a noun.

> *...the thousands whose lives have been damaged.*
> *There was a chap there whose name I've forgotten.*
> *...predictions whose accuracy will have to be confirmed.*
> *...sharks, whose brains are minute.*

Note that *whose* is not restricted to people.

Asking questions: interrogative pronouns

1.151 One way of asking questions is by using an **interrogative pronoun**.

The interrogative pronouns are *who, whose, whom, what,* and *which.* They are used as the subject or object of a clause, or as the object of a preposition. *Whose* and *which* are also determiners. Other words, such as *where, when, why,* and *how,* are also used to ask questions.

Interrogative pronouns are not used as the indirect object of a clause.

> *Who was at the door?*
> *'There's a car outside.' – 'Whose is it?'*
> *Whom do you support?*
> *What are you doing?*
> *Which is best, gas or electric?*

For more information about structures in which interrogative pronouns are used, see paragraphs 5.10 to 5.36.

1.152 Interrogative pronouns refer to the information you are asking for.

Who, whose, and *whom* are used when you think that the answer to the question will be a person.

> *'He lost his wife.' – 'Who? Terry?'*
> *He looked at the cat. Whose is it? Have you ever seen it before?*
> *'To whom, if I may ask, are you engaged to be married?' – 'To Daniel Orton.'*

Which and *what* are used when you think that the answer to the question will be something other than a person.

> *Is there really a difference? Which do you prefer?*
> *'What did he want?' – 'Maurice's address.'*

<code>reported questions</code>

1.153 Interrogative pronouns are also used to introduce reported questions.

> *I asked her who she had been talking to.*
> *He wondered what Daintry would do now.*

For more information about **reported questions**, see paragraphs 7.32 to 7.38.

Other pronouns

1.154 Many other words can be pronouns, provided that it is clear what is being talked about, because it is then unnecessary to repeat the noun.

For example, most **indefinite determiners** can also be pronouns. For more information about indefinite determiners, see paragraphs 1.223 to 1.250.

Here is a list of indefinite determiners that are also pronouns:

all	each	fewer	more	several
another	either	less	most	some
any	enough	little	much	
both	few	many	neither	

Like all noun phrases, they can be used as the subject, direct object, or indirect object of a clause, or the object of a preposition.

Both were offered jobs immediately.
Children? I don't think she has any.
I saw one girl whispering to another.

1.155 Although *a*, *an*, *every*, and *no* are indefinite determiners, they cannot stand alone as pronouns.

To refer back to a noun phrase that includes the determiner *a* or *an*, you can use the pronoun *one*. Similarly, you use *each* to refer back to a noun phrase that includes *every*, and *none* to refer back to a noun phrase that includes *no*.

Note that *another* and *others* are pronouns, but *other* cannot be a pronoun.

all, both, and each for emphasis

1.156 *All*, *both*, and *each* can be used in addition to nouns or personal pronouns for emphasis, in a similar way to the use of **reflexive pronouns** described in paragraphs 1.116 to 1.118.

The brothers all agreed that something more was needed.
He loved them both.
Ford and Duncan each had their chances.

They come after an auxiliary verb, a modal, or *be*.

They were both still working at their universities.
The letters have all been signed.
The older children can all do the same things together.

Each can also come at the end of the clause.

Three others were fined £200 each.

numbers

1.157 **Numbers** can also be pronouns. For example, the answer to the question *How many children do you have?* is usually *Three* rather than *Three children*.

'How many people are there?' – 'Forty-five.'
Of the other women, two are dancers.
They bought eight companies and sold off five.

For more information on numbers, see paragraphs 2.213 to 2.231.

other pronouns

1.158 The number *one* is a special case. Like other numbers, it is sometimes used to refer to one of a group of things.

One is also used to refer back to a noun phrase with the determiner *a*.

Could I have a bigger one, please?

It can also be used for emphasis after another determiner.

There are systems of communication right through the animal world; each one is distinctive.

One can be used as a **personal pronoun**. This use is explained in paragraph 1.121.

1.159 Note that *the one* and *the ones* can be used to refer to a noun alone, rather than to the whole of the noun phrase. They are nearly always used with a modifier such as an adjective, or some form of information after the noun, such as a prepositional phrase.

'Which poem?' – 'The one they were talking about yesterday.'
There are three bedrooms. Mine is the one at the back.
He gave the best seats to the ones who arrived first.

1.160 You use *the other, the others, others*, or *another* to refer to different members of a group of things or people.

Some writers are greater than others.
One runner was way ahead of all the others.

1.161 If you want to say something about a member of a group of people or things you can use *one*. You can then refer to the rest of the group as *the others*.

The bells are carefully installed so that disconnecting one will have no effect on the others.
They had three little daughters, one a baby, the others twins of twelve.

You use *the one* and *the other* to refer to each of a pair of things.

The same factors push wages and prices up together, the one reinforcing the other.

If you do not wish to specify exactly which of a group you are talking about, you refer to *one or other* of them.

It may be that one or other of them had fears for their health.

Definite and indefinite determiners

1.162 In English, there are two main ways in which you can use a **noun phrase**. You can use it to refer to someone or something, knowing that the person you are speaking to understands which person or thing you are talking about.

The man began to run towards the boy.
Young people don't like these operas.
Thank you very much for your comments.
...a visit to the Houses of Parliament.

Alternatively, you can use a noun phrase to refer to someone or something of a particular type, without saying which person or thing you mean.

There was a man in the lift.
I wish I'd bought an umbrella.
Any doctor would say she didn't know what she was doing.

In order to distinguish between these two ways of using a noun phrase, you use a special class of words called **determiners**. There are two types of determiner, **definite determiners** and **indefinite determiners**. You put them at the beginning of a noun phrase.

Using the definite determiner *the*

1.163 *The* is the most common definite determiner; it is sometimes called the **definite article**.

This, that, these, and *those* are often called **demonstratives** or **demonstrative adjectives**. For more information on these, see paragraphs 1.184 to 1.193.

My, *your*, *his*, *her*, *its*, *our* and *their* are **possessive determiners**. They are also sometimes called **possessive adjectives** or just **possessives**. For more information about these, see paragraphs 1.194 to 1.210.

Here is the list of definite determiners:

the	that	~	his	our
~	these	my	her	their
this	those	your	its	

Note that in English you cannot use more than one definite determiner before a noun.

1.164 Because *the* is the most common definite determiner, you can put *the* in front of any common noun.

She dropped the can into the grass.
The girls were not in the house.

In these examples, the use of *the can* means that a can has already been mentioned; *the grass* is definite because it has already been stated that *she* is outside, and the presence of grass may also have been stated or is presumed; *the girls*, like *the can*, must have been mentioned before; and *the house* means the one where the girls were staying at the time.

pronouncing *the*

1.165 *The* always has the same spelling, but it has three different pronunciations:

▶ /ðə/ when the following word begins with a consonant sound

...the dictionary...the first act...the big box.

▶ /ði/ when the following word begins with a vowel sound

...the exhibition... the effect... the impression.

▶ /ði:/ when it is emphasized

You don't mean the Ernest Hemingway?

See paragraph 1.181 for more information about emphatic uses of *the*.

the with a noun

1.166 You can use a noun phrase consisting just of *the* and a noun when you know that the person you are talking or writing to will understand which person, thing, or group you are referring to.

The expedition sailed out into the Pacific.
...the most obnoxious boy in the school.
He stopped the car in front of the bakery.

nouns referring to one thing only

1.167 Some nouns are used with *the* because they refer to only one person, thing, or group. Some of these are specific names or **proper nouns**, for example titles such as *the Pope*, unique things such as *the Eiffel Tower*, and place names such as *the Atlantic*.

...a concert attended by the Queen.
We went on camel rides to the Pyramids.

See paragraphs 1.52 to 1.58 for more information about proper nouns.

Some are **singular nouns**, that is they refer to something of which there is only one in the world, such as *the ground*, or *the moon*.

The sun began to turn red.
In April and May the wind blows steadily.

See paragraphs 1.34 to 1.40 for more information about singular nouns.

specific places and organizations

1.168 Other nouns are used to talk about just one person, thing, or group in a particular place or organization, so that if you are talking about that place or organization or talking to someone in it, you can use just *the* and the noun.

For example, if there is only one station in a town, the people who live in the town will talk about *the station*. Similarly, people living in Britain talk to each other about *the economy*, meaning *the British economy*, and people working for the same organization might talk about *the boss*, *the union*, or *the canteen* without needing to specify the organization.

The church has been broken into.
There's a wind coming off the river.
We had to get rid of the director.
The mayor is a forty-eight-year-old former labourer.
What is the President doing about all this?

generalizing about people and things

1.169 Normally, if you want to talk generally about all people or things of a particular type, you use the plural form of a noun without a determiner.

However, there are some countable nouns that are used in the singular with *the* to refer to something more general.

For example, you can use *the theatre* or *the stage* to talk about all entertainment performed in theatres. Similarly, *the screen* refers to films in general, and *the law* refers to the system of laws in a country.

For him, the stage was just a way of earning a living.
He was as handsome in real life as he was on the screen.
They do not hesitate to break the law.

Some nouns that normally refer to an individual thing or person can be used in the singular with *the* to refer generally to a system or service in a particular place. For example, you can use *the bus* to talk about a bus service and *the phone* to talk about a telephone system.

How long does it take on the train?
We rang for the ambulance.

Nouns referring to musical instruments can be used in the singular with *the* when you are talking about someone playing, or being able to play, a particular kind of instrument.

You play the oboe, I see, said Simon.
I was playing the piano when he phoned.

using adjectives as nouns

1.170 When you want to talk generally about groups of people who share the same characteristic or quality, you often choose an adjective preceded by *the*.

This project is all about giving employment to the unemployed.

See paragraphs 1.66 to 1.72 for more information about using adjectives as nouns.

formal generalizations

1.171 Nouns referring to plants and animals can be used in the singular with *the* when you are making a statement about every member of a species. For example, if you say *The swift has long, narrow wings*, you mean that all swifts have long, narrow wings.

The primrose can grow abundantly on chalk banks.
Australia is the home of the kangaroo.

Similarly, a noun referring to a part of the human body can be used with *the* to refer to that part of anyone's body.

These arteries supply the heart with blood.
...the arteries supplying the kidneys.

The is sometimes used with other nouns in the singular to make a statement about all the members of a group.

The article focuses on how to protect the therapist rather than on how to cure the patient.

These uses are fairly formal. They are not common in ordinary speech. Usually, if you want to make a statement about all the things of a particular kind, you use the plural form of a noun without a determiner. See paragraph 1.227 for more information about this.

ⓘ USAGE NOTE

1.172 Many common time expressions consist of just *the* and a noun.

We wasted a lot of money in the past.
The train leaves Cardiff at four in the afternoon.
...the changes which are taking place at the moment.

See Chapter 4 for more information about time expressions.

referring back

1.173 In each of the paragraphs above showing uses of *the* and a noun, it is possible to understand who or what is being referred to because the noun phrase is commonly accepted as referring to one particular person, thing, or group.

However, you can use *the* with any noun, if it is obvious who or what you are referring to from what has already been said or written.

The usual way of referring back to a noun is to use a pronoun, but if the second reference does not come immediately after the first one, or if it is not immediately obvious which noun is being referred to, you should use *the*, and the noun again. For example, if you have already mentioned that you were in a train, and then continued to tell a story, you can say afterwards *The train suddenly stopped.*

1.174 You can also use *the* and a noun when you are referring to someone or something closely connected with something you have just mentioned.

For example, you do not usually say *We tried to get into the room, but the door of the room was locked.* You say *We tried to get into the room, but the door was locked*, because it is obvious which door you are referring to.

She stopped and lit a match. The wind almost blew out the flame.

the with longer noun phrases

1.175 Although there are many situations where you use just *the* and a noun, there are other occasions when you need to add something else to the noun in order to make it clear which person, thing, or group you are referring to.

adding adjectives

1.176 Sometimes you can show who or what you are referring to by putting an **adjective** between *the* and the noun.

> This is *the main bedroom*.
> Somebody ought to have done it long ago, remarked *the fat man*.

Sometimes you need to use more than one adjective.

> After the crossroads look out for *the large white building*.

For more information about adjectives, see paragraphs 2.2 to 2.168.

adjectives: expanding

1.177 When you use an adjective between *the* and a noun, you do not always do it in order to make clear who or what is being referred to.

For example, you might want to add further information about someone or something that you have already mentioned. So, if you first refer to someone as *a woman* in a sentence such as *A woman came into the room*, you might later want to refer to her as *the unfortunate woman* or *the smiling woman*.

This is a very common use in written English, especially in stories, but it is not often used in conversation.

> *The astonished waiter* was now watching from the other end of the room.
> *The poor woman* had witnessed terrible violence.
> The loss of pressure caused *the speeding car* to go into a skid.

adding clauses or phrases

1.178 Another way of showing who or what you are referring to is by adding extra information after *the* and a noun, for example a prepositional phrase, a relative clause, a *to*-infinitive, an adverb of place or time, or a phrase introduced by a participle.

So you might refer to particular people at a party by using noun phrases such as *the girl in the yellow dress*, *the woman who spilled her drink*, or *the man smoking a cigar*.

> *The cars in the driveways* were all Ferraris and Porsches.
> *The book that I recommend* now costs over twenty pounds.
> *The thing to aim for* is an office of your own.
> Who made the bed in *the room upstairs*?
> It depends on *the person being interviewed*.

For more information about this type of extra information that is added to a noun, see paragraphs 2.272 to 2.302.

the with uncountable nouns

1.179 You do not normally use *the* with **uncountable nouns** because they refer to something in a general way. However, *the* is necessary if the uncountable noun is followed by extra information such as a clause or a phrase that relates it to a particular person, thing, or group.

For example, you cannot say *I am interested in education of young children*. You have to say *I am interested in the education of young children*.

Babies need <u>the comfort of their mother's arms</u>.
Even <u>the honesty of Inspector Butler</u> was in doubt.
I've no idea about <u>the geography of Scotland</u>.

For more information about uncountable nouns, see paragraphs 1.23 to 1.33.

superlatives

1.180 *The* is also used with **superlative adjectives**.

I'm not <u>the best cook in the world</u>.
They went to <u>the most expensive restaurant in town</u>.

See paragraphs 2.112 to 2.122 for more information about superlative adjectives.

emphasizing *the*

1.181 *The* is often used in front of a noun to indicate that someone or something is the best of its kind.

New Zealand is now <u>the place to visit</u>.

You can also use *the* in front of a person's name to show that you are referring to the most famous person with that name.

You actually met <u>the George Harrison</u>?

When you use *the* in either of these ways, you emphasize it and pronounce it /ðiː/.

the with indefinite determiners

1.182 *The* can be used in front of some **indefinite determiners**, usually to give an indication of amount or quantity.

These indefinite determiners are:

few	little	many	other

...pleasures known only to <u>the few</u>.
...a coup under the leadership of <u>the select few</u>.
He was one of <u>the few who knew where to find me</u>.
We have done <u>the little that is in our power</u>.

You use *the* with *other* to refer to the second of two things, when you have just mentioned one of them.

The men sat at one end of the table and the women at <u>the other</u>.

For more information about indefinite determiners, see paragraphs 1.223 to 1.250.

the with numbers

1.183 *The* is used with *one* and *ones*.

I'm going to have <u>the green one</u>.
The shop was different from <u>the ones I remembered</u>.
...a pair of those old glasses, <u>the ones with those funny</u> square lenses.

The is also used with other **numbers**.

It is a mistake to confuse the two.
Why is she so different from the other two?

See paragraphs 2.208 to 2.239 for more information about numbers.

Definite determiners: using *this*, *that*, *these*, and *those*

1.184 You use the **definite determiners** *this*, *that*, *these*, and *those* to talk about people or things in a definite way.

You use *this* and *these* to talk about people and things that are close to you in place or time. When you talk about people or things that are more distant in place or time, you use *that* and *those*.

You put *this* and *that* in front of singular nouns, uncountable nouns, and the singular pronoun *one*. You put *these* and *those* in front of plural nouns and the plural pronoun *ones*.

This, *that*, *these*, and *those* are often called **demonstratives** or **demonstrative adjectives**.

this and these

1.185 *This* and *these* are used to talk about people or things that are very obvious in the situation that you are in. For example, if you are inside a house, you can refer to it as *this house*. If you are holding some keys in your hand, you can refer to them as *these keys*. If you are at a party, you can refer to it as *this party*.

I have lived in this house my entire life.
I am going to walk up these steps towards you.
I'll come as soon as these men have finished their work.
I like this university.
Good evening. In this programme we are going to look at the way in which British music has developed in recent years.

When it is clear who or what you are referring to, you can use *this* and *these* as **pronouns**. This use is explained in paragraphs 1.124 to 1.127.

1.186 *This* and *these* are also used in many expressions that refer to current periods of time, for example *this month*, *this week*, and *these days*. This use is explained in Chapter 4.

that and those

1.187 You use *that* and *those* when you are talking about things or people that you can see but that are not close to you.

How much is it for that big box?
Can I have one of those brochures?
Can you move those books off there?

1.188 When it is clear who or what you are talking about, you can use *that* and *those* as **pronouns**. This use is explained in paragraphs 1.124 to 1.127.

Could you just hold that?
Please don't take those.

 **USAGE NOTE**

1.189 You can show that you are referring to the same person or thing you have just mentioned by using *this*, *that*, *these*, or *those* in front of a noun. For example, if you have just mentioned a girl, you can refer to her as *this girl* or *that girl* the second time you mention her. Normally, you use a **pronoun** to refer to someone or something you have just mentioned, but sometimes you cannot do this because it might not be clear who or what the pronoun refers to.

Students and staff suggest books for the library, and normally we're quite happy to get those books.
Their house is in a valley. The people in that valley speak about the people in the next valley as foreigners.
They had a lot of diamonds, and they asked her if she could possibly get these diamonds to Britain.

The use of *this, that, those,* etc. to refer again to something that has already been mentioned is fully explained in paragraphs 10.7 to 10.10.

1.190   In informal English, you can also use *that* and *those* in front of a noun to talk about people or things that are already known to the person you are speaking or writing to.

That idiot Antonio has gone and locked our cabin door.
Have they found those missing children yet?
Do you remember that funny little apartment?

1.191   You can use *that* in front of a noun when you are talking about something that has just happened.

I knew that meeting would be difficult.

That is used as a **pronoun** to talk about something that has just happened. This use is explained in paragraphs 1.124 to 1.127.

using *those* instead of *the*

1.192   In more formal English, *those* can be used instead of *the* in front of a plural noun when the plural noun is followed by a **relative clause**. In this use, the relative clause specifies exactly which group of people or things are being referred to.

...those workers who are employed in large enterprises.
The parents are not afraid to be firm about those matters that seem important to them.

informal use of *this* and *these*

1.193   In informal spoken English, people sometimes use *this* and *these* in front of nouns even when they are mentioning someone or something for the first time.

And then this woman came up to me and she said, I believe you have a goddaughter called Celia Ravenscroft.
At school we had to wear these awful white cotton hats.

Possessive determiners: *my, your, their,* etc.

1.194   You often want to show that a thing belongs to someone or that it is connected in some way with someone.

One way of doing this is to use a word like *my, your,* and *their,* which tells you who something belongs to. These words are called **possessive determiners**.

Are your children bilingual?
I remember his name now.
They would be welcome to use our library.
I'd been waiting a long time to park my car.

1.195 There are seven possessive determiners in English, and each one is associated with a particular **personal pronoun:**

	singular	plural
1st person	my	our
2nd person	your	
3rd person	his her its	their

Personal pronouns are explained in paragraphs 1.95 to 1.106.

! BE CAREFUL

1.196 You do not spell the possessive *its* with an apostrophe. *It's* is short for *it is*.

position

1.197 Possessive determiners, like other determiners, come after any words like *all* or *some of* (called **predeterminers**), and before any numbers or adjectives.

...all *his* letters.
...*their* next message.
...*my* little finger.
...*our* two lifeboats.

See paragraph 1.251 for more information about predeterminers.

! BE CAREFUL

1.198 In English, you do not use more than one definite determiner before a noun. Therefore, possessive determiners must be used on their own. You cannot say *I took off the my shoes*. You have to choose whether to say *I took off my shoes*, or *I took off the shoes*.

agreement with noun

1.199 You choose which possessive determiner to use according to the identity of the person or thing that owns something. For example, if you want to identify something as belonging to or relating to a particular woman, you always use *her*. The following noun does not affect the choice.

I took off my shoes.
Her husband remained standing. He had his hands in his pockets.
She had to give up her job.
The group held its first meeting last week.
The creature lifted its head.
...the two dark men, glasses in their hands, waiting silently.
...the car companies and their workers.

1.200 When you want to draw attention to the fact that something belongs or relates to a particular person or thing, you can use the word *own* after the possessive determiner.

> I helped him to some more water but left <u>my own glass</u> untouched.
> Residents are allowed to bring <u>their own furniture</u> with them if they wish to do so.
> Make <u>your own decisions</u>.
> I heard it with <u>my own ears</u>.
> She felt in charge of <u>her own affairs</u>.

If you use a number or adjective in this structure, you put the number or adjective after *own*.

> ...their <u>own three children</u>.
> The players provided their <u>own white shorts</u>.

1.201 Possessive determiners do not always show that what follows them is actually possessed (or owned) by someone. Sometimes they just show that what follows is connected or associated with someone in some way.

> They then turned <u>their attention</u> to other things.
> ...the vitality of <u>our music</u> and <u>our culture</u>.
> In summer, hay fever interfered with all <u>her activities</u>.
> It's <u>his brother</u> who has the workshop.

1.202 You can use a possessive determiner in front of a noun that refers to an action, in order to show who or what is doing the action.

> ...not long after <u>our arrival</u>.
> ...<u>his criticism</u> of the Government.
> ...<u>their fight</u> for survival.
> I'm waiting for <u>your explanation</u>.
> Most of <u>their claims</u> were worthy.

In the last example, *their claims* refers to the claims that they have made.

1.203 You can also use a possessive determiner to say who or what is affected by an action.

> <u>My appointment</u> as the first woman chairman symbolizes change.
> ...the redistribution of wealth, rather than <u>its creation</u>.
> They expressed their horror at <u>her dismissal</u>.

In the last example, *her dismissal* refers to the fact that she was dismissed by someone or by a company.

In the first of the following examples, *his supporters* means the people who support him.

> ...Birch and <u>his supporters</u>.
> She returned the ring to <u>its owner</u>.

USAGE NOTE

1.204 Sometimes in English the determiner *the* is used where there is an obvious possessive meaning. In these cases the possession is already made clear by a preceding noun or pronoun. The following paragraphs explain the situations in which you use *the* rather than a possessive determiner.

1.205 When you refer to a specific part of someone's body, you normally use a possessive determiner.

> She has something on her feet and a bag in her hand.
> Nancy suddenly took my arm.
> The children wore nothing on their feet.
> She thanked him shyly and patted his arm.
> I opened the cupboard and they fell on my head.
> He shook his head.

However, when you are describing an action that someone does to a part of someone else's body, you often use the definite article (the), especially when the body part is the object of a preposition and when the object of the verb is a pronoun. For example, if you say She hit me on the head, head is the object of the preposition on and me is the object of the verb hit.

> I patted him on the head.
> He took her by the arm and began drawing her away.

You use the definite article because the owner of the body part has already been identified, and you do not need to repeat this information.

Similarly, if the object of the verb is a **reflexive pronoun** such as myself, yourself, and so on, you use the definite article. This is because the reflexive pronoun already refers to you or to the person who is doing the action, so you do not need to repeat this information by using a possessive determiner.

> I accidentally hit myself on the head with the brush handle.
> We can pat ourselves on the back for bringing up our children.

Uses of reflexive pronouns are explained in paragraphs 1.111 to 1.118.

1.206 If you want to describe something that you do to yourself or that someone else does to themselves, you normally use a possessive determiner.

> She was brushing her hair.
> 'I'm going to brush my teeth,' he said.
> She gritted her teeth and carried on.
> He walked into the kitchen and shook his head.

! | **BE CAREFUL**

1.207 You usually use possessive determiners when you refer to people or animals. You do not usually use them to refer to things that are not alive. It is, for example, more usual to say the door or the door of the room than its door.

generic use

1.208 Possessive determiners are sometimes used to talk about things that belong to or are associated with people in general, in a similar way to generic pronouns. For more information on **generic pronouns**, see paragraphs 1.119 to 1.123.

Your can be used when you are talking about something that belongs to or is associated with people in general, or with a person in a situation that you are imagining.

> Can eating a low-fat diet weaken your hair?
> Going to the gym is good for your general health.
> Part of the process involves discussing your decision with a career counsellor.

In more formal English, one's is sometimes used instead of your.

> A satisfying job can bring structure and meaning to one's life.

Our can be used to talk about all of mankind or society.

Being a child is not easy in our society.

Their can be used to refer to a person when you do not know, or do not want to specify, whether that person is male or female.

The most important asset a person has is their ability to work.
Each winner received a plaque with their award title.

other possessives

1.209 There are other ways of showing that something is owned by or connected with someone or something else. For example, you can use 's (apostrophe s) or a prepositional phrase beginning with *of*.

Mary's daughter is called Elizabeth.
Very often the person appointed has no knowledge of that company's end product.
...the house of a rich banker in Paris.
In the opinion of the team, what would they consider to be absolutely necessary?

possessive determiners used in titles

1.210 Possessive determiners are also sometimes used in titles such as *Your Majesty* and *His Excellency*. This use is explained in paragraph 1.56.

The possessive form: apostrophe s ('s)

1.211 You usually show that something belongs to or is associated with a specific, named person by adding 's to the name of the person, and by placing this possessive form in front of the thing that belongs to them, or is associated with them. For example, if John owns a motorbike, you can refer to it as 'John's motorbike'.

Sylvia put her hand on John's arm.
...the main features of Mr Brown's economic policy.

When you use a noun rather than a name to refer to the person, the noun phrase containing the possessive form also contains a determiner in the usual way.

...his grandmother's house.
Your mother's best handbag.

Note that the determiner applies to the possessive form and not to the noun that is being modified by the possessive.

spelling and pronunciation

1.212 The spelling and pronunciation patterns used to form possessives change according to the spelling and pronunciation of the name or noun. These are explained in the Reference section.

other uses of 's

1.213 Note that in addition to being the possessive form, the pattern 's can also be added to words as a contraction of *is* or *has*. This is explained in the Reference section.

showing close connection

1.214 Apostrophe s ('s) is most often added to a noun referring to a person or an animal.

I wore a pair of my sister's boots.

Philip watched his friend's reaction.
Billy patted the dog's head.

It can also be used to show that something belongs to or is associated with a group of people or an institution.

She runs the foreign exchange desk for the bank's corporate clients.
They also prepare the university's budget.
...the paper's political editor, Mr Fred Emery.
There was a raid on the Democratic Party's headquarters.
What is your government's policy?

1.215 Apostrophe s ('s) is sometimes added to a noun referring to an object when specifying a part of it or a quality or feature that it has.

I like the car's design.
You can predict a computer's behaviour because it follows rules.

Apostrophe s ('s) is used after nouns and names referring to places to specify something in that place.

He is the administrative head of the country's biggest city.
The city's population is in decline.
...Britain's most famous company.

1.216 If you want to emphasize that something belongs or relates to a particular person and nobody else, you use *own*. *Own* can be used after the possessive form of a name or noun, as well as after a possessive determiner.

Professor Wilson's own answer may be unacceptable.
We must depend on David's own assessment.

If you are specifying a number of things, you put the number after *own*.

...the Doctor's own two rooms.

other structures

1.217 When you are talking about two things of the same type that belong to different people you can use the possessive form of a name or noun like a possessive pronoun so that you can avoid repeating the thing itself. In the first example below, *her brother's* is used instead of *her brother's appearance*.

Her appearance is very different to her brother's.
My room is next to Karen's.
It is your responsibility rather than your parents'.

The possessive form can also be used on its own to refer to someone's home or place of work.

He's round at David's.
She stopped off at the butcher's for a piece of steak.
She hasn't been back to the doctor's since.

Possessive pronouns are explained in paragraphs 1.107 to 1.110.

used in prepositional phrases with *of*

1.218 The possessive form can be used in a prepositional phrase beginning with *of* after a noun phrase. You use this structure when you are talking about one of a number of things that belong to someone or are associated with them, rather than about something unique.

Julia, a friend <u>of Jenny's</u>, was there too.
That word was a favourite <u>of your father's</u>.

 USAGE NOTE

1.219 Possessive forms can also be used to refer to things of a particular type that are usually associated with someone.

...a woman dressed in a <u>man's</u> raincoat.
...a <u>policeman's</u> uniform.
...<u>women's</u> magazines.
...the <u>men's</u> lavatory.

1.220 The possessive form can sometimes be used with nouns that refer to an action in order to show who or what is performing the action.

...the <u>banking service's</u> rapid growth.
...<u>Madeleine's</u> arrival at Fairwater House School.

Note that phrases beginning with *of* are used more commonly to do this, and that they are more formal than this use of possessive forms. The use of prepositional phrases beginning with *of* to show who or what is performing an action is explained in paragraph 2.282.

1.221 Sometimes you can add apostrophe s ('s) to a noun referring to the thing affected by the performer of an action and put it in front of the noun referring to that performer. For example, you can talk about *the scheme's supporters*.

...<u>Christ's</u> followers.
...the <u>car's</u> owner.

Sometimes an apostrophe s ('s) structure can be used to refer to the thing affected by an action.

...<u>Capello's</u> appointment as England manager.

Note again that *of* structures are more commonly used to do this.

other ways of showing possession

1.222 It is also possible to show possession by using either a prepositional phrase beginning with *of*, or a structure with a noun modifier in it.

Prepositional phrases beginning with *of* are explained in paragraphs 2.277 to 2.283. Noun modifiers are explained in paragraphs 2.169 to 2.174.

Indefinite determiners: *all*, *some*, *many*, etc.

1.223 **Indefinite determiners** are used in noun phrases when you are talking about people or things in a general way, without identifying them.

Here is a list of indefinite determiners:

a	both	few	much	some
all	each	little	neither	
an	either	many	no	
another	enough	more	other	
any	every	most	several	

A, and *an* are the most common indefinite determiners; they are sometimes called the **indefinite article**. For more information about *a* and *an*, see paragraphs 1.228 to 1.235.

For more information about the other indefinite determiners, see paragraphs 1.236 to 1.250.

with countable nouns

1.224 *A* and *an* are used with singular countable nouns, and show that you are talking about just one person or thing.

Another is used with singular countable nouns and *other* with plural countable nouns, but only after one or more of the same type of person or thing has been mentioned.

Any can be used with singular and plural countable nouns to talk about one or more people or things. You use *enough, few, many, more, most, several*, and *some* with plural countable nouns to show that you are talking about a number of people or things. Each of these determiners indicates a different set or group within the total number. For more information about their meanings, see the section beginning at paragraph 1.236.

All, both, each, either, and *every* show that you are talking about the total number of people or things involved. *Both* and *either* specify that only two people or things are involved. *Both* is used with a plural noun, and *either* with a singular noun. *All, each*, and *every* usually show that there are more than two. *All* is used with a plural noun, and *each* and *every* with a singular noun.

No and *neither* refer to the total number of things involved in negative statements. *No* is used with singular or plural nouns, and *neither* only with singular nouns. *No* and *neither* are covered in the section on **negative words** in Chapter 5.

For more information about **countable nouns**, see paragraphs 1.15 to 1.22.

with uncountable nouns

1.225 For uncountable nouns, *any, enough, little, more, most, much*, and *some* are used to talk about a quantity of something. *No* and *all* indicate the total quantity of it.

For more information about **uncountable nouns**, see paragraphs 1.23 to 1.33.

> ❗ **BE CAREFUL**

1.226 *A, an, another, both, each, either, every, few, many, neither*, and *several* are not usually used with uncountable nouns.

using nouns without determiners

1.227 When you are referring to things or people in an indefinite way, you can sometimes use a noun without a determiner.

...raising money from industry, government, and trusts.
Permission should be asked before visitors are invited.

Uncountable nouns are usually used without a determiner.

Health and education are matters that most voters feel strongly about.
Wealth, like power, tends to corrupt.

Plural nouns are used without a determiner when you are referring to all the people or things of a particular kind.

Dogs need a regular balanced diet, not just meat.
Are there any jobs that *men* can do that *women* can't?

Plural nouns can also be used without a determiner to talk about an unspecified number of things.

Teachers should read <u>stories</u> to children.
Cats and dogs get <u>fleas</u>.

For more information about plural nouns, see paragraphs 1.41 to 1.46.

A and *an*

1.228 A and *an* are the most common **indefinite determiners**. They are used for talking about a person or thing when it is not clear or not important which one is intended. You put *a* or *an* in front of the singular form of a **countable noun**.

He's bought the children <u>a puppy</u>.
He was eating <u>an apple</u>.
<u>An old lady</u> was calling to him.

choosing *a* or *an*

1.229 You use *a* when the following word begins with a consonant sound.

...<u>a</u> piece...<u>a</u> good teacher...<u>a</u> language class.

This includes some words that begin with a vowel in their written form, because the first sound is a *y* sound, /j/.

...<u>a</u> university...<u>a</u> European language.

You use *an* when the following word begins with a vowel sound.

...<u>an</u> example...<u>an</u> art exhibition...<u>an</u> early train.

This includes some words that begin with the letter *h* in their written form, because the *h* is not pronounced.

...<u>an</u> honest politician...quarter of <u>an</u> hour.

A is usually pronounced /ə/. An is usually pronounced /ən/.

not being specific about which person or thing you are referring to

1.230 People often say that you use *a* or *an* when you are mentioning something for the first time, but this is not a very helpful rule because there are so many situations where you use *the* for the first mention of something. See, for example, paragraphs 1.166, 1.167, and 1.168.

You usually use *a* or *an* when it is not clear or not important which specific person or thing is being referred to.

She picked up <u>a book</u>.
After weeks of looking, we eventually bought <u>a house</u>.
<u>A colleague</u> and I got some money to do research on rats.

adding extra information

1.231 Sometimes, *a* or *an* is simply followed by a noun.

I got <u>a postcard</u> from Susan.
The FBI is conducting <u>an investigation</u>.

But if you want to add extra information, you can add an adjective, or a following clause or phrase.

I met a Swedish girl on the train from Copenhagen.
I've been reading an interesting article in The Economist.
We had to write a story about our parents' childhood.
I chose a picture that reminded me of my own country.

a or an after linking verbs

1.232   You can also use *a* or *an* after a **linking verb**.

She is a model and an artist.
His father was an alcoholic.
Noise was considered a nuisance.
His brother was a sensitive child.

For more information about linking verbs, see Chapter 3.

a and an with uncountable nouns

1.233   Sometimes, *a* or *an* are used with an uncountable noun, especially one that relates to human emotions or mental activity. This only happens when the uncountable noun is limited by an adjective, or a phrase or clause giving more information.

A general education is perhaps more important than an exact knowledge of some particular theory.
She had an eagerness for life.

using individuals to generalize

1.234   You can use *a* or *an* with a noun when you are using one individual person or thing to make a general statement about all people or things of that type. For example, if you say *A gun must be kept in a safe place*, you are talking about an individual gun in order to make a general statement about all guns.

A computer can only do what you program it to do.
A dog likes to eat far more meat than a human being.
An unmarried mother was looked down on.

This is not the usual way of referring to groups. Normally, if you want to make a statement about all the people or things of a particular kind, you use the plural form of a noun without a determiner. See paragraph 1.227 for more information about this.

nouns referring to one thing only

1.235   *A* and *an* are sometimes used with **singular nouns** such as *sun*, *moon*, and *sky* that refer to just one thing. You normally use *the* with these nouns, but you use *a* or *an* when you are drawing attention to some special feature by adding a modifier or a following phrase or clause to the noun. This use is particularly common in literature.

We drove under a gloomy sky.
A weak sun shines on the promenade.

For more information on singular nouns, see paragraphs 1.34 to 1.40.

Other indefinite determiners

some

1.236 *Some* is usually used to show that there is a quantity of som things or people, without being precise. It is used with unco plural countable nouns.

Some is usually used in affirmative statements.

There is <u>some</u> evidence that the system works.
There's <u>some</u> chocolate cake over there.
I had <u>some</u> good ideas.

Some can be used in questions, when you expect the answer to be *yes*.

Could you give me <u>some</u> examples?
Would you like <u>some</u> coffee?

Some is also used to mean quite a large amount or number. For example, in *I did not meet her again for some years*, *some* means almost the same as *several* or *many*.

You will be unable to restart the car for <u>some</u> time.
It took <u>some</u> years for Dan to realize the truth.

1.237 You can also use *some* in front of numbers, in slightly more literary English, to show that you are not being totally accurate.

I was <u>some</u> fifteen miles by sea from the nearest village.
...an animal weighing <u>some</u> five tons.

1.238 When you want to emphasize that you do not know the identity of a person or thing, or you think their identity is not important, you can use *some* with a singular countable noun, instead of *a* or *an*.

Most staff members will spend a few weeks in <u>some</u> developing country.
Supposing you had <u>some</u> eccentric who came and offered you a thousand pounds.

any

1.239 *Any* is used before plural nouns and uncountable nouns when you are referring to a quantity of something that may or may not exist.

The patients know their rights like <u>any</u> other consumers.
Check online if you're in <u>any</u> doubt.
You can stop at <u>any</u> time you like.

Any is also used in questions asking whether something exists or not. It is also used in negative statements to say that something does not exist.

Do you have <u>any</u> advice on that?
Do you have <u>any</u> vacancies for bar staff?
It hasn't made <u>any</u> difference.
Nobody in her house knows <u>any</u> English.
I rang up to see if there were <u>any</u> tickets left.

Questions and negative statements are explained further in Chapter 5.

Note that you can use *any* with singular countable nouns to talk about someone or something of a particular type, when you do not want to mention a specific person or thing.

<u>Any</u> big tin container will do.
Cars can be rented at almost <u>any</u> US airport.

...n also be used as a **pronoun**. See paragraphs 1.93 to 1.161 for more information ...out pronouns. It is also used in **if-clauses**. For more information about these, see Chapter 8.

another and other

1.240 *Another* is used with singular countable nouns to talk about an additional person or thing of the same type as you have already mentioned.

> *Could I have another cup of coffee?*
> *He opened another shop last month.*

It can also be used before numbers to talk about more than one additional thing.

> *Margaret staying with us for another ten days.*
> *Five officials were sacked and another four arrested.*

Other is used with plural nouns, or occasionally with uncountable nouns.

> *Other people must have thought like this.*
> *They are either asleep or entirely absorbed in play or other activity.*

selecting from a group

1.241 *Enough* is used to say that there is as much of something as is needed, or as many things as are needed. You can therefore use *enough* in front of uncountable nouns or plural nouns.

> *There's enough space for the children to run around.*
> *They weren't getting enough customers.*

Many indicates that there is a large number of things, without being very precise. You use *many* with a plural countable noun.

> *He spoke many different languages.*

When you want to emphasize that there is only a small number of things of a particular kind, you use *few* with a plural countable noun.

> *There are few drugs that act quickly enough to be effective.*
> *There were few doctors available.*

Few is quite formal. In less formal English, you can use *not many* with the same meaning.

> *There aren't many gardeners like him.*

Most indicates nearly all of a group or amount. You use *most* with an uncountable noun or a plural countable noun.

> *Most people recover but the disease can be fatal.*
> *Most farmers are still using the old methods.*

Several usually indicates an imprecise number that is not very large, but is more than two. You use *several* with a plural countable noun.

> *Several projects had to be postponed.*
> *I had seen her several times before.*
> *There were several reasons for this.*

all, both, and either

1.242 *All* includes every person or thing of a particular kind. You use *all* with an uncountable noun or a plural countable noun.

> *They believe that all prisoners should be treated the same.*

Both is used to say something about two people or things of the same kind. You use *both* with a plural countable noun. The two people or things have usually been mentioned or are obvious from the context. *Both* is sometimes used to emphasize that two people or things are involved, rather than just one.

There were excellent performances from <u>both</u> actresses.
Denis held his cocoa in <u>both</u> hands.

Either is also used to talk about two things, but usually indicates that only one of the two is involved. You use *either* with a singular countable noun. When it is part of the subject of a clause, the verb is in the singular.

No argument could move <u>either</u> old gentleman from this decision.
If <u>either</u> parent has the disease, there is a much higher chance that the child will develop it.

Note that *either* can mean both of two things, especially when it is used with *end* and *side*.

They stood on <u>either</u> side of the bed.

each and every

1.243 You use *each* and *every* when you are talking about all the members of a group of people or things. You use *each* when you are thinking about the members as individuals, and *every* when you are making a general statement about all of them. *Each* and *every* are followed by a singular countable noun.

<u>Each seat</u> was covered with a white lace cover.
They would rush out to meet <u>each visitor</u>.
This new wealth can be seen in <u>every village</u>.
<u>Every child</u> would have milk <u>every day</u>.
<u>Each</u> applicant has five choices.
I agree with <u>every</u> word Peter says.

You can modify *every* but not *each*. You can say things such as *Almost every chair is broken* or *Not every chair is broken* but you cannot say *Almost each chair is broken* or *Not each chair is broken*. This is because *each* is slightly more precise and definite than *every*.

Note that *each* can be used when talking about two people or things, but *every* is only used for numbers larger than two.

little and much

1.244 If you want to emphasize that there is only a small amount of something, you use *little*. You use *much* to emphasize a large amount. *Little* and *much* are used with uncountable nouns.

Little is used only in affirmative statements. It is not used in questions or negatives.

There was <u>little</u> applause.
We've made <u>little</u> progress.
We have very <u>little</u> information.

Little is quite formal. In less formal texts, *not much* is more common. For example, instead of saying *We've made little progress*, you can say *We haven't made much progress*.

Much is usually used in questions and negatives.

Do you watch <u>much</u> television?
He did not speak <u>much</u> English.

Very much is used only in negative statements. For example, *I don't have very much sugar* means *I have only a small quantity of sugar*.

I haven't given very much attention to this problem.

Much is used in affirmative statements when it is modified by an adverb such as *too*, *so* or *as*.

It would take too much time.
Provide as much information as you can about the property.

In more formal English, *much* can be used in affirmative statements without an adverb. This usage is most common with abstract nouns, particularly those relating to discussion, debate and research.

The subject of company annual accounts is generating much debate among accountants and analysts.
The team's findings have caused much excitement among medical experts.
After much speculation, intelligence agencies now believe that he survived.

Usually, though, *much* is not used in affirmative statements. Instead, people generally use *a lot of* and, in less formal texts, *lots of*. For example, people would not usually say *I have much work to do*; instead, they would say *I have a lot of work to do*. For more information on *a lot of*, see 2.176.

certain, numerous, and various

1.245 Some other words can be indefinite determiners, such as *certain*, *numerous*, and *various*. You use *certain*, *numerous* and *various* with a plural countable noun.

Certain is used to refer to some members of a group, without specifying which ones.

We have certain ideas about what topics are suitable.

Numerous, like *many*, indicates a large number in an imprecise way.

I have received numerous requests for information.

Various is used to emphasize that you are referring to several different things or people.

We looked at schools in various European countries.

more, few, and less

1.246 There are three comparatives that are determiners. *More* is used in front of plural and uncountable nouns, usually with *than*, to refer to a quantity or amount of something that is greater than another quantity or amount.

He does more hours than I do.
His visit might do more harm than good.

But *more* is also often used to refer to an additional quantity of something rather than in comparisons.

More teachers need to be recruited.
We need more information.

Less is used to refer to an amount of something that is smaller than another amount. *Fewer* is used to refer to a group of things that is smaller than another group. *Less* is usually used before uncountable nouns and *fewer* before plural nouns, but in informal English *less* is also used before plural nouns.

The poor have less access to education.
...machinery which uses less energy.

As a result, he found <u>less</u> time than he would have hoped for his hobbies.
There are <u>fewer</u> trees here.

For more information about **comparison**, see paragraphs 2.103 to 2.139.

other expressions

1.247 Some other expressions also behave like indefinite determiners: *a few, a little, a good many, a great many*. These have a slightly different meaning from the single word determiners *few, little,* and *many*.

If you are mentioning a small number of things, but without any emphasis, you can use *a few* with plural countable nouns.

They went to San Diego for <u>a few</u> days.
<u>A few</u> years ago we set up a factory.
I usually do <u>a few</u> jobs for him in the house.

Similarly, if you are just mentioning a small amount of something without any emphasis, you can use *a little* with uncountable nouns.

He spread <u>a little</u> honey on a slice of bread.
I have to spend <u>a little</u> time in Oxford.
Charles is having <u>a little</u> trouble.

However, *a good many* and *a great many* are more emphatic forms of *many*.

I haven't seen her for <u>a good many</u> years.
He wrote <u>a great many</u> novels.

modifying determiners: *four more rooms, too much time*

1.248 Some indefinite determiners can be modified by *very, too,* and *far*, or sometimes by another indefinite determiner.

You can modify *more* with numbers or with other indefinite determiners.

Downstairs there are <u>four more rooms</u>.
There had been <u>no more accidents</u>.
You will never have to do <u>any more work</u>.

You can use *too many* or *too much* to say that a quantity is more than is wanted or needed, and *too few* or *too little* if it is not enough.

There were <u>too many</u> competitors.
They gave <u>too much</u> power to the Treasury.
There's <u>too little</u> literature involved.

You can use *very* before *few, little, many,* and *much*. You can also say *a very little* or *a very great many*.

<u>Very many</u> women have made their mark on industry.
<u>Very few</u> cars had reversing lights.
I had <u>very little</u> money left.

using *one*

1.249 You use *one* as a determiner when you have been talking or writing about a group of people or things and you want to say something about a particular member of the group. *One* is used instead of *a* or *an* and is slightly more emphatic.

We had <u>one</u> case that dragged on for a couple of years.
They criticise me all the time, wrote <u>one</u> woman.

I know one household where that happened, actually.

The use of *one* as a **number** is explained in paragraphs 2.214 to 2.215.

1.250 Many determiners are also **pronouns**; that is, they can be used without a following noun. For more information about these, see paragraphs 1.154 to 1.161.

predeterminers: *all the people, quite a long time*

1.251 Normally, a determiner is the first word in a noun phrase. However, there is a class of words called **predeterminers** which can come in front of a determiner.

Here is a list of predeterminers:

all	half	twice	rather
both	many	~	such
double	quarter	quite	what

The first group are used to talk about amounts or quantities. *All* can also be used to refer to every part of something. When used with this meaning it is used with an uncountable noun.

All the boys started to giggle.
He will give you all the information.
All these people knew each other.
I shall miss all my friends.
I invited both the boys.
Both these parties shared one basic belief.
She paid double the sum they asked for.
I'm getting twice the pay I used to get.

In the second group, *quite* and *rather* can be used either to emphasize or to reduce the effect of what is being said. In speech, the meaning is made clear by your tone of voice. In writing, it is sometimes difficult to know which meaning is intended without reading more of the text.

It takes quite a long time to get a divorce.
It was quite a shock.
Seaford is rather a pleasant town.
It was rather a disaster.

Such and *what* are used for emphasis.

He has such a beautiful voice.
What a mess!

Chapter 2

Giving information about people and things: adjectives, numbers, and other modifiers

2 Giving information about people and things: adjectives, numbers, and other modifiers

Introduction

2.1   In the previous chapter the use of nouns, pronouns, and determiners to name and identify people and things was explained. This chapter explains ways of giving more information about the people and things that have already been named or identified.

One way of giving more information within a noun phrase about people or things is by the use of an **adjective**, such as *small*, *political*, or *blue*. Adjectives can be used as modifiers of a noun or after linking verbs. They are explained in paragraphs 2.2 to 2.168.

Sometimes, **nouns**, rather than adjectives, are used to modify the noun. This is explained in paragraphs 2.169 to 2.174.

There are other groups of words that are used before a noun phrase to give more information about people and things. They are linked to the noun phrase by *of*. These include certain **indefinite determiners** such as *many of* and *some of* (explained in paragraphs 2.176 to 2.193), and other expressions that are used for describing a part or amount of something, such as *a piece of* and *a bottle of* (explained in paragraphs 2.194 to 2.207).

Numbers and **fractions** are also used to indicate the amount of people or things you are talking about. Numbers are explained in paragraphs 2.208 to 2.239 and fractions are explained in paragraphs 2.240 to 2.249.

The other way of giving more information within a noun phrase about people or things is by using a **qualifier**, that is, giving extra information in the form of a phrase or a clause after the noun to expand its meaning. This is explained in paragraphs 2.272 to 2.302.

Describing people and things: adjectives

2.2   When you want to give more information about something than you can give by using a noun alone, you can use an **adjective** to identify it or describe it in more detail.

...a new idea.
...new ideas.
...new creative ideas.
Ideas are important.
...to suggest that new ideas are useful.

main points about adjectives

2.3   The most important things to notice about an adjective in English are

▶ what structure it is in (e.g. before a noun or after a linking verb)

▶ what type of adjective it is (e.g. describing a quality or placing the noun in a particular class).

❗ BE CAREFUL

2.4 The form of an adjective does not change: you use the same form for singular and plural and for subject and object.

We were looking for a _good_ place to camp.
The next _good_ place was forty-five miles further on.
Good places to fish were hard to find.
We found hardly any _good_ places.

structure

2.5 Adjectives are nearly always used in connection with a noun or pronoun to give information about the person, thing, or group that is being referred to. When this information is not the main purpose of a statement, adjectives are placed in front of a noun, as in *hot coffee*.

The use of adjectives in a noun phrase is explained in paragraph 2.19.

2.6 Sometimes, however, the main purpose of a statement is to give the information expressed by an adjective. When this happens, adjectives are placed after a **linking verb** such as *be* or *become*, as in *I am cold* and *He became ill*. The use of adjectives after a linking verb is explained in paragraphs 3.122 to 3.137.

types of adjective

2.7 There is a large group of adjectives that identify qualities that someone or something has. This group includes words such as *happy* and *intelligent*. These are called **qualitative adjectives**.

Qualitative adjectives are explained in paragraphs 2.22 to 2.25.

2.8 There is another large group of adjectives that identify someone or something as a member of a class. This group includes words such as *financial* and *intellectual*. These are called **classifying adjectives**.

Classifying adjectives are explained in paragraphs 2.26 to 2.28.

Some adjectives are both qualitative and classifying. These are explained in paragraph 2.29.

2.9 There is a small group of adjectives that identify the colour of something. This group includes words like *blue* and *green*. They are called **colour adjectives**.

Colour adjectives are explained in paragraphs 2.30 to 2.35.

2.10 Another small group of adjectives are used to emphasize your feelings about the person or thing you are talking about. These adjectives are called **emphasizing adjectives**, and they include adjectives such as *complete*, *absolute*, and *utter*.

Emphasizing adjectives are explained in paragraphs 2.36 to 2.39.

2.11 There is a small group of adjectives that are used in a very similar way to **determiners** (see paragraphs 1.162 to 1.251) to make the reference more precise.

These are called **postdeterminers** because their place in a noun phrase is immediately after the determiner, if there is one, and before any other adjectives.

Postdeterminers are explained in paragraph 2.40.

2.12   Most adjectives can be used either before the noun or after a linking verb. However, there are some that can be used only in one position or the other. This is explained in paragraphs 2.41 to 2.53.

2.13   There are a few adjectives that can be used immediately after the noun. They are explained in paragraphs 2.58 to 2.62.

2.14   When two or more adjectives are used in a structure, they usually occur in a particular order. This is explained in paragraphs 2.54 to 2.57.

2.15   There are a large number of English adjectives ending in -*ing*, many of which are related to the **-*ing* participle** of a verb. In this grammar they are called **-*ing* adjectives**.

There are also a large number of English adjectives ending in -*ed*, many of which are related to the **-*ed* participle** of a verb. In this grammar they are called **-*ed* adjectives**.

-*ing* adjectives are explained in paragraphs 2.63 to 2.76. -*ed* adjectives are explained in paragraphs 2.77 to 2.93.

2.16   **Compound adjectives** are made up of two or more words, usually written with hyphens between them.

Compound adjectives are explained in paragraphs 2.94 to 2.102.

2.17   When you want to compare the amount of a quality that two or more people or things have, you can use **comparative** and **superlative** adjectives. There are also some other ways of comparing things.

Comparatives are explained in paragraphs 2.103 to 2.111, and superlatives are explained in paragraphs 2.112 to 2.122. Other ways of comparing things are explained in paragraphs 2.123 to 2.139.

2.18   You can also talk about the amount of a quality that something or someone has by using an adverb like *totally* or *mildly* with an adjective.

This is explained in paragraphs 2.141 to 2.168.

Adjective structures

2.19   Adjectives are used in two main structures. One of them involves adjectives coming before the noun phrase. If you say *Julia was carrying an old suitcase*, your main purpose is to say that Julia was carrying a suitcase. The adjective *old* gives more information about what kind of suitcase it was.

He was wearing a <u>white</u> t-shirt.
...a <u>technical</u> term.
...a <u>pretty little star-shaped</u> flower bed.

Most adjectives can be used in this way.

2.20 The other main structure involves adjectives being used after **linking verbs** such as *be* and *become*. Putting an adjective after a linking verb has the effect of focusing attention on the adjective. If you say *The suitcase she was carrying was old*, your main purpose is to describe the suitcase, so the focus is on the adjective *old*.

The roads are <u>busy</u>.
The house was <u>quiet</u>.
He became <u>angry</u>.
I feel <u>cold</u>.
Nobody seemed <u>amused</u>.

The use of adjectives after linking verbs is explained in paragraphs 3.132 to 3.137.

Most adjectives can be used in this way.

2.21 In the following examples, the first example in each pair shows an adjective being used before the noun, while the second example shows it being used with a linking verb.

There was no <u>clear</u> evidence.
'That's very <u>clear</u>,' I said.
It had been a <u>pleasant</u> evening.
It's not a big stream, but it's very <u>pleasant</u>.
She bought a loaf of <u>white</u> bread.
The walls were <u>white</u>.

Identifying qualities: *a sad story, a pretty girl*

2.22 There are two main types of adjective, **qualitative** and **classifying**. Adjectives that describe a quality that someone or something has, such as *sad*, *pretty*, *small*, *happy*, *healthy*, *wealthy*, and *wise*, are called **qualitative adjectives**.

...a <u>sad</u> story.
...a <u>pretty</u> girl.
...a <u>small</u> child.
...a <u>happy</u> mother with a <u>healthy</u> baby.
...<u>wealthy</u> bankers.
I think it would be <u>wise</u> to give up.

gradability: *very sad, rather funny*

2.23 Adjectives that describe qualities are **gradable**, which means that the person or thing referred to can have more or less of the quality mentioned.

2.24 The usual way in which you show the amount of a quality that something or someone has is by using adverbs like *very* and *rather* in front of qualitative adjectives. This is explained in paragraphs 2.140 to 2.156.

2.25 The other way in which you can talk about the amount of a quality that something or someone has is by using a **comparative**, such as *bigger* and *more interesting*, or a **superlative**, such as *the biggest* and *the most interesting*. Comparatives and superlatives are explained in paragraphs 2.103 to 2.122.

Here is a list of qualitative adjectives:

active	appropriate	beautiful	bright
angry	attractive	big	broad
anxious	bad	brief	busy

calm	firm	nice	small
careful	flat	obvious	soft
cheap	frank	odd	special
clean	free	old	steady
clear	fresh	pale	strange
close	friendly	patient	strong
cold	frightened	plain	stupid
comfortable	funny	pleasant	successful
common	good	poor	suitable
complex	great	popular	sure
cool	happy	powerful	surprised
curious	hard	pretty	sweet
dangerous	heavy	proud	tall
dark	high	quick	terrible
dear	hot	quiet	thick
deep	important	rare	thin
determined	interesting	reasonable	tight
different	kind	rich	tiny
difficult	large	rough	tired
dirty	late	sad	typical
dry	light	safe	understanding
easy	likely	sensible	useful
effective	long	serious	violent
efficient	loose	sharp	warm
expensive	loud	shocked	weak
fair	lovely	short	wet
familiar	low	sick	wide
famous	lucky	significant	wild
fast	narrow	silly	worried
fat	nervous	simple	young
fine	new	slow	

Identifying type: *financial help, abdominal pains*

2.26 The other main type of adjective consists of adjectives that you use to identify the type or *class* that something belongs to. For example, if you say *financial help*, you are using the adjective *financial* to describe what type of help you are talking about (that is, to *classify* help). Adjectives that are used in this way are called **classifying adjectives**.

...*financial* help.
...*abdominal* pains.
...a *medieval* manuscript.
...my *daily* shower.
...an *equal* partnership.
...a *sufficient* amount of milk.

Note that **noun modifiers** (see paragraphs 2.169 to 2.174) are used in a similar way to classifying adjectives. For example, *financial matters* and *money matters* are similar in both structure and meaning.

Here is a list of classifying adjectives:

absolute	double	industrial	official	royal
active	due	inevitable	open	rural
actual	east	intellectual	original	scientific
agricultural	eastern	internal	personal	separate
alternative	economic	international	physical	sexual
annual	educational	legal	political	single
apparent	electric	local	positive	social
available	empty	magic	possible	solid
basic	external	male	potential	south
central	female	medical	private	southern
chemical	financial	mental	professional	standard
civil	foreign	military	proper	straight
commercial	free	modern	psychological	sufficient
communist	full	moral	public	theoretical
conservative	general	national	raw	traditional
cultural	golden	natural	ready	urban
daily	historical	negative	real	west
democratic	human	north	religious	western
direct	ideal	northern	revolutionary	wooden
domestic	independent	nuclear	right	wrong

2.27 Adjectives such as *British*, *American*, and *Australian*, that indicate nationality or origin, are also classifying adjectives. They start with a capital letter because they are related to names of countries.

...*American* citizens.

Some classifying adjectives are formed from people's names, for example *Victorian* and *Shakespearean*. They also start with a capital letter.

...*Victorian* houses.

2.28 Because they put something in a class, classifying adjectives are not **gradable** in the way that qualitative adjectives are. For example, if you do not have to pay for something, you cannot say that it is *very free*, or *rather free*. Things are either in a particular class or not in it. Therefore, classifying adjectives do not have comparatives and superlatives and are not normally used with adverbs like *very* and *rather*.

However, when you want to show that you feel strongly about what you are saying, you can use an *intensifying* adverb such as *absolutely* with a classifying adjective. This is explained in paragraphs 2.147 to 2.148.

adjectives that are of both types

2.29 Some adjectives can be either **qualitative** or **classifying** depending on the meaning. For example, in *an emotional person*, *emotional* is a qualitative adjective meaning *feeling or expressing strong emotions*; it has a comparative and superlative and it can be used with words like *very* and *rather*. Thus, a person can be *very emotional*, *rather emotional*, or *more emotional* than someone else. However, in *the emotional needs of children*, *emotional* is a classifying adjective meaning *relating to a person's emotions*, and so it cannot be used with words like *very* or *rather*, and it does not have a comparative and superlative.

Here is a list of adjectives that are often used both as qualitative adjectives and as classifying adjectives:

academic	effective	modern	regular	scientific
conscious	emotional	moral	religious	secret
dry	extreme	objective	revolutionary	similar
educational	late	ordinary	rural	social

Identifying colours: colour adjectives

2.30   When you want to say what colour something is, you use a **colour adjective**.

...her <u>blue</u> eyes.
...a <u>red</u> ribbon.

Here is a list of the main colour adjectives:

black	cream	orange	red	white
blue	green	pink	scarlet	yellow
brown	grey	purple	violet	

adding extra information to colour adjectives

2.31   If you want to specify a colour more precisely, you use a word such as *light*, *pale*, *dark*, *deep*, or *bright*, in front of a colour adjective.

...<u>light brown</u> hair.
...a <u>pale green</u> suit.
...a <u>dark blue</u> dress.
...<u>deep red</u> dye.
...her <u>bright blue</u> eyes.

These combinations sometimes have hyphens.

...a <u>light-blue</u> suit.
...the plant's tiny <u>pale-pink</u> flowers.

Note that these words cannot be used with the colours *black* or *white*, because you cannot have different shades of black and white.

approximate colours

2.32   If you want to talk about a colour that does not have a definite name you can:

▶ use a colour adjective with *-ish* added to the end

...<u>greenish</u> glass.
...<u>yellowish</u> hair.

▶ combine two colour adjectives, often with *-ish* or *-y* on the end of the first one

...<u>greenish-white</u> flowers.

...a greeny blue line.
...the blue-green waves.

⭐ | **BE CREATIVE**

2.33 You can mix colours in these ways to produce whatever new colour you are trying to describe.

comparison of colour adjectives

2.34 Colour adjectives such as *blue* and *green* occasionally have comparatives and superlatives ending in -*er* and -*est*.

His face was redder than usual.
...the bluest sky I have ever seen.

Comparatives and **superlatives** are explained in paragraphs 2.103 to 2.122.

colour nouns

2.35 Colours can also be nouns, and the main colours can also be plural nouns.

The snow shadows had turned to a deep blue.
They blended in so well with the khaki and reds of the landscape.
...brilliantly coloured in reds, yellows, blacks, and purples.

Showing strong feelings: *complete, absolute,* etc.

2.36 You can emphasize your feelings about something that you mention by putting an adjective such as *complete, absolute,* or *utter* in front of a noun.

He made me feel like a complete idiot.
Some of it was absolute rubbish.
...utter despair.
...pure bliss.

You generally use an adjective of this kind only when the noun shows your opinion about something.

Because they are used to show strong feelings, these adjectives are called **emphasizing adjectives**.

Here is a list of emphasizing adjectives:

absolute	outright	pure	true
complete	perfect	real	utter
entire	positive	total	

adjectives for showing disapproval

2.37 A small group of adjectives ending in -*ing* are used in very informal spoken English for emphasis, usually to show disapproval or contempt.

Everybody in the whole stinking town was loaded with money.
Shut that blinking door!

Here is a list of adjectives used informally for emphasis:

blinking	blundering	freezing	scalding	thundering
blithering	crashing	piddling	stinking	whopping
blooming	flaming	raving	thumping	

! **BE CAREFUL**

2.38 Many of these adjectives are usually used with one particular noun or adjective after them: *blithering idiot, blundering idiot, crashing bore, raving lunatic, thundering nuisance, freezing cold, scalding hot, piddling little ..., thumping great ..., whopping great ....*

He's driving that car like a <u>raving</u> lunatic!
I've got a <u>stinking</u> cold.
...a <u>piddling little</u> car.

very as an emphasizing adjective

2.39 The word *very* is sometimes used to emphasize a noun, in expressions like *the very top* and *the very end*.

...at the <u>very</u> end of the shop.
...the <u>very</u> bottom of the hill.
These molecules were formed at the <u>very</u> beginning of history.

Making the reference more precise: postdeterminers

2.40 There is a small group of adjectives that are used in a very similar way to **determiners** (see paragraphs 1.162 to 1.251) to make the reference more precise. These are called **postdeterminers**, because their place in a noun phrase is immediately after the determiner, if there is one, and before any other adjectives.

...the <u>following</u> brief description.
...<u>certain</u> basic human qualities.
...improvements in the <u>last</u> few years.
...<u>further</u> technological advance.
He wore his <u>usual</u> old white coat....
...the <u>only</u> sensible thing to do.

You often need to make it clear precisely what you are referring to. For example, if you say *Turn left at the tall building* someone might ask which tall building you mean. If you say *Turn left at the next tall building*, there can be no doubt which one you mean. The postdeterminer *next* picks it out precisely.

Here is a list of adjectives that are postdeterminers:

additional	first	next	past	same
certain	following	only	present	special
chief	further	opposite	previous	specific
entire	last	other	principal	usual
existing	main	particular	remaining	

Some of these adjectives are also ordinary classifying adjectives.

He had children from a <u>previous</u> marriage.
There are two <u>main</u> reasons for this.

Here is a list of postdeterminers that are also classifying adjectives:

additional	further	particular	principal
chief	main	past	remaining
existing	other	previous	specific

Adjectives that are used to show the position of something are also used for precise reference.

...the middle button of her black leather coat.
...the top 100 German companies.

Here is a list of adjectives sometimes used to talk about the position of something as well as for precise reference:

left	upper	top	middle	front
right	lower	bottom	end	back

Postdeterminers can also be used with numbers. This is explained in paragraph 2.219.

Special classes of adjectives

2.41 Most adjectives can be used both before the noun and after a linking verb, but there are some that are only used in one position or the other.

There are a few adjectives that are always or almost always used in front of a noun and are never or rarely used after a linking verb. These adjectives are called **attributive adjectives**.

Examples are *atomic* and *outdoor*. You can talk about *an atomic explosion*, but you do not say *The explosion was atomic*. You can talk about *outdoor pursuits*, but you do not say *Their pursuits are outdoor*.

adjectives that are only used in front of a noun

2.42 A few **qualitative adjectives** (see paragraphs 2.22 to 2.25) are only used in front of a noun. Here is a list of qualitative adjectives always used in this way:

adoring	commanding	knotty	scant
belated	fateful	paltry	searing
chequered	flagrant	punishing	thankless
choked	fleeting	ramshackle	unenviable

Most adjectives that are only used in front of a noun are **classifying adjectives** (see paragraphs 2.26 to 2.28). Here is a list of classifying adjectives used attributively:

atomic	federal	neighbouring	smokeless
bridal	forensic	north	south
cardiac	indoor	northern	southern
countless	institutional	occasional	subterranean
cubic	introductory	orchestral	supplementary
digital	investigative	outdoor	underlying
east	judicial	phonetic	west
eastern	lone	preconceived	western
eventual	maximum	remedial	woollen
existing	nationwide	reproductive	

2.43 There are no **colour adjectives** (see paragraphs 2.30 to 2.35) that are restricted to this position.

Emphasizing adjectives (see paragraphs 2.36 to 2.39) are usually used in front of a noun.

adjectives that always follow a linking verb

2.44 Some adjectives are normally used only after a linking verb and not in front of a noun. These adjectives are called **predicative adjectives**.

For example, you can say *She felt glad*, but you do not normally talk about *a glad woman*.

Here is a list of adjectives usually used in this way:

afraid	asleep	due	ready	unable
alive	awake	glad	safe	unlikely
alone	aware	ill	sorry	well
apart	content	likely	sure	

Note that they do not have to be followed by a prepositional phrase.

2.45 Some adjectives are usually followed by a prepositional phrase because their meaning would otherwise be unclear or incomplete. For example, you cannot simply say that someone is *accustomed*. You have to say that they are *accustomed to* something.

The following usage note explains which prepositions you use after a particular adjective.

i USAGE NOTE

2.46 There are a few adjectives that are followed by the preposition *to* when they are used after a linking verb.

She's allergic to cats.
Older people are particularly susceptible to heart problems.

Here is a list of adjectives that are usually or always used after a linking verb and are followed by *to*:

accustomed	close	prone	resistant
adjacent	conducive	proportional	similar
allergic	devoted	proportionate	subject
attributable	impervious	reconciled	subservient
attuned	injurious	related	susceptible
averse	integral	resigned	unaccustomed

2.47 There are a few adjectives that are followed by the preposition *of* when they are used after a linking verb.

He was <u>aware of</u> the danger that faced him.
They seemed <u>capable of</u> winning their first game of the season.
He was <u>devoid of</u> any talent whatsoever.
His mind seemed to have become <u>incapable of</u> any thought.

Here is a list of adjectives that are usually or always used after a linking verb and are followed by *of*:

aware	desirous	heedless	mindful
bereft	devoid	illustrative	reminiscent
capable	fond	incapable	representative
characteristic	full	indicative	

2.48 There are a few adjectives that are followed by the preposition *with* when they are used after a linking verb.

His surprise became <u>tinged with</u> disbelief.
The plastic has to be <u>compatible with</u> the body tissues that make contact with it.
This way of life is <u>fraught with</u> danger.

Here is a list of adjectives that are usually or always used after a linking verb and are followed by *with*:

| compatible | conversant | fraught | tinged |
| consonant | filled | riddled | |

2.49 Some adjectives are followed by other prepositions when they are used after a linking verb.

These ideas are <u>rooted in</u> self-deception.
Didn't you say the raid was <u>contingent on</u> the weather?
Darwin concluded that people were <u>descended from</u> apes.

Here is a list of adjectives that are usually or always used after a linking verb and are followed by the preposition indicated:

| contingent on | inherent in | rooted in | swathed in |
| descended from | lacking in | steeped in | unhampered by |

In some cases, there is a choice between two prepositions.

Many of their courses are <u>connected with</u> industry.
Such names were arbitrarily given and were not <u>connected to</u> any particular event.

Here is a list of adjectives that are usually or always used after a linking verb and that are followed by the prepositions shown:

answerable for	dependent on	incumbent on	parallel to
answerable to	dependent upon	incumbent upon	parallel with
burdened by	immune from	insensible of	reliant on
burdened with	immune to	insensible to	reliant upon
connected to	inclined to	intent on	stricken by
connected with	inclined towards	intent upon	stricken with

2.50 *Different* is most commonly followed by *from*. It is also sometimes followed by *to* in British English or *than* in American English.

Students today are <u>different from</u> the students ten years ago.

adjectives followed by *to*-infinitive clauses

2.51 To complete the meaning of some adjectives that are used predicatively, you need to follow with a clause beginning with a **to-infinitive**. For example, you cannot just say *He is unable.* You have to add a clause beginning with *to*-infinitive such as *to do: He is unable to do it.* **To-infinitive clauses** are explained in the Reference section.

They were <u>unable to help her</u>.
I am <u>willing to try</u>.
She is <u>bound to notice there's something wrong</u>.
I'm <u>inclined to agree with the minister</u>.

Here is a list of adjectives that are always or nearly always followed by a *to*-infinitive clause:

able	doomed	fit	likely	unable
bound	due	inclined	loath	unwilling
destined	fated	liable	prepared	willing

2.52 You can also use a clause beginning with a *to*-infinitive after many other adjectives to give more information about something.

I was <u>afraid to go home</u>.
I was <u>happy to see them again</u>.
He was <u>powerless to prevent it</u>.
I was almost <u>ashamed to tell her</u>.
The path was <u>easy to follow</u>.

Note that the subject of the main clause is also the subject of the *to*-infinitive clause.

adjectives followed by *that*-clauses

2.53 When adjectives that refer to someone's beliefs or feelings are used after a linking verb, they are often followed by a **that-clause** (see paragraphs 8.119 to 8.121). The subject of the *that*-clause is not always the same as the subject of the main clause, so you need to specify it.

She was <u>sure that</u> he meant it.
He was <u>frightened that</u> something terrible might be said.
I'm <u>aware that</u> I reached a rather large audience through the book.

Note that the word *that* is not always used in a *that*-clause.

They were <u>sure</u> she had been born in the city.

Here is a list of common adjectives often followed by a *that*-clause:

afraid	certain	happy	sorry	upset
angry	confident	pleased	sure	worried
anxious	frightened	proud	surprised	
aware	glad	sad	unaware	

Note that all of these adjectives except *angry, aware, unaware, upset,* and *worried* can also be followed by a *to*-infinitive.

I was <u>afraid that she might not be able to bear the strain</u>.
Don't be <u>afraid to ask questions</u>.
She was <u>surprised that I knew about it</u>.
The twins were very <u>surprised to see Ralph</u>.

Position of adjectives in noun phrases

2.54 When you use more than one adjective in a noun phrase, the usual order for the adjectives is: qualitative adjectives, followed by colour adjectives, followed by classifying adjectives.

...a <u>little white wooden</u> house.
...<u>pretty black lacy</u> dresses.
...a <u>large circular</u> pool of water.
...a <u>beautiful pink</u> suit.
...<u>rapid technological</u> advance.
...a <u>nice red</u> apple.
...the <u>black triangular</u> fin.

This order is nearly always followed in English. Occasionally however, when you want to focus on a particular characteristic of the person or thing you are describing, you can vary this order, especially when one of the adjectives refers to colour or size.

...a <u>square black</u> hole.

Note that you sometimes put a comma or *and* between adjectives. This is explained in paragraphs 8.180 to 8.186 and paragraph 8.201.

...the <u>long, low</u> caravan.
It was a <u>long and tedious</u> business.

2.55 **Comparatives** (see paragraphs 2.103 to 2.111) and **superlatives** (see paragraphs 2.112 to 2.122) normally come in front of all other adjectives in a noun phrase.

...<u>better</u> parental control.
...the <u>highest</u> monthly figures on record.

position of noun modifiers and adjectives

2.56 When a noun phrase contains both an adjective and a noun modifier (see paragraphs 2.169 to 2.174) the adjective is placed in front of the noun modifier.

...the booming European <u>car</u> industry.
...the world's biggest and most prestigious <u>book</u> fair.

two or more adjectives after a linking verb

2.57 When you use two adjectives after a linking verb, you use a conjunction, usually *and*, to link them. If you use more than two adjectives, you usually put a conjunction such as *and* between the last two adjectives and commas between the others. This is fully explained in paragraphs 8.180 to 8.186 and paragraph 8.201.

The room was large and square.
We felt hot, tired, and thirsty.

Note that you put the adjectives in the order that you think is the most important.

adjectives after nouns

2.58 There are a few adjectives that are usually or always used after a noun. Here is a list showing the different groups of adjectives used after a noun:

designate	~	old	concerned	~
elect	broad	tall	involved	affected
galore	deep	thick	present	available
incarnate	high	wide	proper	required
manqué	long	~	responsible	suggested

ℹ USAGE NOTE

2.59 The adjectives *designate*, *elect*, *galore*, *incarnate*, and *manqué* are only used immediately after a noun.

She was now president elect.
There are empty houses galore.

2.60 The adjectives *broad*, *deep*, *high*, *long*, *old*, *tall*, *thick*, and *wide* are used immediately after measurement nouns when giving the size, duration, or age of a thing or person. This use is fully explained in paragraph 2.253.

...six feet tall.
...three metres wide.
...twenty five years old.

2.61 The adjectives *concerned*, *involved*, *present*, *responsible*, and *proper* have different meanings depending on whether you put them in front of a noun or immediately after one. For example, *the concerned mother* describes a mother who is anxious, but *the mother concerned* simply refers to a mother who has just been mentioned.

...the approval of interested and concerned parents.
The idea needs to come from the individuals concerned.
All this became a very involved process.
He knew all of the people involved.
...the present international situation.
Of the 18 people present, I know only one.
...parents trying to act in a responsible manner.
...the person responsible for his death.
...a proper training in how to teach.
...the first round proper of the FA Cup.

2.62 The adjectives *affected*, *available*, *required*, and *suggested* can be used in front of a noun or after a noun without any change in meaning.

Newspapers were the only <u>available</u> source of information.
...the number of teachers <u>available</u>.
...the <u>required</u> changes.
You're way below the standard <u>required</u>.
...the cost of the <u>suggested</u> improvements.
The proposals <u>suggested</u> are derived from successful experiments.
Aside from the <u>affected</u> child, the doctor checks every other member of the household.
...the proportion of the population <u>affected</u>.

Special forms: -*ing* adjectives

2.63 There are many adjectives ending in -*ing*. Most of them are related in form to the **-*ing* participles** of verbs. In this grammar they are called **-*ing* adjectives**.

He was an amiable, <u>amusing</u> fellow.
He had been up all night attending a <u>dying</u> man.

The **-*ing* form** is explained in the Reference section.

describing an effect

2.64 One group of -*ing* adjectives describe the effect that something has on your feelings and ideas, or on the feelings and ideas of people in general.

...an <u>alarming</u> increase in burglaries.
A <u>surprising</u> number of men do not marry.
...a <u>charming</u> house on the outskirts of the town.
...a warm <u>welcoming</u> smile.

2.65 These adjectives are normally **qualitative adjectives**. This means that they can be used with a **submodifying adverb** (a word like *very* or *rather*), and have comparatives and superlatives.

...a <u>very convincing</u> example.
There is nothing <u>very surprising</u> in this.
...a <u>very exciting</u> idea.
...a <u>really pleasing</u> evening at the theatre.
When Bernard moans he's much <u>more convincing</u>.
...one of <u>the most boring</u> books I've ever read.

2.66 They can be used in front of a noun or after a linking verb.

They can still show <u>amazing</u> loyalty to their parents.
It's <u>amazing</u> what they can do.
...the most <u>terrifying</u> tale ever written.
The present situation is <u>terrifying</u>.

2.67 These -*ing* adjectives have a related transitive verb that you use to describe the way someone is affected by something. For example, if you speak of *an alarming increase*, you mean that the increase alarms you. If you speak of *a surprising number*, you mean that the number surprises you.

Here is a list of *-ing* adjectives that describe an effect and that have a similar meaning to the usual meaning of the related verb:

alarming	demeaning	harassing	rewarding
amazing	depressing	humiliating	satisfying
amusing	devastating	infuriating	shocking
annoying	disappointing	inspiring	sickening
appalling	disgusting	interesting	startling
astonishing	distracting	intimidating	surprising
astounding	distressing	intriguing	tempting
bewildering	disturbing	menacing	terrifying
boring	embarrassing	misleading	threatening
challenging	enchanting	mocking	thrilling
charming	encouraging	overwhelming	tiring
compelling	entertaining	pleasing	welcoming
confusing	exciting	refreshing	worrying
convincing	frightening	relaxing	

Transitive verbs are explained in paragraphs 3.14 to 3.25.

describing a process or state

2.68 The other main group of *-ing* adjectives are used to describe a process or state that continues over a period of time.

...her *growing* band of supporters.
Oil and gas drillers are doing a *booming* business.
...a life of *increasing* labour and *decreasing* leisure.

2.69 These adjectives are **classifying adjectives**, so they are not used with words like *very* and *rather*. However, adjectives used to identify a process are often modified by adverbs that describe the speed with which the process happens.

...a *fast diminishing* degree of personal freedom.
...*rapidly rising* productivity.

2.70 These *-ing* adjectives have related intransitive verbs.

Here is a list of *-ing* adjectives that describe a continuing process or state and that have a similar meaning to the usual meaning of the related verb:

ageing	bursting	dying	prevailing	resounding
ailing	decreasing	existing	recurring	rising
bleeding	diminishing	increasing	reigning	ruling
booming	dwindling	living	remaining	

Intransitive verbs are explained in paragraphs 3.8 to 3.13.

2.71 These *-ing* adjectives are only used in front of a noun, so when *-ing* forms of intransitive verbs appear after the verb *be* they are actually part of a progressive form.

BE CREATIVE

2.72 | In English, you can make most verbs into adjectives by adding *-ing* to the verb and putting it in front of the noun, to say what someone or something is doing.

...*a* <u>walking</u> *figure.*
...*FIFA, world football's* <u>ruling</u> *body.*
...*bands performing in front of* <u>screaming</u> *crowds.*
...*two years of* <u>falling</u> *employment.*
...*a tremendous noise of* <u>smashing</u> *glass.*

form and meaning

2.73 Most of the *-ing* adjectives talked about so far are related to verbs. Sometimes however, *-ing* adjectives are not related to verbs at all. For example, there is no verb *to neighbour*.

Whole families came from <u>neighbouring</u> *villages.*

Here is a list of *-ing* adjectives that are not related to verbs:

appetizing	enterprising	neighbouring
balding	excruciating	scathing
cunning	impending	unwitting

2.74 Sometimes, an *-ing* adjective is related to an uncommon use of a verb, or appears to be related to a verb but is not related exactly to any current use. For example, the verb *haunt* is most commonly used in connection with ghosts, but the adjective *haunting* is more often used to talk about such things as songs and memories. A *haunting tune* is a tune you cannot forget.

Here is a list of qualitative *-ing* adjectives that are not related to a common transitive use of a verb:

becoming	engaging	penetrating	ravishing	trying
bracing	fetching	piercing	retiring	
cutting	halting	pressing	revolting	
dashing	haunting	promising	searching	
disarming	moving	rambling	taxing	

Here is a list of classifying *-ing* adjectives that are not related to a common intransitive use of a verb:

acting	floating	going	missing
driving	gathering	leading	running

2.75 Some adjectives are derived from a verb and a prefix. For example, *outgoing* is derived from the verb *go* and the prefix *out-*. There is no verb *to outgo*.

Wouldn't that cause a delay in <u>outgoing</u> *mail?*

Here is a list of *-ing* adjectives derived from a verb and a prefix:

forthcoming	outgoing	uplifting
incoming	outstanding	upstanding
oncoming	overarching	
ongoing	overbearing	

2.76   A small group of *-ing* adjectives are used in informal spoken English for emphasis, usually to express disapproval. This use is explained in paragraphs 2.41 to 2.42.

Some **compound adjectives** (see paragraphs 2.94 to 2.102) end in *-ing*.

Special forms: *-ed* adjectives

2.77   A large number of English adjectives end in *-ed*. Many of them have the same form as the **-ed participle** of a verb. Others are formed by adding *-ed* to a noun. Others are not closely related to any other words.

...a <u>disappointed</u> man.
...a <u>bearded</u> man.
...<u>sophisticated</u> electronic devices.

2.78   Adjectives with the same form as irregular **-ed participles** (see the Reference section) that do not end in *-ed* are also included here as *-ed* adjectives.

Was it a <u>broken</u> bone, a <u>torn</u> ligament, or what?

The *-ed* participles of some **phrasal verbs** (see paragraphs 3.83 to 3.116) can also be used as adjectives. When they are used in front of a noun, the two parts of the phrasal verb are usually written with a hyphen between them.

...the <u>built-up</u> urban mass of the city.

2.79   Most *-ed* adjectives are related to a transitive verb and have a passive meaning. They show that something has happened or is happening to the thing being described. For example, *a frightened person* is a person who has been frightened by something. *A known criminal* is a criminal who is known by the police.

We have a long list of <u>satisfied</u> customers.
We cannot refuse to teach children the <u>required</u> subjects.

qualitative *-ed* adjectives

2.80   *-ed* adjectives that refer to a person's mental or emotional reaction to something are generally qualitative.

He was a <u>worried</u> old man.
...a <u>bored</u> old woman.
...an <u>interested</u> student.

These adjectives can be modified by words such as *very* and *extremely*, just like other qualitative adjectives (see paragraphs 2.140 to 2.156).

form and meaning

2.81   Like other adjectives used for talking about feelings, these adjectives are often used to describe the expression, voice, or manner of the person affected, instead of referring directly to that person.

...her big blue <u>frightened</u> eyes.
She could hear his <u>agitated</u> voice.
Barry gave him a <u>worried</u> look.

2.82 Here is a list of qualitative -*ed* adjectives that have a similar meaning to the most common meaning of the related verb:

agitated	confused	disgusted	inhibited	shocked
alarmed	contented	disillusioned	interested	surprised
amused	delighted	distressed	pleased	tired
appalled	depressed	embarrassed	preoccupied	troubled
astonished	deprived	excited	puzzled	worried
bored	disappointed	frightened	satisfied	

Here is a list of qualitative -*ed* adjectives that do not have a similar meaning to the usual meaning of the related verb:

animated	determined	guarded	mixed
attached	disposed	hurt	strained
concerned	disturbed	inclined	

classifying -*ed* adjectives

2.83 Many other -*ed* adjectives are used for classifying, and so cannot be used with words like *very* and *rather*. For example, *a furnished apartment* is one type of apartment, contrasting with *an apartment without furniture*.

...a <u>furnished</u> apartment.
...a <u>painted</u> wooden bowl.
...the <u>closed</u> bedroom door.

Most adjectives that refer to physical distinctions are classifying adjectives.

2.84 Here is a list of classifying -*ed* adjectives that have a similar meaning to the most common meaning of the related verb:

abandoned	closed	established	integrated	reduced
armed	concentrated	fixed	known	required
blocked	condemned	furnished	licensed	torn
boiled	cooked	haunted	loaded	trained
broken	divided	hidden	paid	united
canned	drawn	improved	painted	wasted
classified	dried	infected	processed	

Here is list of -*ed* classifying adjectives that have a different meaning from the most common meaning of the related verb:

advanced	noted	spotted
marked	pointed	veiled

2.85 Classifying -ed adjectives cannot normally be modified with words like *quite* and *very*. However, an **adverb of manner**, (see paragraphs 6.36 to 6.44) or an **adverb of degree**, (see paragraphs 6.45 to 6.52) is often used before an -ed adjective.

For example, *a pleasantly furnished room* is a room that has been furnished with pleasant furniture.

...pleasantly furnished rooms.
...a well-known novelist.

2.86 Some -ed adjectives are not often used on their own, and an adverb is necessary to complete the sense. You do not usually talk about *dressed people*, but you can say that they are *well dressed* or *smartly dressed* for example. The -ed adjectives in the following examples nearly always have an adverb in front of them.

...a cautiously worded statement.
...impeccably dressed men.
It was a richly deserved honour.
...superbly cut clothes.
...the existence of a highly developed national press.
...a well organized campaign.
...a tall, powerfully built man.
She gazed down at his perfectly formed little face.

Note that combinations like this are sometimes hyphenated, making them **compound adjectives**.

...a well-equipped army.

-ed adjectives with an active meaning

2.87 A few -ed adjectives are related to the -ed participle of intransitive verbs and have an active meaning, not a passive meaning. For example, *a fallen tree* is a tree that has fallen.

...a capsized ship.
She is the daughter of a retired army officer.
...an escaped prisoner.

Here is a list of -ed adjectives with an active meaning:

accumulated	escaped	fallen	swollen
dated	faded	retired	wilted

-ed adjectives after linking verbs

2.88 Most -ed adjectives can be used both in front of a noun and after a linking verb.

The worried authorities decided to play safe.
My husband was worried.

A small number of -ed adjectives are normally only used after a linking verb. Often, they are followed by a preposition, a *to*-infinitive, or a *that*-clause.

I was thrilled by the exhibition.
The Brazilians are pleased with the results.
...food destined for areas of south Sudan.
He was always prepared to account for his actions.

Here is a list of *-ed* adjectives often used after a linking verb, with or without a phrase or clause after them:

convinced	intimidated	pleased	thrilled
delighted	intrigued	prepared	tired
interested	involved	scared	touched

Here is a list of *-ed* adjectives normally used after a linking verb with a phrase or clause after them:

agreed	dressed	lost	shut
destined	finished	prepared	stuck

✪ BE CREATIVE

2.89 The *-ed* participle of almost any transitive verb can be used as an adjective, though some are more commonly used than others.

...she said, with a <u>forced</u> smile.
There was one <u>paid</u> tutor and three volunteer tutors.
The <u>recovered</u> animals will be released.
...the final <u>corrected</u> version.

✪ BE CREATIVE

2.90 Some *-ed* adjectives are formed from nouns. For example, if a living thing has wings, you can describe it as *winged*. If someone has skills, you can describe them as *skilled*.

...<u>winged</u> angels.
...a <u>skilled</u> engineer.
She was dressed in black and carried a black <u>beaded</u> purse.
...<u>armoured</u> cars.
...the education of <u>gifted</u> children.

-ed adjectives formed from nouns

2.91 Here is a list of *-ed* adjectives formed from nouns:

armoured	detailed	gloved	principled	striped
barbed	flowered	hooded	salaried	turbaned
beaded	freckled	mannered	skilled	walled
bearded	gifted	pointed	spotted	winged

-ed adjectives formed from nouns are commonly used as the second part of **compound adjectives** (see paragraph 2.94 to 2.102) such as *grey-haired* and *open-minded*.

-ed adjectives unrelated to verbs or nouns

2.92 There are also some *-ed* adjectives in regular use that are not related to verbs or nouns in the ways described above. For example, there are no words *parch* or *belove*. There is a noun *concert*, but the adjective *concerted* does not mean *having a concert*.

He climbed up the dry <u>parched</u> grass to the terrace steps.
...a complex and <u>antiquated</u> system of taxation.
...attempts to mount a <u>concerted</u> campaign.
...the purchase of expensive <u>sophisticated</u> equipment.

2.93   Here is a list of *-ed* adjectives that are not related to verbs or nouns:

antiquated	beloved	crazed	indebted	sophisticated
ashamed	bloated	deceased	parched	tinned
assorted	concerted	doomed	rugged	

Compound adjectives

2.94   **Compound adjectives** are made up of two or more words, usually written with hyphens between them. They may be qualitative, classifying, or colour adjectives.

I was in a <u>light-hearted</u> mood.
She was dressed in a <u>bottle-green</u> party dress.
...the <u>built-up</u> urban mass of the city.
...an <u>air-conditioned</u> restaurant.
...a <u>good-looking</u> girl.
...<u>one-way</u> traffic.
...a <u>part-time</u> job.

formation patterns

2.95   These are the most common and least restricted patterns for forming compound adjectives:

▶ adjective or number plus noun plus *-ed*, e.g. *grey-haired* and *one-sided*

▶ adjective or adverb plus *-ed* participle, e.g. *low-paid* and *well-behaved*

▶ adjective, adverb, or noun plus *-ing* participle, e.g. *good-looking*, *long-lasting* and *man-eating*.

Note that compound adjectives describe simple concepts: a *good-looking* person looks good, and a *man-eating* beast eats humans. More complex descriptions in English need to be given using a following phrase or clause.

2.96   These are less common and more restricted patterns for forming compound adjectives:

▶ noun plus *-ed* participle, e.g. *tongue-tied* and *wind-swept*

▶ noun plus adjective, e.g. *accident-prone*, *trouble-free*

▶ adjective plus noun, e.g. *deep-sea*, *present-day*

▶ *-ed* participle plus adverb, e.g. *run-down*, *cast-off*

▶ number plus singular countable noun, e.g. *five-page*, *four-door*

Note that compound adjectives formed according to the last of these patterns are always used in front of a noun.

compound qualitative adjectives

2.97 Here is a list of compound qualitative adjectives:

able-bodied	laid-back	one-sided	swollen-headed
absent-minded	light-hearted	open-minded	tender-hearted
accident-prone	long-lasting	run-down	thick-skinned
big-headed	long-standing	second-class	tongue-tied
clear-cut	long-suffering	second-rate	top-heavy
close-fitting	low-cut	shop-soiled	trouble-free
cold-blooded	low-paid	short-handed	two-edged
easy-going	low-slung	short-lived	two-faced
far-fetched	mind-blowing	short-sighted	warm-hearted
far-reaching	mouth-watering	short-tempered	well-balanced
good-looking	muddle-headed	slow-witted	well-behaved
good-tempered	narrow-minded	smooth-talking	well-dressed
hard-up	nice-looking	soft-hearted	well-known
hard-wearing	off-colour	starry-eyed	well-off
ill-advised	off-hand	strong-minded	wind-blown
kind-hearted	off-putting	stuck-up	worldly-wise
labour saving	old-fashioned	sun-tanned	wrong-headed

compound classifying adjectives

2.98 Here is a list of compound classifying adjectives:

air-conditioned	deep-seated	full-scale
all-out	double-barrelled	gilt-edged
all-powerful	double-breasted	grey-haired
audio-visual	drip-dry	half-price
blue-blooded	drive-in	half-yearly
bow-legged	duty-bound	hand-picked
brand-new	duty-free	high-heeled
breast-fed	empty-handed	home-made
broken-down	face-saving	ice-cold
broken-hearted	far-flung	interest-free
built-up	first-class	knee-deep
bullet-proof	free-range	last-minute
burnt-out	free-standing	late-night
cast-off	freeze-dried	lead-free
clean-shaven	front-page	left-handed
cross-Channel	full-blown	life-size
cross-country	full-face	long-distance
cut-price	full-grown	long-lost
deep-sea	full-length	long-range

loose-leaf	panic-stricken	so-called
made-up	part-time	so-so
man-eating	present-day	south-east
mass-produced	purpose-built	south-west
middle-aged	ready-made	strong-arm
never-ending	record-breaking	tax-free
north-east	red-brick	tone-deaf
north-west	remote-controlled	top-secret
nuclear-free	right-angled	unheard-of
odds-on	right-handed	wide-awake
off-guard	second-class	world-famous
off-peak	second-hand	worn-out
one-way	see-through	year-long
open-ended	silver-plated	
open-mouthed	single-handed	

compound colour adjectives

2.99 Here is a list of compound colour adjectives:

blood-red	flesh-coloured	navy-blue	royal-blue
blue-black	ice-blue	nut-brown	shocking-pink
bottle-green	iron-grey	off-white	sky-blue
dove-grey	jet-black	pea-green	snow-white
electric-blue	lime-green	pearl-grey	

long compound adjectives

2.100 A few compound adjectives are made up of more than two words. Compounds of three or more words are often written with hyphens when they are used in front of nouns, and without hyphens when they are used after a linking verb.

...the _day-to-day_ chores of life.
...a _down-to-earth_ approach.
...a _free-and-easy_ relationship.
..._life-and-death_ decisions.
...a trip to an _out-of-the-way_ resort.
Their act is _out of date_.

2.101 Some compound adjectives seem rather odd because they contain words that are never used as single words on their own, for example _namby-pamby_, _higgledy-piggledy_, and _topsy-turvy_. Words like these are usually informal.

...all that _artsy-craftsy_ spiritualism.
...his _la-di-da_ family.

2.102 Some compound adjectives are borrowed from foreign languages, especially from French and Latin.

...the arguments once used to defend laissez-faire economics.
...their present per capita fuel consumption.
In the commercial theatre, almost every production is ad hoc.

Here is a list of compound adjectives borrowed from other languages:

à la mode	compos mentis	hors de combat
a posteriori	cordon bleu	infra dig
a priori	de facto	laissez-faire
ad hoc	de jure	non compos mentis
ad lib	de luxe	per capita
au fait	de rigueur	prima facie
avant-garde	de trop	pro rata
bona fide	ex gratia	sub judice

Comparing things: comparatives

2.103 You can describe something by saying that it has more of a quality than something else. You do this by using **comparative adjectives**. Only qualitative adjectives usually have comparatives, but a few colour adjectives also have them. Comparatives normally consist of the usual form of the adjective with either *-er* added to the end, as in *harder* and *smaller*, or *more* placed in front, as in *more interesting* and *more flexible*.

Note that *good* and *bad* have the irregular comparative forms *better* and *worse*.

The patterns for forming regular and irregular comparatives are explained in the Reference section.

2.104 Comparatives can be used as **modifiers** in front of a noun.

The family moved to a smaller home.
He dreams of a better, more exciting life.
A harder mattress often helps with back injuries.

Note that comparatives can also be used as modifiers in front of *one*.

An understanding of this reality provokes a better one.

2.105 Comparatives can also be used after a **linking verb**.

The ball soaked up water and became heavier.
His breath became quieter.
We need to be more flexible.

The use of adjectives after linking verbs is explained in paragraphs 3.132 to 3.137.

structures used after comparatives

2.106 Comparatives are often followed by *than* when you want to specify what the other thing involved in the comparison is. You say exactly what you are comparing by using one of a number of structures after *than*.

These structures can be

▶ noun phrases

Charlie was <u>more honest than his predecessor</u>.
...an area <u>bigger than Mexico</u>.

Note that when *than* is followed by a pronoun on its own, the pronoun must be an object pronoun such as *me*, *him*, or *her*.

My brother is <u>younger than me</u>.
Lamin was <u>shorter than her</u>.

▶ phrases that start with a preposition

The changes will be even <u>more striking</u> in the case of teaching <u>than in medicine</u>.
The odds of surviving childhood in New York City are <u>worse than in some Third World countries</u>.

▶ clauses

I would have done a <u>better job than he did</u>.
I was a <u>better</u> writer <u>than he was</u>.
He's <u>taller than I am</u>.

Note that when a comparative is not followed by a *than* phrase, the other thing in the comparison should be obvious. For example, if someone says *Could I have a bigger one, please?* they are likely to be holding the item that they think is too small.

A mattress would be <u>better</u>.

position of comparatives

2.107 If you choose a phrase or clause beginning with *than* when you are using a comparative in front of a noun, you usually put the phrase or clause after the whole noun phrase, not directly after the comparative.

The world is a <u>more dangerous</u> place <u>than it was</u>.
Willy owned a <u>larger</u> collection of books <u>than anyone else I have ever met</u>.

A comparative can also come immediately after a noun, but only when it is followed by *than* and a noun phrase.

We've got a rat <u>bigger than</u> a cat living in our roof.
...packs of cards <u>larger than</u> he was used to.

more and more than

2.108 *More* is sometimes used in front of a whole noun phrase to show that something has more of the qualities of one thing than another, or is one thing rather than being another.

Music is <u>more</u> a way of life <u>than</u> an interest.
This is <u>more</u> a war movie <u>than</u> a western.

Note that *more than* is used before adjectives for emphasis.

Their life may be horribly dull, but they are <u>more than satisfied</u>.
You would be <u>more than welcome</u>.

comparatives used as nouns

2.109 Comparative adjectives are sometimes used as noun-type words in fairly formal English. In such phrases, you put *the* in front of it, and follow it with *of* and a noun phrase that refers to the two things being compared.

...the shorter of the two lines.
Dorothea was the more beautiful of the two.
There are two windmills, the larger of which stands a hundred feet high.

If it is clear what you are talking about, you can omit *of* and the following noun phrase.

Notice to quit must cover the rental period or four weeks, whichever is the longer.

less

2.110 The form that is used to say that something does not have as much of a quality as something else is *less* followed by an adjective.

The answer had been less truthful than his own.

You can also use *less* and an adjective to say that something does not have as much of a quality as it had before.

As the days went by, Sita became less anxious.

Note that *less than* is used before adjectives to express a negative idea.

It would have been less than fair.

contrasted comparatives

2.111 You show that one amount of a quality or thing is linked to another amount by using two contrasted comparatives preceded by *the*.

The smaller it is, the cheaper it is to post.
The more militant we became, the less confident she became.
The larger the organization, the less scope there is for decision.

Comparing things: superlatives

2.112 Another way of describing something is to say that it has more of a quality than anything else of its kind. You do this by using a **superlative adjective**. Only qualitative adjectives usually have superlatives, but a few colour adjectives also have them. Superlatives normally consist of either *-est* added to the end of an adjective and *the* placed in front of it, as in *the hardest* and *the smallest*, or of *the most* placed in front of the adjective, as in *the most interesting* and *the most flexible*.

Note that *good* and *bad* have the irregular superlative forms *the best* and *the worst*.

The patterns for forming regular and irregular superlatives of adjectives are explained in the Reference section.

Note that superlative adjectives are nearly always preceded by *the*, because you are talking about something definite. Occasionally, when superlatives are used after a linking verb, *the* is omitted (see paragraph 2.117).

❗ BE CAREFUL

2.113 Adjectives with *most* in front of them are not always superlatives. *Most* can also mean *very*.

This book was <u>most interesting</u>.
My grandfather was a <u>most extraordinary</u> man.

Words like *very* and *rather* are called **submodifying adverbs**. These are explained in paragraphs 2.140 to 2.156.

used in front of a noun

2.114 Superlatives can be used as **modifiers** in front of a noun.

He was <u>the cleverest</u> man I ever knew.
It was <u>the most exciting</u> summer of their lives.
She came out of <u>the thickest</u> part of the crowd.
Now we come to <u>the most important</u> thing.
...<u>the oldest</u> rock paintings in North America.
...<u>the most eminent</u> scientists in Britain.

Note that superlatives are also used as modifiers in front of *one*.

No one ever used <u>the smallest</u> one.

used after a linking verb

2.115 Superlatives are also used after a **linking verb**.

He was <u>the youngest</u>.
The sergeant was <u>the tallest</u>.

The use of adjectives after linking verbs is explained in paragraphs 3.132 to 3.137.

structures used after superlatives

2.116 You can use a superlative on its own if it is clear what is being compared. For example, if you say *Paul was the tallest*, you are referring to a group of people that has already been identified.

If you need to refer to the point of the comparison, you use a phrase or clause that consists of

▶ phrases that start with a preposition, usually *in* or *of*

Henry was <u>the biggest of them</u>.
The third requirement is <u>the most important of all</u>.
These cakes are probably <u>the best in the world</u>.

Note that if the superlative is placed in front of a noun, the preposition comes after the noun.

...the <u>best</u> hotel for families.
I'm in <u>the worst</u> business in the world.

▶ a relative clause

It's <u>the best</u> I'm likely to get.
The waiting room was <u>the worst</u> I had seen.

Note that if the superlative is placed in front of a noun, the relative clause comes after the noun.

That's <u>the most convincing</u> answer that you've given me.

USAGE NOTE

2.117 You usually put *the* in front of the superlative, but you can occasionally omit it, especially in informal speech or writing.

> *Wool and cotton blankets are generally <u>cheapest</u>.*
> *It can be used by whoever is <u>closest</u>.*

However, you cannot omit *the* when the superlative is followed by *of* or another structure showing what group of things you are comparing. So, for example, you can say *Amanda was the youngest of our group* or *Amanda was the youngest* or *Amanda was youngest*, but you cannot say *Amanda was youngest of our group*.

You can sometimes use the possessive form of a noun or a possessive determiner instead of *the* in front of a superlative. Often the possessive form of a noun is used instead of a phrase beginning with a preposition. For example, you can say *Britain's oldest man* instead of *the oldest man in Britain*.

> *...<u>the world's most popular</u> cheese.*
> *...<u>my newest</u> assistant.*

The possessive form of nouns is explained in paragraphs 1.211 to 1.222, and possessive determiners are explained in paragraphs 1.194 to 1.210.

used with other adjectives

2.118 A superlative is sometimes accompanied by another adjective ending in *-able* or *-ible*. This second adjective can be placed either between the superlative and the noun or after the noun.

> *...<u>the narrowest imaginable</u> range of interests.*
> *...<u>the most beautiful</u> scenery <u>imaginable</u>.*
> *...<u>the longest possible</u> gap.*
> *I say that in <u>the nicest</u> way <u>possible</u>.*

superlatives used as nouns

2.119 Superlative adjectives are sometimes used like nouns in fairly formal English. When you use a superlative adjective in this way, you put *the* in front of it, and follow it with *of* and a noun or pronoun that refers to the things being compared. When superlative adjectives are used in this way they can refer to one thing or to more than one.

> *They are often too poor to buy or rent even <u>the cheapest</u> of houses.*
> *He made several important discoveries. <u>The most interesting</u> of these came from an examination of an old manuscript.*

If it is clear what you are talking about, you can omit *of* and the following noun phrase.

> *There are three types of ant-eater. <u>The smallest</u> lives entirely in trees.*

 USAGE NOTE

2.120 In informal speech, people often use a superlative rather than a comparative when they are talking about two things. For example, someone might say *The train is quickest* rather than *The train is quicker* when comparing a train service with a bus service. However, some people think that it is better to use superlatives only when comparing more than two things.

used with ordinal numbers: *the second biggest city*

2.121   **Ordinal numbers** are used with superlatives to show that something has more of a quality than nearly all other things of their kind. For example, if you say that a mountain is *the second highest mountain*, you mean that it is higher than any other mountain except the highest one.

> Cancer is *the second biggest* cause of death in Britain.
> ...*the second most important* man in her life, her hairdresser.
> It is Japan's *third largest* city.

Ordinal numbers are explained in paragraphs 2.232 to 2.239.

the least

2.122   When you want to show that something has less of a quality than anything else, you use *the least* followed by an adjective.

> This is *the least popular* branch of medicine.

Similarly, when you are talking about a group of things that have less of a quality than other things of their kind, you use *the least*.

> ...*the least savage* men in the country.

Other ways of comparing things: saying that things are similar

2.123   Another way of describing things is by saying that something is similar in some way to something else.

talking about things with the same quality

2.124   If you want to say that a thing or person has as much of a quality as something or someone else, you can use a structure based on the word *as* in front of a qualitative adjective. Usually this adjective is followed by a phrase or clause that also begins with *as*.

This can be

▶ a phrase beginning with the preposition *as*

> You're just *as bad as your sister*.
> ...huge ponds *as big as tennis courts*.
> Takings were *as high as ever*.

▶ a clause introduced by *as*

> Conversation was not *as slow as I feared it would be*.
> The village gardens aren't *as good as they used to be*.

2.125   When this comparative structure is followed by a phrase consisting of *as* and a pronoun on its own, the pronoun must be an object pronoun such as *me*, *him*, or *her*.

> Jane was not as clever as *him*.

However, when the comparative structure is followed by a clause consisting of *as* and a pronoun that is the subject of a clause, then that pronoun must be a subject pronoun such as *I*, *he* or *she*.

> They aren't as clever as *they appear to be*.

2.126 If it is clear what you are comparing something or someone to, you can omit the phrase or clause.

Frozen peas are just as good.

2.127 You can also use the *as...as...* structure to say that something has much more or less of a quality than something else. You do this by putting an expression such as *twice*, *three times*, *ten times*, or *half* in front of the first *as*. For example, if one building is ten metres high and another building is twenty metres high, you can say that the second building is *twice as high as* the first building or that the first building is *half as high as* the second one.

The grass was twice as tall as in the rest of the field.
Water is eight hundred times as dense as air.

This structure is often used in the same way to refer to qualities that cannot be measured. For example, if you want to say that something is much more useful than something else, you can say that the first thing is *a hundred times as useful as* the second one.

Without this help, rearing our children would be ten times as hard as it is.

USAGE NOTE

2.128 When the *as...as...* structure is preceded by *not*, it has the same meaning as *less...than*. For example, *I am not as tall as George* means the same as *I am less tall than George*. Some people use *not so...as...* instead of *not as...as...*.

The film is not as good as the book.
The young otter is not so handsome as the old.

2.129 Words like *just*, *quite*, *nearly* and *almost* can be used in front of this comparative structure, modifying the comparison with their usual meanings.

Sunburn can be just as severe as a heat burn.

The use of these words in comparison is explained in paragraphs 2.157 to 2.168.

2.130 When you are using the *as...as...* structure you sometimes put a noun after the adjective and before the following phrase or clause. This noun must begin with *a* or *an*. For example, instead of saying *This knife is as good as that one*, you can say *This is as good a knife as that one*.

I'm as good a cook as she is.
This was not as bad a result as they expected.

Sometimes, instead of using *not* before this structure, you use *not such* followed by *a* or *an*, an adjective, a noun, and *as*.

Water is not such a good conductor as metal.

2.131 Instead of using this *as...as...* structure you can use expressions such as *the height of* and *the size of* to show that something is as big as something else, or bigger or smaller.

The tumour was the size of a golf ball.
It is roughly the length of a man's arm.

`like`

2.132 If something has similar qualities or features to something else, instead of using the *as...as...* comparative structure you can say that the first thing is *like* the second one. You do this by using phrases beginning with *like* after **linking verbs**.

He looked like an actor.
That sounds like an exaggeration.
The whole thing is like a bad dream.

Here is a list of the linking verbs used with *like*:

be	look	smell	taste
feel	seem	sound	

When you want to say that one thing resembles another, you can use a phrase beginning with *like* after these linking verbs.

It was like a dream.
Sometimes I feel like a prisoner here.
He looked like a nice man.
The houses seemed like mansions.
You smell like a tramp!
It sounded like a fine idea.

2.133 *Like* has the comparative *more like* and *less like*, and the superlative *most like* and *least like*.

It made her seem less like a child.
Of all his children, she was the one most like me.

ℹ **USAGE NOTE**

2.134 You can use words like *exactly* and *just* in front of *like*.

He looks just like a baby.
She looked like a queen, just exactly like a queen

This is explained in paragraph 2.165.

same as

2.135 If you want to say that one thing is exactly like something else, you can say that it is *the same as* the other thing.

The rich are the same as the rest of us.

The same as can be followed by a noun phrase, a pronoun, or a clause.

24 Spring Terrace was the same as all its neighbours.
Her colouring was the same as mine.
The furnishings are not exactly the same as they were when we lived there.

If two or more things are exactly like each other, you can say that they are *the same*.

Come and look! They're exactly the same.
They both taste the same.

You use *the same* when you are comparing people or things with other people or things that you have just mentioned.

It looks like a calculator and weighs about the same.
The message was the same.
The end result is the same.

Note that you use *the opposite* and *the reverse* in a similar way.

The kind of religious thoughts I had were just the opposite.
Some people think that a healthy diet is expensive, but in fact the reverse is true.

2.136 You can use words like *nearly* and *exactly* in front of *the same as* and *the same*.

They are virtually the same as other single cells.
You two look exactly the same.

Here is a list of words used in the same way with *the same as* and *the same*:

almost	just	much	virtually
exactly	more or less	nearly	

These words are explained in paragraphs 2.140 to 2.168.

2.137 You can put a noun such as *size*, *length*, or *colour* after *the same*. For example, if you want to say that one street is as long as another one, you can say that the first street is *the same length as* the second one, or that the two streets are *the same length*.

Its brain was about the same size as that of a gorilla.
They were almost the same height.

adjectives meaning *the same*

2.138 The adjectives *alike*, *comparable*, *equivalent*, *identical*, and *similar* are also used to say that two or more things are like each other. You can put the preposition *to* after all of them except *alike* in order to mention the second of the things being compared.

They all looked alike.
The houses were all identical.
Flemish is similar to Afrikaans.

modifying adjectives used in comparisons

2.139 When you want to suggest that you are comparing different amounts of a quality, you can use words like *comparatively*, *relatively*, and *equally*.

Psychology's a comparatively new subject.
The costs remained relatively low.
Her technique was less dramatic than Ann's, but equally effective.
He was extra polite to his superiors.

Talking about different amounts of a quality

2.140 When you want to say something more about the quality that an adjective describes, you can use a **submodifying adverb** such as *very* or *rather* with it. You do this in order to indicate the amount of the quality, or to intensify it.

submodifying adverbs: *extremely narrow, slightly different*

2.141 Because qualitative adjectives are **gradable**, allowing you to say how much or how little of the quality is relevant, you are more likely to use **submodifying adverbs** (words like *extremely* or *slightly*) with them than with other types of adjective.

...an extremely narrow road.
...a highly successful company.
...in a slightly different way.
I was extraordinarily happy.
...helping them in a strongly supportive way.

...a very pretty girl.
She seems very pleasant.
...a rather clumsy person.
His hair was rather long.

2.142 You can use words like *very* and *extremely* with some classifying adjectives (see paragraphs 2.146 to 2.148) and with colour adjectives (see paragraph 2.35). Note that most *-ed* adjectives can be modified by words such as *very* and *extremely*, just like other qualitative adjectives.

...a very frightened little girl.
...an extremely disappointed young man.

intensifying qualitative adjectives

2.143 You can use many submodifying adverbs like *very* or *extremely* with qualitative adjectives in order to intensify their meaning.

...extremely high temperatures.
Geoffrey was a deeply religious man.
France is heavily dependent on foreign trade.

Here is a list of words used to intensify the meaning of adjectives:

amazingly	exceedingly	incredibly	suspiciously
awfully	extraordinarily	infinitely	terribly
bitterly	extremely	notably	unbelievably
critically	fantastically	particularly	very
dangerously	greatly	radically	violently
deeply	heavily	really	vitally
delightfully	highly	remarkably	wildly
disturbingly	hopelessly	seriously	wonderfully
dreadfully	horribly	strikingly	
eminently	hugely	supremely	
especially	impossibly	surprisingly	

Note that *very* can be used in front of superlative adjectives when you want to be very emphatic. This is explained in paragraphs 2.167 to 2.168.

2.144 Many of these submodifying adverbs not only intensify the meaning of the adjective but also allow you to express your opinion about what you are saying. For example, if you say that something is *surprisingly large*, you are expressing surprise at how large it is as well as intensifying the meaning of *large*.

He has amazingly long eyelashes.
...a delightfully refreshing taste.
...a shockingly brutal scene.
...a horribly uncomfortable chair.
...incredibly boring documents.

However, you use a few of these submodifying adverbs with no other purpose than to intensify the meaning of the adjective.

They're awfully brave.
The other girls were dreadfully dull companions.

Here is a list of words only used to intensify adjectives:

awfully	especially	greatly	really	terribly
dreadfully	extremely	highly	so	very

Note that *awfully*, *dreadfully*, and *terribly* are used in informal language and *highly* is used in very formal language.

Note also that *so* is normally only used after a linking verb.

I am so sorry.

reducing qualitative adjectives

2.145 Some submodifying adverbs are used to reduce the effect of qualitative adjectives.

The story was mildly amusing.
It's a fairly common feeling.
...moderately rich people.
...his rather large stomach.
My last question is somewhat personal.

Here is a list of words used to reduce the effect of an adjective:

faintly	mildly	pretty	rather	slightly
fairly	moderately	quite	reasonably	somewhat

Note also that *quite* is normally only used with adjectives that are used after a linking verb.

She was quite tall.

talking about extent

2.146 Some modifying adverbs are used to talk about the extent of the quality that you are describing.

Here is a list of words used to talk about the extent of a quality:

almost	nearly	absolutely	quite
exclusively	partly	altogether	simply
fully	predominantly	completely	totally
largely	primarily	entirely	utterly
mainly	roughly	perfectly	
mostly	~	purely	

USAGE NOTE

2.147 The first group in the list above are used almost always just to talk about the extent of a quality. They are most commonly used with classifying adjectives.

It was an almost automatic reflex.
...a shop with an exclusively female clientele.
...the largely rural south east.
The wolf is now nearly extinct.
The reasons for this were partly economic and practical, and partly political and social.

Almost and *nearly* are also used with qualitative adjectives.

The club was <u>almost</u> empty.
It was <u>nearly</u> dark.

Note that *roughly* can be used when you want to say that something is nearly or approximately like something else.

West Germany, Japan and Sweden are at <u>roughly similar</u> levels of economic development.

Note also that *half* is sometimes used in this way. For example, you can describe someone as *half American* if just one of their parents was American.

2.148 The second group in the list above are used not only to talk about the extent of a quality but also to emphasize the adjective. They are used with classifying adjectives as well as qualitative adjectives.

You're <u>absolutely right</u>.
This policy has been <u>completely unsuccessful</u>.
Everyone appeared to be <u>completely unaware</u> of the fact.
The discussion was <u>purely theoretical</u>.
It really is <u>quite astonishing</u>.
...a <u>totally new</u> situation.
We lived <u>totally separate</u> lives.
...<u>utterly trivial</u> matters.

Note that *absolutely* is frequently used with qualitative adjectives that express enthusiasm or lack of enthusiasm. When you use *absolutely* in this way you are emphasizing how strongly you feel about what you are saying.

...an <u>absolutely absurd</u> idea.
I think it's <u>absolutely wonderful</u>.
The enquiry is <u>absolutely crucial</u>.

Here is a list of qualitative adjectives often emphasized by *absolutely*:

absurd	enormous	huge	splendid
awful	essential	impossible	terrible
brilliant	excellent	massive	vital
certain	furious	perfect	wonderful
crucial	hilarious	ridiculous	

Note also that *completely* and *utterly* can also be used in this way.

It is <u>completely</u> impossible to imagine such a world.
He began to feel <u>utterly</u> miserable.

saying that there is enough of something

2.149 You can use submodifying adverbs such as *adequately*, *sufficiently*, and *acceptably* when you want to say that someone or something has enough of the quality you are describing.

The roof is <u>adequately insulated</u>.
We found a bank of snow <u>sufficiently deep</u> to dig a cave.

 USAGE NOTE

2.150 You can also show that you think something is sufficient by using *enough*. *Enough* always comes after the adjective, and never before it.

I was not a good enough rider.
It seemed that Henry had not been careful enough.

Enough can be followed by the preposition *for* to indicate a person involved, or by a *to*-infinitive to indicate a related action.

A girl from the factory wasn't good enough for him.
If you find that the white wine is not cold enough for you, ask for some ice to be put in it.
The children are old enough to travel to school on their own.
None of the fruit was ripe enough to eat.

Note that when *enough* is used after an adjective, you can use *just* in front of the adjective to show that someone or something has enough of the quality described by the adjective, but no more than that.

Some of these creatures are just large enough to see with the naked eye.

2.151 *Enough* is also a determiner (see paragraphs 1.223 to 1.247).

He hasn't had enough exercise.

When *enough* is a determiner, it can have a word like *just* or *almost* in front of it.

There was just enough space for a bed.
I have almost enough tokens for one book.

saying that there is not enough of something

2.152 If you want to show that you think something you are describing is insufficient, you can use submodifying adverbs such as *inadequately*, *insufficiently*, and *unacceptably*.

...people growing up in insufficiently supportive families.
Their publications were inadequately researched.

saying that there is too much of something

2.153 If you want to say that you think someone or something has too much of a quality, you normally use *too* in front of a qualitative adjective that is used after a linking verb.

My feet are too big.
It was too hot.
Dad thought I was too idealistic.

You can emphasize *too* by putting *far* in front of it. In informal English you can also use *way*.

The journey was far too long.
It was far too hot to work in the garden.
The price was way too high.

Too can be followed by the preposition *for* to indicate a person involved or by a *to*-infinitive to indicate a related action.

The shoes were too big for him.
He was too old for that sort of thing.
She was too weak to lift me.
He was too proud to apologize.

Note that you do not usually use *too* with an adjective in front of a noun, although you do use *too* in front of the determiners *many*, *much*, and *few*.

There is too much chance of error.
Too few people nowadays are interested in literature.
You ask too many questions, Sam.

! BE CAREFUL

2.154 *Too* cannot be used instead of *very*. Rather than saying *I am too happy to meet you*, you must say *I am very happy to meet you*.

2.155 Other words that indicate too much of a quality are *excessively*, *overly*, and the prefix *over-*. These can be used, like *too*, with adjectives that come after a linking verb, but they can also be used with adjectives in front of a noun.

> ...*excessively high* accident rates.
> ...an intellectual but *over-cautious* man.
> They were *overly eager*.

★ BE CREATIVE

2.156 As well as adverbs of degree like *excessively* and *insufficiently*, you can use some other types of adverb in front of adjectives to modify their meaning.

> ...the *once elegant* palace.
> ...a *permanently muddy* road.
> ...*internationally famous* golfers.
> ...*naturally blonde* hair.
> ...*coolly elegant* furniture.
> ...*purposely expensive* gadgets.

Adverbs are explained in Chapter 6.

Saying things are different

2.157 When you are using comparative adjectives, you may want to say that something has much more or much less of a quality than something else. You do this by adding words like *much* or *a little*.

> It is a *much better* school than yours.
> These creatures are *much less mobile*.
> There are *far worse* dangers.
> Some children are *a lot more difficult* than others.

You also use these words to say that something has much more or much less of a quality than it had before.

> He had become *much more mature*.
> That's *much less important* than it was.

2.158 Some modifying words and phrases are only used when comparative adjectives are being used after linking verbs.

> You look *a lot better*.
> It would be *a good deal easier* if you came to my place.
> The journey back was *a great deal more unpleasant* than the outward one had been.

Here is a list of modifying words and phrases used in front of comparative adjectives after a linking verb:

a good deal	a great deal	a lot	heaps	lots

Note that *lots* and *heaps* are only used in informal spoken English.

2.159 However, other submodifying adverbs can be used with comparative adjectives that are being used either in front of a noun or after a linking verb.

They are faced with a <u>much harder</u> problem than the rest of us.
The risk from smoking is <u>much greater</u> if you have a weak heart.
Computers can be applied to a <u>far wider</u> range of tasks.
The delay was <u>far longer</u> than they claimed.

Here is a list of submodifying adverbs used with adjectives that are used both in front of a noun and after a linking verb:

considerably	infinitely	vastly
far	much	very much

USAGE NOTE

2.160 If you want to say that something has more of a quality than something else that already has a lot of it, you use *even* or *still* before a comparative adjective, or *still* after it.

She's <u>even lazier</u> than me!
She was <u>even more possessive</u> than Rosamund.
I had a <u>still more recent</u> report.
The text is actually <u>worse still</u>.

Similarly, you use *even* or *still* to say that something has less of a quality than something else that has little of this quality.

This did not happen before the war, and is now <u>even less</u> likely.

You also use *even* or *still* when comparing the amount of a quality that something has at one time with the amount that it has at another.

The flight was <u>even faster</u> coming back.
They will become <u>richer still</u>.

In formal or literary English, *yet* is sometimes used in the same way as *still*.

He would have been <u>yet more alarmed</u> had she withdrawn.
The planes grow <u>mightier yet</u>.

2.161 You can show that something has an increasing or decreasing amount of a quality by repeating comparative adjectives. For example, you can say that something is getting *bigger and bigger*, *more and more difficult*, or *less and less common*.

He's getting <u>taller and taller</u>.
...defences that were proving <u>more and more effective</u>.

Increasingly can be used instead of *more and more* and *decreasingly* instead of *less and less*.

I was becoming <u>increasingly</u> depressed.
It was the first of a number of <u>increasingly</u> frank talks.

2.162 If you want to say that something has a little more or a little less of a quality than something else, you use *rather*, *slightly*, *a bit*, *a little bit*, or *a little* with comparative adjectives.

It's a <u>rather more complicated</u> story than that.
She's only a <u>little bit taller</u> than her sister.

You also use these forms to say that something has a little more or a little less of a quality than it had before.

We must be <u>rather more visible</u> to people in the community.
...the little things that made life <u>slightly less intolerable</u>.

2.163 If you want to say emphatically that something has no more of a quality than something else or than it had before, you can use *no* in front of comparative adjectives.

Some species of dinosaur were no bigger than a chicken.

Any is used for emphasis in front of comparatives in negative clauses, questions, and conditional clauses. For example, *He wasn't any taller than Jane* means the same as *He was no taller than Jane*.

I was ten and didn't look any older.
If it will make you any happier, I'll shave off my beard.
Is that any clearer?

Note that you only use *no* and *any* like this when comparatives are being used after a linking verb. You cannot use *no* and *any* with comparatives when they are being used in front of a noun phrase. For example, you cannot say *It was a no better meal* or *Is that an any faster train?*

2.164 When you use the comparative structure *as ... as ...* (see paragraphs 2.124 to 2.130), submodifying words such as *just*, *quite*, *nearly*, and *almost* can be used in front of it, modifying the comparison with their usual meanings.

Mary was just as pale as he was.
There is nothing quite as lonely as illness.
...a huge bird which was nearly as big as a man.
The land seemed almost as dark as the water.

Nearly is also used when the *as ... as ...* structure is preceded by *not* with the meaning *less......than*. You put it after the *not*. For example, *I am not nearly as tall as George* means the same as *I am much less tall than George*.

This is not nearly as complicated as it sounds.

2.165 When you use *like* to describe someone or something by comparing them with someone or something else (see paragraphs 2.132 to 2.134), you can use a submodifying adverb in front of it.

...animals that looked a little like donkeys.
It's a plane exactly like his.

Here is a list of modifying words and phrases used with *like*:

a bit	exactly	quite	somewhat
a little	just	rather	very

2.166 When you use *the same as* and *the same* to describe someone or something by saying they are identical to someone or something else, you can use a number of submodifying adverbs in front of them, including *just*, *exactly*, *much*, *nearly*, *virtually*, and *more or less*.

I'm just the same as everyone else.
The situation was much the same in Germany.
The moral code would seem to be more or less the same throughout the world.

2.167 When you are using superlative adjectives, you may wish to say that something has much more or much less of a quality than anything else of its kind.

The submodifying adverbs *much*, *quite*, *easily*, *by far*, and *very* can be used with the superlative adjectives.

Much, *quite*, and *easily* are placed in front of *the* and the superlative.

Music may have been much the most respectable of his tastes.
...the most frightening time of my life, and quite the most dishonest.
This is easily the best film of the year.

By far can be placed either in front of *the* and the superlative or after the superlative.

They are by far the most dangerous creatures on the island.
The Union was the largest by far.

2.168 *Very* is only used with superlatives formed by adding *-est* or with irregular superlatives such as *the best* and *the worst*. *Very* is placed between *the* and the superlative.

...the very earliest computers.
It was of the very highest quality.

Very is also used to modify superlative adjectives when you want to be very emphatic. It is placed after a determiner such as *the* or *that* and in front of a superlative adjective or one such as *first* or *last*.

...in the very smallest countries.
...one of the very finest breeds of dogs.
...on the very first day of the war.
He had come at the very last moment.
That very next afternoon he was working in his room.
He spent weeks in that very same basement.

Modifying using nouns: noun modifiers

2.169 Nouns can be used as modifiers in front of other nouns when you want to give more specific information about someone or something.

Sometimes, when nouns are used like this they become fixed expressions called **compound nouns** (see paragraphs 1.83 to 1.92).

When the nouns used in front of other nouns are not in fixed expressions, they are called **noun modifiers**.

...the car door.
...tennis lessons.
...a football player.
...cat food.
...the music industry.
...a surprise announcement.

singular and plural forms

2.170 You normally use the singular form of a **countable noun** (see paragraphs 1.15 to 1.22) as a noun modifier, even when you are referring to more than one thing. For example, you refer to a shop that sells books as *a book shop*, not *a books shop*, even though it sells a large number of books, not just one.

Many **plural nouns** lose their -s endings when used in front of other nouns.

...my trouser pocket.
...pyjama trousers.
...paratroop attacks.

Here is a list of common plural nouns that lose their -s and -es endings when they are used as modifiers:

knickers	pyjamas	spectacles	trousers
paratroops	scissors	troops	

However, some plural nouns keep the same form when used in front of other nouns.

...arms control.
...clothes pegs.

Here is a list of common plural nouns that remain the same when they are used as modifiers:

arms	clothes	jeans
binoculars	glasses	sunglasses

Plural nouns are explained in paragraphs 1.41 to 1.46.

using more than one noun modifier

2.171   If you want to be even more specific, you can use more than one noun modifier. For example, a *car insurance certificate* is a certificate that shows that a car has been insured, and a *state pension scheme* is a scheme that is run by the state and concerns workers' pensions.

...a Careers Information Officer.
...car body repair kits.
...a family dinner party.
...a school medical officer.

used with adjectives

2.172   If you want to give more information about a noun that has a noun modifier in front of it, you can put **adjectives** in front of the noun modifier.

...a long car journey.
...a new scarlet silk handkerchief.
...complex business deals.
...this beautiful morning sunlight.
...the French film industry.

When an adjective comes in front of two nouns, it is usually obvious whether it is modifying the two nouns combined or only the noun modifier.

For example, in *an electric can opener*, the adjective *electric* is modifying the combination *can opener*; whereas in *electric shock treatment*, *electric* is modifying the noun *shock* and then both the adjective and the noun modifier are modifying the noun *treatment*.

Adjectives are explained in paragraphs 2.2 to 2.102.

use of proper nouns

2.173   **Proper nouns** can also be used as noun modifiers. For example, if you want to show that something is connected with a place, organization, or institution, you put the name of the place, organization, or institution in front of all other noun modifiers. You also put them in front of classifying adjectives.

...Brighton Technical College.

...the Cambridge House Literacy Scheme.

Proper nouns are explained in paragraphs 1.52 to 1.58.

⊗ BE CREATIVE

2.174 The use of noun modifiers in English is very common indeed. In fact, when the context makes it clear what you mean, you can use almost any noun to modify any other noun. You can use noun modifiers to talk about a wide range of relationships between the two nouns.

For example, you can say what something is made of, as in *cotton socks*. You can also say what is made in a particular place, as in *a glass factory*. You can say what someone does, as in *a football player*, or you can say where something is, as in *my bedroom curtains*.

You can say when something happens, as in *the morning mist* and *her wartime activities*. You can also describe the nature or size of something, as in *a surprise attack* and *a pocket chess-set*.

Talking about quantities and amounts

2.175 This section deals with ways of talking about quantities and amounts of things. You often refer to quantities by using a number, but sometimes in everyday situations you can do this by using a word or a phrase such as *several* or *a lot* and link it with *of* to the following noun. Quantity expressions like these are explained in paragraphs 2.176 to 2.193. When phrases such as *a bottle* are used like this, they are called **partitives**. Partitives are explained in paragraphs 2.194 to 2.207.

When you want to be very precise about the quantity or amount of something, you can use **numbers** (see paragraphs 2.208 to 2.239) or **fractions** (see paragraphs 2.240 to 2.249).

Numbers, fractions, and quantity expressions are also used in expressions of measurement to indicate the size, weight, length, and so on, of something. Ways of talking about **measurements** are explained in paragraphs 2.250 to 2.257. Approximate measurements are explained in paragraphs 2.264 to 2.271. Numbers are also used to say how old someone or something is. This is explained in paragraphs 2.258 to 2.263.

Talking about amounts of things: *a lot of ideas, plenty of shops*

2.176 When you want to talk about a quantity of things or an amount of something, you can use the pronoun form of some indefinite determiners (such as *all* or *both*) followed by *of* and a noun phrase.

I am sure both of you agree with me.
Most of the population have fled.
All of her children live abroad.

2.177 Here is the list of indefinite determiners that can be used in this way. *Of* is given after each as a reminder.

all of	either of	(a) little of	much of	some of
another of	enough of	lots of	neither of	
any of	(a) few of	many of	none of	
both of	fewer of	more of	one of	
each of	less of	most of	several of	

You can also use a phrase such as *a lot of* or *a number of* to talk about quantity in the same way.

...a house with <u>lots of</u> *windows.*
I make <u>a lot of</u> *mistakes.*
In Tunis there are <u>a number of</u> *art galleries.*
I never found <u>the rest of</u> *my relatives.*

2.178 Here is a list of phrases that can be used to talk about quantity.

an amount of	a good many of	the majority of	~
a bit of	a great many of	a minority of	gobs of (American)
a little bit of	a number of	~	heaps of
a couple of	plenty of	part of	loads of
a good deal of	a quantity of	the remainder of	masses of
a great deal of	~	the rest of	tons of
a lot of	a majority of	the whole of	

Note that the words in the last group in this list are used in informal speech only.

only with definite determiners

2.179 Some of these quantity expressions are linked by *of* only to noun phrases that begin with a definite determiner such as *the*, *these*, or *my*. A pronoun such as *us*, *them*, or *these* can also be used after *of*.

Nearly <u>all of the increase</u> *has been caused by inflation.*
<u>Part of the farm</u> *lay close to the river bank.*
Only <u>a few of them</u> *were armed.*

Here is a list of quantity expressions with *of* that are usually or always followed by noun phrases beginning with definite determiners:

all of	few of	neither of	a few of
another of	fewer of	none of	a little of
any of	less of	one of	a good many of
both of	little of	part of	a great many of
certain of	many of	several of	~
each of	more of	some of	the remainder of
either of	most of	various of	the rest of
enough of	much of	~	the whole of

with place names

2.180 Some of these quantity expressions can also be used with place names.

<u>Much of America</u> *will be shocked by what happened.*
...involving <u>most of Africa</u> *and* <u>a lot of South America</u>.

Here is a list of quantity expressions used with place names:

all of	part of	a great deal of
less of	some of	a lot of
more of	~	~
most of	a bit of	the rest of
much of	a little bit of	the whole of
none of	a good deal of	

verb agreement

2.181 When you use a quantity expression as the subject of a verb, the verb is singular or plural depending on whether the quantity expression refers to one thing or to more than one thing.

Some of the information <u>has</u> already been analysed.
Some of my best friends <u>are</u> policemen.

with plural nouns

2.182 Many quantity expressions can only be used in front of plural noun phrases.

I am sure <u>both of</u> you agree with me.
Start by looking through their papers for <u>either of</u> the two documents mentioned below.
<u>Few of</u> these organizations survive for long.
<u>Several of</u> his best books are about space flight.
I would like to ask you <u>a couple of</u> questions.
The report contained large <u>numbers of</u> inaccuracies.

Here is a list of quantity expressions that are only used with plural noun phrases:

another of	few of	one of	a few of
both of	fewer of	several of	a good many of
certain of	many of	various of	a great many of
each of	neither of	~	a number of
either of	numbers of	a couple of	

For more information about *each of* see paragraphs 2.186 to 2.187, about *fewer of* see paragraph 2.189, and about *a number of* see paragraphs 2.191 to 2.192.

Note that *neither of* is used in a similar way to *either of* when you are talking about two things in negative clauses. This is explained in paragraph 5.81.

with uncountable nouns and singular nouns

2.183 A few quantity expressions are only used with uncountable nouns and singular noun phrases.

<u>Much of</u> the day was taken up with classes.
This is <u>a bit of</u> a change.
There was <u>a good deal of</u> smoke.
If you use rich milk, pour off <u>a little of</u> the cream.
I spent <u>the whole of</u> last year working there.

Here is a list of quantity expressions only used with uncountable nouns and singular noun phrases:

less of	part of	a little bit of	a little of
little of	~	a good deal of	~
much of	a bit of	a great deal of	the whole of

For more information about *less of* see paragraph 2.189.

with plural nouns and uncountable nouns

2.184 A very few quantity expressions are used only with plural noun phrases and uncountable nouns.

...the seizure of vast <u>quantities of</u> illegal weapons.
Very large <u>quantities of</u> aid were needed.
They had <u>loads of</u> things to say about each other.
We had <u>loads of</u> room.
...<u>plenty of</u> the men.
Make sure you give <u>plenty of</u> notice.

Here is a list of quantity expressions that are only used with plural noun phrases and uncountable nouns:

plenty of	~	heaps of	masses of
quantities of	gobs of *(American)*	loads of	tons of

Note that when the second group in this list are used with an uncountable noun as the subject of a verb, the verb is singular, even though the quantity expression looks plural.

Masses and <u>masses of</u> food <u>was</u> left over.

with all types of noun

2.185 Some quantity expressions can be used with plural nouns, with singular nouns, or with uncountable nouns.

...<u>some of</u> the most distinguished men of our time.
We did <u>some of</u> the journey by night.
<u>Some of</u> the gossip was surprisingly accurate.

Here is a list of quantity expressions that are used with plural nouns, singular nouns, or uncountable nouns:

all of	more of	~	~
any of	most of	an amount of	the remainder of
enough of	none of	a lot of	the rest of
lots of	some of	a quantity of	

Note that *an amount of* is nearly always used with an adjective such as *small*: *a small amount of*. This is explained in paragraph 2.191.

Note also that when *lots of* is used with an uncountable noun as the subject of a verb, the verb is singular, even though the quantity expression looks plural.

He thought that *lots of* lovely money *was* the source of happiness.

Any of is explained more fully in paragraph 2.188.

USAGE NOTE

2.186 When you want to refer to each member of a particular group, you can use *each of* and a plural noun phrase.

Each of the drawings is slightly different.
We feel quite differently about each of our children.
Work out how much you can afford to pay each of them.

Note that *each one* and *every one* can be used before *of* instead of *each*, for emphasis.

This view of poverty influences each one of us.
Every one of them is given a financial target.

BE CAREFUL

2.187 When the quantity expression *each of* is used with a plural noun phrase, the verb after the noun phrase is always singular.

USAGE NOTE

2.188 *Any of* can refer to one or several people or things, or to part of something. Note that if it is the subject of a verb, when it refers to several things, the verb is plural, and when it refers to a part of something, the verb is singular.

She has those coats. She might have been wearing any of them.
Hardly any of these find their way into consumer products.
Has any of this been helpful?
It was more expensive than any of the other magazines we were normally able to afford.

2.189 There are three comparative quantity expressions that can be used before noun phrases. *Less of* is usually used with singular nouns and uncountable nouns, *fewer of* is usually used with plural nouns, and *more of* is used with all three types of noun.

I enjoy cooking far more now, because I do less of it.
Fewer of these children will become bored.
He was far more of an existentialist.

Note that *more of* is sometimes used in front of a noun phrase to intensify it.

He could hardly have felt more of a fool than he did at that moment.
She was more of a flirt than ever.
America is much more of a classless society.

Note also that *less of* is sometimes used instead of *fewer of*, but many people think that this is not correct.

omitting *of*

2.190 When the context makes it clear, or when you think that the person you are talking to will understand what you mean, you can sometimes reduce the structure to the quantity word only. For example, if you are talking about applications for a job and there were twenty candidates, you can say *Some were very good* rather than *Some of them were very good*.

A few crossed over the bridge.
Some parts can be separated from the whole.

I have four bins. I keep one in the kitchen and the rest *in the dustbin area.*
Most of the books had been packed into an enormous trunk and the remainder *piled on top of it.*

i | **USAGE NOTE**

2.191 You can add adjectives to *a number of* and *a quantity of* to say how large or small an amount or number of things is.

The city attracts a large number of *tourists.*
We had a limited number of *people to choose from.*
The novel provides an enormous quantity of *information.*
... a tiny quantity of *acid.*

An *amount of* is always used with adjectives, and is usually used with uncountable nouns.

Pour a small amount of *the sauce over the chicken.*
He has a large amount of *responsibility.*
It only involves a small amount of *time.*
There has to be a certain amount of *sacrifice.*
They have done a vast amount of *hard work.*

The plural forms of *quantity*, *number*, and *amount* are used, especially when referring to separate amounts.

...groups that employ large numbers of *low-paid workers.*
Enormous amounts of *money are spent on advertising.*

modifying quantity expressions

2.192 When a quantity expression contains an adjective, you can put *very* in front of the adjective.

... a very great deal of *work.*
... a very large amount of *money.*

2.193 Some quantity expressions can be modified using *quite*.

I've wasted quite enough of *my life here.*
Quite a few of *the employees are beginning to realise the truth.*
Most of them have had quite a lot of *experience.*
... quite a large amount of *industry.*

Here is a list of quantity expressions that can be modified by *quite*:

enough	a large amount of	a large number of
a few	a small amount of	
a lot of	a number of	

Talking about particular amounts of things: *a piece of paper, a drop of water*

2.194 When you want to talk about a particular quantity of something, you can use a **partitive** structure that consists of a particular partitive (e.g. *piece*) linked by *of* to another noun. Partitives are always countable nouns.

Who owns this bit of *land?*
... portions of *mashed potato.*

If the partitive is singular, then the verb used with it is usually singular. If it is plural, the verb is also plural.

A piece of paper <u>is</u> lifeless.
Two pieces of metal <u>were</u> being rubbed together.

Note that all partitives consist of two or more words, because *of* is needed in every case. *Of* is printed in the lists below as a reminder.

partitives with uncountable nouns

2.195 When the noun after the partitive is an uncountable noun, you use countable nouns such as *bit*, *drop*, *lump*, or *piece* as the partitive.

Here's a <u>bit of</u> paper.
...a <u>drop of</u> blood.
<u>Drops of</u> sweat dripped from his forehead.
...a tiny <u>piece of</u> material.
...a <u>pinch of</u> salt.
...<u>specks of</u> dust.

These partitives can be used without *of* when it is obvious what you are talking about.

He sat down in the kitchen before a plate of cold ham, but he had only eaten one <u>piece</u> when the phone rang.

2.196 Here is a list of partitives used with uncountable nouns:

amount of	grain of	piece of	shred of
bit of	heap of	pile of	slice of
blob of	knob of	pinch of	speck of
chunk of	lump of	pool of	spot of
clump of	mass of	portion of	touch of
dash of	morsel of	scrap of	trace of
drop of	mountain of	sheet of	

Some of these partitives are also used with plural nouns referring to things that together form a mass.

...a huge <u>heap of</u> stones.
...a <u>pile of</u> newspapers.

Here is a list of partitives used with both uncountable and plural nouns:

amount of	heap of	mountain of	portion of
clump of	mass of	pile of	

⊘ BE CREATIVE

2.197 Many nouns that refer to the shape of an amount of something can also be partitives with uncountable or plural nouns.

...a <u>ball of</u> wool.
...<u>columns of</u> smoke.
...a <u>ring of</u> excited faces.

Here is a list of partitives used for talking about the shape of an amount of something:

ball of	ring of	square of	strip of	tuft of
column of	shaft of	stick of	thread of	wall of

Many nouns that refer to both shape and movement can also be used as partitives.

It blew a _jet of_ water into the air.
...a constant _stream of_ children passing through the door.

Here is a list of partitives used for talking about both shape and movement:

dribble of	gust of	shower of	stream of
gush of	jet of	spurt of	torrent of

✪ BE CREATIVE

You can use any noun to describe shape in this way. For example you can talk about a triangle of snooker balls.

2.198 There are many nouns that refer to groups that can be used as partitives. They are linked by _of_ to plural nouns that indicate what the group consists of.

It was evaluated by an independent _team of_ inspectors.
A _group of_ journalists gathered at the airport to watch us take off.
...a _bunch of_ flowers.

Here is a list of partitives referring to groups:

audience of	company of	gang of	team of
bunch of	family of	group of	troupe of
clump of	flock of	herd of	

✪ BE CREATIVE

You can use any noun referring to a group of people or things in this way. For example, you can talk about an army of volunteers.

measurement nouns

2.199 Nouns referring to measurements are often used in partitive structures to talk about an amount of something that is a particular length, area, volume, or weight. Uncountable nouns are used after _of_ in structures referring to length, and both uncountable and plural nouns are used in structures referring to weight.

...ten _yards of_ velvet.
Thousands of _square miles of_ land have been contaminated.
I drink a _pint of_ milk a day.
...three _pounds of_ strawberries.
...10 _ounces of_ cheese.

Nouns referring to measurements are explained in paragraphs 2.250 to 2.257.

referring to contents and containers

2.200 You use partitives when you want to talk about the contents of a container as well as to the container itself. For example, you can refer to a carton filled with milk as *a carton of milk*.

> I went to buy a <u>bag of</u> chips.
> The waiter appeared with a <u>bottle of</u> red wine.
> ...a <u>packet of</u> cigarettes.
> ...a <u>pot of</u> honey.
> ...<u>tubes of</u> glue.

You can also use partitives to refer to the contents only.

> They drank another <u>bottle of</u> champagne.
> She ate a whole <u>box of</u> chocolates.

Here is a list of partitives referring to containers:

bag of	bucket of	glass of	pot of	tub of
barrel of	can of	jar of	sack of	tube of
basin of	carton of	jug of	spoon of	tumbler of
basket of	case of	mug of	tablespoon of	
bottle of	cask of	pack of	tank of	
bowl of	crate of	packet of	teaspoon of	
box of	cup of	plate of	tin of	

ending in -ful

2.201 You can add *-ful* to these partitives referring to containers.

> He brought me a <u>bagful of</u> sweets.
> Pour a <u>bucketful of</u> cold water on the ash.
> ...a <u>cupful of</u> boiled water.
> ...a <u>tankful of</u> petrol.

Here is a list of partitives referring to containers that are very commonly used with *-ful*:

bag	box	cup	spoon	tank
basket	bucket	plate	tablespoon	teaspoon

When people want to make a noun ending in *-ful* plural, they usually add an *-s* to the end of the word, as in *bucketfuls*. However some people put the *-s* in front of *-ful*, as in *bucketsful*.

> She ladled three <u>spoonfuls of</u> sugar into my tea.
> They were collecting <u>basketfuls of</u> apples.
> ...two <u>teaspoonfuls of</u> powder.
> ...2 <u>teaspoonsful of</u> milk.

⭐ BE CREATIVE

2.202 You can also add *-ful* to other partitives.

> Eleanor was holding an <u>armful of</u> red roses.
> I went outside to throw a <u>handful of</u> bread to the birds.

He took another <u>mouthful of</u> whisky.
...a <u>houseful of</u> children.

 USAGE NOTE

2.203 You sometimes use a mass noun instead of a partitive structure. For example, *two teas* means the same as *two cups of tea*, and *two sugars* means *two spoonfuls of sugar*.

We drank a couple of <u>beers</u>.
I asked for two <u>coffees</u> with milk.

Mass nouns are explained in paragraphs 1.28 to 1.31.

referring to parts and fractions

2.204 You use a partitive when you want to talk about a part or a fraction of a particular thing.

I spent a large <u>part of</u> my life in broadcasting.
The system is breaking down in many <u>parts of</u> Africa.
A large <u>portion of</u> the university budget goes into the Community Services area.
...a mass movement involving all <u>segments of</u> society.

Here is a list of partitives referring to a part of something:

part of	portion of	section of	segment of

referring to individual items

2.205 You use a partitive with an uncountable noun referring to things of a certain type when you want to refer to one particular thing of that type.

...an <u>article of</u> clothing.
I bought a few <u>bits of</u> furniture.
Any <u>item of</u> information can be accessed.

Here is a list of partitives referring to one thing of a particular type:

article of	bit of	item of	piece of

Here is a list of uncountable nouns referring to things of a certain type that are often used with the partitives listed above:

advice	clothing	homework	luggage	research
apparatus	equipment	information	machinery	
baggage	furniture	knowledge	news	

pair of

2.206 Some plural nouns refer to things that are normally thought to consist of two parts, such as trousers or scissors. Some others refer to things that are made in twos, such as shoes or socks. When you want to talk about one of these two-part items, or two-item sets, you use the partitive *pair* linked to these plural nouns by *of*.

...a <u>pair of</u> jeans.
...a <u>pair of</u> tights.
...a dozen <u>pairs of</u> sunglasses.

I bought a <u>pair of</u> tennis shoes.
I smashed three <u>pairs of</u> skis.

These **plural nouns** are explained in paragraphs 1.41 to 1.46.

⭐ **BE CREATIVE**

2.207 Whenever you want to (i) talk about a limited amount of something, (ii) indicate the area that something occupies, or (iii) specify a particular feature that something has, you can use a noun that indicates the amount or the nature of the thing (e.g. *a bottle*), linked by *of* to a noun that indicates what the thing is (e.g. *water*).

For example, if you say *a forest of pines*, you are talking about a large area of trees. Similarly, you can talk about *a border of roses*.

This structure can be extended very widely, so that you can talk about *a city of dreaming spires*, for example.

Referring to an exact number of things: numbers

cardinal numbers

2.208 When you want to refer to an exact number of things, you use numbers such as *two*, *thirty*, and *777*, which are called **cardinal numbers**, or sometimes **cardinals**.

I'm going to ask you <u>thirty</u> questions.
...<u>two hundred and sixty</u> copies of the record.

The cardinal numbers are listed in the Reference section and their use is explained in paragraphs 2.213 to 2.231.

ordinal numbers

2.209 When you want to identify or describe something by showing where it comes in a series or sequence, you use an **ordinal number**, or an **ordinal**, such as *first*, *second*, *fourteenth*, or *twenty-seventh*.

She received a video camera for her <u>fourteenth</u> birthday.
I repeated my story for the <u>third</u> time that day.

The ordinal numbers are listed in the Reference section and their use is explained in paragraphs 2.232 to 2.239.

fractions

2.210 When you want to show how large a part of something is compared to the whole of it, you use a **fraction** such as *a third* or *three-quarters*.

A <u>third</u> of the American forces were involved.
The bottle was about <u>three-quarters</u> full when he started.

Fractions are explained in paragraphs 2.240 to 2.249.

measuring things

2.211 When you want to talk about a size, distance, area, volume, weight, speed, or temperature, you can do so by using a number or quantity expression in front of a **measurement noun** such as *feet* and *miles*.

He was about six <u>feet</u> tall.

It's four miles to the city centre from here.

Measurement nouns are explained in paragraphs 2.250 to 2.257.

If you do not know the exact number, size, or quantity of something, you can give an approximate amount or measurement using one of a group of special words and expressions. These are explained in paragraphs 2.264 to 2.271.

`age`

2.212 When you want to say how old someone or something is, you have a choice of ways in which to do it. These are explained in paragraphs 2.258 to 2.263.

Talking about the number of things: cardinal numbers

2.213 If you want to talk about some or all of the things in a group, you can show how many things you are talking about by using a **cardinal number**.

The cardinal numbers are listed in the Reference section.

By Christmas, we had ten cows.

When you use a determiner and a number in front of a noun, you put the determiner in front of the number.

...the three young men.
...my two daughters.
Watch the eyes of any two people engrossed in conversation.
All three candidates are coming to Blackpool later this week.

When you put a number and an adjective in front of a noun, you usually put the number in front of the adjective.

...two small children.
...fifteen hundred local residents.
...three beautiful young girls.

`one`

2.214 *One* is used as a number in front of a noun to emphasize that there is only one thing, to show that you are being precise, or to contrast one thing with another. *One* is followed by a singular noun.

That is the one big reservation I've got.
He balanced himself on one foot.
There was only one gate into the palace.
This treaty was signed one year after the Suez Crisis.
It was negative in one respect but positive in another.

One is also used, like other numbers, as a quantity expression.

One of my students sold me her ticket.
...one of the few great novels of the century.
It's one of the best films I've ever seen.

One also has special uses as a determiner and a pronoun. These are explained in paragraph 1.249 and paragraphs 1.158 to 1.161.

2.215 When a large number begins with the figure 1, the 1 can be said or written as *a* or *one*. *One* is more formal.

...a million dollars.
...a hundred and fifty miles.
Over one million pounds has been raised.

talking about negative amounts

2.216 The number 0 is not used in ordinary English to say that the number of things you are talking about is zero. Instead the negative determiner *no* or the negative pronoun *none* is used, or *any* is used with a negative. These are explained in paragraphs 5.51 and 5.71 to 5.73.

numbers and agreement

2.217 When you use any number except *one* in front of a noun, you use a plural noun.

There were ten people there, all men.
...a hundred years.
...a hundred and one things.

2.218 When you use a number and a plural noun to talk about two or more things, you usually use a plural verb. You use a singular verb with *one*.

Seven guerrillas were wounded.
There is one clue.

However, when you are talking about an amount of money or time, or a distance, speed, or weight, you usually use a number, a plural noun, and a singular verb.

Three hundred pounds is a lot of money.
Ten years is a long time.
Twenty six miles is a long way to run.
90 miles an hour is much too fast.
Ninety pounds is all she weighs.

Ways of measuring things are explained in paragraphs 2.250 to 2.257.

numbers with ordinals and postdeterminers

2.219 You can use cardinal numbers with both **ordinals** (see paragraphs 2.232 to 2.239) and **postdeterminers** (see paragraph 2.40). When you use a cardinal number with a determiner followed by an ordinal number or a postdeterminer, the cardinal number usually comes after the determiner and the ordinal or postdeterminer.

The first two years have been very successful.
...throughout the first four months of this year.
...the last two volumes of the encyclopedia.
...in the previous three years of his reign.

Note that some postdeterminers can be used like ordinary **classifying adjectives** (see paragraph 2.40). When they are used like this, the cardinal number comes before them.

He has written two previous novels.
...two further examples.

numbers as pronouns

2.220 When either the context makes it clear, or you think that your listener already knows something, you can use the cardinal number without a noun.

These two are quite different.

When cardinal numbers are used like this, you can put ordinal numbers, postdeterminers, or superlative adjectives in between the determiner and the cardinal number.

I want to tell you about the programmes. The first four are devoted to universities.
The other six are masterpieces.
The best thirty have the potential to be successful journalists.

expressing large numbers

2.221 When you use *dozen, hundred, thousand, million*, or *billion* to indicate exact numbers, you put *a* or another number in front of them.

...a hundred dollars.
...six hundred and ten miles.
...a thousand billion pounds.
...two dozen diapers.

!   **BE CAREFUL**

2.222   When you use *dozen, hundred, thousand, million*, or *billion* they remain singular even when the number in front of them is greater than one.

!   **BE CAREFUL**

2.223   You can use *dozen, hundred, thousand, million*, or *billion* without *of* in a less precise way by putting *several, a few*, and *a couple of* in front of them.

...several hundred people.
A few thousand cars have gone.
...life a couple of hundred years ago.

approximate quantities

2.224 When you want to emphasize how large a number is without stating it precisely, you can use *dozens, hundreds, thousands, millions*, and *billions* in the same way as cardinals followed by *of*.

That's going to take hundreds of years.
...hundreds of dollars.
We travelled thousands of miles across Europe.
...languages spoken by millions of people.
We have dozens of friends in the community.

You can put *many* in front of these plural forms.

I have travelled many hundreds of miles with them.

𝒊   **USAGE NOTE**

2.225   People often use the plural forms when they are exaggerating.

I was meeting thousands of people.
Do you have to fill in hundreds of forms before you go?

You can also emphasize or exaggerate a large number by using these words in phrases beginning with *by*.

...a book which sells by the million.
...people who give injections by the dozen.
Videos of the royal wedding sold by the hundred thousand.

numbers as labels

2.226 Cardinal numbers are used to label or identify things.

Room 777 of the Stanley Hotel.
Number 11 Downing Street.

numbers as quantity expressions

2.227 You can also use cardinal numbers as quantity expressions linked by *of* to a noun phrase referring to a group. You do this when you want to emphasize that you are talking about a part or all of a group.

I saw four of these programmes.
Three of the questions today have been about democracy.
I use plastic kitchen bins. I have four of them.
All eight of my great-grandparents lived in the city.
All four of us wanted to get away from the Earl's Court area.
The clerk looked at the six of them and said, All of you?
I find it less worrying than the two of you are suggesting.

Quantity expressions are explained in paragraphs 2.176 to 2.193.

number quantity expressions as pronouns

2.228 Cardinal numbers are used to quantify something without the *of* and the noun phrase, when it is clear what you are referring to.

...a group of painters, nine or ten in all.
Of the other wives, two are dancers and one is a singer.
...the taller student of the two.
...breakfast for two.

numbers after subject pronouns

2.229 Cardinal numbers are also used after subject pronouns.

In the fall we two are going to England.
You four, come with me.

numbers in compound adjectives

2.230 Cardinal numbers can be used as part of a **compound adjective** (see paragraphs 2.94 to 2.102). The cardinal number is used in front of a noun to form a compound adjective that is usually hyphenated

He took out a five-dollar bill.
I wrote a five-page summary of the situation.

Note that the noun remains singular even when the number is two or more, and that compound adjectives that are formed like this cannot be used after a linking verb. For example, you cannot say *My essay is five-hundred-word*. Instead you would probably say *My essay is five hundred words long*.

numbers with time expressions

2.231 Cardinal numbers are sometimes used with general time words such as *month* and *week*. You do this when you want to describe something by saying how long it lasts.

If the thing is referred to with an uncountable noun, you use the **possessive form** (see paragraphs 1.211 to 1.222) of the general time word.

She's already had at least <u>nine months'</u> experience.
On Friday she had been given <u>two weeks'</u> notice.

Sometimes the apostrophe is omitted.

They wanted <u>three weeks</u> holiday and <u>three weeks</u> pay.

The determiner *a* is usually used when you are talking about a single period of time, although *one* can be used instead when you want to be more formal.

She's on <u>a year's</u> leave from Hunter College.
He was only given <u>one week's</u> notice.

Cardinal numbers are also used with general time words as modifiers of adjectives.

She was <u>four months</u> pregnant.
The rains are <u>two months</u> late.
His rent was <u>three weeks</u> overdue.

Referring to things in a sequence: ordinal numbers

2.232 If you want to identify or describe something by saying where it comes in a series or sequence, you use an **ordinal number**.

Quietly they took their seats in the <u>first</u> three rows.
Flora's flat is on the <u>fourth</u> floor of this five-storey block.
They stopped at the <u>first</u> of the trees.

Note that you can also use *following, last, next, preceding, previous*, and *subsequent* like ordinal numbers to say where something comes in a series or sequence.

The <u>following</u> morning he checked out of the hotel.
...the <u>last</u> rungs of the fire-escape.
...at the <u>next</u> general election.
The <u>preceding</u> text has been professionally transcribed.
I mentioned this in a <u>previous</u> programme.
...the <u>subsequent</u> career patterns of those taking degrees.

Following, subsequent, previous, and *preceding* are only used to indicate the position of something in a sequence in time or in a piece of writing. *Next* and *last* are used more generally, for example to refer to things in rows or lists.

The ordinal numbers are listed in the Reference section.

as modifiers

2.233 Ordinals are often used in front of nouns. They are not usually used after linking verbs like *be*. They are usually preceded by a determiner.

...the <u>first</u> day of autumn.
He took the lift to the <u>sixteenth</u> floor.
...on her <u>twenty-first</u> birthday.
...his father's <u>second</u> marriage.

In some idiomatic phrases ordinals are used without determiners.

The picture seems <u>at first glance</u> chaotic.
I might. <u>On second thoughts</u>, no.
<u>First children</u> usually get a lot of attention.

written forms

2.234 Ordinals can be written in abbreviated form, for example in dates or headings or in very informal writing. You write the last two letters of the ordinal after the number expressed in figures. For example, *first* can be written as *1st*, *twenty-second* as *22nd*, *hundred and third* as *103rd*, and *fourteenth* as *14th*.

> ...on August <u>2nd</u>.
> ...the <u>1st</u> Division of the Sovereign's Escort.
> ...the <u>11th</u> Cavalry.

ordinals with *of*

2.235 You can specify which group the thing referred to by an ordinal belongs to by using the preposition *of* after the ordinal.

> It is <u>the third of</u> a series of eight programmes.
> Tony was <u>the second of</u> four sons.

When ordinals are used like this, they usually refer to one person or thing. However, when they are used with a *to*-infinitive, or another phrase or clause after them, they can refer to one person or thing or to more than one. *First* is used like this more than the other ordinals.

> I was <u>the first to recover</u>.
> They had to be <u>the first to go</u>.
> The proposals – <u>the first for 22 years</u> – amount to a new charter for the mentally ill.
> The withdrawals were <u>the first that the army agreed to</u>.

as pronouns

2.236 You can use an ordinal to refer to a member of a group that you have already mentioned or to something of the kind already mentioned, and you can omit the noun that identifies the thing.

> In August 1932 two of the group's members were expelled from the party and <u>a third</u> was suspended.
> The third child tries to outdo <u>the first and second</u>.
> A second pheasant flew up. Then <u>a third</u> and <u>a fourth</u>.

2.237 The adjectives *next* and *last* can be used, like ordinals, by themselves when the context makes the meaning clear.

> You missed one meal. <u>The next</u> is on the table in half an hour.
> Smithy removed <u>the last</u> of the screws.

ordinals used as adverbs

2.238 The ordinal *first* is also used as an adverb to show that something is done before other things. Other ordinals are also sometimes used to show the order in which things are done, especially in informal English. People also use ordinals as adverbs when they are giving a list of points, reasons, or items. This is explained fully in paragraph 10.54.

other uses of ordinals

2.239 The use of ordinals in expressing fractions is explained in paragraphs 2.241 and 2.243. The use of ordinals to express dates, as in *the seventeenth of June*, is explained in paragraph 4.88.

Ordinal numbers can be used in front of cardinal numbers. This is explained in paragraphs 2.219 to 2.220.

Talking about an exact part of something: fractions

2.240 When you want to show how small or large a part of something is compared to the whole of it, you use a **fraction**, such as *a third*, followed by *of* and a noun referring to the whole thing. Fractions can also be written in figures (see paragraph 2.248).

singular fractions

2.241 When you express a fraction in words, the way you do so depends on whether the fraction is singular or plural. If it is singular, you write or say an **ordinal number** or the special fraction terms *half* or *quarter*, with either the number *one* or a determiner such as *a* in front of them. The fraction is linked to a noun by *of*.

This state produces a third of the nation's oil.
...a quarter of an inch.
You can take a fifth of your money out on demand.
A tenth of our budget goes on fuel.
Forests cover one third of the country.
...one thousandth of a degree.
...one quarter of the total population.

An adjective can also be placed after the determiner and before the fraction.

...the first half of the twentieth century.
I read the first half of the book.
...the southern half of England.
...in the first quarter of 2004.

☐ USAGE NOTE

2.242 If you are using *half* in front of a pronoun, you still use *of* after the *half*.

Nearly half of it comes from the Middle East.
More than half of them have gone home.
Half of us have lost our jobs.

Note that when the fraction *a half* is used with *of*, you usually write or say it as *half* without a determiner. *A half* and *one half* are rarely used.

They lost half of their pay.
Half of the people went to private schools.
I had crossed more than half of America.

plural fractions

2.243 If the fraction is plural, you put a **cardinal number** in front of a plural form of the **ordinal number** or special fraction word *quarter*.

...the poorer two thirds of the world.
The journey is going to take three quarters of an hour.
...four fifths of the money.
Nine tenths of them live on the land.
...3 millionths of a centimetre.

When *half* is used with whole numbers or amounts, it is used with the determiner *a*.

...one and a half acres of land.
...four and a half centuries.

agreement with verb

2.244 When you talk about fractions of a single thing, you use a singular form of a verb afterwards.

Half of our work is to design programmes.
Two thirds of the planet's surface is covered with water.
Two fifths of the forest was removed.

However, when you talk about fractions of a number of things, you use a plural form of a verb afterwards.

Two thirds of Chad's exports were cotton.
A quarter of the students were seen individually.
More than half of these photographs are of her.

fractions as pronouns

2.245 When it is clear to your listener or reader who or what you are referring to, either because of the context or because you and your listener or reader know what is meant, you can use fractions as pronouns without the *of* and noun after them.

Of the people who work here, half are French and half are English.
Two thirds were sterilized.
One sixth are disappointed with the service.

numbers followed by fractions

2.246 Besides their use as quantity expressions linked by *of* to a noun phrase, fractions can also be used after a whole number or amount plus *and*, with a noun placed after the fraction. The noun must be plural even if the number is *one*.

You've got to sit there for one and a half hours.
...five and a quarter days.
...more than four and a half centuries ago

If you are using *a* instead of *one*, the *and* and the fraction come after the noun.

...a mile and a half below the surface.
...a mile and a quarter of motorway.

half as predeterminer

2.247 Besides being used with *of* as a quantity expression, *half* is also used as a **predeterminer** (see paragraph 1.251), directly in front of a determiner.

I met half the girls at the conference.
The farmers sold off half their land.
...half a pound of coffee.
...half a bottle of milk.

Note that *half* is always used with *of* before a pronoun (see paragraph 2.242).

fractions expressed in figures

2.248 You can write a fraction in figures, for example 1/2, 1/4, 3/4, and 2/3. These correspond to *a half*, *a quarter*, *three quarters* and *two thirds* respectively.

2.249 Fractions are often given in a special form as a number of hundredths. This type of fraction is called a **percentage**. For example, *three hundredths*, expressed as a percentage, is *three per cent*. It can also be written as *three percent* or *3%*. *A half* can be expressed as *fifty per cent*, *fifty percent*, or *50%*.

90 percent of most food is water.
About 20 per cent of student accountants are women.
Before 1960 45% of British trade was with the Commonwealth.

You use percentages on their own as noun phrases when it is clear what they refer to.

Ninety per cent were self employed.
...interest at 10% per annum.

Talking about measurements

2.250 You can refer to a size, distance, area, volume, weight, speed, or temperature by using a number or quantity expression in front of a **measurement noun**. Measurement nouns are countable.

They grow to twenty feet.
...blocks of stone weighing up to a hundred tons.
Reduce the temperature by a few degrees.
Average annual temperatures exceed 20° centigrade.

Other ways of expressing distance are explained in paragraphs 6.91 to 6.92. Measurement nouns referring to size, area, volume, and weight are often used in **partitive structures** (see paragraphs 2.194 to 2.207) such as *a pint of milk* and *a pound of onions*. They are also used in phrases beginning with *of* (see paragraph 2.283).

2.251 There are two systems of measurement used in Britain – the **imperial system** and the **metric system**. Each system has its own measurement nouns.

Here is a list of the imperial units of measurement indicating size, distance, area, volume, and weight:

inch	~	quart	pound
foot	acre	gallon	stone
yard	~	~	hundredweight
mile	pint	ounce	ton

Note that the plural of *foot* is *feet*, but *foot* can also be used with numbers. Similarly *stone* is usually used instead of *stones*.

Here is a list of the metric units of measurement indicating size, distance, area, volume, and weight:

millimetre	kilometre	~	litre	gram
centimetre	~	millilitre	~	kilogram
metre	hectare	centilitre	milligram	tonne

after linking verbs

2.252 Measurement nouns are often used after **linking verbs** such as *be*, *measure* and *weigh*.

> *The fish <u>was</u> about eight feet long.*
> *It <u>measures</u> approximately 26 inches wide x 25 inches long.*
> *...a square area <u>measuring</u> 900 metres on each side.*
> *It <u>weighs</u> fifty or more kilos.*

The use of adjectives after linking verbs is explained in paragraphs 3.132 to 3.137.

adjectives after measurements

2.253 When measurement nouns that give the size of something are used after a linking verb, they are often followed by an adjective that makes it clear exactly what the measurement refers to

> *He was about <u>six feet tall</u>.*
> *The spears were about <u>six foot long</u>.*
> *...a room <u>2 metres wide</u>.*
> *The water was <u>fifteen feet deep</u>.*
> *...a layer of stone <u>four metres thick</u>.*

Here is a list of the adjectives that follow measurement nouns indicating size:

broad	high	tall	wide
deep	long	thick	

Note that you do not say *two pounds heavy* but *two pounds in weight* instead.

phrases beginning with in after measurements

2.254 Similarly, some measurement nouns can be followed by prepositional phrases beginning with *in*.

> *...a block of ice one cubic foot <u>in size</u>.*
> *I put on nearly a stone <u>in weight</u>.*
> *They are thirty centimetres <u>in length</u>.*
> *...deposits measuring up to a kilometre <u>in thickness</u>.*
> *It was close to ten feet <u>in height</u>.*

Here is a list of phrases beginning with *in* used after measurements:

in area	in distance	in size	in weight
in breadth	in height	in thickness	in width
in depth	in length	in volume	

measurement nouns used as modifiers

2.255 Measurement nouns can also be used as modifiers in front of a noun when you want to describe things in terms of their measurements.

> *...a <u>5 foot 9 inch</u> bed.*
> *...<u>70 foot high</u> mounds of dust.*

...12 x 12 inch tiles.
...a five-pound bag of lentils.

Note that the measurement noun is singular.

2.256 If you want to describe fully the size of an object or area, you can give its dimensions; that is, you give measurements of its length and width, or length, width, and depth. When you give the dimensions of an object, you separate the figures using *and*, *by*, or the multiplication sign *x*.

...planks of wood about three inches thick and two feet wide.
The island measures about 25 miles by 12 miles.
Lake Nyasa is 450 miles long by about 50 miles wide.
The box measures approximately 26 inches wide x 25 inches deep x 16 inches high.

If you are talking about a square object or area, you give the length of each side followed by the word *square*.

Each family has only one room eight or ten feet square.
The site measures roughly 35 feet square.

Square is used in front of units of length when expressing area. *Cubic* is used in front of units of length when expressing volume.

...a farm covering 300 square miles.
The brain of the first ape-men was about the same size as that of a gorilla, around 500 cubic centimetres.

You express temperature in degrees, using either degrees centigrade, or degrees Fahrenheit. Note that in everyday language the metric term *centigrade* is used to indicate temperature, whereas in scientific language the term *Celsius* is used which refers to exactly the same scale of measurement.

2.257 You talk about the speed of something by saying how far it can travel in a particular unit of time. To do this, you use a noun such as *mile* or *kilometre*, followed by *per*, *a*, or *an*, and a time noun.

The car could do only forty-five miles per hour.
Wind speeds at the airport were 160 kilometres per hour.
Warships move at about 500 miles per day.

Talking about age

2.258 When you want to say how old someone is, you have a choice of ways in which to do it. You can be exact or approximate. Similarly, when you want to say how old something is, you can use different ways, some exact, and some approximate.

talking about exact age

2.259 When you want to talk about a person's exact age, you can do so by using

▶ *be* followed by a number, and sometimes *years old* after the number

I was nineteen, and he was twenty-one.
I'm only 63.
She is twenty-five years old.
I am forty years old.

▶ *of* (or less commonly *aged*) and a number after a noun

...a child of six.

...two little boys aged about nine and eleven.

▶ a compound adjective, usually hyphenated, consisting of a number, followed by a singular noun referring to a period of time, followed by *old*

...a twenty-two-year-old student.
...a five-month-old baby.
...a pretty 350-year-old cottage.
...a violation of a six-year-old agreement.

▶ a compound noun consisting of a number followed by *-year-old*

The servant was a pale little fourteen-year-old who looked hardly more than ten.
All the six-year-olds are taught by one teacher.
...Melvin Kalkhoven, a tall, thin thirty-five-year-old.

talking about approximate age

2.260 When you want to talk about a person's age in an approximate way, you can do so by using

▶ *in*, followed by a possessive determiner, followed by a plural noun referring to a particular range of years such as *twenties* and *teens*

He was in his sixties.
I didn't mature till I was in my forties.
...the groups who are now in their thirties.
...when I was in my teens.

Note that you can use *early*, *mid-*, *middle*, or *late* to indicate approximately where someone's age comes in a particular range of years.

He was then in his late seventies.
She was in her mid-twenties.
Jane is only in her early forties.

▶ *over* or *under* followed by a number

She was well over fifty.
She was only a little over forty years old.
There weren't enough people who were under 25.

Note that you can also use *above* or *below* followed by *the age of* and a number.

55 per cent of them were below the age of twenty-one.

▶ a compound noun referring to a group of people whose age is more or less than a particular number, which consists of *over* or *under* followed by the plural form of the particular number.

The over-sixties do not want to be turned out of their homes.
Schooling for under-fives should be expanded.

 This construction is not common in American English.

2.261 You can put several of the above structures after a noun to talk about the age of a person or thing.

...a woman in her early thirties.
...help for elderly ladies over 65.
She had four children under the age of five.

2.262 If you want to say that someone's age is similar to someone else's age, you use structures such as *of his age* and *of her parents' age* after a noun. The *of* is often dropped.

A lot of girls <u>of Helen's age</u> are interested in clothes.
It's easy to make friends because you're with people <u>of your own age</u>.
She will have a tough time when she plays with children <u>her own age</u>.

talking about the age of a thing

2.263 If you want to say what the age of a thing is, you can use

▶ *be* followed by a number followed by *years old*

It'<u>s</u> at least <u>a thousand million years old</u>.
The house <u>was</u> about <u>thirty years old</u>.

Note that you can also use this pattern after a noun.

...rocks <u>200 million years old</u>.

▶ a compound adjective indicating the century when something existed or was made, which consists of an ordinal number and *century*

...a <u>sixth-century</u> church.
...life in <u>fifth-century</u> Athens.

▶ a compound adjective, usually hyphenated, consisting of a number, followed by a singular noun referring to a period of time, followed by *old*

...a <u>1,000-year-old</u> temple.

Approximate amounts and measurements

2.264 If you do not know the exact number, size, or quantity of something, you can give an approximate amount or measurement using one of a group of special words and expressions. Some of these words and expressions are put in front of a quantity and some are put after it.

Here is a list of some of the words and expressions used to give approximate amounts and measurements:

about	at most	nearly	or under
almost	at the maximum	no more than	over
a maximum of	at the most	odd	roughly
a minimum of	less than	or less	some
approximately	maximum	or more	something like
around	minimum	or so	under
at least	more than	or thereabouts	up to

expressing minimum amounts

2.265 Some of these expressions indicate that a number is a minimum figure and that the actual figure is or may be larger.

Here is a list of expressions that indicate a minimum number:

a minimum of	minimum	or more	plus
at least	more than	over	

_i_ **USAGE NOTE**

2.266 You put _a minimum of_, _more than_, and _over_ in front of a number.

He needed a minimum of 26 Democratic votes.
...a school with more than 1300 pupils.
The British have been on the island for over a thousand years.

You put _or more_ and _plus_ after a number or amount, and _minimum_ after an amount.

...a choice of three or more possibilities.
This is the worst disaster I can remember in my 25 years plus as a police officer.
He does an hour's homework per night minimum.

You put _at least_ in front of a number or after a number or amount.

She had at least a dozen brandies.
I must have slept twelve hours at least!

expressing maximum amounts

2.267 Some of these expressions are used to indicate that a number is a maximum figure and that the actual figure is or may be smaller.

Here is a list of expressions that indicate a maximum number:

almost	at the most	nearly	under
a maximum of	fewer than	no more than	up to
at most	less than	or less	
at the maximum	maximum	or under	

_i_ **USAGE NOTE**

2.268 You put _almost_, _a maximum of_, _fewer than_, _less than_, _nearly_, _no more than_, _under_ and _up to_ in front of a number.

Fewer than and _less than_ mean the same, but _fewer than_ is more formal.

There were fewer than 20 people at the event.
The puppy's less than seven weeks old.
The company now supplies almost 100 of the city's restaurants.
These loans must be repaid over a maximum of three years.
She had nearly fifty dollars.
We managed to finish the entire job in under three months.
Their bodies might be up to a metre wide.

You put _at the maximum_, _at most_, _at the most_, _maximum_, _or less_, and _or under_ after a number.

Classes are of eight at the maximum.
The images take thirty-six hours maximum.
The area would yield only 200 pounds of rice or less.
...12 hours a week or under.

expressing approximate amounts

2.269 Some of these expressions are used to show that a number is approximate and that the actual figure could be larger or smaller.

Here is a list of the expressions showing that a number is approximate:

about	odd	roughly
approximately	or so	some
around	or thereabouts	something like

🇮 **USAGE NOTE**

2.270 You put *about*, *approximately*, *around*, *roughly*, *some*, and *something like* in front of a number.

About 85 students were there.
Every year we have approximately 40 pupils who take mathematics.
It would cost around 35 million pounds.
A loft conversion costs roughly £12,000.
They have to pay America some $683,000 this year.
Harrington has cheated us out of something like thirty thousand quid over the past two years.

You put *odd* and *or so* after a number or amount, and *or thereabouts* after an amount.

...a hundred odd acres.
For half a minute or so, neither of them spoke.
Get the temperature to 30°C or thereabouts.

2.271 You show a range of numbers using *between* and *and*, or *from* and *to*, or just *to*.

Most of the farms around here are between four and five hundred years old.
My hospital groups contain from ten to twenty patients.
...peasants owning two to five acres of land.

Note the use of *anything* before *between* and *from*, to emphasize how great the range is.

An average rate of anything between 25 and 60 per cent is usual.
It is a job that takes anything from two to five weeks.

Expanding the noun phrase

2.272 This section deals with structures that are used to add further information about the person or thing referred to. These are called **qualifiers**. The word that is qualified is usually a noun but can be an indefinite pronoun or *those*.

possible structures

2.273 The structures that are dealt with in this section are

▶ prepositional phrases

...a girl with red hair.
...the man in the dark glasses.

The use of prepositional phrases to expand the noun phrase is explained in paragraphs 2.275 to 2.290.

▶ adjectives followed by phrases or clauses

...machinery capable of clearing rubble off the main roads.
...the type of comments likely to provoke criticism.
...a concept inconceivable a hundred years earlier.

The use of adjectives followed by phrases or clauses to expand the noun phrase is explained in paragraphs 2.291 to 2.292.

▶ non-finite clauses

...a simple device <u>to test lung function</u>.
...two of the problems <u>mentioned above</u>.
He gestured towards the three cards <u>lying on the table</u>.

The use of non-finite clauses to expand the noun phrase is explained in paragraphs 2.293 to 2.301.

▶ noun phrases giving further information about other noun phrases. This is explained in paragraph 2.302.

2.274 Some other structures are also used. These are explained fully in other sections. They include

▶ single words such as *galore* and *concerned*, which are explained in paragraphs 2.58 to 2.62.

▶ relative clauses

Shortly after the shooting, the man <u>who had done it</u> was arrested.
Where's that cake <u>your mother made</u>?

Relative clauses are explained in paragraphs 8.83 to 8.116.

▶ place adverbs and time adverbials

...down in the dungeon <u>beneath</u>.
...a reflection of life <u>today</u> in England.

Time adverbials are explained in Chapter 4 and adverbs of place are explained in paragraphs 6.53 to 6.72.

Nouns with prepositional phrases

2.275 In general, any prepositional phrase that describes or classifies something can be used directly after a noun or pronoun.

...the man <u>in charge</u>.
...a film about four men <u>on holiday</u>.
She reached into the room <u>behind her</u>.

2.276 In particular, there are several kinds of prepositional phrase that are usually only used in this way. Of these, prepositional phrases beginning with *of* are the most numerous. Others include certain uses of *with, in* and *by*.

2.277 Many nouns referring to things and actions can be expanded by using prepositional phrases beginning with *of* after them. This allows the noun to be expanded with a wide range of meanings. You can use *of* with nouns referring to feelings such as *love* and *fear* to show what the feeling relates to; for example, *fear of flying* and *love of animals*. Further meanings are described in the following paragraphs.

! BE CAREFUL

2.278 **Personal pronouns** are not usually placed after *of*. For example, you cannot say *Joyce was the daughter of him* or *the pages of it*. **Possessive determiners** are used instead to show possession. These are explained in paragraphs 1.194 to 1.210.

2.279 Prepositional phrases beginning with *of* can be used to show what something consists of.

...a letter of confirmation.
...strong feelings of jealousy.

They can also be used to show what the subject matter of something is.

...a picture of a house.
...Gretchen's account of her interview with Nichols.
...the idea of death.

2.280 Prepositional phrases beginning with *of* can be used to say that something belongs to or is associated with someone or something.

Cental is a trademark of Monotore Ltd.
No.28 was the town house of Sir Winston Churchill.
James is the son of a Methodist minister.
The acting ability of the pupils is admirable.
...the beauty of the Welsh landscape.
Four boys sat on the floor of the living room.
Ellen aimlessly turned the pages of her magazine.

Note that apostrophe s ('s) structures are much more frequently used to say that something belongs to someone or something. **Apostrophe s ('s)** is explained in paragraphs 1.211 to 1.222.

2.281 Prepositional phrases beginning with *of* can be used to say that someone or something has a particular quality.

...a woman of energy and ambition.
...problems of varying complexity.
...a flower of monstrous proportions.
A household of this size inevitably has problems.

Of can also be used in front of a number to indicate someone's age.

...a woman of twenty-two.
...a child of six.

Other ways of talking about age are explained in paragraphs 2.258 to 2.263.

2.282 Prepositional phrases beginning with *of* can be used with nouns referring to an action to show who or what is performing the action.

...the arrival of the police.
...the growth of modern industry.

They are also used to show who or what someone does something to. For example, if you are talking about people who support a scheme, you can call them *the supporters of the scheme*.

...supporters of the hunger strike.
...critics of the Trade Union Movement.
...the creator of the universe.
...a student of English.
...the cause of the tragedy.

Of structures are also used to indicate the thing affected by an action.

...the destruction of their city.
...the dismissal of hundreds of workers.

2.283 Prepositional phrases beginning with *of* and containing measurement are used to show how great an area, speed, distance, or temperature is.

There were fires burning over a total area of about 600 square miles.
It can barely maintain a speed of 25 kilometres an hour.

...an average annual temperature <u>of 20°</u>.

Ways of measuring things are explained in paragraphs 2.250 to 2.257.

2.284 Prepositional phrases beginning with *with* can be used to say that someone or something has a particular characteristic, feature, or possession.

...a girl <u>with red hair</u>.
...a girl <u>with a foreign accent</u>.
...a big car <u>with reclining seats</u>.
...a man <u>with a violent temper</u>.
...the man <u>with the gun</u>.
...those <u>with large families</u>.

They are also used to indicate what something has on or in it.

...a sheet of paper <u>with writing on it</u>.
...a round box <u>with some buttons in it</u>.
...a white, plain envelope <u>with her name printed on it</u>.
...fragments of wrapping paper <u>with bits of sticky tape still adhering to them</u>.

in

2.285 Prepositional phrases beginning with *in* can be used to say what someone is wearing.

...a grey-haired man <u>in a raincoat</u>.
...the man <u>in the dark glasses</u>.
...little groups of people <u>in black</u>.

by

2.286 Prepositional phrases beginning with *by* can be used after a noun referring to an action to say who or what is performing it.

...his appointment <u>by the King</u>.
...the compression of air <u>by the piston</u>.

with prepositional phrases

2.287 Some nouns, especially abstract nouns, need to be followed by a prepositional phrase to show what they relate to. There is often little or no choice about which preposition to use after a particular noun.

He has an allergy <u>to peanuts</u>.
...his authority <u>over them</u>.
...the solution <u>to our energy problem</u>.
...the bond <u>between mother and child</u>.

2.288 Here is a list of nouns that usually or often have *to* after them:

access	answer	disloyalty	reference	testimony
addiction	antidote	exception	relevance	threat
adherence	approach	fidelity	reply	vulnerability
affront	attachment	incitement	resistance	witness
allegiance	aversion	introduction	return	
allergy	contribution	preface	sequel	
allusion	damage	prelude	solution	
alternative	devotion	recourse	susceptibility	

Here is a list of nouns that usually or often have *for* after them:

admiration	cure	disrespect	recipe	search
appetite	demand	hunger	regard	substitute
aptitude	desire	love	remedy	sympathy
bid	disdain	need	respect	synonym
craving	dislike	provision	responsibility	taste
credit	disregard	quest	room	thirst

Here is a list of nouns that usually or often have *on* after them:

assault	concentration	effect	reliance
attack	constraint	embargo	restriction
ban	crackdown	hold	stance
claim	curb	insistence	tax
comment	dependence	reflection	

Here is a list of nouns that usually or often have *with* after them:

affinity	correspondence	familiarity	link
collision	date	identification	parity
collusion	dealings	intersection	quarrel
connection	dissatisfaction	intimacy	relationship
contrast	encounter	involvement	sympathy

Here is a list of nouns that are usually followed by one of two prepositions. The list indicates the choice of prepositions available:

agreement about	battle against	debate about	transition from
agreement on	battle for	debate on	transition to
argument against	case against	decision about	
argument for	case for	decision on	

Here is a list of other nouns that are usually followed by a preposition.

complex about	anger at	quotation from
crime against	bond between	foray into
grudge against	departure from	relapse into
insurance against	escape from	awareness of
reaction against	excerpt from	authority over
safeguard against	freedom from	control over

As you can see from the lists and examples given above, it is often the case that words with a similar meaning are typically followed by the same preposition. For example, *appetite*, *craving*, *desire*, *hunger*, and *thirst* are all followed by *for*.

🛈 **USAGE NOTE**

2.289 Some nouns are related to verbs that are always or often followed by a particular preposition. These nouns are followed by the same preposition as their related verbs, and they are used to indicate the thing that is affected by the action. For example, *to* is used after both the verb *refer* and the related noun *reference*.

We have already referred to this phenomenon.
...reverent references to the importance of home.
They swim about busily searching for food.
...the search for food.
I want to escape from here.
...an escape from reality.

2.290 Some nouns referring to a feeling or state are related to an adjective that is usually followed by a preposition. These nouns are followed by the same preposition as their related adjectives. For example, *of* is used after the adjective *aware* and the related noun *awareness*.

She was quite aware of her current situation.
...the public's increasing awareness of the problems.
He was angry at Sally Gardner for accusing him.
...her anger at the kids.

Nouns with adjectives

2.291 When adjectives are used in clauses after nouns or pronouns to expand their meaning they can be followed by

▶ prepositional phrases

...a warning to people eager for a quick cure.
those responsible for the project.

▶ a *to*-infinitive

...remarks likely to cause offence.
It has been directed against those least able to retaliate.

▶ expressions of time or place

...a concept inconceivable a hundred years earlier.
For the facilities available here, I must ask for a fee.

Note that you can use adjectives as qualifiers when they are preceded by time or measurement expressions.

...those <u>still alive</u>.
...a small hill <u>about 400 feet high</u>.

Note also that a few adjectives, such as *present* and *responsible*, can be used on their own after a noun or pronoun. The use of these adjectives is explained in paragraphs 2.58 to 2.62.

other structures

2.292 There are some other structures, especially those that indicate comparison, degree, or result, that often involve a qualifying structure. In particular, some words that modify adjectives, such as *more*, *too*, or *so*, often have a qualifying structure to complete their meaning.

Peter came in, <u>more excited than anyone had seen him before</u>.
Ralph was <u>too angry to think clearly</u>.
...steel cylinders <u>strong enough to survive a nuclear catastrophe</u>.
...a grand piano <u>as big as two coffins</u>.
She was <u>so ill that she couldn't eat</u>.
Technology has made <u>such spectacular advances that it is difficult to keep up</u>.

The use of comparative adjectives plus *than* after noun phrases is explained in paragraphs 2.106 to 2.108. Other ways of comparing things are explained in paragraphs 2.123 to 2.139. The use of *so...that* and *such...that* is explained in paragraphs 8.58 to 8.63.

Nouns followed by *to*-infinitive, *-ed* participle, or *-ing* participle: *something to eat, a girl called Patricia, a basket containing eggs*

2.293 The following **non-finite** clauses (= clauses containing a verb that has no tense) can be used to expand the meaning of a noun: *to*-infinitive clauses (see paragraphs 2.294 to 2.299), *-ed* participle clauses (see paragraph 2.300), and *-ing* participle clauses (see paragraph 2.301).

nouns followed by *to*-infinitive clauses

2.294 A *to*-infinitive clause is often placed after nouns in order to show what the thing referred to is intended to do.

The government of Mexico set up a programme <u>to develop new varieties of wheat</u>.
They need people <u>to work in the factories</u>.

2.295 You can refer to something or someone that should or can have something done to them by using a clause containing a *to*-infinitive after a noun or indefinite pronoun.

I make notes in the back of my diary of things <u>to be mended or replaced</u>.
...when I've had something <u>to eat</u>.

You can also use a clause consisting of a *to*-infinitive followed by a preposition.

There wasn't even a chair <u>to sit on</u>.
He had nothing <u>to write with</u>.

2.296 You can also use a *to*-infinitive clause when you want to say that you are talking about, for example, the first, oldest, or only person who did something.

...the first woman <u>to be elected to the council</u>.

2.297 A clause containing a *to*-infinitive is used after some abstract nouns to show what action they relate to.

...people who didn't have the opportunity <u>to go to university</u>.

ℹ USAGE NOTE

2.298 Many of these nouns are related to verbs or adjectives that are also often followed by *to*-infinitive clauses. For example, a *to*-infinitive clause is used after both the verb *need* and the noun *need*, and after both the adjective *able* and the related noun *ability*.

I *need to borrow* five thousand dollars.
...the *need to preserve* secrecy about their intentions.
It *failed to grow*.

2.299 Here is a list of nouns that usually or often have a *to*-infinitive clause after them:

ability	desire	need	unwillingness
attempt	disinclination	opportunity	urge
bid	failure	readiness	way
chance	inability	reason	willingness
compulsion	inclination	refusal	

nouns followed by *-ed* participle clauses

2.300 A clause containing an *-ed* participle can be used directly after a noun to show that something has been produced or affected by an action.

...a girl *called Patricia*.
...dresses *made of paper*.
...two of the problems *mentioned above*.
...a story *written by a nine-year-old girl*.

nouns followed by *-ing* participle clauses

2.301 A clause containing an *-ing* participle can be used directly after a noun to show that someone or something is doing something.

He gestured towards the three cards *lying on the table*.
...a wicker shopping-basket *containing groceries*.

with an identifying noun phrase

2.302 You can give further information about someone or something by using a noun phrase that describes them or identifies them.

If you put this noun phrase after the main noun phrase, a comma is almost always put after the main noun phrase because the second noun phrase is separate from it, not part of it.

...the bald eagle, *the symbol of America*.
...David Beckham, *a first-class football player*.
Her mother, *a Canadian*, died when she was six.

If you put this noun phrase before the main noun phrase, you can sometimes choose whether to use a comma to separate the two noun phrases or not.

...Joan's husband, *Jim Inglis*.
...*my husband* George.

Chapter 3

Making a message: types of verb

3   Making a message: types of verb

3.1   When you make a statement, you use a **clause**. A clause that is used to make a statement contains a **noun phrase**, which refers to the person or thing that you are talking about, and a **verb phrase**, which shows what sort of action, process, or state you are talking about.

The noun phrase, which usually comes in front of the verb, is called the **subject** of the verb or the clause. For example, in the clause *Ellen laughed*, *Ellen* is the subject. The formation of noun phrases is explained in Chapters 1 and 2.

A verb phrase used in a statement has a particular form, and shows agreement with number and person. The formation of verb phrases is explained in the Reference section. Quite often in statements the verb phrase is a single word, and it is quite common to talk about the *verb* of a clause.

This chapter deals mainly with the use of verbs in **active** clauses, where the subject is the performer of an action rather than the person or thing affected by an action. The use of verbs in **passive** clauses, where the subject is the person or thing affected, is explained in paragraphs 9.8 to 9.24.

Showing who is involved

intransitive verbs

3.2   If an action or event involves only one person or thing, you mention only the performer of the action (the subject) and the action (the verb).

The girl screamed.
I waited.
An awful thing has happened.

Verbs like this are called **intransitive verbs**.

However, you can then mention another person or thing that is involved using a **prepositional phrase**.

She walked across the street.

Intransitive verbs are explained in paragraphs 3.8 to 3.13.

transitive verbs

3.3   If the action or event involves another person or thing that the action affects, relates to, or produces, you put a noun phrase referring to them after the verb. This is called the **object** of the verb. If it is necessary to distinguish it from other objects, it is called the **direct object**.

He closed the door.
I hate sport.
Some of the women noticed me.

Verbs like this are called **transitive verbs**. Transitive verbs are explained in paragraphs 3.14 to 3.25.

Reflexive verbs and **delexical verbs** are special kinds of transitive verbs. They are explained in paragraphs 3.26 to 3.31 and 3.32 to 3.45.

intransitive or transitive verbs

3.4 The majority of verbs in English give you the option of presenting an event either as involving the subject only, or as involving the subject and someone or something else as a direct object.

She paints by holding the brush in her teeth.
Yarkov paints vivid portraits of friends and acquaintances.
Gus asked me whether I'd like to have dinner with him. I accepted.
I accepted the invitation.

This means that most verbs can be used with or without an object. Verbs that can be used like this are explained in paragraphs 3.46 to 3.54.

With some verbs, the thing affected by the action can be put as the object of the verb or as the object of a preposition after the verb. These verbs are explained in paragraphs 3.55 to 3.58.

Ergative verbs are a special kind of verb that can be used with or without an object. They are explained in paragraphs 3.59 to 3.67.

reciprocal verbs

3.5 **Reciprocal verbs** refer to actions that involve people affecting each other in the same way with the same action. There are two types of **reciprocal verb**. One type is used either with or without an object.

We met at Hargreaves' place.
I had met him in Zermatt.

The other type is used without an object, and with or without a prepositional phrase mentioning one of the participants.

We argued over this question for a long time.
I argued with this man for half an hour.

Reciprocal verbs are explained in paragraphs 3.68 to 3.72.

verbs with two objects

3.6 Some transitive verbs also allow you to mention a person who benefits from an action or receives something as a result. The verb is then followed by both a direct object and an **indirect object**.

Hand me my bag.
His uncle had given him books on India.
She sends you her love.
She passed him his cup.

Verbs that can take an indirect object as well as a direct object are explained in paragraphs 3.73 to 3.82.

phrasal verbs, compound verbs

3.7 Some verbs have two or three parts. These are **phrasal verbs** and **compound verbs**. Phrasal verbs are explained in paragraphs 3.83 to 3.116, and compound verbs are explained in paragraphs 3.117 to 3.125.

Intransitive verbs: talking about events that involve only the subject

3.8   When you are talking about an action or event that does not have an object, you use an **intransitive verb**.

Her whole body <u>ached</u>.
Such people still <u>exist</u>.
My condition <u>deteriorated</u>.

Many intransitive verbs describe physical behaviour or the making of sounds.

Bob <u>coughed</u>.
Vicki <u>wept</u> bitterly.
The gate <u>squeaked</u>.

3.9   Here is a list of verbs that are normally used without an object and that usually or often have no adverb or prepositional phrase after them:

ache	disappear	fluctuate	rise	squeal
advance	disintegrate	gleam	roar	stink
arise	doze	growl	scream	subside
arrive	droop	happen	shine	sulk
bleed	economize	hesitate	shiver	surrender
blush	elapse	howl	sigh	swim
cease	ensue	itch	sleep	throb
collapse	erupt	kneel	slip	tingle
cough	evaporate	laugh	smile	vanish
crackle	exist	moan	snarl	vary
cry	expire	occur	sneeze	vibrate
decay	faint	pause	snore	wait
depart	fall	persist	snort	waver
deteriorate	falter	prosper	sob	weep
die	fidget	quiver	sparkle	wilt
digress	flinch	recede	speak	work
dine	flourish	relent	squeak	yawn

A few of these verbs are used with an object in idioms or with very specific objects, but they are intransitive in all their common meanings.

intransitive verbs followed by phrases that begin with a preposition

3.10   Many intransitive verbs always or typically have an adverb or prepositional phrase after them. With some, only a prepositional phrase beginning with a particular preposition is possible. This use of a preposition allows something affected by the action to be mentioned, as the object of the preposition.

Everything you see here <u>belongs to</u> me.
Landlords often <u>resorted to</u> violence.
I <u>sympathized with</u> them.
I'm <u>relying on</u> Bill.
He <u>strives for</u> excellence in all things.

3.11   Here is a list of verbs that always or typically have a particular preposition after them
        when they are used with a particular meaning:

rave about	stem from	adhere to
~	suffer from	allude to
insure against	~	amount to
plot against	believe in	appeal to
react against	consist in	aspire to
~	culminate in	assent to
hint at	dabble in	attend to
~	indulge in	belong to
alternate between	invest in	bow to
differentiate between	result in	cling to
oscillate between	wallow in	defer to
~	~	dictate to
appeal for	lapse into	lead to
atone for	~	listen to
care for	complain of	object to
clamour for	conceive of	refer to
hope for	consist of	relate to
long for	despair of	resort to
opt for	learn of	revert to
pay for	smack of	stoop to
qualify for	think of	~
strive for	tire of	alternate with
yearn for	~	associate with
~	bet on	consort with
detract from	feed on	contend with
emanate from	insist on	flirt with
emerge from	spy on	grapple with
radiate from	trample on	sympathize with
shrink from	~	teem with

Here is a list of verbs that can have either of two prepositions after them with the
same or very similar meaning:

abound in	depend on	engage in
abound with	depend upon	engage on
cater for	dote on	enthuse about
cater to	dote upon	enthuse over
conform to	embark on	gravitate to
conform with	embark upon	gravitate towards
contribute to	end in	hunger after
contribute towards	end with	hunger for

improve on	prevail on	revolve around
improve upon	prevail upon	revolve round
liaise between	profit by	spring from
liaise with	profit from	spring out of
lust after	rely on	
lust for	rely upon	

Note that some intransitive verbs can be used in the passive when they are followed by a preposition. See paragraph 9.23.

intransitive verbs followed by an adverb or prepositional phrase

3.12 Other verbs can be followed by a variety of prepositional phrases, or an adverb, often relating to time or place.

Verbs of movement are usually or often followed by adverbs or phrases relating to direction.

He went back to his own room.
I travelled south.

Here is a list of verbs of movement:

come	flow	hurtle	spring
crawl	gallop	plunge	stroll
creep	glide	run	travel
drift	go	soar	walk

Look, *gaze*, *glance*, and *stare* are also followed by adverbs or phrases relating to direction.

Verbs of position are usually followed by adverbs or phrases relating to position.

Donald was lying on the bed.
She lives in Lausanne.
I used to live here.

Here is a list of verbs of position:

be	lie	remain	stand
belong	live	sit	stay
hang	be located	be situated	

Verbs such as *extend* or *stretch* are followed by adverbs or phrases relating to extent.

...an area stretching from London to Cambridge.

There are a few verbs that are always followed by other types of adverb or phrase.

It behaves rather like a squirrel.
My brother agreed to act as a go-between.
I hoped that the absorption of poison hadn't progressed too far.

Here is a list of verbs that are always followed by other types of adverb or phrase:

act	behave	campaign	progress

verbs that are occasionally transitive

3.13   There are a few verbs that are usually intransitive but that can be transitive when they are used with one particular object. The object is usually directly related to the verb. For example, *smile* is usually used without an object, but you can use it with the noun *smile*. For example, *He smiled a patient smile* is a literary alternative to saying *He smiled patiently*. The focus is on the type of smile rather than on the act of smiling.

Steve smiled his thin, cruel smile.
He appears to have lived the life of any other rich gentleman.
Alice laughed a scornful laugh.
I once dreamed a very nice dream about you.

Here is a list of verbs that can only be used with an object when the object is directly related to the verb:

dance (a dance)	dream (a dream)	live (a life)	smile (a smile)
die (a death)	laugh (a laugh)	sigh (a sigh)	

A more common way of focusing on the noun phrase is to use a **delexical verb** such as *give*, *take*, or *have*, as in *Mary gave him a really lovely smile*. See paragraphs 3.32 to 3.45 for more information about the use of delexical verbs.

Transitive verbs: involving someone or something other than the subject

3.14   Many verbs describe events that must, in addition to the subject, involve someone or something else. Some of these verbs can only be used with a following object.

The extra profit justifies the investment.
He had committed a disgraceful action.
They are employing more staff.

This means that they are followed by a direct object.

She had friends.
Children seek independence.
The trial raised a number of questions.

different types of object

3.15   Many verbs that are only used with an object can take a large range of objects. For example, there are many things you can *want*: money, a rest, success, and so on.

She wanted some help.
I put my hand on the door.
She described her background.
I still support the government.
He had always liked Mr Phillips.
Japan has a population of about a hundred million.

Some transitive verbs have a restricted range of objects, because of their meaning. For example, the object of the verb *kill* must be something that is alive. The object of the verb *waste* must be something you can use, such as time, money, or food.

They killed huge elephants with tiny poisoned darts.
Why waste money on them?

3.16 Here is a list of verbs that are transitive:

achieve	cut	get	maintain	rent
address	damage	give	make	report
admire	defy	grant	mean	respect
affect	demand	guard	mention	reveal
afford	describe	handle	name	risk
avoid	design	hate	need	see
bear	desire	have	own	seek
believe	destroy	hear	plant	sell
blame	discover	heat	please	shock
build	discuss	hire	prefer	specify
buy	display	hit	prevent	spot
calm	do	include	process	support
carry	dread	influence	produce	take
catch	enjoy	introduce	pronounce	tease
claim	equal	issue	protect	test
commit	exchange	justify	provide	threaten
complete	expect	keep	raise	trust
concern	experience	kill	reach	upset
consider	express	know	receive	use
control	favour	lack	recommend	value
convince	fear	like	record	want
correct	fill	list	release	waste
cover	find	love	remember	wear
create	free	lower	remove	welcome

Note that *do* and *have* are also very often used as **auxiliaries**. See the Reference section for this use.

Have got and *has got* are often used instead of the present tense of *have* when talking about possession. The forms of *have* behave like auxiliaries when used like this before *got*.

I've got an umbrella.
She's got a degree.

Measure and *weigh* are sometimes considered to be transitive verbs when used to state measurements and weights. This use is explained in paragraph 2.252. *Cost* is used to state the cost of something, as in *An adult ticket costs 90p.*

human objects

3.17 When you are talking about something that affects a person rather than a thing, it is normal in English to say who that person is. Therefore, verbs such as *anger*, *thank*, and *warn*, which involve affecting people, usually have a human object.

I tried to comfort her.
Her sudden death had surprised everybody.

Blue suits you.
Money did not interest him very much.
Lebel briefed Caron on the events of the afternoon.

3.18 Here is a list of verbs that usually have a human object:

anger	contact	suit	thank
brief	frighten	surprise	trouble
comfort	interest	tease	warn

transitive verbs that need to be followed by an adverb or prepositional phrase

3.19 With some transitive verbs, you have to give additional information about what is going on by using an adverb or prepositional phrase after the object.

Some verbs typically have a prepositional phrase beginning with a particular preposition after their object.

The judge based his decision on constitutional rights.
He had subjected me to the pressure of financial ruin.
My parents still view me as a little boy.

Here is a list of verbs that always or usually have a particular preposition after their object:

regard as	deprive of	condemn to	subordinate to
view as	remind of	confine to	~
~	rid of	consign to	acquaint with
mistake for	rob of	dedicate to	associate with
swap for	~	entitle to	confront with
~	accustom to	liken to	engrave with
dissociate from	ascribe to	owe to	pelt with
prevent from	attribute to	return to	ply with
~	compare to	subject to	trust with

With the following verbs, there is a choice of preposition:

divide by	~	~	present to
divide into	base on	entrust to	present with
~	base upon	entrust with	supply to
incorporate in	lavish on	equate to	supply with
incorporate into	lavish upon	equate with	

3.20 Other verbs are typically followed by an adverb or prepositional phrase, but not one containing a particular preposition. The adverb or phrase often relates to place.

He placed the baby on the woman's lap.
I positioned my chair outside the room.
He never puts anything away.
He treated his labourers with kindness.

Here is a list of verbs that usually have some kind of adverb or prepositional phrase after their object:

bring	escort	lead	rip	store
chuck	fling	place	send	throw
convey	hoist	point	set	thrust
cram	jab	position	shove	tie
direct	jot	prop	smear	treat
drag	lay	put	stick	

For more on adverbs and phrases that follow verbs, see Chapter 6.

transitive verbs of position and movement

3.21 Note that some verbs of movement and position are transitive, not intransitive; they are followed by nouns referring to places rather than by adverbs or prepositional phrases. This is because the verbs themselves show that you are talking about movement or position of a particular kind. For example, *enter* implies movement *into* a place and *occupy* implies position *in* a place.

He approached the house nervously.
It was dark by the time they reached their house.
A small ornamental pool occupied the centre of the room.
Everyone had left the room.

Here is a list of transitive verbs of movement:

approach	leave	reach
enter	near	round

Here is a list of transitive verbs of position:

cover	fill	occupy
crowd	inhabit	throng

Some verbs of movement can be followed either by a noun phrase or by a prepositional phrase. See paragraph 3.58.

USAGE NOTE

3.22 Note that even verbs that are almost always followed by an object can occasionally be used without an object. This is possible in very restricted contexts. For example, if you are contrasting two actions, it is not necessary to say what else is involved.

Money markets are the places where people with money buy and sell.
Some people build while others destroy.
We gave, they took.

If you use a list of different verbs for emphasis, you do not need to name the object.

They set out to be rude; to defy, threaten, or tease.

If you repeat a verb in order to contrast it with a similar action, or to emphasize it, the object can be omitted.

She had ceased to love as she had once loved.

3.23 Verbs that describe feelings and attitudes are sometimes used without an object, particularly in the **to-infinitive** form. This is because the object is assumed to be people in general. For example, *please* usually requires an object, but you can say *He likes to please*, meaning he likes to please people.

He likes to shock.
She was anxious to please.
He must be convinced if he is to convince.
I have a tendency to tease.

reporting verbs

3.24 There is a large group of verbs, such as *say*, *suggest*, and *think*, which are used to report what people say or think. They are called **reporting verbs**. They are followed by a *that*-clause which is called the **reported clause**.

She said that she would come.

The reported clause is often thought of as being an object, and so these verbs are usually said to be transitive verbs. In this book, reporting verbs are explained in Chapter 7.

Reporting verbs such as *advise* and *persuade*, which have an object that refers to the person being addressed, are explained in paragraphs 7.75 and 7.76.

Some reporting verbs can take as their object a noun such as *question* or *story* that refers to something that is said or written. These verbs are listed in paragraph 7.82. Some take an object that refers to an event or fact, and is therefore closely related to a *that*-clause. These are listed in paragraph 7.83.

Verbs such as *believe* and *know* that can be used as reporting verbs, but that are ordinary transitive verbs when used with another common meaning, are included in the lists of transitive verbs given above.

3.25 Most transitive verbs can be used in the passive. See paragraphs 9.9 to 9.21.

Reflexive verbs: verbs where the object refers back to the subject

 BE CREATIVE

3.26 If you want to talk about a situation where the same person is involved as both the subject and the object of an action, you use a **reflexive pronoun** as the object of a clause. For example, it is common to blame someone else if something goes wrong, but you say *I blame myself for what happened* if you think that the mistake was your own fault.

Although a few verbs are typically used with reflexive pronouns, you can actually use a reflexive pronoun as the object of any transitive verb, when the meaning allows you to do so.

I blame myself for not paying attention.
She freed herself from my embrace.
After the meeting, he introduced himself to me.
Why not buy a book and teach yourself?
Don't deceive yourself.
We must ask ourselves several questions.
Every country has the right to defend itself.

Reflexive pronouns are explained in paragraphs 1.111 to 1.118.

true reflexive verbs

3.27 Note that the verbs *busy*, *content*, and *pride* are true reflexive verbs: they must be used with a reflexive pronoun.

He had busied himself in the laboratory.
Many scholars contented themselves with writing textbooks.
He prides himself on his tidiness.

3.28 Another small group of verbs only take an object that refers to a person when the object is a reflexive pronoun. For example, you can *express an opinion* and you can *express yourself* (meaning that you can put ideas into words), but you cannot *express a person*.

Professor Baxendale expressed himself very forcibly.
She enjoyed herself enormously.
He applied himself to learning how Parliament worked.

Here is a list of verbs that take a reflexive pronoun as their object when you refer to a person:

apply	distance	excel	express
compose	enjoy	exert	strain

reflexive pronouns used for emphasis

3.29 Some verbs that normally do not have objects, because they involve only the performer of the action, can have a reflexive pronoun as their object if you want to emphasize that the subject is doing something that affects himself or herself. You can therefore say *Bill washed himself* rather than *Bill washed*.

I always wash five times a day.
Children were encouraged to wash themselves.
I stood in the kitchen while he shaved.
He prefers to shave himself before breakfast.
Ashton had behaved abominably.
He is old enough to behave himself.
Successful companies know how to adapt to change.
You've got to be willing to adapt yourself.

Here is a list of verbs that have senses in which you can use a reflexive pronoun for emphasis:

acclimatize	commit	move	undress
adapt	dress	readjust	wash
behave	hide	shave	

! **BE CAREFUL**

3.30 Note that reflexive pronouns are not used as much in English as in some other languages when talking about actions that you do to yourself. As mentioned above, you would usually say *I washed* rather than *I washed myself* in English. Sometimes a noun with a possessive is used instead. For example, you would say *I combed my hair* rather than *I combed myself*.

3.31 Note that reflexive verbs are not used in the passive.

Delexical verbs: verbs with little meaning

3.32 There are some very common verbs that are used with nouns as their object to show simply that someone performs an action, not that someone affects or creates something. These verbs have very little meaning when they are used in this way.

For example, *had* in *She had a shower* has very little meaning in itself. Most of the meaning of the sentence is carried by the noun *shower*.

We <u>were having a joke</u>.
Roger <u>gave a grin</u> of sheer delight.
He <u>took a step</u> towards Jack.

verbs that are often delexical

3.33 This section focuses on the very common verbs that are used in this transitive structure. They are called **delexical verbs**.

Here is a list of verbs that are used as delexical verbs. The first four are very commonly used in this way.

give	take	hold
have	~	keep
make	do	set

Note that *have got* is not used as a delexical verb.

Structures containing delexical verbs are very common in English. Although the total number of delexical verbs is small, it includes some of the most common words in the language.

3.34 In many cases, there is a verb that has a similar meaning to the meaning of the delexical verb + noun. For example, the verb *look* means almost the same as *have a look*. When *look* is a verb, as in *I looked round the room*, you are focusing on the action of looking. When you use *look* as a noun in a delexical structure, you are naming an event, something that is complete. This structure often seems to be preferred. Note that the verb corresponding to the delexical structure is often intransitive.

She <u>made a signal</u>.
She <u>signalled</u> for a taxi.
A couple <u>were having a drink</u> at a table by the window.
A few students <u>were drinking</u> at the bar.
She <u>gave an amused laugh</u>.
They both <u>laughed</u>.
He <u>gave a vague reply</u>.
They <u>replied</u> to his letter.

There are also some verbs that are transitive.

Fans tried to <u>get a glimpse</u> of the singer.
I <u>glimpsed</u> a bright flash of gold on the left.
He <u>gave a little sniff</u>.
She <u>sniffed</u> the air.
Comis <u>took a photograph</u> of her.
They <u>photographed</u> the pigeons in Trafalgar Square.

with singular noun

3.36 The noun that is the object of the delexical verb is often in the singular and is usually preceded by *a* or *an*.

She made a remark about the weather.
She gave a cry when I came in.
I might take a stroll.

There are some countable nouns that are almost always used in the singular after a delexical verb. Here is a list of these nouns:

cry	grumble	smell
feel	need	taste
grouse	read	try

Note that these words are more commonly used as verbs in the language as a whole.

with plural noun

3.36 You can also use a delexical verb followed by a plural noun.

She took little sips of the cold drink.
He took photographs of Vita in her summer house.
The newspaper made unpleasant remarks about his wife.

with uncountable noun

3.37 It is also occasionally possible to follow a delexical verb with an uncountable noun.

We have made progress in both science and art.
Cal took charge of this side of their education.

talking about a brief event

3.38 One difference in meaning between using a structure containing a delexical verb and a verb with a similar meaning is that the delexical structure can give the impression that the event you are describing is brief. For example, *She gave a scream* suggests that there was only one quick scream, whereas *She screamed* does not suggest that the event was brief.

Mr. Sutton gave a shout of triumph.
Zoe gave a sigh of relief.
He gave a laugh.

using adjectives

3.39 Another reason for choosing a delexical structure is that you can add further details about the event by using adjectives in front of the noun, rather than by using adverbs. It is more natural, for example, to say *He gave a quick furtive glance round the room* than to say *He glanced quickly and furtively round the room*.

He gave a long lecture about Roosevelt.
She had a good cry.
He was forced to make a humiliating apology.
These legends hold a romantic fascination for many Japanese.

nouns with no equivalent verb

3.40 There are some nouns used in delexical structures that do not correspond in form to a verb that has a similar meaning to the delexical structure. Sometimes there is such a verb, but the form is slightly different.

Work experience allows students to make more effective career decisions.
I decided I wouldn't resign after all.
He made the shortest speech I've ever heard.
Iain spoke candidly about the crash.

In other cases, there is no corresponding verb with a similar meaning at all and so there is no other structure that can be used.

He had been out all day taking pictures of the fighting.
That is a very foolish attitude to take.
She made a number of relevant points.
Try not to make so much noise.

nouns used with *have*

3.41 In most cases, only one delexical verb is used with any particular noun.

The following examples show nouns that are used after *have*.

They have a desperate need to communicate.
They had a fundamental belief in their own superiority.
She had a good cry.
Let's not have a quarrel.
We should have a talk.

Here is a list of nouns that are used after *have*:

argument	dance	grouse	respect
belief	disagreement	grumble	sleep
chat	fall	need	talk
cry	fight	quarrel	

nouns used with *take*

3.42 The following examples show nouns that are used after *take*.

He takes no interest in his children.
...kids taking turns to use a playground slide.
He was taking no chances.
She was prepared to take great risks.
Davis took the lead in blaming the pilots.
The Government fought against suggestions that it should take full blame for the affair.

Here is a list of nouns that are used after *take*. The first set of nouns are countable nouns; the second set of nouns are uncountable nouns or always either singular or plural:

attitude	picture	charge	power
chance	risk	consequences	responsibility
decision	turn	form	shape
interest	~	lead	time
photo	blame	offence	trouble
photograph	care	office	

nouns used with *give*

3.43 Many nouns can be used after *give*.

Some of these nouns refer to noises that people make, or expressions they make with their face. Using *give* with one of these nouns often suggests that the action is involuntary or that it is not necessarily directed at other people. For example, *She gave a scream* suggests that she could not help screaming.

The young cashier gave a patient sigh.
Roger gave a grin of sheer delight.
He gave a shrill gasp of shock.
Both of them gave an involuntary little giggle.
He gave a soft chuckle.

Here is a list of nouns that refer to noises people make, or expressions they make with their face:

chuckle	grin	scream	smile	yell
cry	groan	shout	sniff	
gasp	laugh	shriek	snigger	
giggle	scowl	sigh	whistle	

Another group of nouns are often preceded by an indirect object (that is, an object that refers to the person or thing that received the action) because they describe activities that involve someone else, apart from the subject.

They gave us a wonderfully warm welcome.
Elaine gave him a hug.
He gave her hand a squeeze.
He gave him a good kick.
She gave him a long kiss.

Here is a list of nouns that can be preceded by an indirect object:

clue	hug	look	ring	squeeze
glance	kick	punch	shove	welcome
hint	kiss	push	slap	

A third group of nouns refer to actions involving something being said.

The poetry professor is required to give a lecture every term.
Lord Young will be giving a first-hand account of the economic difficulties the Russians are struggling to overcome.
Senator Brown has given warning that conflict over the plans could lead to a constitutional crisis.

Here is a list of nouns that refer to actions involving something being said:

account	example	lecture	report	talk
advice	information	news	speech	thought
answer	interview	reason	summary	warning

nouns used with *make*

3.44 Many nouns can be used after *make*.

The delexical structures using a lot of these nouns are closely related to **reporting structures**, which are explained in Chapter 7. There is usually a related verb that can be used followed by a reported clause.

She made a remark about the weather.
Allen remarked that at times he thought he was back in America.
Now and then she makes a comment on something.
He commented that he was only doing his job.
I haven't made a full confession, sir.
Fox confessed that he had stolen the money.
The cricketers made a public protest against apartheid.
She protested that his comments were sexist.
I made a secret signal to him.
The Bank of England signalled that there would be no change in interest rates.
You made the right decision.
One candidate resigned, deciding that banking was not for her.

Here is a list of nouns that are used after *make* and have a related reporting verb:

arrangement	confession	protest	suggestion
claim	decision	remark	
comment	promise	signal	

Other nouns used with *make* express actions involving something being said, or describe change, results, effort, and so on.

I'll make some enquiries for you.
They agreed to make a few minor changes.
They made an emotional appeal for their daughter's safe return.
He made an attempt to calm down.
He has made a significant contribution to the success of the business.

Here is a list of other nouns that are used after *make*:

appeal	contribution	noise	sound
attempt	effort	point	speech
change	enquiry	progress	start
charge	impression	recovery	success

Note that, unlike the other nouns in this list, *progress* is uncountable.

nouns used with *have* and *take*

3.45 There are some nouns that can be used after either *have* or *take*. In general *have* is more common with these nouns in British English and *take* is more common in

American English. There is sometimes a slight difference in emphasis: using *have* puts more emphasis on the experience, and using *take* puts more emphasis on the performer of the action.

One group of these nouns refer to physical activities.

I'd rather have a swim.
Have a drink.
She decided to take a stroll along the beach.
I took a bath, my second that day.

Here is a list of nouns that refer to physical activities:

bath	jog	shower	walk
break	paddle	stroll	
drink	rest	swim	
holiday	run	vacation *(American)*	

Another group refer to actions that involve using our senses.

She should let a doctor have a look at you.
Even Sally had a little sip of wine.
A Harvard scientist was once allowed in to have a peep.
Mark took a bite of meat.

Here is a list of nouns that refer to such actions:

bite	look	sip	sniff
feel	peep	smell	taste

Verbs that can be used both with and without an object

3.46   There are several reasons why you can use verbs both with and without an object.

different meanings

3.47   One important reason for using verbs both with and without an object is that many verbs have more than one common meaning. For example, the verb *run* is used without an object when it is used in the sense *to move quickly*. But *run* has an object when it is used in the sense *to manage* or *operate*.

She runs in order to keep fit.
She runs a hotel.
She reflected for a moment and then decided to back out.
The figures reflected the company's attempts to increase its profile.
I can manage perfectly well on my own.
I can no longer manage my life.
She moved rather gracefully.
The whole incident had moved her profoundly.

3.48 Here is a list of verbs that can be used both with and without an object, depending on which meaning you are using:

add	dress	hold	play	spread
aim	drive	hurt	point	stand
beat	escape	leak	press	stretch
blow	exercise	lose	propose	strike
call	fit	manage	reflect	study
change	fly	meet	run	tend
cheat	follow	miss	shoot	touch
count	hang	move	show	turn
draw	head	pass	sink	win

verbs that do not always need an object

3.49 Many verbs in English can be used with or without an object, with the same basic meaning. The object is not needed when it is obvious what type of thing you are talking about.

For example, you could say either *She eats food slowly* or *She eats slowly*. It is obvious in this context that what she eats is food, and so you only mention food if you want to emphasize the fact (which is unlikely), or if you want to say what kind of food she eats.

With verbs like these, you normally use an object only when you want to be specific or when you want to contrast what happened on one specific occasion with what happens normally. For example, you would say *I've been studying history*, as opposed to *I've been studying*, only if you want or need to mention the subject specifically, or if you normally study something else.

...a healthy person who eats sensibly.
Twice a week he eats an apple for lunch.
He raised his own glass and drank.
He drank a good deal of coffee.
He had won, and she had helped.
She could help him to escape.
I cooked for about eight directors.
She had never cooked dinner for anyone.
I washed and ironed for them.
She ironed my shirt.
Rudolph waved and went into the house.
She smiled and waved her hand.
She sat and typed.
She typed a letter to the paper in question.

You need to give the object when it is different from the one that people would normally associate with the verb. For example, *to wave* is usually interpreted as meaning *to wave your hand*, so if something else is being waved, you have to mention it.

He waved a piece of paper in his left hand.
Charlie washed Susan's feet.

You also mention the object when you want to say something specific about it.

He washed his summer clothes and put them away.
Bond waved a cheerful hand.
I could save quite a lot of money.

3.50 Here is a list of verbs that can be used without an object when it is obvious what sort of thing is involved:

borrow	drive	learn	read	steal
change	dust	lend	ride	study
clean	eat	marry	save	type
cook	film	paint	sing	wash
draw	help	park	smoke	wave
drink	iron	point	spend	write

object already mentioned

3.51 There is another group of verbs that usually have an object but that can be used without an object with the same meaning. These are verbs where the object is obvious because it has already been mentioned. For example, if you have already mentioned the place where something happened, you can say *I left*, without naming the place again.

At last she thanked them and <u>left</u>.
He turned away and walked quickly up the passage. I locked the door and <u>followed</u>.
I was in the middle of a quiet meal when the tanks <u>attacked</u>.
She did not look round when he <u>entered</u>.
The sentry fired at the doctor and fortunately <u>missed</u>.
Only two or three hundred men belonged to the Union before the war, now thousands <u>joined</u>.

3.52 Here is a list of verbs that can be used without an object when the object has already been mentioned:

accept	check	guess	notice	ring
aim	choose	improve	observe	rule
answer	consider	join	offer	search
approach	direct	judge	order	serve
ask	dry	know	pass	share
attack	enter	lead	phone	sign
begin	explain	leave	play	strike
bite	fit	lose	produce	telephone
blow	follow	mind	pull	understand
board	forget	miss	push	watch
call	gain	move	remember	win

3.53 If you think that the object may not be obvious from what has been said or if you particularly want to draw attention to it, you mention it.

All I know is that Michael and I never <u>left the house</u>.
Miss Lindley <u>followed Rose</u> into the shop.
They were unaware they had <u>attacked a British warship</u>.
A man <u>entered the shop</u> and demanded money.
She threw the first dart and <u>missed the board</u> altogether.
I <u>had joined an athletic club</u> in Chicago.

3.54 There are not many verbs that always have an object or never have an object. The decision about whether or not to mention an object is left to the users. If they think that the people reading or listening to them will have no difficulty in working out what person or thing is affected by the action, then they can leave out the object. If they think that this will not be clear, they will use an object in order to prevent misunderstanding. The main reasons for omitting the object are that it is obvious from the meaning of the verb itself, or that it is obvious from what has already been said.

Verbs that can take an object or a prepositional phrase

3.55 There is a small group of verbs that can be followed by either an object or a prepositional phrase. The verb *fight* is one of these verbs, so that, for example, you can say *He fought the enemy* or *He fought against the enemy*.

The Polish Army fought the Germans for nearly five weeks.
He was fighting against history.
The New Zealand rugby team played South Africa's Springboks.
In his youth, Thomas played against Glamorgan.

3.56 There is usually little difference in meaning between using the verb on its own and following it with a preposition. For example, there is very little difference in meaning between *brush* and *brush against*, *gnaw* and *gnaw at*, and *hiss* and *hiss at* in the following examples.

Her arm brushed my cheek.
Something brushed against the back of the shelter.
Rabbits often gnaw the woodwork of their cages.
Insects had been gnawing at the wood.
They hissed the Mayor at the ceremony.
Frederica hissed at him.

3.57 Here is a list of verbs that can be used with an object or a prepositional phrase, with little difference in meaning:

boo (at)	fight (against)	jeer (at)	rule (over)
brush (against)	fight (with)	juggle (with)	sip (at)
check (on)	gain (in)	mock (at)	
distinguish	gnaw (at)	mourn (for)	sniff (at)
(between)	hiss (at)	nibble (at)	tug (at)
enter (for)	infiltrate (into)	play (against)	twiddle (with)

3.58 Many of the verbs that can take an object or a prepositional phrase are verbs, such as *wander* and *cross*, that describe physical movement. The preposition is one that indicates place, and so allows you to emphasize the physical position of the subject in relation to the object.

He wandered the halls of the Art Institute.
He wandered through the streets of New York.
I crossed the Mississippi.
The car had crossed over the river to Long Island.
We climbed the mountain.
I climbed up the tree.

Here is a list of verbs that describe movement, and examples of the prepositions that can follow them:

chase (after)	jump (over)	roam (over)	skirt (round)
climb (up)	leap (over)	roam (through)	walk (through)
cross (over)	reach (across)	run (across)	wander (through)

Changing your focus by changing the subject: *I opened the door, The door opened*

3.59 Some verbs allow you to describe an action from the point of view of the performer of the action or from the point of view of something that is affected by the action. This means that the same verb can be used with an object, or without an object, and without the original performer being mentioned.

In the first example below, *the door* is the object of the verb *opened*, but in the second example *the door* is the subject of *opened* and there is no mention of who opened the door.

I opened the door and peered into the room.
Suddenly the door opened.
An explosion shook the rooms.
The whole room shook.

Note that the object of the transitive verb, which is the subject of the intransitive verb, usually refers to a thing, not a person.

Verbs that can have the same thing as their object, when transitive, or their subject, when intransitive, are called **ergative verbs**. There are several hundred ergative verbs in regular use in current English.

<hr/>

changes

3.60 Many ergative verbs describe events that involve a change from one state to another.

He was slowing his pace.
She was aware that the aircraft's taxiing pace had slowed.
I shattered the glass.
Wine bottles had shattered all over the pavement.
They have closed the town's only pub.
The street markets have closed.
The firm has changed its name.
Over the next few months their work pattern changed.
The driver stopped the car.
A big car stopped.

3.61 Here is a list of ergative verbs that describe events involving a change of some kind:

age	continue	empty	rot	stop
begin	crack	end	shatter	stretch
bend	darken	fade	shrink	tear
bleach	decrease	finish	shut	thicken
break	diminish	grow	slow	widen
burn	disperse	improve	split	worsen
burst	double	increase	spread	
change	drown	open	start	
close	dry	quicken	stick	

food, movement, vehicles

3.62 There are many other ergative verbs that relate specifically to certain areas of meaning. For example, some relate to food and cooking, others describe physical movement, and others involve a vehicle as the object of the transitive verb or the subject of the intransitive verb.

I've *boiled* an egg.
The porridge *is boiling*.
I'm *cooking* spaghetti.
The rice *is cooking*.
The birds *turned* their heads sharply at the sound.
Vorster's head *turned*.
She *rested* her head on his shoulder.
Her head *rested* on the edge of the table.
She *had crashed* the car twice.
Pollock's car *crashed* into a clump of trees.

3.63 Here is a list of verbs relating to food, physical movement, and vehicles:

bake	roast	move	steady	drive
boil	simmer	rest	swing	fly
cook	thicken	rock	turn	park
defrost	~	shake	~	reverse
fry	balance	spin	back	run
melt	drop	stand	crash	sail

restrictions on ergative subjects

3.64 Note that some verbs are used ergatively with one or two nouns only. For example, you can say *He fired a gun* or *The gun fired*. You can also say *He fired a bullet*, but you would not normally say *The bullet fired*.

I *rang* the bell.
The bell *rang*.
A car *was sounding* its horn.
A horn *sounded* in the night.
He *had caught* his sleeve on a splinter of wood.
The hat *caught* on a bolt and tore.

3.65 Here is a list of verbs that can be used ergatively with the noun, or type of noun, that is given:

catch (an article of clothing)	ring (a bell, the alarm)
fire (a gun, rifle, pistol)	show (an emotion such as fear, anger)
play (music)	sound (a horn, the alarm)

ergative verbs that need extra information

3.66 There are a few ergative verbs that usually have an adverb or some other phrase or clause when they are used intransitively. This is because you choose this structure when you want to emphasize how something behaves when affected in some way, and so the person who does the action is not important.

I like the new Range Rover. It handles beautifully.
Wool washes well if you treat it carefully.

Here is a list of ergative verbs that are usually followed by some extra information when they are used intransitively:

clean	handle	polish	stain
freeze	mark	sell	wash

comparison of passive and ergative use

3.67 Note that ergative verbs perform a similar function to the **passive** because they allow you to avoid mentioning who or what does the action. For example, you could say *Jane froze a lot of peas from the garden*. If you were not interested in who froze them but in what she froze, you could say *A lot of peas were frozen*, using the passive. If you were interested in how they froze, you could say, *The peas from the garden froze really well*, making use of the fact that the verb is ergative.

For information about the **passive**, see 9.8 to 9.24.

Verbs that involve people affecting each other with the same action: *John and Mary argued*

3.68 Some verbs can describe processes that involve two people or two groups of people doing the same thing to each other. For example, *John and Mary argued* means that John argued with Mary and Mary argued with John.

The pair of you have argued about that for years.
He came out and we hugged.
They competed furiously.

These verbs are called **reciprocal verbs**.

reciprocal verbs with plural subject

3.69 One of the structures in which you use reciprocal verbs is where the two groups are put together in a plural subject and the verb is then used without an object.

Their faces touched.
Their children are always fighting.
They kissed.

emphasizing equal involvement

3.70 When you want to emphasize that both participants are equally involved in the action, you put *each other* or *one another* after the verb.

We embraced each other.
They kissed each other in greeting.
They fought each other desperately for it.
The two boys started hitting one another.

Here is a list of reciprocal verbs that are used transitively with the pronouns *each other* and *one another*:

consult	engage	kiss	meet
cuddle	fight	marry	touch
embrace	hug	match	

With some verbs you need to use a preposition, usually *with*, in front of *each other* or *one another*.

You've got to be able to communicate with each other.
Third World countries are competing with each other for a restricted market.
The two actors began to engage with one another.

Here is a list of reciprocal verbs that must be followed by *with* before the pronouns *each other* and *one another*:

agree	coincide	consult	disagree	mix
alternate	collide	contend	engage	quarrel
argue	combine	contrast	integrate	struggle
balance	communicate	converse	mate	
clash	conflict	co-operate	merge	

Here is a list of verbs that can be used with a preposition other than *with*:

compete (against)	correspond (with)	part (from)	talk (to)
compete (with)	fight (against)	relate (to)	talk (with)
correspond (to)	fight (with)	separate (from)	

Note that *consult*, *engage*, and *fight* can be used either with an object or with a preposition.

showing unequal involvement

3.71 In the examples given above, the speaker or writer believes that both people or groups are equally involved in the event, because both are the subject. However, the user may want to focus on one person more than the other. In this case, a noun that refers to that person is put in subject position.

If the verb can be used with an object, a noun referring to the other participant is used as the object of the verb.

He embraced her.
She married a young engineer.
You could meet me at a restaurant.
He is responsible for killing many people.

If the verb needs a preposition after it, the other noun is used as the object of the preposition.

Our return coincided <u>with the arrival of bad weather</u>.
Youths clashed <u>with police</u> in Belfast.
The distribution of aid corresponds <u>to need</u>.

3.72 People sometimes make one person or group the subject when the event is a violent or unpleasant one, in order to make them appear aggressive or responsible for the violence. For example, the headline *Police clash with youths* might suggest that the police were responsible for the clash, even though the youths also clashed with the police.

<u>Paul</u> collided with a large man in a sweat-stained shirt.
<u>The role of worker</u> conflicts with the role of parent.
She liked him even when <u>she</u> was quarrelling with him.

Verbs that can have two objects: *give someone something*

3.73 Sometimes you may want to talk about an event that involves someone in addition to the people or things that are the subject and object of the clause. This third participant is someone who benefits from the action or receives something as a result. They become the **indirect object** of the clause. The **direct object**, as usual, is the person or thing that something is done to. For example, in *I gave John a book*, *John* is the indirect object and *the book* is the direct object.

The indirect object is put immediately after the verb, in front of the direct object.

Dad gave <u>me a car</u>.
Can you pass <u>me the sugar</u> please?
She brought <u>me a boiled egg and toast</u>.
He had lent <u>Tim the money</u>.
A man promised <u>him a job</u>.
The distraction provided <u>us a chance to relax</u>. (Am)

indirect objects in phrases that begin with a preposition

3.74 Instead of putting the indirect object in front of the direct object, it is possible to put it in a phrase beginning with *to* or *for* that comes after the direct object.

He handed his room key <u>to the receptionist</u>.
Ralph passed a message <u>to Jack</u>.
He gave it <u>to me</u>.

This structure is used particularly in cases where you want to focus on the indirect object. You can use it, for example, when the indirect object is significantly longer than the direct object.

He had taught English <u>to all the youth of Ceylon and India</u>.
He copied the e-mail to <u>every single one of his staff</u>.

pronouns as objects

3.75 It is normal to use this prepositional structure when the direct object is a pronoun such as *it* or *them*.

I took the bottle and offered <u>it to Oakley</u>.
Woodward finished the second page and passed <u>it to the editor</u>.
It was the only pound he had and he gave <u>it to the little boy</u>.
God has sent <u>you to me</u>.

Note that in informal spoken English, some people put the indirect object in front of the direct object when both objects are pronouns. For example, some people say *He gave me it* rather than *He gave it to me*. Both pronouns are unstressed and both refer to information that is already known, and so it does not matter what order they come in.

indirect objects with *to*

3.76 If you want to put the indirect object in a phrase that begins with a preposition, you use the preposition *to* with some verbs, especially ones where the direct object is something that is transferred from one person to another.

Mr Schell wrote a letter the other day to the New York Times.
I had lent my apartment to a friend for the weekend.
I took out the black box and handed it to her.

Here is a list of verbs that can have an indirect object introduced by *to*:

accord	give	mail	quote	show
advance	grant	offer	read	sing
award	hand	owe	rent	take
bring	lease	pass	repay	teach
deal	leave	pay	sell	tell
feed	lend	play	send	write
forward	loan	post	serve	

indirect objects with *for*

3.77 If the action you are describing involves one person doing something that will benefit another person, you can use the preposition *for* to introduce the indirect object.

He left a note for her on the table.
He poured more champagne for the three of them.
She brought presents for the children.

Here is a list of verbs that can have an indirect object introduced by *for*:

book	design	leave	pour	spare
bring	fetch	make	prepare	take
build	find	mix	reserve	win
buy	fix	order	save	write
cash	get	paint	secure	
cook	guarantee	pick	set	
cut	keep	play	sing	

 USAGE NOTE

3.78 Note that the verbs *bring*, *leave*, *play*, *sing*, *take*, and *write* are in both of the lists (3.76 and 3.77). That is because there are a few verbs that can take either *to* or *for* in front of the indirect object, depending on the meaning you want to express. For example, *Karen wrote a letter to her boyfriend* means that the letter was addressed to her boyfriend and was for him to read. *Karen wrote a letter for her boyfriend* means that her boyfriend wanted to send someone else a letter and Karen was the person who actually wrote it.

ⓘ USAGE NOTE

3.79   There are some verbs that take two objects where the indirect object almost always comes in front of the direct object rather than being introduced by *to* or *for*.
For example, you say *He begrudged his daughter the bread she ate* and *She allowed her son only two pounds a week*. It would be very unusual to say *She allowed two pounds a week to her son*.

Here is a list of verbs that do not usually have their indirect object introduced by *to* or *for*:

allow	bet	cost	envy	promise
ask	cause	deny	forgive	refuse
begrudge	charge	draw	grudge	

Note that *wish* can be used as this sort of verb when its direct object is a word or phrase like *luck*, *good luck*, or *happy birthday*.

3.80   When you use a passive form of a verb with two objects, either the direct object or the indirect object can become the subject. See 9.20 for full information.

ⓘ USAGE NOTE

3.81   When the subject and the indirect object refer to the same person, you can use a **reflexive pronoun** as the indirect object.

I'm going to buy myself some new clothes.
He had got himself a car.
He cooked himself an omelette.

Reflexive pronouns are explained in paragraphs 1.111 to 1.118.

verbs that usually have both a direct object and an indirect object

3.82   Most of the verbs listed above as verbs that take two objects can be used with the same meaning with just a direct object.

He left a note.
She fetched a jug from the kitchen.

However, the following verbs always or usually have both a direct object and an indirect object:

accord	allow	give	lend	show
advance	deny	hand	loan	tell

A few verbs can be used with the person who benefits from the action, or receives something, as the direct object.

I fed the baby when she woke.
I forgive you.

Here is a list of these verbs:

ask	envy	feed	forgive	pay	teach

Phrasal verbs: *I sat down, She woke me up*

3.83 There is a special group of verbs that consist of two or three words. These are called **phrasal verbs**. They consist of

▶ a verb followed by an adverb:

He sat down.
The noise gradually died away.
The cold weather set in.

▶ a verb followed by a preposition (sometimes called a **prepositional verb**):

She looked after her invalid mother.
She sailed through her exams.
She fell down the steps and broke her ankle.

▶ or a verb followed by an adverb and a preposition:

You may come up against unexpected difficulties.
I look forward to reading it.
Fame has crept up on her almost by accident.

By combining a verb and an adverb or preposition in this way, you can extend the usual meaning of the verb or create a new meaning, different from any that the verb has on its own. You cannot, therefore, always guess the meaning of a phrasal verb from the usual meanings of the verb and the adverb or preposition. For example, if someone says *I give up* they do not give anything to anyone, nor is there any upward movement involved.

In the case of a few phrasal verbs, the first part is not found independently as a verb at all. For example, there are phrasal verbs *sum up*, *tamper with*, and *zero in on*, but no verbs *sum*, *tamper*, or *zero*.

Note that phrasal verbs are never written as a single word or with a hyphen.

3.84 Most phrasal verbs consist of two words. These are explained below in paragraphs 3.85 to 3.110. Three-word phrasal verbs are explained in paragraphs 3.111 to 3.113.

intransitive phrasal verbs with adverbs

3.85 Some phrasal verbs are used without an object. These phrasal verbs are generally verb plus adverb combinations.

Rosamund went away for a few days.
The boys were fooling around.
She must have dozed off.

3.86 Here is a list of phrasal verbs that consist of a verb and an adverb with no object:

back away	branch out	chip in	come down	crop up
back down	break away	climb down	come forward	cry off
back off	break out	close in	come in	cuddle up
balance out	butt in	cloud over	come on	curl up
barge in	camp out	club together	come out	cut in
bear up	cast about	come about	come round	die away
boil over	catch on	come along	come to	die down
bounce back	change down	come apart	come up	die out
bow down	change up	come away	cool off	dine out
bow out	check up	come back	creep in	double back

doze off	give in	make off	run out	step aside
drag on	glaze over	meet up	rush in	step back
drop back	go ahead	melt away	seize up	step down
drop by	go along	mount up	sell up	step in
drop out	go around	move off	set in	stick around
ease up	go away	move over	settle down	stock up
ebb away	go back	nod off	settle in	stop by
end up	go down	opt out	settle up	stop off
fade away	go on	own up	shop around	stop over
fade out	go out	pass away	simmer down	tag along
fall apart	go under	pay up	sink in	tail away
fall away	go up	pine away	sit around	tail off
fall back	grow up	play around	sit back	taper off
fall behind	hang back	pop up	sit down	tick over
fall out	hang together	press ahead	slip up	touch down
fall over	hit out	press on	speak up	tune in
fall through	hold on	push ahead	splash out	wade in
fight back	land up	push on	spring up	wait about
fizzle out	lash out	rear up	stand back	wait up
flare up	let up	ride up	stand down	walk out
fool around	lie back	ring off	stand in	waste away
forge ahead	lie down	rise up	stand out	watch out
get about	live in	roll about	start out	wear off
get ahead	look ahead	roll in	stay in	weigh in
get along	look back	roll over	stay on	
get by	look in	rot away	stay up	
get up	loom up	run away	steam up	

intransitive phrasal verbs with prepositions: *look after, call on*

3.87   Other phrasal verbs used in intransitive clauses are verb plus preposition combinations. These are sometimes called **prepositional verbs**.

Ski trips now <u>account for</u> nearly half of all school visits.
I'm just <u>asking for</u> information.
...the arguments that <u>stem from</u> gossip.

Note that the nouns at the end of the above examples (*nearly half of all school visits, information*, and *gossip*) are objects of the prepositions and not direct objects of the verbs.

3.88 Here is a list of phrasal verbs that consist of a verb with no object and a preposition:

abide by	draw on	leap at	romp through
account for	drink to	level with	run across
allow for	dwell on	lie behind	run into
answer for	eat into	live for	run to
ask after	embark on	live off	sail through
ask for	enter into	live with	see to
bank on	expand on	look after	seize on
bargain for	fall for	look into	set about
break into	fall into	look to	settle for
break with	fall on	make for	settle on
brood on	feel for	meet with	skate over
bump into	flick through	part with	smile on
burst into	frown upon	pick at	stand for
call for	get at	pick on	stem from
call on	get into	pitch into	stick at
care for	get over	plan for	stick by
come across	go about	plan on	stumble across
come between	go against	play at	stumble on
come by	go for	play on	take after
come for	grow on	poke at	take against
come from	hang onto	pore over	tamper with
come into	head for	provide for	tangle with
come under	hit on	puzzle over	trifle with
come upon	hold with	rattle through	tumble to
count on	jump at	reason with	wade through
cut across	keep to	reckon on	wait on
dawn on	laugh at	reckon with	walk into
deal with	launch into	reckon without	watch for
dispose of	lay into	rise above	worry at

preposition or adverb: *We looked around the old town, Would you like to look around?*

3.89 In the case of some intransitive phrasal verbs, the second word (*across, around, down,* etc) is a preposition if the second thing involved needs to be mentioned, or can be an adverb if the second thing involved is clear from the context.

I could hang around your office.
We'll have to hang around for a while.
They all crowded around the table.
Everyone crowded around to see him jump into the water.

3.90 Here is a list of intransitive phrasal verbs whose second word is a preposition if the other thing involved needs to be mentioned, or an adverb if it does not:

ask around	crowd around	go up	push through
bend over	do without	go without	rally round
break through	fall behind	hang around	run around
bustle about	fall down	join in	run down
come across	fall off	knock about	run up
come after	gather around	lag behind	scrape through
come along	get in	lean over	see round
come by	get off	lie about	shine through
come down	get on	look round	show through
come in	get round	look through	sit around
come off	go about	lounge about	spill over
come on	go along	move about	stand around
come over	go down	pass by	stop by
come through	go in	pass over	trip over
come up	go round	push by	
cross over	go through	push past	

transitive phrasal verbs: *look something up, let someone down*

3.91 Some phrasal verbs are nearly always used with an object.

We put our drinks down on the bar.
I finished my meal off as quickly as I could.
She read the poem out quietly.

3.92 Here is a list of phrasal verbs that consist of a transitive verb and an adverb:

add on	carry out	drag up	give off
beat up	cast aside	dream up	hammer out
blot out	catch out	drink in	hand down
board up	chase up	drive out	hand in
bring about	chat up	drum up	hand on
bring along	clean out	eat away	hand out
bring back	conjure up	eat up	hand over
bring down	count out	explain away	hand round
bring forward	cross off	fight off	have on
bring in	cross out	fill in	hire out
bring off	cut back	fill up	hold down
bring out	cut down	filter out	hold up
bring round	cut off	find out	hunt down
bring up	cut up	fix up	hush up
buy out	deal out	follow up	keep back
buy up	dig up	frighten away	kick out
call off	do up	gather up	knock down
call up	drag in	give away	knock out
carry off	drag out	give back	knock over

lap up	pull apart	set aside	tell off
lay down	pull down	set back	think over
lay on	push about	set down	think through
lay out	push around	shake off	think up
leave behind	push over	shake up	thrash out
leave out	put about	shoot down	throw away
let down	put across	shrug off	throw off
let in	put around	shut away	throw on
let off	put away	shut in	throw out
let out	put down	shut off	tidy away
lift up	put forward	shut out	tie down
live down	put off	size up	tie up
melt down	put on	smooth over	tip off
mess up	put out	snap up	tip up
mix up	put through	soak up	tire out
nail down	put together	sort out	tone down
note down	put up	sound out	top up
order about	read out	spell out	track down
pack off	reason out	spin out	trade in
pass down	reel off	stamp out	try on
pass over	rinse out	step up	try out
pass round	rip off	stick down	turn down
patch up	rip up	summon up	turn on
pay back	rope in	switch on	use up
pay out	rope off	take apart	warn off
phase in	rub in	take away	wash away
phase out	rub out	take back	weed out
pick off	rule out	take down	weigh out
pick out	rush through	take in	weigh up
piece together	scale down	take on	whip up
pin down	screen off	take up	win back
pin up	seal off	talk over	win over
play back	see off	talk round	wipe away
play down	seek out	tear apart	wipe out
plug in	sell off	tear down	wipe up
point out	send up	tear up	
print out	set apart	tell apart	

Phrasal verbs that consist of a transitive verb and a preposition are explained in paragraphs 3.107 to 3.110.

phrasal

3.93   A large group of phrasal verbs can be used both with and without an object.

Often this is because a phrasal verb has more than one meaning. For example, *break in* does not have an object when it is used in the sense of *get into a place by force*. But *break in* does take an object when it is used in the sense of *get someone used to a new situation*.

If the door is locked, I will try to <u>break in</u>.
He believes in <u>breaking in</u> his staff gradually.
A plane <u>took off</u>.
Gretchen <u>took off</u> her coat.
The engine <u>cut out</u>.
She <u>cut out</u> some coloured photographs from a magazine.

3.94   Here is a list of phrasal verbs that can be used both with and without an object, depending on which meaning is being used:

add up	get down	kick off	put in	sum up
bail out	get in	knock about	roll up	switch off
black out	get out	knock off	run down	take off
break in	get together	lay off	run off	tear off
call in	give up	leave off	run over	throw up
carry on	hang out	look out	set forth	tuck in
clear out	hold off	look up	set off	turn away
cut out	hold out	make out	set out	turn back
draw on	join up	make up	show off	turn in
draw out	keep away	mess about	show up	turn out
draw up	keep down	miss out	split up	turn round
dress up	keep in	pass off	stick out	turn up
drop off	keep off	pass on	stick up	wind down
drop round	keep on	pay off	stow away	wind up
fight back	keep out	pick up	strike out	work out
finish up	keep up	pull in	string along	wrap up

3.95   There are a few phrasal verbs that have only one meaning, but that can be used either with or without an object. It is possible to use them without an object because the object is either obvious or can be guessed in a particular context.

It won't take me a moment to <u>clear away</u>.
I'll help you <u>clear away</u> the dishes.

3.96   Here is a list of phrasal verbs that have only one meaning but that can be used with or without an object:

answer back	call back	cover up	open up	wash up
breathe in	clear away	drink up	take over	
breathe out	clear up	help out	tidy away	

3.97 Just as with ordinary verbs, some phrasal verbs are **ergative verbs**; that is, you can use the object of the transitive verb as the subject of the intransitive verb.

> The guerrillas blew up the restaurant.
> The gasworks blew up.
> I won't wake him up just yet.
> He woke up in the middle of the night.

See paragraphs 3.59 to 3.67 for information about ergative verbs.

3.98 Here is a list of ergative phrasal verbs:

back up	build up	get off	pull through	thaw out
block up	burn up	heat up	rub off	wake up
blow up	check in	hurry up	shut up	warm up
book in	check out	line up	sign up	wear down
break off	cheer up	move on	slow down	wear out
break up	close down	open up	spread out	
buck up	dry up	peel off	start off	

3.99 In the case of some ergative phrasal verbs, the second word can be a preposition if the other thing involved needs to be mentioned, or can be an adverb if the other thing involved is clear from the context.

> ...leaves that had been blown off the trees.
> My hat blew off.

3.100 Here is a list of ergative phrasal verbs whose second word can be a preposition or an adverb:

blow off	get through	move up	stick in
chip off	get up	peel off	stick on
get down	move down	poke through	

position of the object

3.101 When you are using a phrasal verb with an object that is a short noun phrase, you usually have a choice as to where you put the object. It can be placed either after the second word of the phrasal verb or after the first word and before the second word.

> He filled up his car with petrol.
> She filled my glass up.
> He handed over the box.
> Mrs Kaul handed the flowers over to Judy.

3.102 However, when the object consists of a long noun phrase, it is more likely to come after the second word of the phrasal verb, so that the two parts of the phrasal verb are not separated too widely. In this way, attention is focused on the information contained in the noun phrase, rather than on the second word of the phrasal verb.

> Police have been told to turn back all refugees who try to cross the border.

when the object is a pronoun

3.103   When the object is a pronoun such as *me*, *her*, or *it*, it usually comes before the second word of the phrasal verb. This is because it is not new information, and so it is not put in a position of prominence at the end of the clause.

I waited until he had <u>filled</u> it <u>up</u>.
He <u>tied</u> her <u>up</u> and bundled her into the car.

when the object is an abstract noun

3.104   If the object of a phrasal verb is an abstract noun such as *hope*, *confidence*, or *support*, it usually comes after the second word of the phrasal verb. So, although you can say *He built his business up*, you usually say *We are trying to build up trust with the residents*. Similarly, although you can say *He put my parents up for the night*, you normally say *The peasants are putting up a lot of resistance*.

The newspapers <u>whipped up</u> sympathy for them.
They attempted to <u>drum up</u> support from the students.
He didn't <u>hold out</u> much hope for them.

cases where the object is always placed after the first word of the verb

3.105   With a small number of phrasal verbs, the object is always placed between the first and the second words of the verb. For example, you can say *I can't tell your brothers apart* but not *I can't tell apart your brothers*.

Captain Dean <u>was</u> still <u>ordering</u> everybody <u>about</u>.
I <u>answered</u> my father <u>back</u> and took my chances.

Note that most of these verbs take a human object.

Here is a list of phrasal verbs that always belong in this group when they are used with an object:

answer back	churn up	invite over	pull to	slap around
ask in	count in	jolly along	push about	stand up
bash about	drag down	keep under	push around	stare out
bind over	dress down	knock about	push to	string along
book in	drop round	mess about	run through	talk round
bring round	feel out	move about	see through	tear apart
bring to	get away	muck about	send ahead	tell apart
brush off	hear out	order about	send away	tip off
call back	help along	play along	send up	truss up
carry back	invite in	play through	shut up	turf out
catch out	invite out	pull about	sit down	

Some phrasal verbs have more than one transitive sense, but belong in this group when they are used with one particular meaning. For example, *take back* belongs in this group when it means *remind someone of something* but not when it means *regain something*.

The smell of chalk <u>took</u> us all <u>back</u> to our schooldays.
...his ambition of <u>taking back</u> disputed territory.

Here is a list of phrasal verbs that belong in this group when used with a particular meaning:

bowl over	get out	nail down	set up	take in
bring down	give up	pass on	shake up	take off
bring out	have on	pin down	show around	throw about
buoy up	hurry up	pull apart	show up	toss about
cut off	keep up	push around	start off	trip up
do over	kick around	put down	straighten	turn on
draw out	knock out	put out	out	ward off
get back	knock up	see out	take back	wind up

objects with prepositions

3.106 Remember that when a phrasal verb consists of an intransitive verb followed by a preposition, the noun phrase always comes after the preposition, even when it is a pronoun.

A number of reasons <u>can account for</u> this change.
They <u>had dealt with</u> the problem intelligently.
If I went away and left you in the flat, would you <u>look after</u> it?

There is a list of phrasal verbs that consist of an intransitive verb and a preposition in paragraph 3.88.

transitive phrasal verbs with prepositions: *She talked me into buying it*

3.107 Some phrasal verbs consist of a transitive verb and a preposition. They have one noun phrase after the first word, as the object of the verb, and a second noun phrase after the second word, as the object of the preposition.

They agreed to <u>let</u> him <u>into</u> their secret.
The farmer threatened to <u>set</u> his dogs <u>on</u> them.
They'll <u>hold</u> that <u>against</u> you when you apply next time.

3.108 Here is a list of phrasal verbs that consist of a transitive verb and a preposition:

build into	hold against	lumber with	read into	thrust upon
build on	keep to	make of	set against	write into
draw into	lay before	put on	set back	
drum into	leave off	put onto	set on	
frighten into	let into	put through	talk into	

preposition or adverb: *I'll cross you off, I'll cross you off the list*

3.109 In the case of some transitive phrasal verbs, the second word is a preposition if the third thing involved needs to be mentioned, but it is an adverb if the third thing involved is clear from the context.

Rudolph <u>showed them around the theatre</u>.
Rudolph <u>showed them around</u>.

3.110 Here is a list of transitive phrasal verbs whose second word can be a preposition or an adverb:

cross off	hurl about	lop off	show around
dab on	keep off	push around	shut in
hawk around	knock off	scrub off	sink in

intransitive three-word phrasal verbs: *look forward to, catch up with*

3.111   Most phrasal verbs consist of two words: a verb and an adverb, or a verb and a preposition. However, some phrasal verbs consist of three words: a verb, an adverb, and a preposition. This type of verb is sometimes called a **phrasal-prepositional verb**.

Most three-word phrasal verbs are intransitive. The preposition at the end is followed by its own object.

His girlfriend <u>walked out on</u> him.
You're not going to <u>get away with</u> this!
She sometimes finds it hard to <u>keep up with</u> her classmates.
The local people have to <u>put up with</u> a lot of tourists.
Terry Holbrook <u>caught up with</u> me.

3.112   Here is a list of intransitive three-word phrasal verbs:

be in for	come up with	go down with	play along with
be on to	crack down on	go in for	play around with
bear down on	creep up on	go off with	put up with
boil down to	crowd in on	go over to	read up on
break out of	cry out against	go through with	run away with
brush up on	cry out for	grow out of	run off with
bump up against	cut back on	keep in with	run up against
burst in on	date back to	keep on at	shy away from
call out for	do away with	keep up with	sit in on
catch up with	double back on	kick out against	snap out of
chime in with	face up to	lead up to	stick out for
clamp down on	fall back on	live up to	stick up for
clean up after	fall in with	look down on	suck up to
come across as	get away with	look forward to	take up with
come down on	get down to	look out for	talk down to
come down to	get in on	look up to	tie in with
come down with	get off with	make away with	walk away from
come in for	get on to	make off with	walk away with
come on to	get on with	make up to	walk off with
come out in	get round to	match up to	walk out on
come out of	get up to	measure up to	wriggle out of
come out with	give up on	miss out on	zero in on
come up against	go along with	monkey about with	
come up to	go back on		

transitive three-word phrasal verbs: *He talked me out of buying the car*

3.113 A few three-word phrasal verbs are transitive. The direct object of the verb comes immediately after the verb. A second noun phrase is put after the preposition, as normal.

I'll let you in on a secret.
Kroop tried to talk her out of it.
They put their success down to hard work.

Here is a list of transitive three-word phrasal verbs:

do out of	let in on	put down to	take up on
frighten out of	play off against	put up to	talk out of
let in for	put down as	take out on	

! **BE CAREFUL**

3.114 In standard written English it is not possible to have indirect objects with phrasal verbs. The only objects you can have are direct objects of the verb and objects of prepositions. In informal spoken English, however, a few phrasal verbs do have both a direct and an indirect object. In such cases, the indirect object is placed between the verb and the particle, and the direct object follows.

Would you break me off a piece of chocolate, please?
We brought her back some special cookies from Germany.

phrasal verbs in questions and relative clauses

3.115 There is one way in which a preposition that is part of a phrasal verb behaves differently from an ordinary preposition.

Normally, when the object of a preposition is put at the beginning of a question or a relative clause, it can be preceded by the preposition, especially in formal speech or writing. For example, you can say *From which student did you get the book?* and *the document on which he put his signature.*

However, if the preposition is part of a phrasal verb, it cannot be put before its object in such structures. You have to say *What are you getting at?* not *At what are you getting?*, and *the difficulties which he ran up against* not *the difficulties against which he ran up.*

Who were they laughing at?
This was one complication he had not bargained for.

3.116 Most phrasal verbs that contain a transitive verb can be used in the **passive**. So can a few phrasal verbs that contain an intransitive verb and a preposition. See paragraphs 9.17 and 9.23.

Compound verbs: *ice-skate, baby-sit*

3.117 Some verbs, such as *cross-examine* and *test-drive*, consist of two words. They are sometimes called **compound verbs**.

He would have been cross-examined on any evidence he gave.
He asked to test-drive a top-of-the-range vehicle.
It is not wise to hitch-hike on your own.

! **BE CAREFUL**

3.118 It is important to realize that you cannot always guess the meaning of a compound verb if you are not already familiar with it. For example, to *soft-soap* does not mean to use soap that is soft; it means to flatter someone in order to persuade them to do something for you.

written forms of compound verbs

3.119 Compound verbs are usually written with a hyphen.

No one had <u>cross-referenced</u> the forms before.
Children <u>ice-skated</u> on the sidewalks.

However, some compound verbs may be written with a space between the words and some may be written as single words. For example, both *roller-skate* and *roller skate* are used, as are *baby-sit* and *babysit*.

forms of compound verbs

3.120 Many compound verbs consist of a noun plus a verb.

It may soon become economically attractive to <u>mass-produce</u> hepatitis vaccines.

Others consist of an adjective plus a verb.

Somebody had <u>short-changed</u> him.

3.121 A few compound verbs consist of words that seem strange because they are not normally used as single words on their own, for example *pooh-pooh* and *shilly-shally*. These verbs are usually used in informal conversation rather than formal writing.

Sally had <u>pooh-poohed</u> the idea of three good meals a day.
Come on, don't <u>shilly-shally</u>. I want an answer.

Other compound verbs look strange because they have been borrowed from foreign languages, for example *ad-lib* and *kow-tow*.

They <u>ad-libbed</u> so much that the writers despaired of them.
He resents having to <u>kow-tow</u> to anyone or anything.

intransitive compound verbs

3.122 Some compound verbs do not have an object.

Many people <u>window-shopped</u> in the glass of the great store.
If you keep to the rules, you may <u>roller-skate</u>.
He has learned to <u>lip-read</u>.
I'm learning to <u>water-ski</u>.

Here is a list of compound verbs that do not have an object:

baby-sit	ice-skate	lip-read	roller-skate	water-ski
back-pedal	jack-knife	name-drop	shilly-shally	window-shop
hitch-hike	kow-tow	play-act	touch-type	wolf-whistle

3.123 Other compound verbs typically have an object:

You can spin-dry it and it will still retain its shape.
I didn't have time to blow-dry my hair.
At first we cold-shouldered him.
They ill-treated our ancestors.

Here is a list of compound verbs that typically have an object:

back-comb	cross-reference	ghost-write	soft-soap
blow-dry	double-cross	ill-treat	spin-dry
cold-shoulder	double-glaze	pooh-pooh	spoon-feed
court-martial	dry-clean	proof-read	stage-manage
cross-check	field-test	rubber-stamp	tape-record
cross-examine	force-feed	short-change	toilet-train
cross-question	frog-march	short-weight	wrong-foot

3.124 A third group of compound verbs may be used with or without an object.

Kate had to double-park outside the flat.
Murray double-parked his car and jumped out.
I tried to ad-lib a joke.
The commentator decided to ad-lib.

Here is a list of compound verbs that can be transitive or intransitive:

ad-lib	chain-smoke	double-park	spring-clean
bottle-feed	criss-cross	mass-produce	stir-fry
breast-feed	deep-fry	short-circuit	tie-dye
bulk-buy	double-check	sight-read	

3.125 Only the second part of a compound verb inflects. If the second part is used on its own as a verb, the compound verb usually inflects in the same way as the verb on its own.

See the Reference section for an explanation of how to inflect verbs.

Linking verbs

3.126 If you want to describe someone or something, for example to say who or what they are or what qualities they have, you use one of a special set of verbs. These verbs are called **linking verbs**.

Cigarette smoking is dangerous to your health.
The station seemed a very small one.
He looked English.
I became enormously fond of her.

The most common linking verbs are *be*, *become*, *look*, *remain*, and *seem*.

3.127 A linking verb links a subject and an adjective or a noun phrase (called a **complement**). The subject, as usual, comes first and the adjective or noun phrase comes after the verb. The adjective or noun phrase describes or identifies the subject.

> Her general knowledge is amazing.
> The children seemed frightened.
> That's a very difficult question.
> She's the head of a large primary school.
> Suleiman Salle became the first President of Eritrea.

Linking verbs are explained in paragraphs 3.132 to 3.154.

Some other intransitive verbs are sometimes used in a similar way to linking verbs. See paragraphs 3.155 to 3.160.

verbs with object complements: *The film made me sad*

3.128 Some verbs, such as *make* and *find*, are used with an **object complement**, that is, both an object and an adjective or a noun phrase. The adjective or noun phrase describes the object.

> The lights made me sleepy.
> I found the forest quite frightening.

These verbs are explained in paragraphs 3.161 to 3.171.

phrases that begin with a preposition

3.129 You can often use a phrase beginning with a preposition after a linking verb.

> The first-aid box is on the top shelf.
> I began to get in a panic.

For more information about phrases and clauses that can be used after linking verbs, see paragraphs 3.172 to 3.181.

it* with *be

3.130 *Be* is often used with *it* as an impersonal subject. This structure is used to comment on places, situations, actions, experiences, and facts.

> It was very quiet in the hut.
> It was awkward keeping my news from Ted.
> It's strange you should come today.

Some other linking verbs are occasionally used in a similar way.

The use of *it* as an impersonal subject is explained in paragraphs 9.31 to 9.45.

there* with *be

3.131 *Be* is often used with *there* as its subject to indicate the existence of something.

> There is another explanation.
> There is a rear bathroom with a panelled bath.

This use of *there* is explained in paragraphs 9.46 to 9.55.

Adjectives after linking verbs: *He seems happy, I'm tired*

3.132 Many **adjectives** can be used after linking verbs.

I am proud of these people.
They seemed happy.
You don't want them to become suspicious.
They have remained loyal to the Government.

They can be modified in various ways or have various structures after them.

We were very happy.
Your suspicions are entirely correct.
Their hall was larger than his whole flat.
He was capable of extraordinary kindness.

Adjectives used after linking verbs, and the structures used with them, are explained in paragraphs 2.41 to 2.53.

3.133 Here is a list of verbs that can be used as linking verbs with a following adjective:

be	prove	~	go	turn
~	seem	become	grow	
appear	smell	come	keep	
feel	sound	fall	remain	
look	taste	get	stay	

Note that the verbs in third group refer to changing or to staying the same.

ⓘ USAGE NOTE

3.134 Some verbs in the second group listed above have special features.

Appear, *prove*, and *seem* are often followed by *to be* and an adjective, instead of directly by an adjective.

Mary was breathing quietly and seemed to be asleep.
Some people appeared to be immune to the virus.

See paragraph 3.192 for information on using a *to*-infinitive after these verbs.

3.135 With some verbs in the second group, especially *feel*, *look*, and *seem*, you can use the *-ed* participle of a verb as an adjective.

The other child looked neglected.
The quarrel of the night before seemed forgotten.

3.136 When you are using the second group of verbs to say what qualities someone or something seems to have, you may want to mention the person whose viewpoint you are giving. You can do this by using a phrase beginning with the preposition *to*. It usually comes after the adjective.

They looked all right to me.
It sounds unnatural to you, I expect.

❗ BE CAREFUL

3.137 You cannot use all adjectives with all linking verbs. Some verbs, such as *be* and *look*, are used with a wide range of adjectives and some are used with a restricted range. For example, *taste* is used only with adjectives that describe the taste of something;

go is used mainly with adjectives that indicate colour or a negative state; and *fall* is used mainly with *asleep*, *ill*, and *silent*.

Sea water <u>tastes nasty</u>.
It <u>tasted sweet</u> like fruit juice.
Jack <u>went red</u>.
It all <u>went horribly wrong</u>.
The world <u>has gone crazy</u>.
He <u>fell asleep</u> at the table.
The courtroom <u>fell silent</u>.

Nouns after linking verbs: *She is a teacher, It remained a secret*

3.138 **Nouns** can be used after the following linking verbs:

be	feel	sound	represent
become	look	~	~
remain	prove	constitute	comprise
~	seem	make	form

qualities

3.139 You can use descriptive nouns or noun phrases after *be*, *become*, *remain*, *feel*, *look*, *prove*, *seem*, *sound*, *constitute*, and *represent* to say what qualities someone or something has.

Their policy on higher education is <u>an unmitigated disaster</u>.
He always seemed <u>a controlled sort of man</u>.
I feel <u>a bit of a fraud</u>.
The results of these experiments remain <u>a secret</u>.
Any change would represent <u>a turnaround</u>.

Make is only used as a linking verb with a noun that indicates whether someone is good at a particular job.

He'll make <u>a good president</u>.

using one: *That's a nice one*

3.140 With *be*, *become*, *remain*, *feel*, *look*, *prove*, *seem*, and *sound*, you can use a noun phrase based on *one*.

The noun phrase consists of *a* or *an* followed by the adjective and *one*, if the subject is singular. For example, instead of saying *The school is large*, you can say *The school is a large one*.

The sound is <u>a familiar one</u>.
The impression the region gives is still <u>a rural one</u>.

If the subject is plural, you can use the adjective followed by *ones*.

My memories of a London childhood are <u>happy ones</u>.

One can also be followed by a **prepositional phrase** or a **relative clause**.

Their story was indeed <u>one of passion</u>.
The problem is <u>one that always faces a society when it finds itself threatened</u>.

size, age, colour, shape

3.141 If you want to make a statement about the size, age, colour, or shape of something, you can use a noun phrase based on *size*, *age*, *colour*, or *shape* after the linking verbs mentioned in the previous paragraph. The noun phrase begins with a determiner and has an adjective in front of the noun or the preposition *of* after it.

It's just the right shape.
The opposing force would be about the same size.
The walls are a delicate pale cream colour.
His body was the colour of bronze.
It is only the size of a mouse.

types of people and things

3.142 You can use noun phrases beginning with *a* or *an*, or plural noun phrases without a determiner, after *be*, *become*, *remain*, *comprise*, and *form*, to say what type of person or thing someone or something is.

He is a geologist.
I'm not an unreasonable person.
He is now a teenager.
The air moved a little faster and became a light wind.
They became farmers.
Promises by MPs remained just promises.
These arches formed a barrier to the tide.

talking about identity

3.143 You can use names or noun phrases referring to a particular person or thing after *be*, *become*, *remain*, *constitute*, *represent*, *comprise*, and *form* to talk about exactly who or what someone or something is.

This is Desiree, my father's second wife.
He's now the Director of the Office of Management and Budget.
The winner of the competition was Ross Lambert of Forest Hill Primary School.
The downstairs television room became my room for receiving visitors.
...the four young men who comprised the TV crew.

ℹ️   USAGE NOTE

3.144 When you use a noun indicating a unique job or position within an organization, you do not have to put a determiner in front of the noun.

At one time you wanted to be President.
He went on to become head of one of the company's largest divisions.

pronouns after linking verbs

3.145 **Personal pronouns** are sometimes used after linking verbs to indicate identity. Note that the object pronouns are used, except in very formal speech or writing.

It's me again.

Possessive pronouns are also used after linking verbs, to indicate identity or to describe something.

This one is yours.
This place is mine.

Indefinite pronouns are sometimes used to describe something, usually with a qualifying structure after them.

It's _nothing serious_.
You're _someone who does what she wants_.

When pronouns are used after linking verbs, the linking verb is usually _be_.

other structures that follow linking verbs

3.146 The use of noun phrases containing **measurement nouns** after _be_ and other verbs is explained in paragraphs 2.252 to 2.254.

combinations of verbs and prepositions

3.147 Some verbs function as linking verbs when they are followed by a particular preposition.

The object of the preposition describes or classifies the subject of the verb.

His fear _turned into unreasoning panic_.
Taylor's fascination with bees _developed into an obsession_.
An autobiography really _amounts to a whole explanation of yourself_.

Here is a list of verb and preposition combinations that function as linking verbs:

amount to	change to	grow into	turn into
change into	develop into	morph into	turn to

These all have the same basic meaning as _become_, except for _amount to_, which has a similar meaning to _constitute_.

The phrasal verb _make up_ also functions as a linking verb.

Wood _made up 65% of the Congo's exports_.

Commenting

3.148 There are several ways in which a **to-infinitive** can be used to comment on someone or something in relation to an action.

commenting on behaviour: _You're crazy to do that_

3.149 If you want to say that someone shows a particular quality when they do something, you can use the structure: subject + linking verb + adjective or noun phrase + _to_-infinitive.

Most people think I am _brave to do this_.
I think my father was _a brave man to do what he did_.

commenting on suitability: _She's the right person to do the job_

3.150 You can use a similar structure to say that someone or something would do a particular task better than anyone or anything else.

He was absolutely _the right man to go to Paris and negotiate_.
She may be _an ideal person to look after the children_.
He is _just the man to calm everyone down_.

You cannot use adjectives alone in constructions of this kind. You use a noun phrase containing an adjective such as *right*, *ideal*, or *best*, or *just the* followed by the noun *person*, *man*, or *woman*. For example, you can say *He was the ideal person to lead the expedition*, but you cannot say *He was ideal to lead the expedition*.

Instead of a *to*-infinitive, you can sometimes use a phrase beginning with the preposition *for*. In this structure, an adjective can be used alone.

He's not the right man for it.
They are ideal for this job.

commenting on an event: *That was an awful thing to happen*

3.151 If you want to express your feeling about an event, you can use a *to*-infinitive after a noun phrase that follows a linking verb.

It seemed such a terrible thing to happen.

The *to*-infinitive consists of *to* and an intransitive verb, usually *happen*.

You cannot use an adjective alone in constructions of this type. For example, you can say *It was a wonderful thing to happen*, but you cannot say *It was wonderful to happen*.

commenting on willingness: *Chris is anxious to meet you*

3.152 If you want to say that someone is willing or unwilling to do something, you can use a *to*-infinitive after an adjective that follows a linking verb.

They were willing to risk losing their jobs.
I am anxious to meet Mrs Burton-Cox.
She is eager to succeed.
He is unwilling to answer questions.
I was reluctant to involve myself in this private fight.

You cannot use nouns in constructions of this type. For example, you can say *He was willing to come*, but you cannot say *He was a willing person to come*.

commenting on something: *This case is easy to carry*

3.153 If you want to show your opinion of something by describing what the experience of doing something to it is like, you can use a *to*-infinitive after an adjective or noun phrase that follows a linking verb.

Silk is comfortable to wear.
It's a nice thing to have.
Telling someone they smell is a hard thing to do.
She was easy to talk to.

Note that the *to*-infinitive must be the *to*-infinitive of a transitive verb or of an intransitive verb followed by a preposition.

commenting on an action: *That was a silly thing to do*

3.154 If you want to show your opinion of an action, you can use a *to*-infinitive that has an object.

They thought this was a sensible thing to do.
This is a very foolish attitude to take.

The *to*-infinitive is usually *to do*, *to make*, or *to take*.

You cannot use an adjective alone in constructions of this kind. For example, you can say *It was a silly thing to do*, but you cannot say *It was silly to do*.

Other verbs with following adjectives: *He stood still*

3.155 Some intransitive verbs can be followed by adjectives in the same way as linking verbs.

George stood motionless for at least a minute.
Pugin died insane at the early age of forty.

However, it is clear that these verbs are not just linking verbs. *George stood motionless* does not mean the same as *George was motionless*. In the sentence *George stood motionless*, the verb *stand* is performing two functions: it is telling us that George was standing, and it is also acting as a linking verb between *George* and the adjective *motionless*.

Here is a list of verbs that can be used in this way:

hang	gaze	go	flame	be born
lie	stare	pass	gleam	die
sit	~	survive	glow	return
stand	emerge	~	run	
~	escape	blush	~	

Ways in which these verbs can be used with following adjectives are discussed in the following paragraphs.

Adjectives are sometimes used in combination with other verbs, but are separated from the main clause by a comma. This use is dealt with in paragraph 8.147.

 USAGE NOTE

3.156 You can use adjectives describing states after *hang*, *lie*, *sit*, and *stand*.

I used to lie awake watching the rain seep through the roof.
A sparrow lies dead in the snow.
Francis Marroux sat ashen-faced behind the wheel.
She stood quite still, facing him.

Gaze and *stare* can be used in a similar way with a limited set of adjectives.

She stared at him wide-eyed.

3.157 You can use some combinations of verbs and adjectives to say that something does not happen to someone or something, or that someone does not have something.

Go, *pass*, *emerge*, *escape*, and *survive* are often used in combinations like these. The adjectives they combine with are often formed by adding *un-* to *-ed* participles.

Your efforts won't go unnoticed.
The guilty went unpunished.
Somehow, his reputation emerged unblemished.
Fortunately we all escaped unscathed.
Mostly, they go unarmed.
The children always went barefoot.

3.158 Verbs such as *blush*, *flame*, *gleam*, *glow*, and *run* can be used with colour adjectives after them to say what colour something is or what colour it becomes.

They blew into the charcoal until it glowed red.
The trees flamed scarlet against the grass.

3.159 *Die*, *return*, and the passive verb *be born* can be followed by either adjectives or noun phrases.

> *She died young.*
> *He died a disappointed man.*
> *At the end of the war, he returned a slightly different man.*
> *He was born a slave.*

fixed phrases

3.160 Some combinations of verb and adjective are fixed phrases. You cannot use the verb in front of any other adjective.

> *I wanted to travel light.*
> *The children ran wild.*
> *The joke was wearing thin with use.*

Describing the object of a verb

3.161 You can put an adjective after the object of some transitive verbs. This adjective describes the object, and is often called an **object complement**.

> *Willie's remarks made her uneasy.*
> *I find the British legal system extremely complicated.*

Some of these verbs are used to say that someone or something is changed or that someone is given a new job. Others are used to describe a person's opinion of someone or something.

For information on how to use these verbs in the passive, see paragraph 9.21.

verbs that relate to causing something to happen: *Their comments made me angry*

3.162 If you want to say that someone or something causes a person or thing to have a particular quality, you can use one of a group of transitive verbs, followed by an adjective.

> *He said waltzes made him dizzy.*
> *They're driving me crazy.*
> *Then his captor had knocked him unconscious.*
> *She painted her eyelids deep blue.*
> *He wiped the bottle dry.*

Here is a list of verbs that can be used in this way:

cut	make	plane	shoot
drive	paint	render	sweep
get	pat	rub	turn
knock	pick	send	wipe

Most of these verbs can be followed by only one adjective or a very small range of adjectives. However *make* and *render* can be used with a wide range of adjectives.

keep, hold, leave

3.163 You can also use *keep*, *hold*, and *leave* with an object followed by an adjective, to say that someone or something is caused to remain in a particular state.

The light through the thin curtains had kept her awake.
Leave the door open.
Hold it straight.

verbs that relate to giving someone a job or role

3.164 If you want to say that someone is given an important job, you can use *make*, *appoint*, *crown*, or *elect* with an object followed by a noun phrase referring to the job.

In 1910 Asquith made him a junior minister.

The noun used in this way does not usually have a determiner when it refers to a unique job.

Ramsay MacDonald appointed him Secretary of State for India.

verbs of opinion

3.165 Some transitive verbs with the general meaning *consider* can be used with an adjective or noun phrase to say what someone's opinion of a person or thing is.

They consider him an embarrassment.
Do you find his view of America interesting?

Here is a list of these verbs:

account	consider	find	judge	reckon
believe	deem	hold	presume	think

Prove can also be followed by an object complement, although it means *show*, not *consider*.

He had proved them wrong.

3.166 These verbs are often used in the passive. *Believe, presume, reckon,* and *think* are nearly always used in the passive in these structures.

Her body was never found and she was presumed dead.
30 bombers were believed shot down.

3.167 All the verbs listed in paragraph 3.165 except *account* can also be used with a *to*-infinitive clause after their object showing what someone thinks a person or thing is like or does.

We believed him to be innocent.

See paragraph 3.206 for information about using a *to*-infinitive clause after the object of these verbs.

3.168 You can use the verbs listed in 3.165 with *it* as their object followed by an object complement and a *to*-infinitive clause to show someone's opinion of an action. For example, instead of saying *She found breathing difficult*, you can say *She found it difficult to breathe.*

Gretchen found it difficult to speak.
He thought it right to resign.
He considered it his duty to go.

These are examples of *it* being used in an impersonal way. For more information about the impersonal use of *it*, see paragraphs 9.31 to 9.45.

describing and naming

3.169 If you want to say that people use a particular word, word group, or name to describe or refer to someone or something, you can use the word, word group, or name after one of a group of transitive verbs.

People who did not like him called him dull.
They called him an idiot.
Everyone called her Molly.
He was declared innocent.
They named the place Tumbo Kutu.

Here is a list of verbs that can be used in this way. The first group is followed by an adjective; the second group is followed by a noun phrase; and the third group is followed by a name.

call	pronounce	call	proclaim	christen
certify	term	declare	term	dub
declare	~	designate	~	name
label	brand	label	call	nickname

titles

3.170 The passive verbs *be entitled*, *be headed*, and *be inscribed* are followed by a title or inscription.

The draft document was entitled 'A way forward'.

describing states

3.171 A few transitive verbs can be followed by an adjective to say that someone or something is in a particular state when something happens to them, or is preferred to be in that state.

More than forty people were burned alive.
...a soup that can be served cold.
They found it dead.
Do you want it white or black?

Here is a list of verbs that can be used in this way:

burn	find	like	serve	want
eat	leave	prefer	show	

Sometimes an *-ed* participle or an *-ing* participle describing a state is used.

She found herself caught in a strong tidal current.
Maureen came in and found Kate sitting on a chair staring at the window.

Using a prepositional phrase after a linking verb

3.172 When you want to give information about someone or something by describing their circumstances, you can sometimes use a **prepositional phrase** after a linking verb.

3.173　You can use many kinds of prepositional phrase after *be*.

> He was still *in a state of shock*.
> I walked home with Bill, who was *in a very good mood*.
> She had an older brother who was *in the army*.
> I'm *from Dortmund* originally.
> ...people who are *under pressure*.
> Your comments are *of great interest to me*.
> This book is *for any woman who has a child*.

use after other verbs

3.174　Some other linking verbs can be used with a more restricted range of prepositional phrases.

> He *seemed in excellent health*.
> We do ask people to *keep in touch* with us.
> These methods have gradually *fallen into disuse*.
> He *got into trouble* with the police.

Here is a list of other linking verbs that are used with prepositional phrases:

appear	feel	keep	seem
fall	get	remain	stay

referring to place

3.175　Some verbs that are always or often followed by an adjective can also be used with prepositional phrases relating to place.

> She's *in California*.
> I'll stay *here* with the children.
> The cat was now lying *on the sofa*.

Here is a list of these verbs:

be	remain	~	lie	stand
keep	stay	hang	sit	

For more information about prepositional phrases and adverbs relating to place, see paragraphs 6.73 to 6.92 and 6.53 to 6.72.

referring to time

3.176　*Be* can be used with time expressions to say when something took place or will take place.

> That final meeting was *on 3 November*.

For more information about time expressions, see paragraphs 4.85 to 4.111.

3.177 Prepositional phrases can also be used in transitive structures to say that someone or something is caused to be in a particular state.

They'll get me out of trouble.
The fear of being discovered kept me on the alert.

Talking about what role something has or how it is perceived: the preposition *as*

3.178 Prepositional phrases beginning with *as* can be used after some verbs.

3.179 Prepositional phrases beginning with *as* are used after certain intransitive verbs to show what role or function the subject has, or what identity they pretend to have.

Bleach removes colour and acts as an antiseptic and deodoriser.
He served as Kennedy's ambassador to India.
The sitting room doubles as her office.

Here is a list of verbs that can be followed by *as* in this way:

act	double	pass	serve
come	function	pose	

Work can also be used in this way, when it has a human subject.

She works as a counsellor with an AIDS charity.

3.180 A number of transitive verbs can be used with *as* after their object.

With some, a noun phrase is used after *as*. The *as* phrase describes the role of the object or what it is thought to be.

I wanted to use him as an agent.
I treated business as a game.

Here is a list of transitive verbs that can be used with *as* and a noun phrase:

brand	condemn	elect	label	suggest
cast	consider	establish	name	take
categorize	define	give	perceive	treat
certify	denounce	hail	recognize	use
characterize	depict	identify	regard	view
choose	describe	intend	scorn	
class	diagnose	interpret	see	

With others, an adjective is used after *as*. The adjective indicates what quality or characteristic the object is thought to have.

Party members and officials described him as brilliant.
They regarded manual work as degrading.

Here is a list of transitive verbs that can be used with *as* and an adjective:

brand	class	depict	label	see
categorize	condemn	describe	perceive	view
certify	define	diagnose	regard	
characterize	denounce	establish	scorn	

3.181 *Look upon*, *refer to*, and *think of* are also used with *as* in this way. *As* must be followed by a noun when used with *refer to*.

In some households the man <u>was referred to as</u> the master.

Talking about closely linked actions: using two main verbs together

3.182 This section describes the ways in which you use two main verbs together to talk about two actions or states that are closely linked.

These two actions may be performed by the same person. See paragraphs 3.189 to 3.201.

She <u>stopped speaking</u>.
Davis <u>likes to talk</u> about horses.

Alternatively, the actions may be performed by different people. If they are, the performer of the second action is the object of the first verb. See paragraphs 3.202 to 3.212.

I don't <u>want them to feel</u> I've slighted them.
One of the group began pumping her chest to <u>help her breathe</u>.

3.183 Note that the first verb needs the second verb after it because it does not give enough information on its own. For example, *I want* does not give enough information to be a useful statement, but *I want to talk to you* does.

Some of the verbs dealt with below, for example *want* and *like*, can also be ordinary transitive verbs, with a noun phrase after them. Transitive verbs are explained in paragraphs 3.14 to 3.25.

3.184 If you want to talk about two actions that are less closely linked, you refer to each action in a separate clause. Ways of combining clauses are explained in Chapter 8.

verb forms

3.185 The first verb involved in this type of structure is the main verb of the structure. It usually inflects for tense and agrees in number with the subject; it is **finite**.

I <u>wanted</u> to come home.
Lonnie <u>wants</u> to say sorry.
More and more people <u>are coming</u> to appreciate the contribution that these people make to our society.

3.186 The second verb in the combination does not inflect for tense or change its form at all; it is **non-finite**.

She tried <u>to read</u>.
They had been trying <u>to read</u>.

Information about finite and non-finite forms can be found in the Reference section.

3.187 There are four non-finite verb forms that are used for the second verb in this type of structure:

▶ the -*ing* participle
▶ the *to*-infinitive
▶ the infinitive without *to*
▶ the -*ed* participle

Note that the infinitive without *to* and the -*ed* participle form of the verb are used in only a few combinations.

Other kinds of -*ing* form and infinitive are also sometimes used.

Those very close to the blast risk being burnt.
Neither Rita nor I recalled ever having seen her.
She wanted to be reassured.
They claimed to have shot down 22 planes.

3.188 The position of *not* in negative structures of this type is explained in paragraphs 5.59 and 5.60.

Talking about two actions done by the same person

3.189 When you are talking about two actions that are done by the same person, you use the second verb directly after the first.

Children enjoy playing alongside each other.
You deserve to know the truth.

verbs followed by an -*ing* participle

3.190 Some verbs are always followed by an -*ing* participle clause in structures of this kind.

She admitted lying to him.
Have you finished reading the paper?
He missed having someone to dislike.
I recall being very impressed with the official anthems.

Here is a list of verbs that are used with an -*ing* participle, but not a *to*-infinitive:

admit	defer	endure	loathe	resent
adore	delay	enjoy	mention	resist
appreciate	deny	fancy	mind	risk
avoid	describe	finish	miss	sit
celebrate	detest	go	postpone	stand
commence	discontinue	imagine	practise	stop
consider	dislike	keep	recall	suggest
contemplate	dread	lie	report	

These verbs are also sometimes used with a passive -*ing* form.

They enjoy being praised.

Admit, *celebrate*, *deny*, *mention*, and *recall* are quite often used with a perfect -*ing* form.

Carmichael had denied having seen him.

USAGE NOTE

3.191 Note that *need* can be used with an *-ing* participle after it, but the *-ing* participle then has the same meaning as a passive *to*-infinitive. For example, *The house needs cleaning* means the same as *The house needs to be cleaned*.

Require and *want* are also occasionally used in the same way, although some people do not like this use of *want*.

verbs followed by a *to*-infinitive

3.192 Other verbs are used with a *to*-infinitive.

Mrs Babcock had always longed to go to Ireland.
She forgot to bring a suitcase.
She wishes to ask a favour of you.

Here is a list of verbs that are used with a *to*-infinitive, and rarely or never with an *-ing* participle:

ache	decide	hesitate	plan	swear
afford	demand	hope	pledge	tend
agree	deserve	intend	prepare	threaten
aim	desire	learn	pretend	trouble
appear	disdain	live	promise	venture
arrange	endeavour	long	prove	volunteer
ask	expect	manage	reckon	vote
attempt	fail	mean	refuse	vow
care	fight	need	resolve	wait
choose	forget	neglect	scorn	want
claim	grow	offer	seek	wish
consent	happen	opt	seem	
dare	help	pay	survive	

Most of these verbs can be used with a passive infinitive.

She refused to be photographed.
He deserves to be shot.

The following verbs from the above list are not usually used with a passive infinitive, because of their meanings:

claim	intend	mean	threaten
dare	learn	neglect	trouble
forget	manage	pretend	venture

Appear, claim, happen, pretend, prove, seem, and *tend* are quite often used with a perfect infinitive.

They seemed to have disappeared.

Note that *help* is also followed by the infinitive without *to*.

Coffee helped keep him alert.

i **USAGE NOTE**

3.193 Note that *afford* is always preceded by a modal, and that *care* is normally used with a negative.

Can we afford to ignore this source of power as other sources of energy are diminishing?
...a kitchen for someone who doesn't care to cook.

3.194 The use of *have* followed by a *to*-infinitive clause is explained in paragraph 5.244.

verbs used with either form

3.195 A few verbs can be used with either an *-ing* participle or a *to*-infinitive without changing the meaning of the verb.

It started raining.
A very cold wind had started to blow.
We both love dancing.
He loves to talk about his work.

Here is a list of verbs that can be followed either by an *-ing* participle or a *to*-infinitive without greatly changing the meaning:

attempt	cease	fear	love
begin	continue	hate	prefer
bother	deserve	like	start

Note that *bother* is often used with a negative or a broad negative.

He didn't bother complaining about it.
We hardly even bother to clean it.

i **USAGE NOTE**

3.196 With a few verbs, the meaning is altered depending on whether you use an *-ing* participle or a *to*-infinitive . These verbs are *come, go on, remember, try,* and *regret.*

If someone *comes running, flying,* or *hurtling* somewhere, they move in that way. If you *come to do something,* you gradually start doing it.

When they heard I was leaving, they both came running out.
People came to believe that all things were possible.

If you *try to do something,* you attempt it, to see if you can do it. If you *try doing something,* you do it in order to find out if it is effective.

She tried to think calmly.
Try lying down in a dark room for a while. That usually helps.

With the other verbs, the difference in meaning relates to the timing of the action.

If you *go on doing something,* you continue to do it, but if you *go on to do something,* you subsequently start doing it.

They went on arguing into the night.
She went on to talk about the political consequences.

If you *remember doing something,* you did it in the past, but if you *remember to do something,* you do it at the present time.

I remember promising that I would try.
We must remember to say thank you.

Similarly, if you *regret doing something*, you have already done it, but if you *regret to do something*, you have to do it at the present time.

She did not <u>regret accepting</u> his offer.
I <u>regret to say</u> rents went up.

Regret is only used with the *to*-infinitive of a small number of verbs that share the meaning of giving or receiving information. These verbs are:

announce	learn	see
inform	say	tell

! **BE CAREFUL**

3.197 When you have a choice between an *-ing* participle and a *to*-infinitive, you do not use the *-ing* participle if the first verb is in a progressive form.

The Third World <u>is beginning to export</u> to the West.
The big clouds <u>were starting to cover</u> the sun.
Educational budgets <u>are continuing to increase</u>.

With verbs that cannot be followed by a *to*-infinitive, you normally use a noun phrase instead of the *-ing* participle.

I knew Miss Head would just be finishing <u>her cello practice</u>.

3.198 Note that a few verbs, principally *need*, *want*, *have*, *buy*, and *choose*, are used with an object and a *to*-infinitive when talking about two actions performed by the same person. The *to*-infinitive must be transitive. It is understood as relating to the noun, rather than being closely connected with the first verb.

I <u>need a car to drive</u> to work.
She <u>chose the correct one to put</u> in her bag.

to-infinitive showing purpose

3.199 Note that verbs that refer to a deliberate action are sometimes followed by a clause expressing purpose. Here, *to* means *in order to*.

Several women <u>moved to help</u> her.
The captain <u>stopped to reload</u> the machine-gun.

Note that the first verb has a complete meaning of its own; the second verb is giving a reason for the first action, not completing the information about it.

See paragraphs 8.43 to 8.46 for more details on expressing purpose.

ℹ **USAGE NOTE**

3.200 When the base form of *try* is used, for example as an **imperative** or with a **modal**, it is sometimes used with *and* followed by the base form of the second verb, rather than with a *to*-infinitive. The two actions seem to be separate, because of the *and*, but are in fact very closely linked.

<u>Try and get</u> a torch or a light, it's terribly dark down here.
I'll <u>try and answer</u> the question.

Some speakers consider this to be informal or incorrect.

Come and *go* are often used in a similar way with *and*, in simple forms as well as in the base form. The verb after *and* can also inflect.

Come and see me whenever you feel depressed.
I went and fetched another glass.

get with an -ed participle

3.201 In informal spoken English, *get* is sometimes used with an *-ed* participle directly after it, in a structure with a passive meaning.

Then he got killed in a plane crash.

When *get* is used to form passives in the past and present perfect, American English normally uses the participle *gotten*, rather than *got*.

Her foot had gotten caught between some rocks. (Am)

Talking about two actions done by different people

3.202 If you want to talk about two closely linked actions that are performed by different people, you follow the first verb with an object. This object then functions as the subject of the second verb. For example, in *She asked Ginny to collect the book*, Ginny is the person who is asked, and she is also the person who performs the action of collecting the book.

I saw him looking at my name on the door.
You can't stop me seeing him!

use of possessive determiner

3.203 Note that when the second verb is an *-ing* participle, a possessive determiner is sometimes used in front of it, instead of a pronoun. This is rather formal.

These professional ethics prevent their discussing their clients with the public.
She did not like my living in London.

Note that a possessive determiner is only used in this way when the second verb can have a human subject.

transitive verbs with an -ing participle

3.204 Some verbs are used with an object and an *-ing* participle.

He caught Hooper looking at him.

Here is a list of verbs that are used with an object and an *-ing* participle:

catch	hear	like	prevent	spot
describe	imagine	notice	save	stop
feel	keep	observe	see	want
find	leave	picture	send	watch

Listen to also belongs in this group. The object after it is the object of the preposition *to*.

I listened to Kaspar talking.

These verbs are sometimes used with a passive *-ing* form, but not usually with a perfect *-ing* form.

She felt herself being spun around.

verbs with an infinitive without *to*

3.205 Some of the verbs in the above paragraph can also be used with an infinitive without *to*.

She felt her hair rise on the back of her neck
Dr Hochstadt heard her gasp.

There is a slight change of meaning depending on which form is used. If you choose the *-ing* participle, you emphasize that the action continued happening for a period of time.

But I stayed there, listening to her singing.
I looked over and saw Joe staring at me.

If you choose the infinitive without *to*, you emphasize that the action was completed.

We listened to Jenny finish the sonnet.
It was the first time she had heard him speak of his life.

Here is a list of verbs that can be used with an *-ing* participle or an infinitive without *to*, with the change of meaning described above:

feel	listen to	observe	watch
hear	notice	see	

Note that these verbs can be used in the active only when they are followed by an infinitive without *to*. See also paragraph 3.208.

transitive verbs with a *to*-infinitive

3.206 Other verbs are used with an object and a *to*-infinitive clause.

His sister had taught him to sew.
I encourage students to do these exercises at home.

Here is a list of verbs that are used with an object and a *to*-infinitive:

advise	defy	instruct	pay	tell
allow	enable	intend	permit	train
ask	encourage	invite	persuade	trust
beg	expect	lead	prefer	urge
cause	forbid	leave	press	use
challenge	force	like	programme	want
choose	get	mean	prompt	warn
command	help	move	recruit	
compel	induce	oblige	remind	
dare	inspire	order	teach	

Note that some of the verbs in the above list are used for reporting orders, requests, and advice. For more information on this use, see paragraph 7.39.

Here is a list of verbs that are always or usually used in the passive when followed by a *to*-infinitive:

allege	deem	know	require	understand
assume	discover	learn	rumour	
believe	estimate	prove	say	
claim	feel	reckon	see	
consider	find	report	think	

They refer to saying, thinking, or discovering. The *to*-infinitive that follows them is most commonly *be* or *have*, or a perfect infinitive.

The house was believed to be haunted.
He was proved to be wrong.

using the passive

3.207 If you do not know who the subject of the second verb is, or you do not want to mention them, you can use a passive construction.

A gardener was immediately sacked if he was caught smoking.
I was asked to come for a few days to help them.

The following verbs are not usually used in the passive when followed by an *-ing* participle:

feel	like	prevent	stop
imagine	listen to	save	want

The following verbs are not usually used in the passive when followed by a *to*-infinitive:

defy	get	like	prefer	want

USAGE NOTE

3.208 *Hear*, *observe*, and *see* are not used with a *to*-infinitive when they are active but they can be used with either an *-ing* participle or a *to*-infinitive when they are passive.

You use them with an *-ing* participle when you want to show that the action described by the second verb took place over a period of time.

A terrorist was seen standing in the middle of the road.
Her companions could be heard playing games.

If a *to*-infinitive is used, you are implying that the action was completed.

She could distinctly be seen to hesitate.
The baby was seldom heard to cry.

See also paragraph 3.205.

verbs followed by *for* and a *to*-infinitive

3.209 There are some verbs used with another verb with a *to*-infinitive that are followed by the preposition *for* and its object, rather than by a direct object. The object of *for* is the performer of the second action.

They called for action to be taken against the unions.
I waited for him to speak.

Note that the *to*-infinitive is often a passive one.

Here is a list of verbs that can be used in this way:

appeal	ask	long	plead	wait
apply	call	opt	press	wish
arrange	clamour	pay	vote	yearn

transitive verbs with an infinitive without *to*

3.210 A few verbs are followed by an object and an infinitive without *to*, not an -*ing* participle or a *to*-infinitive. They are *let*, *make*, and *have* in the sense of *cause to happen* or *experience*.

Jenny let him talk.
My father made me go for the interview.
He lay in a darkened room and had her bring him meals on trays.

Verbs that can be used either with an infinitive without *to* or with an -*ing* participle are explained in paragraph 3.205.

have and *get* used for showing cause

3.211 A special use of *have* when used with another verb is to say that the subject causes something to be dealt with by someone else. In this case, *have* is followed by an object referring to the thing dealt with, and then by the -*ed* participle of a transitive verb or of an intransitive verb followed by a preposition.

I have my hair cut every six weeks.

This structure is also used to say that something belonging to the subject of *have* is affected in some way.

She'd just lost her job and had some money stolen.

If you want to mention the performer of the second action, you use *by* followed by a noun.

He had to have his leg massaged by his trainer.

Get can also be used with an object and an -*ed* participle to talk about causing something to be dealt with or affected in some way.

We must get the car repaired.

want and *need* with an -*ed* participle

3.212 *Want* is also used with an object and an -*ed* participle, to show that you would like something to be done.

I want the whole approach changed.
I don't want you hurt.

Need is used in a similar way, usually when the object is something that belongs to the subject.

You need your eyes tested.

Chapter 4

Expressing time: tenses and time adverbials

4 Expressing time: tenses and time adverbials

Introduction

4.1 When you are making a statement, you usually need to make it clear whether you are talking about a situation that exists now, existed in the past, or is likely to exist in the future. There are different ways of expressing time: **tense** is one; the use of **time adverbials** is another.

A tense is a verb form that indicates a particular point in time or period of time.

The form belonging to a particular tense is obtained by the addition of **inflections** to the base form of the verb. In English, time is also indicated by the inclusion of **auxiliaries** or **modals** in the verb phrase.

smile...smiled
was smiling...has been smiling...had smiled
will smile...may smile

Some verbs have irregular forms for past tenses.

fight...fought
go...went

For information about all these forms, see the Reference section.

4.2 Sometimes the point in time is clear from the tense of the verb, and no other time reference is required. However, if you want to draw attention to the time of the action, you use a **time adverbial**.

A time adverbial may be (i) an adverb (e.g. *afterwards, immediately*), (ii) a prepositional phrase (e.g. *at eight o' clock, on Monday*), or (iii) a noun phrase (e.g. *the next day, last week*).

She's moving <u>tomorrow</u>.
He was better after undergoing surgery <u>on Saturday</u>.
Record profits were announced <u>last week</u>.

For more general information about adverbials, see the beginning of Chapter 6.

position of time adverbial

4.3 Time adverbials normally come at the end of a clause, after the verb or after its object if there is one. You can put more focus on the time by placing the adverbial at the beginning of the clause.

We're getting married <u>next year</u>.
<u>Next year</u>, the museum is expecting even more visitors.
I was playing golf <u>yesterday</u>.
<u>Yesterday</u> the atmosphere at the factory was tense.

If the time adverbial is an adverb, it can also come immediately after *be* or after the first auxiliary in a verb phrase.

She <u>is now</u> pretty well-known in this country.
Cooper <u>had originally</u> been due to retire last week.
Public advertisements for the post <u>will soon</u> appear in the national press.

duration and frequency

4.4   Some verb forms are used to say that an event takes place continuously over a period of time, or is repeated several times. You may also want to say how long something lasts, or how often it happens. To do this, **adverbials of duration** (e.g. *for a long time*) and **adverbials of frequency** (e.g. *often*, *every year*) are used.

America has <u>always</u> been highly influential.
People are <u>sometimes</u> scared to say what they really think.
Hundreds of people are killed <u>every year</u> in fires.
They would go on talking <u>for hours</u>.

Adverbials of frequency are explained and listed in paragraphs 4.114 to 4.122.
Adverbials of duration are explained and listed in paragraphs 4.123 to 4.144.

4.5   The following paragraphs describe the ways in which you can talk about the present, the past, and the future. After each of these, there is a section on the ways in which you use time adverbials with each tense.

There are some time adverbials that are used mainly with the past tenses. These are explained in paragraph 4.41. Time adverbials that are used with future forms can be found in paragraphs 4.60 to 4.62.

subordinate clauses

4.6   This chapter deals only with the choice of tense in **main clauses**.

Sometimes, the point in time is not indicated by a time adverbial, but by a **subordinate clause**. Subordinate clauses of time are introduced by conjunctions that refer to time, such as *since*, *until*, *before*, and *after*.

For information about the tense of the verb in the subordinate clause, see paragraph 8.9.

The present

4.7   In situations where you are discussing an existing state of affairs, you use a verb that is in the present tense. Usually, the verb tense is sufficient to show that you are referring to the present. You normally only use a time adverbial for emphasis, or to refer to something that is unrelated to the present moment.

The present in general: the present simple

the present moment

4.8   If you want to talk about your thoughts and feelings at the present moment, or about your immediate reactions to something, you use the **present simple**.

I'<u>m</u> awfully busy.
They both <u>taste</u> the same.
Gosh, he <u>looks</u> awful.
I <u>want</u> a breath of fresh air.

You can also use the present simple to talk about a physical feeling that is affecting you or someone else.

I <u>feel</u> heavy. I do. I <u>feel</u> drowsy.
My stomach <u>hurts</u>.

Note, however, that if you are talking about physical perceptions such as seeing

and hearing, you normally use the modal *can*, although the present simple is
occasionally used.

I can see the fishing boats coming in.
I can smell it. Can't you?
I see a flat stretch of ground.
I hear approaching feet.

general present including present moment

4.9 If you want to talk about a settled state of affairs that includes the present moment
but where the particular time reference is not important, you use the present simple.

My dad works in Saudi Arabia.
He lives in the French Alps near the Swiss border.
He is a very good brother. We love him.
She's a doctor's daughter.
Meanwhile, Atlantic City faces another dilemma.

general truths

4.10 If you want to say that something is always or generally true, you use the present
simple.

Near the equator, the sun evaporates greater quantities of water.
A molecule of water has two atoms of hydrogen and one of oxygen.
A chemical reaction occurs in the fuel cell.

regular or habitual actions

4.11 If you want to talk about something that a particular person or thing does regularly
or habitually, you use the present simple.

Do you smoke?
I get up early and eat my breakfast listening to the radio.

used in reviews

4.12 You usually use the present simple when you are discussing what happens in a book,
play, or film.

In the film he plays the central character of Charles Smithson.
In those early chapters, he keeps himself very much in the background.

USAGE NOTE

4.13 You can use the present simple of the verb *say* when you are describing something
you have read in a book.

The criminal justice system, the author says, has failed to keep pace with the drug problem.
The Bible says love of money is the root of all evil.

used in commentaries

4.14 On radio and television, commentators often use the present simple when they
are describing an event such as a sports match or a ceremony at the time that it is
happening.

He turns, he shoots, he scores!

4.15 When you are reporting what someone said to you at a point in the recent past, you can use the present simple of a reporting verb such as *hear* or *tell*.

> *I've never been paragliding myself, but they <u>tell</u> me it's a really exciting sport.*
> *Tamsin's a good cook, I <u>hear</u>.*
> *Grace <u>says</u> you told her to come over here.*

For more detailed information about reporting verbs, see Chapter 7.

used in commenting

4.16 When you are commenting on what you are saying or doing, you use the present simple of a verb such as *admit, promise, reject,* or *enclose*. For more information on this type of verb, see paragraphs 7.64 to 7.67.

> *This, I <u>admit</u>, was my favourite activity.*
> *I <u>enclose</u> a small cheque which may come in handy.*
> *I <u>leave</u> it for you to decide.*

The present progressive

the moment of speaking

4.17 If you want to talk about an activity that is in progress, you use the **present progressive**.

> *We're <u>having</u> a meeting. Come and join in.*
> *What <u>am</u> I <u>doing</u>? I'm <u>looking</u> out of the window.*
> *My head <u>is aching</u>.*
> *I'm already <u>feeling</u> tense.*

emphasizing the present moment

4.18 If you want to emphasize the present moment or to indicate that a situation is temporary, you use the present progressive.

> *Only one hospital, at Angal, <u>is functioning</u>.*
> *We're <u>trying</u> to create a more democratic society.*
> *She's <u>spending</u> the summer in Europe.*
> *I'm <u>working</u> as a British Council Officer.*

progressive change

4.19 You also use the present progressive to talk about changes, trends, development, and progress.

> *The village <u>is changing</u> but it is still undisturbed.*
> *His handwriting <u>is improving</u>.*
> *World energy demand <u>is increasing</u> at a rate of about 3% per year.*

habitual actions

4.20 If you want to talk about a habitual action that takes place regularly, especially one that is new or temporary, you use the present progressive.

> *You're <u>going</u> out a lot these days.*
> *Do you know if she's still <u>playing</u> these days?*
> *She's <u>seeing</u> a lot more of them.*

Time adverbials with reference to the present

4.21 You do not normally need to use an additional time adverbial with present forms of verbs, but you can add them in order to emphasize the immediate present or general present, or to contrast the present with the past or future.

They're getting on quite well at the moment.
We're safe now.
What's the matter with you today, Marnie?
I haven't got a grant this year.

general truths

4.22 If you are using the present simple to talk about something that is always or generally true, you can reinforce or weaken your statement by using an adverb.

Babies normally lose weight in the beginning.
The attitude is usually one of ridicule.
Traditionally, the Japanese prefer good quality clothes.

Here is a list of common adverbs that can be used to modify your statement in this way:

always	mainly	often	usually
generally	normally	traditionally	

The use of the present simple to talk about general truths is explained in paragraph 4.10.

regular actions

4.23 When you use the present simple to say that an action takes place regularly, you can use an **adverbial of frequency** such as *often* or *sometimes* to be more specific about how often it happens.

Several groups meet weekly.
I visit her about once every six months.
It seldom rains there.
I never drink alone.

The use of the present simple to talk about regular activities is explained in paragraph 4.11.

More information about adverbials of frequency, including a list of the most common ones, can be found in paragraphs 4.114 to 4.122.

frequent actions

4.24 The present progressive is also used with words like *always* and *forever* when you want to emphasize how often the action takes place. This use expresses disapproval or annoyance. The adverb is placed after the auxiliary verb.

You're always looking for faults.
It's always raining.
And she's always talking to him on the telephone.
They are forever being knocked down by cars.

The use of the present progressive to talk about frequent, habitual actions is explained in paragraph 4.20.

time adverbials with present verb forms

4.25 Note that some adverbs that refer to the present time, such as *now* and *today*, are also used to express past time. However, there are a few adverbs and other time adverbials that are almost always used with present verb forms.

I'm not planning on having children at present.
...the camping craze that is currently sweeping America.
Nowadays fitness is becoming a generally accepted principle of life.

The following is a list of time adverbials that are normally only used with present verb forms:

at present	in this day and	nowadays	these days
currently	age	presently	

Note that in this list the word *presently* means *now*.

The past

4.26 When you are talking about the past, a time adverbial is necessary to specify the particular time in the past you are referring to. The time reference can be established in a previous clause, and the verbs in the following clauses are therefore put in the past tense.

It was very cold that night. Over my head was a gap in the reed matting of the roof.
The house was damaged by fire yesterday. No-one was injured.

Stating a definite time in the past: the past simple

4.27 If you want to say that an event occurred or that something was the case at a particular time in the past, you use the **past simple**.

The Israeli Prime Minister flew into New York yesterday to start his visit to the US.
Our regular window cleaner went off to Canada last year.
On 1 February 1968 he introduced the Industrial Expansion Bill.
They gave me medication to help me relax.

past situations

4.28 If you want to say that a situation existed over a period of time in the past, you also use the past simple.

He lived in Paris during his last years.
Throughout his life he suffered from epilepsy

4.29 If you are talking about something that happened in the past, and you mention a situation that existed at that time, you use the past simple. You can do this whether or not the situation still exists.

All the streets in this part of Watford looked alike.
About fifty miles from the university there was one of India's most famous and ancient Hindu temples.

habitual and regular actions

4.30 If you want to talk about an activity that took place regularly or repeatedly in the past, but that no longer occurs, you use the past simple.

We walked a great deal when I was a boy.
Each week we trekked to the big house.

Would and *used to* can also be used to say that something happened regularly in the past but no longer does so. See paragraphs 5.114 and 5.255 for more information.

Actions in progress in the past: the past progressive

repeated actions

4.31   If you want to focus on action in progress or repeated actions that occurred in the past, you use the **past progressive**.

Her tooth was aching, her burnt finger was hurting.
He was looking ill.
Everyone was begging the captain to surrender.
I was meeting thousands of people and getting to know no one.

contrasting events

4.32   If you want to contrast a situation with an event that happened just after that situation existed, you use the past progressive to describe the first situation. You then use the past simple to describe and draw attention to the event that occurred after it.

We were all sitting round the fire waiting for my brother to come home. He arrived about six in the evening.
I was waiting angrily on Monday morning when I saw Mrs. Miller.

The past in relation to the present: the present perfect

4.33   If you want to mention something that happened in the past but you do not want to state a specific time, you use the **present perfect**.

They have raised £180 for a swimming pool.
I have noticed this trait in many photographers.

!   **BE CAREFUL**

4.34   You cannot use time adverbials that place the action at a definite time in the past with the present perfect. For example, you cannot say *I have done it yesterday*.

You can, however, use an **adverbial of duration**.

The settlers have left the bay forever.
I ate brown rice, which I have always hated, and vegetables from my garden.

Adverbials of duration are explained and listed in paragraphs 4.123 to 4.142.

You can also use *since* and *for* with the present perfect because when they are used in this way they refer to a definite time.

They have been back every year since then.
She has worked for him for ten years.

For more information on *since* see paragraph 4.137. Other uses of *for* are explained in paragraphs 4.125 to 4.128.

situations that still exist

4.35   If you want to talk about an activity or situation that started at some time in the past, continued, and is still happening now, you use the present perfect or the **present perfect progressive**.

All my adult life I *have waited* for the emergence of a strong centre party.
She's *always felt* that films should be entertaining.
National productivity *has been declining*.
I *have been dancing* since I was a child.

emphasizing duration of event

4.36 If you want to emphasize the duration of a recent event, you use the present perfect progressive.

> She's *been crying*.
> Some people will say that what I *have been describing* is not a crisis of industry.
> The Department of Aboriginal Affairs *has* recently *been conducting* a survey of Australian Aborigines.

Events before a particular time in the past: the past perfect

4.37 If you want to talk about a past event or situation that occurred before a particular time in the past, you use the **past perfect**.

> One day he noticed that a culture plate *had become* contaminated by a mould.
> Before the war, he *had worked* as a bank manager.
> She *had lost* her job as a real estate agent and was working as a waitress.
> I detested games and *had* always *managed* to avoid children's parties.

emphasizing time and duration

4.38 If you want to emphasize the recentness and the duration of a continuous activity that took place before a particular time in the past, you use the **past perfect progressive**.

> Until now the rumours that *had been circulating* were exaggerated versions of the truth.
> The doctor *had been working* alone.
> He died in hospital where he *had been receiving* treatment for cancer.
> They *had been hitting* our trucks regularly.

expectations and wishes

4.39 If you want to say that something was expected, wished for, or intended before a particular time in the past, you use the past perfect or the past perfect progressive.

> She *had* naturally *assumed* that once there was a theatre everybody would want to go.
> It was the remains of a ten-rupee note which she *had hoped* would last till the end of the week.
> It was not as nice on the terrace as Clarissa *had expected*.
> I *had been expecting* some miraculous obvious change.

Time adverbials with reference to the past

4.40 When you are using past verb forms, you normally use a time adverbial to indicate that you are talking about the past.

> *At one time* the arts of reading and writing were classed among the great mysteries of life for the majority of people.
> I've made some poor decisions *lately*, but I'm feeling much better now.
> It was very splendid *once*, but it's only a ruin now.
> It's Mark who lost his wife. *A year last January*.
> It was terribly hot *yesterday*.

types of time adverbial

4.41 Time adverbials can refer either to a specific time, or to a more general indefinite period of time.

The lists below give the most common indefinite time adverbials that are used mainly with past verb forms. With the exception of *since* and *ever since*, which come at the end of a clause, you put them after the auxiliary or modal in a verb phrase that has more than one word; if you use them with the past simple you put them in front of the verb.

The words in the following list can be used with all past verb forms:

again	ever since	in the past	previously
already	finally	just	recently
earlier	first	last	since

The words in the following list can be used with all past verb forms except the present perfect:

afterwards	formerly	once
at one time	immediately	originally
eventually	next	subsequently

Note that *once* here means *at some time in the past*. For its uses as an adverb of frequency, see paragraph 4.115.

For the uses of *since* as a preposition in time adverbials, see paragraph 4.137.

Some time adverbials used with past verb forms are more specific. They include words like *yesterday*, *ago*, *other*, and *last*. Note that *ago* is placed after the noun phrase.

I saw him yesterday evening.
We bought the house from her the day before yesterday.
Three weeks ago I was staying in San Francisco.
I saw my goddaughter the other day.
It all happened a long time ago.

! **BE CAREFUL**

4.42 You say *last night*, not *yesterday night*.

used for emphasis

4.43 There are some cases where you have to specify the time reference. In other cases, you may simply want to make the timing of the action clear, or emphatic. These cases are described below.

used with the past simple

4.44 When you use the past simple to describe habitual or regular activities, you can use an **adverbial of frequency** to indicate the regularity or repetition of the activity.

He often agreed to work quite cheaply.
Sometimes he read so much that he became confused.
Etta phoned Guppy every day.

The use of the past simple to describe habitual actions is explained in paragraph 4.30.

used with the past progressive

4.45   If you are using the past progressive to talk about repeated actions, you can add an adverb of frequency such as *always* or *forever* after the auxiliary to emphasize the frequency of the action or to express your annoyance about it.

> *In the immense shed where we worked, something <u>was always going</u> wrong.*
> *She <u>was always knitting</u> – making sweaters or baby clothes.*
> *Our builder <u>was forever going</u> on skiing holidays.*

The use of the past progressive to describe repeated actions is explained in paragraph 4.31.

used with the present perfect

4.46   When you use the present perfect to mention something that is still relevant to the present, you can add an adverb of frequency to show that the action was repeated.

> *I've <u>often</u> wondered why we didn't move years ago.*
> *Political tensions have <u>frequently</u> spilled over into violence.*

The use of the present perfect to talk about situations that are still relevant is explained in paragraph 4.33.

4.47   Note that if you are talking about a quality, attitude, or possession that still exists or is still relevant, you need to use the present perfect with an adverbial of duration.

> *We've had it <u>for fifteen years</u>.*
> *He's <u>always</u> liked you, you know.*
> *I <u>have known</u> him <u>for years</u>.*
> *My people <u>have been</u> at war <u>since 1917</u>.*

4.48   If you use the present perfect and the present perfect progressive to mention a continuing activity that began in the past, you can add an adverbial of duration to show how long it has been going on.

> *<u>For about a week</u> he had been complaining of a bad headache.*
> *They <u>have been meeting</u> regularly <u>for two years</u>.*
> *He <u>has looked</u> after me well <u>since his mother died</u>.*

The use of the present perfect and the present perfect progressive to talk about activities that began in the past is explained in paragraph 4.35.

used with the past perfect

4.49   When you use the past perfect to describe a repeated event that took place before a particular time in the past, you use an adverbial of frequency to show how often it was repeated.

> *Posy <u>had always sought</u> her out even then.*
> *The housekeeper mentioned that the dog <u>had attacked</u> its mistress <u>more than once</u>.*

The use of the past perfect to describe events that occurred before a particular time in the past are explained in paragraph 4.37.

4.50   If you are using the past perfect to talk about a situation that did not change in the past, you use an adverbial of duration to emphasize the length of time during which it existed.

> *They weren't really our aunt and uncle, but we <u>had always known</u> them.*
> *All through those many years he <u>had never ever lost track of</u> my father.*
> *His parents <u>had been married for twelve years</u> when he was born.*

4.51   If you are using the past perfect progressive to mention a recent, continuous activity, you can specify when it began.

The Home Office had until now been insisting on giving the officers only ten days to reach a settlement.
Since then, the mother had been living with her daughter.

Adverbials of frequency or duration can also be added for emphasis.

The drive increased the fatigue she had been feeling for hours.
The rain had been pouring all night.

The use of the past perfect progressive to talk about a recent, continuous activity is explained in paragraph 4.38.

Expressing future time

4.52   It is not possible to talk with as much certainty about the future as it is about the present or the past. Any reference you make to future events is therefore usually an expression of what you think might happen or what you intend to happen.

Indicating the future using *will*

4.53   If you want to say that something is planned to happen, or that you think it is likely to happen in the future, you use the **modal** *will* in front of the base form of the verb.

Nancy will arrange it.
These will be dealt with in chapter 7.
'I will check,' said Brody.
When will I see them?
What do you think Sally will do?
You will come back, won't you?

If the subject is *I* or *we*, the modal *shall* is sometimes used instead of *will* to talk about future events.

I shall do everything I can to help you.
You will stay at home and I shall go to your office.
'We shall give him some tea,' Naomi said.

 This is not common in modern American English.

The modals *will* and *shall* are used in several other ways, usually with some element of future time. For more information, see Chapter 5.

general truths

4.54   If you want to talk about general truths and to say what can be expected to happen if a particular situation arises, you use *will*.

When peace is available, people will go for it.
An attack of malaria can keep a man off work for three days. He will earn nothing and his family will go hungry.

indicating certainty

4.55   If you are sure that something will happen because arrangements have been made, you can use the **future progressive**.

I'll be seeing them when I've finished with you.
She'll be appearing tomorrow and Sunday at the Royal Festival Hall.

I'll be waiting for you outside.
I understand you'll be moving into our area soon.
They'll spoil our picnic. I'll be wondering all the time what's happening.
Our people will be going to their country more.

Note that a time adverbial or an adverbial of frequency is normally required with the future progressive.

4.56 If you are referring to something that has not happened yet but will happen before a particular time in the future, you can use the **future perfect**.

By the time you get to the school, the concert will have finished.
Maybe by the time we get there he'll already have started.
By then, maybe you'll have heard from your sister.

Note that you must indicate the specific future time referred to by using a time adverbial or another clause.

indicating duration

4.57 If you want to indicate the duration of an event at a specific time in the future, you can use the **future perfect progressive**.

By the time the season ends, I will have been playing for fifteen months without a break.
The register will have been running for a year in May.

Note that you need to use a time adverbial to indicate the future time and an adverbial of duration to state how long the event will last.

Other ways of talking about the future

be going to

4.58 If you are stating an intention that something will happen, or if you have some immediate evidence that something will happen fairly soon, you can use *be going to* followed by an **infinitive**.

I'm going to explore the neighbourhood.
Evans knows lots of people. He's going to help me. He's going to take me there.
You're going to have a heart attack if you're not careful.
We're going to see a change in the law next year.

planned events

4.59 You can use *be due to* and *be about to* to refer to planned future events that you expect to happen soon. They are followed by infinitive clauses.

He is due to start as a courier shortly.
The work is due to be started in the summer.
Another 385 people are about to lose their jobs.
Are we about to be taken over by the machine?

Time adverbials with reference to the future

firm plans for the future

4.60 The **present simple** is used to talk about timetabled or scheduled events. The **present progressive** is used to state firm plans that you have for the future. A time adverbial is necessary unless you are sure that the hearer or reader knows that you are talking about the future.

My last train <u>leaves</u> Euston <u>at 11.30</u>.
The UN General Assembly <u>opens</u> in New York <u>later this month</u>.
<u>Tomorrow morning</u> we meet up to <u>exchange</u> contracts.
<u>I'm leaving</u> at the end of this week.
My mum <u>is coming</u> to help look after the new baby

vague time reference

4.61   When you want to make a general or vague reference to future time, you use an adverbial that refers to indefinite time.

I'll drop by <u>sometime</u>.
<u>Sooner or later</u> he'll ask you to join him there.
<u>In future</u> she'll have to take sedentary work of some sort.

Here is a list of indefinite time adverbials that are used mainly with future forms:

in future	one of these days	sometime
in the future	some day	sooner or later

tomorrow

4.62   Adverbials that include the word *tomorrow* are mainly used with references to future time.

We'll try somewhere else <u>tomorrow</u>.
Shall I come <u>tomorrow night</u>?
He'll be here <u>the day after tomorrow</u>.
<u>This time tomorrow</u> I'll be in New York.

next

4.63   Some adverbials that are mainly used with reference to future time include the word *next*. If you are using a specific day or month such as *Saturday* or *October*, you can put *next* either before or after the day or month. Otherwise, *next* is placed in front of the time reference.

<u>Next week</u> Michael Hall will be talking about music.
<u>Next summer</u> your crops will be very much better.
I think we'll definitely be going <u>next year</u>.
Will your accommodation be available <u>next October</u>?
The boots will be ready by <u>Wednesday next</u>.
A post mortem examination will be held on <u>Monday next</u>.
She won't be able to do it <u>the week after next</u>.

 In American English, *next* is always placed in front of the time reference.

Other uses of verb forms

4.64   So far in this chapter, the commonest and simplest uses of the various verb forms have been dealt with. However, there are also some less common uses of tenses.

Vivid narrative

4.65 Stories are normally told using the past. However, if you want to make a story seem vivid, as if it were happening now, you can use the **present simple** for actions and states and the **present progressive** for situations.

There's a loud explosion behind us. Then I <u>hear</u> Chris giggling. Sylvia <u>is</u> upset.
The helicopter <u>climbs over</u> the frozen wasteland.
Chris <u>is crying</u> hard and others <u>look</u> over from the other tables.
He <u>sits down</u> at his desk chair, <u>reaches</u> for the telephone and <u>dials</u> a number.

Forward planning from a time in the past

4.66 There are several ways of talking about an event that was in the future at a particular time in the past, or that was expected to occur. These are described in the following paragraphs.

events planned in the past

4.67 The **past progressive** can be used to talk about events planned in the past, especially with some common verbs such as *come* and *go*.

Four of them <u>were coming</u> for Sunday lunch.
Her daughter <u>was going</u> to a summer camp tomorrow.
My wife <u>was joining</u> me later with the two children.

4.68 The **past simple** of *be* can be used in structures used to express future events, such as *be going to*, *be about to*, and *be due to*. The implication is usually that the expected event has not happened or will not happen. For more information on *be going to*, see paragraph 5.233.

I thought for a moment that she <u>was going to cry</u>.
He <u>was about to raise</u> his voice at me but stopped himself.
The ship <u>was due to sail</u> the following morning.

Referring to states rather than activities

4.69 Certain verbs are mainly used in the present simple or past simple rather than the present progressive or past progressive. These are called **stative verbs**. The most common stative verbs are listed in the Reference section. They include verbs that refer to lasting emotions and mental states, such as *love*, *like*, *want* and *know*; verbs that refer to the senses, such as *see* and *hear*; and verbs that refer to permanent states, such as *keep*, *fit* and *belong*.

Do you <u>like</u> football?
I <u>want</u> to come with you.
Where <u>do you keep</u> your keys?
Then I <u>heard</u> a noise.

Generally, these sentences cannot be expressed as, for example, *Are you liking football?*, *I'm wanting to come with you*, *Where are you keeping your keys?* or *Then I was hearing a noise.*

 However, a few of these verbs are sometimes used with present and past progressive forms, particularly in informal spoken English. You can use the progressive form with these verbs when you want to emphasize that a state is new or temporary, or when you want to focus on the present moment.

Rachel <u>is loving</u> one benefit of the job – the new clothes.

I'm liking grapes these days too.
I'm wanting the film to be deliberately old-fashioned.

Some people think this usage is incorrect, and it is usually avoided in formal texts.

Here is a list of verbs that are traditionally considered to be stative verbs, but that are sometimes used with present and past progressive forms:

forget	imagine	like	remember
guess	lack	love	want

You can use the present perfect progressive or past perfect progressive with some stative verbs in both formal and informal contexts.

I've been wanting to speak to you about this for some time.
John has been keeping birds for about three years now.
Then she heard it. The sound she had been hearing in her head for weeks.

Using time adverbials to indicate past, present, or future

4.70 In many statements, it is the time adverbial rather than the verb form that carries the time reference.

For example, a common use is to put time adverbials that normally refer to future time with the present simple or present progressive when it is used to refer to future actions. They can also be used with references to the future that are made in the past.

The company celebrates its 50th anniversary this year.
After all, you're coming back next week.
The farmer just laughed and rode away. So the next week I tried my luck at another farm.
We arranged to meet in three weeks' time.

The adverbs *now*, *today*, *tonight*, and expressions involving *this* refer to a period of time that includes the present moment. They are used fairly commonly with all verb forms. This is because an event can be located before, during, or after the time specified by the verb form.

I was now in a Scottish regiment.
Your boss will now have no alternative but to go to his superiors and explain the situation.
One of my children wrote to me today.
I will ski no more today.
It's dark today.
'I went to the doctor this morning,' she said.
He won't be able to fight this Friday.
I'm doing my ironing this afternoon.

referring to an earlier or a later time

4.71 If you want to refer to time that follows a particular event or period of time, you use an adverb such as *soon* or *later*. You can use an adverb such as *beforehand* or *earlier* to refer to time that preceded a particular period of time or an event.

Sita was delighted with the house and soon began to look on it as home.
It'll have to be replaced soon.
He later settled in Peddle, a small town near Grahamstown.
I'll explain later.
I was very nervous beforehand.

You'll be having a bath and going to the hairdresser's beforehand.
She had seen him only five hours earlier.

This type of time reference is common with past and future forms. It is sometimes used with present forms when they are used to refer to past, future, or habitual actions.

Sometimes I know beforehand what I'm going to talk about.
I remember the next day at school going round asking the boys if they'd ever seen a ghost.
But afterwards, as you read on, you relate back to it.

Here is a list of adverbials that are used to refer to time in a relative way:

afterwards	suddenly	the week after
at once	within minutes	the month after
before long	within the hour	the year after
eventually	~	~
finally	the next day	beforehand
immediately	the next week	early
in a moment	the next month	earlier
instantly	the next year	earlier on
later	the following day	in advance
later on	the following week	late
presently	the following month	one day
shortly	the following year	on time
soon	the day after	punctually

Note that in this list *presently* means *soon*.

You can use *early* to show that something happens before the expected or planned time, and *late* to indicate that it happens after that time. *On time* and *punctually* are used to show that something happens at the planned time.

These adverbs come after the verb or at the end of the clause.

Tired out, he had gone to bed early.
If you get to work early, you can get a lot done.
He had come to the political arena late, at the age of 62.
We went quite late in the afternoon.
If Atkinson phoned on time, he'd be out of the house in well under an hour.
He arrived punctually.

With *early* and *late* you can also use the comparative forms *earlier* and *later*.

I woke earlier than usual.
Later, the dealer saw that it had been sold.

Note that *early*, *late*, and *on time* are also used after linking verbs.

The door bell rang. Barbara was appalled. 'They're early.'
The Paris train was slightly late.
What time is it now? This bus is usually on time.

For more information on **linking verbs**, see paragraphs 3.126 to 3.181.

4.72 You can also specify a time by relating it to an event, using a qualifying expression or a relative clause after the time adverbial.

I didn't sleep well the night before the prosecution.
I called him the day I got back.

4.73   You can also use some prepositions to relate events to each other, or to particular periods of time. These prepositions are listed in paragraph 4.100, and there is a full explanation in paragraphs 4.103 to 4.108.

After the war, he returned to teaching.
Joseph had been married prior to his marriage to Mary.
Wages have fallen during the last two months.

necessary time

4.74   If you want to refer to a *necessary time*, beyond which an event will no longer be relevant, useful, or successful, you can use *in time*.

I had to walk fast to reach the restaurant in time.
He leapt back, in time to dodge the train.

If something happens before the necessary time, you can use *too early*, and if it happens after the necessary time, you can use *too late*.

Today they grow up too early.
It's much too early to assess the community service scheme.
They arrived too late for the information to be any good.
It's too late to change that now.

previously mentioned time

4.75   If the time you are referring to in the past or future has already been mentioned, you can use the adverb *then*.

We kept three monkeys then.
We were all so patriotic then.
It'll be too late then.

To be more specific, you can use *that* with the name of a day, month, season, and so on, or with a general time word.

William didn't come in that Tuesday.
So many people will be pursuing other activities that night.

Emphasizing the unexpected: continuing, stopping, or not happening

4.76   If you want to comment on the existence of the relationship between past, present, and future situations, you can use one of the following adverbials:

already	any more	no longer	still	up to now
any longer	as yet	so far	up till now	yet

still for existing situations

4.77   If you want to say that a situation exists up to the present time, you use *still*. If you use *be* as a main verb or an auxiliary verb, you put *still* after *be* or the auxiliary. If you use any simple verb except *be* you put *still* in front of the verb. *Still* often suggests that the continuation of the situation is surprising or undesirable.

It's a marvel that I'm still alive to tell the tale.
Male prejudice still exists in certain quarters.

Years had passed and they were still paying off their debts.

In negative statements that use the *n't* contraction, *still* is placed in front of *be* or the auxiliary.

We've been working on it for over two years now. And it still isn't finished.
We still don't know where we're going.

still for expected situations

4.78 You can also use *still* in front of a *to*-infinitive to say that something has not happened yet, although it is expected to, or you feel that it should.

The Government had still to agree on the provisions of the bill.
The problems were still to come.
There are many other questions still to be answered.

Still is not used in negative statements in this way; see paragraph 4.79 for a similar use of *yet*.

yet for expected situations

4.79 If you want to indicate that something has not happened up to the present time, but is likely to happen in the future, you use *yet* with a negative. *Yet* usually comes at the end of the clause.

We don't know the terms yet.
I haven't set any work yet. I suppose I shall some day.
They haven't heard yet.

If you want to sound more emphatic, you can put *yet* before a simple verb or after the auxiliary and negative word.

No one yet knows exactly what it means.
Her style had not yet matured.

Yet can also be used in questions, where it is usually put at the end of the clause.

Has she had the baby yet?
Has Mr. Harris arrived yet?

In American English, when asking whether something has happened, it is more usual to use the past simple with *yet*.

Did you eat yet?
Did the kids see that movie yet?

4.80 You can also use *yet* in affirmative statements to say that something that is expected has not happened up to the present time. In this case, *yet* is followed by a *to*-infinitive clause.

The true history of art in post-war America is yet to be written.
He had yet to attempt to put principles into practice.

4.81 *Yet* is also used in affirmative statements with superlatives to show that the statement applies up to the present, but may not apply in the future. *Yet* normally comes at the end of the clause.

This is the best museum we've visited yet.
Mr. Fowler said that February had produced the best results yet.
This is the biggest and best version yet.

likely change

4.82   If you want to say that a situation that has existed up to the present time may change in the future, you can use *as yet*, *so far*, *up to now*, or *up till now*. They are normally placed either at the beginning or the end of the clause. They are also occasionally placed after an auxiliary verb.

> *As yet*, *no group has claimed responsibility for the attack.*
> *Only Mother knows as yet.*
> *So far, the terms of the treaty have been carried out according to schedule.*
> *You've done well so far, Mrs Rutland.*
> *Up till now, the most extraordinary remark I remember was made by you.*
> *...something he had up to now been reluctant to provide.*
> *It's been quiet so far.*
> *You haven't once up till now come into real contact with our authorities.*

Note that these expressions can be used in affirmative and negative statements.

a past situation that has stopped existing

4.83   If you want to say that a past situation does not exist in the present, you can use *no longer*, or a negative with *any longer* or *any more*.

> *She was no longer content with a handful of coins.*
> *They didn't know any longer what was funny and what was entertaining.*
> *They don't live together any more.*

already for emphasizing occurrence

4.84   If you want to emphasize that a situation exists, rather than not yet having occurred, you use *already*. It is usually put in front of any simple verb except *be*, or after *be* as a main verb, or following an auxiliary verb.

> *The energy already exists in the ground.*
> *Senegal already has a well established film industry.*
> *He was just a year younger than Rudolph, but was already as tall and much stockier.*
> *My watch says nine o'clock. And it's already too hot to sleep.*
> *Britain is already exporting a little coal.*
> *We have already advertised your post in the papers.*

In American English, when stating that something has happened, it is more usual to use the past simple with *already*.

> *We already advertised your post in the papers.*
> *The kids already saw that movie.*

You can put *already* at the beginning or the end of the clause for emphasis.

> *Already robberies and lootings have increased.*
> *I was happy for her; she looked better already.*

Already is not often used with the past simple, except with the verbs *be*, *have*, and *know*.

Note that *already* cannot normally be used in negative statements, but can be used in negative *if*-clauses, negative questions, and relative clauses.

> *Refer certain types of death to the coroner if this has not already been done.*
> *Those who have not already left are being advised to do so.*
> *What does it show us that we haven't already felt?*

Time adverbials and prepositional phrases

Specific times

4.85 Specific time adverbials are used after the verb *be* when you want to state the current time, day, or year.

> 'Well what time is it now?' – 'It's one o'clock'.
> It was a perfect May morning.
> Six weeks isn't all that long ago, it's January.

They are also often used in prepositional phrases to say when something happened, or when it is expected to happen.

> I got there at about 8 o'clock.
> The submarine caught fire on Friday morning.
> That train gets in at 1800 hours.

clock times

4.86 Clock times are usually expressed in terms of hours and parts of an hour or minutes, for example *one o'clock, five minutes past one, one twenty, half past one*. The day is usually divided into two sets of twelve hours, so it is sometimes necessary to specify which set you mean by adding *a.m.*, *p.m.*, or a prepositional phrase such as *in the morning* or *in the evening*.

In many official contexts, a twenty-four hour system is used.

If the hour is known, only the minutes are specified: *five past, ten to, quarter to, half past* and so on. *Midday* and *noon* are occasionally used.

times of the day

4.87 The most frequently used words for periods of the day are *morning, afternoon, evening,* and *night*. There are also some words that refer to the rising and setting of the sun, such as *dusk* and *sunset*, and others that refer to mealtimes.

> On a warm, cloudy evening, Colin went down to the river.
> They seem to be working from dawn to dusk.
> Most of the trouble comes outside the classroom, at break-time and dinnertime.

Here is a list of words that are used to talk about periods of the day:

morning	daybreak	~	teatime
afternoon	first light	daytime	dinnertime
evening	sunrise	night-time	suppertime
night	dusk	breakfast-time	bedtime
~	sunset	break-time	
dawn	nightfall	lunchtime	

naming days

4.88 The seven days of the week are **proper nouns:**

Monday	Wednesday	Friday	Sunday
Tuesday	Thursday	Saturday	

Saturday and Sunday are often referred to as *the weekend*, and the other days as *weekdays*.

A few days in the year have special names, for example:

New Year's Day	Fourth of July	Christmas Day
Valentine's Day	Labor Day	Boxing Day
Presidents' Day	Halloween	New Year's Eve
Good Friday	Thanksgiving	
Easter Monday	Christmas Eve	

You can also name a day by giving its date using an **ordinal** number.

'When does your term end?' – 'First of July'.
The Grand Prix is to be held here on the 18th July.
Her season of films continues until October the ninth.

You can omit the month if it is clear from the context which month you are referring to.

So Monday will be the seventeenth.
St Valentine's Day is on the fourteenth.

There is more information about ordinals in the Reference section.

months, seasons, and dates

4.89   The twelve months of the year are **proper nouns:**

January	April	July	October
February	May	August	November
March	June	September	December

There are four seasons: *spring*, *summer*, *autumn* (usually *fall* in American English) and *winter*. *Springtime*, *summertime*, and *wintertime* are also used.

Some periods of the year have special names; for example, *Christmas*, *Easter*, and *the New Year*.

years, decades, and centuries

4.90   Years are referred to in English by numbers. When you are speaking, you refer to years before 2000 as *nineteen sixty-seven* (1967), or *seventeen hundred* (1700), for example.

...the eleventh of January, 1967.
A second conference was held in February 1988.
My mother died in 1945.

When you are speaking, you refer to years between 2000 and 2009 as *two thousand* (2000) or *two thousand and eight* (2008), for example.

Years after 2009 are said as either *two thousand and ten* (2010), *two thousand and eleven* (2011), etc. or as *twenty ten* (2010), *twenty eleven* (2011), etc.

To refer to periods longer than a year, decades (ten years) and centuries (a hundred years) are used. Decades start with a year ending in zero and finish with a year ending in nine: *the 1960s* (1960 to 1969), *the 1820s* (1820 to 1829). If the century is already known, it can be omitted: *the 20s, the twenties, the Twenties*.

To be more specific, for example in historical dates, *AD* is added before or after the numbers for years or centuries after Jesus is believed to have been born: *1650 AD, AD 1650, AD 1650-53, 1650-53 AD*. Some writers who prefer to avoid referring to religion use *CE*, which stands for *the Common Era*: *1650 CE*.

BC (which stands for *Before Christ*) is added after the numbers for years or centuries before Jesus is believed to have been born: *1500 BC, 15–1200 BC*. An alternative abbreviation that does not refer to religion is *BCE*, which stands for *Before the Common Era*.

Centuries start with a year ending in two zeroes and finish with a year ending in two nines. Ordinals are used to refer to them. The *first century* was from *0 AD to 99 AD*, the *second century* was *100–199 AD*, and so on, so the period *1800–1899 AD* was the *nineteenth century* and the current century is the *twenty-first century* (*2000–2099 AD*). Centuries can also be written using numbers: *the 21st century*.

at for specific times

4.91 If you want to say when something happens, you use *at* with clock times, periods of the year, and periods of the day except for *morning*, *evening*, *afternoon*, and *daytime*.

> Our train went *at 2.25*.
> I got up *at eight o'clock*.
> The train should arrive *at a quarter to one*.
> We go to church *at Easter* and *Christmas*.
> I went down and fetched her back *at the weekend*.
> On Tuesday evening, just *at dusk*, Brody had received an anonymous phone call.
> He regarded it as his duty to come and read to me *at bedtime*.
> *At night* we kept them shut up in a wire enclosure.
> Let the fire burn out now. Who would see smoke *at night-time* anyway?

You can also use *at* with *time* and similar words such as *moment* and *juncture* and with units of clock time such as *hour* and *minute*.

> General de Gaulle duly attended the military ceremony *at the appointed time*.
> It was *at this juncture* that his luck temporarily deserted him.
> If I could have done it *at that minute* I would have killed him.
> There were no lights *at this hour*, and roads, bungalows, and gardens lay quiet.

at for relating events

4.92 You can also use *at* when you want to relate the time of one event to another event such as a party, journey, election, and so on.

> I had first met Kruger *at a party* at the British Embassy.
> She represented the Association *at the annual meeting* of the American Medical Association in Chicago.
> It is to be reopened *at the annual conference* in three weeks' time.

4.93 *At* is also used with ages, stages of development, and points within a larger period of time.

> *At the age of twenty*, she married another Spanish dancer.
> He left school *at seventeen*.
> *At an early stage of the war* the British Government began recruiting a team of top mathematicians and electronics experts.
> We were due to return to the United Kingdom *at the beginning of March*.

in for periods of time

4.94   If you want to mention the period of time in which something happens, you use *in* with centuries, years, seasons, months, and the periods of the day *morning*, *afternoon*, and *evening*. You also use *in* with *daytime* and *night-time*.

> *In the sixteenth century* there were three tennis courts.
> It's true that we expected a great deal *in the sixties*.
> Americans visiting Sweden *in the early 1950s* were astounded by its cleanliness.
> If you were to go on holiday on the continent *in wintertime* what sport could you take part in?
> To be in Cornwall at any time is a pleasure; to be here *in summer* is a bonus.
> It's a lot cooler *in the autumn*.
> She will preside over the annual meeting of the Court *in December*.
> *In September* I travelled to California to see the finished film.
> I'll ring the agent *in the morning*.
> Well, she does come in to clean the rooms *in the day-time*.

Note that if *morning*, *afternoon*, and *evening* are used with a modifier or a following phrase or clause, you use *on*. See paragraph 4.96 for details.

in for specific time

4.95   *In* is also used when you want to specify a period of time, minutes, hours, days, and so on, using an **ordinal**.

> Vehicle sales *in the first eight months* of the year have plunged by 24.4 per cent.
> ...*in the early hours* of the morning.

In is also used with some other nouns referring to events and periods of time.

> My father was killed *in the war*.
> Everyone does unusual jobs *in wartime*.
> *In winter*, we tend to get up later.
> Two people came to check my room *in my absence*.

Ordinals are explained in paragraphs 2.232 to 2.239.

on for short periods of time

4.96   If you want to mention the day when something happens, you use *on*. You can do this with named days, with days referred to by ordinals, and with days referred to by a special term such as *birthday* or *anniversary*.

> I'll send the cheque round *on Monday*.
> Everybody went to church *on Christmas Day*.
> I hear you have bingo *on Wednesday*.
> Pentonville Prison was set up *on Boxing Day*, 1842.
> He was born *on 3 April 1925* at 40 Grosvenor Road.
> ...the grey suit Elsa had bought for him *on his birthday*.
> Many of Eisenhower's most cautious commanders were even prepared to risk attack *on the eighth or ninth*.
> ...addressing Parliament *on the 36th anniversary* of his country's independence.

You can use *the* with named days for emphasis or contrast, and *a* to indicate any day of that name.

> He died *on the Friday* and was buried *on the Sunday*.
> We get a lot of calls *on a Friday*.

You also use *on* with *morning, afternoon, evening*, and *night* when they are modified or when they are followed by extra information in the form of a phrase or a clause.

...at 2.30 p.m. <u>on a calm afternoon</u>.
There was another important opening <u>on the same evening</u>.
Tickets will be available <u>on the morning of the performance</u>.
It's terribly good of you to turn out <u>on a night like this</u>.

on for longer periods of time

4.97 *On* is also used with words referring to travel such as *journey, trip, voyage, flight*, and *way* to say when something happened.

But <u>on that journey</u>, for the first time, Luce's faith in the eventual outcome was shaken.
Eileen was accompanying her father to visit friends made <u>on a camping trip</u> the year before.

on for subsequent events

4.98 *On* can be used in a slightly formal way with nouns and *-ing* forms referring to actions or activities to show that one event occurs after another.

I shall bring the remaining seven hundred pounds <u>on my return</u> in eleven days.

ordering of time adverbials

4.99 On the few occasions when people have to specify a time and date exactly, for example in legal English or formal documents, the usual order is: clock time, followed by period of day, day of the week, and date.

...at eight o'clock on the morning of 29 October 1618.
...on the night of Thursday July 16.

Non-specific times

approximate times

4.100 If you want to be less precise about when something happened, you can use a word like *around* or *about*.

At <u>about</u> four o'clock in the morning, we were awoken by a noise.
The device that exploded at <u>around</u> midnight on Wednesday severely damaged the fourth-floor bar.
The supply of servants continued until <u>about</u> 1950, then abruptly dried up.
The attack began <u>shortly before</u> dawn.

Here is a list of words and expressions that you can use if you want to be less precise about when something happened:

about	just after	round about	soon after
almost	just before	shortly after	thereabouts
around	nearly	shortly before	

About, almost, around, nearly, and *round about* are usually used with clock times or years. With *about, around*, and *round about*, the preposition *at* can often be omitted in informal English.

Then quite suddenly, <u>round about</u> midday, my mood began to change.
<u>About</u> nine o'clock he went out to the kitchen.

It is also possible to use prepositions to relate events to less specific points or periods of time, for example when the exact time of an event is not known, or when events happen gradually, continuously, or several times.

He developed central chest pain <u>during the night</u>.
For, also <u>over the summer</u>, his book had come out.

Here is a list of prepositions that are used to relate events to a non-specific time:

after	by	following	prior to
before	during	over	

❗ BE CAREFUL

4.101 *Almost* or *nearly* can only be used after the verb *be*.

4.102 You can also use *or thereabouts* after the time adverbial.

> *Back in 1975 <u>or thereabouts</u> someone lent me an article about education.*
> *...at four o'clock <u>or thereabouts</u>.*

during for periods of time

4.103 *During* can be used instead of *in* with periods of the day, months, seasons, years, decades, and centuries.

> *We try to keep people informed by post <u>during September</u>.*
> *She heated the place <u>during the winter</u> with a huge wood furnace.*
> *<u>During 1973</u> an Anti-Imperialist Alliance was formed.*
> *<u>During the Sixties</u> various levies were imposed.*
> *<u>During the seventh century</u> incendiary weapons were invented.*
> *They used to spend the whole Sunday at chapel but most of them behaved shockingly <u>during the week</u>.*

4.104 *During* is used with most event nouns to show that one event takes place while another is occurring.

> *<u>During his stay in prison</u>, he has written many essays and poems.*
> *...trying to boost police morale <u>during a heated battle with rioters</u>.*
> *The young princes were protected from press intrusion <u>during their education</u>.*
> *Some families live in the kitchen <u>during a power cut</u>.*
> *<u>During the journey</u> I came to like and respect them.*

❗ BE CAREFUL

4.105 *During the week* means on weekdays, in contrast to the weekend.

over for events

4.106 *Over* can be used with *winter*, *summer*, and special periods of the year to show that an event occurred throughout the period or at an unspecified time during it.

> *...to help keep their families going <u>over the winter</u>.*
> *My friends had a marvellous time <u>over the New Year</u>.*

Over is also used when referring to a period of time immediately before or after the time of speaking or the time being talked about.

> *The number will increase considerably <u>over the next decade</u>.*
> *They have been doing all they can <u>over the past twenty-four hours</u>.*

We packed up the things I had accumulated over the last four years.

Over can be used with meals and items of food or drink to show that something happens while people are eating or drinking.

Davis said he wanted to read it over lunch.
Can we discuss it over a cup of coffee?

relating events and times

4.107 You can also be more general by stating the relationship between an event and a period of time or specific point in time.

Before, *prior to*, and *after* are used to relate events to a time.

She gets up before six.
If you're stuck, come back and see me before Thursday.
...the construction of warships by the major powers prior to 1914.
City Music Hall is going to close down after Easter.
He will announce his plans after the holidays.

They can also be used to relate one event to another.

I was in a bank for a while before the war.
She gave me much helpful advice prior to my visit to Turkey.
Jack left after breakfast.
He was killed in a car accident four years after their marriage.
After much discussion, they had decided to take the coin to a jeweller.

Following, *previous to* and *subsequent to* can also be used with events.

He has regained consciousness following a stroke.
He suggests that Ross was prompted previous to the parade.
The testimony and description of one witness would be supplied prior to the interview; those of the other two subsequent to it.

order of events

4.108 *Before* and *after* can also be used to show the order of events when the same person does two actions or two people do the same action.

I should have talked about that before anything else.
He knew Nell would probably be home before him.
I do the floor after the washing-up.

You can also sometimes use *earlier than* or *later than*.

Smiling develops earlier than laughing.

events that happen at the same time

4.109 To indicate that two or more events happen at the same time, the adverbs *together* and *simultaneously*, or the adverbials *at the same time* and *at once* can be used:

Everything had happened together.
His fear and his hate grew simultaneously.
Can you love two women at the same time?
I can't be everywhere at once.

linking adverbs

4.110 You can also show what order things happen in using adverbs such as *first, next,* and *finally. Simultaneously* and *at the same time* are used in a similar way to link clauses. This is dealt with in paragraph 10.53.

by for specific time

4.111 *By* is used to emphasize that an event occurs at some time before a specific time, but not later. *By* is also used to indicate that a process is completed or reaches a particular stage not later than a specific time.

> *By eleven o'clock,* Brody was back in his office.
> The theory was that *by Monday* their tempers would have cooled.
> *By next week,* there will be no supplies left.
> Do you think we'll get to the top of this canyon *by tomorrow?*
> *By now* the moon was up.
> But *by then* he was bored with the project.

Extended uses of time adverbials

4.112 Time adverbials can be used after the noun phrase to specify events or periods of time.

> I'm afraid the meeting *this afternoon* exhausted me.
> The sudden death of his father *on 17 November 1960* was not a surprise.
> ...until I started to recall the years *after the Second World War.*
> No admissions are permitted in the hour *before closing time.*

Clock times, periods of the day, days of the week, months, dates, seasons, special periods of the year, years, decades, and centuries can be used as modifiers before the noun phrase to specify things.

> Every morning he would set off right after the *eight o'clock* news.
> Castle was usually able to catch the *six thirty-five* train from Euston.
> He boiled the kettle for his *morning* tea.
> He learned that he had missed the *Monday* flight.
> I had *summer* clothes and *winter* clothes.
> Ash had spent the *Christmas* holidays at Pelham Abbas.

Possessive forms can also be used.

> ...a discussion of *the day's events.*
> It was Jim Griffiths, who knew nothing of *the morning's happenings.*
> The story will appear in *tomorrow's paper.*
> *This week's batch of government statistics* added to the general confusion over the state of the economy.

Frequency and duration

4.113 Here is a list of units of time that are used when you are showing how often something happens, or how long it lasts or takes:

moment	hour	week	year
second	day	fortnight	decade
minute	night	month	century

Fortnight is used only in the singular. *Moment* is not used with numbers because it does not refer to a precise period of time, so you cannot say for example *It took five moments*.

 Fortnight is not used in American English, where *two weeks* is used instead.

Words for periods of the day, days of the week, months of the year, and seasons are also used, such as *morning*, *Friday*, *July*, and *winter*.

Clock times may also be used.

Talking about how frequently something happens

4.114 Some adverbials show approximately how many times something happens:

again and again	ever	never	regularly
a lot	frequently	normally	repeatedly
all the time	from time to time	occasionally	seldom
always	hardly ever	often	sometimes
constantly	infrequently	over and over	sporadically
continually	intermittently	periodically	usually
continuously	much	rarely	

I never did my homework on time.
Sometimes I wish I was back in Africa.
We were always being sent home.
He laughed a lot.

Never is a negative adverb.

She never goes abroad.

Ever is only used in questions, negative clauses, and *if*-clauses.

Have you ever been to a concert?

Much is usually used with *not*.

The men didn't talk much to each other.

Some adverbs of frequency such as *often* and *frequently* can also be used in the comparative and superlative.

Disasters can be prevented more often than in the past.
I preached much more often than that.
They cried for their mothers less often than might have been expected.
...the mistakes that we make most frequently.

 USAGE NOTE

4.115 To show how many times something happens, you can use a specific number, *several*, or *many* followed by *times*.

We had to ask three times.
It's an experience I've repeated many times since.
He carefully aimed his rifle and fired several times.

If the number you are using is *one* you use *once* (not *one time*) in this structure. If it is *two* you can use *twice*.

I've been out with him once, that's all.
The car broke down twice.

If something happens regularly, you can say how many times it happens within a period of time by adding *a* and a word referring to a period of time.

The group met <u>once a week</u>.
You only have a meal <u>three times a day</u>.
The committee meets <u>twice a year</u>.

You can also use an adverb of frequency such as *once* with a unit of time preceded by *every* to say that something happens a specified number of times regularly within that unit of time.

The average Briton moves house <u>once every seven and a half years</u>.
We meet <u>twice every Sunday</u>.
<u>Three times every day</u>, he would come to the kiosk to check that we were all right.

If an event happens regularly during a specific period of the day, you can use the period of day instead of *times*:

I used to go in <u>three mornings a week</u>.
He was going out <u>five nights a week</u>.

A regular rate or quantity can also be expressed by adding *a* and a general time word. *Per* is sometimes used instead of *a*, especially in technical contexts.

He earns about £1000 a week.
I was only getting <u>three hours of sleep a night</u>.
...rising upwards at the rate of <u>300 feet per second</u>.
He hurtles through the air at <u>600 miles per hour</u>.

estimating frequency

4.116 If you want to be less precise about how frequently something happens, you can use one of the following words or expressions: *almost*, *about*, *nearly*, *or so*, *or less*, and *or more*.

You can use *almost* and *about* in front of *every*.

In the last month of her pregnancy, we went out <u>almost</u> every evening.

You can also use *almost* in front of *-ly* time adverbs derived from general time words, for example *monthly*, *weekly* and *daily*.

Small scale confrontations occur <u>almost</u> daily in many states.

Or so, *or less*, and *or more* are used after frequency expressions, but not after adverbs of frequency.

Every hour <u>or so</u>, my shoulders would tighten.
If the delay is two hours <u>or more</u>, the whole cost of the journey should be refunded.

regular intervals

4.117 If you want to say that something happens at regular intervals, you can use *every* followed by either a general or a specific unit of time. *Each* is sometimes used instead of *every*.

We'll go hunting <u>every day</u>.
You get a lump sum and you get a pension <u>each week</u>.
Some people write out a new address book <u>every January</u>.

Every can also be used with a number and the plural of the unit of time.

<u>Every five minutes</u> the phone would ring.

The regular or average rate or quantity of something can also be expressed using *every* and *each*.

One fighter jet was shot down every hour.
...the 300,000 garments the factory produces each year.

ⓘ USAGE NOTE

4.118 If something happens during one period of time but not during the next period, then happens again during the next, and so on, you can use *every other* followed by a unit of time or a specific time word. *Every second* is sometimes used instead of *every other*.

We wrote to our parents every other day.
Their local committees are usually held every other month.
He used to come and take them out every other Sunday.
It seemed easier to shave only every second day.

Prepositional phrases with *alternate* and a plural time word can also be used.

On alternate Sunday nights, I tell the younger children a story.
Just do some exercises on alternate days at first.

particular occurrences of an event

4.119 The adverbs *first*, *next*, and *last* are used to show the stage at which an event takes place.

First, *the first time*, and *for the first time* can indicate the first occurrence of an event.

He was, I think, in his early sixties when I first encountered him.
They had seen each other first a week before, outside this hotel.
...the tactical war games which were first fought in Ancient Greece.
It rained heavily twice while I was out. The first time I sheltered under a tree, but the second time I walked through it.
For the first time Anne Marie felt frightened.

The repetition of an event or situation that has not happened for a long time can be indicated by using *for the first time* with *in* and the plural form of a general time word.

He was happy and relaxed for the first time in years.

A future occurrence is indicated by *next time* or *the next time*.

Don't do it again. I might not forgive you next time.
The next time I come here, I'm going to be better.

The use of *next* with statements referring to the future is described in paragraph 4.63.

The most recent occurrence of an event can be indicated by using *last* as an adverb or the noun phrases *last time* or *the last time*.

He seemed to have grown a lot since he last wore it.
He could not remember when he had last eaten.
When did you last see him?
You did so well last time.

The final occurrence can be indicated by *for the last time*.

For the last time he waved to the three friends who watched from above.

The use of *last* in statements about the past is described in paragraph 4.41.

You can also use *before*, *again*, and noun phrases with an ordinal and *time* to say whether an event is a first occurrence, or one that has happened before.

You can use *before* with a perfect form of a verb to show whether something is happening for the first time or whether it is a repeated occurrence.

I've never been in a policeman's house before.
He's done it before.

The adverb *again* is used to talk about a second or subsequent occurrence of an event. Ordinals can be used with *time*, in noun phrases or in more formal prepositional phrases with *for*, to specify a particular occurrence of a repeated event.

Someone rang the front door bell. He stood and listened and heard it ring again and then a third time.
We have no reliable information about that yet, he found himself saying for the third time.

-ly time adverbs

4.120 Some general time words can be changed into adverbs by adding *-ly* and used to show the frequency of an event.

hourly	weekly	monthly	yearly
daily	fortnightly	quarterly	

Note the spelling of *daily*. The adverb *annually* and the adjective *annual* have the same meaning as *yearly*.

It was suggested that we give each child an allowance yearly or monthly to cover all he or she spends.
She phones me up hourly.

The same words can be used as adjectives.

To this, we add a yearly allowance of £65.00 towards repairs.
The media gave us hourly updates.
They had a long-standing commitment to making a weekly cash payment to mothers.

prepositional phrases

4.121 Prepositional phrases with plural forms of specific time words can also be used to indicate frequency. For example, *on* is used with days of the week; *during* and *at* are used with *weekends*.

We've had teaching practice on Tuesdays and lectures on Thursdays.
She does not need help with the children during weekends.
We see each other at weekends.

 In American English, and in informal British English, you can use the plural forms of specific time words without *on*.

She only works Wednesdays and Fridays.
Thursday mornings I volunteer at the local senior center.
His radio program broadcasts Friday nights at nine.

In is used with periods of the day, except *night*.

I can't work full time. I only work in the afternoons, I have lectures in the mornings.
Harry Truman loved to sit in an old rocking chair in the evenings and face the lawns behind the White House.

development and regular occurrence

4.122 To show that something develops gradually, or happens at regular intervals, you can use a general time word with *by* followed by the same general time word.

She was getting older year by year, and lonelier, and more ridiculous.
Millions of citizens follow, day by day, the unfolding of the drama.

Gradual development can also be indicated by the adverbs *increasingly* and *progressively*.

...the computers and information banks on which our world will increasingly depend.
His conduct became increasingly eccentric.
As disposable income rises, people become progressively less concerned with price.

Talking about how long something lasts

4.123 The following section explains ways of showing how long something lasts or takes.

Some adverbs and adverbial expressions are used to show how long an event or state lasts. Here is a list of adverbs that are used to show duration:

always	forever	long	permanently
briefly	indefinitely	overnight	temporarily

She glanced briefly at Lucas Simmonds.
You won't live forever.
The gates are kept permanently closed.

Briefly and *permanently* can be used in the comparative.

This new revelation had much the same outward effect, though more briefly.
This is something I would like to do more permanently.

The form *long* is only used as an adverb in negatives and questions.

I haven't been in England long.
How long does it take on the train?

In affirmative clauses, it is used in expressions such as *a long time* and prepositional phrases such as *for a long time*. However, the comparative and superlative forms *longer* and *longest* can be used in affirmative and negative clauses.

Then of course you'll go with Parry. She's been your friend longer.
I've been thinking about it a lot longer than you.
She remained the longest.

In affirmative and negative if-clauses, you can use *for long*.

If she's away for long we won't be able to wait.

prepositional phrases

4.124 However, prepositional phrases are more commonly used. The following prepositions are used in adverbials of duration:

after	for	in	throughout	until
before	from	since	to	

The prepositional object can be a noun phrase referring to a specific period of time. This can be in the singular after the determiner *a* (or *one* for emphasis), or in the plural after a number or quantity expression.

The noun phrase can also refer to an indefinite period, for example expressions such as *a long time*, *a short while*, *a while*, or *ages*, or plural time words such as *hours*.

for *for length of time*

4.125 The preposition *for* indicates how long something continues to happen.

Is he still thinking of going away to Italy for a month?
The initial battle continued for an hour.
This precious happy time lasted for a month or two.
For the next week, she did not contact him.
We were married for fifteen years.
I didn't speak for a long time.
She would have liked to sit for a while and think.

You use *the* instead of *a* when the period of time is already known, with seasons, periods of the day, and *weekend*, or when you modify the time word with words like *past*, *coming*, *following*, *next*, *last*, or an **ordinal**.

Tell Aunt Elizabeth you're off for the day.
We've been living together for the past year.
For the first month or two I was bullied constantly.
For the next few days he had to stay in bed.
Put them in cold storage for the winter.
I said I'm off to Brighton for the weekend.

Remember that you do not use a determiner with special periods of the year.

At least come for Christmas.

4.126 *For* can also be used with specific time adverbials to show the time when something is to be used, not how long it takes or lasts.

Everything was placed exactly where I wanted it for the morning.

4.127 *For* can also be used in negative statements when you want to say that something need not or will not happen until a certain period of time has passed. *Yet* is often added.

It won't be ready to sail for another three weeks.
I don't have to decide for a month yet.

for *for emphasis*

4.128 *For* is used with a plural noun phrase to emphasize how long something lasts.

Settlers have been coming here for centuries.
I don't think he's practised much for years.
I've been asking you about these doors for months.

ⓘ USAGE NOTE

4.129 You can also use a general time word with *after* followed by the same general time word to emphasize that a state continues for a long time or that an action is repeated continuously for a long time.

I wondered what kept her in Paris decade after decade.
They can go on making losses, year after year, without fearing that they will go bust.

in and within for end of a period

4.130 *In* is used to indicate that something happens or will happen before the end of a certain period of time. In more formal English *within* is used.

> *Can we get to the airport in an hour?*
> *That coat must have cost you more than I earn in a year.*
> *The face of a city can change completely in a year.*
> *They should get the job finished within a few days.*

4.131 *In* and *within* are also used to show that something only took or takes a short time.

> *The clouds evaporated in seconds.*
> *What an expert can do in minutes may take you hours to accomplish.*
> *Within a few months, the barnyard had been abandoned.*

for and in with general or specific time

4.132 *For* and *in* can be used in negative statements to say that something does not happen during a period of time. You can use them in this way with specific units of time, and with more general time references.

> *He hadn't had a proper night's sleep for a month.*
> *I haven't seen a chart for forty years!*
> *The team had not heard from Stabler in a month.*
> *He hasn't slept in a month.*
> *I haven't seen him for years.*
> *Let's have a dinner party. We haven't had one in years.*
> *I haven't fired a gun in years.*

noun phrases that express duration

4.133 Note that with the verbs *last*, *wait*, and *stay*, which have duration as part of their meaning, the adverbial can be a noun phrase instead of a prepositional phrase with *for*.

> *The campaign lasts four weeks at most.*
> *His speech lasted for exactly 14 and a half minutes.*
> *'Wait a minute,' the voice said.*
> *He stayed a month, five weeks, six weeks.*

The verbs *take* and *spend* can also indicate duration but the adverbial can only be a noun phrase.

> *It took me a month to lose that feeling of being a spectator.*
> *What once took a century now took only ten months.*
> *He spent five minutes washing and shaving.*

approximate duration

4.134 If you want to be less precise about how long something lasts, you can use one of the following words or expressions: *about, almost, nearly, around, more than, less than,* and so on.

> *They've lived there for more than thirty years.*
> *They have not been allowed to form unions for almost a decade.*
> *The three of us travelled around together for about a month that summer.*
> *In less than a year, I learned enough Latin to pass the entrance exam.*
> *He had been in command of HMS Churchill for nearly a year.*

When you make a general statement about the duration of something, you can indicate the maximum period of time that it will last or take by using *up to*.

Refresher training for up to one month each year was the rule for all.

You can also use expressions such as *or so*, *or more*, *or less*, and *or thereabouts* to make the duration less specific.

He has been writing about tennis and golf for forty years or so.
Our species probably practised it for a million years or more.
...hopes which have prevailed so strongly for a century or more.

Almost, *about*, *nearly*, and *thereabouts* are also used when talking about when an event takes place; see paragraph 4.100 for details of this.

Talking about the whole of a period

4.135   If you want to emphasize that something lasts for the whole of a period of time, you can use *all* as a determiner with many general time words.

'I've been wanting to do this all day,' she said.
I've been here all night.
They said you were out all afternoon.
We've not seen them all summer.

You can also use *whole* as a modifier in front of a general time word.

It took me the whole of my first year to adjust.
...scientists who are monitoring food safety the whole time.
...people who have not worked for a whole year.

You can also use *all through*, *right through*, and *throughout* with *the* and many general time words, or with a specific decade, year, month, or special period.

Discussions and arguments continued all through the day.
Right through the summer months they are rarely out of sight.
Throughout the Sixties, man's first voyage to other worlds came closer.

Words referring to events are sometimes used instead of the time words to emphasize that something happened for the entire duration of the event.

He wore an expression of angry contempt throughout the interrogation.
A patient reported a dream that had recurred throughout her life.
All through the cruelly long journey home, he lay utterly motionless.

4.136   If you want to emphasize that something happens all the time, you can list periods of the day or seasons of the year, or mention contrasting ones.

...people coming in morning, noon, and night.
I've worn the same suit summer, winter, autumn and spring, for five years.
Thousands of slave labourers worked night and day to build the fortifications.
Ten gardeners used to work this land, winter and summer.
Each family was filmed 24/7 for six weeks.

24/7 is an abbreviation of *24 hours a day, 7 days a week*. It is used in informal English and in journalism.

Showing the start or end of a period

start time

4.137   You can also show how long a situation lasts by using prepositional phrases to give the time when it begins or the time when it ends, or both.

If you want to talk about a situation that began in the past and is continuing now, or to consider a period of it from a time in the past to the present, you use the preposition *since* with a time adverbial or an event to show when the situation began. The verb is in the present perfect.

I've been here since twelve o'clock.
I haven't had a new customer in here since Sunday.
Since January, there hasn't been any more trouble.
I haven't been out since Christmas.
The situation has not changed since 2001.
There has been no word of my friend since the revolution.

Since is also used to indicate the beginning of situations that ended in the past. The verb is in the past perfect.

I'd been working in London since January at a firm called Kendalls.
He hadn't prayed once since the morning.
I'd only had two sandwiches since breakfast.

Since can also be used with other prepositional phrases that indicate a point in time.

I haven't seen you since before the summer.

The noun phrase after *since* can sometimes refer to a person or thing rather than a time or event, especially when used with a superlative, *first*, or *only*, or with a negative.

They hadn't seen each other since Majorca.
I have never had another dog since Jonnie.
Ever since London, I've been working towards this.

4.138 The time when a situation began can also be shown by using the preposition *from* and adding the adverb *on* or *onwards*. The noun phrase can be a date, an event, or a period. The verb can be in the past simple or in a perfect form.

...the history of British industry from the mid sixties on.
From the eighteenth century on, great private palaces went up.
But from the mid-1960s onwards the rate of public welfare spending has tended to accelerate.
The family size starts to influence development from birth.
They never perceived that they themselves had forced women into this role from childhood.
...the guide who had been with us from the beginning.

4.139 You can also use the preposition *after* to give the time when a situation began.

They don't let anybody in after six o'clock.
After 1929 I concentrated on canvas work.
He'd have a number of boys to help him through the summertime but after October he'd just have the one.

end time

4.140 Similarly, if you want to say that a situation continues for some time and then stops, you can indicate the time when it stops by using the preposition *until* with a time adverbial or an event.

The school was kept open until ten o'clock five nights a week.
They danced and laughed and talked until dawn.
She walked back again and sat in her room until dinner.
I've just discovered she's only here until Sunday.
He had been willing to wait until the following summer.
Until the end of the 18th century little had been known about Persia.

Until that meeting, most of us knew very little about him.

Until can also be used in negative clauses to say that something did not or will not happen before a particular time.

We won't get them until September.
My plane does not leave until tomorrow morning.

Until is also used with other prepositional phrases that indicate a point in time.

I decided to wait until after Easter to visit John.

Some people use *till* instead of *until*, especially in informal English.

Sometimes I lie in bed till nine o'clock.

Up to and *up till* are also sometimes used, mainly before *now* and *then*.

Up to now, I have been happy with his work.
It was something he had never even considered up till now.
I had a three-wheel bike up to a few years ago but it got harder and harder to push it along.
Up to 1989, growth averaged 1 per cent.

4.141 You can also use the preposition *before* to indicate when a situation ends.

Before 1716 Cheltenham had been a small market town.

start and end times

4.142 The duration of a situation or event can be shown by saying when it begins and when it ends. You can use *from* to show when it begins and *to*, *till*, or *until* to show when it ends.

The Blitz on London began with nightly bombings from 7 September to 2 November.
They are active in the line from about January until October.
They seem to be working from dawn till dusk.

You can also use *between* and *and* instead of *from* and *to*.

The car is usually in the garage between Sunday and Thursday in winter.

 In American English, *through* is often placed between the two times:

The chat show goes out midnight through six a.m.

If you are using figures to refer to two times or years, you can separate them with a dash, instead of using *from* and *to*.

...open 10–5 weekdays, 10–6 Saturdays and 2–6 Sundays.

Using time expressions to modify nouns

4.143 You can also use time expressions involving a **cardinal number** and a general time word to modify nouns. Note that an apostrophe is added to the time word.

Four of those were sentenced to 15 days' detention.
They want to take on staff with two years' experience.

This use of cardinal numbers is described in paragraph 2.231.

4.144 Time expressions are also used as **compound adjectives** to modify countable nouns.

They all have to start off with a six-month course in German.
I arrived at the University for a three-month stint as a visiting lecturer.

Compound adjectives are explained in paragraphs 2.94 to 2.102.

Chapter 5

Varying the message: modals, negatives, and ways of forming sentences

5 Varying the message: modals, negatives, and ways of forming sentences

5.1 This chapter deals with three different ways in which the meaning of a sentence can be varied, by altering the order of words or by adding other words to the verb phrase.

Paragraphs 5.2 to 5.48 explain how to form statements, questions, orders, and suggestions.

Paragraphs 5.49 to 5.93 explain how **negative words** are used to talk about the opposite of something or the absence of something.

Paragraphs 5.94 to 5.258 explain how **modals** are used to talk about possibility, or to show the attitude of the speaker.

Statements, questions, orders, and suggestions

5.2 Sentences are used to do many different things.

The most common use is to give information.

I went to Glasgow University.
Carol was one of my sister's best friends.

Sometimes you use a sentence to obtain information, rather than to give it.

Where is my father?
What did you say to Myra?
How long have you been out of this country?

At other times you want to express an opinion, give an order, make a suggestion, or make a promise.

That's an excellent idea.
Go away, all of you.
Shall we listen to the news?
If you have any questions, I'll do my best to answer them.

When someone says or writes a sentence, they need to show what they are trying to do with it, so that it will be clear, for example, that they are asking a question and not making a statement.

`word order`

5.3 Often it is the order of words that indicates which way a sentence is being used. For example, if you say *He is Norwegian*, the word order makes it clear that you are making a statement. If you say *Is he Norwegian?*, the word order indicates that you are asking a question.

Another way of showing which way a sentence is being used is to begin it with a verb, rather than with the subject. For example, if you say *Give this book to Michael*, it is clear that you are giving an order or instruction, rather than making a statement or asking a question.

5.4 There are three main ways of showing what type of sentence is being used in English. These sentence-types are used for forming statements, questions, and orders.

The **declarative** form is used in most main clauses. Statements are almost always made using the declarative form. When a clause is in the declarative, the subject is placed in front of the verb.

The declarative is sometimes called the **indicative**.

I want to talk to Mr Castle.
Gertrude looked at Anne.
We'll give you fifteen pounds now.

The **interrogative** form is usually used in questions. In clauses, the subject is often placed after the main verb or after an auxiliary verb.

Is she very upset?
Where is my father?
Have you met Harry?
Did you give him my letter?

The **imperative** is used to try to direct someone's actions. In clauses, the subject is usually omitted and the **base form** of the verb is used.

Come back this minute.
Show me the complete manuscript.

There is a fourth form called the **subjunctive**. This is a feature of English verbs that sometimes occurs in subordinate clauses. The subjunctive is not used to distinguish between different uses of language, and is therefore not dealt with in this chapter. Clauses in which the subjunctive occurs are explained in paragraphs 7.43, 8.41, and 8.48.

5.5 The ways in which these different structures are used are explained in the following paragraphs.

Paragraphs 5.6 to 5.9 explain how the declarative is used to make statements. Paragraphs 5.10 to 5.36 explain how the interrogative is used to ask questions. Paragraphs 5.37 to 5.41 explain how the imperative is used to try to direct someone's actions.

Other uses of the declarative, interrogative, and imperative are explained in paragraphs 5.42 to 5.48.

Making statements: the declarative form

5.6 When you are giving information, you use the **declarative** form.

We ate dinner at six.
I like reading poetry.
Officials have refused to comment.

5.7 When you are expressing an opinion, you usually use the declarative form.

I think she is a brilliant writer.
It's a good thing Father is deaf.
He ought to have let me know he was going out.

making promises

5.8   When you make a promise, you use the declarative form.

> *I shall do everything I can to help you.*
> *I'll have it sent down by special delivery.*

emphasis

5.9   You can emphasize a statement by putting *do*, *does*, or *did* in front of the **base form** of the verb.

> *I do feel sorry for Roger.*
> *A little knowledge does seem to be a dangerous thing.*
> *He had no time to spend time with his family, but he did bring home a regular salary.*

Asking questions: the interrogative form

5.10   When you ask a question, you usually use the **interrogative** form.

types of question

5.11   There are two main types of question.

Questions that can be answered by *yes* or *no* are called *yes/no*-questions.

> *'Is he your only child?'* – *'Yes.'*
> *'Are you planning to marry soon?'* – *'No.'*
> *'Can I help you?'* – *'Yes, I'd like to book a single room, please.'*
> *'Are you interested in racing?'* – *'Yes, I love it.'*
> *'Are you a singer as well as an actress?'* – *'No, I'm not a singer at all.'*
> *'Do you like it?'* – *'Yes, I really like it.'*

The actual answer to a *yes/no*-question is not always *yes* or *no*. For example, if you ask someone *Do you read in bed?*, they might say *Sometimes* or *Never*. If you say to someone *Do you like jazz?*, they might say *I think it's great*. But the questions *Do you read in bed?* and *Do you like jazz?* are still *yes/no*-questions, because *yes* and *no* are the type of answers the questioner expects. *Sometimes* will be interpreted as a weak *yes* answer, *never* as a strong *no* answer, and *I think it's great* as a strong *yes* answer.

Yes/no-questions are fully explained in paragraphs 5.12 to 5.22.

The other main type of question begins with a *wh*-word such as *what*, *where*, or *when*. When you ask a question of this type, the answer cannot be *yes* or *no*.

> *'Who gave you my number?'* – *'Your mother did.'*
> *'Why didn't you ask me?'* – *'I was afraid to.'*
> *'Where is he now?'* – *'He's at university.'*

This type of question is called a *wh*-question. When *wh*-words are used as pronouns or adverbs at the beginning of a *wh*-question, they are called **interrogative pronouns** or **interrogative adverbs**.

Wh-questions are explained in paragraphs 5.23 to 5.36.

Yes/no-questions

position of auxiliary verbs

5.12   In a *yes/no*-question, if there is an auxiliary verb, the auxiliary verb comes first, followed by the subject, then the main verb.

Are you staying here, by any chance?
Will they win again?
Will they like my garden?
Can he read yet?

If there is more than one auxiliary verb, the first auxiliary verb comes at the beginning of the clause, followed by the subject, followed by the other verbs.

Had he been murdered?
Has it been thrown away, perhaps?

For information about auxiliaries, see the Reference section.

5.13 If there is no auxiliary verb, you put *do*, *does*, or *did* at the beginning of the clause, in front of the subject, followed by the base form of the main verb.

Do you understand what I'm saying?
Does it hurt much?
Did you meet George in France?

Note that if the main verb is *do*, you still put *do*, *does*, or *did* at the beginning of the clause, in front of the subject.

Do they do the work themselves?
Does David do this sort of thing often?

be and have as main verbs

5.14 If the verb is *be*, you do not use *do*. You simply put the verb at the beginning of the clause, followed by the subject.

Are you okay?
Is she Ricky's sister?
Am I right?
Was it lonely without us?

If the verb is *have*, you usually put *do*, *does*, or *did* at the beginning of the clause, in front of the subject.

Do passengers have rights?
Does anyone have a question?
Did you have a good flight?

However, when you use *have* in the sense of *own* or *possess*, you do not need to use *do*, *does*, or *did*. You can simply put *have*, *has*, or *had* at the beginning of the clause. This is a slightly formal use.

Have we anything else we ought to talk about first?
Has he any idea what it's like?

If you use *have got* or *has got* in a *yes/no*-question, you put *have* or *has* at the beginning of the clause, followed by the subject, followed by *got*.

Have you got any brochures on Holland?
Has she got a car?

Have got and *has got* are explained in paragraph 3.15.

Making a question more polite

5.15 You can make a question or request softer or more polite by beginning with an expression like *Do you know ...* or *Could you tell me ....* This type of question is called an **indirect question**.

Here are some expressions you can use to make questions more polite:

Could you tell me …	Do you have any idea …
Do you know …	Would you mind telling me …

When one of these introductory expressions is used, the word order of the rest of the sentence is the same as in an affirmative statement.

Could you tell me what time <u>the train leaves</u>?
Do you know where <u>he lives</u>?
Do you have any idea <u>what's happening</u>?
Would you mind telling me how old <u>you are</u>?

When you answer a question of this type, the answer is usually *yes* or *no*, followed by the information asked for.

'Could you tell me what time the train leaves?' — 'Yes, <u>it leaves at three o'clock</u>.'
'Do you know where he lives?' — 'Yes, <u>in the farm up on the hill</u>.'
'Do you have any idea what's happening?' — '<u>No, I'm afraid not!</u>'
'Would you mind telling me how old you are? — '<u>Not at all. I'm 52.</u>'

Note that the 'positive' answer to a question beginning *Would you mind telling me …* is *No* or *Not at all*. It means *No, I wouldn't mind* (= *Yes, that's fine*).

Making a statement into a question: question tags

5.16 You can ask for confirmation that something is true by making a statement in the declarative, then adding an expression such as *isn't it?* or *was she?* Constructions like these are called **question tags**. Question tags are most often used in spoken English.

forming question tags

5.17 Question tags are formed using an auxiliary or a form of *be* or *do*, followed by a personal pronoun referring to the subject.

If the main clause is in the affirmative, you use a negative tag. Negative tags are always contracted, except in old-fashioned or very formal English.

<u>It is</u> quite warm, <u>isn't it?</u>

If the main clause is in the negative, you use an affirmative tag.

<u>You didn't</u> know I was an artist, <u>did you?</u>

If the main clause of your statement has an auxiliary in it, you use the same auxiliary in the tag.

<u>You will</u> stay in touch, <u>won't you?</u>

If the main clause has the past simple or present simple form of *be* as the main verb, you use this in the tag.

<u>They are</u>, <u>aren't they?</u>

If the main clause does not have an auxiliary or the verb *be*, you use *do*, *does*, or *did* in the tag.

After a couple of years <u>the heat gets</u> too much, <u>doesn't it?</u>
<u>He played</u> for Ireland, <u>didn't he?</u>

Note that the negative tag with *I* is *aren't I*, even though *am* is the auxiliary or main verb in the main clause.

<u>I'm</u> controlling it, <u>aren't I?</u>

checking statements

5.18 If you have an opinion or belief about something and you want to check that it is
true, or to find out if someone agrees with you, you can make a statement and add a
question tag after it to make it into a question.

If you are making an affirmative statement and you want to check that it is true, you
use a negative question tag.

You like Ralph a lot, don't you?
They are beautiful places, aren't they?

If you are making a negative statement and want to check that it is true, you use an
affirmative tag.

It doesn't work, does it?
You won't tell anyone else all this, will you?

You can also use an affirmative tag if your statement contains a broad negative, a
negative adverb, or a negative pronoun.

That hardly counts, does it?
You've never been to Benidorm, have you?
Nothing had changed, had it?

replying to tags

5.19 The person you are speaking to replies to the content of your statement rather than
to the tag, and confirms an affirmative statement with *yes* and a negative statement
with *no*.

'It became stronger, didn't it?' – 'Yes it did.'
'You didn't know that, did you?' – 'No.'

other uses of question tags

5.20 If you are making a statement about yourself and you want to check if the person
you are talking to has the same opinion or feeling, you can put a tag with *you* after
your statement.

I think this is the best thing, don't you?
I love tea, don't you?

Question tags can also be used to show your reaction to something that someone
has just said or implied, for example to show interest, surprise, or anger. Note that
you use an affirmative tag after an affirmative statement.

You fell on your back, did you?
You've been to North America before, have you?
Oh, he wants us to make films as well, does he?

When using *let's* to suggest doing something, you can add the tag *shall we* to check
that the people you are talking to agree with you.

Let's forget it, shall we?

If you are suggesting that you do something and you want to check that the person
you are speaking to agrees, you can add the tag *shall I?*

I'll call the doctor, shall I?

If you are telling someone to do something and you want to make your order sound
less forceful, you can do so by adding a question tag. The tag is usually *will you*, but
won't you and *can't you* are also used.

Come into the kitchen, <u>will you?</u>
Look at that, <u>will you?</u>
See that she gets safely back, <u>won't you?</u>

When you are using a negative imperative, you can only use *will you* as a tag.

Don't tell Howard, <u>will you?</u>

You can also add an affirmative tag such as *are you?* to an affirmative statement if you want to show interest in a piece of information.

So, you're leaving us, <u>are you?</u>
He's a friend of yours, <u>is he?</u>

all-purpose question tags

5.21 In informal spoken English, you can use a one-word all-purpose question tag such as *right?* or *eh?*

You're American, <u>right?</u>
He's a lawyer, <u>right?</u>
Let's talk about something else, <u>eh?</u>
Not good, <u>eh?</u>

In some varieties of English, particularly those spoken in India, Singapore and Malaysia, *isn't it?* is used as an all-purpose question tag.

We've seen that film already, <u>isn't it?</u>
They're arriving tomorrow, <u>isn't it?</u>

Informal multicultural British English uses the common all-purpose question tag *innit* (a shortened form of *isn't it*), both with and without a rising question mark.

It makes you think though, <u>innit?</u>
It's all just a bit of fun, <u>innit?</u>
So eventually he gave me the sack, <u>innit</u>.

Either/or-questions

5.22 You sometimes ask a question in which you mention two or more possible answers. You link the possible answers with *or*. For example, you might say *Is he awake or asleep?* or *Do you like your coffee white or black?* You expect the actual answer to your question to be one of the answers you have mentioned.

Words, phrases, and clauses can all be linked in this way.

Questions like these are sometimes called *either/or*-questions.

'Is it <u>a boy or a girl?</u>' – 'A beautiful <u>boy</u>.'
'Was it <u>healthy or diseased?</u>' – '<u>Diseased</u>, I'm afraid.'
'Shall we take the bus or do you want to walk?' – 'Let's <u>walk</u>, shall we?'

Wh-questions

5.23 When you ask someone a *wh*-question, you want them to specify a particular person, thing, place, reason, method, time, or amount. You do not expect them to answer *yes* or *no*.

wh-words

5.24 *Wh*-questions begin with a *wh*-word.

Wh-words are a set of pronouns, adverbs, and determiners which all, with the exception of *how*, begin with *wh*-. Here is a list of the main *wh*-words:

how	when	which	whom	why
what	where	who	whose	

wh-word as subject

5.25   When a wh-word is the subject of a verb, or when it forms part of the subject, the word order of the clause is the same as that of a clause in the declarative, i.e. the subject is put first, followed by the verb.

Who invited you?
And then what happened?
Which mattress is best?

wh-word as object or adverb

5.26   When a wh-word is the object of a verb or preposition, or when it forms part of the object, or when it is an adverb, the position of the subject is the usual one in the interrogative form; that is, it comes after the first verb in the clause.

What am I going to do without you?
Which graph are you going to use?
Why would Stephen lie to me?
When would you be coming down?

If you are using the **present simple** or the **past simple** of any verb except *be*, you put *do*, *does*, or *did* in front of the subject.

What do you really think?
Which department do you want?
Where does she live?
How do you know what it's like?
When did you last see John Cartwright?

If you are using the present simple or the past simple of *be*, the main verb goes in front of the subject. You do not use *do*, *does*, or *did*.

Where is the station?
How was your meeting?
When was the last time you cleaned the garage?

questions without a verb

5.27   In conversation, a wh-question sometimes consists of a wh-word on its own. For example, if you say to someone *I'm learning to type*, they might say *Why?*, meaning *Why are you learning to type?*

'He saw a snake.' – 'Where?'
'I have to go to Germany.' – 'When?'
'I knew you were landing today.' – 'How?'

A wh-question can also consist of a noun phrase containing a wh-word. For example, if you say to someone *I gave your book to that girl*, they might say *Which girl?*, meaning *Which girl did you give my book to?*

'He knew my cousin.' – 'Which cousin?'
'Who was your friend?' – 'What friend?'

who and whom

5.28 The pronoun *who* is used to ask questions about a person's identity. *Who* can be the subject or object of a verb.

Who discovered this?
Who were her friends?
Who is Michael Howard?
Who did he marry?

In more formal English, *whom* is sometimes used instead of *who* as the object of a verb.

Whom shall we call?
Whom did you see?

Who and *whom* can also be the object of a preposition. When *who* is the object of a preposition, the preposition is put at the end of the clause.

Who did you dance with?
Who do I pay this to?

When *whom* is the object of a preposition, the preposition is put at the beginning of the clause, in front of *whom*.

For whom was he working while in Baghdad?
To whom is a broadcaster responsible?

 In informal spoken English, *who* is sometimes used after a preposition.

So you report to who?

This use is especially common when you leave out part of the question.

'They were saying horrible things.' – 'Really? To who?'
'It could be difficult.' – 'For who?'

whose

5.29 *Whose* is used as a determiner or pronoun to ask which person something belongs to or is associated with.

Whose children did you think they were?
Whose coat was it?
Whose is that?

which

5.30 *Which* is used as a pronoun or determiner to ask someone to identify a specific person or thing out of a number of people or things.

Which is the best restaurant?
Which is her room?
Which do you like best?
Which doctor do you want to see?

When *which* is a determiner, it can be part of the object of a preposition. The preposition is usually put at the end of the question.

Which station did you come from?
Which character did you like most?

when and where

5.31 When is used to ask questions about the time something happened, happens, or will happen.

> When did you find her?
> When do we have supper?
> Ginny, when are you coming home?

Where is used to ask questions about place, position, or direction.

> Where does she live?
> Where are you going?
> Where do you go to complain?

why

5.32 Why is used to ask a question about the reason for something.

> Why are you here?
> Why does Amy want to go and see his grave?
> Why does she treat me like that when we're such old friends?

Why is sometimes used without a subject and with the base form of a verb, usually to ask why an action is or was necessary.

> Why wake me up?
> Why bother about me?
> Why make a point of it?

Why not can be used with the base form of a verb, in order to make a suggestion or to ask why a particular action has not been taken.

> Why not end it now?
> Why not read a book?
> If you have money in the bank, why not use it?

how

5.33 How is usually used to ask about the method used for doing something, or about the way in which something can be achieved.

> How do we open it?
> How are you going to get that?
> How could he explain it to her?
> How did he know when you were coming?

How is also used to ask questions about the way a person feels, about the way someone or something looks, or about the way something sounds, feels, or tastes.

> How are you feeling today?
> 'How do I look?' – 'Very nice.'
> How did you feel when you stood up in front of the class?

how with other words

5.34 How can be combined with other words at the beginning of questions.

How many and how much are used to ask what number of things there are or what amount of something there is.

How many is followed by a plural countable noun.

How many people are there?
How many languages can you speak?
How many times have you been?

How much is followed by an uncountable noun.

How much money have we got in the bank?
Just how much time have you been devoting to this?

How many and *how much* can be used without a following noun when you do not need to make it clear what sort of thing you are talking about.

How many did you find?
How much did he tell you?
How much does it cost?
How much do they really understand?

How long is used to ask about the length of a period of time.

How long have you lived here? ·
How long will it take?
How long can she live like this?
How long ago was that?

How long is also used to ask questions about the length of something.

How long is this road?

How far is used in questions about distance and extent.

How far can we see?
How far is it to Montreal from here?
How far have you got with your homework?

You can combine *how* with an adjective when you are asking to what extent something has a particular quality or feature.

How big is your flat?
How old are your children?

 How come? is an informal way of asking *why?* It is normally used only in speech.

How come you know so much about Linda?

5.35   *What* can be a pronoun or determiner, or it can be used in combination with *if* or *for*.

What is used as a pronoun to find out various kinds of specific information, for example details of an event, the meaning of a word or expression, or the reason for something.

What's wrong with his mother?
What has happened to him?
What is obesity?
What keeps you hanging around here?

What can be used to ask someone's opinion of something.

What do you think about the present political situation?

What is often used as the object of a preposition. The preposition usually goes at the end of the question.

What are you interested in?
What did he die of?
What do you want to talk about?

What is used as a determiner to find out the identity of something or to ask what kind of thing it is.

What books does she read?
What church did you say you attend?

What if goes in front of a clause in the declarative. It is used to ask what should be done if a particular difficulty occurs.

What if it's really bad weather?
What if they didn't want to part with it, what would you do then?

You put *what* at the beginning of a question and *for* at the end of it when you want to know the reason for something or the purpose of something. *What are you staring for?* means the same as *Why are you staring? What is this handle for?* means *What is the purpose of this handle?*

What are you going for?
What are those lights for?

 In informal spoken English, you can also say *What for?* when someone says what they have done, or what they intend to do, and you want to know the reason for their actions.

'I've bought you a present.' – 'What for?'

What can also be used in combination with *about* or *of*. This use is explained in paragraph 5.47.

whatever, wherever, and whoever

5.36   If you want a question to sound more emphatic, you can use *whatever* instead of *what*, *wherever* instead of *where*, or *whoever* instead of *who*.

Whatever is the matter?
Wherever did you get this?
Whoever heard of a bishop resigning?

Directing other people's actions: the imperative

orders and instructions

5.37   When someone gives a very clear order or instruction, they usually use the **imperative**.

Discard any clothes you have not worn for more than a year.
Put that gun down.
Tell your mother as soon as possible.

Written instructions are given in the imperative.

Boil up a little water with washing up liquid in it.
Fry the chopped onion and pepper in the oil.

   USAGE NOTE

When they are followed by a second verb, the imperative forms of *come* and *go* are used with *and*, followed by the base form of the second verb, rather than a to-infinitive. The two actions seem to be separate, because of the *and*, but they are in fact very closely linked.

Come and see me whenever you need help.

In spoken American English, the imperative forms of *come* and *go* can be followed directly by the base form of the verb.

Come see what the dog did to the couch. (Am)
Go get some sleep. (Am)

An order can be made more forceful by putting *you* in front of the verb.

You get in the car.
You shut up!

advice and warnings

5.38   You can use the imperative when you are giving advice or a warning.

Be sensible.
You *be* careful.

Often advice or a warning is expressed in a negative form. You form a negative imperative by putting *don't* or *do not* in front of the base form of the verb.

Don't be afraid of them.
Don't be discouraged.
Do not approach this man under any circumstances.

You can also form a negative imperative by putting *never* in front of the base form of a verb.

Never make a social phone call after 9.30 p.m.

Another way of giving advice or a warning is to use one of the modals *should* or *ought to* in a declarative sentence.

You *should get* to know him better.
You *shouldn't keep* eggs in the refrigerator.

This use is explained in detail in paragraph 5.215.

appeals

5.39   You use the imperative when you are trying to get someone to do something.

Come quickly... *Come* quickly... *Hurry!*

You can make an appeal more forceful by putting *do* in front of the verb.

Oh *do stop* whining!
Do come and stay with us in Barbados for the winter.

explanations

5.40   You can use the imperative with some verbs when you are explaining something and you want the listener or reader to think about a particular thing or possibility, or to compare two things.

Take, for instance, the new proposals for student loans.
Imagine, for example, an assembly line worker in a factory making children's blocks.
But *suppose* for a moment that the automobile industry had developed at the same rate as computers.
For example, *compare* a typical poor country like Indonesia with a rich one like Canada.
Consider, for example, the contrast between the way schools today treat space and time.

Here is a list of verbs that are used in this way:

compare	contrast	look at	picture	take
consider	imagine	note	suppose	

5.41 *Let* is used in imperative sentences in four different ways:

▶ it is used to give an order or instruction

Let Phillip have a look at it.

▶ you use it followed by *us* when you are making a suggestion about what you and someone else should do. *Let us* is almost always shortened to *Let's*

Let's go outside.
Let's creep forward on hands and knees.

▶ you use it followed by *me* when you are offering to do something

Let me take your coat.

▶ in very formal English, it is used to express a wish.

Let the joy be universal.
Let confusion live!
Let the best man or woman win.

To make a negative suggestion you use *Let's not* or, in informal American English, *Let's don't*.

Let's not stay till the end.
Let's don't ask about the missing books. (Am, informal)

Other uses of the declarative, the interrogative, and the imperative

confirming

5.42 You can confirm that something is true by asking a question using the **declarative** form.

So you admit something is wrong?
Then you think we can keep it?

When you ask a question using the declarative form, you expect a *yes*-type answer, unless you use a negative construction, in which case you expect the answer *no*.

'You mean it's still here?' – *'Of course.'*
'Your parents don't mind you being out so late?' – *'No, they don't'.*

Questions expressed in the declarative form often begin with a conjunction.

So you're satisfied?
And you think that's a good idea?

instructing

5.43 In informal spoken English, you can give an instruction by using a declarative sentence with *you* as the subject.

You put the month and the temperature on the top line.
You take the bus up to the landing stage at twelve-thirty.
You just put it straight in the oven.

offers and invitations

5.44 When you are making an offer or an invitation, you usually use a *yes/no*-question beginning with a modal such as *can* or *would*. This use is explained in detail in paragraphs 5.173 to 5.178.

Can I help you?
Can I give you a lift?
Would you like me to get something for you?
Would you like some coffee?
Would you like to go to Ernie's for dinner?

You can also make an offer or invitation in a more informal way by using the **imperative** form. Note that you can only do this when it is clear that you are not giving an order.

Have a cigar.
Come to my place.
Come in, Mrs Kintner.

You add emphasis by putting *do* in front of the verb.

Do have a chocolate biscuit.
Do help yourselves.

requests, orders, and instructions

5.45 When you are making a request, you usually use a *yes/no*-question beginning with one of the modals *could*, *can*, or *would*.

Could I ask you a few questions?
Can I have my hat back, please?
Would you mind having a word with my husband?

You can also give an order or instruction using a *yes/no*-question beginning with a modal.

Will you tell Watson I shall be in a little late?

These uses are explained in detail in paragraphs 5.156 to 5.166.

questions that do not expect an answer

5.46 When you use a *yes/no*-question to offer help or to make a request, you still expect the answer *yes* or *no*. However, people sometimes say things that seem like *yes/no*-questions, although they do not expect an answer at all. They are using the *yes/no*-question form to express a strong feeling, opinion, or impression.

For example, instead of saying *That's an ugly building*, someone might say *Isn't that an ugly building?* Or instead of saying *You never seem to get upset*, someone might say *Don't you ever get upset?*

Questions like these are called **rhetorical questions**.

Is there nothing she won't do?
Can't you see that I'm busy?
Hasn't anyone round here got any sense?
Does nothing ever worry you?

Another kind of rhetorical question consists of a statement followed by a question tag such as *are you?* or *is it?* For example, someone might say *So you are the new assistant, are you?* or *So they're coming to tea, are they?*

So you want to be an actress, do you?
So they're moving house again, are they?

Rhetorical questions can also begin with *how*. They usually express a feeling of shock or indignation. For example, instead of saying *You are very cruel*, someone might say *How can you be so cruel?*

How can you say such things?
How dare you speak to me like that?

Rhetorical questions are dealt with fully in paragraph 9.94.

questions without a verb

5.47 You can ask a question consisting of *what about* or *what of* in front of a noun phrase, without a verb. You ask a question like this to remind someone of something, or to draw their attention to something. With this type of question, you often expect an action, rather than a reply.

What about the others on the list?
What about your breakfast?
But what of the women themselves?

suggestions

5.48 There are several ways in which you can make a suggestion:

▶ you can use the modal *could* in a declarative sentence (see paragraph 5.183)

We could have tea.
You could get someone to dress up as a pirate.

▶ you can use a negative wh-question beginning with *why*

Why don't we just give them what they want?
Why don't you write to her yourself?

▶ you can use a question consisting of *what about* or *how about* in front of an *-ing* form

What about becoming an actor?
How about using makeup to dramatize your features?

▶ you can use the imperative.

'Give them a reward each,' I suggested.

You can also make a suggestion about what you and someone else might do by using *let's*. This use is explained in paragraph 5.41.

Forming negative statements

5.49 When you want to say that something is not true, is not happening, or is not the case, you normally use a **negative statement**. Negative statements contain words like *not*, *never*, or *nowhere*. These are called **negative words**.

Here is the list of negative words in English:

neither	no	none	nor	nothing
never	nobody	no one	not	nowhere

Negative words indicate the opposite of something or an absence of something.

5.50 Another group of words such as *scarcely* and *seldom* can be used to make a statement almost negative. These words are called **broad negatives**. They are explained in paragraphs 5.82 to 5.89.

5.51 If a statement about the existence of something has a negative word in it, you use *any* (not *no*) as a determiner in front of the following noun phrase. You can also use a word beginning with *any-* such as *anyone* or *anywhere*.

> We didn't have *any* money.
> He writes poetry and *never* shows it to *anyone*.
> It is *impossible* to park the car *anywhere*.

For another use of *any* see paragraph 2.163.

> **!** **BE CAREFUL**

5.52 In standard English, it is almost always unacceptable to use two negative words in the same clause. For example, you do not say, *I don't never go there*, or *I don't know nothing*.

5.53 The use of negatives in **reported speech** is explained in paragraph 7.13. The use of negatives with **modals** is explained in paragraph 5.104.

> *not*

5.54 The most commonly used negative word is *not*. Its use with different verbs corresponds to the way these verbs are used in **yes/no-questions** (see paragraphs 5.12 to 5.14).

> **position in verb phrases**

5.55 When *not* is used with a verb phrase that contains an auxiliary verb, it comes after the first verb in the phrase.

> They *could not exist* in their present form.
> They *might not* even *notice*.
> The White House *has not commented* on the report.
> He *had not attended* many meetings.
> I *was not smiling*.
> Her teachers *were not impressed* with her excuses.

> **adding *do***

5.56 If there is no auxiliary verb, you put *do*, *does*, or *did* after the subject, followed by *not* or *-n't*, followed by the base form of the main verb.

> They *do not need* to talk.
> He *does not speak* English very well.
> I *didn't know* that.

Be and *have* are exceptions to this; this is explained in the following paragraphs 5.57 and 5.58. The shortening of *not* to *-n't* is explained in paragraphs 5.61 and 5.62.

> **not with *be***

5.57 If the verb is *be*, you do not use *do*. You simply put *not* or *-n't* after the verb.

> It *is not* difficult to see why they were unsuccessful.
> There *is not* much point in heading south.
> This *isn't* my first choice of restaurant.

not with *have* and *have got*

5.58 If the verb is *have*, you usually put *do*, *does*, or *did* after the subject, followed by *not* or *-n't*, followed by the base form *have*.

The organization <u>does not have</u> a good track record.
He <u>didn't have</u> a very grand salary.

 You can simply put *not* or *-n't* after the verb, but this use is less common, and almost never used in modern American English.

He <u>hadn't</u> enough money.
I <u>haven't</u> any papers to say that I have been trained.

If you use *have got*, you put *not* or *-n't* after *have*, followed by *got*.

I <u>haven't got</u> the latest figures.
He <u>hasn't got</u> a daughter.

Have got is explained in paragraph 3.15.

position with *-ing* forms and *to*-infinitives

5.59 When *not* is used with an *-ing* form or a *to*-infinitive clause, it is placed in front of the *-ing* form or *to*-infinitive.

We stood there, <u>not knowing</u> what was expected of us.
He lost out by <u>not taking</u> a degree at another university.
Try <u>not to worry</u>.
It took a vast amount of patience <u>not to strangle</u> him.

with an inflected form and an *-ing* form or *to*-infinitive

5.60 When a clause contains an inflected verb and an *-ing* form or *to*-infinitive, you put *not* either with the inflected form or with the *-ing* form or *to*-infinitive, depending on the meaning you want to express.

For example, you can say either *Mary tried not to smile* or *Mary did not try to smile*, but they express different meanings. The first means that Mary tried to avoid smiling. The second means that Mary did not even try to smile.

However, with some verbs that are used with *to*-infinitives, the meaning is the same whether *not* is placed with the main verb or with the *to*-infinitive.

She <u>did not appear</u> to have done anything.
Henry <u>appears not to appreciate</u> my explanation.
It <u>didn't seem</u> to bother them at all.
They <u>seemed not to notice</u> me.

Here is a list of verbs that are used with *to*-infinitives. With all of these, the meaning of the clause is the same, whether *not* is put in front of the verb or in front of the *to*-infinitive:

appear	happen	plan	tend	wish
expect	intend	seem	want	

The use of two verbs in a clause to talk about two actions or states is dealt with in paragraphs 3.182 to 3.212.

Note that with some **reporting verbs** the meaning is the same whether you put *not* in front of the reporting verb or in front of the main verb. This is explained in paragraph 7.13.

contractions of *not*

5.61 In spoken English and in informal written English, *not* is often shortened to *-n't* after *be* or *have* or after an auxiliary. *-n't* is attached to the end of the verb.

Maria isn't really my aunt at all.
He doesn't believe in anything.
I haven't heard from her recently.

Note that *cannot* is shortened to *can't*, *shall not* is shortened to *shan't*, and *will not* is shortened to *won't*.

Here is a complete list of the shortened forms you can use:

aren't	doesn't	can't	shan't
isn't	don't	couldn't	shouldn't
wasn't	hadn't	mightn't	won't
weren't	hasn't	mustn't	wouldn't
didn't	haven't	oughtn't	

USAGE NOTE

5.62 Note that if the verb is already shortened and added to its subject, you cannot shorten *not* to *-n't*. This means, for example, that you can shorten *she is not* to *she isn't* or *she's not*, but not to *she'sn't*.

It isn't easy.
It's not easy.
I haven't had time.
I've not had time.

Note that you cannot add *-n't* to *am*. You can only use *I'm not* as the shortened form.

I'm not excited.

The form *aren't I* is used in questions.

In questions, *not* is usually shortened to *-n't* and added to the first verb in the verb phrase.

Didn't she win at the Olympics?
Hasn't he put on weight?
Aren't you bored?

However, in formal English, it is also possible to put *not* after the subject.

Did he not have brothers?
Was it not rather absurd?

other uses of *not*

5.63 You can also use *not* with almost any word or word group in a clause. For example, you can use it with nouns, adjectives, adverbs, prepositional phrases, and some quantity expressions such as *a lot of*. You usually do this in order to be more forceful, careful, polite, hesitant, and so on. The following paragraphs 5.64 and 5.65 describe some of these uses.

5.64 *Very* is often used after *not* to soften the negative meaning of a clause. This sounds more polite or hesitant than using *not* without *very*.

His attitude is not very logical.
It's not very strong tea; it won't stain.

He wasn't a very good actor.
She shook her head, but not very convincingly.

You can use *not* with *absolutely*, *altogether*, *entirely*, or *necessarily* in a similar way. You do this in order to sound more polite or less critical.

Previous experience isn't absolutely necessary, but it helps.
I was not altogether sure.
They are not entirely reliable.
Science is not necessarily hostile to human values.

You use *not* to show that the thing you are describing does in fact have some good qualities, although you do not want to make them sound better than they really are. This structure is often used with words that have a negative prefix such as *un-* or *-less*.

She's not an unattractive woman.
It's not a bad start.
It's a small point, but not an unimportant one.
America is very well developed, but not limitless.

not used for contrast

5.65 *Not* is sometimes used to contrast one part of a clause with another. Using *not* in this way emphasizes the positive part of a statement.

He held her arm in his hand, not hard, but firmly.
We move steadily, not fast, not slow.
'Were they still interested?' – 'Not just interested. Overjoyed.'
I will move eventually, but not from Suffolk.
It's not a huge hotel, but it's very nice.

never

5.66 *Never* is used to say that something was not or will not ever be the case.

When it is used with a verb phrase that contains an auxiliary verb, *never* is put after the first verb in the verb phrase and in front of the main verb.

I would never trust my judgement again.
...a type of glass that is rare and is never used.
The number of people who died will never be known.
Fifty years ago, men were never expected to wash the dishes or help with the children.
I had never been to this big town before.
I've never done so much work in all my life.

However, you can put *never* in front of the first word in the verb phrase in order to emphasize the negative aspect of a statement.

I never would have guessed if he hadn't told me.
There was no such person–there never had been.

with simple forms of be

5.67 If the main verb is the present simple or past simple of *be*, *never* usually comes after the verb.

She was never too proud to learn.
I'm never very keen on keeping a car for more than a year.
There were never any people in the house.

However, you can put *never* in front of a simple form of *be* for emphasis.

There never was enough hot water at home.
It never was very clear.
There never is any great change.

with simple forms of other verbs

5.68 If the main verb is the present simple or past simple of any verb except *be*, *never* comes in front of the verb.

I never want to see you in my classes again.
She never goes abroad.
He never went to university.
He never did any homework.

emphasis

5.69 You can make a negative statement more emphatic by using *never* followed by *do*, *does*, or *did* in front of the base form of the verb. For example, instead of saying *I never met him*, you can say *I never did meet him*.

They never did get their money back.
She never did find her real mother.
Some people never do adjust to life here.

never in imperatives

5.70 *Never* can be used at the beginning of imperative structures.

Never change a wheel near a drain.
Never dry clothes in front of an open fire.

Imperative structures are explained in paragraph 5.4 and in paragraphs 5.37 to 5.41.

no

5.71 *No* is an indefinite determiner that is used in front of singular and plural nouns to say that something does not exist or is not available.

There was no money for an operation.
We had no parents, nobody to look after us.
He has no ambition.
I could see no tracks.

Indefinite determiners are explained in paragraphs 1.223 to 1.250.

5.72 In spoken English, *-n't* is often used with *any* instead of *no*. For example, instead of saying *I had no money*, you can say *I didn't have any money*.

They hadn't meant any harm to her.
I can't see any hope in it.

none

5.73 The pronoun *none* is used to say that there is not a single thing or person, or not even a small amount of a particular thing.

I waited for comments but none came.
The entire area is covered with shallow lakes, none more than a few yards in depth.
We have been seeing difficulties where none exist.

For another use of *none* see paragraph 1.155.

none of

5.74 *None of* is a quantity expression.

None of the townspeople had ever seen such weather.
None of this has happened without our consent.

For an explanation of *none of* see paragraphs 2.179 and 2.185.

words beginning with *no-*

5.75 There are four words beginning with *no-* that are used in negative statements. *Nothing*, *no one*, and *nobody* are **indefinite pronouns**. *Nowhere* is an **indefinite place adverb**.

There's nothing you can do.
Nobody in her house knows any English.
There's almost nowhere left to go.

Indefinite pronouns are explained in paragraphs 1.128 to 1.141.

Indefinite place adverbs are explained in paragraphs 6.61 and 6.71.

followed by *but*

5.76 *Nothing*, *no one*, *nobody*, and *nowhere* can be followed by *but* to mean *only*. For example, *There was nothing but cheese* means that there was only cheese.

I look back on this period with nothing but pleasure.
He heard no one but his uncles.

Indefinite pronouns and adverbs that begin with *any* can be used in similar structures. However, in these structures *but* means *except*, rather than *only*.

I could never speak about anything but business to Ivan.
He never spoke to anyone but his wife.

neither and *nor*

5.77 *Neither* and *nor* are used together to say that two alternatives are not possible, likely, or true. *Neither* goes in front of the first alternative and *nor* goes in front of the second one.

Neither Margaret nor John was there.
They had neither food nor money until the end of the week.

neither in replies

5.78 *Neither* can be used on its own as a reply, to refer to two alternatives that have already been mentioned.

'Does that mean yes or no?' – *'Neither'.*

5.79 If a clause contains a negative word, particularly *not*, you can use *neither* or *nor* to negate a second clause. In the second clause, you put *neither* or *nor* first, followed by the verb, followed by the subject.

This isn't a dazzling achievement, but neither is it a negligible one.
These people are not insane, nor are they fools.

If there is an auxiliary, it is placed in front of the subject in the second clause.

The organization had broken no rules, but neither had it acted responsibly.
I don't feel any shame. Neither do I think I should.

neither with singular nouns

5.80 *Neither* can be used on its own in front of a singular noun referring to each of two things when you are making a negative statement about both of them. For example, *Neither partner benefited from the agreement* means that there were two partners and the negative statement applies to both of them.

Neither report mentioned the Americans.
Neither film was particularly good.
Neither sex has a monopoly on thought or emotion.
Neither parent is the good one or the bad one.

Note that in this structure *neither* is used with a singular verb.

neither of

5.81 When *neither* is followed by *of*, it makes a set of two things negative. *Neither of* is followed by a plural noun phrase.

Neither of us was having any luck.
Neither of the boys screamed.
Neither of them was making any sound.

Neither of is normally used with a singular verb.

Neither of these extremes is desirable.
Neither of these opinions proves anything.

However, it is also possible to use a plural verb.

Neither of the children were there.

Broad negatives: *hardly, seldom*, etc.

5.82 Another way in which you can make a statement negative is by using a **broad negative**. Broad negatives are adverbs like *rarely* and *seldom*, which are used to make a statement almost totally negative.

The estimated sales will hardly *cover the cost of making the film.*
We were scarcely *able to move.*
Kuwait lies barely *30 miles from the Iranian coast.*

Here is a list of the most common broad negatives:

barely	hardly	rarely	scarcely	seldom

position in clause

5.83 The position of a broad negative within a clause is similar to that of *never* (see paragraphs 5.66 to 5.68).

5.84 When you use a broad negative with a verb phrase that contains an auxiliary verb, you put it after the first word in the verb phrase and in front of the main verb.

I could scarcely believe my eyes.
Religion was rarely discussed in our house.
His eyes had hardly closed.

with simple form of be

5.85 If the verb is the present simple or past simple of *be*, the broad negative usually comes after the verb.

Change is seldom easy.
The new pressure group is barely six months old.
The office was hardly ever empty.
The lagoons are rarely deep.
The results were scarcely encouraging.

with other verbs

5.86 If the verb is the present simple or past simple of any verb except *be*, the broad
negative usually comes in front of the verb.

He seldom bathed.
Marsha rarely felt hungry.
John hardly ever spoke to the Press.

It is also possible to put a broad negative after the verb, but this is less common.

Such moments happen rarely in life.
They met so seldom.

as first word in the clause

5.87 In formal or literary English, a broad negative is sometimes placed at the beginning
of a clause for emphasis. If you are using a verb phrase with an auxiliary, the first
word in the verb phrase is placed after the broad negative, followed by the subject
and then the remainder of the verb phrase.

Seldom has society offered so wide a range of leisure time activities.
Hardly had he settled into his seat when Adam charged in.

If there is no auxiliary, you put the present simple or past simple of *do* after the broad
negative, followed by the subject, followed by the base form of the main verb.

Seldom did a week pass without a request for assessment.
Rarely do local matches live up to expectations.

Note that *barely* and *scarcely* are not often used in this way.

USAGE NOTE

5.88 If you make a **question tag** out of a statement that contains a broad negative, the
tag on the end of the statement is normally in the affirmative, as it is with other
negatives. Question tags are explained in paragraphs 5.16 to 5.20.

She's hardly the right person for the job, is she?
You seldom see that sort of thing these days, do you?

You can modify *rarely* and *seldom* by putting *so*, *very*, *too*, or *pretty* in front of them. You
can also modify *rarely* by using *only*.

It happens so rarely.
Women were very seldom convicted.
He too seldom makes the first greeting.
Most people go to church only rarely.

If you want to say there is very little of something, you can use a broad negative with
any or with a word that begins with *any-*.

The bonds show barely any interest.
Hardly anybody came.
In fact, it is seldom any of these.
With scarcely any warning, the soldiers charged.
Sometimes two or three relatives are admitted, but rarely any friends.

almost

5.89 Instead of using a broad negative, you can use *almost* followed by a negative word such as *no* or *never*. For example, *There was almost no food left* means the same as *There was hardly any food left*.

> They've <u>almost no</u> money for anything.
> The cars thinned out to <u>almost none</u>.
> They were very private people, with <u>almost no</u> friends.
> Children <u>almost never</u> began conversations.

Emphasizing the negative aspect of a statement

at all

5.90 You can add *at all* to a negative statement in order to make it more emphatic. You use *at all* with any negative word, with *without*, or with a **broad negative**.

> She had <u>no</u> writing ability <u>at all</u>.
> 'There's no need,' said Jimmie. '<u>None at all</u>'.
> He did it <u>without</u> any help <u>at all</u>.
> He <u>hardly</u> read anything <u>at all</u>.

Broad negatives are explained in paragraphs 5.82 to 5.88.

whatsoever

5.91 You can put *whatsoever* after *none* and *nothing* in order to emphasize the negative aspect of a statement.

> 'You don't think he has any chance of winning?' – '<u>None whatsoever</u>.'
> There is absolutely no enjoyment in that, <u>none whatsoever</u>.
> You'll find yourself thinking about <u>nothing whatsoever</u>.

If *no* is used as a determiner in a noun phrase, you can put *whatsoever* after the noun phrase.

> There is <u>no</u> need <u>whatsoever</u> to teach children how to behave.
> There was <u>no</u> debate <u>whatsoever</u>, not even in Parliament.

You can also use *whatsoever* in negative statements that contain *any* or a word that begins with *any-*.

> You are not entitled to <u>any</u> aid <u>whatsoever</u>.
> He was devoid of <u>any</u> talent <u>whatsoever</u>.
> I knew I wasn't learning <u>anything whatsoever</u>.

ever

5.92 You can put *ever* after negative words in order to emphasize the negative aspect of a statement.

> I can't say I <u>ever</u> had much interest in fishing.
> Nobody <u>ever</u> leaves the airport.
> I never <u>ever</u> believed we would have such success.

other expressions

5.93 There are several expressions that are used to emphasize a negative statement that contains *not*. These include *in the least*, *the least bit*, *in the slightest*, and *a bit*.

I don't mind in the least, I really don't.
Neither of the managers was the least bit repentant afterwards.
I don't really envy you in the slightest.
They're not a bit interested.

If *in the least* and *in the slightest* are used with verbs, they are placed either immediately after the verb or after the object, if there is one.

I wouldn't have objected in the least.
She did not worry Billy in the least.
The weather hadn't improved in the slightest.

If *in the least* is used with an adjective, it is put in front of it. *In the slightest* usually comes after an adjective.

I wasn't in the least surprised.
She wasn't worried in the slightest.

The least bit and *a bit* are used only with adjectives and are placed in front of the adjective.

I'm not the least bit worried.
They're not a bit interested.

Using modals

5.94 Language is not always used just to exchange information by making simple statements and asking questions. Sometimes we want to make requests, offers, or suggestions, or to express our wishes or intentions. We may want to be polite or tactful, or to indicate our feelings about what we are saying.

We can do all these things by using a set of verbs called **modals**. Modals are always used with other verbs. They are a special kind of **auxiliary verb**.

Here is a list of the modals used in English:

can	may	must	shall	will
could	might	ought to	should	would

In some grammars, *dare*, *need*, and *used to* are also referred to as modals. In this grammar, we call these words **semi-modals**. They are dealt with separately in paragraphs 5.248 to 5.258.

Ought is sometimes regarded as a modal, rather than *ought to*. For a further note about this, see paragraph 5.101.

Modals are sometimes called **modal verbs** or **modal auxiliaries**.

5.95 The main uses of modals are explained in paragraphs 5.96 to 5.100. Special features of modals are described in paragraphs 5.101 to 5.108.

Ways of referring to time when using modals are explained in paragraphs 5.109 to 5.116. Ways of using modals to say whether something is possible are explained in paragraphs 5.117 to 5.153. Ways of using modals when interacting with other people are explained in paragraphs 5.154 to 5.222.

Expressions that can be used instead of modals are described in paragraphs 5.223 to 5.247. **Semi-modals** are explained in paragraphs 5.248 to 5.258.

The main uses of modals

5.96   Modals are mainly used when you want to show your attitude towards what you are saying, or when you are concerned about the effect of what you are saying on the person you are speaking or writing to.

attitude to information

5.97   When you are giving information, you sometimes use modals to show how certain you are that what you are saying is true or correct.

For example, if you say *Mr Wilkins is the oldest person in the village*, you are giving a definite statement of fact. If you say *Mr Wilkins must be the oldest person in the village*, the modal *must* shows that you think Mr Wilkins is the oldest person, because you cannot think of anyone in the village who is older than Mr Wilkins. If you say *Mr Wilkins might be the oldest person in the village*, the modal *might* shows that you think it is possible that Mr Wilkins is the oldest person, because he is very old.

attitude to intentions

5.98   You can use modals to show your attitude towards the things you intend to do, or intend not to do. For example, if you say *I won't go without Simon*, you are expressing strong unwillingness to go without Simon. If you say *I can't go without Simon*, you are saying that there is a special reason for not going without him. If you say *I couldn't go without Simon*, you are saying that you are unwilling to go without Simon, because to do so would be wrong, or impossible because of the circumstances.

attitude to people

5.99   When you use language, you are affecting and responding to a particular person or audience. Modals are often used to produce a particular effect, and the modal you choose depends on several factors, such as the relationship you have with your listener, the formality or informality of the situation, and the importance of what you are saying.

For example, it would normally be rude to say to a stranger *Open the door*, although you might say it in an emergency, or you might say it to a close friend or a child. Normally, you would say to a stranger *Will you open the door?*, *Would you open the door?*, or *Could you open the door?*, depending on how polite you want to be.

use in sentences containing more than one clause

5.100   Modals have special uses in three kinds of sentence containing more than one clause:

▶ they are used in **reported clauses**

Wilson dropped a hint that he might come.
I felt that I would like to wake her up.

For more information about reported clauses see Chapter 7.

▶ they are used in **conditional statements**

If he had died when he was 50, he would have died healthy.
If only things had been different, she would have been far happier with George.

For more information about conditionals see paragraphs 8.25 to 8.42.

▸ they are used in **purpose clauses**.

He stole under the very noses of the store detectives in order that he might be arrested and punished.
He resigned so that he could spend more time with his family.

For more information about purpose clauses see paragraphs 8.47 and 8.48.

Special features of modals

form of following verb

5.101 Modals are followed by the **base form** of a verb.

I must leave fairly soon.
I think it will be rather nice.
They ought to give you your money back.

Note that *ought* is sometimes regarded as a modal, rather than *ought to*. *Ought* is then said to be followed by a *to*-infinitive.

5.102 Sometimes a modal is followed by the base form of one of the auxiliary verbs *have* or *be*, followed by a participle.

When a modal is followed by *be* and an *-ing* participle, this shows that you are talking about the present or the future.

People may be watching.
You ought to be doing this.
The play will be starting soon.

When a modal is followed by *have* and an *-ed* participle, this shows that you are talking about the past.

You must have heard of him.
She may have gone already.
I ought to have sent the money.

In passive structures, a modal is followed by *be* or *have been* and an *-ed* participle.

The name of the winner will be announced.
They ought to be treated fairly.
Such charges may have been justified.

A modal is never followed by the auxiliary verb *do*, or by another modal.

no inflections

5.103 Modals do not inflect. This means there is no *-s* form in the third person singular, and there are no *-ing* or *-ed* forms.

There's nothing I can do about it.
I am sure he can do it.
I must leave fairly soon.

Could is sometimes thought to be the past tense of *can*. This is discussed in paragraphs 5.112 and 5.113.

negatives

5.104 Negatives are formed by putting a **negative word** such as *not* immediately after the modal. *Can not* is usually written as one word, *cannot*.

You must not worry.
I cannot go back.

In the case of *ought to*, you put the negative word after *ought*.

He <u>ought not to</u> have done so.

 In American English, the *to* of *ought to* is optional in negative statements.

News organizations <u>ought not</u> treat them so poorly. (American)

After *could, might, must, ought, should*, and *would*, *not* is often shortened to *-n't* and is added to the modal.

You <u>mustn't</u> talk about Ron like this.
Perhaps I <u>oughtn't to</u> confess this.
He <u>oughtn't</u> turn away from those who have supported him. (American)

Shall not, will not, and *cannot* are shortened to *shan't, won't,* and *can't. May not* is not shortened at all.

I <u>shan't</u> get much work done tonight.
He <u>won't</u> be finished for at least another half an hour.
I <u>can't</u> go with you.

questions

5.105 Questions are formed by putting the modal in front of the subject. In the case of *ought to*, you put *ought* in front of the subject and *to* after it.

<u>Could you</u> give me an example?
<u>Ought we to</u> tell someone about it?
<u>Mightn't it</u> be better to leave things as they are?
Why <u>could they</u> not leave her alone?
<u>Must we</u> explain everything we do in such detail?

question tags

5.106 Modals are used in **question tags**.

They can't all be right, <u>can they</u>?
You won't tell anyone, <u>will you</u>?

With a negative tag, the shortened form of the negative is used.

It would be handy, <u>wouldn't it</u>?
It'll give you time to think about it, <u>won't it</u>?

Question tags are explained in paragraphs 5.16 to 5.20.

contractions

5.107 In spoken English, when *will* and *would* are used after a pronoun, they are often shortened to *-'ll* and *-'d* and added to the pronoun.

I hope you'<u>ll</u> agree.
She'<u>ll</u> be all right.
They'<u>d</u> both call each other horrible names.
If I went back on the train, it'<u>d</u> be better.

Will and *would* cannot be shortened like this when they are used on their own, without a following verb. For example, you can say *Paul said he would come, and I hope he will*, but you cannot say *Paul said he would come, and I hope he'll*.

USAGE NOTE

5.108 You sometimes use a modal on its own, without a following verb. You do this when you are repeating a modal. For example, if someone says *I expect Margaret will come tonight*, you can say *I hope she will*, meaning *I hope she will come*.

'I *must go*.' – 'I *suppose you must*.'
'You *should have become an archaeologist*.' – 'You're dead right, I *should*.'
If you *can't do it*, we'll find someone who *can*.

You also omit the verb following a modal when this verb has just been used without a modal, or with a different modal. For example, if someone says *George has failed his exam*, you can say *I thought he would*, meaning *I thought he would fail his exam*.

I *love* him and I always *will*.
They had come to believe that it not only *must go on for ever* but that it *should*.

However you cannot omit the verb *be* after a modal when you have just used it without a modal. For example, if someone says *Is he a teacher?*, you cannot say *I think he might*. You must say *I think he might be*.

Weather forecasts *aren't* very reliable and never *will be*.
The Board's methods *are* not as stringent as they *could be*.
Relations between the two countries *have not been* as smooth as they *might have been*.

For more information on leaving out words in verb phrases see paragraphs 10.60 to 10.81.

Referring to time

5.109 Modals do not usually show whether you are talking about the past, the present, or the future. Usually you indicate this in other ways, for example by putting an auxiliary verb and a participle after the modal. Sometimes the general context makes it clear whether you are talking about a past, present, or future event or situation.

the future: *shall* and *will*

5.110 *Shall* and *will* are exceptions to this.

Shall always indicates that you are talking about a future event or situation.

I *shall* do what you suggested.
Eventually we *shall* find a solution.

Will usually shows that you are talking about a future event or situation.

The farmer *will* feel more responsible towards his workers.
He *will* not return for many hours.

However, *will* is sometimes used to talk about present situations.

You *will* not feel much love for him at the moment.

This use of *will* is described in paragraph 5.123.

5.111 *Could* and *would* are sometimes described as past tense forms of *can* and *will*. However, this is true in only a few minor ways. These are explained in the following paragraphs.

ability in the past: *could*

5.112 *Could* can be regarded as the past tense of *can* if you are simply talking about the ability of a person or thing to do something.

For example, if you are talking about a living person, you can say *He can speak Russian and Finnish*. If you are talking about a dead person, you can say *He could speak Russian and Finnish*.

For a fuller explanation of these uses see paragraphs 5.118 to 5.120.

reported speech

5.113 *Could* and *would* are sometimes used in place of *can* and *will* when you are reporting what someone has said.

For example, if your friend has said *I can come*, you might report this as *He said that he could come*. Similarly, if he has said, *I will come*, you might report this as *He said that he would come*.

For a full explanation of **reported speech** see Chapter 7.

things that happened regularly in the past: *would*

5.114 *Would* is used to talk about something that happened regularly in the past, but no longer happens.

The other children would tease me and call me names.
A man with a list would come round and say you could go off duty.

When you use *would* like this, you often add a time expression.

She would often hear him grumbling.
Once in a while she'd give me some lilac to take home.
Every day I'd ring up home and ask if they'd changed their minds.

You can use *used to* instead of *would*. *Used to* is explained in paragraphs 5.254 to 5.258.

thinking about the future: *would*

5.115 *Would* is also used in stories to talk about the thoughts that someone is having about the future. For example, if a character in a story is thinking that she will see a girl called Jane the next day, the author might simply say *She would see Jane the next day*.

He would recognize it when he heard it again.
They would reach the castle some time.

refusing to do something: *would not*

5.116 When *would* is used with *not* to talk about something that happened in the past, it has a special meaning. It is used to say that someone refused to do something.

They just would not believe what we told them.
After all this, I wouldn't come back to the farm.

The use of modals to express a refusal is explained in paragraphs 5.196 to 5.201.

Talking about possibility

5.117   The following four sections explain the different ways in which modals are used to talk about the possibility of something happening or being done.

Paragraphs 5.118 to 5.121 explain how *can* and *could* are used to talk about the ability of a person or thing to do something.

Paragraphs 5.122 to 5.141 explain how modals are used to express degrees of certainty about past, present, and future situations and events.

Paragraphs 5.142 to 5.145 explain how modals are used to say that something is permissible.

Paragraphs 5.146 to 5.153 explain how modals are used to say that something is forbidden or unacceptable.

Talking about ability

skills and abilities: *can* and *could*

5.118   *Can* is used to say that someone has a particular skill or ability.

> You *can* all read and write.
> Some people *can* ski better than others.
> He *cannot* dance.
> ...the girl who *can't* act.

Could is used to say that someone had a skill or ability in the past.

> When I arrived, I *could* speak only a little English.
> I *could* barely walk.
> He *could* kick goals from anywhere.

awareness: *can* and *could*

5.119   *Can* is also used to say that someone is aware of something through one of their senses.

> I *can* see you.
> I *can* smell it. *Can't* you?

Could is used to say that someone was aware of something through one of their senses on a particular occasion in the past.

> I *could* see a few faint stars in a clear patch of sky.
> I *could* feel my heart bumping.
> Police said they *could* smell alcohol on his breath.

general truths: *can* and *could*

5.120   *Can* and *could* are also used to express facts that are generally the case, particularly when they relate to something or someone being capable of having a particular effect, or of behaving in a particular way.

> It *can* be very unpleasant.
> Art *can* be used to communicate.
> Throwing parties *can* be hard work.
> He *could* be very stiff, could Haggerty.
> He *could* really frighten me, and yet at the same time he *could* be the most gentle and courteous of men.

!

5.121   You cannot use *can* or *could* to say that someone or something will have a particular ability in the future. Instead you use *be able to* or *be possible to*.

Be able to and be possible to can also be used to talk about someone's ability to do something in the present or the past.

Be able to and *be possible to* are dealt with in paragraphs 5.224 to 5.231.

Talking about likelihood

5.122   The following paragraphs explain how modals are used to express different degrees of certainty about past, present, and future situations and events.

Paragraphs 5.123 to 5.129 explain the main ways in which modals are used to express degrees of certainty.

Paragraphs 5.130 to 5.134 explain special uses of modals when talking about possible future situations.

Paragraphs 5.135 to 5.141 explain special uses of modals when talking about possible situations in the past.

assuming that something is the case: *will* and *would*

5.123   You use *will* when you are assuming that something is the case, and you do not think there is any reason to doubt it.

Those of you who are familiar with the game will know this.
He will be a little out of touch, although he's a rapid learner.
She will have forgotten all about it by now.

Similarly, you use *will not* or *won't* when you are assuming that something is not the case.

The audience will not be aware of such exact details.
You won't know Gordon. He's our new doctor.

After *you*, you can use *would* instead of *will*, if you want to be more polite.

You would agree that the United States should be involved in assisting these countries.

certainty: *would* and *should*

5.124   You also use *would* to say that something is certain to happen in particular circumstances.

Even an illiterate person would understand that.
Few people would agree with this as a general principle.
A picnic wouldn't be any fun without you.

After *I*, you can use *should* instead of *would*.

The very first thing I should do would be to teach you how to cook.
I should be very unhappy on the continent.

 This is unusual in American English, which normally uses *would* after *I*.

belief: *must* and *cannot*

5.125 You use *must* to show that you believe something is the case, because of particular facts or circumstances.

> *Oh, you must be Sylvia's husband.*
> *Fashion must account for a small percentage of sales.*
> *This article must have been written by a woman.*

When you are indicating that something is not the case, you use *cannot*. You do not use *must not*. (See paragraph 5.128.)

> *The two conflicting messages cannot possibly both be true.*
> *You can't have forgotten me.*
> *He can't have said that. He just can't.*

present possibility: *could*, *might*, and *may*

5.126 You use *could*, *might*, or *may* to say that there is a possibility of something happening or being the case. *May* is slightly more formal than *could* or *might*; otherwise there is very little difference in meaning between these modals.

> *Don't eat it. It could be poisonous.*
> *His route from the bus stop might be the same as yours.*
> *In rare cases the jaw may be broken during extraction.*

If you put *well* after *could*, *might*, or *may*, you are saying that it is fairly likely that something is the case.

> *It could well be that the economic situation is getting better.*
> *His predictions could well have come true.*
> *You might well be right.*
> *I think that may well have been the intention.*

negative possibility: *might not* and *may not*

5.127 You use *might not* or *may not* to say that it is possible that something is not the case.

> *He might not be in England at all.*
> *That mightn't be true.*
> *That may not sound very imposing.*

impossibility: *could not* and *cannot*

5.128 You use *could not* or *cannot* to say that it is impossible that something is the case.

> *...knowledge which could not have been gained in any other way.*
> *It couldn't possibly be poison.*
> *He cannot know everything that is going on.*
> *You can't talk to the dead.*

strong assertion: *could not* with comparatives

5.129 *Could* is sometimes used in negative constructions with the comparative form of an adjective. You use *could* like this to say that it is not possible for someone or something to have more of a particular quality.

> *I couldn't be happier.*
> *You couldn't be more wrong.*
> *The setting couldn't have been lovelier.*
> *He could hardly have felt more ashamed of himself.*

talking about the future

5.130 The following paragraphs explain how modals are used when you are talking about possible future situations. The uses of *must*, *cannot*, *could*, *might*, and *may* are similar to their uses when you are talking about possible situations in the present.

certainty: *will*

5.131 You use *will* to say that something is certain to happen or be the case in the future.

> They *will* see everything.
> The price of food *will* go up.
> The service *will* have been running for a year in May.

Be going to can also be used to say that something is certain to happen in the future. This use of *be going to* is dealt with in paragraph 5.233.

certainty: *shall*, *must*, and *cannot*

5.132 *Shall* is also used to say that something is certain to happen. You usually use *shall* when you are talking about events and situations over which you have some control. For example, you can use *shall* when you are making a resolution or a promise.

> I *shall* be leaving as soon as I am ready.
> Very well, my dear. You *shall* have the coat.
> Of course he *shall* have water.
> 'You'll make a lot of money.' – 'I *shall* one day.'

 This usage is considered very formal in American English and is not often used.

You use *must* to say that something is certain to happen because of particular facts or circumstances.

> This research *must* eventually lead to computer decision-making.

You use *cannot* to say that something is certain not to happen because of particular facts or circumstances. You do not use *must not*.

> A team *cannot* hope to win consistently without a good coach.
> The bad weather *can't* last.

expectation: *should* and *ought to*

5.133 You use *should* or *ought to* to say that you expect something to happen.

> She *should* be back any time now.
> This course *should* be quite interesting for you.
> The Court of Appeal *ought to* be able to help you.
> It *ought to* get better as it goes along.

Should and *ought to* are also used when you are talking about the importance of doing something. This use is explained in paragraph 5.215.

future possibility: *could*, *might*, and *may*

5.134 You use *could*, *might*, or *may* to say that it is possible that a particular thing will happen.

> England's next fixture in Salzburg *could* be the decisive match.
> The river *could* easily overflow.

They might be able to remember what he said.
Clerical work may be available for two students who want to learn about publishing.

If you put *well* after *could*, *might*, or *may*, you are indicating that it is fairly likely that something will happen or be the case.

When it is finished it may well be the largest cathedral in the world.
We might well get injured.

If you put *possibly* or *conceivably* after *could*, *might*, or *may*, you are indicating that it is possible, but fairly unlikely, that something will happen or be the case.

These conditions could possibly be accepted.
Rates could conceivably rise by as much as a whole percentage point.

talking about the past

5.135 The following paragraphs explain how you use modals when you are talking about possible situations in the past.

expectation: *should have, ought to have*

5.136 You use *should* or *ought to* with *have* to say that you expect something to have happened already.

Dear Mom, you should have heard by now that I'm O.K.

You also use *should* or *ought to* with *have* to say that something was expected to happen, although it has not in fact happened.

Muskie should have won by a huge margin.
She ought to have been home by now.

possibility: *would have*

5.137 You use *would* with *have* to talk about actions and events that were possible in the past, although they did not in fact happen.

Denial would have been useless.
I would have said yes, but Julie persuaded us to stay at home.
You wouldn't have pushed him, would you?

possibility: *could have, might have*

5.138 You use *could* or *might* with *have* to say that there was a possibility of something happening in the past, although it did not in fact happen.

It could have been awful.
I could easily have spent the whole year on it.
You could have got a job last year.
A lot of men died who might have been saved.
You might have found it very difficult.

uncertainty: *could have, might have, may have*

5.139 You also use *could*, *might*, or *may* with *have* to say that it is possible that something was the case, but you do not know whether it was the case or not.

It is just possible that such a small creature could have preyed on dinosaur eggs.
They might have moved house by now.
I may have seemed to be overreacting.

negative possibility: *might not have, may not have*

5.140   You use *might not* or *may not* with *have* to say that it is possible that something did not happen or was not the case.

> They *might not have* considered me as their friend.
> My father *mightn't have* been to blame.
> The parents *may not have* been ready for this news.

impossibility: *could have* with negative

5.141   You use *could* with a negative and *have* to say that it is impossible that something happened or was the case.

> It *couldn't have* been wrong.
> The money was not, and *never could have* been, the property of the organization.

Talking about permission

permission: *can*

5.142   *Can* is used to say that someone is allowed to do something.

> You *can* drive a van up to 3-ton capacity using an ordinary driving licence.

If you are giving permission for something, you use *can*.

> You *can* borrow that pen if you want to.
> You *can* go off duty now.
> She *can* go with you.

formal permission: *may*

5.143   In more formal situations, *may* is used to give permission.

> You *may* speak now.
> They *may* do exactly as they like.

permission in the past: *could*

5.144   *Could* is used to say that someone was allowed to do something in the past.

> We *could* go to any part of the island we wanted to.

!   **BE CAREFUL**

5.145   You cannot use *can* or *could* to say that someone will be allowed to do something in the future. Instead you use *be able to*.

> *Be able to* is dealt with in paragraphs 5.224 to 5.231.

Saying that something is unacceptable

5.146   Modals are often used in negative structures to say that an action is forbidden or unacceptable.

saying that something is forbidden: *cannot*

5.147 *Cannot* is used to say that something is forbidden, for example because of a rule or law.

> *Children <u>cannot</u> bathe except in the presence of two lifesavers.*
> *We're awfully sorry we <u>can't</u> let you stay here.*

saying that something is forbidden: *may not*

5.148 *May not* is used in a similar way to *cannot*, but is more formal.

> *You <u>may not</u> make amendments to your application once we have received it.*
> *This material <u>may not</u> be published, broadcast, or redistributed in any manner.*

saying that something is forbidden: *will not*

5.149 *Will not* is used to tell someone very firmly that they are not allowed to do a particular thing. Usually, the speaker has the power to prevent the hearer from doing this thing.

> *'I'll just go upstairs.' – 'You <u>will not</u>.'*
> *Until we have cured you, you <u>won't</u> be leaving here.*

saying that something is forbidden: *shall not*

5.150 *Shall not* is used to say formally that a particular thing is not allowed. *Shall not* is often used in written rules, laws, and agreements.

> *Persons under 18 <u>shall not</u> be employed in nightwork.*
> *Equality of rights under the law <u>shall not</u> be denied or abridged by the United States or by any State.*

> *Shan't* is used in a similar way to *will not* and *won't*.

> *You <u>shan't</u> leave without my permission.*

saying that something is forbidden: imperatives

5.151 You can also say that something is not allowed by using an **imperative** sentence. Imperative sentences are explained in paragraph 5.4 and in paragraphs 5.37 to 5.41.

undesirable actions: *should not*

5.152 *Should not* is used to tell someone that an action is unacceptable or undesirable.

> *You <u>should not</u> take her help for granted.*
> *You <u>shouldn't</u> do that.*
> *You <u>shouldn't</u> be so unfriendly.*

undesirable actions: *must not*

5.153 *Must not* is used to say much more firmly that something is unacceptable or undesirable.

> *You <u>must not</u> accept it.*
> *You <u>mustn't</u> do that.*
> *You <u>mustn't</u> breathe a word of this to anyone.*

Interacting with other people

5.154 You often say things in order to get someone to behave in a particular way. For example, you may want someone to take a particular action, to accept an offer, or to give their permission for something to be done.

In these situations, modals are often used. The modal you choose depends on several factors. The main ones are:

▶ the formality or informality of the situation

▶ the relationship between yourself and the person you are speaking to

▶ the degree of politeness you want to show.

In particular situations, other factors can be important. For example, if you are making an offer or suggestion, the modal you choose may depend on how persuasive you want to be.

5.155 The following sections explain how to use modals in different situations.

Paragraphs 5.156 to 5.172 explain how to give instructions and make requests.

Paragraphs 5.173 to 5.181 explain how to make an offer or an invitation.

Paragraphs 5.182 to 5.189 explain how to make suggestions.

Paragraphs 5.190 to 5.195 explain how to state an intention.

Paragraphs 5.196 to 5.201 explain how to express unwillingness or a refusal to do something.

Paragraphs 5.202 to 5.210 explain how to express a wish.

Paragraphs 5.211 to 5.215 explain how to indicate the importance of doing something.

Paragraphs 5.216 to 5.222 explain various ways of introducing what you are going to say.

Giving instructions and making requests

5.156 When you give an instruction or make a request, you usually use a modal in an interrogative sentence.

You use *will*, *would*, *can*, or *could* with *you* to tell someone to do something, or to ask someone to do something.

You use *can*, *could*, *may*, or *might* with *I* or *we* or with other personal pronouns or noun phrases to ask someone's permission to do something.

Instructions and requests are always made more polite by adding *please*. *Please* and other markers of politeness are explained in paragraph 5.172.

instructions and appeals for help

5.157 *Will*, *would*, and *could* are used with *you* in two ways:

▶ you use them to give an instruction or an order

▶ you use them to ask for help or assistance.

instructions and appeals for help: *will*

5.158 *Will* is used to give an instruction or order in a fairly direct way. It is slightly less forceful than using the imperative.

Will you pick those toys up please?
Will you pack up and leave at once, please.

Will is used to ask for help in fairly informal situations.

Mummy, will you help me?

instructions and appeals for help: *would*

5.159 When *would* is used to give an instruction or order, it is more polite than *will*.

Would you tell her that Adrian phoned?
Would you ask them to leave, please?

When *would* is used to ask for help, it is less informal and more polite than *will*.

Would you do me a favour?

instructions and appeals for help: *could*

5.160 When *could* is used to give an instruction or order, it is more polite than *would*.

Could you follow me please?
Could you just switch the projector on behind you?

When *could* is used to ask for help, it is more polite than *would*.

Could you show me how to do this?

appeals for help: *can*

5.161 *Can* can be used with *you* to ask for help. You usually use *can* when you are not sure whether someone will be able to help you or not.

Oh hello. Can you help me? I've been trying this number for ten minutes and I can't get through.

requests

5.162 *Can*, *could*, *may*, and *might* are used with *I* or *we* when you are asking for something, or are asking permission to do something.

These modals can also be used with *he*, *she*, or *they*, or with other noun phrases, when you are asking for something on behalf of someone else. For example, you can say *Can she borrow your car?* or *Could my mother use your telephone?*

requests: *can*

5.163 *Can* is used to make a request in a simple and direct way.

Can I ask a question?
'Can I change this?' I asked the box office lady, offering her my ticket.

requests: *could*

5.164 *Could* is more polite than *can*.

Could I have a bottle of lemonade, please?
Could I just interrupt a minute?

requests: *can't* and *couldn't*

5.165 You can make a request sound more persuasive by using *can't* or *couldn't* instead of *can* or *could*. For example, you can say *Can't I come with you?* instead of *Can I come with you?*

Can't we have some music?
Couldn't we stay here?

requests: *may* and *might*

5.166 *May* and *might* are more formal than *can* and *could*. In the past, people were taught that, when asking for something, it was correct to say *may* rather than *can*, and *might* rather than *could*. However *can* and *could* are now generally used. Requests beginning with *might* are unusual, and are considered by most people to be old-fashioned.

May I have a cigarette?
May we have something to eat?
May I ask what your name is?
Might I inquire if you are the owner?

instructions: *would like*

5.167 *Would like* can be used with *I* or *we* in a declarative sentence to give an instruction or order. It is followed by *you* and a *to*-infinitive clause.

OK, everyone, I would like you to get into a circle.

Want can be used in a similar way to *would like*. This use of *want* is dealt with in paragraph 5.236.

firm instructions: *will*

5.168 An instruction or order can also be given using *will* in a declarative sentence. This form is used when the speaker is angry or impatient.

You will go and get one of your parents immediately.
You will give me those now.

formal instructions: *shall*

5.169 *Shall* is sometimes used in a declarative sentence to give an instruction or order. This is a very formal use.

There shall be no further communication between you.

imperatives

5.170 The **imperative** can also be used to give an instruction or order. This use is explained in paragraph 5.37.

requests: *would like, should like*

5.171 You can use *would like* or (in British English only) *should like* in a declarative sentence to make a request. *Would like* and *should like* are followed by a *to*-infinitive clause or a noun phrase.

I would like to ask you one question.

I'd like to have a little talk with you.
I should like a list of your customers over the past year.

polite additions to requests

5.172 All the ways of giving instructions or making requests described above can be made more polite by using *please*.

Can I speak to Nicola, please?
Please may I have the key?

You can also make a request more polite by adding the name of the person you are addressing at the beginning or end of your question.

Martin, could you make us a drink?
Can I talk to you, Howard?

Another way of making a request more polite is to add an adverb such as *perhaps* or *possibly* after the subject of the verb.

Could I perhaps bring a friend with me?
May I possibly have a word with you?

 In spoken English, you can make a request more polite by adding *just* after the subject of the verb.

Could you just come into my office for a minute?

Making an offer or an invitation

5.173 Modals are often used to make an offer or an invitation.

You use *will* or *would* with *you* to ask someone to accept something, or to make an invitation.

You use *can, may, shall,* or *should* with *I* or *we* when you are offering to help someone.

Some of these structures are similar to those described in the previous section.

offers and invitations: *will*

5.174 *Will* is used with *you* in an interrogative sentence to offer something to someone, or to make an invitation in a fairly informal way. You use *will* when you know the person you are talking to quite well.

Will you have a whisky, Doctor?
Will you stay for lunch?

offers and invitations: *would* and *wouldn't*

5.175 A more polite way of offering something or making an invitation is to use *would* with a verb that means *to like*.

Would you like a drink?
Would you care to stay with us?

If you want to sound more persuasive without seeming impolite or insistent, you can use *wouldn't* instead of *would*.

Wouldn't you like to come with me?
Wouldn't you care for some more coffee?

offers of help: *can*

5.176 When you are offering to do something for someone, you usually use *can* followed by *I* or *we*.

> <u>Can</u> I help you with the dishes?
> <u>Can</u> we give you a lift into town?

offers of help: *may*

5.177 *May* is also used when you are offering to do something for someone. It is less common than *can*, and is rather formal and old-fashioned.

> <u>May</u> I help you?
> <u>May</u> I take your coat?

offers of help: *shall* and *should*

5.178 You can also use *shall* or *should* when you are offering to do something.

If you are offering to do something that you can do immediately, or you are fairly confident that your offer will be accepted, you use *shall*.

> <u>Shall</u> I shut the door?
> <u>Shall</u> I spell that for you?

If you talking about a less likely or less immediate situation, or if you are uncertain whether your offer will be accepted, you use *should*.

> <u>Should</u> I give her a ring?
> <u>Should</u> I put all these meetings on my calendar?

emphasizing ability: *can*

5.179 If you want to emphasize your ability to help, you can make an offer using *can* in a declarative sentence.

> I have a car. I <u>can</u> drop you off on my way home.
> I <u>can</u> pop in at the shop tomorrow.

persuasive invitations: *must* and *have to*

5.180 If you want to make an invitation in a very persuasive way, you can use a declarative sentence beginning with *you* and *must* or *have to*. *Have to* is more common in American English.

> You <u>must</u> join us for drinks this evening.
> You <u>have to</u> come and visit me.

You only use *must* and *have to* like this with people who you know well.

5.181 Other ways of making an offer or invitation are dealt with in paragraph 5.44.

Making suggestions

5.182 Suggestions can be made by using a modal in a declarative or interrogative sentence. The subject of the sentence is usually *we* or *you*.

suggesting: *could*

5.183 You can make a suggestion by using *could* in a declarative sentence or *couldn't* in an interrogative sentence.

If the business doesn't work out we could sell it.
You could have a nursery there.
Couldn't you just build more factories?
Couldn't some international agreement be concluded to ban these weapons?

suggesting: *should* and *ought to*

5.184 If you are making a suggestion and you want to indicate that you feel strongly that it is a good idea, you can use *should* or *ought to*.

You should ask Norry about this.
I think you should get in touch with your solicitor.
We ought to celebrate. Let's get a bottle of champagne.
I think you ought to try a different approach.

A more polite way of making a suggestion that you feel strongly about is to use *shouldn't* or *oughtn't to* in an interrogative sentence.

Shouldn't we at least give her a chance?
Oughtn't we to phone the police?

persuading: *must*

5.185 If you are suggesting an action and you are trying to persuade someone that it should be done, you use *must*. You only use *must* like this when you are talking to someone you know well.

You must say hello to your daughter.
We must go to the place, perhaps have a weekend there.

polite suggestions: *might*

5.186 If you want to make a suggestion in a very polite way, you can use *might* with *you* in a declarative sentence. *Might* is followed by a verb meaning *to like* or *to want*.

You might want to comment on his latest proposal.
I thought perhaps you might like to come along with me.

You can also make a polite suggestion by using a sentence beginning with *It might be*, followed by a noun phrase or adjective and a *to*-infinitive clause.

I think it might be a good idea to stop now.
It might be better to wait a while.

suggesting: *might as well*, *may as well*

5.187 You can also make suggestions using the expressions *might as well* and *may as well*.

You use *might as well* when what you are suggesting seems to be the only sensible course of action, although you are not enthusiastic about it.

He might as well take the car.
We might as well call the whole thing off.

You use *may as well* to show that it is not important to you whether your suggestion is accepted or not.

You <u>may as well</u> open them all.
We <u>may as well</u> give her a copy.

suggesting: *shall*

5.188 You can make a suggestion about what you and someone else could do by using an interrogative sentence beginning with *shall* and *we*.

<u>Shall</u> we go and see a film?
<u>Shall</u> we go on to question number six?
<u>Shall</u> we talk about something different now?

5.189 Other ways of making suggestions are described in paragraph 5.48.

Stating an intention

5.190 Intentions are usually stated by using *will*, *shall*, or *must* in a declarative sentence. The subject is *I* or *we*.

intentions: *will*

5.191 The usual way to state an intention is to use *I* or *we* with *will*. The shortened forms *I'll* and *we'll* are very common.

I <u>will</u> call you when I am ready.
We <u>will</u> stay here.
I'<u>ll</u> write again some time.
We'<u>ll</u> discuss that later.

You state your intention not to do something using *will not* or *won't*.

I <u>will not</u> follow her.
I <u>won't</u> keep you any longer.
We <u>won't</u> let them through the gate.

5.192 You can show that you are very determined to do something by using the full form *I will* or *we will* and stressing *will*.

You can show that you are very determined not to do something either by using *I won't* or *we won't* and stressing *won't*, or by using *I will not* or *we will not* and stressing *not*.

intentions: *shall*

5.193 Another way of stating an intention is to use *I* or *we* with *shall*.

I <u>shall</u> be leaving soon.
I <u>shall</u> make some enquiries and call you back.
We <u>shall</u> continue to monitor his progress.

 This use is slightly old-fashioned, rather formal, and uncommon in American English.

You can show that you are very determined not to do something by using *shall not* or *shan't*. This is more emphatic than using *will not* or *won't*.

I <u>shall not</u> disclose his name.
I <u>shan't</u> go back there.

 The form *shan't* is not used in American English.

intentions: *must*

5.194 If you want to show that it is important that you do something, you can use *I must*.

> I <u>must</u> leave fairly soon.
> I <u>must</u> ask her about that.
> I <u>must</u> call my mum–it's her birthday today.

5.195 Ways of stating an intention without using a modal are explained in paragraphs 5.237 to 5.240.

Expressing unwillingness or refusal

5.196 A refusal can be expressed by using a modal in a negative declarative sentence. The subject is usually *I* or *we*, but other personal pronouns or noun phrases can be used.

refusal: *will not* and *won't*

5.197 If you want to say firmly that you refuse to do something, you use *will not* or *won't*.

> I <u>will not</u> hear a word said against the National Health Service.
> I <u>won't</u> let this happen.

You can just say *I won't*.

> 'Tell me your secret.' – '<u>I won't</u>. It wouldn't be a secret if I told you.'
> It isn't that I <u>won't</u>. I can't.

You can use *won't* to say that someone else is refusing to do something.

> He <u>won't</u> give her the money.

refusal: *would not*

5.198 If you want to say that you refused to do something in the past, you use *would not* or *wouldn't*.

> He thought I was a freak because I <u>wouldn't</u> carry a weapon.

unwillingness: *cannot*

5.199 If you want to show that you have strong feelings that prevent you from doing something, you use *cannot* or *can't*.

> I <u>cannot</u> leave everything for him.
> I <u>can't</u> give you up.

unwillingness: *couldn't*

5.200 *Couldn't* is used in two ways to express unwillingness to do something.

You use it to show that you are unwilling to do something because you are afraid, embarrassed, or disgusted.

> I <u>couldn't</u> possibly go out now.
> I <u>couldn't</u> let him touch me.

You use it to indicate that you are unwilling to do something because you think it would be unfair or morally wrong.

> I <u>couldn't</u> leave Hilary to cope on her own.
> I <u>couldn't</u> take your last chocolate.

5.201 Other ways of expressing refusal and unwillingness are described in paragraphs 5.241 to 5.243.

Expressing a wish

5.202 Wishes can be expressed by using a modal in a declarative sentence.

wishes: *would*

5.203 You can say what someone wants by using *would* followed by a verb meaning *to like*. After the verb meaning *to like* you put a *to*-infinitive clause or a noun phrase.

> I _would_ like to know the date.
> I _would_ prefer to say nothing about this problem.
> We'_d_ like to keep you here.
> Oh, I hope it will be twins. I'_d_ love twins.

5.204 You can say what someone does not want by using *would not*.

> I _would not_ like to see it.
> We _wouldn't_ like to lose you.

Normally, when you are using *would* with *like* to say what someone does not want, you put *not* after *would*. If you put *not* after *like*, you change the meaning slightly.

For example, if you say I would not like to be a student, you mean you are not a student and do not want to be one. But if you say I would like not to be a student, you mean you are a student and do not want to be one.

> They _would like not_ to have to go through all that.

You can also say what someone does not want by using *would* with *hate*.

> I _would_ hate to move to another house now.
> Personally, I _would_ hate to be dragged into this dispute.

wishes: *should*

5.205 You can also say what someone wants or does not want by using *should*. *Should* is less common than *would*, and is slightly more formal.

> I _should_ like to live in the country.
> I _should_ hate to see them disappear.

preference: *would rather, would sooner*

5.206 You can say that someone prefers one situation to another by using *would rather* or *would sooner*.

> He _would rather_ have left it.
> She'_d rather_ be left alone.
> I'_d sooner_ walk than do any of these things.

wishes: *would have*

5.207 If you want to say that someone wanted something to happen, although it did not happen, you use *would have* and an -*ed* participle.

> I _would have_ liked to hear more from the patient.
> She _would have_ liked to remain just where she was.

USAGE NOTE

5.208 Another way of saying that you want something is to use *wouldn't* with a verb or expression that is normally used to refuse something, such as *mind* or *object to*.

> *I wouldn't mind being a manager of a store.*
> *'Drink, Ted?' – 'I wouldn't say no, Bryan.'*

regret: *would that*

5.209 In very old-fashioned English, *would* is used without a subject to express a wish that a situation might be different, or to express regret that something did not happen in the past. *Would* is followed by a *that*-clause.

> *'Are they better off now than they were two years ago?' – 'Would that they were.'*
> *Would that the developments had been so easy.*

When *I*, *he*, *she*, or *it* is the subject of the *that*-clause, the verb is usually *were*, not *was*.

> *Would that you were here tonight.*
> *Two years ago we were told that they would be much better off by now. Would that they were.*

hopes and wishes: *may*

5.210 In very formal English, *may* is used to express a hope or wish.

> *Long may they continue to do it.*
> *May he justify our hopes and rise to the top.*

Indicating importance

5.211 Modals can be used in declarative sentences to say that it is important that something is done. Different modals indicate different degrees of importance.

importance: *must*

5.212 *Must* is used in three common ways to talk about the importance of doing something.

You use *must* with *you* or *we* to urge someone to do something, because you feel it is important. *Must not* is used to urge someone not to do something.

> *You must come at once.*
> *We must accept the truth about ourselves.*
> *You must not worry.*
> *You mustn't let her suffer for it.*

Have to, *have got to*, and *need to* can be used instead of *must* to talk about the importance of doing something. This is explained in paragraphs 5.244 and 5.245.

You use *must* to say that something is required by a rule or law.

> *People who qualify must apply within six months.*
> *European Community standards must be met.*

You use *must* to say that it is necessary that something happens or is done, in order that something else can happen.

> *Meadows must have rain.*
> *To travel properly you must have a valid ticket.*

necessity: *will have to, will need to*

5.213 If you want to say that an action will be necessary in the future, you use *will have to* or *will need to*.

> They <u>will have to</u> pay for the repairs.
> Mr Smith <u>will have to</u> make the funeral arrangements.
> You <u>will need to</u> cover it with some kind of sheeting.
> Electric clocks <u>will need to</u> be reset.

necessity: *shall have to*

5.214 *Shall have to* is sometimes used instead of *will have to* after *I* or *we*.

> I <u>shall have to</u> speak about that to Peter.
> We <u>shall have to</u> assume that you are right.

 This is a slightly formal use, and is rarely used in American English.

importance: *should* and *ought to*

5.215 *Should* and *ought to* are used in three different ways when you are talking about the importance of doing something.

You use *should* or *ought to* when you are trying to help someone by advising them to do something.

> Carbon steel knives <u>should</u> be wiped clean after use.
> You <u>should</u> claim your pension 3-4 months before you retire.
> You <u>ought to</u> try a different approach.

You use *should* or *ought to* when you are saying that something is the right or correct thing to do.

> We <u>should</u> send her a postcard.
> The judges <u>should</u> offer constructive criticism.
> We <u>ought to</u> stay with him.
> You <u>ought</u> not <u>to</u> do that.

You use *should* or *ought to* with *have* and an *-ed* participle to say that something was desirable in the past, although it did not in fact happen.

> One sailor <u>should have</u> been asleep and one on watch.
> We <u>ought to have</u> stayed in tonight.
> A more junior member of staff <u>ought to have</u> done the work.

You also use *should* and *ought to* to say that you expect something to happen. This use is explained in paragraph 5.133.

Introducing what you are going to say

5.216 Sometimes you introduce what you are going to say by using a modal followed by a verb such as *say* or *ask* that refers to the act of saying something. You can also combine a modal with a verb such as *think* or *believe* that refers to the holding of an opinion.

You use a modal in order to sound more polite, or to show your feelings about what you are going to say.

In structures like these, the subject is usually *I*. Sometimes you use an impersonal structure beginning with *it* or *you*. For example, instead of saying *I ought to mention that he had never been there*, you can say *It ought to be mentioned that he had never been there*.

importance: *must*

5.217 If you feel strongly that what you are saying is important, you use *must*.

I must apologize to you.
I must object.
It must be said that he has a point.

importance: *should* and *ought to*

5.218 If you feel that it is important or appropriate that something is said, you indicate that you are going to say it by using *should* or *ought to*.

I should explain at this point that there are two different sorts of microscope.
It should also be said that I learned a great deal from the experience.
I ought to stress that this was not a trial.
Perhaps I ought to conclude with a slightly more light-hearted question.

politeness: *can* and *could*

5.219 If you want to say something during a discussion, you can indicate politely that you are going to say it by using *can*.

Perhaps I can mention another possibility.
If I can just intervene for one moment...

If you want to be even more polite, you use *could*.

Perhaps I could just illustrate this by mentioning two cases that I know of personally.
Perhaps I could just ask you this...

5.220 You also use *can* and *could* when you are mentioning an opinion or a way of describing something.

Can suggests that you approve of the opinion or description.

Such behaviour can be a reaction to deep emotional upset.

Could is more neutral.

You could argue that this is irrelevant.
You could call it a political offence.

approval: *may* and *might*

5.221 *May* and *might* can also be used to mention an opinion or a way of describing something.

May suggests that you approve of the opinion or description. It is more formal than *can*.

This, it may be added, greatly strengthened him in his resolve.

Might also suggests that you approve of the opinion or description. You use *might* when you think there is a possibility that the person you are talking to will disagree with you.

You might say she's entitled to get angry.
That, one might argue, is not too terrible.

5.222 If you are stating an opinion of your own, you can show politely that you are going to state it by using *should*.

I should think it would last quite a long time.

Would is used in a similar way, but is less common.

I would guess it may well come down to cost.

Expressions used instead of modals

5.223 Several ordinary verbs and fixed expressions are used to express the same attitudes and ideas as modals. These verbs and expressions are explained in the following paragraphs. Each group of paragraphs corresponds to an earlier section in the chapter dealing with the use of modals in a particular type of situation.

saying whether something is possible

5.224 *Be able to* and *be possible to* can be used instead of *can* and *could* to say whether or not something is possible.

The subject of *be able to* and *be unable to* usually refers to a person or group of people, but it can refer to any living thing. It can also refer to something organized or operated by people, such as a company, a country, or a machine.

The subject of *be possible to* is always the impersonal pronoun *it*.

5.225 If you want to say that it is possible for someone or something to do something, you can use *be able to*.

All members are able to claim travelling expenses.
The college is able to offer a wide choice of subjects.

You use *be able to* with a negative to say that it is not possible for someone or something to do something.

They are not able to run fast or throw a ball.

5.226 You also use *be unable to* to say that it is not possible for someone or something to do something.

I am having medical treatment and I'm unable to work.
We are unable to comment on this.

5.227 You also use *be possible to* with *it* as the subject to say that something is possible. You usually use this expression to say that something is possible for people in general, rather than for an individual person.

It is possible to insure against loss of earnings.
Is it possible to programme a computer to speak?

If you use *be possible to* to say that something is possible for a particular person or group, you put *for* and a noun phrase after *possible*.

It is possible for us to measure his progress.
It's possible for each department to support new members.

You use *be possible to* with a negative to say that something is not possible.

It is not possible to quantify the effect.

5.228 You can also use *be impossible to* to say that something is not possible.

> *It is impossible to fix the exact moment in time when it happened.*
> *It is impossible for him to watch TV and talk.*

5.229 To change the tense of *be able to*, *be unable to*, *be possible to*, or *be impossible to*, you simply change the form of *be* to an appropriate simple form.

> *The doctor will be able to spend more time with the patient.*
> *Their parents were unable to send them any money.*
> *It was not possible to dismiss his behaviour as a contributing factor.*
> *It was impossible for her to obey this order.*

5.230 All modals except *can* and *could* can be used with these expressions.

> *A machine ought to be able to do this.*
> *The United States would be unable to produce any wood.*
> *It may be impossible to predict which way things will develop.*

5.231 *Used to* can be used with *be able to* and *be possible to*.

> *You used to be able to go to the doctor for that.*
> *It used to be possible to buy second-hand wigs.*

For more information about *used to*, see paragraphs 5.254 to 5.258.

saying how likely something is

5.232 You can use *have to* or *have got to* instead of *must* to show that you think something is the case, because of particular facts or circumstances.

> *'That looks about right.' – 'It has to be.'*
> *Money has got to be the reason.*

5.233 You can use *be going to* instead of *will* to say that something is certain to happen or be the case in the future.

> *The children are going to be fishermen or farmers.*
> *Life is going to be a bit easier from now on.*

5.234 You can use *be bound to* or *be sure to* to say emphatically that something is certain to happen in the future.

> *Marion's bound to be back soon.*
> *It was bound to happen sooner or later.*
> *The roads are sure to be busy this weekend.*

giving instructions and making requests

5.235 Instead of beginning a question with *can* or *could* when you are making a request, you can begin it with *is* and the impersonal pronoun *it*. After *it*, you put an expression such as *all right* and either a *to*-infinitive clause or an *if*-clause.

> *Is it all right for him to come in and sit and read his paper?*
> *Is it okay if we have lunch here?*

5.236 You can use *want* instead of *would like* to give an instruction or make a request. *Want* is more direct and less polite than *would like*.

> *I want you to turn to the front of the atlas.*
> *I want to know what you think about this.*
> *I want to speak to the manager.*

Wanted is also sometimes used. It is more polite than *want*.

I wanted to ask if you could give us any advice.
Good morning, I wanted to book a holiday in the South of France.

stating an intention

5.237 You can use *be going to* instead of *will* to state an intention.

I am going to talk to Boris.
I'm going to show you our little school.

5.238 You use *intend to* to state a fairly strong intention.

I intend to go to Cannes for a month in August.
I don't intend to stay very long.

5.239 You use *be determined to* or *be resolved to* to indicate a very strong intention to do something. *Be resolved to* is rather formal.

I'm determined to try.
She was resolved to marry a rich American.

5.240 You can use *have to* or *have got to* instead of *must* to show that it is important that you do something.

I have to get home now.
It's something I have got to overcome.

expressing unwillingness

5.241 You can use *I am not* instead of *I will not* to say firmly that you are unwilling to do or accept something. *I am not* is followed by an *-ing* participle.

I am not staying in this hospital.
I'm not having dirty rugs.

5.242 You can use *refuse* instead of *will not* when you are refusing to do something. *Refuse* is followed by a *to*-infinitive clause.

I refuse to list possible reasons.
I refuse to pay.

5.243 You can use *unwilling* or *reluctant* with a *to*-infinitive clause to say that someone is not willing to do or accept something.

He is unwilling to answer the questions.
They seemed reluctant to talk about what had happened.

You can use several adjectives after *not* to say that someone is unwilling to do or accept something.

Exporters are not willing to supply goods on credit.
I'm not prepared to teach him anything.
Thompson is not keen to see history repeat itself.

indicating importance

5.244 You can use *have to* or *have got to* instead of *must* to say that something is necessary or extremely important.

We have to look more closely at the record of their work together.
This has got to be put right.
You've got to be able to communicate.

5.245 *Need to* can also be used instead of *must* or *have to*.

> *We need to change the balance of power.*
> *You do not need to worry.*

5.246 You can also say that something is important or necessary by using a sentence beginning with the impersonal pronoun *it*, followed by *is*, an adjective such as *important* or *necessary*, and a *that*-clause.

> *It is important that you should know precisely what is going on.*
> *It is essential that immediate action should be taken.*
> *It is vital that a mother takes time to get to know her baby.*

Important and *necessary* can also be followed by a *to*-infinitive clause.

> *It's important to recognize what industry needs at this moment.*
> *It is necessary to examine this claim before we proceed any further.*

5.247 You can use *had better* instead of *should* or *ought to* to say that something is the right or correct thing to do. You use *had better* with *I* or *we* to show an intention. You use it with *you* when you are giving advice or a warning.

> *I think I had better show this to my brother.*
> *He decided that we had better meet.*
> *You'd better go.*

Semi-modals

5.248 *Dare*, *need*, and *used to* can be used as modals, or they can be used in other ways. When they are used as modals, they have some characteristics that other modals do not have. For these reasons, they are sometimes called **semi-modals**.

The use of *dare* and *need* as modals is explained in paragraphs 5.249 to 5.253.

The use of *used to* as a modal is explained in paragraphs 5.254 to 5.258.

dare and need

5.249 When *dare* and *need* are used as modals, they have the same meaning as when they are followed by a *to*-infinitive clause. However, they are normally used as modals only in negative sentences and in questions.

> *Nobody dare disturb him.*
> *No parent dare let their child roam free.*
> *He told her that she need not worry.*
> *How dare you speak to me like that?*
> *Need you go so soon?*

 Need not is often shortened to *needn't*. *Dare not* is sometimes shortened to *daren't* in British English but this contraction is very rare in American English.

> *I daren't ring Jeremy again.*
> *We needn't worry about that.*

inflected forms

5.250 Unlike other modals, *dare* has some inflected forms that are occasionally used.

In the present simple, the third person singular form can be either *dare* or *dares*.

> *He dare not admit he had forgotten her name.*
> *What nobody dares suggest is that the children are simply spoilt.*

In the past simple, either *dare* or *dared* can be used. *Dare* is more formal than *dared*.

He dare not take his eyes off his assailant.
He dared not show he was pleased.

Need is not inflected when it is used as a modal.

use with other modals

5.251 Normally, modals cannot be used with other modals. However *dare* can be used with *will*, *would*, *should*, and *might*.

No one will dare override what the towns decide.
I wouldn't dare go to there alone.

use with *do*

5.252 Unlike other modals, *dare* can be used with the auxiliary verb *do*.

We do not dare examine it.
Don't you ever dare come here again!

In ordinary speech, *did not dare* and *didn't dare* are much more common than *dared not* or *dare not*.

She did not dare leave the path.
I didn't dare speak or move.
We didn't dare say that we would prefer to go home.

other uses of *dare* and *need*

5.253 Besides being used as modals, *dare* and *need* are used in other ways in which they are not followed by the base form of another verb. Both verbs can be followed by a *to*-infinitive clause, and *need* is a common transitive verb.

used to

5.254 *Used to* cannot be used with other modals.

She used to get quite cross with Lily.
...these Westerns that used to do so well in Hollywood.
What did we use to call it?

However, *used to* can be used with the auxiliary verb *do*. This is explained in paragraphs 5.257 and 5.258.

Used is sometimes regarded as a modal, rather than *used to*. *Used* is then said to be followed by a *to*-infinitive.

5.255 *Used to* is used to say that something happened regularly or existed in the past, although it no longer happens or exists.

Used to is similar to *would* when it is used to describe repeated actions in the past. However, unlike *would*, *used to* can also describe past states and situations.

I'm not quite as mad as I used to be.
You used to bring me flowers all the time.

The use of *would* to talk about things that happened regularly in the past is dealt with in paragraph 5.114.

omitting the following verb phrase

5.256 *Used to* can be used on its own without a following verb phrase when it is clear from the context what the subject matter is.

People don't work as hard as they <u>used to</u>.
I don't feel British any more. Not as much as I <u>used to</u>.

negatives

5.257 *Used to* is not common in negative structures.

 In informal speech, people sometimes make negative statements by putting *didn't* in front of *used to*. This is sometimes represented as *use to*.

They <u>didn't use to</u> mind what we did.

However, many people consider this use to be incorrect.

Another way to form the negative is to put *never* in front of *used to*.

Where I was before, we <u>never used to</u> have posters on the walls.

Sometimes *not* is put between *used* and *to*. This is a fairly formal use.

It <u>used not to</u> be taxable.

Some grammar books give a contracted form for the negative, *usedn't to* or *usen't to*. This is now rarely used, and is thought to be very old-fashioned.

questions

5.258 You normally form questions with *used to* by putting *did* in front of the subject, followed by *used to* or *use to*. Wh-questions are formed by putting the *wh*-word at the beginning, followed by *used to*.

<u>Did she used</u> to be nice?
<u>What used to</u> annoy you most about him?

You can form negative questions by putting *didn't* in front of the subject, followed by the subject and *used to* or *use to*.

<u>Didn't they use to</u> mind?

In more formal English, *did* is put in front of the subject and *not* after it, followed by *used to* or *use to*.

<u>Did she not use to</u> smile?

Chapter 6

Expressing manner and place: other adverbials

6 Expressing manner and place: other adverbials

Introduction

6.1 When you are talking about an event or a situation, you sometimes want to say something about it that has not been indicated by the subject, verb, object, or complement. You do this by using an **adverbial**.

An adverbial is a word or group of words that you use when you want to say when an event or situation occurs, how it occurs, how much it occurs, or where it occurs.

I was <u>soon</u> lost.
She laughed <u>quietly</u>.
She was <u>tremendously</u> impressed.
He fumbled <u>in his pocket</u>.

adverb phrases

6.2 The two main types of adverbial are **adverb phrases** and **prepositional phrases**.

He acted <u>very clumsily</u>.
I cannot speak <u>too highly</u> of their courage and skill.
He takes his job <u>very seriously indeed</u>.
He did not play <u>well enough</u> throughout the week to deserve to win.

However, adverbs very often occur on their own.

I shook her <u>gently</u>.
He <u>greatly</u> admired Cezanne.
He <u>scarcely</u> knew his aunt
The number will <u>probably</u> be higher than we expected.

For more information about adverbs, see the section beginning at paragraph 6.16.

prepositional phrases

6.3 Adverbials that consist of a preposition and a noun, such as *in a box* and *to the station*, are called **prepositional phrases**. These are dealt with in detail in the section beginning at paragraph 6.73.

Large cushions lay <u>on the floor</u>.
The voice was coming <u>from my apartment</u>.

noun phrases

6.4 Occasionally, **noun phrases** can also be used as adverbials.

He was looking really ill <u>this time yesterday</u>.
I'm going to handle this <u>my way</u>.

When noun phrases are used as adverbials, they most often relate to time. Time adverbials are dealt with in Chapter 4. Noun phrases that relate to place are dealt with at paragraph 6.72; those that relate to manner are dealt with at paragraph 6.44, and those that relate to degree at paragraph 6.52.

For more information on noun phrases in general, see Chapters 1 and 2.

adding meaning to verb phrases

6.5   The most common way in which adverb phrases give additional information is by adding something to the meaning of a verb phrase.

He nodded and smiled warmly.
The report says that hospitals and rescue services coped extremely well.
I could find that out fairly easily.

Prepositional phrases have a wider range of meanings.

It was estimated that at least 2,000 people were on the two trains.
Kenny Stuart came second, knocking two minutes off his previous best time.
For the first time since I'd been pregnant I felt well.

Many **intransitive verbs** normally require an adverbial. See paragraph 3.10 for more information about these.

Ashton had behaved abominably.
She turned and rushed out of the room.

Some **transitive verbs** normally require an adverbial after the object of the verb. For more information about these, see paragraph 3.19.

I put my hand on the door.

adding meaning to clauses

6.6   Adverbials can also add meaning to a whole clause, for example by giving the writer's or speaker's comment on it. For more information, see the section on **sentence adverbials** beginning at paragraph 9.56.

Obviously crime is going to be squeezed in a variety of ways.
Fortunately, the damage had been slight.
Ideally the dairy should have a concrete or tiled floor.
No doubt she loves Gertrude too.

They can also show the way in which one sentence is linked to another clause. For more information, see the section on **sentence connectors** beginning at paragraph 10.48.

The second paragraph repeats the information given in the first paragraph. Therefore, it isn't necessary.

Position of adverbials

6.7   The position of adverbials within clauses is flexible, allowing many changes of emphasis and focus.

Adverbials are normally placed at the end of the clause after the verb phrase, or after an object if there is one.

She packed carefully.
They would go on talking for hours.
I enjoyed the course immensely.

beginning of clause for emphasis

6.8   You can emphasize the adverbial by placing it at the beginning of the clause, in front of the subject.

Gently Fiona leaned forward and wiped the old lady's tears away.
In his excitement Billy had forgotten the letter.

The adverbial is often separated by a comma from the rest of the clause.

After much discussion, they had decided to take the coin to the jeweller.

This position is often used in written stories to draw attention to the adverbial. For more information, see paragraph 9.70.

Note that adverbs of degree are rarely used at the beginning of a clause: see paragraph 6.45.

between subject and verb

6.9 Adverbials can also be placed between the subject and the main verb. This focuses on the adverbial more than when it is at the end of the clause, but not as much as putting it at the beginning of the clause. However, this position is much more common with adverbs than with prepositional phrases.

I quickly became aware that she was looking at me.
We often swam in the surf.
He carefully wrapped each component in several layers of foam rubber.
He noisily opened the fridge and took out a carton of milk.

Note that in verb phrases containing auxiliaries, the adverbial is still placed in front of the main verb.

I had almost forgotten about the trip.
We will never have enough money to provide all the services that people want.
It would not in any case be for him.

Long adverbials in this position are usually separated by commas from the rest of the clause.

Fred, in his own way, was a great actor.

Adverbials of place rarely occur in this position. For more information about adverbials of place, see the section beginning at paragraph 6.53.

6.10 Some adverbials are often placed in front of the main verb:

most adverbs of indefinite frequency (see paragraph 4.114)

always	ever	normally	regularly	usually
constantly	frequently	occasionally	repeatedly	
continually	hardly ever	often	seldom	
continuously	never	rarely	sometimes	

some adverbs of indefinite time (see paragraph 4.41)

again	earlier	first	last	recently
already	finally	just	previously	since

some adverbs of degree (see paragraph 6.45), especially emphasizing adverbs (see paragraph 6.49)

absolutely	completely	greatly	quite	totally
almost	deeply	largely	rather	utterly
altogether	entirely	nearly	really	virtually
badly	fairly	perfectly	somewhat	well

focusing adverbs, when modifying a verb (see paragraph 9.67)

even	just	merely	only	really	simply

Note that some adverbs have a different reference when they are placed in front of the main verb rather than at the end of the clause:

The Trade Unions have acted foolishly.
Baldwin had foolishly opened the door.

The first example means that the Unions acted in a foolish way. The second example means that opening the door was a foolish action, and not that the door was opened in a foolish way.

Americans always tip generously.
He generously offered to drive me home.

The first example tells us how well Americans tip, the second example indicates that his offer was a generous action.

USAGE NOTE

6.11 If the verb is a *to*-infinitive, you usually put an adverb after it, or after the object if there is one.

He tried to leave quietly.
Thomas made an appointment to see him immediately.

Some people, however, particularly when they are speaking, do put adverbs between the *to* and the infinitive. This use is considered to be incorrect by some speakers of English.

My wife told me to probably expect you, he said.
Vauxhall are attempting to really break into the market.

Sometimes, however, if you avoid putting the adverb between the *to* and the infinitive, you change the emphasis of the sentence, or it can sound clumsy. In such cases, *splitting the infinitive*, as it is called, is now generally considered acceptable.

Participants will be encouraged to actively participate in the workshop.
I want you to really enjoy yourself.

Note that the second example above means *I want you to enjoy yourself very much*. If you said *I really want you to enjoy yourself*, you would mean *It is very important for me that you enjoy yourself*.

minor points about position

6.12 If a clause has two adverbials, and one is an adverb and the other is a prepositional phrase, you can usually place either of them first.

Miss Burns looked calmly at Marianne.
They were sitting happily in the car.
The women shouted at me savagely.
He got into the car quickly and drove off.

However, if the prepositional phrase is rather long, it is more common to place the adverb first, immediately after the verb.

He listened calmly to the report of his aides.
She would sit cross-legged in her red robes.

Similarly, if the verb phrase is followed by a long object, the adverb comes after the verb and before the object.

She sang <u>beautifully</u> a school song the children had taught her when they were little.

6.13   In clauses with more than one adverbial, the meaning of the adverbials can also affect their order. The usual order is adverbial of manner, then adverbial of place, then time adverbial.

They knelt <u>quietly in the shadow of the rock</u>.
I tried to reach you <u>at home several times</u>.
He was imprisoned <u>in Cairo in January 1945</u>.
Parents may complain that their child eats <u>badly at meals</u>.
The youngsters repeat this <u>in unison at the beginning of each session</u>.

However, if a clause contains an adverb of manner and an adverb of direction such as *down*, *out*, or *home*, the adverb of direction is usually put in front of the adverb of manner.

Lomax drove <u>home fast</u>.
I reached <u>down slowly</u>.

6.14   Adverbials of different types can be placed together, sometimes separated by a comma, but adverbials of the same type, for example two adverbials of manner, are usually linked by conjunctions such as *and* and *but*, or structures such as *rather than*. For more information about how to link adverbials using conjunctions, see paragraph 8.188.

She sang <u>clearly</u> and <u>beautifully</u>.
They help to combat the problem <u>at source</u>, rather than <u>superficially</u>.

6.15   When clauses begin with an adverbial, the normal order of subject and verb is sometimes changed. For example, after adverbials of place, the verb usually comes before the subject. For more information about adverbials of place, see the section beginning at paragraph 6.53.

<u>Next to it</u> stood a pile of paper cups.
<u>Beyond them</u> lay the fields.

This also happens when **broad negative** adverbs such as *hardly* and *barely*, and some other **negative words** are placed at the beginning of the clause. For more information about these, see paragraphs 5.49 to 5.93.

<u>Never</u> in history had technology made such spectacular advances.
<u>Seldom</u> can there have been such a happy meeting.

Both of these cases are particularly common in written stories. A change in the normal order of subject and verb can occur after other adverbs, but only in poetry or old-fashioned English. The following example is from a Christmas carol written in 1843:

<u>Brightly</u> shone the moon that night, though the frost was cruel.

Adverbs

Types of adverb

6.16   There are several types of adverb:

> ▶ **adverbs of time**, **frequency**, and **duration**, for example *soon*, *often*, and *always*. Because these are all related to time, they are dealt with fully in Chapter 4.

> ▶ **adverbs of place**, for example *around*, *downstairs*, and *underneath*. These are dealt with in the section on **place** beginning at paragraph 6.53.

> ▶ **adverbs of manner**, for example *beautifully*, *carefully*, and *silently*. See the section beginning at paragraph 6.36 for more information about these.

> ▶ **adverbs of degree**, for example *almost*, *badly*, *terribly*, and *well*. See the section beginning at paragraph 6.45 for more information about these.

> ▶ **sentence connectors**, for example *consequently*, *furthermore*, and *however*. These are dealt with in paragraphs 10.48 to 10.56.

> ▶ **sentence adverbs**, for example *alas*, *apparently*, *chiefly*, and *interestingly*. See the section beginning at paragraph 9.79 for more information on these.

> ▶ **broad negative adverbs**, for example *barely*, *hardly*, *rarely*, *scarcely*, and *seldom*. These are dealt with at paragraphs 5.82 to 5.89.

> ▶ **focusing adverbs**, for example *especially* and *only*. These are dealt with in the section beginning at paragraph 9.64.

Adverb forms and meanings related to adjectives

-ly adverbs

6.17   Many adverbs are related to adjectives. The main relationships and rules of formation are explained below.

Many adverbs are formed by adding *-ly* to an adjective. For example, the adverbs *quietly* and *badly* are formed by adding *-ly* to the adjectives *quiet* and *bad*.

Most of the adverbs formed in this way are **adverbs of manner**, so some people refer to adverbs of manner as *-ly* adverbs.

Sit there quietly, and listen to this music.
I didn't play badly.
He reported accurately what they said.
He nodded and smiled warmly.

For more information about adjectives, see Chapter 2.

spelling

6.18   Some *-ly* adverbs have slightly different spellings from the adjectives they are related to, for example *nastily*, *gently*, *terribly*, *academically*, *truly*, and *fully*. For information about these adverbs, see the Reference section.

6.19   Not all adverbs ending in *-ly* are adverbs of manner. Some are adverbs of degree, such as *extremely* and *slightly*: see the list at paragraph 6.45.

I enjoyed the course immensely.
Sales fell slightly last month.

A few are adverbs of time, duration, or frequency, such as *presently*, *briefly*, and *weekly*: see the lists of these in Chapter 4.

At 10.15 a.m. soldiers <u>briefly</u> opened fire again.
These allegations are <u>currently</u> being investigated by my legal team.

Others are adverbs of place, such as *locally* and *internationally*, linking adverbs such as *consequently*, or sentence adverbs such as *actually*. For lists of adverbs of place, see the section beginning at paragraph 6.53. For lists of sentence adverbs, see Chapter 9.

They live <u>locally</u> and they have never caused any bother.
These efforts have received little credit <u>internationally</u>.
They did not preach. <u>Consequently</u>, they reached a vastly wider audience.
There still remains something to say. Several things, <u>actually</u>.

adverb meaning

6.20   Most adverbs formed by adding -*ly* to an adjective have a similar meaning to the adjective, for example *quietly* and *beautifully* have similar meanings to *quiet* and *beautiful*.

She is thoughtful, <u>quiet</u> and controlled.
'I'm going to do it,' I said <u>quietly</u>.
His costumes are <u>beautiful</u>, a big improvement on the previous ones.
The girls had dressed more <u>beautifully</u> than ever, for him.

6.21   Some -*ly* adverbs have a different meaning from the meanings of their related adjectives. For example, *hardly* means *not very much* or *almost not at all* and is not used with any of the meanings of the adjective *hard*.

This has been a long <u>hard</u> day.
Her bedroom was so small she could <u>hardly</u> move in it.

Here is a list of adverbs ending in -*ly* that have a different meaning from the meanings of their related adjectives:

barely	lately	scarcely
hardly	presently	shortly

6.22   Some -*ly* adverbs are not related to adjectives, for example *accordingly*. Some are related to nouns, for example *bodily*, *purposely*, *daily* and *weekly*. For lists of these, see the Reference section.

6.23   Adverbs ending in -*ly* are very rarely formed from some types of adjective:

▶ most classifying adjectives, for example *racist*, *eastern*, *female*, *urban*, *foreign*, and *available*. See Chapter 2 for lists of classifying adjectives.

▶ most colour adjectives, although -*ly* adverbs from these are occasionally found in works of literature.

The hills rise <u>greenly</u> to the deep-blue sky.
He lay still, staring <u>blackly</u> up at the ceiling.

▶ some very common qualitative adjectives that refer to basic qualities:

big	old	tall	wet
fat	small	tiny	young

▶ adjectives that already end in -*ly*, for example *friendly*, *lively*, *cowardly*, *ugly*, and *silly*.

▶ most adjectives that end in -*ed*, such as *frightened* and *surprised*. See the Reference section for a list of the common ones that do form -*ly* adverbs, such as *excitedly* and *hurriedly*.

same form as adjective: *a fast car, drive fast*

6.24 In some cases, an adverb has the same form as an adjective and is similar in meaning. For example, *fast* is an adverb in the sentence *News travels fast* and an adjective in the sentence *She likes fast cars*.

...a fast rail link from London to the Channel Tunnel.
The driver was driving too fast for the conditions.

In these cases, the adverb is usually placed immediately after the verb or object, and rarely in front of the verb.

alike	far	long	overseas	through
downtown	fast	next	past	
extra	inside	outside	straight	

Some words ending in -ly are both adverbs and adjectives, for example *daily*, *monthly*, and *yearly*. These relate to frequency and are explained in paragraph 4.120.

6.25 Several postdeterminers, including *further*, *next*, *only*, *opposite*, and *same*, have the same form as adverbs but no direct relation in meaning. Note that *well* is an adverb and adjective, but usually means *not ill* as an adjective, and *with skill or success* as an adverb.

He has done well.

two forms: *dear/dearly, hard/hardly*, etc.

6.26 Sometimes, two adverbs are related to the same adjective. One adverb has the same form as the adjective, and the other is formed by adding -ly.

He closed his eyes tight.
He closed his eyes tightly.
Failure may yet cost his country dear.
Holes in the road are a menace which costs this country dearly in lost man hours every year.
The German manufacturer was urging me to cut out the middle man and deal with him direct.
The trend in recent years has been to deal directly with the supplier.

Here is a list of common adverbs that have both these forms:

clear	deep	fine	high	thick
clearly	deeply	finely	highly	thickly
close	direct	first	last	thin
closely	directly	firstly	lastly	thin
dear	easy	hard	late	tight
dearly	easily	hardly	lately	tightly

Note that the -ly adverb often has a different meaning from the adverb with the same form as the adjective,

The river was running high and swiftly.
I thought highly of the idea.
He has worked hard.
Border could hardly make himself heard above the din.
When the snake strikes, its mouth opens wide.
Closing dates for applications vary widely.

Note that, with some words that are adverbs and adjectives, the addition of *-ly* forms a new adverb and a new adjective, for example *dead* and *deadly*, *low* and *lowly*.

no adverb from adjective

6.27 Some adjectives do not form adverbs at all. These include the common qualitative adjectives listed in paragraph 6.23, such as *big* and *old*.

Here is a list of some more adjectives that do not form adverbs:

afraid	awake	foreign	little
alive	content	good	long
alone	difficult	hurt	sorry
asleep	drunk	ill	standard

Note that the adverbs relating to *content* and *drunk* are formed by adding *-ly* to the forms *contented* and *drunken*, thus giving *contentedly* and *drunkenly*.

USAGE NOTE

6.28 If there is no adverb related to an adjective, and you want to give additional information about an event or situation, you can often use a prepositional phrase.

In some cases, the prepositional phrase involves a noun that is related to the adjective. For example, there is no adverb related to the adjective *difficult*, but you can use the related noun *difficulty* in the prepositional phrase *with difficulty* instead.

He stood up slowly and <u>with difficulty</u>.

In other cases, for example with adjectives that end in *-ly*, a general noun such as *way*, *manner*, or *fashion* is used.

He walks <u>in a funny way</u>.
He greeted us <u>in his usual friendly fashion</u>.

Prepositional phrases may be used even if an adverb does exist, for example when you want to add more detailed information or to add emphasis.

She comforted the bereaved relatives <u>in a dignified, compassionate and personalized manner</u>.
At these extreme velocities, materials behave <u>in a totally different manner from normal</u>.

adverbs not related to adjectives

6.29 Some adverbs are not related to adjectives at all. This is especially true of adverbs of time and place. See Chapter 4 for adverbs of time, and the section beginning at paragraph 6.53 for adverbs of place.

It will <u>soon</u> be Christmas.

There are also some other adverbs that are not related to adjectives.

For a list of the common adverbs that are not related to adjectives, see the Reference section.

Comparative and superlative adverbs

6.30 You may want to say how something happens or is done in relation to how it happens on a different occasion, or how it was done by someone or something else. You can do this by using adverbs in the **comparative** or **superlative**.

He began to speak <u>*more quickly*</u>.
This form of treatment is <u>*most commonly*</u> *used in younger patients.*

Most **adverbs of manner** (see paragraph 6.36) have comparatives and superlatives.

A few other adverbs also have comparatives and superlatives: some adverbs of **time** (*early* and *late*, see paragraph 4.71), **frequency** (*often* and *frequently*, see paragraph 4.114), **duration** (*briefly*, *permanently*, and *long*, see paragraph 4.123), and **place** (*near*, *close*, *deep*, *high*, *far*, and *low*, see paragraphs 6.88 and 6.60).

6.31 The forms and uses of comparative and superlative adverbs are generally similar to those of adjectives. For more information about comparatives and superlatives of adjectives, see paragraphs 2.103 to 2.122.

However, unlike adjectives, the comparative of an adverb is usually formed with *more* and the superlative with *most*, and not by adding -*er* and -*est*.

The people needed business skills so that they could manage themselves <u>*more effectively*</u>.
...the text that Professor Williams's work <u>*most closely*</u> *resembles.*
Valium is <u>*most often*</u> *prescribed as an anti-anxiety drug.*

irregular forms

6.32 Some very common adverbs have comparatives and superlatives that are single words and not formed using *more* and *most*. Note that adverbs that have irregular comparatives also have irregular superlatives.

Well has the comparative *better* and the superlative *best*.

She would ask him later, when she knew him <u>*better*</u>.
I have to find out what I can do <u>*best*</u>.

Badly has the comparative *worse* and the superlative *worst*.

'I don't think the crowd helped her,' Gordon admitted. 'She played <u>*worse*</u>.'
The expedition from Mozambique fared <u>*worst*</u>.

Note that *worse* and *worst* are also the comparative and superlative of *ill* when it is an adverb or adjective.

6.33 Adverbs that have the same form as adjectives also have the same comparatives and superlatives as the adjectives. For example, *fast* has *faster* and *fastest*, and *hard* has *harder* and *hardest*. For a list of common adverbs that have the same form as adjectives, see paragraph 6.24.

They worked <u>*harder*</u>, *they were more honest.*
The winning blow is the one that strikes <u>*hardest*</u>.
This would enable claims to be dealt with <u>*faster*</u>.
This type of sugar dissolves <u>*fastest*</u>.

6.34 Some adverbs have comparatives and superlatives with *more* and *most*, but also have single-word comparatives and superlatives.

They can be built <u>*more quickly*</u>.
You probably learn <u>*quicker*</u> *by having lessons.*
Those women treated <u>*quickest*</u> *were those most likely to die.*
The American computer firm will be relying <u>*more heavily*</u> *on its new Scottish plant.*
It seems that the rights of soldiers weigh <u>*heavier*</u> *than the rights of those killed.*
The burden fell <u>*most heavily*</u> *on Kanhai.*
Illiteracy weighs <u>*heaviest*</u> *on the groups who are already disadvantaged in other ways.*

📋 **USAGE NOTE**

6.35 The structures involving comparatives and superlatives are generally the same for adverbs as for adjectives:

▶ the use of *no* and *any* with comparatives: see paragraph 2.163

He began to behave <u>more and more erratically</u>.
Omoro didn't want to express it <u>any more strongly</u>.

▶ the optional use of *the* with superlatives: see paragraph 2.117

His shoulders hurt <u>the worst</u>.
Old people work <u>hardest</u>.

▶ the use of words like *much* or *a little* with comparatives and superlatives: see the section beginning at paragraph 2.157

The situation resolved itself <u>much more easily</u> than I had expected.
There the process progresses <u>even more rapidly</u>.

▶ the use of *than* after comparatives: see paragraph 2.106

This class continues to grow <u>more rapidly than any other group</u>.
Prices have been rising <u>faster than incomes</u>.
You might know this <u>better than me</u>.

▶ repeating comparatives to show changes in extent: see paragraph 2.161

He began to behave <u>more and more erratically</u>.

Adverbs of manner

adverbs of manner

6.36 You often want to say something about the way something is done or about the circumstances of an event or situation. The most common way of doing this is by using **adverbs of manner**. Adverbs of manner give more information about the way in which an event or action takes place.

He nodded and smiled <u>warmly</u>.
She <u>accidentally</u> shot herself in the foot.

how something is done: *sing beautifully, walk briskly*

6.37 Many adverbs of manner are used to describe the way in which something is done. For example, in the sentence *He did it carefully*, *carefully* means *in a careful way*.

They think, dress and live <u>differently</u>.
He acted very <u>clumsily</u>.
You must be able to speak <u>fluently</u> and <u>correctly</u>.

6.38 Here is a list of common -*ly* adverbs that describe the way in which something is done:

abruptly	brightly	casually	comfortably
accurately	brilliantly	cheaply	consistently
awkwardly	briskly	clearly	conveniently
badly	carefully	closely	correctly
beautifully	carelessly	clumsily	dangerously

delicately	gracefully	rapidly	superbly
differently	hastily	readily	swiftly
discreetly	heavily	richly	systematically
distinctly	honestly	rigidly	tenderly
dramatically	hurriedly	roughly	thickly
easily	intently	ruthlessly	thinly
economically	meticulously	securely	thoroughly
effectively	neatly	sensibly	thoughtfully
efficiently	nicely	sharply	tightly
evenly	oddly	silently	truthfully
explicitly	patiently	simply	uncomfortably
faintly	peacefully	smoothly	urgently
faithfully	peculiarly	softly	vaguely
fiercely	perfectly	solidly	vigorously
finely	plainly	specifically	violently
firmly	pleasantly	splendidly	vividly
fluently	politely	steadily	voluntarily
formally	poorly	steeply	warmly
frankly	professionally	stiffly	widely
freely	properly	strangely	willingly
gently	quietly	subtly	wonderfully

feelings and manner: *smile happily, walk wearily*

6.39 Adverbs formed from adjectives that describe people's feelings, for example *happily* or *nervously*, indicate both the way in which something is done and the feelings of the person who does it.

For example, the sentence *She laughed happily* means both that she laughed in a happy way and that she was feeling happy.

We laughed and chatted <u>happily</u> together.
Gaskell got up <u>wearily</u> and headed for the stairs.
They looked <u>anxiously</u> at each other.
The children waited <u>eagerly</u> for their presents.
The children smiled <u>shyly</u>.

6.40 Here is a list of adverbs that describe the feelings of the person who does something as well as the way in which it is done:

angrily	eagerly	hopefully	sadly
anxiously	excitedly	hopelessly	shyly
bitterly	furiously	impatiently	sincerely
boldly	gladly	miserably	uncomfortably
calmly	gloomily	nervously	uneasily
cheerfully	gratefully	passionately	unhappily
confidently	happily	proudly	wearily
desperately	helplessly	reluctantly	

6.41   Adverbs of manner can also indicate the circumstances in which something is done, rather than how it is done. For example, in the sentence *He spoke to me privately*, *privately* means *when no one else was present* rather than *in a private way*.

I need to speak to you <u>privately</u>.
He had <u>publicly</u> called for an investigation of the entire school system.
Britain and France <u>jointly</u> suggested a plan in 1954.
I have undertaken all the enquiries <u>personally</u>.

6.42   Here is a list of adverbs that are used to show the circumstances in which an action takes place:

accidentally	first-class	legally	privately
alone	full-time	logically	publicly
artificially	illegally	mechanically	regardless
automatically	independently	naturally	retail
bodily	indirectly	officially	scientifically
collectively	individually	openly	secretly
commercially	innocently	overtly	solo
deliberately	instinctively	part-time	specially
directly	involuntarily	personally	symbolically
duly	jointly	politically	wholesale

forms

6.43   Most adverbs of manner are formed from qualitative adjectives, for example *stupidly* from *stupid*, and *angrily* from *angry*. For more information about the forms of adverbs, see paragraph 6.17.

i   **USAGE NOTE**

6.44   Instead of using an adverb of manner, you can sometimes use prepositional phrases or noun phrases to give more information about the manner or circumstances of an action.

'Come here', he said <u>in a low voice</u>.
I know I have to do it <u>this way</u>.

In some cases you may have to do this, because there is no adverb. See paragraph 6.23.

Adverbs of degree

6.45   When you want to give more information about the extent of an action or the degree to which an action is performed, you often use an **adverb of degree**.

I enjoyed the course <u>immensely</u>.
I had <u>almost</u> forgotten about the trip.
A change of one word can <u>radically</u> alter the meaning of a statement.

6.46 Here is a list of adverbs of degree:

absolutely	extraordinarily	partly	somewhat
adequately	extremely	perfectly	soundly
almost	fairly	poorly	strongly
altogether	fantastically	positively	sufficiently
amazingly	fully	powerfully	supremely
awfully	greatly	practically	surprisingly
badly	half	pretty	suspiciously
completely	hard	profoundly	terribly
considerably	hugely	purely	totally
dearly	immensely	quite	tremendously
deeply	incredibly	radically	truly
drastically	intensely	rather	unbelievably
dreadfully	just	really	utterly
enormously	largely	reasonably	very
entirely	moderately	remarkably	virtually
exceedingly	nearly	significantly	well
excessively	noticeably	simply	wonderfully
extensively	outright	slightly	

from adjectives

6.47 Adverbs of degree are often formed from adjectives by adding -ly. Some are formed from qualitative adjectives, for example *deeply*, *hugely*, and *strongly*, and some from classifying adjectives, for example *absolutely*, *perfectly*, and *utterly*.

A few adverbs of degree are formed from postdeterminers, such as *entirely*.

See Chapter 2 for more information about types of adjectives.

position in clause

6.48 You can use adverbs of degree in the usual positions for adverbials.

I admired him greatly.
I greatly enjoyed working with them.
Yoga can greatly diminish stress levels.

However, you rarely use an adverb of degree at the beginning of a clause. For example, you do not usually say *Greatly I admired him*. For more information about placing adverbs at the beginning of a clause, see paragraph 9.70.

A few adverbs of degree are nearly always used in front of the main verb:

almost	largely	nearly	really	virtually

For example, you usually say *He almost got there*, not *He got there almost*.

This type of institution has largely disappeared now.
He really enjoyed talking about flying.
The result virtually ensures Scotland's place in the finals.

Some adverbs of degree are almost always used after the main verb:

altogether	hard	somewhat	well
enormously	outright	tremendously	

This was a different level of communication <u>altogether</u>.
The proposal was rejected <u>outright</u>.
I enjoyed the book <u>enormously</u>.

emphasizing adverbs

6.49 A group of adverbs of degree are called **emphasizing adverbs**. These are formed from emphasizing adjectives (see paragraph 2.36).

absolutely	just	positively	really	truly
completely	outright	purely	simply	utterly
entirely	perfectly	quite	totally	

Note that the emphasizing adverb *outright* has the same form as an adjective, an adverb of manner, and an adverb of degree.

6.50 You use an emphasizing adverb such as *absolutely*, *just*, *quite*, or *simply* to add emphasis to the action described by a verb. Emphasizing adverbs usually come in front of verbs.

I <u>quite</u> agree.
I <u>absolutely</u> agree.
I <u>just</u> know I'm going to be late.
I <u>simply</u> adore this flat.

In a verb phrase, the emphasizing adverb comes after the auxiliary or modal and in front of the verb.

Someone had <u>simply</u> appeared.
I was <u>absolutely</u> amazed.

However, *absolutely* is occasionally used after verbs as well.

I <u>agree absolutely</u> with what Geoffrey has said.

For other uses of emphasizing adverbs, see paragraphs 9.62 to 9.63.

adverbs of degree in front of other adverbs: *very carefully, fairly easily*

6.51 You can use some adverbs of degree such as *very* and *rather* in front of other adverbs. When adverbs of degree are used like this they are called **submodifying adverbs**.

They can also be used in front of adjectives; this use is explained in paragraphs 2.140 to 2.168, where lists of submodifying adverbs and their meanings are also given.

He prepared his speech <u>very</u> carefully.
He was having to work <u>awfully</u> hard.
Things changed <u>really</u> dramatically.
We get on <u>extremely</u> well with our neighbours.
We were able to hear everything <u>pretty</u> clearly.
The paper disintegrated <u>fairly</u> easily.
He dressed <u>rather</u> formally.
Every child reacts <u>somewhat</u> differently.

Note that *moderately* and *reasonably* are mainly used in front of adverbs that do not end in *-ly*.

He works reasonably hard.

A few adverbs of degree can be used as in this way with comparatives: see the section beginning at paragraph 2.157.

This could all be done very much more quickly.
I thanked him again, even more profusely than before.
I hope you can see slightly more clearly what is going on.

Note that *still* can also be placed after the comparative.

They're doing better in some respects now. Of course they've got to do better still.

other adverbs of degree

6.52 There are some special adverbs of degree. These include *much*, which is used as an adverb of degree in negative clauses, and in reported questions after *how*.

She was difficult as a child and hasn't changed much.
These definitions do not help much.
Have you told him how much you love him?

Very much is also used in a similar way.

She is charming. We like her very much.

The comparative adverbs *better* and *worse* and the superlative adverbs *best* and *worst* are also adverbs of degree.

You know him better than anyone else.
It is the land itself which suffers worst.

More and *less* can be used as comparative adverbs of degree.

Her tears frightened him more than anything that had ever happened to him before.
The ground heats up less there.

Most and *least* can be used as superlative adverbs of degree.

She gave me the opportunity to do what I wanted to do most.
They staged some of his least known operas.

Comparative adverbs and superlative adverbs are explained in the section beginning at paragraph 6.30.

The noun phrases *a bit*, *a great deal*, *a little*, and *a lot* are also used as adverbs of degree.

I don't like this a bit.
The situation's changed a great deal since then.

Adverbs of place

6.53 Adverbs are also used after verbs to give information about place.

No birds or animals came near.
Seagulls were circling overhead.

In many cases the same word can be used as a preposition and as an adverb.

The limb was severed below the elbow.
This information is summarized below.

6.54 Here is a list of words that are used as adverbs to show position. Note that some adverbs consist of more than one word, for example, *out of doors*.

abroad	downwind	northward	underground
ahead	eastward	offshore	underwater
aloft	halfway	outdoors	upstairs
ashore	here	out of doors	upstream
away	indoors	overhead	uptown
close to	inland	overseas	upwind
downstairs	midway	southward	westward
downstream	nearby	there	yonder *(American)*
downtown	next door	underfoot	

The common adverbs of place that are used as adverbs and as prepositions are sometimes called **adverb particles** or **adverbial particles**. The following words are used as adverbs to show position, and can also be used as prepositions:

aboard	below	down	off	throughout
about	beneath	in	opposite	underneath
above	beside	in between	outside	up
alongside	beyond	inside	over	
behind	close by	near	round	

6.55 An adverb can be used alone after a verb to show place or direction.

The young men hated working underground.
The engine droned on as we flew northward.

You can also use an adverb showing place or direction when it is clear from the context what place or direction you are referring to. For example, you may have mentioned the place earlier, or the adverb may refer to your own location, or to the location of the person or thing being talked about.

He moved to Portugal, and it was there where he learnt to do the samba.
She walked away and my mother stood in the middle of the road, watching.
They spent the autumn of 1855 in Japan. It was here that Hilary wrote her first novel.

i **USAGE NOTE**

6.56 A few adverbs of position are used to show the area in which a situation exists:

globally	nationally	worldwide
internationally	universally	
locally	widely	

Everything we used was bought locally.

Unlike most other adverbs of position, they cannot be used after *be* to state the position of something.

6.57 A few other adverbs are used to show where two or more people or things are in relation to each other: *together*, *apart*, *side by side* and *abreast*.

All the villagers and visitors would sit together round the fire.
A figure stood at the window holding the curtains apart.

adverbs of position with a following adverbial

6.58 Some adverbs of position are normally followed by another adverbial of position. This is particularly common when the verb *be* is used as a main verb.

Barbara's down at the cottage.
Adam was halfway up the stairs.
Out on the quiet surface of the river, something moved.
She is up in her own bedroom.

deep, far, high, low

6.59 The adverbs *deep*, *far*, *high*, and *low*, which indicate distance as well as position, are also usually followed by another adverbial of position, or are modified or qualified in some other way.

Many of the eggs remain buried deep among the sand grains.
One plane, flying very low, swept back and forth.

Deep down, *far away*, *high up*, and *low down* are often used instead of the adverbs on their own.

The window was high up, miles above the rocks.
Sita scraped a shallow cavity low down in the wall.

Far and *far away* are often qualified by a prepositional phrase beginning with *from*.

I was standing far away from the ball.
We lived far from the nearest village.

adverbs of position: comparatives and superlatives

6.60 Some adverbs have comparative and superlative forms. The superlative form is not used to show position, but to specify which of several things you are talking about.

Deeper, *further* (or *farther*), *higher*, and *lower* are usually followed by a prepositional phrase showing position.

Further along the beach, a thin trickle of smoke was climbing into the sky.
The beans are a bit higher on the stalk this year.

Nearer can be used as an adverb as well as a preposition (see paragraph 6.88). *Closer* can only be used as an adverb.

The hills were nearer now.
Thousands of tourists stood watching or milled around trying to get closer.

anywhere, everywhere, somewhere, nowhere

6.61 There are four indefinite adverbs of position: *anywhere*, *everywhere*, *nowhere*, and *somewhere*. They are used to talk about a position that is not definite or that is very general.

I dropped my cigar <u>somewhere</u> round here.
I thought I'd seen you <u>somewhere</u>.
There were bicycles <u>everywhere</u>.
No-one can find Howard or Barbara <u>anywhere</u>.

Nowhere makes a clause negative.

There was <u>nowhere</u> to hide.

If *nowhere* is at the beginning of a clause, the subject of the verb must be placed after an auxiliary or a form of *be* or *have*.

<u>Nowhere have I seen</u> any serious mention of this.
<u>Nowhere are they</u> overwhelmingly numerous.

 American English has informal variants for all four of these adverbs in which the word *place* replaces *-where*. These can be written as one or two words.

Haven't you got <u>some place</u> to go?
Video-conferencing can connect anyone, anytime, <u>anyplace</u>.

adding information

6.62 There are several structures you can use with indefinite place adverbs in order to give more information. You can use:

▶ an adverb of place:

I would like to work <u>somewhere abroad</u>.
We're certainly <u>nowhere near</u>.

▶ an adjective:

We could go to Majorca if you want <u>somewhere lively</u>.
Are you going <u>somewhere nice</u>?

▶ a prepositional phrase:

The waiter wasn't <u>anywhere in sight</u>.
In 1917, Kollontai was the only woman in any government <u>anywhere in the world</u>.

▶ or a *to*-infinitive clause:

We mentioned that we were looking for <u>somewhere to live</u>.
I wanted to have <u>somewhere to put it</u>.

You can also use a relative clause. Note that the relative pronoun is usually omitted.

Was there <u>anywhere you wanted to go</u>?
<u>Everywhere I went</u>, people were angry or suspicious.

different or additional places

6.63 *Else* is used after the indefinite place adverb to indicate a different or additional place.

We could hold the meeting <u>somewhere else</u>.
More people die in bed than <u>anywhere else</u>.

Elsewhere can be used instead of *somewhere else*.

Gwen sat next to the window. The other girls had found seats <u>elsewhere</u>.

6.64 *Everywhere* and *anywhere* can also be used as the subjects of verbs, especially *be*.

Sometimes I feel that <u>anywhere</u>, just <u>anywhere</u>, would be better than this.
I looked around for a shop, but <u>everywhere</u> was closed.

Destinations and directions

adverbs indicating destinations and targets

6.65 Adverbs can be used to indicate destinations and targets.

I have expected you, she said, inviting him <u>inside</u>.
No birds or animals came <u>near</u>.

The following adverbs are used to indicate destinations or targets:

aboard	home	inwards	skyward
abroad	homeward	near	there
ashore	in	next door	underground
close	indoors	outdoors	upstairs
downstairs	inland	out of doors	uptown
downtown	inside	outside	
heavenward	inward	overseas	

The comparative forms *nearer* and *closer* are more commonly used than *near* or *close*.

Come <u>nearer</u>.

Deep, far, high, and *low* are also used as adverbs showing a destination or target but only when they are modified in some other way.

The dancers sprang <u>high into the air</u> brandishing their spears.

The comparative forms *deeper, further* (or *farther*), *higher*, and *lower* are also used, and so is the superlative form *furthest* (or *farthest*). These do not have to be modified in any way.

We left the waterfall and climbed <u>higher</u>.
People have to trek <u>further and further</u>.

relative direction

6.66 Adverbs can be used to show direction in relation to the particular position of the person or thing you are talking about. For more information on **phrasal verbs**, see paragraphs 3.83 to 3.116.

Go <u>north</u> from Leicester Square up Wardour Street.
Don't look <u>down</u>.
...the part of the engine that was spinning <u>around</u>.
Mrs James gave a little cry and hurried <u>on</u>.
They grabbed him and pulled him <u>backwards</u>.
He turned <u>left</u> and began strolling slowly down the street.

They can also show the direction in which someone or something is facing in relation to the front of the place they are in.

The seats face <u>forward</u>.

The following adverbs are used to show direction of this sort:

ahead	sideways	eastward	south-west
along	~	eastwards	round
back	anti-clockwise	north	up
backward	around	northward	
backwards	clockwise	northwards	upward
forward	counterclockwise	north-east	upwards
forwards	(American)	north-west	west
left	down	south	westward
on	downward	southward	westwards
onward	downwards	southwards	
right	east	south-east	

movement in several directions

6.67 The adverbs *round*, *about*, and *around* show movement in several directions within a place.

Stop rushing about!
They won't want anyone else trampling around.

The following adverbial expressions are used to talk about repeated movement in different directions:

back and forth	in and out	up and down
backwards and forwards	round and round	
from side to side	to and fro	

At other times she would pace up and down outside the trailer.
Burke was walking back and forth as he spoke.

movement away

6.68 The following adverbs are used to talk about movement away from someone or something:

aside	away	off	out	outward

The farmer just laughed and rode away.
It took just one tug to pull them out.

The adverb *apart* indicates that two or more things move away from each other.

I rushed in and tried to pull the dogs apart.

movement along a path

6.69 The following adverbs are used to talk about movement along a road, path, or line:

alongside	downhill	uphill
beside	downstream	upstream

Going downhill was easy.
It wasn't the moving that kept me warm; it was the effort of pushing Daisy uphill.

6.70 The following adverbs are used to talk about movement across or past something:

across	over	past	through
by	overhead	round	

There's an aircraft coming over.
'Where are you going?' demanded Miss Craig as Florrie rushed by.

6.71 The indefinite place adverbs are used to talk about a destination or direction when you want to be more general or vague.

He went off somewhere for a shooting weekend.
Dust blew everywhere, swirling over dry caked mountains.
There was hardly anywhere to go.
Can't you play elsewhere?

Nowhere is mainly used metaphorically, to indicate lack of progress.

They were getting nowhere and had other things to do.

See paragraph 6.61 for more information on these indefinite adverbs.

6.72 Like prepositional phrases, adverbs can also be placed after nouns.

They watched him from the terrace above.
The man opposite got up.
People everywhere are becoming aware of the problem.
We took the road south.

Prepositions

6.73 This section explains how **prepositional phrases** are used to show the place where an action occurs, the place where someone or something is, the place they are going to or coming from, or the direction they are moving in.

A **prepositional phrase** consists of a **preposition** and its **object**, which is nearly always a noun.

The most basic use of most prepositions is to indicate position and direction.

He fumbled in his pocket.
On your left is the river.
Why did he not drive to Valence?
The voice was coming from my apartment.
I ran inside and bounded up the stairs.

6.74 A **preposition** is a word that allows you to say more about a thing or an action, because you can choose any appropriate noun after it as its object. Most prepositions are single words, although there are some that consist of more than one word, such as *out of* and *in between*.

Here is a list of common one-word prepositions that are used to talk about place or destination:

about	before	down	opposite	toward (Am)
above	behind	from	outside	towards
across	below	in	over	under
along	beneath	inside	past	underneath
alongside	beside	into	round	up
among	between	near	through	within
around	beyond	off	throughout	
at	by	on	to	

 Note that *toward* and *towards* are both used in American English, with no difference in meaning.

Here is a list of prepositions that consist of more than one word and that are used to talk about place or destination:

across from	away from	in between	next to
ahead of	close by	in front of	on top of
all over	close to	near to	out of

6.75 Many prepositions can also be adverbs; that is, they can be used without an object. See paragraph 6.54 for a list of these.

! | **BE CAREFUL**

6.76 Because English has a large number of prepositions, some of them, such as *beside*, *by*, *near*, and *next to*, are very close in meaning. Other prepositions, for example *at* and *in*, have several different meanings. The meaning and usage of prepositions should be checked where possible in a dictionary.

6.77 Prepositions have an **object**, which comes after the preposition.

The switch is by <u>the door</u>.
Look behind <u>you</u>, Willie!

Note that if a personal pronoun is used as the object of a preposition, it must be the object pronoun: *me, you, him, her, it, us, them*.

Prepositions also combine with complex noun phrases to describe places in some detail. See paragraph 2.280 for information on the use of *of* in noun phrases.

I stood alone <u>in the middle of the yard</u>.
He was sitting <u>towards the end of the room</u>.
He went <u>to the back of the store</u>.

Position of prepositional phrases

after verbs showing position

6.78 Prepositional phrases are most commonly used after verbs. They are used after verbs that indicate position in order to specify where something is.

She <u>lives</u> in Newcastle.
An old piano <u>stood</u> in the corner of the room.

You ought to stay *out of the sun.*

The following verbs are often used to show position:

be	hang	live	sit	stand
belong	lie	remain	be situated	stay

After verbs indicating movement

6.79 Prepositional phrases are used after verbs indicating movement to specify the direction of movement.

I went *into the kitchen and began to make the dinner.*
Mrs Kaul was leading *him to his seat.*
The others burst *from their tents.*
The storm had uprooted *trees from the ground.*
He took *her to Edinburgh.*

after verbs indicating activities

6.80 Prepositional phrases are used after verbs indicating activities to specify where an activity takes place.

...children playing *in the street.*
The meeting was held *at a community centre in Logan Heights.*
He was practising *high jumps in the garden.*

6.81 Prepositional phrases usually come at the end of the clause, after the verb, or after the object of the verb if there is one.

We landed at a small airport.
We put the children's toys in a big box.

at the beginning of a clause: for emphasis or contrast

6.82 If you want to focus on the prepositional phrase for emphasis or contrast, it can be placed at the beginning of the clause. This ordering is mainly used in descriptive writing or reports.

In the garden *everything was peaceful.*
At the top of the tree *was a brown cat.*

at the beginning of a clause: verb before subject

6.83 If you put a prepositional phrase that refers to the position of something at the beginning of the clause when you are using a verb with no object, the normal word order after it is often changed, and the verb is placed before the subject.

On the ceiling hung dustpans and brushes.
Inside the box lie the group's US mining assets.
Beyond them lay the fields.

If you are using *be* as a main verb, the verb always comes before the subject; so, for example, you cannot say *Under her chin a colossal brooch was.*

Under her chin was a colossal brooch.
Next to it is a different sign *which says simply Beware.*
Alongside him will be Mr Mitchell Fromstein.

Showing position

6.84 The prepositional phrases in the following examples show the place where an action occurs, or the place where someone or something is.

The children shouted, waving leafy branches above their heads.
The whole play takes place at a beach club.
Two minutes later we were safely inside the taxi.
He stood near the door.
She kept his picture on her bedside table.

prepositions showing position

6.85 The following prepositions are used to show position:

aboard	among	between	near	through
about	around	beyond	near to	under
above	astride	by	next to	underneath
across	at	close by	off	up
against	away from	close to	on	upon
ahead of	before	down	on top of	with
all over	behind	in	opposite	within
along	below	in between	out of	
alongside	beneath	in front of	outside	
amidst	beside	inside	past	

USAGE NOTE

6.86 Some prepositions are only used with a restricted group of nouns.

For example, *aboard* is used with a noun referring to a form of transport, such as *ship*, *plane*, *train*, or *bus*, or with the name of a particular ship, the flight number for a particular plane journey, and so on.

There's something terribly wrong aboard this ship, Dr Marlowe.
More than 1500 people died aboard the Titanic.
...getting aboard that flight to Rome.
He climbed aboard a truck.

Here is a list of nouns that you use with *aboard* to indicate position:

aircraft carrier	jet	sledge	wagon
boat	plane	space shuttle	yacht
bus	rocket	train	
coach	ship	trawler	
ferry	sled (American)	truck	

Astride is mainly used to say that a person has one leg on each side of something, usually sitting on it or riding it.

He whipped out a chair and sat astride it.
He spotted a man sitting astride a horse.

When *before* is used to show position, the object is usually a person or group of people.

Leading representatives were interviewed <u>before a live television audience</u>.
He appeared <u>before a disciplinary committee</u>.

All over usually has a large or indefinite area as its object.

Through the site, thousands of people <u>all over the world</u> are being reunited with old friends.
There were pieces of ship <u>all over the place</u>.

USAGE NOTE

6.87 Some prepositions have several meanings. For example, *on* can be used to say that someone or something is resting on a horizontal surface or is attached to something, or that someone's place of work is an area such as a farm or a building site.

The phone was <u>on</u> the floor in the hallway.
I lowered myself down <u>on</u> a rope.
My father worked <u>on</u> a farm.

prepositions with comparative forms

6.88 *Near*, *near to*, and *close to* have comparative forms that can also be used as prepositions.

We're moving <u>nearer my parents</u>.
Venus is much <u>nearer to the Sun</u> than the Earth.
The judge's bench was <u>closer to me</u> than Ruchell's chair.

more specific position

6.89 If you want to say more exactly which part of the other thing an object is nearest to, or exactly which part of an area or room it is in, you can use one of the following prepositions: *at*, *by*, *in*, *near*, *on*, *round*. *To* and *towards*, usually used to indicate direction, are used to express position in a more approximate way.

The objects of the prepositions are nouns referring to parts of an object or place, such as *top*, *bottom*, and *edge*. Here is a list of words that are used to talk about parts of an object or place:

back	top	west	mountainside
bottom	~	~	poolside
edge	east	bankside	quayside
end	north	bedside	ringside
front	north-east	dockside	roadside
left	north-west	graveside	seaside
middle	south	hillside	waterside
right	south-east	kerbside	
side	south-west	lakeside	

 Note that the compound direction prepositions (*northeast*, *southwest*, etc.) may be spelled either with or without a hyphen in British English. They are hardly ever spelled with a hyphen in American English.

When the place that you are referring to is obvious or has been stated earlier, you use the nouns in the singular with the determiner *the*.

I ran inside and bounded up the stairs. Wendy was standing at the top.
He was sitting towards the rear.
To the north are the main gardens.
We found him sitting by the fireside.

Other determiners, for example *this* and *each*, are used with nouns such as *side*, *end*, and *edge*, because an object or place may have several sides, ends, or edges.

Loosen the two screws at each end of the fuse.
Standing on either side of him were two younger men.

If the person or thing has been mentioned or is obvious, a possessive determiner can be used.

...a doll that turns brown in the sun, except for under its swimsuit.
There was a gate on our left.

6.90 Note that two- or three-word prepositions that include the word *of* are more specific because *of* can be followed by any noun.

She turned and rushed out of the room.
There was a man standing in front of me.
My sister started piling the books on top of each other.

specific distances

6.91 The place where an action occurs, or where someone or something is, can also be shown by stating its distance from another object or place.

You mention the actual distance before a prepositional phrase with *from* or *away from*.

Here he sat on the terrace a few feet from the roaring traffic.
The ball swerved two feet away from her.

Distance is also expressed in terms of the time taken to travel it.

My house is only 20 minutes from where I work.
They lived only two or three days away from Juffure.

The method of travelling can be stated to be even more precise.

It is less than an hour's drive from here.
It's about five minutes' walk from the bus stop.

showing position and distance

6.92 To show both where something is and how far from another object or place it is, the distance is stated before the following prepositions:

above	below	down	past
along	beneath	inside	under
behind	beyond	outside	up

The volcano is only a few hundred metres below sea level.

The distance can also be stated before prepositional phrases including *left* and *right* or points of the compass such as *north* and *south-east*.

We lived forty miles to the east of Ottawa.

Showing direction

6.93 The prepositional phrases in the following examples show the place that someone or something is going to, or the place that they are moving towards.

I'm going with her to Australia.
They jumped into the water.
He saw his mother running towards him.
He screwed the lid tightly onto the top of the jar.
She stuck her knitting needles into a ball of wool.

prepositions used

6.94 The following prepositions are used to show destinations and targets:

aboard	at	inside	out of	towards
all over	away from	into	round	up
along	beside	near	to	
alongside	down	off	toward	
around	from	onto	*(American)*	

Note that *onto* is sometimes written as two words.

The bird hopped up on to a higher branch.

In American English and some varieties of British English, *out* is used as a preposition without *of* to show direction.

He walked out the door for the last time.

The prepositional phrases *to the left* and *to the right* are also used to indicate direction, from your own viewpoint or that of someone else. See paragraph 6.96.

ℹ️ USAGE NOTE

6.95 There are some restrictions in the choice of preposition.

At is not usually used to show the place that the subject of the verb is moving to or towards. It is used to show what someone is looking at, or what they cause an object to move towards.

They were staring at a garage roof.
Supporters threw petals at his car.

After is used to show that someone or something is following another moving person or thing, or is moving in the same direction but behind them.

He hurried after his men.
...dragging the sacks after us along the ground.

direction relative to the front

6.96 You use the prepositional phrases *to the left* and *to the right* to say which direction someone or something is moving in relation to the direction they are facing.

They turned to the left and drove away.

6.97 The prepositions *about*, *round*, *around*, and *all over* are used to show movement in several directions within a place.

> I wandered <u>round the garden</u>.
> She jumped <u>around the room</u> in front of the children as she acted out her story.
> The boys began climbing <u>all over the ship</u>.

 Round is not used as a preposition in American English; *around* is always used instead.

6.98 Prepositional phrases show the place or object that is the starting point of a movement.

The following prepositions are used: *away from*, *from*, *off*, and *out of*.

> The coffee was sent up by the caterer <u>from the kitchens</u> below.
> She turned and rushed <u>out of the room</u>.
> He took his hand <u>off her arm</u>.

6.99 *From* is also used before another preposition or before some adverbs to talk about the starting point of a movement.

> I had taken his drinking bowl <u>from beneath the kitchen table</u>.
> ...goods imported <u>from abroad</u>.
> Thomas had stopped bringing his lunch <u>from home</u>.

From is used before the following adverbs:

above	beneath	home	overseas
abroad	downstairs	inside	somewhere
anywhere	elsewhere	next door	there
behind	everywhere	nowhere	underneath
below	here	outside	upstairs

Prepositional phrases after nouns

6.100 As well as being used after verbs, prepositional phrases can be used after nouns to give information about place.

> The muscles <u>below Peter's knees</u> were beginning to ache a little.
> The chestnut trees <u>in the back garden</u> were a blazing orange.
> They stood and watched the boats <u>on the river</u>.
> ...the clock <u>in her bedroom</u>.
> ...the low wall <u>round the garden</u>.
> ...the black shapeless masses <u>to the left and right of the road</u>.

6.101 Prepositional phrases can be added after roads, routes, and so on, to specify them by indicating their destination or direction.

> ...the main road <u>from Paris to Marseilles</u>.
> ...the road <u>between the camp and the hospital</u>.
> ...the road <u>through the canyon</u>.

Similarly, doors, entrances, and so on can be specified by adding prepositional phrases indicating where you get to by going through them.

He opened the door to his room.
...at the entrance to the library.

Prepositional phrases are also used after nouns to say where someone or something comes from.

...a veterinary officer from Singapore.
...an engineer from Hertfordshire.

Other uses of prepositional phrases

6.102 Prepositions are often used to talk about things other than place as well, for example to talk about a time, a way of doing something, or a feeling or quality. The following paragraphs from 6.103 to 6.110 describe these uses briefly, and give cross references to fuller explanations elsewhere.

The following prepositions are only or mainly used to indicate things other than place:

after	despite	except	like	since
as	during	for	of	until

referring to time

6.103 Although the main use of prepositional phrases is to talk about position or direction, they are also used to refer to time.

I'll see you on Monday.
They are expecting to announce the sale within the next few days.

The use of prepositions to talk about time is explained in paragraphs 4.100 to 4.108.

referring to the way something is done

6.104 Prepositional phrases are also used to say something more about the way in which an action was performed, or the way in which it should be done.

'Oh yes,' Etta sneered in an offensive way.
A bird can change direction by dipping one wing and lifting the other.
He brushed back his hair with his hand.

Prepositional phrases such as *on foot* or *by bus* can be used to talk about a method of travelling.

I usually go to work on foot.
I travelled home by bus.

The use of adverbs to talk about the way things are done is explained in the section beginning at paragraph 6.36.

6.105 You can also use prepositional phrases to give more information about the feelings of the person performing the action.

Fanny saw with amazement that the letter was addressed to herself.

like and as in comparison

6.106 You can use the preposition *like* to show that someone or something behaves in a similar way to someone or something else.

She treated me like a servant.
She shuffled like an old lady.

There is more information about comparison in general in the section beginning at paragraph 2.103.

6.107 You can also use *like* and *as* to say that someone or something is treated in a similar way to someone or something else. The noun phrase after *like* or *as* describes the person or thing affected by the action, not the person or thing doing the action.

My parents dressed me like a little doll.
Their parents continue to treat them as children.
She treated her more like a daughter than a companion.

You can also use expressions such as *like this* or *like that* to refer to a particular manner of doing something.

If you're going to behave like this, the best thing you can do is to go back to bed.
How dare you speak to me like that?

The use of *like* and *as* in subordinate clauses is explained in paragraphs 8.78 to 8.80.

6.108 You can say that one way of doing something has as much of a quality as another way of doing something, by using *as* followed by an adverb followed by another *as*. The second *as* is followed by a noun phrase, a pronoun, an adverbial, or a clause.

The company has not grown as quickly as many of its rivals.
She wanted someone to talk to as badly as I did.

circumstances of an action

6.109 You use prepositional phrases to say something about the circumstances of an action.

'No,' she said with a defiant look.
...struggling to establish democracy under adverse conditions.

reason, cause, or purpose

6.110 Prepositional phrases can also be used to say something about the reason for an action, or the cause or purpose of it.

In 1923, the Prime Minister resigned because of ill health.
He was dying of pneumonia.

As is used to show the function or purpose of something.

He worked as a truck driver.
During the war they used the theatre as a warehouse.

Prepositions used with verbs

in phrasal verbs

6.111 Some verbs always have a prepositional phrase after them in particular meanings. They are called **phrasal verbs**, and information about them can be found in paragraphs 3.83 to 3.116.

She sailed through her exams.
What are you getting at?

verbs with optional prepositional phrases

6.112 Some verbs can have a prepositional phrase instead of a direct object. For more information on these verbs, see paragraph 3.10.

The Polish Army fought the Germans for nearly five weeks.
She was fighting against history.
We climbed the mountain.
I climbed up the tree.

indirect objects of verbs with two objects

6.113 A prepositional phrase is used as an indirect object when the indirect object comes after the direct object.

For information on verbs with two objects, see paragraphs 3.73 to 3.82.

If the action described by the verb involves the transfer of something from one person or thing to another, the preposition *to* is used.

I passed the letter to my husband.
The recovered animals will be given to zoos.

If the action involves a person doing something for the benefit of another person, the preposition *for* is used.

She left a note for her on the table.

with reciprocal verbs

6.114 Some **reciprocal verbs** require a prepositional phrase when a second noun phrase is mentioned.

For information on reciprocal verbs, see paragraphs 3.68 to 3.72.

Our return coincided with the arrival of bad weather.
She has refused to cooperate with investigators.

with passive verbs

6.115 Prepositional phrases are used after verbs in the **passive**.

Ninety men were cut off by storms.
Moisture is drawn out with salt.

The use of prepositional phrases after passive verbs is explained in paragraphs 9.14 to 9.16.

position of prepositional phrases and adverbs after verbs

6.116 When verbs are followed by prepositional phrases and adverbs, a long prepositional phrase is usually placed after the adverb.

He listened calmly to the report of his aides.

A short prepositional phrase can come before or after the adverb.

The women shouted at me savagely.
Miss Burns looked calmly at Marianne.

Prepositional phrases after nouns and adjectives

6.117 Prepositional phrases are sometimes used after nouns and adjectives to describe the subject or object of a clause rather than the manner of an action or situation. See the section beginning at paragraph 2.275 for more information.

...a girl in a dark grey dress.
...a man with a quick temper.

particular prepositions after nouns and adjectives

6.118 Particular prepositions are used after some nouns and adjectives when you are adding information. See paragraphs 2.45 to 2.50 and 2.287 to 2.290.

My respect <u>for her</u> is absolutely enormous.
Women's tennis puts an emphasis <u>on technique</u>, not strength.
He is responsible <u>for pursuing the claim</u>.

comparisons with *than* and *like*

6.119 A prepositional phrase with *than* often shows the person or thing that is the basis of a comparison.

He was smarter <u>than you</u>.
She was more refined <u>than her husband</u>.

For more information on **comparisons**, see the section beginning at paragraph 2.103.

The preposition *like* is used to show that someone or something is similar to someone or something else, without comparing any specific quality.

The British forces are <u>like permanent tourists</u>.
We need many more people <u>like these</u>.

of

6.120 *Of* is used in prepositional phrases after any noun to indicate various relationships between one noun phrase and another, especially belonging, possession, and connection. It can be used to state what something is, what it contains, what it is made from, or how much of it there is.

He was a member <u>of the golf club</u>.
She's a friend <u>of Stephen's</u>.
...the Mayor <u>of Moscow</u>.

Extended meanings of prepositions

6.121 The uses of prepositional phrases to express time and manner are really extended or metaphorical uses that cover a wide range of prepositions and are part of a metaphor that affects many other aspects of language as well. For example, when you talk about *approaching a point in time*, *a short stretch of time*, and so on, you are using words that refer to space to talk about time.

However, there are also extended meanings that apply only to small groups of prepositions, or sometimes only to individual prepositions.

For example, *in* basically indicates position inside a container.

What's that <u>in your bag</u>?
It will end up <u>in the dustbin</u>.

However, it is often used with reference to areas rather than containers.

Emma sat <u>in an armchair</u> with her legs crossed.
Then we were told what had happened <u>in Sheffield</u>.

In is also used to talk about relative position.

We had to do something <u>in the centre</u> of the town to attract visitors.

However, *in* is also used in ways that extend its meaning further away from physical position. For example, it can be used to say that someone is involved in a particular situation, group, or activity.

They were in no danger.
The child was in trouble with the police.
This government won't be in power for ever.
Mr Matthews has remained in office but the island has no Parliament.

It can show inclusion in a more abstract way.

Some of her early Hollywood experiences were used in her 1923 film, Mary of the Movies.
In any book, there is a moral purpose.

It can also indicate that something has reached a particular stage, or appears in a particular way.

The first primroses are in flower.
Her hair was in pigtails over either shoulder.

A few other prepositions with a basic meaning relating to containers are used in similar ways: for example *within, into, out of*.

Anything within reason should be considered.
When we get those men into the police force, they are going to be real heroes.
Heroines who were considered attractive by earlier generations now seem hopelessly out of touch.

Other ways of giving information about place

noun phrases referring to place: place names

6.122 Some verbs of position and movement are followed by noun phrases referring to places. These are described in paragraph 3.21.

Peel approached the building.

6.123 Instead of using a noun phrase to refer to a place, you can use the name of the place.

This great block of land became Antarctica.
...an island roughly the size of Martha's Vineyard.
Her work is on show at the National Museum of Film and Photography in Bradford.

verbs after place names

6.124 Most place names are singular nouns, although some look like plural nouns, for example *The Netherlands*. Some place names, for example those referring to groups of islands or mountains, are plural nouns. Verbs used with place names follow the normal rules, so a singular verb form is used with a singular noun and a plural verb form with a plural noun.

Milan is a very interesting city.
The Andes split the country down the middle.

place names used for talking about people

6.125 The name of a place can be used to talk about the people who live there. If the place name is a singular noun, a singular verb form is still used, even though the noun is being used to refer to a plural concept.

Europe was sick of war.

The name of a country or its capital city is often used to talk about the government of that country.

Britain and *France* jointly suggested a plan.
Washington put a great deal of pressure on *Tokyo*.

place names used for talking about events

6.126 Place names are also used to talk about a well-known historical or recent event that occurred there, such as a battle, a disaster, an international sports competition, a scandal, or an important political meeting.

After *Waterloo*, *trade and industry surged again.*
What was the effect of *Chernobyl* *on British agriculture?*
...the chain of events that led to *Watergate*.

place names used as modifiers before nouns

6.127 Many place names can be used as modifiers, to show where things come from or are characteristic of, as well as where things are.

...a *London* *hotel.*
...the *New Zealand* *rugby team.*

If a place name begins with *the*, you omit it when you use the name as a modifier.

... *Arctic* *explorers.*
She has a *Midlands* *accent.*

Note that the names of continents and of many countries cannot be used as modifiers. Instead, you use classifying adjectives such as *African* and *Italian*.

Chapter 7

Reporting what people say or think

7 Reporting what people say or think

7.1 This chapter explains the different ways of reporting what people say or think.

7.2 One way of reporting what someone has said is to repeat their actual words.

'I don't know much about music,' Judy said.

Repeating someone's actual words like this is called **direct speech**.

Instead of repeating Judy's words, the writer could say, *Judy said that she didn't know much about music*. This is called **reported speech**. Some grammars called this **indirect speech**.

Direct speech and reported speech both consist of two clauses. The main clause is called a **reporting clause**. The other clause shows what someone said or thought.

In **direct speech**, this other clause is called the **quote**.

'Have you met him?' I asked.
'I'll see you tomorrow,' said Tom.

In **reported speech**, the other clause is called the **reported clause**.

He mentioned that he had a brother living in London.
He asked if you would be able to call and see him.
He promised to give me the money.

Note that the reported clause can begin with a *to*-infinitive.

7.3 In ordinary conversation, we use **reported speech** much more often than **direct speech**. This is because we usually do not know, or cannot remember, the exact words that someone has said. Direct speech is mainly used in written stories.

When we report people's thoughts, we almost always use reported speech, because thoughts do not usually exist in the form of words, so we cannot quote them exactly. Reported speech can be used to report almost any kind of thought.

7.4 Paragraphs 7.5 to 7.15 explain verbs used in **reporting clauses**. Paragraphs 7.16 to 7.26 explain **direct speech**. Paragraphs 7.27 to 7.71 explain **reported speech**. Paragraphs 7.72 to 7.81 explain how to refer to the speaker and hearer in direct speech or reported speech. Paragraphs 7.82 to 7.85 explain other ways of indicating what someone says or talks about.

Showing that you are reporting: using reporting verbs

7.5 You show that you are quoting or reporting what someone has said or thought by using a **reporting verb**. Every reporting clause contains a reporting verb.

'I don't see what you are getting at,' Jeremy said.
He looked old, Harold thought, and sick.
They were complaining that Canton was hot and noisy.

basic reporting verbs

7.6 You use *say* when you are simply reporting what someone said and do not want to add any more information about what you are reporting.

She said that she didn't want to know.

You use *ask* when you are reporting a question.

'How's it all going?' Derek asked.

showing the purpose of speaking

7.7   Some reporting verbs such as *answer*, *complain*, and *explain* tell you what purpose an utterance was intended to serve. For example, *answer* tells you that a statement was intended as an answer, and *complain* tells you that a statement was intended as a complaint.

He answered *that the price would be three pounds.*
He never told me, sir, Watson complained.
'Please don't,' I begged.
I suggested *that it was time to leave.*

Some reporting verbs used in direct speech show the manner of speaking.
See paragraph 7.19.

Here is a list of reporting verbs that can be used to report what people say:

acknowledge	convince	murmur	reply
add	cry	muse	report
admit	declare	mutter	request
advise	decree	note	respond
agree	demand	notify	reveal
allege	deny	object	rule
announce	describe	observe	say
answer	direct	order	scream
argue	discuss	persuade	shout
ask	dispute	plead	shriek
assert	enquire	pledge	state
assure	explain	pray	stipulate
beg	forbid	predict	storm
begin	grumble	proclaim	suggest
boast	guarantee	promise	swear
call	hint	prophesy	teach
chorus	imply	propose	tell
claim	inform	reassure	threaten
command	inquire	recall	thunder
comment	insist	recite	urge
complain	instruct	recommend	vow
concede	invite	record	wail
confess	lament	refuse	warn
confirm	maintain	remark	whisper
contend	mention	remind	write
continue	mumble	repeat	yell

 **BE CAREFUL**

7.8 | Note that the verbs *address*, *converse*, *lecture*, *speak*, and *talk*, although they mean *to say something*, cannot be used as reporting verbs.

verbs of thinking and knowing

7.9   Many reporting verbs are used to talk about people's thoughts, rather than what they say. Reporting verbs are used to talk about many different kinds of thought, including beliefs, wishes, hopes, intentions, and decisions. They can also be used to talk about remembering and forgetting.

We both <u>knew</u> that he was lying.
'I'll go to him in a minute,' she <u>thought</u>.
I <u>had</u> always <u>believed</u> that one day I would see him again.

Here is a list of reporting verbs that can be used to report people's thoughts:

accept	feel	mean	regret
agree	figure	muse	remember
assume	foresee	note	resolve
believe	forget	plan	suppose
consider	guess	ponder	think
decide	hold	pray	understand
determine	hope	prefer	vow
doubt	imagine	propose	want
dream	intend	reason	wish
estimate	judge	recall	wonder
expect	know	reckon	worry
fear	long	reflect	

verbs of learning and perceiving

7.10   Some reporting verbs are used for talking about learning and perceiving facts.

I have since <u>learned</u> that the writer of the letter is now dead.
Then she <u>saw</u> that he was sleeping.

Here is a list of reporting verbs that refer to learning and perceiving facts:

conclude	gather	note	read
discover	hear	notice	realize
elicit	infer	observe	see
find	learn	perceive	sense

7.11   Some of the verbs in the above lists, such as *tell* and *promise*, must be or can be followed by an object showing who the hearer is. See paragraphs 7.75 to 7.76.

Note that some verbs appear in more than one list, because they have more than one meaning.

indicating the way that something is said

7.12 When you use direct speech or reported speech, you can give more information about the way that something is said by putting an adverb or a prepositional phrase after the reporting verb.

'I've got the key!' he announced <u>triumphantly</u>.
His secretary explained <u>patiently</u> that this was the only time he could spare.
I know what you mean, Carrie replied <u>with feeling</u>.

You show how the thing that is said fits into the conversation by using a prepositional phrase.

A gift from my mother, he added <u>in explanation</u>.

negatives in reporting clauses

7.13 With a small number of reporting verbs, the negative is often expressed in the reporting clause rather than in the reported clause. *I don't think Mary is at home* means the same as *I think Mary is not at home*, and *She doesn't want to see him* means *She wants not to see him*.

I <u>do not think</u> she suspects me.
She <u>didn't believe</u> she would ever see him again.
He <u>didn't want</u> to go.
We <u>don't intend</u> to put him on trial.

Here is a list of reporting verbs that are often used with a negative in this way:

believe	imagine	propose	think
expect	intend	reckon	want
feel	plan	suppose	wish

reporting speech and thought in informal spoken English

7.14 In informal spoken English, the reporting verb *go* is sometimes used to introduce direct speech. The reporting clause with *go* always comes before the quote.

I said, 'Well, what do you want to talk about?' He <u>goes</u>, 'I don't care.'
I told her what I'd heard and she <u>went</u>, 'Oh, my gosh.'
When I heard that I'd got the job I <u>went</u>, 'Oh, no, what have I done?'

Note that you cannot add an adverb after *go*. For example, you cannot say, *He went angrily, 'Be quiet!'*

7.15 Another reporting structure that is used in informal spoken English is *be like*. *Be like* can represent either speech or thought. In writing, *be like* is usually followed by a comma. The quote is sometimes in quotation marks, and sometimes not.

He got a call from Oprah, and he <u>was like</u>, 'Of course I'll go on your show.'
He's <u>like</u>, 'It's boring! I hate chess!' And I'm <u>like</u>, 'Please teach me!'
The minute I met him, I <u>was like</u>, he's perfect.

As with other reporting verbs, you can use *be like* with a noun or a personal pronoun: for example, you can say *She was like, ...*, *The doctor was like, ...* or *Jane was like, ...*, followed by the thing that she/the doctor/Jane said or thought.

Unlike other reporting verbs, you can also use *be like* after the pronoun *it*. This structure is often used to present a mixture of speech and thought, or a general situation. For example, if you say *It was like, Oh wow!* it is possible that nobody actually said or thought *Oh wow!* Rather, the sentence gives us an idea of the situation and means something like *It was amazing/surprising*.

So I get back in the bus, quarter of an hour passes and <u>it's like</u>, Where's Graham? When that happened <u>it was like</u>, Oh, no, not again.

Be like always comes before the reported clause.

Reporting someone's actual words: direct speech

7.16   When you want to say that a person used particular words, you use **direct speech**. You can do this even if you do not know, or do not remember, the exact words that were spoken. When you use direct speech, you report what someone said as if you were using their own words.

Direct speech consists of two clauses. One clause is the **reporting clause**, which contains the reporting verb.

'I knew I'd seen you,' <u>I said</u>.
Yes please, <u>replied John</u>.

The other part is the **quote**, which represents what someone says or has said.

'<u>Let's go and have a look at the swimming pool</u>,' she suggested.
'<u>Leave me alone</u>,' I snarled.

You can quote anything that someone says – statements, questions, orders, suggestions, and exclamations. In writing, you use quotation marks (also called *inverted commas* in British English) (' ') or (" ") at the beginning and end of a quote.

'Thank you,' I said.
After a long silence he asked: 'What is your name?'

Note that, in written stories, quotes are sometimes used without reporting clauses if the speakers have been established, and if you do not wish to indicate whether the quotes are questions, suggestions, exclamations, etc.

'When do you leave?' – 'I should be gone now.' – 'Well, good-bye, Hamo.'

7.17   Thinking is sometimes represented as speaking to oneself. You can therefore use some verbs that refer to thinking as reporting verbs in **direct speech**.

I must go and see Lynn, Marsha thought.

When you are using direct speech to say what someone thought, you usually omit the quotation marks at the beginning and end of the quote.

How much should he tell her? Not much, he decided.
Perhaps that's no accident, he reasoned.
Why, she wondered, was the flag at half mast?

7.18   Here is a list of reporting verbs that are often used with direct speech:

add	assert	complain	grumble	pray
admit	assure	conclude	inquire	proclaim
advise	beg	confess	insist	promise
agree	begin	continue	muse	read
announce	boast	decide	observe	reason
answer	claim	declare	order	recite
argue	command	demand	plead	reflect
ask	comment	explain	ponder	remark

reply	say	tell	vow	write
report	state	think	warn	
respond	suggest	urge	wonder	

A few of these verbs can or must be used with an object that refers to the hearer. See paragraphs 7.75 to 7.76.

verbs that describe the way in which something is said

7.19   If you want to indicate the way in which something was said, you can use a reporting verb such as *shout*, *wail*, or *scream*. Verbs like these usually occur only in written stories.

Jump! shouted *the old woman.*
Oh, poor little thing, she wailed.
Get out of there, I screamed.

Here is a list of verbs that indicate the way in which something is said:

bellow	cry	mutter	shriek	wail
call	mumble	scream	storm	whisper
chorus	murmur	shout	thunder	yell

⭐ **BE CREATIVE**

7.20   Another way of describing the way in which something is said is to use a verb that is usually used to describe the sound made by a particular kind of animal.

Excuse me! Susannah barked.

You can use a verb such as *smile*, *grin*, or *frown* to indicate the expression on someone's face while they are speaking.

'I'm awfully sorry.' – 'Not at all,' I smiled.
It was a joke, he grinned.

⭐ **BE CREATIVE**

7.21   You use verbs like *bark* and *smile* in direct speech when you want to create a particular effect, especially in writing.

position of reporting verb

7.22   There are several positions in which you can put the reporting verb in relation to a quote. The usual position is after the quote, but it can also go in front of the quote or in the middle of the quote.

You have to keep trying, he said.
He stepped back and said, Now look at that.
You see, he said, my father was an inventor.

7.23   If you put the reporting verb in the middle of a quote, it must go in one of the following positions:

▸ after a **noun phrase**

That man, I said, never opened a window in his life.

▶ after a **vocative** such as *darling* or *Dad*

'Darling', Max said to her, 'don't say it's not possible.'

▶ after a **sentence adverb**

Maybe, he said hesitantly, maybe there is a beast.

▶ after a **clause**

'I know you don't remember your father,' said James, 'but he was a kind and generous man.'

7.24   You can use most reporting verbs in front of a quote.

She replied, My first thought was to protect him.
One student commented: He seems to know his subject very well.

However, the reporting verbs *agree*, *command*, *promise*, and *wonder* are hardly ever used in front of a quote.

changing the order of the subject and the reporting verb

7.25   When a reporting verb comes after a quote, the subject is often put after the verb.

'Perhaps he isn't a bad sort of chap after all,' <u>remarked Dave</u>.
I see, <u>said John</u>.
I am aware of that, <u>replied the Englishman</u>.

Note that this is not done when the subject is a pronoun, except in some literary contexts.

punctuation of quotes

7.26   The following examples show how you punctuate quotes in British English. You can use either single quotation marks (' ') or double quotation marks (" "). The ones used to begin a quote are called **opening** quotation marks, and the ones used to end a quote are called **closing** quotation marks.

'Let's go,' I whispered.
"We have to go home," she told him.
Mona's mother answered: 'Oh yes, she's in.'
He nodded and said, 'Yes, he's my son.'
'Margaret', I said to her, 'I'm so glad you came.'
What are you doing? Sarah asked.
'Of course it's awful!' shouted Clarissa.
What do they mean, she demanded, by a "population problem"?

Note that in the last example shown above, there is a quote within a quote. If you are using single quotation marks for the main quote, the quoted words within the main quote are enclosed in double quotation marks. If you are using double quotation marks for the main quote, the quoted words within the main quote are enclosed in single quotation marks.

 In American English, you always use double quotation marks (" "), except where you have a quote within a quote. In such cases, the quoted words within the main quote are enclosed in single quotation marks (' '). This is shown in the second example below.

"What are you doing?" Sarah asked.
"What do they mean," she demanded, "by a 'population problem'?"

If you are quoting more than one paragraph, you put opening quotation marks at the beginning of each paragraph, but you put closing quotation marks only at the end of the last paragraph.

Reporting in your own words: reported speech

7.27 When you report what people have said using your own words rather than the words they actually used, you use **reported speech**.

The woman said she had seen nothing.
I replied that I had not read it yet.

You usually use a reported speech structure when you report what someone thinks.

He thought she was worried.

Reported speech is sometimes called **indirect speech**. Reported speech consists of two parts. One part is the **reporting clause**, which contains the reporting verb.

I told him that nothing was going to happen to me.
I have agreed that he should do it.
I wanted to be alone.

The other part is the **reported clause**.

He answered that he thought the story was extremely interesting.
He felt that he had to do something.
He wondered where they could have come from.

You usually put the reporting clause first, in order to make it clear that you are reporting rather than speaking directly yourself.

Henry said that he wanted to go home.

The exact words that Henry used are unlikely to have been *I want to go home*, although they might have been. It is more likely that he said something like *I think I should be going now*. You are more likely to report what he meant rather than what he actually said.

There are many reasons why you do not quote a person's exact words. Often you cannot remember exactly what was said. At other times, the exact words are not important or not appropriate in the situation in which you are reporting.

types of reported clause

7.28 There are several types of **reported clause**. The type you use depends on whether you are reporting a statement, a question, an order, or a suggestion.

Most reported clauses either are *that*-clauses or begin with a *to*-infinitive. When a question is being reported, the reported clause begins with *if*, *whether*, or a *wh*-word. The use of *that*-clauses as reported clauses is discussed in paragraphs 7.29 to 7.31. **Reported questions** are discussed in paragraphs 7.32 to 7.38. The use of *to*-infinitive clauses in reported speech is discussed in paragraphs 7.39 to 7.48.

Reporting statements and thoughts

7.29 If you want to report a statement or someone's thoughts, you use a reported clause beginning with the conjunction *that*.

He said that the police had directed him to the wrong room.
He wrote me a letter saying that he understood what I was doing.
Mrs Kaul announced that the lecture would now begin.

In informal speech and writing, the conjunction *that* is commonly omitted.

They said I had to see a doctor first.
She says she wants to see you this afternoon.
He knew the attempt was hopeless.
I think there's something wrong.

In each of these sentences, *that* could have been used. For example, you can say either *They said I had to see a doctor first* or *They said that I had to see a doctor first*.

That is often omitted when the reporting verb refers simply to the act of saying or thinking. You usually include *that* after a verb that gives more information, such as *complain* or *explain*.

The FBI <u>confirmed that</u> the substance was an explosive.
I <u>explained that</u> she would have to stay in bed.

This kind of reported clause is often called a *that*-clause, even though many occur without *that*.

Note that some relative clauses also begin with *that*. In such clauses, *that* is a relative pronoun, not a conjunction. **Relative clauses** are explained in paragraphs 8.83 to 8.116.

verbs used with *that*-clauses

7.30 Here is a list of verbs that are often used as reporting verbs with *that*-clauses:

accept	contend	guess	persuade	say
acknowledge	convince	hear	pledge	see
add	decide	hold	pray	sense
admit	deny	hope	predict	speculate
agree	determine	imagine	promise	state
allege	discover	imply	prophesy	suggest
announce	dispute	inform	read	suppose
answer	doubt	insist	realize	suspect
argue	dream	judge	reason	swear
assert	elicit	know	reassure	teach
assume	estimate	lament	recall	tell
assure	expect	learn	reckon	think
believe	explain	maintain	record	threaten
boast	fear	mean	reflect	understand
claim	feel	mention	remark	vow
comment	figure	note	remember	warn
complain	find	notice	repeat	wish
concede	foresee	notify	reply	worry
conclude	forget	object	report	write
confirm	gather	observe	resolve	
consider	guarantee	perceive	reveal	

Note that some of these verbs are only used in reported speech in some of their senses. For example, if you say *He accepted a present* you are using *accept* as an ordinary verb.

A few of these verbs can or must be used with an object that refers to the hearer. See paragraphs 7.75 to 7.76.

Some of these verbs, such as *decide* and *promise*, can also be used with a *to*-infinitive. See paragraphs 7.39 and 7.45.

Some other verbs, such as *advise* and *order*, can be used as reporting verbs with *that*-clauses only if the *that*-clause contains a **modal** or a **subjunctive**. *That*-clauses of this kind are discussed in paragraph 7.43.

position of reported clauses

7.31   You usually put the reporting clause before the *that*-clause, in order to make it clear that you are reporting rather than speaking directly yourself.

I said that I would rather work at home.
Georgina said she was going to bed.

However, if you want to emphasize the statement contained in the reported clause, you can change the order and put the reported clause first, with a comma after it. You do not use *that* to introduce the clause.

All these things were trivial, he said.
She was worried, he thought.

If the reported clause is long, you can put the reporting clause in the middle.

Ten years ago, Moumoni explained, some government people had come to inspect the village.

Reporting questions

7.32   As well as reporting what someone says or thinks, you can also report a question that they ask or wonder about.

Questions in reported speech are sometimes called **reported questions** or **indirect questions**.

the reporting verb

7.33   The reporting verb most often used for reporting questions is *ask*. Questions can be reported in a more formal way using *enquire* or *inquire*.

I asked if I could stay with them.
He asked me where I was going.
She inquired how Ibrahim was getting on.

❗   BE CAREFUL

7.34   When you report a question:

▶ you do not use interrogative word order

▶ you do not use a question mark.

So the question *Did you enjoy it?* could be reported: *I asked her if she had enjoyed it.*

Questions are explained in paragraphs 5.10 to 5.36.

yes/no questions

7.35   There are two main types of question, and so two main types of reported speech structure for questions.

One type of question is called a *yes/no* question. These are questions that can be answered simply with *yes* or *no*.

When you report a *yes/no* question, you use an *if*-clause beginning with the conjunction *if*, or a *whether*-clause beginning with the conjunction *whether*.

You use *if* when the speaker has suggested one possibility that be true. *Do you know my name?* could be reported as *A woman asked if I knew her name.*

She asked him if his parents spoke French.
Someone asked me if the work was going well.
He inquired if her hair had always been that colour.

You use *whether* when the speaker has suggested one possibility but has left open the question of other possibilities. After *whether*, you can suggest another possibility, or you can leave it unstated.

I was asked whether I wanted to stay at a hotel or at his home.
She asked whether the servants were still there.
I asked Professor Fred Bailey whether he agreed.
A policeman asked me whether he could be of help.

Sometimes the alternative possibility is represented by *or not*.

The barman didn't ask whether or not they were over eighteen.
They asked whether Britain was or was not a Christian country.

For more information about **yes/no questions**, see paragraphs 5.12 to 5.14.

7.36   There are a few other verbs that can be used before *if*-clauses or *whether*-clauses, because they refer to being unsure of facts or to discovering facts.

I didn't know whether to believe him or not.
Simon wondered if he should make conversation.
She didn't say whether he was still alive.

Here is a list of other verbs that can be used before *if*-clauses and *whether*-clauses:

consider	discover	know	say	tell
determine	doubt	remember	see	wonder

Note that *know*, *remember*, *say*, *see*, and *tell* are usually used in a negative or interrogative clause, or a clause with a modal.

All the verbs in the list, except *wonder*, can also be used with *that*-clauses: see paragraph 7.30. They can all also be used with clauses beginning with *wh*-words: see paragraph 7.38.

wh-questions

7.37   The other type of question is called a *wh*-question. These are questions in which someone asks for information about an event or situation. *Wh*-questions cannot be answered with *yes* or *no*.

When you report a *wh*-question, you use a *wh*-word at the beginning of the reported clause.

He asked where I was going.
She enquired why I was so late.
She started to ask what had happened, then decided against it.
I asked how they had got there so quickly.
I never thought to ask who put it there.

 When the details of the question are clear from the context, you can sometimes leave out everything except the *wh*-word. This happens mostly in spoken English, especially with *why*.

I asked why.
They enquired how.

For more information about **wh-questions** see paragraphs 5.23 to 5.36.

7.38 Other verbs can be used before clauses beginning with *wh*-words, because they refer to knowing, learning, or mentioning one of the circumstances of an event or situation.

She doesn't know <u>what we were talking about</u>.
They couldn't see <u>how they would manage without her</u>.
I wonder <u>what's happened</u>.

Here is a list of other verbs that can be used before clauses beginning with *wh*-words:

decide	explain	know	say	test
describe	forget	learn	see	think
determine	guess	realize	suggest	understand
discover	imagine	remember	teach	wonder
discuss	judge	reveal	tell	

Note that *imagine*, *say*, *see*, *suggest*, and *think* are usually used in a negative or interrogative clause, or a clause with a modal.

All the verbs in the list, except *describe*, *discuss*, and *wonder*, can also be used with *that*-clauses: see paragraph 7.30.

Reporting orders, requests, advice, and intentions

reporting requests

7.39 If someone orders, requests, or advises someone else to do something, this can be reported by using a *to*-infinitive after a reporting verb such as *tell*. The person being addressed, who is going to perform the action, is mentioned as the object of the reporting verb.

He told her to wait there for him.
He commanded his men to retreat
He ordered me to fetch the books.
My doctor advised me to see a neurologist.

For more on this type of structure, see paragraphs 3.202 and 3.206.

Here is a list of reporting verbs that can be used with a person as object followed by a *to*-infinitive:

advise	command	invite	remind	urge
ask	forbid	order	teach	warn
beg	instruct	persuade	tell	

 USAGE NOTE

7.40 A few verbs can be used with a *to*-infinitive to report requests when the hearer is mentioned in a prepositional phrase.

An officer shouted <u>to us</u> to stop all the noise.
I pleaded <u>with him</u> to tell me.

Here is a list of these verbs and the prepositions used with them:

appeal to	plead with	shout at	shout to	whisper to	yell at

7.41 In ordinary conversation, requests are often put in the form of a question. For example, you might say *Will you help me?* instead of *Help me*. Similarly, reported requests often look like reported questions.

He asked me if I could lend him fifty dollars.

When you report a request like this, you can mention both the person receiving it and the person making it.

She asked me whether I would help her.

Alternatively, you can just mention the person making it.

He asked if I would answer some questions.

7.42 You can report a request in which someone asks for permission to do something by using a *to*-infinitive after *ask* or *demand*.

I asked to see the manager.

reporting suggestions

7.43 When someone makes a suggestion about what someone else (not their hearer) should do, you report it by using a *that*-clause. In British English, this clause often contains a **modal**, usually *should*.

He proposes that the Government should hold an inquiry.
Travel agents advise that people should change their money before they travel.

Note that this structure can also be used to report a suggestion about what the hearer should do. Consider the example: *Her father had suggested that she ought to see a doctor*; her father might have suggested it directly to her.

 If you do not use a modal, the result is considered more formal in British English. In American English, however, this is the usual verb form that is used after suggesting verbs.

Someone suggested that they break into small groups.

Note that when you leave out the modal, the verb in the reported clause still has the form it would have if the modal were present. This verb form is called the **subjunctive**.

It was his doctor who advised that he change his job.
I suggested that he bring them all up to the house.
He urges that the restrictions be lifted.

Here is a list of reporting verbs that can be followed by a *that*-clause containing a modal or a subjunctive:

advise	decree	order	recommend	urge
agree	demand	plead	request	
ask	direct	pray	rule	
beg	insist	prefer	stipulate	
command	intend	propose	suggest	

Note that *advise, ask, beg, command, order,* and *urge* can also be used with an object and a *to*-infinitive, and *agree, pray,* and *suggest* can also be used with *that*-clauses without a modal.

7.44 When someone makes a suggestion about what someone else should do, or about what they themselves and someone else should do, you can report this using one of the reporting verbs *suggest, advise, propose,* or *recommend* followed by an *-ing* participle.

Barbara suggested going to another coffee-house.
Deirdre proposed moving to New York.

reporting intentions and hopes

7.45 When you are reporting an action that the speaker (the subject of the reporting verb) intends to perform, you can report it in two ways. You can either report it simply as an action, using a *to*-infinitive clause, or you can report it as a statement or fact, using a *that*-clause.

For example, promises relate to actions (eg *He promised to phone her*) but they can also be seen as relating to facts (eg *He promised that he would phone her*).

The verb phrase in the *that*-clause always contains a **modal**.

I promised to come back.
She promised that she would not leave hospital until she was better.
I decided to withhold the information till later.
She decided that she would leave her money to him.
I had vowed to fight for their freedom.
She vowed that she would not leave her home.

Here is a list of verbs that can be used either with a *to*-infinitive or with a *that*-clause containing a modal:

decide	hope	propose	threaten
expect	pledge	resolve	vow
guarantee	promise	swear	

USAGE NOTE

7.46 *Claim* and *pretend* can also be used with these two structures, when you are saying that someone is claiming or pretending something about himself or herself. For example, *He claimed to be a genius* has the same meaning as *He claimed that he was a genius*.

He claimed to have witnessed the accident.
He claimed that he had found the money in the forest.

Note that the *to*-infinitive can be in the perfect form: *to have* + *-ed* participle, when you are referring to a past event or situation.

7.47 Note that a few verbs that indicate personal intentions can be used only with a *to*-infinitive.

I intend to say nothing for the present.
They are planning to move to the country.
I don't want to die yet.

Here is a list of these verbs:

intend	long	mean	plan	refuse	want

Reporting uncertain things

7.48 When you are reporting an action that someone is wondering about doing themselves, you can use a *to*-infinitive beginning with *whether*.

I've been wondering <u>whether to retire</u>.
He didn't know <u>whether to feel glad or sorry at his dismissal</u>.

Here is a list of verbs that can be used with *to*-infinitive clauses of this kind:

choose	debate	decide	know	wonder

Note that *choose*, *decide*, and *know* are usually used in a negative or interrogative clause, or a clause with a modal.

When you are mentioning information about something involved in an action, you can use a *to*-infinitive after a *wh*-word as the reported clause.

I asked him <u>what to do</u>.
I shall teach you <u>how to cook</u>.

Here is a list of verbs that can be used with *to*-infinitives of this kind:

describe	forget	learn	say	tell
discover	guess	realize	see	think
discuss	imagine	remember	suggest	understand
explain	know	reveal	teach	wonder

As an alternative to both kinds of *to*-infinitive, you can use a clause containing *should*.

I wondered <u>whether I should call for help</u>.
He began to wonder <u>what he should do now</u>.

All the verbs in the above lists, except *choose* and *debate*, can also be used with ordinary clauses beginning with *whether* or *wh*-words. See paragraphs 7.35 to 7.38.

Time reference in reported speech

7.49 This section explains how to show time reference in reported speech. Descriptions of time reference in reported speech often give a simplified system that involves changing the tense in the actual words spoken, so that a present tense would be changed to a past tense, and a past tense would be changed to the past perfect. In fact, tense changes in reported speech are affected by several factors other than time, such as whether you wish to distance yourself from what was said, or whether you want to emphasize the fact that a statement is still true.

past tense for both verbs

7.50 If you are reporting something that was said or believed in the past, or if you want to distance yourself from what the other person said, you usually use a past tense for both the reporting verb and the verb in the reported clause.

She <u>said</u> you <u>threw</u> away her sweets.
Brody <u>asked</u> what <u>happened</u>.
In the Middle Ages, people <u>thought</u> the world <u>was</u> flat.

reporting verb in other tenses

7.51 If you are reporting something that someone says or believes at the time that you are speaking, you use a present tense of the reporting verb.

A third of adults <u>say</u> that work is bad for your health.
I <u>think</u> it's going to rain.

However, you can also use a present tense of the reporting verb when you are reporting something said in the past, especially if you are reporting something that someone often says or that is still true.

She says she wants to see you this afternoon.
My doctor says it's nothing to worry about.

If you are predicting what people will say or think, you use a future form of the reporting verb.

No doubt he will claim that his car broke down.
They will think we are making a fuss.

tense of verb in reported clause

7.52 Whatever the tense of your reporting verb, you put the verb in the reported clause into a tense that is appropriate at the time that you are speaking.

If the event or situation described in the reported clause is in the past at the time that you are speaking, you generally use the past simple, the past progressive, or the present perfect: *She said she enjoyed the course*, *She said she was enjoying the course*, or *She said she has enjoyed the course*. See Chapter 4 for information on when to use these forms.

Dad explained that he had no money.
She added that she was working too much.
He says he has never seen a live shark in his life.

When the reporting verb is in a past tense, a past tense is also usually used for the verb in the reported clause even if the reported situation still exists. For example, you could say *I told him I was eighteen* even if you are still eighteen. You are concentrating on the situation at the past time that you are talking about.

He said he was English.

A present form is sometimes used instead, to emphasize that the situation still exists.

I told him that I don't eat more than anyone else.

If the event or situation was in the past at the time that the reported statement was made, or had existed up to that time, you use the past perfect: *She said she had enjoyed the course*.

He knew he had behaved badly.
Mr Benn said that he had been in hospital at the time.

If the event or situation is still going on, you use a present form if you are using a present form of the reporting verb: *She says she's enjoying the course*.

Don't assume I'm a complete fool.
He knows he's being watched.

If the event or situation was in the future at the time of the statement or is still in the future, you use a modal. See paragraphs 7.53 to 7.56, below.

modals in reported clauses

7.53 The basic rules for using modals in reported clauses are as follows.

If the verb in the reporting clause is in a past form or has *could* or *would* as an auxiliary, you usually use *could*, *might*, or *would* in the reported clause.

If, as is less common, the verb in the reporting clause is in the present or has *can* or *will* as an auxiliary, you usually use *can*, *may*, or *will* in the reported clause.

7.54 When you want to report a statement or question about someone's ability to do something, you normally use *could*.

They believed that war could be avoided.
Nell would not admit that she could not cope.

If you want to report a statement about possibility, you normally use *might*.

They told me it might flood here.
He said you might need money.

If the possibility is a strong one, you use *must*.

I told her she must be out of her mind.

When you want to report a statement giving permission or a request for permission, you normally use *could*. *Might* is used in more formal English.

I told him he couldn't have it.
Madeleine asked if she might borrow a pen and some paper.

When you want to report a prediction, promise, or expectation, or a question about the future, you normally use *would*.

She said they would all miss us.
He insisted that reforms would save the system, not destroy it.

7.55 If the reported event or situation still exists or is still in the future, and you are using a present tense of the reporting verb, you use *can* instead of *could*, *may* instead of *might*, and *will* or *shall* instead of *would*.

Helen says I can share her apartment.
I think the weather may change soon.
I don't believe he will come.

Note that you cannot use *can have* instead of *could have*, or *will have* instead of *would have*. You cannot use *may have* instead of *might have* if you are using it like *could have* to talk about something that did not happen.

You can also use *can*, *may*, *will*, and *shall* when you are using a past tense of the reporting verb, if you want to emphasize that the situation still exists or is still in the future.

He claimed that the child's early experiences may cause psychological distress in later life.

If you are using a present reporting verb and want to indicate that the reported event or situation is hypothetical or very unlikely, you can use the modals *could*, *might*, or *would*.

I believe that I could live very comfortably here.

7.56 When you want to report a statement about obligation, it is possible to use *must*, but the expression *had to* (see paragraph 5.244) is more common.

He said he really had to go back inside.
Sita told him that he must be especially kind to the little girl.

You use *have to*, *has to*, or *must* if the reported situation still exists or is in the future.

When you want to report a statement prohibiting something, you normally use *mustn't*.

He said they mustn't get us into trouble.

When you want to report a strong recommendation, you can use *ought to*. You can also use *should*.

He knew he *ought to* be helping Harold.
I felt I *should* consult my family.

7.57 When you want to report a habitual past action or a past situation, you can use the semi-modal *used to*.

I wish I knew what his favourite dishes *used to* be.

7.58 The use of **modals** in reported clauses can be compared with the ordinary use of modals (see paragraphs 5.94 to 5.258). Many of the functions are similar, but some are rarely or never found in reported clauses.

reporting conditional statements

7.59 When you are reporting a **conditional statement**, the tenses of the verbs are, in most cases, the same as they would be normally. However, they are different if you are using the past simple form of a reporting verb, and reporting a conditional statement such as *If there is no water in the radiator, the engine will overheat*. In this case, you can use the past simple instead of the present simple and *would* instead of *will* in the reported conditional statement: *She said that if there was no water in the radiator, the engine would overheat*.

For information about conditional statements, see paragraphs 8.25 to 8.42.

Making your reference appropriate

7.60 People, things, times, and places can be referred to in different ways, depending on who is speaking or on when or where they are speaking. For example, the same person can be referred to as *I*, *you*, or *she*, and the same place can be referred to as *over there* or *just here*.

If you use **reported speech** to report what someone has said, the words you use to refer to things must be appropriate in relation to yourself, the time when you are speaking, and the place in which you are speaking. The words you use may well be different from the words originally spoken, which were appropriate from the point of view of the speaker at the time.

referring to people and things

7.61 For example, if a man is talking to someone about a woman called Jenny, and he says, *I saw her in the High Street*, there are several ways in which this statement can be reported. If the original speaker repeats what he said, he could say, *I said I saw her in the High Street*. *I* and *her* do not change, because they still refer to the same people.

If the original listener reports what was said, he or she could say, *He said he saw her in the High Street*. *I* becomes *he*, because the statement is reported from the point of view of a third person, not from the point of view of the original speaker.

If the original listener reports the statement to Jenny, *her* becomes *you*: *He said he saw you in the High Street*.

The original listener might report the statement to the original speaker. This time, *I* has to change to *you*: *You said you saw her in the High Street*.

You're crazy.
I told him *he* was crazy.

Possessive determiners and pronouns change in the same way as personal pronouns in order to keep the same reference. So the following sentences could all report the same question: *She asked if he was my brother, She asked if you were my brother, I asked if he was her brother*. The original question might have been expressed as *Is he your brother?*

7.62   When reporting, you may need to change **time adverbials** such as *today*, *yesterday*, or *next week*.

For example, if someone called Jill says *I will come tomorrow*, you could report this statement the following day as *Jill said she would come today*. At a later time, you could report the same statement as *Jill said she would come the next day* or *Jill said she would come the following day*.

We decided to leave the city <u>the next day</u>.
I was afraid people might think I'd been asleep during <u>the previous twenty-four hours</u>.

7.63   You may need to change words that relate to position or place.

For example, if you are talking to a man about a restaurant, he might say *I go there every day*. If you report his statement while you are actually in the restaurant, you could say *He said he comes here every day*.

Using reporting verbs to perform an action

7.64   Reporting verbs are often used when people explicitly say what function their statement is performing. They do this using *I* and the present simple of a verb such as *admit* or *promise* that refers to something that is done with words. For example, instead of saying *I'll be there* you could say *I promise I'll be there*, which makes the statement stronger.

<u>I suggest</u> we draw up a document.
I'll be back at one, <u>I promise</u>.
I was somewhat shocked, <u>I admit</u>, by these events.

The following verbs can be used in this way:

acknowledge	contend	pledge	say	vow
admit	demand	predict	submit	warn
assure	deny	promise	suggest	
claim	guarantee	prophesy	swear	
concede	maintain	propose	tell	

7.65   Some other verbs that refer to doing something with words are used without a *that*-clause after them. When used without a *that*-clause, the use of the present simple with *I* performs the function of a statement in itself, rather than commenting on another statement.

I apologize for any delay.
I congratulate you with all my heart.
I forgive you.

The following verbs are commonly used in this way:

absolve	authorize	declare	nominate	renounce
accept	baptize	dedicate	object	resign
accuse	challenge	defy	order	second
advise	confess	forbid	pronounce	sentence
agree	congratulate	forgive	protest	
apologize	consent	name	refuse	

7.66 The verbs in the above lists are sometimes called **performative verbs** or **performatives**, because they perform the action they refer to.

🔲 **USAGE NOTE**

7.67 Some of these verbs are used with modals when people want to be emphatic, polite, or tentative.

I must apologize for Mayfield.
I would agree with a lot of their points.
She was very thoroughly checked, I can assure you.
May I congratulate you again on your excellent performance.

Avoiding mention of the person speaking or thinking

7.68 There are several reporting structures that you can use if you want to avoid saying whose opinion or statement you are giving.

use of passives to express general beliefs

7.69 If you want to show or suggest that something is an opinion held by an unspecified group of people, you can use a passive form of a reporting verb with *it* as the **impersonal** subject.

It is assumed that the government will remain in power.
In former times it was believed that all enlarged tonsils should be removed.
It is now believed that foreign languages are most easily taught to young children.
It was said that half a million dollars had been spent on the search.

Here is a list of reporting verbs that are used in the passive with *it* as their subject:

accept	concede	find	observe	rule
acknowledge	conclude	foresee	predict	rumour
admit	confirm	forget	propose	say
agree	consider	guarantee	realize	state
allege	decide	hold	recall	stipulate
announce	decree	hope	reckon	suggest
argue	discover	imply	recommend	suppose
assert	estimate	know	record	think
assume	expect	mention	remember	understand
believe	explain	note	report	
claim	fear	notice	request	
comment	feel	object	reveal	

This structure has much in common with a structure using a passive reporting verb and a *to*-infinitive clause. In this structure, the main person or thing involved in the reported opinion is put as the subject of the reporting verb.

Intelligence is assumed to be important.
He is said to have died a natural death.
He is believed to have fled to France.

Note that the *to*-infinitive is most commonly *be* or *have*, or a perfect infinitive.

Here is a list of reporting verbs, from the list above, that are also used in this type of structure:

agree	claim	expect	hold	understand
allege	consider	feel	know	
assume	discover	find	observe	
believe	estimate	guarantee	think	

seem **and** appear

7.70 If you want to say that something appears to be the case, you can use either of the verbs *seem* and *appear*. These verbs can be used as reporting verbs followed by a *that*-clause or they can be used with a *to*-infinitive. You can use this structure to give your own opinion or that of someone else. The subject of *seem* or *appear* is *it*, used impersonally.

It seemed that she had not been careful enough
It seemed that he had lost his chance to win.
It appears that he followed my advice.

Alternatively, you can use a structure involving *seem* or *appear* and a *to*-infinitive clause. The main person or thing involved in the fact that appears to be true is put as the subject of the reporting verb.

She seemed to like me.
He appears to have been an interesting man.
The system appears to work well.

If you want to mention the person whose viewpoint you are giving, you can add a prepositional phrase beginning with *to* after *seem* or *appear*.

It seemed <u>to Jane</u> that everyone was against her.

ℹ️ USAGE NOTE

7.71 There are a few expressions containing impersonal *it* that are used as reporting clauses before *that*-clauses to show that someone suddenly thought of something: *It occurred to me, It struck me*, and *It crossed my mind*.

<u>*It occurred to her*</u> *that someone was missing.*
<u>*It crossed my mind*</u> *that somebody must have been keeping things secret.*

Referring to the speaker and hearer

referring to the speaker

7.72 You usually use a reporting verb to report what one person has said or thought, so the subject of a reporting verb is usually a singular noun.

Henry said that he wanted to go home.
He claimed his health had been checked several times at a clinic.

When you report the statements, opinions, orders, or questions of a group of people, you can use a plural noun or a collective noun as the subject of the reporting verb.

The judges demanded that the race be run again.
The committee noted that this was not the first case of its kind.

When you report what was said on television or radio, or what is printed or written in a newspaper or other document, you can mention the source or means of communication as the subject of a reporting verb.

The newspaper said he was hiding somewhere near Kabul.
His contract stated that his salary would be £50,000 a year.

Note that you can also use *say* with nouns such as *sign, notice, clock,* and *map* as the subject.

The notice said that attendants should not be tipped.
A sign over the door said Dreamland Cafe.
The road map said it was 210 kilometres to the French frontier.

use of the passive

7.73   As explained in paragraph 7.69, when you want to avoid mentioning the person who said something, you can use a reporting verb in the passive.

It was said that some of them had become insane.
He was said to be the oldest man in the firm.

If you want to avoid mentioning the person giving an order or giving advice, you use a passive reporting verb with the person who receives the order or advice as the subject.

Harriet was ordered to keep away from my room.

USAGE NOTE

7.74   If you want to distance yourself from a statement you are making, you can show that you are reporting what someone else has said by using a phrase beginning with *according to*, rather than using reported speech.

According to Dime, he had strangled Jed in the course of a struggle.

referring to the hearer

7.75   After some reporting verbs that refer to speech, you have to mention the hearer as a direct object. *Tell* is the most common of these verbs.

I told them you were at the dentist.
I informed her that I was unwell and could not come.
Smith persuaded them that they must support the strike.

You can use these verbs in the passive, with the hearer as the subject.

She had been told she could leave hospital.
Members had been informed that the purpose of the meeting was to elect a new chairman.
She was persuaded to look again.

Here is a list of reporting verbs that must have the hearer as the direct object when they are used with a *that*-clause:

assure	inform	persuade	remind
convince	notify	reassure	tell

Here is a list of reporting verbs that must have the hearer as the direct object when they are used with a *to*-infinitive clause:

advise	forbid	order	teach	warn
beg	instruct	persuade	tell	
command	invite	remind	urge	

verbs with or without the hearer as object

7.76   After a few reporting verbs that refer to speech, you can choose whether or not to mention the hearer.

I promised that I would try to phone her.
I promised Myra I'd be home at seven.
The physicians warned that, without the operation, the child would die.
Thomas warned her that his mother was slightly deaf.

Here is a list of reporting verbs that can be used with or without the hearer as object when used with a *that*-clause:

ask	promise	teach	warn

Promise can also be used with or without an object when it is used with a *to*-infinitive. *Ask* has to be used with an object when it is used with a *to*-infinitive clause to report a request for the hearer to do something, but it is used without an object when the request is for permission to do something (see paragraphs 7.39 and 7.42).

the hearer in prepositional phrases

7.77   With many other reporting verbs, if you want to mention the hearer, you do so in a prepositional phrase beginning with *to*.

I explained to her that I had to go home.
'Margaret', I said to her, 'I'm so glad you came.'

Here is a list of reporting verbs that are used with *that*-clauses or quotes and that need the preposition *to* if you mention the hearer:

admit	confess	insist	report	suggest
announce	declare	mention	reveal	swear
boast	explain	murmur	say	whisper
complain	hint	propose	shout	

Propose and *swear* can also be used with a *to*-infinitive, but not if you mention the hearer.

I propose to mention this at the next meeting.

7.78   When you are describing a situation in which a speaker is speaking forcefully to a hearer, you can mention the hearer in a prepositional phrase beginning with *at*.

The tall boy shouted <u>at them</u>, Choir! Stand still!
Shut up! he bellowed <u>at me</u>.

Here is a list of reporting verbs that are used to describe forceful speech. If you want to mention the hearer, you use a prepositional phrase beginning with *at*:

bark	grumble	scream	snap	wail
bellow	howl	shout	storm	yell
growl	roar	shriek	thunder	

7.79 With verbs that describe situations where both the speaker and the hearer are involved in the speech activity, you can mention the hearer in a prepositional phrase beginning with *with*.

He agreed <u>with us</u> that it would be better to have no break.
Can you confirm <u>with Ray</u> that this date is ok?

Here is a list of reporting verbs that take the preposition *with* if you mention the hearer:

agree	argue	confirm	plead	reason

7.80 With verbs that describe situations where someone is getting information from someone or something, you use a prepositional phrase beginning with *from* to mention the source of the information.

I discovered <u>from her</u> that a woman prisoner had killed herself.

Here is a list of reporting verbs where the source of the information is mentioned using *from*:

discover	gather	infer	see
elicit	hear	learn	

reflexive pronouns

7.81 A **reflexive pronoun** is sometimes used as the object of a reporting verb or preposition in order to say what someone is thinking. For example, *to say something to yourself* means to think it rather than to say it aloud.

I told <u>myself</u> that he was crazy.
It will soon be over, I kept saying to <u>myself</u>.

Other ways of indicating what is said

objects with reporting verbs

7.82 Sometimes you use a noun such as *question*, *story*, or *apology* to refer to what someone has said or written. You can use a reporting verb with one of these nouns as its object instead of a reported clause.

He asked <u>a number of questions</u>.
Simon whispered <u>his answer</u>.
He told <u>funny stories</u> and made everyone laugh.
Philip repeated <u>his invitation</u>.

Here is a list of reporting verbs that are often used with nouns that refer to something spoken or written:

accept	explain	mutter	shout
acknowledge	forget	note	state
ask	guess	notice	suggest
begin	hear	promise	tell
believe	imagine	refuse	understand
continue	know	remember	whisper
demand	lay out	repeat	write
deny	learn	report	
expect	mention	set down	

7.83 Some reporting verbs can have as their objects nouns that refer to events or facts. These nouns are often closely related to verbs. For example, *loss* is closely related to *lose*, and instead of saying *He admitted that he had lost his passport*, you can say *He admitted the loss of his passport*.

British Airways announce the arrival of flight BA 5531 from Glasgow.
The company reported a 45 per cent drop in profits.

Here is a list of reporting verbs that are often used with nouns that refer to events or facts:

accept	discuss	imagine	prefer	sense
acknowledge	doubt	mean	promise	suggest
admit	expect	mention	recommend	urge
announce	explain	note	record	
demand	fear	notice	remember	
describe	foresee	observe	report	
discover	forget	predict	see	

USAGE NOTE

7.84 Note that *say* is usually only used with an object if the object is a very general word such as *something, anything,* or *nothing*.

I must have said something wrong.
The man nodded but said nothing.

prepositional phrases with reporting verbs

7.85 A few verbs referring to speech and thought can be used with a prepositional phrase rather than a reported clause, to indicate the general subject matter of a statement or thought.

Thomas explained about the request from Paris.

Here are three lists of verbs that can be used with a prepositional phrase referring to a fact or subject. In each list, the verbs in the first group are used without an object, and the verbs in the second group are used with an object referring to the hearer. Note that *ask* and *warn* can be used with or without an object.

The following verbs are used with *about*:

agree	dream	inquire	wonder	teach
ask	explain	know	worry	tell
boast	forget	learn	write	warn
complain	grumble	mutter	~	
decide	hear	read	ask	

No one knew <u>about my interest in mathematics</u>.
I asked him <u>about the horses</u>.

The following verbs are used with *of*:

complain	learn	write	inform	remind
dream	read	~	notify	warn
hear	think	assure	persuade	
know	warn	convince	reassure	

They never complained <u>of the incessant rain</u>.
No one had warned us <u>of the dangers</u>.

The following verbs are used with *on*. None of them take an object referring to the hearer.

agree	decide	insist	report
comment	determine	remark	write

He had already decided <u>on his story</u>.
They are insisting <u>on the release of all political prisoners</u>.

Note that *speak* and *talk* are used with *about* and *of* but not with reported clauses.

Other ways of using reported clauses

nouns used with reported clauses

7.86 There are many nouns, such as *statement*, *advice*, and *opinion*, that refer to what someone says or thinks. Many of the nouns used in this way are related to reporting verbs. For example, *information* is related to *inform*, and *decision* is related to *decide*. These nouns can be used in reporting structures in a similar way to reporting verbs. They are usually followed by a reported clause beginning with *that*.

He referred to <u>Copernicus' statement that the Earth moves around the sun</u>.
They expressed <u>the opinion that I must be misinformed</u>.
There was <u>little hope that he would survive</u>.

Here is a list of nouns that have related reporting verbs and that can be used with *that*-clauses:

admission	answer	belief	declaration
advice	argument	claim	dream
agreement	assertion	conclusion	expectation
announcement	assumption	decision	explanation

feeling	reply	saying	warning
guess	report	sense	wish
hope	response	statement	
information	revelation	thought	
knowledge	rule	threat	
promise	rumour	understanding	

Some of these nouns can also be followed by a *to*-infinitive clause:

agreement	decision	promise	warning
claim	hope	threat	wish

The decision to go had not been an easy one to make.
Barnaby's father had fulfilled *his promise to buy his son a horse*.

Note that some nouns that are not related to reporting verbs can be followed by *that*-clauses, because they refer or relate to facts or beliefs. Here is a list of some of these nouns:

advantage	evidence	news	story
benefit	experience	opinion	tradition
confidence	fact	possibility	view
danger	faith	principle	vision
disadvantage	idea	risk	word
effect	impression	sign	

He didn't want her to get *the idea that he was rich*.
She can't accept *the fact that he's gone*.
Eventually a distraught McCoo turned up with *the news that his house had just burned down*.

Chapter 8

Combining messages

8 Combining messages

8.1   Sometimes a statement is too complex or detailed to be expressed in a single clause. You make statements of this kind by putting two or more clauses together in one sentence.

There are two ways in which you can do this. One way is to use one clause as a main clause and to add other **subordinate** clauses. A **subordinate clause** is a clause that depends on the main clause to complete its meaning, and that cannot form a sentence on its own. For this reason, in some grammars, it is called a **dependent clause**.

I came because I want you to help me.
I didn't like the man who did the gardening for them.
You have no right to keep people off your land unless they are doing damage.
When he had gone, Valentina sighed.

The other way is simply to link clauses together.

I'm an old man and I'm sick.
I like films but I don't go to the cinema very often.

Questions and orders can also consist of more than one clause.

What will I do if he doesn't come?
If she is ambitious, don't try to hold her back.

Clauses are explained in Chapters 3 and 5.

conjunctions

8.2   When you put two clauses into one sentence, you use a **conjunction** to link them and to show the relationship between them.

When he stopped, no one said anything.
They were going by car because it was more comfortable.
The telephone rang and Judy picked it up.
The food looked good, but I was too full to eat.

8.3   There are two types of conjunction. They show the different types of relationship between clauses in a sentence.

subordinating conjunctions

8.4   When you are adding a clause in order to develop an aspect of what you are saying, you use a **subordinating conjunction**.

The cat jumped onto my father's lap while he was reading his letters.
He had cancer although it was detected at an early stage.
When the jar was full, he turned the water off.

A clause that begins with a subordinating conjunction is called a **subordinate clause**.

When an atom is split, it releases neutrons.
If he had won, he would have shared the money.
The house was called Sea View, although there were no sea anywhere in sight.

You can also add subordinate clauses to questions and imperative clauses.

How long is it since you've actually taught?

Make a plan before you start.

Sentences containing a main clause and one or more subordinate clauses are often called **complex sentences**.

There are three main kinds of subordinate clause:

Adverbial clauses: these are dealt with in paragraphs 8.6 to 8.82.

Relative clauses: these are dealt with in paragraphs 8.83 to 8.116.

Nominal *that*-clauses: those relating to reported speech and thought are referred to as **reported clauses**, and are dealt with in Chapter 7; those relating to facts are dealt with in paragraphs 8.117 to 8.128.

coordinating conjunctions

8.5   If you are simply linking clauses, you use a **coordinating conjunction**.

Her son lives at home and has a steady job.
He's a shy man, but he's not scared of anything or anyone.

You can also put coordinating conjunctions between questions and between imperative clauses.

Did you buy those curtains or do you make your own?
Visit your local dealer or phone for a brochure.

Clauses joined by a coordinating conjunction are called **coordinate clauses**.

She turned and left the room.

Sentences that contain coordinate clauses are sometimes called **compound sentences**.

A full explanation of **coordinate clauses** is given in paragraphs 8.149 to 8.163. Other uses of **coordinating conjunctions** are explained in paragraphs 8.164 to 8.201.

Adverbial clauses

8.6   There are eight types of **adverbial clause**:

type of clause	usual conjunction	paragraphs
time clauses	when, before, after since, while, as, until	paragraphs 8.8 to 8.24
conditional clauses	if, unless	paragraphs 8.25 to 8.42
purpose clauses	in order to, so that	paragraphs 8.43 to 8.48
reason clauses	because, since, as	paragraphs 8.49 to 8.53
result clauses	so that	paragraphs 8.54 to 8.64
concessive clauses	although, though, while	paragraphs 8.65 to 8.72
place clauses	where, wherever	paragraphs 8.73 to 8.77
clauses of manner	as, like, the way	paragraphs 8.78 to 8.82

Non-finite clauses, when they begin with a subordinating conjunction, are dealt with in the sections dealing with adverbial clauses. Non-finite clauses that do not begin with a subordinating conjunction are dealt with separately in paragraphs 8.129 to 8.145. Other structures that function like non-finite clauses are described in paragraphs 8.146 to 8.148.

position of adverbial clause

8.7   The usual position for an adverbial clause is just after the main clause.

I couldn't think of a single thing to say <u>after he'd replied like that</u>.
The performances were cancelled <u>because the leading man was ill</u>.

However, most types of adverbial clause can be put in front of a main clause.

<u>When the city is dark</u>, we can move around easily.
<u>Although crocodiles are inactive for long periods</u>, on occasion they can run very fast indeed.

Occasionally, you can put an adverbial clause in the middle of another clause.

They make allegations which, <u>when you analyse them</u>, do not have too many facts behind them.

There are a few types of adverbial clause that always go after a main clause; other types always go in front of one. This is explained in the sections dealing with the different types of clause.

Time clauses: *When I was young, ...*

8.8   **Time clauses** are used for saying when something happens, by referring to a period of time or to another event.

Her father died <u>when she was young</u>.
Stocks of food cannot be brought in <u>before the rains start</u>.
He was detained last Monday <u>after he returned from a business trip overseas</u>.
<u>When I first arrived</u> I didn't know anyone.

Time clauses can be used after **time adverbials**.

We'll give him his presents <u>tomorrow, before he goes to school</u>.
I want to see you for a few minutes <u>at twelve o'clock, when you go to lunch</u>.

Time adverbials are explained in Chapter 4.

tenses in time clauses

8.9   When you are talking about the past or the present, the verb in a time clause has the same tense that it would have in a main clause or in a simple sentence.

I was standing by the window when I <u>heard</u> her speak.
I look after the children while she <u>goes</u> to Denver.

However, if the time clause refers to something that will happen or exist in the future, you use the **present simple**, not the future.

For example, you say *When he comes, I will show him the book*, not *When he will come, I will show him the book*.

As soon as we <u>get</u> the tickets, we'll send them to you.
He wants to see you before he <u>dies</u>.
Let me stay here till Jeannie <u>comes</u> home.

If you mention an event in a time clause that will happen before an event referred to in the main clause, you use the **present perfect** in the time clause, not the future perfect.

For example, you say *When you have had your supper, come and see me*, not *When you will have had your supper, come and see me*.

We won't be getting married until we've saved enough money.
Come and tell me when you have finished.

8.10 The most common conjunction in time clauses is *when*. *When* is used to say that something happened, happens, or will happen on a particular occasion.

When the telegram came and I read of his death, I couldn't believe it.
He didn't know how to behave when they next met.

8.11 You can mention the circumstances in which something happens or happened by using *when*, *while*, or *as*.

The train has automatic doors that only open when the train is stationary.
While he was still in the stable, there was a loud knock at the front door.
He would swim beside me as I rowed in the little dinghy.

Whilst is a more formal form of *while*.

We chatted whilst the children played in the crèche.

🇺🇸 *Whilst* is not used in modern American English.

 USAGE NOTE

8.12 If you want to emphasize that something happened at a particular time, you can use *It was* followed by an expression such as *six o'clock* or *three hours later*, followed by a *when*-clause.

For example, instead of saying *I left at six o'clock*, you say *It was six o'clock when I left*.

It was about half past eight when he arrived at Gatwick.
It was late when he returned.

This is an example of a **split sentence**. Split sentences are explained in paragraphs 9.25 to 9.30.

 repeated events

8.13 If you want to say that something always happened or happens in particular circumstances, you use *when*, *whenever*, *every time*, or *each time*.

When he talks about Ireland, he does sound like an outsider.
Whenever she had a cold, she ate only fruit.
Every time I go to that class I panic.
He looked away each time she spoke to him.

8.14 You use an expression such as *the first time*, *the next time*, or *the third time* to say that something happened during one occurrence of an event.

The last time we talked he said he needed another two days.
The next time I come here, I'm going to be better.

events in sequence

8.15 You can also use *when*, *after*, or *once* to talk about one event happening immediately after another.

When his wife left him he suffered terribly.
Stop me when you've had enough.
The turtle returns to the sea after it has laid its eggs.
Once the damage is done, it takes many years for the system to recover.

If you want to say how long one event happened after another, you put a noun phrase such as *two days* or *three years* in front of *after*.

Exactly six weeks after she had arrived, she sent a cable to her husband and caught the plane back to New York.

As soon as, *directly*, *immediately*, *the moment*, *the minute*, and *the instant* are all used to talk about one event happening a very short time after another.

They heard voices as soon as they pushed open the door.
The minute someone left the room, the others started talking about them.
Immediately the meal was over, it was time for prayer.

 The words *directly* and *immediately* are not used as conjunctions in American English.

8.16 When you want to say that something happened, happens, or will happen at an earlier time than something else, you use *before*.

It was necessary for them to find a home before the cold weather arrived.
Before they moved to the city she had never seen a car.

If you want to say how long one event happened before another, you put a noun phrase such as *three weeks* or *a short time* in front of *before*.

He had a review with the second organiser, about a month before the report was written.
Long before you return she will have forgotten you.

8.17 When you are telling a story, you sometimes want to say what was happening when a particular event occurred. You first say what was happening, then add a clause beginning with *when* in which you mention the event.

I had just finished my meal when I heard voices.
He was having his dinner when the telephone rang.

If you want to say that one event happened a very short time after another, you use a clause in the past perfect, followed by a time clause in the past simple. After *had* in the first clause, you put *no sooner* or *hardly*.

When you use *no sooner*, the time clause begins with *than*.

I had no sooner checked into the hotel than he arrived with the appropriate documents.

When you use *hardly*, the time clause begins with *when* or *before*.

He had hardly got his eyes open before she told him that they were leaving.

No sooner or, less frequently, *hardly* can be put at the beginning of the first clause, followed by *had* and the subject.

No sooner had he asked the question than the answer came to him.
Hardly had he settled into his seat when Alan came bursting in.
Hardly had he got on his horse before people started firing at him.

8.18 When something is the case because of a new situation, you can say what is the case and then add a subordinate clause saying what the new situation is. The subordinate clause begins with *now that*. In British English you can leave out *that*.

He could travel much faster now that he was alone.
I feel better now I've talked to you.

saying when a situation began

8.19 If you want to say that a situation started to exist at a particular time and still exists, you use *since* or *ever since*. In the time clause, you use the **past simple**.

I've been in politics since I was at university.
It's been making money ever since it opened.

You also use *since* or *ever since* to say that a situation started to exist at a particular time, and still existed at a later time. In the time clause, you use the **past simple** or the **past perfect**.

He had been tired <u>ever since</u> he <u>started</u> work.
Janine had been busy <u>ever since</u> she <u>had heard</u> the news.

If you are mentioning someone's age at the time when a situation started, you always use the **past simple**.

I was seven years older than Wendy and had known her <u>since</u> she <u>was</u> twelve.

Since is also used in **reason clauses**. This is explained in paragraph 8.50.

saying when a situation ends

8.20 If you want to say that a situation stopped when something happened, you use *until* or *till*.

I stayed there talking to them <u>until</u> I saw Sam Ward leave the building.
We waited <u>till</u> they arrived.

You also use *until* or *till* to say that a situation will stop when something happens in the future. In the time clause you use the **present simple** or the **present perfect**.

Stay with me <u>until</u> I <u>go</u>.
We'll support them <u>till</u> they <u>find</u> work.
Tell him I won't discuss anything <u>until</u> I<u>'ve spoken</u> to my wife.

8.21 *By which time, at which point, after which, whereupon*, and *upon which* are also used at the beginning of time clauses.

You use *by which time* to say that something had already happened or will already have happened before the event you have just mentioned.

He was diagnosed in 1999, <u>by which time</u> he was already very ill.

You use *at which point* to say that something happened immediately after the event you have just mentioned.

The company closed in the late seventies, <u>at which point</u> he retired.

You use *after which* to say that a situation started to exist or will start to exist after the event you have just mentioned.

The items were removed for chemical analysis, <u>after which</u> they were never seen again.

You use *whereupon* or *upon which* to say that something happened immediately after the event you have just mentioned and was a result of it. Both of these uses are rather formal.

His department was shut down, <u>whereupon</u> he returned to Calcutta.
I told Dr Johnson of this, <u>upon which</u> he called for Joseph.

ℹ️ USAGE NOTE

8.22 You can use a clause beginning with *when* after a question beginning with *why*. For example, you can say *Why should I help her when she never helps me?* However this clause is not a time clause. In your question, you are expressing surprise or disagreement at something that has been said, and the *when*-clause indicates the reason for your surprise or disagreement.

Why should he do me an injury <u>when</u> he has already saved my life?
Why worry her <u>when</u> it's all over?

8.23   Instead of using a finite time clause, you can often use a **non-finite clause**, that is, a clause that contains an *-ing* or *-ed* participle.

For example, you can say *I often read a book when travelling by train*, meaning *I often read a book when I am travelling by train*, and you can say *When finished, the building will be opened by the Prince of Wales*, meaning *When it is finished, the building will be opened by the Prince of Wales*.

Adults sometimes do not realize their own strength when dealing with children.
Mark watched us while pretending not to.
I deliberately didn't read the book before going to see the film.
After complaining of a headache for a few days, Gerry agreed to see a doctor.
They had not spoken a word since leaving the party.
Michael used to look surprised when praised.
Once convinced about an idea, he pursued it relentlessly.

Note that you can only use a clause like this when it does not need to have a new subject, that is, when it is about the same thing as the main clause.

8.24   For some statements about time, you can use a phrase consisting of *when*, *while*, *once*, *until*, or *till*, followed by a **prepositional phrase** or an **adjective**.

For example, you can say, *When in Paris, you should visit the Louvre*, meaning *When you are in Paris, you should visit the Louvre*.

He had read of her experiences while at Oxford.
When under threat, they can become violent.
Steam or boil them until just tender.

You can use a phrase consisting of *when*, *whenever*, *where*, or *wherever* and an adjective such as *necessary* or *possible*.

For example, you can say *You should take exercise whenever possible*, meaning *You should take exercise whenever it is possible*.

She spoke rarely, and then only when necessary.
Try to speak the truth whenever possible.
Help must be given where necessary.
All experts agree that, wherever possible, children should learn to read in their own way.

Conditional clauses: *If I had more money, ...*

8.25   When you want to talk about a possible situation and its consequences, you use a **conditional clause**.

Conditional clauses are used:

▶ to talk about a situation that sometimes exists or existed

If they lose weight during an illness, they soon regain it afterwards.
Government cannot operate effectively unless it is free to take its own decisions.
If I saw him in the street, he'd just say Good morning.

▶ to talk about a situation that you know does not exist

If England had a hot climate, the attitude would be different.
If I could afford it I would buy a boat.

▶ to talk about a situation when you do not know whether it exists or not

If he is right it would be possible once more to manage the economy in the old way.
The interval seemed unnecessary, <u>unless it was to give them a break</u>.

▶ to talk about a situation that may exist in the future.

<u>If I leave my job</u> I'll have no money to live on.
<u>If I went back on the train</u> it'd be cheaper.
Don't bring her <u>unless she's ready</u>.

8.26 Conditional clauses usually begin with *if* or *unless*.

You use *if* to say that a consequence of something happening or being the case would be that something else would happen or be the case.

<u>If you do that</u> I shall be very pleased.
<u>If I asked for something</u> I got it.
They will even clean your car <u>if you ask them to</u>.

When an if-clause is put first, *then* is sometimes put at the beginning of the main clause.

If this is what was happening in the Sixties, <u>then</u> I'm glad I wasn't around then.

Unless means *except if*. For example, *You will fail your exams unless you work harder* means *You will fail your exams except if you work harder*.

There can be no new growth <u>unless</u> the ground is cleared.
Nobody gets anything <u>unless</u> they ask for it.

Clauses beginning with *unless* usually go after a main clause.

modals and imperatives

8.27 When you are using a conditional clause, you often use a **modal** in the main clause.

You always use a modal in the main clause when you are talking about a situation that does not exist.

If you weren't here, she <u>would</u> get rid of me in no time.
If anybody had asked me, I <u>could</u> have told them what happened.

Modals are explained in paragraphs 5.94 to 5.258.

Conditional clauses are often used with **imperative** structures.

If you dry your washing outdoors, wipe the line first.
If it's four o'clock in the morning, don't expect them to be pleased to see you.

Imperative structures are explained in paragraphs 5.4 and 5.37 to 5.41.

verb forms in conditional sentences

8.28 There are special rules about which verb form to use in conditional sentences.

People often describe conditional structures in terms of three, or sometimes four (see **zero conditional** below), categories:

▶ the **first conditional**, in which the verb in the main clause is *will* or *shall* and the verb in the conditional clause is in the **present simple**.

I'll scream if you say that again.

▶ the **second conditional**, in which the verb in the main clause is *would* or *should* and the verb in the conditional clause is in the **past simple**.

If I had more time, I would happily offer to help.

▶ the **third conditional**, in which the verb in the main clause is *would have* or *should* *have* and the verb in the conditional clause is in the **past perfect**.

If I had tried a bit harder, I would have passed that exam.

▶ the **zero conditional**, in which the verb in both clauses is in the **present simple**.

Water boils if you heat it to 100°C.

Many conditionals do follow these patterns. There are, however, various other normal patterns of tense in conditional clauses, which are set out in the following paragraphs.

talking about things that often happen

8.29　When you are talking about something that often happens, you use the **present simple** or the **present progressive** in the conditional clause and in the main clause.

If a big dog approaches me, I panic.
He never rings me up unless he wants something.
If the baby's crying, she probably needs feeding.
If an advertisement conveys information which is false or misleading, the advertiser is committing an offence.

talking about things that often happened in the past

8.30　When you are talking about something that often happened in the past, you use the **past simple** or the **past progressive** in the conditional clause. In the main clause, you use the **past simple** or a **modal**.

They sat on the grass if it was fine.
If it was raining, we usually stayed indoors.
If anyone came, they'd say How are you?
If they wanted to go out, I would stay with the baby.
I could not fall asleep unless I did an hour of yoga.

possible situations

8.31　When you are talking about a possible situation in the present, you usually use the **present simple** or the **present perfect** in the conditional clause. In the main clause you usually use a **modal**.

If anyone doubts this, they should look at the facts.
Unless you've tried it, you can't imagine how pleasant it is.

If-clauses of this kind are sometimes used when you are offering to do something, or giving permission for something to be done. You use a modal in the main clause, and the subordinate clause consists of *if*, a pronoun, and *want*, *like*, or *wish*.

I'll teach you, if you want.
You can leave if you like.

things that might happen in the future

8.32　When you are talking about something that might happen in the future, you use the **present simple** in the conditional clause, and **will** or **shall** in the main clause.

If I survive this experience, I'll never leave you again.

Willie will never achieve anything unless he is pushed.

USAGE NOTE

8.33 A more formal way of talking about a possible future situation is to use *should* in the conditional clause. For example, instead of saying *If anything happens, I will return immediately*, you can say *If anything should happen, I will return immediately*. In the main clause you use a modal, usually *will* or *would*.

> *If that should happen, you will be blamed.*

Another way of talking about a possible future situation is to use *were* and a *to*-infinitive in a conditional clause. For example, instead of saying *If he goes, I will go too*, you can say *If he were to go, I would go too*. In the main clause you use *would*, *should*, or *might*.

> *If we were to move north, we would be able to buy a bigger house.*

unlikely situations

8.34 When you are talking about an unlikely situation, you use the **past simple** in the conditional clause, and *would*, *should*, or *might* in the main clause.

> *The older men would find it difficult to get a job if they left the farm.*
> *I should be surprised if it was less than five pounds.*
> *If I frightened them, they might run away and I would never see them again.*

In the conditional clause, *were* is sometimes used instead of *was*, especially after *I*.

> *If I were a guy, I would look like my dad.*
> *If I were asked to define my condition, I'd say bored.*

what might have been

8.35 When you are talking about something that might have happened in the past but did not happen, you use the **past perfect** in the conditional clause. In the main clause, you use *would have*, *could have*, *should have*, or *might have*.

> *Perhaps if he had realized that, he would have run away while there was still time.*
> *If she had not been ill, she would probably have won that race.*

putting the verb first

8.36 In formal or literary English, if the first verb in an *if*-clause is *should*, *were*, or *had*, this verb is sometimes put at the beginning of the clause and *if* is omitted. For example, instead of saying *If any visitors should come, I will say you are not here*, someone might say *Should any visitors come, I will say you are not here*.

> *Should ministers demand an inquiry, we would welcome it.*
> *Were it all true, it would still not excuse their actions.*
> *Were they to stop advertising, prices would be significantly reduced.*
> *Had I known how important it was, I would have filmed the occasion.*

 USAGE NOTE

8.37 Instead of using a conditional clause containing the word *be*, you can sometimes use a phrase consisting of *if* followed by an adjective or a prepositional phrase. For example, instead of saying *We will sell the car, if it is necessary*, you can say *We will sell the car, if necessary*.

> *This unfortunate situation is to be avoided if possible.*
> *If I were innocent, I'd rather be tried here; if guilty, in America.*
> *If in doubt, ask at your local library.*

necessary conditions

8.38 If you want to say that one situation is necessary for another, you use *provided*, *providing*, *as long as*, *so long as*, or *only if*. *Provided* and *providing* are often followed by *that*.

Ordering is quick and easy <u>provided</u> you have access to the internet.
<u>Provided that</u> it's not too much money I'd love to come to Spain.
The oven bakes magnificent bread <u>providing</u> it is hot enough.
They are happy for the world to stay as it is, <u>as long as</u> they are comfortable.
These activities can flourish <u>only if</u> agriculture and rural industry are flourishing.

When you are using *only if*, you can put the *only* in the main clause, separated from the *if*. For example, instead of saying *I will come only if he wants me*, you can say *I will only come if he wants me*.

He told them that disarmament was <u>only</u> possible <u>if</u> Britain changed her foreign policy.

Another way of saying that one situation is necessary for another is to use a **conditional clause** consisting of *if* followed by the subject, a form of *be*, and a *to*-infinitive clause. In the main clause, you say what is necessary using *must*.

It's late, and <u>if I am to get any sleep</u> I <u>must</u> go.
<u>If you are to escape</u>, you <u>must</u> leave me and go on alone.

8.39 If you want to say that one situation would not affect another, you can use *even if*.

I would have married her <u>even if</u> she had been penniless.
<u>Even if</u> you don't get the job this time, there will be many exciting opportunities in the future.

Even if is also used in **concessive clauses**. This is explained in paragraph 8.67.

8.40 If you want to say that a situation would not be affected by any of two or more things, you use *whether*. You put *or* between the different possibilities.

Catching a frog can be a difficult business, <u>whether</u> you're a human <u>or</u> a bird <u>or</u> a reptile.
<u>Whether</u> you go to a launderette <u>or</u> do your washing at home, the routine is the same.

If you want to say that what happens would not be affected by either of two opposite situations, you use a clause beginning with *whether or not*.

<u>Whether or not</u> people have religious faith, they can believe in the power of love.
I get an electrician to check all my electrical appliances every autumn, <u>whether or not</u> they are giving trouble.

Or not can be put at the end of the clause.

<u>Whether</u> I agreed <u>or not</u>, the search would take place.

  USAGE NOTE

8.41 When the verb in a *whether*-clause is *be*, the **subjunctive** is sometimes used. When you use the subjunctive, you use the **base form** of a verb rather than the third person singular. This is considered rather formal in British English, but is common in American English.

Always report such behaviour to the nearest person in authority, whether it <u>be</u> a school teacher or a policeman, or anyone else.

When the verb in a *whether*-clause is *be* and the subject is a personal pronoun such as *they* or *it*, you can omit *be* and the pronoun. For example, instead of saying *All the villagers, whether they are young or old, help with the harvest*, you can say *All the villagers, whether young or old, help with the harvest*.

A fresh pepper, <u>whether</u> red <u>or</u> green, lasts about three weeks.
They help people, <u>whether</u> tourists <u>or</u> students, to learn more of our past.

8.42 When you want to say that something is the case and that it does not matter which person, place, cause, method, or thing is involved, you use *whoever*, *wherever*, *however*, *whatever*, or *whichever*.

Whoever wins this civil war, there will be little rejoicing at the victory.
Wherever it is, you aren't going.
However it began, the battle would always develop into a large-scale conflict.

Whatever and *whichever* are used either as determiners or pronouns.

Whatever car you drive, keep fixing it and keep it forever.
The deficit is extremely important this year, whatever they say.
Whichever way you do it, it's hard work.
Whichever you decide, I'm sure it will be just fine.

Another way of saying that it does not matter who or what is involved is to use *no matter* followed by *who*, *where*, *how*, *what*, or *which*.

Most people, no matter who they are, seem to have at least one.
Our aim is to recruit the best person for the job, no matter where they are from.
No matter how I'm playing, I always get that special feeling.

Purpose clauses: *He did it in order to make her happy*

8.43 When you want to talk about the purpose of an action, you use a **purpose clause**.

Here is a list of the most common conjunctions used in purpose clauses:

in order that	so	so that
in order to	so as to	to

types of purpose clause

8.44 There are two kinds of purpose clause.

Clauses containing a *to*-infinitive are the most common.

They had to take some of his land in order to extend the churchyard.
Farmers have put up barricades to prevent people moving on to their land.

The subject of this type of purpose clause is always the same as the subject of the main clause.

This type of purpose clause is explained in paragraphs 8.45 to 8.46.

Other purpose clauses usually contain *that*.

Be as clear and factual as possible in order that there may be no misunderstanding.

This type of purpose clause is explained in paragraphs 8.47 to 8.48.

***to*-infinitive clauses**

8.45 *To*-infinitive purpose clauses usually begin with *in order to* or *so as to*.

They were pushing in order to get to the front.
We had to borrow money in order to buy the house.
We fixed up a screen so as to let in the fresh air and keep out the flies.

If you want to make one of these clauses negative, you put *not* in front of the *to*.

Rose trod with care in order not to spread the dirt.
When removing a stain, work from the edge inwards so as not to enlarge the area affected.

8.46 Some purpose clauses can simply be *to*-infinitive clauses.

People would stroll down the path to admire the garden.
The children sleep together to keep warm.
To understand what is happening now, we need to think about what has been achieved.

However, you cannot use a negative with one of these structures. You cannot say, for example, *We keep the window shut not to let the flies in*. You would have to say, *We keep the window shut in order not to let the flies in*.

that-clauses

8.47 Other purpose clauses usually begin with *in order that*, *so that*, or *so*. They usually contain a **modal**.

If the verb in the main clause is in the **present** or in the **present perfect**, you usually use one of the modals *can*, *may*, *will*, or *shall* in the purpose clause.

...people who are learning English in order that they can study a particular subject.

If the verb in the main clause is in the **past**, you usually use *could*, *might*, *should*, or *would* in the purpose clause.

A stranger had lifted Philip up on his shoulder so that he could see better.
I bought six cows so that we would have some milk to sell.
She wanted the meal ready at six so she could go out at eight.

Ordinary verbs are occasionally used instead of modals, especially in negative purpose clauses.

Make sure you get plenty of rest, so that you don't fall asleep at work.

So that is also used in **result clauses**. This use is explained in paragraphs 8.55 and 8.56.

8.48 In formal or old-fashioned English, *lest* is sometimes used at the beginning of a purpose clause to say what an action is intended to prevent.

For example, *They built a statue of him lest people should forget what he had done* means the same as *They built a statue of him so that people would not forget what he had done*.

He spoke in whispers lest the servants should hear him.

In clauses beginning with *lest*, you use either the **subjunctive** or a **modal**.

Reason clauses: ... *because I wanted to win*

8.49 When you want to give the reason for something, you use a **reason clause**.

Here is a list of the main conjunctions used in reason clauses:

as	because	in case	just in case	since

8.50 If you are simply giving the reason for something, you use *because*, *since*, or *as*.

I couldn't be angry with him because I liked him too much.
I didn't know that she was married, since she rarely talked about herself.
As we had plenty of time, we decided to go for a coffee.

8.51 You use *in case* or *just in case* when you are mentioning a possible future situation which is someone's reason for doing something. In the reason clause, you use the **present simple**.

Mr Woods, I am here just in case anything out of the ordinary happens.

When you are talking about someone's reason for doing something in the past, you use the **past simple** in the reason clause.

He did not sit down in case his trousers got creased.

8.52 In that, inasmuch as, insofar as, and to the extent that are used to say why a statement you have just made is true. These are formal expressions.

I'm in a difficult situation in that I have been offered two jobs and they both sound interesting.
Censorship is ineffective inasmuch as it does not protect anyone.
We are traditional insofar as we write traditional-style songs, but we try and write about modern issues.
He feels himself to be dependent to the extent that he is not free to make his own decisions.

Inasmuch as is sometimes written as *In as much as*, and *insofar as* is sometimes written as *in so far as*.

8.53 People sometimes use reason clauses beginning with *for* or *seeing that*. *For* means the same as *because*. Its use in reason clauses is now considered to be old-fashioned.

I hesitate, for I am not quite sure of my facts.

 *Seeing that* means the same as *since*. It is used only in informal speech.

Seeing that you're the guest on this little trip, I won't tell you what I think of your behaviour last night.

Now and *now that* are used to say that a new situation is the reason for something. Clauses beginning with *now* or *now that* are dealt with as **time clauses**. They are explained in paragraph 8.18.

Result clauses: *I'll drive you there so that you won't be late*

8.54 When you want to talk about the result of something, you use a **result clause**.

Result clauses always come after the main clause.

8.55 Result clauses usually begin with *so that*.

You can use *so that* simply to say what the result of an event or situation was.

My suitcase had become damaged, so that the lid would not stay closed.
A storm had brought the sea into the house, so that they had been forced to escape by a window.
There's a window above the bath so that when I'm relaxing here I can watch the sky.

So, *and so*, and *and* can also be used.

She was having great difficulty getting her car out, and so I had to move my car to let her out.
He was shot in the chest and died.

With these result clauses, you usually put a comma after the main clause.

8.56 You can also use *so that* to say that something is or was done in a particular way to achieve a desired result.

For example, *He fixed the bell so that it would ring when anyone came in* means *He fixed the bell in such a way that it would ring when anyone came in.*

Explain it so that a 10-year-old could understand it.
They arranged things so that they never met.

With these result clauses, you do not put a comma after the main clause.

8.57 *So that* is also used in **purpose clauses**. This use is explained in paragraph 8.47.

8.58 *So* and *that* are also used in a special kind of structure to say that a result happens because something has a quality to a particular extent, or because something is done in an extreme way.

In these structures, *so* is used in front of an adjective or adverb. A *that*-clause is then added.

The crowd was <u>so</u> large <u>that it overflowed the auditorium</u>.
They were <u>so</u> surprised <u>they didn't try to stop him</u>.
He dressed <u>so</u> quickly <u>that he put his boots on the wrong feet</u>.
She had fallen down <u>so</u> often <u>that she was covered in mud</u>.

Sometimes *as* is used instead of *that*. *As* is followed by a *to*-infinitive clause.

...small beaches of sand <u>so</u> white <u>as to dazzle the eye</u>.
I hope that nobody was <u>so</u> stupid <u>as to go around saying those things</u>.

8.59 *So* and *that* can also be used in this way with *many*, *few*, *much*, and *little*.

We found <u>so much</u> to talk about <u>that it was late at night when we remembered the time</u>.
There were <u>so many children you could hardly get in the room</u>.

8.60 When the verb in the main clause is *be* or when an auxiliary is used, the normal order of words is often changed for greater emphasis. *So* is put at the beginning of the sentence, followed by the adjective, adverb, or noun. *Be* or the auxiliary is placed in front of the subject.

For example, instead of saying *The room was so tiny that you could not get a bed into it*, you can say *So tiny was the room that you could not get a bed into it*.

<u>So</u> successful have they been <u>that they are moving to Bond Street</u>.
<u>So</u> rapid is the rate of progress <u>that advance seems to be following advance on almost a monthly basis</u>.

8.61 *Such* and *that* are also used to say that a result happens because something has a quality to a particular extent. You put *such* in front of a noun, and then add a *that*-clause.

If the noun is a singular countable noun, you put *a* or *an* in front of it.

I slapped her hand and she got <u>such</u> a shock <u>that she dropped the bag</u>.
She was in <u>such</u> pain <u>that she almost collapsed</u>.
These birds have <u>such</u> small wings <u>that they cannot get into the air</u>.

8.62 *Such* is sometimes used in a similar structure as an adjective with the meaning *so great*. The *that*-clause goes immediately after it.

The extent of the disaster was <u>such that the local authorities were quite unable to cope</u>.

Sometimes *such* is put at the beginning of a sentence, followed by *be*, a noun phrase, and the *that*-clause. For example, instead of saying *Her beauty was such that they could only stare*, you can say *Such was her beauty that they could only stare*.

<u>Such</u> is the power of suggestion <u>that within a very few minutes she fell asleep</u>.

8.63 You can also use *such* as an adjective to say that a result is obtained by something being of a particular kind. *Such* is followed by a *that*-clause or by *as* and a *to*-infinitive clause.

The dangers are <u>such that an organized tour is a more sensible option</u>.
Conditions in prison should be <u>such as to lessen the chances of prisoners reoffending</u>.

You can use the expression *in such a way* to say that a result is obtained by something being done in a particular way. It is followed by a *that*-clause or by *as* and a *to*-infinitive clause.

She had been taught to behave <u>in such a way that her parents would have as quiet a life as possible</u>.
Is it right that this high tax should be spent <u>in such a way as to give benefit mainly to the motorist</u>?

8.64 You use *otherwise*, *else*, or *or else* to say that a result of something not happening or not being the case would be that something else would happen or be the case.

For example, *Give me back my money, otherwise I'll ring the police* means *If you don't give me back my money, I'll ring the police*.

I want a house I'll like, <u>otherwise</u> I'll get depressed.
I must have done something wrong, <u>or else</u> they wouldn't have kept me here.

Concessive clauses: *I love books, although I don't read much*

8.65 Sometimes you want to make two statements, one of which contrasts with the other or makes it seem surprising. You can put both statements into one sentence by using a **concessive clause**.

Here is a list of conjunctions used in concessive clauses:

although	even though	much as	whereas
despite	except that	not that	while
even if	in spite of	though	whilst

contrast

8.66 If you simply want to contrast two statements, you use *although*, *though*, *even though*, or *while*.

I used to read a lot <u>although</u> I don't get much time for books now.
<u>Though</u> he has lived for years in London, he writes in German.
I used to love listening to her, <u>even though</u> I couldn't understand what she said.
<u>While</u> I did well in class, I was a poor performer at games.

The fairly formal words *whilst* and *whereas* can also be used.

Raspberries have a hairy surface <u>whilst</u> blackberries have a shiny skin.
To every child, adult approval means love, <u>whereas</u> disapproval can cause strong feelings of rejection.

 Whilst is not used in American English.

8.67 If you want to say that something which is probably true does not affect the truth of something else, you use *even if*.

All this is part of modern commercial life (<u>even if</u> it is an essential activity).
He's beginning to be a different person, <u>even if</u> he doesn't realize it.

Even if is also used in **conditional clauses**. This use is explained in paragraph 8.39.

8.68 You can use *not that* instead of using *although* and a negative. For example, instead of saying *I have decided to leave, although no one will miss me*, you can say *I have decided to leave, not that anyone will miss me*.

Clauses beginning with *not that* always go after a main clause.

He's got a new girlfriend, <u>not that</u> I care.
I think I looked very chic for the party, <u>not that</u> anyone noticed.

8.69 If you want to mention an exception to a statement that you have just made, you use *except that*.

> *She treats her daughter the same as her younger boy <u>except that</u> she takes her several times a week to a special clinic.*
> *Nobody said a thing <u>except that</u> one or two asked me if I was better.*

This kind of clause is sometimes called an **exception clause**.

 **USAGE NOTE**

8.70 When a clause beginning with *though* ends with a **linking verb** like *be* or *seem* and a noun or an adjective (= a **complement**), the complement can be brought forward to the beginning of the clause. For example, instead of saying *Though he was tired, he insisted on coming to the meeting*, you can say *Tired though he was, he insisted on coming to the meeting*.

> *<u>Tempting though it may be to discuss this point</u>, it is not really relevant.*
> *I had to accept the fact, <u>improbable though it was</u>.*
> *<u>Astute business man though he was</u>, Philip was capable of making mistakes.*

When the complement is an adjective, you can use *as* instead of *though*.

> *<u>Stupid as it sounds</u>, I believed her.*

When a clause beginning with *though* ends with an adverb, you can often put the adverb at the beginning of the clause.

> *Some members of staff couldn't handle Murray's condition, <u>hard though they tried</u>.*

When you are talking about a strong feeling or desire, you can use *much as* instead of *although*. For example, instead of saying *Although I like Venice, I couldn't live there* you can say *Much as I like Venice, I couldn't live there*.

> *<u>Much as he admired her</u>, he had no wish to marry her.*

-*ing* participle clauses

8.71 *Although*, *though*, *while*, and *whilst* are sometimes used in -*ing* participle clauses. For example, instead of saying *While he liked cats, he never let them come into his house*, you can say *While liking cats, he never let them come into his house*.

> *<u>While</u> accepting the importance of freedom of speech, I believe it must be exercised with responsibility.*

Despite and *in spite of* can also be used at the beginning of -*ing* participle clauses. *Despite working hard, I failed my exams* means *Although I worked hard, I failed my exams*.

> *Sensible, interested parents still play a big part in their children's lives, <u>despite</u> working long hours.*
> *We had two more years of profit <u>in spite of</u> paying higher wages than the previous owner.*

8.72 *Although*, *though*, *while*, and *whilst* are also used in front of noun, adjective, and adverb phrases. For example, instead of saying *Although she was fond of Gregory, she did not love him*, you can say *Although fond of Gregory, she did not love him*. Similarly, instead of saying *They agreed to his proposal, though they had many reservations*, you can say *They agreed to his proposal, though with many reservations*.

> *It was an unequal marriage, <u>although</u> a stable and long-lasting one.*
> *<u>Though</u> not very attractive physically, she possessed a sense of humour.*
> *They had followed her suggestion, <u>though</u> without much enthusiasm.*

Even if, if, and *albeit* can also be used in this way. *Albeit* is a formal word.

Other species have cognitive abilities, <u>even if</u> not as developed as our own.
...a pleasant, <u>if</u> unexciting, novel.
Like mercury, lead affects the brain, <u>albeit</u> in different ways.

Place clauses: *Stay where you are*

8.73 Sometimes, when you want to talk about the location or position of something, you need to use a clause. The kind of clause you use is called a **place clause**.

8.74 Place clauses usually begin with *where*.

He said he was happy <u>where</u> he was.
He left it <u>where</u> it lay.
Stay <u>where</u> you are.

Where is also used in **relative clauses**. This use is explained in paragraphs 8.104 to 8.106.

8.75 In formal or literary English, *where*-clauses are sometimes put in front of a main clause.

<u>Where</u> Kate had stood last night, Maureen now stood.
<u>Where</u> the pink cliffs rose out of the ground there were often narrow tracks winding upwards.

8.76 When you want to say that something happens or will happen in every place where something else happens, you use *wherever*.

Soft ferns spread across the ground <u>wherever</u> there was enough light.
In Bali, <u>wherever</u> you go, you come across ceremonies.
<u>Wherever</u> I looked, I found patterns.

Everywhere can be used instead of *wherever*.

<u>Everywhere</u> I went, people were angry or suspicious.

8.77 *Where* and *wherever* are sometimes used in front of adjectives such as *possible* and *necessary*. When they are used like this, they mean *when* or *whenever*, rather than *where*. For a full explanation of this use, see paragraph 8.24.

Clauses of manner: *I don't know why he behaves as he does*

8.78 When you want to talk about someone's behaviour or the way something is done, you use a **clause of manner**.

Here is a list of conjunctions used in clauses of manner:

as	like	just as
as though	as if	much as

The way, in a way, and *in the way* are also used in clauses of manner in a similar way to conjunctions. These expressions are often followed by *that*.

saying how something is done

8.79 If you simply want to talk about someone's behaviour or the way something is done, you use *like, as, the way, in a way,* or *in the way*.

Is she often rude and cross <u>like</u> she's been this last month?
I don't understand why he behaves <u>as</u> he does.
I was never allowed to do things <u>the way</u> I wanted to do them.
He was looking at her <u>in a way</u> she did not recognize.
We have to make it work <u>in the way</u> that we want it to.

making comparisons

8.80 You can also use these expressions to compare the way something is done with the way someone or something else does it.

Surely you don't intend to live by yourself <u>like</u> she does?
Joyce looked at her <u>the way</u> a lot of girls did.

If you want to make a strong comparison, you use *just as*.

You can think of him and feel proud, <u>just</u> as I do.

If you want to make a fairly weak comparison, you use *much as*.

These tanks speed across the desert, <u>much as</u> they did in World War II.

8.81 You sometimes want to say that something is done in the way that it would be done if something were the case. You do this by using *as if* or *as though*. You use a past tense in the clause of manner.

He holds his head forward <u>as if</u> he <u>has hit</u> it too often on low doorways.
Presidents can't dispose of companies <u>as if</u> people <u>didn't exist</u>.
I put some water on my clothes to make it look <u>as though</u> I <u>had been</u> sweating.
He behaved <u>as though</u> it <u>was</u> nothing to be ashamed of.

You also use *as if* or *as though* after linking verbs such as *feel* or *look*. You do this when you are comparing someone's feelings or appearance to the feelings or appearance they would have if something were the case.

She felt <u>as if</u> she <u>had</u> a fever.
His hair looked <u>as if</u> it <u>had been combed</u> with his fingers.
Her pink dress and her frilly umbrella made her look <u>as though</u> she had <u>come</u> to a garden party.

In formal English, *were* is sometimes used instead of *was* in clauses beginning with *as if* or *as though*.

She shook as if she <u>were</u> crying, but she made no sound.
I felt as if I <u>were</u> the centre of the universe.
You talk as though he <u>were</u> already dead.

You can use *just* in front of *as if* or *as though* for emphasis.

He shouldn't have left her alone, <u>just as if</u> she was someone of no importance at all.

8.82 You can also use *as if* and *as though* in clauses that begin with a *to*-infinitive or a participle.

For a few moments, he sat <u>as if</u> stunned.
He ran off to the house <u>as if</u> escaping.
He shook his head <u>as though</u> dazzled by his own vision.

You can also use *as if* and *as though* in front of adjectives and prepositional phrases.

One must row steadily onwards <u>as if</u> intent on one's own business.
He shivered <u>as though</u> with cold.

Relative clauses

8.83 When you mention someone or something in a sentence, you often want to give further information about them. One way to do this is to use a **relative clause**.

You put a relative clause immediately after the noun that refers to the person, thing, or group you are talking about.

The man <u>who came into the room</u> was small and slender.
Opposite is St. Paul's Church, <u>where you can hear some lovely music</u>.

Relative clauses have a similar function to adjectives, and they are sometimes called **adjectival clauses**.

Nominal relative clauses, which have a similar function to noun phrases, are explained in paragraphs 8.112 to 8.116.

relative pronouns

8.84 Many relative clauses begin with a **relative pronoun**. The relative pronoun usually acts as the subject or object of the verb in the relative clause.

He is the only person who might be able to help.
Most of them have a job, which they take both for the money and the company.

Here is a list of the most common relative pronouns:

that	which	who	whom	whose

Relative pronouns do not have masculine, feminine, or plural forms. The same pronoun can be used to refer to a man, a woman, or a group of people.

She didn't recognize the man who had spoken.
I met a girl who knew Mrs Townsend.
There are many people who find this intolerable.

Some relative clauses do not have a relative pronoun.

Nearly all the people I used to know have gone.

This is explained in paragraphs 8.90, 8.91, and 8.96.

types of relative clause

8.85 There are two types of relative clause.

Some relative clauses explain which person or thing you are talking about. For example, if you say *I met the woman*, it might not be clear who you mean, so you might say, *I met the woman who lives next door*. In this sentence, *who lives next door* is called a **defining relative clause**.

Shortly after the shooting, the man who had done it was arrested.
Mooresville is the town that John Dillinger came from.

Other relative clauses give further information that is not needed to identify the person, thing, or group you are talking about. For example, if you say *I saw Miley Cyrus*, it is clear who you mean. But you might want to add more information about Miley Cyrus, so you might say, for example, *I saw Miley Cyrus, who was staying at the hotel opposite*. In this sentence, *who was staying at the hotel opposite* is called a **non-defining relative clause**.

He was waving to the girl, who was running along the platform.
He walked down to Broadway, the main street of the town, which ran parallel to the river.

This type of relative clause is used mainly in writing rather than speech.

Note that you cannot begin a non-defining relative clause with *that*.

punctuation

8.86 A relative clause that simply gives extra information usually has a comma in front of it and a comma after it, unless it is at the end of a sentence, in which case you just put a full stop. Dashes are sometimes used instead of commas.

My son, who is four, loves Spiderman.

You never put a comma or a dash in front of a defining relative clause.

The woman who owns this cabin will come back in the autumn.

use after pronouns

8.87   Relative clauses that distinguish one noun from all others can be used after some pronouns.

They are used after **indefinite pronouns** such as *someone*, *anyone*, and *everything*.

This is something that I'm very proud of.
In theory anyone who lives or works in the area may be at risk.
We want to thank everyone who supported us through this.

They are sometimes used after *some*, *many*, *much*, *several*, *all*, or *those*.

Like many who met him I was soon in love.
...the feelings of those who have suffered from the effects of crime.

They can also be used after **personal pronouns**, but only in formal or old-fashioned English.

He who is not for reform is against it.
...we who are supposed to be so good at writing.

-ing participle clauses

8.88   Relative clauses can sometimes be reduced to *-ing* participle clauses.

For example, instead of saying *Give it to the man who is wearing the sunglasses*, you can say *Give it to the man wearing the sunglasses*. Similarly, instead of saying *The bride, who was smiling happily, chatted to the guests*, you can say *The bride, smiling happily, chatted to the guests*.

These uses are explained in paragraphs 8.129 to 8.145. See also paragraphs 2.300 and 2.301.

Using relative pronouns in defining clauses

8.89   The following paragraphs explain which pronouns you use in **defining relative clauses**.

referring to people

8.90   When you are referring to a person or group of people, you use *who* or *that* as the **subject** of a defining clause. *Who* is more common than *that*.

The man who employed me was called Tom.
...the people who live in the cottage.
...somebody who is really ill.
...the man that made it.

You use *who*, *that*, or *whom* as the **object** of a defining clause, or you do not use a pronoun at all.

...someone who I haven't seen for a long time.
...a woman that I dislike.
...distant relatives whom he had never seen.
...a man I know.

You use *that* as the **complement** of a defining clause, or you do not use a pronoun.

...the distinguished actress that she later became.
Little is known about the kind of person she was.

After a **superlative**, you do not usually use a pronoun.

He was the cleverest man I ever knew.
...the best thing I ever did.

For more information about **superlatives** see paragraphs 2.112 to 2.122.

referring to things

8.91 When you are referring to a thing or group of things, you use *which* or *that* as the **subject** of a defining clause. *That* is much more common than *which* in American English.

...pasta which came from Milan.
We need to understand the things which are important to people.
There are a lot of things that are wrong.

You use *which* or *that* as the **object** of a defining clause, or you do not use a pronoun.

...shells which my sister had collected.
...the oxygen that it needs.
...one of the things I'll never forget.

After *much* or *all*, you use *that*. You do not use *which*.

There was not much that the military men could do.
Happiness is all that matters.

Using relative pronouns in non-defining clauses

8.92 The following paragraphs explain which pronouns you use in **non- defining relative clauses**.

These clauses cannot be used without a relative pronoun.

referring to people

8.93 When you are referring to a person or group of people, you use *who* as the **subject** of a non-defining clause.

Heath Robinson, who died in 1944, was a graphic artist and cartoonist.
The horse's rider, who has not been named, was too distressed to talk to police.

You use *who* or *whom* as the **object** of a non-defining clause.

Brian, who I do not like, had no idea how to behave properly.
He then became involved in a row with the party chairman, whom he accused of lying.

referring to things

8.94 When you are referring to a thing or group of things, you use *which* as the subject or object of a non-defining clause.

The treatment, which is being tried by researchers, has helped a large number of patients.
The company, which has about 160 shops, is in financial trouble.
He was a man of considerable wealth, which he spent on his experiments.
...this offer, which few can resist.

Using relative pronouns with prepositions

8.95   A relative pronoun can be the object of a preposition. Usually the preposition goes towards the end of the clause, and not in front of the pronoun.

...the job which I'd been training for.
...the universe that we live in.
...the woman who Muller left his money to.

no pronoun

8.96   Often, in ordinary speech, no pronoun is used.

   Angela was the only person I could talk to.
...that place I used to go to last term.
That's all we have time for this week.

indirect objects

8.97   When a relative pronoun is the indirect object of a verb, you use *to* or *for*. For example, you say *the man that she wrote the letter to*, not *the man that she wrote the letter*.

...pieces of work that we give a mark to.

You also use *to* or *for* when there is no relative pronoun.

...the girl I sang the song for.

formal use

8.98   In formal English, the preposition can go at the beginning of a clause in front of *whom* or *which*.

These are the people to whom Catherine was referring.
...a woman friend with whom Rose used to go for walks.
...questions to which there were no answers.

Note however that you cannot put the preposition at the beginning of a clause in front of *who* or *that*.

phrasal verbs

8.99   If the verb in a relative clause is a **phrasal verb** ending with a preposition, you cannot move the preposition to the beginning of the clause.

...all the things I've had to put up with.
...the kind of life he was looking forward to.
There are other problems, which I don't propose to go into at the moment.

☑ USAGE NOTE

8.100   Words such as *some*, *many*, and *most* can be put in front of *of whom* or *of which* at the beginning of a non-defining relative clause.

At the school we were greeted by the teachers, most of whom were women.
It is a language shared by several quite diverse cultures, each of which uses it differently.

Numbers can be put before or after *of whom*.

They act mostly on suggestions from present members (four of whom are women).
There were 80 patients, of whom only one died.

Using *whose*

8.101 If you want to talk about something relating to the person, thing, or group you are talking about, you use a relative clause beginning with *whose* and a noun or noun phrase.

For example, instead of saying *I am writing a letter to Nigel. His father is ill*, you can say *I am writing a letter to Nigel, whose father is ill.*

Whose can be used in defining or non-defining clauses.

...workers whose bargaining power is weak.
...anyone whose credit card is stolen.
She asked friends whose opinion she respected.
...a country whose population was growing.
The man, whose identity was not released, was attacked at 10 p.m. last night.

The noun after *whose* can be the subject or object of the verb in the clause, or it can be the object of a preposition. If it is the object of a preposition, the preposition can come at the beginning or end of the clause.

...the governments in whose territories they operate.
...writers whose company he did not care for.

8.102 In written English, *of which* and *of whom* are sometimes used instead of *whose*. You put these expressions after a noun phrase beginning with *the*.

For example, instead of writing *a town whose inhabitants speak French*, you can write *a town the inhabitants of which speak French.*

...a competition the results of which will be announced today.
I travelled in a lorry the back of which the owner had loaded with yams.

Using other relative pronouns

8.103 Some other words and expressions can be used as relative pronouns.

non-defining clauses

8.104 *When* and *where* are used in **non-defining clauses** (that is, clauses that simply add extra information).

I want to see you at 12 o'clock, when you go to your lunch.
My favourite holiday was in 2009, when I went to Jamaica.
He came from Brighton, where Lisa had once spent a holiday.
She took them up the stairs to the art room, where the brushes and paints had been set out.

defining clauses

8.105 *When* and *where* can also be used in **defining clauses** (that is, clauses that distinguish one noun from all others), but only when the clause is preceded by a particular kind of noun.

When-clauses must be preceded by the word *time* or by the name of a period of time such as *day* or *year*.

There was a time when she thought they were wonderful.
This is the year when the profits should start.

Where-clauses must be preceded by the word *place* or by the name of a kind of place such as *room* or *street*.

...the place where they work.

...the room where I did my homework.
...the street where my grandmother had lived.

Note that place names such as *China* are **proper nouns** and so do not need to have defining relative clauses after them.

8.106 *Where* can also be used in defining clauses after words such as *circumstances, point, situation* and *stage*.

Increasing poverty has led to a situation where the poorest cannot afford to have children.
In time we reached a stage where we had more male readers than female ones.
There comes a point where it's impossible to answer.
Compensation was sometimes granted even in circumstances where no injury had occurred.

8.107 *Why* is used in defining clauses after the word *reason*.

That is a major reason why they were such poor countries.

Whereby is used in defining clauses after words such as *arrangement* and *system*.

...the new system whereby everyone pays a fixed amount.
Counselling is a process whereby the person concerned can learn to manage the emotional realities that face them.

 USAGE NOTE

8.108 Other expressions can be used in defining clauses in place of *when, where, why,* and *whereby*.

After *time* you can use *at which* instead of *when*.

...the time at which the original mineral was formed.

After *place, room, street,* and words such as *year* and *month*, you can use *in which* instead of *where* or *when*.

...the place in which they found themselves.
...the room in which the meeting would be held.
...the year in which Lloyd George lost power.

After *day* you can use *on which* instead of *when*.

Sunday was the day on which we were expected to spend some time with my father.

After *reason* you can use *that* or no pronoun instead of *why*.

...the reason that non-violence is considered to be a virtue.
That's the reason I'm checking it now.

After words such as *situation, stage, arrangement,* or *system* you can use *in which* instead of *where* or *whereby*.

...a situation in which there's a real political vacuum.

Additional points about non-defining relative clauses

8.109 In written English, you can use a non-defining clause, that is, a clause that simply gives extra information, to say that one event happened after another.

For example, instead of saying *I gave the book to George. George then gave it to Mary*, you can say *I gave the book to George, who gave it to Mary*.

I sold my car to a garage, who sold it to a customer at twice the price.
The hot water ran on to the ice, which promptly melted.
Later he went to New Zealand, where he became a teacher.

commenting on a fact

8.110 You can use a non-defining clause beginning with *which* to say something about the whole situation described in a main clause, rather than about someone or something mentioned in it.

> *These computers need only tiny amounts of power, which means that they will run on small batteries.*
> *I never met Brando again, which was a pity.*
> *Before the exam she was a little tense, which was understandable.*

commenting on a time or situation

8.111 When you want to add something to what you have said, you sometimes use a non-defining clause beginning with a preposition, *which*, and a noun, to add extra information. The noun is often a word like *time* or *point*, or a very general word for a situation like *case* or *event*.

> *They remain in the pouch for some seven weeks, by which time they are about 10 cm long.*
> *I was told my work was not good enough, at which point I decided to get another job.*
> *Sometimes you may feel too weak to cope with things, in which case do them as soon as it is convenient.*

Nominal relative clauses: *What you need is ...*

8.112 When it is difficult to refer to something by using a noun phrase, you can sometimes use a special type of relative clause called a **nominal relative clause**.

> *What he really needs is a nice cup of tea.*
> *Whatever she does will affect the whole family.*

8.113 Nominal relative clauses that begin with *what* can be used. *What* can mean either *the thing that* or *the things that*.

> *What he said was perfectly true.*
> *They did not like what he wrote.*
> *I believe that is a very good account of what happened.*
> *I'm what's generally called a dustman.*

People often use a *what*-clause in front of *is* or *was* to say what kind of thing they are about to mention.

> *What I need is a lawyer.*
> *What you have to do is to choose five companies to invest in.*

These structures are explained in paragraphs 9.28 to 9.30.

For another use of *what* in nominal relative clauses see paragraph 8.116.

8.114 Nominal relative clauses that begin with *where* are usually used after a preposition or after the verb *be*. *Where* means *the place where*.

> *I crossed the room to where she was sitting.*
> *He lives two streets down from where Mr Sutton works.*
> *This is where I crashed the car.*

8.115 Nominal relative clauses beginning with *whatever*, *whoever*, or *whichever* are used to refer to something or someone that is unknown or indefinite.

Whatever is used only to refer to things. *Whoever* is used to refer to people. *Whichever* is used to refer to either things or people.

Whatever, *whoever*, and *whichever* can be used as pronouns. *Whichever* is often followed by *of*.

I'll do whatever you want.
I want to do whatever I can to help them.
You'll need written permission from whoever is in charge.
People will choose whichever of these systems they find suits them best.

Whatever and *whichever* can also be used as determiners.

She had had to rely on whatever books were lying around there.
Choose whichever one of the three methods you fancy.

For more information about *whatever*, *whoever*, and *whichever* see paragraph 8.42.

8.116 *What* can be used with the same meaning as *whatever*, both as a pronoun and a determiner.

Do what you like.
We give what help we can.

The main use of *what* in nominal relative clauses is explained in paragraph 8.113.

Nominal *that*-clauses

8.117 A **nominal *that*-clause** is a type of subordinate clause that functions like a noun, and is introduced by *that*. When this type of clause is used to say what someone says or thinks (e.g. *She said (that) she was leaving*), this grammar refers to it as a **reported clause**.

There are some verbs and adjectives, however, that do not refer to saying or thinking, but that are followed by *that*-clauses because they refer to actions relating to facts: for example, checking or proving facts.

He checked that both rear doors were safely shut.
Research with animals shows that males will mother an infant as well as any female.

Here is a list of verbs that are not verbs of speech or thought, but can be followed by a *that*-clause:

arrange	determine	pretend	reveal
check	ensure	prove	show
demonstrate	indicate	require	

Note that *determine* can also be a verb of thought, and *reveal* can also be a verb of speech. See paragraphs 7.30, 7.38, and 7.48.

Arrange and *require* are used with a *that*-clause containing a modal or a subjunctive. *Arrange* can also be used with a *to*-infinitive.

They had arranged that I would spend Christmas with them.
They'd arranged to leave at four o'clock.

Demonstrate, *prove*, *reveal*, and *show* can also be followed by a clause beginning with a *wh*-word that refers to a circumstance involved in a fact.

She took the gun and showed how the cylinder slotted into the barrel.

Prove, *require*, and *show* can also be used in the passive followed by a *to*-infinitive.

No place on Earth can be shown to be safe.

If you want to mention another person involved in these actions, you can put an object after *show*, use *to* after *demonstrate*, *indicate*, *prove*, and *reveal*, and use *with* after *arrange* and *check*.

The children's attitude <u>showed me</u> *that watching violence can affect a child's behaviour.*
This incident <u>proved to me</u> *that Ian cannot be trusted.*
She <u>arranged with the principal of her school</u> *to take some time off.*

8.118 If you want to say that something happens, that something is the case, or that something becomes known, you can use a *that*-clause after *happen*, *transpire*, or *emerge*. The subject of the main clause is **impersonal *it***.

It often happens that someone asks for advice and does not get it.
It just happened that he had a client who rather liked that sort of thing.
It transpired that there was not a word of truth in the letter.
It emerged that, during the afternoon, she had gone home unwell.

Note that the *that*-clause must be introduced by *that*.

adjectives with nominal *that*-clauses: *I was afraid that he would fall*

8.119 There are many adjectives that can be followed by *that*-clauses when they come after a linking verb, usually *be*.

mentioning the cause of a feeling

8.120 If you want to say what causes someone to have a particular feeling, you can mention the cause of the feeling in a *that*-clause after an adjective describing the feeling.

Everybody was sad <u>that she had to return to America</u>.
I am confident <u>that I shall be able to persuade them to go</u>.
I was worried <u>that she'd say no</u>.

Here is a list of adjectives describing feelings:

afraid	frightened	proud	upset
angry	glad	sad	worried
anxious	happy	sorry	
confident	pleased	surprised	

saying what someone knows

8.121 If you want to say that someone knows something, you can say what they know in a *that*-clause after an adjective such as *aware* or *conscious*.

He was aware <u>that he had eaten too much</u>.
She is conscious <u>that some people might be offended</u>.

Here is a list of adjectives indicating knowledge:

aware	conscious	positive	unaware
certain	convinced	sure	

Aware is occasionally used with a *that*-clause beginning with a *wh*-word.

None of our staff were aware <u>what was going on</u>.

commenting on a fact

8.122 If you want to comment on a fact, you can use an adjective describing the fact followed by a *that*-clause. The linking verb has **impersonal *it*** as its subject.

It was sad that people had reacted in the way they did.
It is true that the authority of parliament has declined.
It seems probable that the world can go on producing enough food for everyone.

Here is a list of adjectives used to comment on facts:

apparent	extraordinary	likely	sad
appropriate	fair	lucky	true
awful	funny	natural	unlikely
bad	good	obvious	
clear	important	plain	
essential	inevitable	possible	
evident	interesting	probable	

After a few adjectives, a clause beginning with a *wh*-word can be used.

It's funny how they don't get on.
It was never clear why she took a different route that night.

For more information, see paragraph 9.43.

commenting on a fact or idea

8.123 *That*-clauses can be used after *be* to refer to a fact or idea. The subject is usually one of the nouns listed in paragraph 7.86.

The fact is that a happy person makes a better worker.
The answer is simply that they are interested in doing it.
The most favoured explanation was that he was finally getting tired.
Our hope is that this time all parties will cooperate.

8.124 In formal English, *that*-clauses are sometimes used as the subject of a verb, when people want to comment on a fact.

That she is not stupid is self-evident.
That he is a troubled man is obvious.

In less formal English, *the fact* plus a *that*-clause is often used as a subject instead of a simple *that*-clause.

The fact that what they are doing is dangerous is not important here.
The fact that your boss is offering to do your job for you worries me.

The normal way of commenting on a fact is to use an impersonal *it* structure. See paragraph 8.122.

8.125 People also use *the fact* plus a *that*-clause as the object of prepositions and of verbs that cannot be followed by a simple *that*-clause.

He is proud of the fact that all his children went to university.
We missed the fact that the children were struggling to understand the exercise.

8.126 When you want to talk about something that is not certain or definite, or about which a choice has to be made, you can use clauses beginning with a *wh*-word or *whether*, like the clauses used for **reported questions**. They can be used after prepositions, and as the subject of verbs such as *be*, *depend*, and *matter*.

...the question of who should be President.
The teacher is uncertain about what she wants students to do.
What you get depends on how badly you were injured.
Whether I went twice or not doesn't matter.
Whether you think they are good or not is not important.

8.127 Structures consisting of a *wh*-word plus a *to*-infinitive, which refer to a possible course of action, are used after prepositions but not usually as subjects.

...the problem of what to tell the adopted child.
...a book on how to avoid having a heart attack.
People are worried about how to fill their increased leisure time.

! **BE CAREFUL**

8.128 Note that *if*-clauses, which are used for reported questions, cannot be used after prepositions or as the subject of a verb.

Non-finite clauses

8.129 A **non-finite clause** is a subordinate clause that contains a participle or an infinitive, and that does not contain a stated subject.

There are two types of non-finite clause. One type begins with a **subordinating conjunction**.

She fainted while giving evidence in court.
You've got to do something in depth in order to understand it.

This type of clause is dealt with in the sections on **adverbial clauses** (paragraphs 8.6 to 8.82).

The other type of non-finite clause does not begin with a subordinating conjunction.

He pranced about, feeling very important indeed.
I wanted to talk to her.

This type of clause sometimes consists of a participle and nothing else.

Ellen shook her head, smiling.
Rosie, grumbling, had gone to her piano lesson.

Clauses that contain a participle and do not begin with a subordinating conjunction are explained in the following paragraphs.

8.130 The non-finite clauses discussed in this section work in a similar way to **relative clauses**, and, like relative clauses, they may be used for distinguishing a noun from others or they may simply add extra information.

Some clauses simply add extra information. These are called **non-defining clauses**. They are dealt with in paragraphs 8.132 to 8.143. These clauses are often used in writing, but are not usually used in spoken English.

Others are used to distinguish a noun from all other possibilities. These are called **defining clauses**. They are dealt with in paragraphs 8.144 and 8.145. These clauses are occasionally used in both written and spoken English.

position of non-defining clauses

8.131 Non-defining clauses can go in front of a main clause, after a main clause, or in the middle of one. A non-defining clause is usually separated by a comma from the words in front of it and after it.

Using non-defining clauses

8.132 Non-defining clauses give further information that is not needed to identify the person, thing, or group you are talking about.

The following paragraphs 8.133 to 8.138 explain how these clauses are used when they relate to the **subject** of the verb in a main clause. The subject is not mentioned in the non-defining clause.

-*ing* participle: events happening at the same time

8.133 If you want to say that someone is doing or experiencing two things at the same time, you mention one of them in the main clause and the other in a clause containing an -*ing* participle.

Laughing and shrieking, the crowd rushed under the nearest trees.
Jane watched, _weeping_, from the doorway.
Feeling a little foolish, Pluskat hung up.
Walking about, you notice something is different.
People stared at her. _Seeing herself in a shop window_, she could understand why.

! **BE CAREFUL**

Note that the -*ing* participle should always describe an action performed by the subject of the main part of the sentence. So, for example, you should not say _Going to school, it started to rain_. Instead, you should say _Going to school, I noticed that it had started to rain_.

-*ing* participle: one action after another

8.134 If you want to say that someone did one thing immediately after another, you mention the first action in a clause containing an -*ing* participle and the second one in the main clause.

Leaping out of bed, he dressed so quickly that he put his boots on the wrong feet.

-*ing* participle: reasons

8.135 If you want to explain why someone does something or why something happens, you say what happens in the main clause and give the reason in a clause containing an -*ing* participle.

At one point I decided to go and talk to Uncle Sam. Then I changed my mind, realising that he could do nothing to help.
The puppy would probably not live to grow up, being a tiny, weak little thing.

8.136 You can also use an -*ing* participle directly after a verb in a sentence such as _I stood shivering at the roadside_. This use is explained in paragraphs 3.189 to 3.201.

having and -ed participle: results

8.137 If you want to say that someone did or experienced one thing before another, you mention the first thing in a clause containing *having* and an *-ed* participle. Often this kind of construction shows that the second event was a result of the first one.

I did not feel terribly shocked, <u>having expected him to take the easiest way out</u>.
<u>Having admitted he was wrong</u>, my husband suddenly fell silent.

-ed participle: earlier events

8.138 If you want to say what happened to someone or something before a situation or event described in the main clause, you say what happened in a clause containing an *-ed* participle on its own.

<u>Angered by the policies of the union</u>, she wrote a letter to the General Secretary.

mentioning the subject

8.139 Sometimes you want to use a non-defining clause that has a different subject from the subject of the main clause. These clauses are explained in the following paragraphs 8.140 to 8.143.

8.140 In this kind of non-defining clause, you usually have to mention the subject.

<u>Jack being gone</u>, Stephen opened his second letter.

However, if the non-defining clause comes after the main clause, and it is clear from the context that it relates to the object of the main clause, you do not need to mention the object again.

They picked me up, <u>kicking and screaming</u>, and carried me up to the road.

-ing participle

8.141 You use a non-defining clause containing a subject and an *-ing* participle:

▶ when you want to mention something that is happening at the same time as the event or situation described in the main clause

The embarrassed young man stared at me, <u>his face reddening</u>.

▶ when you want to mention a fact that is relevant to the fact stated in the main clause.

Bats are surprisingly long-lived creatures, <u>some having a life-expectancy of around twenty years</u>.

With is sometimes added at the beginning of the non-finite clause.

The old man stood up <u>with tears running down his face</u>.

-ed participle

8.142 You use *having* and an *-ed* participle to mention something that happened before the thing described in the main clause.

<u>The argument having finished</u>, Mr Lucas was ready to leave.
<u>George having gone to bed</u>, Mick had started watching a movie.
<u>The question having been asked</u>, he had to deal with it.

You use an *-ed* participle on its own to say that something was done or completed before the event or situation described in the main clause.

He proceeded to light his pipe. <u>That done</u>, he put on his woollen scarf and went out.

USAGE NOTE

8.143 In a negative non-defining clause, you put *not* in front of the participle, or in front of *having*.

He paused, not wishing to boast.
He didn't recognize her at first, not having seen her for fifteen years or so.
He began to shout, their reply not having come as quickly as he wanted.

Using defining clauses

8.144 **Defining non-finite clauses** explain which person or thing you are talking about. They are always placed after the noun in a noun phrase.

The old lady driving the horse was dressed in black.
The bus carrying the musicians arrived just before noon.

use after pronouns

8.145 Defining clauses can be used after indefinite pronouns such as *anyone*.

Anyone following this advice could get in trouble.
Ask anybody nearing the age of retirement what they think.

Other structures used like non-finite clauses

8.146 Phrases that do not contain a verb are sometimes used in writing in a similar way to non-finite clauses.

8.147 In writing, you can add a phrase containing one or more adjectives to a sentence. This is another way of making two statements in one sentence.

For example, instead of writing *We were tired and hungry. We reached the farm*, you could write *Tired and hungry, we reached the farm*.

Surprised at my reaction, she tried to console me.
Much discouraged, I moved on to Philadelphia.
The boy nodded, pale and scared.
He knocked at the door, sick with fear.
Of course, said Alison, astonished.

8.148 In a similar way, you can use a phrase to describe something that is connected with the subject of a sentence. The phrase consists of a noun, followed by an adjective, an adverbial, or another noun.

For example, instead of writing *He came into the room. His hat was in his hand*, you could write *He came into the room, his hat in his hand*.

What do you mean by that? said Hugh, his face pale.
She stood very straight, her body absolutely stiff with fury.
He was waiting, drumming with his fingers, his eyes on his napkin.

With is sometimes added at the beginning of a phrase.

She walked on, with her eyes straight ahead.
It was a hot, calm day, with every object visible for miles.

Linking words, phrases, and clauses together

8.149 When you say or write something, you often want to put together two or more clauses of equal importance. You do this by using a **coordinating conjunction**.

Anna had to go into town <u>and</u> she wanted to go to Bride Street.
I asked if I could borrow her bicycle <u>but</u> she refused.
He was a great player, <u>yet</u> he never played for Ireland.

Here is a list of the most common coordinating conjunctions:

and	but	nor	or	then	yet

Coordinating conjunctions are also used to link words and phrases.

The boys shouted <u>and</u> rushed forward.
...domestic animals such as dogs <u>and</u> cats.
Her manner was hurried <u>yet</u> polite.
She spoke slowly <u>but</u> firmly.

Sometimes coordinating conjunctions are used together.

The software is quite sophisticated <u>and yet</u> easy to use.
Eric moaned something <u>and then</u> lay still.

The linking of clauses, words, or phrases using coordinating conjunctions is called **coordination**. Coordinating conjunctions are sometimes called **coordinators**.

8.150 The different uses of coordinating conjunctions are explained in the following paragraphs:

clauses	paragraphs 8.151 to 8.163
verbs	paragraphs 8.164 to 8.170
noun phrases	paragraphs 8.171 to 8.179
adjectives and adverbs	paragraphs 8.180 to 8.189
other words and phrases	paragraphs 8.190 to 8.193

Ways of emphasizing coordinating conjunctions are described in paragraphs 8.194 to 8.199.

The linking of more than two clauses, words, or phrases is explained in paragraphs 8.200 and 8.201.

Linking clauses

8.151 You can use a coordinating conjunction to link clauses that have the same subject, or clauses that have different subjects.

omitting words in the second clause

8.152 When you link clauses that have the same subject, you do not always need to repeat the subject in the second clause.

If the conjunction is *and*, *or*, or *then*, you do not usually repeat the subject.

I picked up the glass <u>and</u> raised it to my lips.
It's a long time since you've bought them a drink <u>or talked to them</u>.
When she recognized Morris she went pale, <u>then blushed</u>.

If the conjunction is *but*, *so*, or *yet*, it is usual to repeat the subject.

I try and see it their way, <u>but I can't</u>.
I had no car, <u>so I hired one for the journey</u>.
He lost the fight, <u>yet somehow he emerged with his dignity</u>.

When you link clauses that have different subjects but that have some common elements, you do not need to repeat all the elements in the second clause.

For example, instead of saying *Some of them went to one restaurant and some of them went to the other restaurant* , you can say *Some of them went to one restaurant and some to the other*.

One soldier was killed <u>and another wounded</u>.
One side was painted black <u>and the other white</u>.

functions of coordinating conjunctions

8.153 A coordinating conjunction can be used simply to link clauses, or it can be used in addition to indicate a relationship between them. These uses are explained in the following paragraphs.

related facts

8.154 If you simply want to mention two related facts, you use *and*.

He has been successful in Hollywood <u>and</u> has worked with such directors as Mike Leigh and Richard Attenborough.
The company will not close <u>and</u> will continue to operate from Belfast.
He gained a B in English <u>and</u> now plans to study languages.

You also use *and* to show that two things happened or are happening at the same time.

I sat <u>and</u> watched him.

Other uses of *and* are explained in the following paragraphs.

sequence

8.155 If you use *and* between two clauses that describe events, you are saying that the event described in the first clause happens or happened before the event described in the second one.

She was born in Budapest <u>and</u> raised in Manhattan.
He opened the car door <u>and</u> got out.

Then can be used in the same way, but it is less common.

We finished our drinks <u>then</u> left.

two negative facts

8.156 When you want to link two negative clauses, you usually use *and*.

When his contract ended he did not return home <u>and</u> he has not been there since 1979.

However, you can use *or* when the clauses have the same subject and the same auxiliaries. In the second clause, you omit the subject, the auxiliaries, and *not*.

For example, instead of saying *She doesn't eat meat and she doesn't eat fish*, you can say *She doesn't eat meat or fish*.

We will not damage <u>or</u> destroy the samples.

He didn't yell <u>or</u> scream.

You can also link negative clauses by using *and neither*, *and nor*, or *nor*. You put *be* or the auxiliary at the beginning of the second clause, in front of the subject.

For example, instead of saying *My sister doesn't like him, and I don't like him*, you can say *My sister doesn't like him, and neither do I*.

I was not happy <u>and neither were they</u>.
I could not afford to eat in restaurants <u>and nor could anyone else I knew</u>.
These people are not crazy, <u>nor are they fools</u>.

But *neither* and *but nor* can also be used.

This isn't a great movie, <u>but neither is it rubbish</u>.
I don't want to marry him <u>but nor do I want anyone else to</u>.

When you use *and* to link two negative statements, you can put *either* after the second statement.

I hadn't been to a rock festival before <u>and</u> Mike hadn't <u>either</u>.
Electricity didn't come into Blackball Farm until recently <u>and</u> they hadn't any hot water <u>either</u>.

For emphasis, you can join two negative clauses by using *neither* and *nor*. This use is explained in paragraph 8.198.

contrast

8.157 When you are adding a contrasting fact, you usually use *but*.

I'm only 63, <u>but</u> I feel a hundred.
It costs quite a lot <u>but</u> it's worth it.
I've had a very pleasant two years, <u>but</u> I can't wait to get back to the city.

If you want to add a fact that contrasts strongly with what you have just said, you use *yet* or *and yet*.

Everything around him was destroyed, <u>yet</u> the minister escaped without a scratch.
I want to leave, <u>and yet</u> I feel I should to stay.

You usually put a comma in front of *but*, *yet*, or *and yet*.

alternatives

8.158 When you want to mention two alternatives, you use *or*.

We could take a picnic <u>or</u> we could find a restaurant when we're out.
Did he jump, <u>or</u> was he pushed?

 USAGE NOTE

8.159 When you are giving advice, you sometimes want to tell someone what will happen if they do a particular thing. You do this by using an imperative clause, followed by *and* and a clause containing a verb in a form that expresses future time.

For example, instead of saying *If you go by train, you'll get there quicker*, you can say *Go by train and you'll get there quicker*.

Do as you are told <u>and</u> you'll be alright.
You speak to me again like that <u>and</u> you're going to be in serious trouble.

When you are giving advice, a warning, or an order, you sometimes want to tell someone what will happen if they do not do what you say. You do this by using an imperative clause, followed by *or* and a clause containing a verb in a form that expresses future time.

For example, instead of saying *Go away! If you don't go away, I'll scream*, you can say *Go away, or I'll scream.*

Hurry up, <u>or</u> you're going to be late for school.
Don't fight <u>or</u> you'll get hurt.

ℹ️ USAGE NOTE

8.160 In writing, you can sometimes begin a sentence with a coordinating conjunction. You do this to make the sentence seem more dramatic or forceful. Some people think this use is incorrect.

The villagers had become accustomed to minor earth tremors. <u>But</u> everyone knew that something unusual had woken them on Monday.
Do you think there is something wrong with her? <u>Or</u> do you just not like her?
Go now. <u>And</u> close that door.

ℹ️ USAGE NOTE

8.161 Sometimes, in writing, two clauses can be made into one sentence without a coordinating conjunction being used. Instead, a semicolon or a dash is put between the clauses. This is a way of expressing two statements in one sentence when no particular coordinating conjunction seems appropriate.

The neighbours drove by; they couldn't bear to look.
I couldn't say thank you–those words were far too small for someone who had risked her life to save mine.

non-finite clauses

8.162 Coordinating conjunctions can be used to link **non-finite clauses**.

To-infinitive clauses can be linked by *and* or *or*.

We need to persuade drivers to leave their cars at home <u>and</u> to use the train instead.
She may decide to remarry <u>or</u> to live with one of her sisters.

Sometimes the second *to* is omitted.

They tried to clear the road <u>and</u> remove discarded objects.

When the second clause is negative, you can use *not* instead of *and not*.

I am paid to treat people, <u>not</u> to interrogate them.

Clauses beginning with a participle can be linked by *and* or *or*.

She lay on the bed gazing at the child <u>and</u> smiling at him.
You may be more comfortable wearing a cotton dress or shirt <u>or</u> sleeping under a cotton blanket.

However, if the first clause begins with *standing*, *sitting*, or *lying*, you do not usually put *and* between the clauses.

Inside were two lines of old people sitting facing each other.

8.163 For information on how to coordinate more than two clauses, see paragraph 8.200.

Linking verbs together

8.164 When you are talking about two actions performed by the same person, thing, or group, you can use a coordinating conjunction to link two verbs.

intransitive verbs

8.165 Coordinating conjunctions can be used to link **intransitive** verbs.

> *Mostly, they just <u>sat</u> and <u>chatted</u>.*
> *We both <u>shrugged</u> and <u>laughed</u>.*

transitive verbs

8.166 When you are describing actions involving the same subject and object, you can link two **transitive** verbs. You put the object after the second verb only.

For example, instead of saying *He swept the floor and polished the floor*, you say *He swept and polished the floor*.

> *<u>Wash</u> and <u>trim</u> the leeks.*

Similarly, instead of saying *They walk to work or cycle to work*, you can say *They walk or cycle to work*.

> *I <u>shouted</u> and <u>waved</u> at them.*

leaving out the auxiliary

8.167 When you are linking verb phrases that contain the same auxiliary, you do not need to repeat the auxiliary in the second clause.

> *Someone <u>may be killed</u> or <u>seriously injured</u>.*
> *Now he <u>is praised</u> rather than <u>criticized</u>.*
> *He knew a lot about horses, <u>having lived</u> and <u>worked</u> with them all his life.*

emphasizing repetition or duration

8.168 If you want to say that someone does something repeatedly or for a long time, you can use *and* to link two identical verbs.

> *They <u>laughed</u> and <u>laughed</u>.*
> *He <u>tried</u> and <u>tried</u>, but in the end he had to give up.*

 USAGE NOTE

8.169 In informal speech, *and* is often used between *try* and another verb. For example, someone might say *I'll try and get a newspaper*. However, this means the same as *I'll try to get a newspaper*.

For more information about this use see paragraph 3.200.

8.170 For information on how to coordinate more than two verbs, see paragraph 8.200.

Linking noun phrases

8.171 When you are talking about two people or things, you can use a coordinating conjunction to link two noun phrases.

8.172 In simple statements about two people or things, you use *and*.

> *There were men <u>and</u> women working in the fields.*
> *I'll give you a nice cup of tea <u>and</u> a biscuit.*
> *...a friendship between a boy <u>and</u> a girl.*

Instead of *and not*, you use *not* with a comma in front of it.

> *I prefer romantic comedies, <u>not</u> action movies.*

If both people or things are the object of the verb in a negative sentence, you use *or*.

We didn't play cricket or football.

alternatives

8.173 When you are giving alternatives, you use *or*.

Serve fruit or cheese afterwards.
Do you have any brothers or sisters?

omitting determiners

8.174 When you refer to two people or things using *and* or *or*, you usually repeat the determiner.

He was holding a suitcase and a birdcage.

However, if the people or things are closely associated in some way, you do not need to repeat the determiner.

My mother and father worked hard.
The jacket and skirt were skilfully designed.
...a man in a suit and tie.

Sometimes both determiners are omitted.

Mother and baby are doing well.
All this had of course been discussed between husband and wife.

referring to one person or thing

8.175 You can sometimes use noun phrases linked by *and* to refer to just one person or thing.

He's a racist and a sexist.
...the novelist and playwright, Somerset Maugham.

omitting adjectives

8.176 When you are linking two nouns, an adjective in front of the first noun usually applies to both nouns.

...the young men and women of America.
...a house crammed with beautiful furniture and china.

verb agreement

8.177 When the subject of a clause consists of two or more nouns linked by *and*, you use a plural verb.

My mother and father are ill.
Time, money and effort were needed.

However, you do not use a plural verb if the nouns refer to the same person or thing.

The writer and filmmaker Michael Hey disagrees.

You also do not use a plural verb with uncountable nouns preceded by *all*, or with singular countable nouns preceded by *each* or *every*.

All this effort and sacrifice has not helped to alleviate poverty.
It became necessary to involve every man, woman and child who was willing to help.

When you link two or more nouns with *or*, you use a plural verb after plural nouns, and a singular verb after singular nouns or uncountable nouns.

One generation's problems or successes <u>are</u> passed to the next.
Can you say No to a friend or relative who <u>wants</u> to insist?

When you link two or more nouns with *or*, and the nouns would take different verb forms if they were used alone, a plural verb is generally used.

It's fine if your parents or brother <u>want</u> to come.

linking pronouns together

8.178 You can put *and*, *or*, or *not* between a pronoun and a noun, or between two pronouns.

Howard <u>and</u> I are planning a party.
She <u>and</u> I have a very good relationship.
Do you <u>or</u> your partner speak German?
I'm talking to you, <u>not</u> her.

When you say something about yourself and someone else, you usually put the pronoun or noun referring to the other person first, and the pronoun referring to yourself second.

My sister <u>and</u> I lived totally different kinds of lives.
You <u>and</u> I must have a talk together.
...a difference of opinion between John <u>and</u> me.
The first people to hear were the Foreign Secretary <u>and</u> myself.

8.179 For information on how to coordinate more than two noun phrases, see paragraph 8.200.

Linking adjectives and adverbs

8.180 When you use two adjectives to describe someone or something, you sometimes put a conjunction between them. This is explained in the following paragraphs 8.181 to 8.187. Conjunctions are also sometimes placed between adverbs. This is explained in paragraph 8.188.

qualitative adjectives

8.181 When you put two **qualitative adjectives** in front of a noun, you put *and* or a comma between the adjectives.

...an <u>intelligent and ambitious</u> woman.
...an <u>intelligent, generous</u> man.

colour adjectives

8.182 When you put two **colour adjectives** in front of a noun, you put *and* between them.

...a <u>black and white</u> swimming suit.

classifying adjectives

8.183 When you put two **classifying adjectives** in front of a noun, you have to decide whether the adjectives relate to the same system of classification or to different systems.

For example, *geographical* and *geological* relate to the same system; *British* and *industrial* relate to different systems.

When you put two classifying adjectives in front of a noun, and the adjectives relate to the same classifying system, you put *and* between them.

...*a social and educational* dilemma.

When the adjectives relate to different classifying systems, you do not put *and* between them, or use a comma.

...the *French classical* pianists Katia and Marielle Labeque.
...*medieval Muslim* philosophers.
...*a square wooden* table.
...*American agricultural* exports.

different types of adjective

8.184 When you put two adjectives of different types in front of a noun, for example a qualitative adjective and a classifying adjective, you do not put *and* between them or use a comma.

...*a large circular* pool of water.
...*a beautiful pink* suit.
...*rapid technological* advance.

adjectives with plural nouns

8.185 When you put two adjectives in front of a plural noun in order to talk about two groups of things that have different or opposite qualities, you put *and* between the adjectives.

...business people from *large and small* companies.
...*European and American* traditions.

adjectives after verbs

8.186 When you use two adjectives after a **linking verb**, you put *and* between them.

Mrs Scott's house was *large and imposing*.
The room was *large and square*.
On this point we can be *clear and precise*.

using other conjunctions

8.187 You can also put *but*, *yet*, or *or* between adjectives.

When you link contrasting adjectives, you put *but* or *yet* between them.

...*a small but comfortable* hotel.
We are *poor but happy*.
...*a firm yet gentle* hand.

When you want to say that either of two adjectives could apply, or to ask which adjective applies, you use *or*.

You can use *red or black* paint.
Call me if you feel *lonely or bored*.
Is this *good or bad*?

If you want to say that neither of two adjectives applies, you use *or* in a negative sentence.

He was *not exciting or good-looking*.

Another way of saying that neither of two adjectives applies is to put *neither* in front of the first one and *nor* in front of the second one.

He is <u>neither young nor handsome</u>.
Their diet is <u>neither healthy nor varied</u>.

linking adverbs together

8.188 You can put *and* between **adverbs**.

Mary was breathing <u>quietly and evenly</u>.
We have to keep airports running <u>smoothly and efficiently</u>.
They walk <u>up and down</u>, smiling.

When you link contrasting adverbs, you put *but* or *yet* between them.

<u>Quickly but silently</u> she darted out of the cell.

If you want to say that neither of two adverbs applies, you use a negative sentence with *or* between the adverbs, or you put *neither* in front of the first adverb and *nor* in front of the second one.

Giving birth does not happen <u>easily or painlessly</u>.
The story ends <u>neither happily nor unhappily</u>.

8.189 For information on how to coordinate more than two adjectives, see paragraph 8.201.

Linking other words and phrases

8.190 Coordinating conjunctions can also be used to link **prepositions**, **prepositional phrases**, **modifiers**, and **determiners**.

linking prepositions together

8.191 You can use *and* to link **prepositions** that apply to the same noun.

We see them on their way <u>to and from</u> school.
You should take the tablets <u>during and after</u> your visit.

linking prepositional phrases together

8.192 You can use *and* to link **prepositional phrases** when you are describing similar actions, situations, or things.

They walked <u>across the lawn and down the garden path</u>.
They had crumbs <u>around their mouths and under their chins</u>.

However, if the phrases describe the same action, situation, or thing, you do not put *and* between them.

Her husband was hit <u>over the head with a mallet</u>.
They walked <u>down the drive between the chestnut trees</u>.
...a man <u>of about forty with wide staring eyes</u>.

linking modifiers and determiners together

8.193 You can use *and* or *or* to link **modifiers**.

...the largest <u>fridge and freezer</u> manufacturer in Germany.
This would not apply to a <u>coal or oil</u> supplier.

You can use *or* to link the **determiners** *his* and *her*.

Your child's school will play an important part in shaping the rest of <u>his or her</u> life.

Emphasizing coordinating conjunctions

8.194 When you are using coordinating conjunctions, you sometimes want to emphasize that what you are saying applies to both the words or phrases linked by the conjunction. You usually do this by putting a word such as *both* or *neither* in front of the first word or phrase.

8.195 When you are using *and*, the most common way of emphasizing that what you are saying applies to two phrases is to put *both* in front of the first phrase.

> By that time <u>both</u> Robin <u>and</u> Drew were overseas.
> They feel <u>both</u> anxiety <u>and</u> joy.
> These headlines <u>both</u> mystified <u>and</u> infuriated him.
> Investment continues <u>both</u> at home <u>and</u> abroad.
> The medicine is <u>both</u> expensive <u>and</u> in great demand.

Another way is to use *and also* instead of *and*.

> Wilkins drove racing cars himself <u>and also</u> raced powerboats.
> The job of the library is to get books to people <u>and also</u> to get information to them.

8.196 For stronger emphasis, you can put *not only* or *not just* in front of the first word or phrase, and *but* or *but also* between the two words or phrases.

> The team is playing really well, <u>not only</u> in England <u>but</u> now in Europe.
> Employers need to think more seriously <u>not only</u> of attracting staff <u>but</u> of keeping them.

8.197 When you are using *or*, the most common way of emphasizing that what you are saying applies to two words or phrases is to put *either* in front of the first word or phrase.

> Sentences can be <u>either</u> true <u>or</u> false.
> You can <u>either</u> buy a special insecticide <u>or</u> get help from an expert.
> <u>Either</u> Margaret <u>or</u> John should certainly have come to see me by now.
> <u>Either</u> we raise money from outside <u>or</u> we close part of the museum.

When you are linking clauses in this way, you can use *or else*, instead of *or*.

> They should <u>either</u> formally charge the men <u>or else</u> let them go.

8.198 If you want to emphasize that a negative statement applies to two words or phrases, you put *neither* in front of the first word or phrase and *nor* in front of the second word or phrase.

For example, instead of saying *The girl did not speak or look up*, you say *The girl neither spoke nor looked up*.

> The thought <u>neither</u> upset <u>nor</u> delighted her.
> She had <u>neither</u> received <u>nor</u> read the letter.
> <u>Neither</u> Margaret <u>nor</u> John was there.

Note that you use a singular verb after singular noun phrases and a plural verb after plural noun phrases.

> Neither Belinda nor anyone else <u>was</u> going to speak.
> Neither city councils nor wealthy manufacturers <u>have</u> much need of painters or sculptors.

8.199 Sometimes you want to draw attention to an element of a sentence by contrasting it with something different. One way to do this is to link the two elements by putting *but* between them. You put *not* in front of the first element.

> I wasn't smiling, <u>not</u> because I was angry <u>but</u> because it was painful to move my face.
> I felt <u>not</u> joy <u>but</u> sadness.
> The upright chairs were <u>not</u> polished <u>but</u> painted.

Linking more than two clauses, phrases, or words

8.200 You can link more than two clauses, words, or phrases using *and* or *or*. Usually you use the conjunction only once, putting it between the last two clauses, words, or phrases. After each of the others you put a comma.

Harrison marched him to the door, threw him out and returned.
...courses in accountancy, science, maths or engineering.

You can also put a comma in front of the conjunction; this usually makes the sentence easier to read, especially if the separated elements contain more than one word or are not completely similar.

Mrs Roberts cooked meals, cleaned, mended clothes, and went to meetings of the sewing club.

 In informal speech, people sometimes put *and* or *or* between each pair of clauses, words, or phrases. Occasionally, you do this in writing when you want to emphasize that all the statements you are making are true.

Mrs Barnett has a gate and it's not locked and that's how they get out.

linking adjectives together

8.201 There are special rules for linking more than two adjectives.

When you put more than two **qualitative adjectives** in front of a noun, you put commas between the adjectives and do not use a conjunction.

...a large, airy, comfortable room.

When you put more than two **classifying adjectives** in front of a noun, you have to decide whether the adjectives relate to the same system of classification or to different systems. (This is explained in paragraph 8.183.)

If the classifying adjectives relate to the same system, you put *and* between the last two adjectives and a comma after each of the others.

...the country's social, economic and political crisis.

If the classifying adjectives relate to different systems of classification, you do not put anything between any of the adjectives.

...an unknown medieval French poet.

When you put both qualitative and classifying adjectives in front of a noun, you do not put anything between them.

...a little white wooden house.

When you put more than two adjectives after a **linking verb**, you put *and* between the last two adjectives and a comma after each of the others.

He was big, dark and mysterious.
We felt hot, tired and thirsty.

Chapter 9

Changing the focus in a sentence

9 Changing the focus in a sentence

Introduction

9.1 The structure of a statement usually follows the sequence *subject, verb, object, complement, adverbial*. The subject, which is what you are going to talk about, comes first. If you do not want to draw special attention to any part of the clause, then you follow this sequence.

subject	verb	adverbial		
Donald	*was lying*	*on the bed.*		

subject	verb	object	adverbial	
She	*has brought*	*the tape*	*with her.*	

subject	verb	object	complement	adverbial
He	*wiped*	*the glass*	*dry*	*with a tea-towel.*

The examples above are in the **declarative** form. Chapter 5 explains how meanings can be expressed using the **declarative**, the **interrogative** and the **imperative** forms. These other forms involve regular changes in the sequence of elements in the clause.

Is he ill?
Put it on the table.

9.2 However, there are other ways of putting the parts of a clause in a different sequence, in order to give special emphasis or meaning.

adverbial	subject	verb	object
In his enthusiasm,	*he*	*overlooked*	*a few big problems.*

object	subject	verb	adverbial
The third sheet	*he*	*placed*	*in his pocket.*

This applies mainly to **main clauses**. This chapter shows how you can change the word order in a main clause when you want to give special force to the whole clause or to one of its elements.

In most **subordinate clauses**, you have no choice about the order of the clause elements (see Chapter 8).

the passive

9.3 One way of changing word order in order to change the focus in a clause is to use the **passive** form. The passive allows you to talk about an event from the point of view of the thing or person affected, and even to avoid mentioning who or what was responsible for the action.

A girl from my class was chosen to do the reading.

The **passive** is explained in paragraphs 9.8 to 9.24.

9.4 Another way of varying the sequence of elements in the clause is to use a **split sentence**. There are three different types.

One type allows you to focus on the person or thing you are talking about, as in *It was Jason who told them*.

The second type allows you to focus on an action, as in *What they did was break a window and get in that way* or *All I could do was cry*.

The third type allows you to focus on the circumstances of an action, for example the time or the place, as in *It was one o'clock when they left*, or *It was in Paris that they met for the first time*.

Split sentences are dealt with in the section beginning at paragraph 9.25.

impersonal *it*

9.5 When you want to say something about a fact, an action, or a particular state, you can use a structure beginning with *it*, for example *It's strange that he didn't call*, *It's easy to laugh*, and *It's no fun being stupid*.

You also use an *it* structure to talk about the weather or the time, for example *It's raining*, *It's a nice day*, and *It's two o'clock*.

It structures are dealt with in the section beginning at paragraph 9.31.

there with *be*

9.6 *There* is used followed by *be* and a noun phrase to introduce the idea of the existence or presence of something. This makes the noun phrase, which is new information, the focus of the clause. For more information, see paragraphs 9.46 to 9.55.

There is someone in the bushes.

adverbials

9.7 There are also two types of adverbial that you can use to focus on a clause as a whole, or on different elements of the clause. These include **sentence adverbials** (see the section beginning at paragraph 9.56) and **focusing adverbials** (see paragraphs 9.79 to 9.90).

He never writes, of course.
Frankly, I don't really care what they think.
As a child she was particularly close to her elder sister.

Focusing on the thing affected: the passive

9.8 Many actions involve two people or things – one that performs the action and one that is affected by the action. These actions are typically referred to using **transitive verbs**, that is, verbs that have an object. **Transitive verbs** are explained fully in Chapter 3.

In English the person or thing you want to talk about is usually put first as the subject of the clause. So, when you want to talk about someone or something that is the **performer** of an action, you make them the subject of the verb and you use an **active** form of the verb. The other person or thing is made the **object** of the verb.

However, you may want to focus on the person or thing affected by an action, which would be the object of an active form of the verb. In that case, you make that person or thing the subject of a **passive** form of the verb.

For example, you could report the same event by using an active form of a verb, as in *The dog has eaten our dinner* or by using a passive form of a verb, as in *Our dinner has been eaten by the dog*, depending on whether you wanted to focus on the dog or your dinner.

formation of the passive

9.9 Passive forms consist of an appropriate form of *be* followed by the *-ed* participle of the verb. For example, the passive form of the present simple of *eat* is the present simple of *be* followed by *eaten*: *It is eaten*.

She escaped uninjured but her boyfriend was shot in the chest.
He was being treated for a stomach ulcer.
He thinks such events could have been avoided.

For details of **passive forms of verbs**, see the Reference section.

not mentioning the person or thing that performed the action

9.10 When you use the passive form of a verb, you do not have to mention the person or thing responsible for the action (the **performer**).

You may want to do this for one of these reasons:

▶ because you do not know who or what the performer is

He's almost certainly been delayed.
The fence between the two properties had been removed.

▶ because it is not important who or what the performer is

I was told that it would be perfectly quiet.
Such items should be carefully packed in boxes.

▶ because it is obvious who or what the performer is

She found that she wasn't being paid the same salary as him.
...the number of children who have been vaccinated against measles.

▶ because the performer has already been mentioned

His pictures of dogs were drawn with great humour.
The government responded quickly, and new measures were passed which strengthened their powers.

▶ because people in general are the performers

Both of these books can be obtained from the public library.
It is very strange and has never been clearly explained.

▶ because you do not want to say who performed an action, or you want to distance yourself from your own action.

The original has been destroyed.
I've been told you wished to see me.

9.11 In accounts of processes and scientific experiments, the passive is used without the performer being mentioned because the focus is on what happens and not on who or what makes it happen.

The principle of bottling is very simple. Food is put in jars, the jars and their contents are heated to a temperature which is maintained long enough to ensure that all bacteria, moulds and viruses are destroyed.

9.12 The passive form of reporting verbs is often used in an impersonal *it* structure, when it is clear whose words or thoughts you are giving or when you are giving the words or thoughts of people in general. See 9.45 in the section on **impersonal *it*** structures.

It was agreed that he would come and see us again the next day.
It was rumoured that he had been sentenced to life imprisonment, but had escaped.

USAGE NOTE

9.13 When people in general are the performers of the action, an **active** form of the verb is sometimes used instead, with the **generic pronouns** *you* or *they* as the subject. *One* is used as the subject in this kind of clause in formal speech and writing.

You can't buy iron now, only steel.
They say she's very bright.
If one decides to live in the country then one should be prepared for the unexpected.

For more information about **generic pronouns**, see paragraphs 1.119 to 1.123.

You can also use the **indefinite pronouns** *someone* or *something*. This allows you to mention a performer, without specifying who or what they are. For more information about **indefinite pronouns**, see paragraphs 1.128 to 1.141.

I think someone's calling you.
Something has upset him.

Ergative verbs can also enable you to avoid mentioning the performer of an action. For example, instead of saying *She opened the door*, you can say *The door opened*. See the section on **ergative verbs** in paragraphs 3.59 to 3.67.

mentioning the performer with *by*

9.14 When you use the passive, you can mention the person or thing that performed the action at the end of the clause by using *by*. This puts emphasis on the performer because the end of the clause is an important position.

His best friend was killed by a grenade, which exploded under his car.
Some of the children were adopted by local couples.
This view has been challenged by a number of workers.

mentioning things or methods used

9.15 As with active forms of verbs, you can mention something that the performer used to perform the action after the preposition *with*.

A circle was drawn in the dirt with a stick.
Moisture must be drawn out first with salt.

You can mention the method using an *-ing* form after *by*.

The strong taste can be removed by changing the cooking water.

passive of verbs referring to states

9.16 A few transitive verbs refer to states rather than actions. When some of these verbs are used in the passive, the person or thing that creates that state is put after the preposition *with*.

The room was filled with people.
The railings were decorated with thousands of bouquets.

Here is a list of transitive verbs referring to states that are used with *with* in the passive:

cover	decorate	ornament	teem
cram	fill	pack	throng
crowd	litter	stuff	

However, *by* is used with some verbs that describe a state.

The building was illuminated by thousands of lights.

Here is a list of transitive verbs referring to states that are used with *by* in the passive:

conceal	illuminate	occupy
exceed	inhabit	overshadow

Some verbs, such as *adorn* and *surround* can be used with *with* or *by* after them.

Her right hand was covered with blood.
One entire wall was covered by a gigantic chart of the English Channel.
The house was surrounded with policemen.
The building was surrounded by a deep green lawn.

Here is a list of transitive verbs that can be used with either *with* or *by* in the passive:

adorn	besiege	cover	encircle	overrun	surround

There are also several verbs that are used with *in*.

She claimed that the drug was contained in a cold cure given to her by the team doctor.
Free transport was not included in the contract.
The walls of her flat are covered in dirt.

Here is a list of transitive verbs that can be used with *in* in the passive:

contain	cover	embody	include	involve	subsume

Note that *cover* can be used with *in*, *by*, or *with*.

phrasal verbs

9.17 **Phrasal verbs** that consist of a transitive verb followed by an adverb or preposition, or by an adverb and a preposition, can be used in the passive. Lists of **phrasal verbs** are given in paragraphs 3.83 to 3.116.

Two totally opposing views have been put forward to explain this phenomenon.
Millions of tons of good earth are being washed away each year.
I was talked into meeting Norman Granz at a posh London restaurant.
Such expectations are drummed into every growing child.

verbs usually used in the passive

9.18 Because of their meaning, some transitive verbs are usually used in the passive. The performer of the action is usually thought to be not worth mentioning or is not known.

He <u>was deemed</u> to be the guardian of the child.
The meeting <u>is scheduled</u> for February 14.
The young men <u>were alleged</u> to have rampaged through the hotel.

The following transitive verbs are usually used in the passive:

be acclaimed	be empowered	be punctuated
be alleged	be fined	be rationed
be annihilated	be gutted	be reconciled
be baffled	be headed	be reprieved
be born	be horrified	be reunited
be compressed	be hospitalized	be rumoured
be conditioned	be indicted	be scheduled
be construed	be inundated	be shipped
be couched	be jailed	be shipwrecked
be cremated	be mesmerized	be short-listed
be dazed	be misdirected	be shrouded
be deafened	be overcome	be staffed
be debased	be paralysed	be stranded
be deemed	be penalized	be strewn
be disconcerted	be perpetrated	be subsumed
be dubbed	be pilloried	be suspended
be dwarfed	be populated	be swamped
be earmarked	be prized	be wounded

The following phrasal verbs are usually used in the passive:

be bowled over	be ploughed up	be sworn in
be caught up	be rained off	be taken aback
be handed down	be scaled down	be written into
be pensioned off	be struck off	

They <u>were bowled over</u> by the number of visitors who came to the show.
The journalists <u>were taken aback</u> by the ferocity of the language.

verbs that are rarely used in the passive

9.19 A few transitive verbs are rarely used in the passive because the thing affected by the action they describe is rarely the thing you are interested in.

The following transitive verbs are rarely used in the passive:

elude	flee	have	like	resemble	survive
escape	get	let	race	suit	

The following phrasal verbs containing a transitive verb are rarely used in the passive:

band together	eke out	jab at	sob out
bite back	flick over	jack in	stand off
boom out	get back	jerk out	tide over
brush up	get down	let through	wait out
call down on	give over	pace out	walk off
cast back	have on	phone back	while away
chuck in	have out	ring back	
cry out	heave up	ring out	
ease off	hunt up	sit out	

verbs with two objects

9.20 In the case of verbs that can have an indirect object as well as a direct object such as *give*, *teach*, and *show*, either object can be the subject of a passive clause.

For example, instead of *He gave the receptionist the key*, you can say *The key was given to the receptionist*, where the direct object of the active clause is the subject of the passive clause. The indirect object can be mentioned after *to* or *for*.

The building had been given to the town by an investment banker.
Shelter had been found for most people.

Sometimes it is unnecessary to mention the indirect object at all.

The vaccine can be given at the same time as other injections.
Interest is charged at 2% a month.

But you can also say *The receptionist was given the key*, where the indirect object of the active clause is the subject of the passive clause. Note that the direct object is still mentioned after the verb.

They were given a pint of water every day.
He had been offered drugs by an older student.

For lists of verbs that can have an indirect object as well as a direct object, see paragraphs 3.73 to 3.82.

transitive verbs with object complement: *The wall was painted blue*

9.21 There is a group of transitive verbs that can have a complement after their object. They are listed and described in paragraphs 3.161 to 3.171. When these verbs are used in the passive, the complement is put directly after the verb.

He was shot dead in San Francisco.
If a person today talks about ghosts, he is considered ignorant or crazy.

reflexive verbs

9.22 **Reflexive verbs**, whose object is a reflexive pronoun referring to the subject of the verb, are not used in the passive. For more information on **reflexive verbs**, see the section beginning at paragraph 3.26.

9.23 Many intransitive phrasal verbs can be used in the passive. The verbs are followed by a preposition and a noun phrase referring to the thing affected by the action the verb describes. The object of the preposition can be made the subject of the passive form of the verb. The preposition remains after the verb, with no object after it.

In some households, the man was referred to as the master.
Two people at the head of the line were being dealt with by a couple of clerks.
The performance had been paid for by a local cultural society.
The children were being looked after by family friends.

The following is a list of intransitive phrasal verbs with prepositions that are often used in the passive:

accede to	enter into	look to	resort to
account for	frown upon	meddle with	rush into
act on	fuss over	minister to	see through
adhere to	get at	mourn for	see to
aim at	get round	object to	seize on
allow for	gloss over	operate on	send for
allude to	guess at	pander to	set on
approve of	hear of	paper over	settle on
ask for	hint at	pay for	shoot at
aspire to	hope for	pick on	skate over
attend to	impose on	plan for	stamp on
bargain for	improve on	plan on	stare at
bite into	indulge in	play with	subscribe to
break into	inquire into	plot against	talk about
budget for	insist on	point to	talk to
build on	jump on	pore over	tamper with
call for	keep to	pounce on	tinker with
call on	laugh at	preside over	touch on
care for	lean on	prevail on	trample on
cater for	leap on	prey on	trifle with
count on	light upon	provide for	wait on
deal with	listen to	put upon	watch over
decide on	long for	puzzle over	wonder at
despair of	look after	reason with	work on
dictate to	look at	refer to	
dispense with	look into	rely on	
dispose of	look through	remark on	

A few three-word phrasal verbs are used in the passive.

He longs to be looked up to.
I was afraid of being done away with.

The following list contains three-word phrasal verbs used in the passive:

do away with	look forward to	play around with
live up to	look out for	talk down to
look down on	look up to	

USAGE NOTE

9.24 Note that in informal spoken English, *get* is sometimes used instead of *be* to form the passive.

> Our car *gets cleaned* about once every two months.
> Before that, I'd *got arrested* by the police.

In present perfect passive and past perfect passive sentences formed with *get*, American English uses *gotten* rather than *got*.

> I had cheated and lied, and I'd *gotten caught*. (American)

Selecting focus: split sentences

9.25 One way of focusing on a particular part of a sentence is to use a **split sentence**. This involves using the verb *be*, either with *it* as an impersonal subject or with a clause such as a relative clause or a *to*-infinitive clause. Other grammars sometimes refer to split sentences as **cleft sentences**.

it as the subject: *It was Fiona who told me*

9.26 If you want to emphasize one noun phrase, you can use *It is* ... or *It was* ... and follow it with a relative clause.

For example, instead of saying *George found the right answer*, you may want to stress the fact that George did it by saying *It was George who found the right answer*.

> *It was* Ted who broke the news to me.
> *It is* usually the other vehicle that suffers most.

Similarly, instead of saying *Henry makes clocks*, you can say *It's clocks that Henry makes*.

> *It's money* that they want.
> *It was me* who David wanted.

other kinds of focus

9.27 In a split sentence, you usually focus on a noun phrase. However, you can focus on other clause elements or even on a whole clause. You then use a relative clause beginning with *that*.

You can make a prepositional phrase, a time adverbial or an adverb of place the focus of a split sentence in order to stress the circumstances of an event.

> *It was from Francis* that she first heard the news.
> *It was then* that I realized I'd forgotten my wallet.
> *It was in Paris* that I first saw these films.

You can also focus on an *-ing* form if you are stressing an action.

> *It was meeting Peter* that really started me off on this new line of work.

You can focus on a clause beginning with *because* to stress the reason for something.

> Perhaps it's *because he's different* that I get along with him.

---

what or all to focus on an action

9.28 If you want to focus on an action performed by someone, you can use a split sentence consisting of *what* followed by the subject, the verb *do*, the verb *be*, and an **infinitive** with or without *to*.

For example, instead of saying *I wrote to George immediately*, you can say *What I did was to write to George immediately*.

What I did was to make a plan.
What you have to do is to choose five companies to invest in.
What it does is draw out all the vitamins from the body.

You can use *all* instead of *what* if you want to emphasize that just one thing is done and nothing else.

All he did was shake hands and wish me good luck.
All she ever does is make jam.

---

focusing on the topic

9.29 Clauses with *what* as their subject are sometimes used to focus on the thing you are talking about. They can be put after the verb *be* as well as in front of it. For example, you can say *Its originality was what appealed to me*, as well as *What appealed to me was its originality*.

What impressed me most was their sincerity.
These six factors are what constitutes intelligence.

---

focusing on what someone wants or needs: *What I want is a holiday, All I need is to win this game*

9.30 If you want to focus on the thing that someone wants, needs, or likes, you can use a split sentence beginning with a clause consisting of *what* followed by the subject and a verb such as *want* or *need*. After this clause, you use the verb *be* and a noun phrase referring to the thing wanted, needed, or liked.

For example, instead of saying *We need a bigger garden*, you can say *What we need is a bigger garden*.

What we as a nation want is not words but deeds.
What you need is a doctor.
What he needed was an excuse to talk.

Here is a list of verbs that can be used with *what* in this structure:

adore	enjoy	like	love	prefer
dislike	hate	loathe	need	want

You can use *all* instead of *what* with the verbs *want* or *need* if you want to emphasize that someone wants or needs a particular thing and nothing else.

All they want is a holiday.
All a prisoner needed was a pass.

If you do not want to mention the performer in the above structures, you can use a passive form of the verb, after *what* or *all that*.

What was needed was a revolution.

Taking the focus off the subject: using impersonal *it*

9.31 You often want to mention only one thing or fact in a clause. For example, you often want to focus on the type of information that is normally expressed by an adjective. But an adjective cannot stand alone as the subject of a clause. A common way of presenting information of this type is to put the adjective after *be*, with *it* as the subject.

If you do not want to choose any of the clause elements as the thing you are going to talk about, you can use several structures with *it* as subject.

It can be used:

▶ to describe a place or situation

It's lovely here.

▶ to talk about the weather or to say what the time is.

It had been raining all day.
It is seven o'clock.

These uses are often called the **impersonal** uses of *it*.

9.32 In these uses, *it* does not refer back to anything earlier in the speech or writing, and so it is different from the **personal pronoun**, which usually refers back to a particular noun phrase:

The ending, when it arrives, is completely unexpected.
Paris is special, isn't it?

For more information about **personal pronouns**, see the section beginning at paragraph 1.95.

Note that the pronoun *it* is also used to refer to a whole situation or fact that has been described or implied.

He's never come to see his son. It's most peculiar, isn't it?
It doesn't matter.
It's my fault.

9.33 *It* is also used to introduce a comment on an action, activity, or experience. The subject *it* refers forward.

It costs so much to get there.
It was amazing that audiences came to the theatre at all.

This structure with *it* allows you to avoid having a long subject, and to put what you are talking about in a more prominent position at the end of the sentence.

Describing a place or situation

9.34 If you want to describe the experience of being in a particular place, you can use *it* followed by a **linking verb** such as *be*, an adjective, and an **adverbial of place**.

It was very hard in Germany after the war.
It was terribly cold in the trucks.
It's nice down there.

For more information about how to talk about place, see the section beginning at paragraph 6.53.

Similarly, you can indicate your opinion of a situation using *it*, *be*, an adjective, and a clause beginning with *when* or *if*.

It's so nice when it's hot, isn't it?
Won't it seem odd if I have no luggage?

9.35 You can also use *it* as the object of verbs such as *like* and *hate* to describe your feelings about a place or situation.

> *I like it here.*
> *He knew that he would hate it if they said no.*

Here is a list of common verbs that are used in this way:

adore	enjoy	like	love
dislike	hate	loathe	prefer

Talking about the weather and the time

describing the weather: *It's raining, It's sunny*

9.36 You can describe the weather by using *it* as the subject of a verb.

> *It's still raining.*
> *It was pouring with rain.*
> *It snowed steadily throughout the night.*

The following verbs are used after *it* to talk about the weather:

drizzle	pour	sleet	thunder
hail	rain	snow	

You can also describe the weather by using *it* followed by *be* and an adjective by itself, or an adjective followed by a noun referring to a period of time.

> *'Can I go swimming?' – 'No, it's too cold.'*
> *It was very windy.*
> *It was a warm, sunny evening.*
> *It's a lovely day, isn't it?*

Here is a list of common adjectives that are used to describe the weather:

bitter	cold	freezing	misty	thundery
blowy	cool	frosty	muggy	warm
blustery	damp	hot	nasty	wet
boiling	dark	humid	rainy	windy
breezy	dry	icy	showery	
chilly	fine	light	stormy	
cloudy	foggy	lovely	sunny	

Note that you can describe a change in the weather or light by using *it* followed by *get* and an adjective.

> *It's getting cold. Shall we go inside?*
> *It's getting dark.*

9.37 You can say what the time, day, or date is by using *it* followed by *be* and an adjective or noun phrase referring to time.

> *It's eight o'clock.*
> *It's Saturday afternoon and all my friends are out.*
> *It was July, but freezing cold.*

9.38 You can form many useful time expressions using a structure with *It is* ... or *It was* ... and an adjective or noun phrase referring to time. The use of this structure puts emphasis on the time of the event.

You can say when something happened using *when*.

> *It was 11 o'clock at night <u>when</u> 16 armed men came to my house.*
> *It was nearly midnight <u>when</u> Kunta finally slept.*

You can say how long ago something happened using *since*.

> *It's two weeks now <u>since</u> I wrote to you.*
> *It was forty years <u>since</u> the war.*

You can say how long the period was between one event and another using *before*.

> *It was ninety days <u>before</u> the search was over.*
> *It was four minutes <u>before</u> half-time.*

You can say how soon something will happen using *to*.

> *It was only two days <u>to</u> the wedding.*

Commenting on an action, activity, or experience

9.39 A common way of commenting on what you are doing or experiencing is to use *it* followed by a **linking verb** and an adjective or noun phrase. This is followed by an *-ing* participle or a *to*-infinitive.

> *It's fun working for him.*
> *It was difficult trying to talk to her.*
> *It's nice to see you with your books for a change.*
> *It will be a stimulating experience to see Mrs Oliver.*

If you want to mention the person who performs the action or has the experience, you use a **prepositional phrase** beginning with *for* and a *to*-infinitive.

> *It becomes hard for a child to develop a sense of identity.*

You can also use the structure with a *to*-infinitive when you are recommending a course of action or saying that something is necessary.

> *Its important to know your own limitations.*
> *It's a good idea to have a little notebook handy.*
> *It is necessary to examine this claim before we proceed any further.*

9.40   Similar structures can be used with verbs other than linking verbs.

If you want to say what effect an experience has on someone, you can use *it* with a verb such as *please*, *surprise*, or *shock*, followed by a noun phrase and a *to*-infinitive. For a list of these verbs, see paragraph 9.44.

It always pleased him to think of his father.
It shocked me to see how much weight he'd lost.
It interests him to hear what you've been buying.

You can use *it* with *take* and a *to*-infinitive clause to indicate what is used in a particular action or activity, or is needed for it, for example the amount of time or the type of person that is needed.

It takes an hour to get to Northampton.
It takes an exceptional parent to cope with a child like that.
It took a lot of work to put it together.

If there is also an **indirect object**, this can be placed immediately after the verb.

It took me a year to save up for a new camera.

If the indirect object is expressed by a prepositional phrase, usually beginning with *for*, it is placed after the direct object.

It took some time for him to realize what was required.
It takes a lot more time for an adult to pick up a language than for a child.

Cost can be used in similar structures when talking about the amount of something, usually money, that is used in an activity.

It costs about £150 a week to keep someone in prison.

With *find* and *think*, you can use *it* as the object, followed by an adjective, and either a *to*-infinitive or a *that*-clause.

He found it hard to make friends.
He thought it right to resign immediately.

9.41   If you want to focus on a clause that starts with a participle or a *to*-infinitive, you can use this clause as the subject of the main clause, instead of *it*. For example, instead of saying *It's fun working for him* you can say *Working for him is fun*.

Measuring the water correctly is most important.

In formal English, *to*-infinitive clauses are sometimes used.

To sell your story to the papers is a risky strategy.

Commenting on a fact that you are about to mention

9.42   When you want to comment on a fact, event, or situation, you can use *it* followed by a **linking verb**, an adjective or a noun phrase, and a *that*-clause giving the fact.

It is strange that it hasn't been noticed before.
It's a shame he didn't come.
From the photographs it seems clear my mother was no beauty.

Here is a list of adjectives used in this structure:

amazing	extraordinary	natural	strange
apparent	fair	obvious	surprising
appropriate	funny	odd	true
awful	good	plain	unbelievable
bad	important	possible	unlikely
clear	inevitable	probable	wonderful
doubtful	interesting	queer	
essential	likely	sad	
evident	lucky	shocking	

Here is a list of nouns used in this structure:

disgrace	nuisance	shame	wonder
marvel	pity	surprise	

USAGE NOTE

9.43 After adjectives like *funny*, *odd*, and *strange*, a clause beginning with *how* is sometimes used instead of a *that*-clause, with the same meaning.

It's funny how they don't get on.
It's strange how life turns out.
It is astonishing how he has changed.

What-clauses can be used after similar adjectives when you want to comment on something that is the object of an action.

It's surprising what you can dig up.
It's amazing what some of them would do for a little publicity.

Why-clauses can be used after adjectives such as *obvious* and *clear* when you want to comment on how clear the reason for something is.

Looking back on these cases, it is clear why the unions distrust the law.

Whether-clauses can be used after adjectives such as *doubtful* and *irrelevant* when you want to comment on something that may or may not be true.

It is doubtful whether supply could ever have kept up with consumption.

other verbs

9.44 If you want to say what someone thinks about a fact, you can use *it* followed by a verb such as *please* or *surprise*. The verb is followed by a noun phrase and a *that*-clause.

It won't surprise you that I stuck it in my pocket.
It bothered her that Alice wasn't interested in going out.

Here is a list of verbs that can be used in this way:

amaze	astonish	delight	horrify	surprise
amuse	astound	disgust	interest	upset
annoy	bewilder	distress	please	worry
appal	bother	grieve	shock	

passive of reporting verbs

9.45 If you want to say what is said, thought, or discovered by a group of people, you can use *it* as the subject of the passive form of a **reporting verb**, followed by a *that*-clause.

It was agreed that the plan should be kept secret.
It was felt that there had been some dishonest behaviour.
It was found that no cases of hypothermia had been recorded.

For a list of verbs that can be used in this way, see paragraph 7.69.

Introducing something new: *there* as subject

saying that something exists: *There are four people in my family*

9.46 When you want to say that something exists, or when you want to mention the presence of something, you can use *there* followed by *be* and a noun phrase.

 In this context, *there* does not refer to a place. In spoken English, the difference is often clearer, because this use of *there* is often pronounced without stress as /ðə/ (American English ðər), whereas the adverb of place is almost always pronounced fully as /ðeə/ (American English ðeər).

There has very little meaning in the structures that are being explained here. For example, the sentence *There is a good reason for this* just means *A good reason for this exists*.

9.47 The noun phrase is usually followed by an adverb or prepositional phrase, a *wh*-clause, or one of the adjectives *available*, *present*, or *free*.

There were thirty boys in the class.
There are three reasons why we should support this action.
There were no other jobs available.

Prepositional phrases relating to place can be put either in front of *there* or after the noun phrase.

On a small table there was a white china mug.
There was a box in the middle of the room.

saying that something happened: *There was a sudden noise*

9.48 You can also use *there* followed by *be* and a noun phrase referring to an event to say that something happened or will happen.

There was a knock at his door.
There were two general elections that year.
There will be trouble tonight.

describing something that is happening: *There was a man standing next to her*

9.49 When you are describing a scene or situation, you can use a structure consisting of *there* followed by *be*, a noun phrase, and an *-ing* participle.

For example, instead of saying *Flames were coming out of it*, you can say *There were flames coming out of it*.

There was a storm raging outside.
There were men and women working in the fields with horses.
There was a revolver lying there.

verb agreement

9.50 Usually a plural form of *be* is used if the noun phrase after it is plural.

There were two men in the room.

You use a singular form of *be* when you are giving a list of items and the first noun in the list is singular or uncountable.

There was a sofa and two chairs.

Note that you use a plural form of *be* in front of plural quantity expressions beginning with *a*, such as *a lot of*, and *a few of*.

There were a lot of people there.

You also use a plural form of *be* in front of numbers beginning with *a*, such as *a hundred*, *a thousand*, and *a dozen*.

There were a dozen reasons why a man might disappear.

contractions with *there*

9.51 In spoken and informal written English, *there is* and *there has* are often contracted to *there's*; *there had* and *there would* to *there'd*; and *there will* to *there'll*.

There's no danger.
I didn't even know there'd been a fire.

there with adjectives

9.52 *There* is also used with adjectives such as *likely*, *unlikely*, *sure*, and *certain* to indicate the likelihood of something occurring.

There are unlikely to be any problems with the timetable.

there with other verbs

9.53 A few other verbs can be used after *there* in a similar way to *be*. If you want to say that something seems to be the case or that something seems to have happened, you can use *there* with *seem* or *appear* followed by *to be* or *to have been*.

There seems to have been some carelessness recently.
There appears to be a lot of confusion on this point.

To be is sometimes omitted, especially in front of an uncountable noun.

There seems little doubt that he was hiding something.

There is sometimes used followed by a passive form of a **reporting verb** and the infinitive *to be* to indicate that people say or think that something exists. For more information on **reporting verbs**, see the section beginning at paragraph 7.5.

There is expected to be an announcement about the proposed building.
Behind the scenes, there is said to be intense conflict.

Happen is used in the same type of structure to indicate that a situation exists by chance.

There happened to be a roll of sticky tape lying on the desk.

You can also use *tend* in this kind of structure to say that something generally happens or exists.

There tend to be a lot of parties at this time of year.

formal and literary uses

9.54 *Exist, remain, arise, follow,* and *come* are sometimes used after *there* to say that something exists or happens. These structures occur only in formal English or literary writing.

There remained a risk of war.
There followed a few seconds' silence.
There comes a time when you have to make a choice.

9.55 Another construction commonly used in literary writing is to begin a sentence with a prepositional phrase relating to place followed by *there* and a verb of position or motion.

For example, instead of saying *The old church stands at the top of the hill*, a writer might say *At the top of the hill there stands the old church*.

From the hook <u>there hung</u> a long black coat.
Beside them <u>there rises</u> a twist of blue smoke.

Focusing using adverbials

Commenting on your statement: sentence adverbials

9.56 There are many adverbials that are used to show your attitude to what you are saying or to make your hearer have a particular attitude to what you are saying. These are dealt with in paragraphs 9.57 to 9.63.

There are also some that are used to make a statement narrower or to focus attention on a particular thing that it applies to. These are dealt with in paragraphs 9.64 to 9.68.

All these adverbials are called **sentence adverbials** because they apply to the whole sentence they are in. They are sometimes called **disjuncts** in other grammars.

Sentence adverbials are often placed at the beginning of a sentence. Some are also used in other positions, as shown in the examples given below, but they are usually separated from the words around them by intonation or by commas, to show that they apply to the whole sentence.

For more general information about **adverbials**, see Chapter 6.

Stating what area you are referring to

being specific: *financially,..., politically speaking,...*

9.57 When you are making it clear what aspect of something you are talking about, you use sentence adverbials formed from classifying adjectives. For example, if you want to say that something is important in the field of politics or from a political point of view, you can say that it is *politically important*. These adverbials often come in front of an adjective, or at the beginning or end of a clause.

It would have been <u>politically</u> damaging for him to retreat.
<u>Biologically</u> we are not designed for eight hours' sleep in one block.
We've had a very bad year <u>financially</u>.

The following is a list of adverbials that can refer to a particular aspect of something:

academically	financially	politically
aesthetically	geographically	psychologically
biologically	ideologically	racially
chemically	intellectually	scientifically
commercially	legally	sexually
constitutionally	logically	socially
culturally	mechanically	spiritually
ecologically	mentally	statistically
economically	morally	superficially
emotionally	numerically	technically
environmentally	outwardly	technologically
ethically	physically	visually

 BE CREATIVE

9.58 *Speaking* is sometimes added to these adverbials. For example, *technically speaking* can be used to mean *from a technical point of view*.

He's not a doctor, <u>technically speaking</u>.
He and Malcolm decided that, <u>politically speaking</u>, they were in complete agreement.

generalizing: *basically*, *on the whole*, etc.

9.59 You often want to avoid making a firm, forceful statement, because you are aware of facts that do not quite fit in with what you are saying.

One way of doing this is to use a sentence adverbial that shows that you are making a general, basic, or approximate statement.

<u>Basically</u>, the older you get, the harder it becomes.
<u>By and large</u> we were allowed to do as we wished.
I think <u>on the whole</u> we don't do too badly.

The following adverbials are used like this:

all in all	by and large	on average
all things considered	essentially	on balance
altogether	for the most part	on the whole
as a rule	fundamentally	overall
at a rough estimate	generally	ultimately
basically	in essence	
broadly	in general	

Note that you can also use the expressions *broadly speaking*, *generally speaking*, and *roughly speaking*.

We are all, broadly speaking, middle class.
Roughly speaking, the problem appears to be confined to the tropics.

⊗ **BE CREATIVE**

9.60 You can also use prepositional phrases formed with classifying adjectives, such as *in financial terms* or *from a political point of view*. Similar prepositional phrases can be formed using the nouns related to these adjectives, for example using *money* instead of *financial*: *in money terms*, *in terms of money*, *with regard to money*, or *from the money point of view*.

Life is going to be a little easier in economic terms.
That is the beginning of a very big step forward in educational terms.
This state was a late developer in terms of commerce.

⊗ **BE CREATIVE**

9.61 Another way of saying something like *with regard to money* is *money-wise*. You add the suffix *-wise* to a noun referring to the aspect you mean. This is generally used to avoid the creation of long phrases.

What do you want to do job-wise when the time comes?
We are mostly Socialists vote-wise.

Emphasizing

9.62 You may want to emphasize the truth of your statement or to stress the seriousness of the situation you are describing. You can do this using the following sentence adverbials:

above all	for heaven's sake	surely
actually	indeed	to put it mildly
at all	positively	to say the least
believe me	really	truly
by all means	simply	without exception
even	so	

Sometimes we actually dared to penetrate their territory.
Above all, do not be too proud to ask for advice.
Eight years was indeed a short span of time.
I really am sorry.
Believe me, if you get robbed, the best thing to do is forget about it.

Note that *indeed* is often used after adjectives with *very*.

I think she is a very stupid person indeed.

At all is used for emphasis in negative clauses, usually at the end.

I didn't like it at all.
I would not be at all surprised if they turned out to be the same person.

Surely is used when you are appealing for agreement.

Surely it is better to know the truth.
Here, surely, is a case for treating people as individuals.

Even is placed in front of a word or group to draw attention to a surprising part of what you are saying.

Even at midday the air was chilly.
Some men were even singing.
There was no one in the cafe, not even a waiter.

So is used as an emphatic introduction when agreeing or commenting.

'Derek! It's raining!' – 'So it is.'
'He's very grateful!' – 'So he should be.'

By all means is used for emphasis when giving permission.

If your baby likes water, by all means give it to him.

For heaven's sake is used when making a request or asking a question.

For heaven's sake, stop doing that, Chris.
What are you staring at, for heaven's sake?

emphasizing that something is exact: *exactly, just, precisely*, etc.

9.63 You may want to emphasize that your statement is not only generally true, but that it is true in all its details. The adverbs *exactly*, *just*, and *precisely* are used for this.

They'd always treated her exactly as if she were their own daughter.
Their decor was exactly right.
I know just how you feel.
The peasants are weak precisely because they are poor.

Focusing on the most important thing

9.64 There are certain adverbials you can use if you want to focus on the most important thing in what you are saying, for example the main reason for something or the main quality of something.

I'm particularly interested in classical music.
They have been used in certain countries, notably in South America.
We want especially to thank all our friends for their support.

The following adverbials can be used like this:

chiefly	mostly	predominantly	specially
especially	notably	primarily	specifically
mainly	particularly	principally	

restricting: *only, just*, etc.

9.65 Some of these adverbials can be used to emphasize that only one particular thing is involved in what you are saying.

The drug is given only to seriously ill patients.
This is solely a matter of money.
It's a large canvas covered with just one colour.

The following adverbials can be used like this:

alone	just	purely	solely
exclusively	only	simply	

9.66 Adverbials for focusing can be used to add a further piece of information that selects a particular group of people or things from a larger set. They can be used in this way with noun phrases, prepositional phrases, adjectives, and subordinate clauses.

I enjoy the company of young people, especially my grandchildren.
In some communities, notably the inner cities, the treatment has backfired.
They were mostly professional people.
You'll enjoy it down in LA, especially if you get a job.

position of focusing adverbials

9.67 In careful writing, adverbials that are used for focusing are usually put immediately in front of the word or clause element they apply to, in order to avoid ambiguity. In speech, it is usually clear from the intonation of the speaker what they apply to.

However, in many cases the focusing adverbial does not necessarily focus on the word or element immediately after it. For example, in the sentence *He mainly reads articles about mechanical things* the word *mainly* almost certainly applies to *about mechanical things*, not to *reads*.

Focusing adverbials are not normally used at the beginning of a sentence. However, you can use *only* to begin a sentence when it focuses on the thing that follows it.

Only thirty-five per cent of four-year-olds get nursery education.
Only in science fiction is the topic touched on.

You can use *just* and *simply* at the beginning of sentences giving instructions.

Just add boiling water.
Simply remove the packaging, and plug the machine in.

Alone is always used after the element that it focuses on. *Only* is sometimes used in this position.

People don't work for money alone.
They were identified by their first names only.

In informal speech and writing, other focusing adverbials are sometimes used after the element they focus on. For example, you can say *We talked about me mostly* instead of *We talked mostly about me*.

We have talked about France mainly.
Chocolate, particularly, is suspected of causing decay of the teeth.
In the early years, especially, a child may be afraid of many things.

This position can also be used when adding a piece of information.

He liked America, New York particularly.
She was busy writing, poetry mostly.

> **USAGE NOTE**

9.68 Some other adverbials can be used to focus on additional information. The adverbs of degree *largely*, *partly*, and *entirely*, and adverbs of frequency such as *usually* and *often* can be used.

The situation had been created largely by the press.
The house was cheap partly because it was falling down and partly because it was in a dangerous area.
The females care for their young entirely by themselves.

They often fought each other, <u>usually</u> as a result of arguments over money.
Some people refuse to give evidence, <u>often</u> because they feel intimidated.

The phrase *in particular*, which has a similar meaning to *particularly*, can be used in the positions shown in the examples below.

Wednesday <u>in particular</u> is very busy.
Next week we shall be taking a look at education and <u>in particular</u> primary schools.
He shouted at the children and at Otto <u>in particular</u>.
<u>In particular</u>, I'm going to concentrate on hydro-electricity.

Other information structures

Putting something first: *In his pocket was a pen, Why she's here I don't know*

9.69   In English, the first element in a declarative clause is usually the subject of the verb. However, if you want to emphasize another element, you can put that first instead.

Sometimes when this takes place the normal order of subject and verb is changed.

adverbials first

9.70   Adverbs and prepositional phrases can often be put first. This is the normal position for **sentence adverbials** (see paragraph 9.56), so they are not particularly emphatic in this position. Other phrases are sometimes placed first, usually to make descriptions more dramatic or vivid in stories and accounts.

<u>At eight o'clock</u> I went down for my breakfast.
<u>For years</u> I'd had to hide what I was thinking.

The subject and verb often change place after prepositional phrases relating to place, and after negative adverbials.

In his pocket <u>was a bag of money</u>.
On no account <u>must they be let in</u>.

For general information on **adverbials**, see Chapter 6. **Negative adverbials** are dealt with in Chapter 5.

reported question first

9.71   When you are saying that you do not know something, you can put the **reported question** first.

<u>What I'm going to do next</u> I don't quite know.
<u>How he escaped serious injury</u> I can't imagine.

For more information on **reported questions**, see paragraphs 7.32 to 7.38.

other parts of the clause

9.72   An adjective or noun phrase can occasionally be put before a linking verb, but this is not common.

<u>Noreen</u>, she was called. She came from the village.
<u>Rare</u> is the individual who does not belong to one of these groups.

The object of a verb is sometimes put first, usually in formal or literary uses. Note that the subject still has to be mentioned.

The money I gave to the agent.
If they sensed my fear, they would attack. This I knew.

Introducing your statement: *The problem is..., The thing is...*

9.73 People often use structures that point forward to what they are going to say and classify or label it in some way. These are sometimes called **prefacing structures** or **prefaces**.

A preface usually introduces the second part of the same sentence, usually a *that*-clause or a *wh*-clause. However, you can also use a whole sentence as the preface to another sentence (see paragraph 9.78).

(see paragraph 9.78)

pointing forward to the second part of sentence

9.74 A common prefacing structure is *the* and a noun, followed by *is*; e.g. *The answer is ....* The noun is sometimes modified by an adjective, or there is sometimes extra information in the form of a phrase or a clause after it. The nouns most commonly used in this structure are:

answer	point	rule	tragedy	wonder
conclusion	problem	solution	trouble	
fact	question	thing	truth	

The fact is, the point is, and *the thing is* are used to show that what you are about to say is important.

The simple fact is that if you get ill, you may be unable to take the examination.
The point is to find out who was responsible.
The thing is, how are we to get her out?

classifying

9.75 Some of these nouns are used in to indicate what sort of thing you are about to say.

The rule is: if in doubt, dry clean.
Is photography an art or a science? The answer is that it is both.
The obvious conclusion is that man is not responsible for what he does.

labelling

9.76 Some of these nouns are used to label what you are going to talk about.

The problem is that the demand for health care is unlimited.
The only solution is to approach each culture with an open mind.
The answer is planning, timing, and, above all, practical experience.

other ways of labelling

9.77 **Split sentences** (see paragraphs 9.25 to 9.30) can be used in labelling.

What we need is law and order.

Impersonal *it* structures with adjectives followed by a *that*-clause are a less emphatic way of prefacing (see paragraph 9.42).

It is interesting that the new products sell better on the web than in shops.

You can use the sentence adverbials *at any rate*, *at least*, and *rather* as prefaces when you are slightly correcting a previous statement, often after *or*.

This had saved her life; or at any rate her sanity.

Anyway can also be used, usually after the correction.

It is, for most of its length anyway, a romantic comedy.

using whole sentences to point forward

9.78 A whole sentence can be used to point forward to the sentence or sentences that follow it. For example, a sentence containing an adjective like *interesting*, *remarkable*, or *funny*, or a general abstract word such as *reason* or *factor* (see paragraphs 10.19 to 10.23), is often used as a preface.

It was a bit strange. Nobody was talking to each other.
This has had very interesting effects on different people.
There were other factors, of course: I too was tired of Miami.
But there were problems. How could we get to Edinburgh without a car?

Focusing on the speaker's attitude

9.79 There are several ways that speakers can focus on their attitude towards what they are saying, and who they are talking to.

Certain adverbials indicate your attitude to what you are saying. These are explained in paragraphs 9.80 to 9.90.

Other structures can be used to show strong reactions, or exclamations. These are explained in paragraph 9.91 to 9.94.

Finally, you can show the way you feel towards people, and indicate your relationship to them by the way you address them. Different ways of addressing people are explained in paragraphs 9.95 to 9.99.

Indicating your attitude to what you are saying

indicating your opinion

9.80 One way of showing your reaction to, or your opinion of, the fact or event you are talking about is by using **commenting adverbials**, which comment on the whole message given in a sentence.

Surprisingly, I found myself enjoying the play.
Luckily, I had seen the play before so I knew what it was about.
It was, fortunately, not a bad accident, and Henry is only slightly hurt.
Interestingly, the solution adopted in these two countries was the same.

The following adverbials are commonly used in this way:

absurdly	coincidentally	ironically	of course
admittedly	conveniently	luckily	paradoxically
alas	curiously	mercifully	please
anyway	fortunately	miraculously	predictably
astonishingly	happily	mysteriously	remarkably
at least	incredibly	naturally	sadly
characteristically	interestingly	oddly	significantly

strangely	typically	unexpectedly	unnecessarily
surprisingly	unbelievably	unfortunately	
true	understandably	unhappily	

One of the uses of *at least* and *anyway* is to show that you are pleased about a particular fact, although there may be other less desirable facts.

At least we're agreed on something.
I like a challenge anyway, so that's not a problem.

 USAGE NOTE

9.81 There are a few commenting adverbials that are often followed by *enough* when used to show your opinion of what you are talking about:

curiously	interestingly	strangely
funnily	oddly	

Oddly enough, she'd never been abroad.
Funnily enough, I was there last week.

distancing and being more specific

9.82 There are several commenting adverbials that have the effect of showing that you are not completely committed to the truth of your statement.

Rats eat practically anything.
It was almost a relief when the race was over.
They are, in effect, prisoners in their own homes.
In a way I liked her better than Mark.

The following adverbials are used in this way:

almost	so to speak
in a manner of speaking	to all intents and purposes
in a way	to some extent
in effect	up to a point
more or less	virtually
practically	

Note that *almost*, *practically*, and *virtually* are not used at the beginning of a clause.

Expressions such as *I think*, *I believe*, and *I suppose* are also used to show your lack of commitment to the truth of what you are saying.

indicating your point of view

9.83 With adverbs such as *luckily*, *fortunately*, *happily*, and *unfortunately*, you can show whose point of view you are giving by adding *for* and a noun phrase referring to the person.

'Does he do his fair share of the household chores?' – *'Oh yes, fortunately for me.'*
Luckily for me and them, love did eventually grow and flourish.

indicating a quality shown by the performer of an action

9.84 Another group of commenting adverbials is used to show a quality you think
someone showed by doing an action. They are formed from adjectives that can be
used to describe people, and are often placed after the subject of the sentence and
in front of the verb.

The League of Friends generously provided about five thousand pounds.
The doctor had wisely sent her straight to hospital.
She very kindly arranged a delicious lunch.
Foolishly, we had said we would do the decorating.

The following adverbials are used in this way:

bravely	correctly	helpfully	wisely
carelessly	foolishly	kindly	wrongly
cleverly	generously	rightly	

mentioning your justification for a statement

9.85 If you are basing your statement on something that you have seen, heard, or read,
you can use a commenting adverbial to show this. For example, if you can see that
an object has been made by hand, you might say *It is obviously made by hand*.

His friend was obviously impressed.
Higgins evidently knew nothing about their efforts.
Apparently they had a row.

These are some common adverbials used in this way:

apparently	evidently	obviously	unmistakably
clearly	manifestly	plainly	visibly

showing that you assume your hearer agrees

9.86 People often use commenting adverbials to persuade someone to agree with them.
In this way, they show that they are assuming that what they are saying is obvious.

Obviously I can't do the whole lot myself.
Price, of course, is an important factor.

The following adverbials are often used in this way:

clearly	naturally	obviously	of course	plainly

indicating reality or possibility

9.87 Some adverbials are used to show whether a situation actually exists or whether it
seems to exist, or might exist.

She seems confident but actually she's quite shy.
They could, conceivably, be right.
Extra cash is probably the best present.

The following adverbials are used like this:

actually	in reality	probably	potentially
certainly	in theory	really	seemingly
conceivably	maybe	unofficially	supposedly
definitely	no doubt	~	theoretically
doubtless	officially	allegedly	undoubtedly
hopefully	perhaps	apparently	
in fact	possibly	nominally	
in practice	presumably	ostensibly	

The adverbials in the second group are often used in front of adjectives.

We drove along apparently empty streets.
It would be theoretically possible to lay a cable from a satellite to Earth.

indicating your attitude

9.88 If you want to make it clear what your attitude is to what you are saying, you can use a commenting adverbial.

Frankly, the more I hear about him, the less I like him.
In my opinion it was probably a mistake.
In fairness, she is not a bad mother.

Here is a list of some of the common adverbials used in this way:

as far as I'm concerned	in fairness	on reflection
frankly	in my opinion	personally
honestly	in my view	seriously
in all honesty	in retrospect	to my mind

using infinitive clauses

9.89 Another way of showing the sort of statement you are making is to use *to be* followed by an adjective, or *to put it* followed by an adverb.

I don't really know, to be honest.
To put it bluntly, someone is lying.

politeness

9.90 When someone who is making a request wants to be polite, they use the adverb *please*.

May I have a word with you, please?
Would you please remove your glasses?
Please be careful.

Exclamations

9.91 **Exclamations** are words and structures that express your reactions emphatically. You usually show this in speech by your intonation and in writing by the use of an **exclamation mark** (usually called an **exclamation point** in American English) at the end of the sentence, although full stops are often used instead. If the exclamation is only a part of a sentence, it is separated from the rest of the sentence by a comma.

showing your reactions

9.92   There are various ways of showing your reaction to something that you are experiencing or looking at, or that you have just been told. One way is to use an exclamation such as *bother*, *good heavens*, *oh dear*, or *ouch*.

Ow! That hurt.
'Margaret Ravenscroft may have been responsible for the fire.' – *'Good heavens!' said Dr Willoughby.*
'She died last autumn.' – *'Oh dear, I'm so sorry.'*

Some exclamations are used only to show reactions. Here is a list of some common ones:

aha	good grief	oh	well I never
blast	good heavens	oh dear	what
blimey	good lord	ooh	whoops
bother	goodness me	oops	wow
bravo	golly	ouch	yippee
crikey	gosh	ow	you're joking
damn	hallelujah	really	yuk
eek	honestly	sheesh	
good gracious	hurray	ugh	

other clause elements

9.93   Other clause elements or clauses can be used in exclamations.

Noun phrases are sometimes used to show your reaction to something. Some nouns, for example *rubbish* and *nonsense*, can be used on their own to express strong disagreement.

'No-one would want to go out with me.' – *'Nonsense. You're a very attractive man.'*

Predeterminers, especially *what*, are often used before the noun.

What a pleasant surprise!
Such an intelligent family!
Quite a show!

Qualitative adjectives are sometimes used on their own, or with *how* in front of them, usually to show a positive reaction to a statement.

'I've arranged a surprise party for him.' – *'Lovely.'*
Oh! Look! How sweet!

A prepositional phrase with *of* can be used to specify a person, and a *to*-infinitive clause to refer to the action.

How nice of you to come!
How nice to see you.

Sentences with *how* and an adjective or adverb, or *what* and a noun phrase, can also be used as exclamations. The adjective, adverb, or noun phrase comes before the subject.

How nice you look!
How cleverly you hid your feelings!
What an idiot I am.
What negative thoughts we're having.

How can be placed at the beginning of an ordinary sentence to show the intensity of a feeling or action.

How I hate posters.
How he talked!

questions that do not expect an answer

9.94 People often use questions as a way of making a comment or exclamation. They do not expect an answer. Questions like this are called **rhetorical questions**.

You can use a negative *yes/no*-question, if you want to encourage other people to agree with you.

Oh Andy, isn't she lovely?
Wouldn't it be awful with no Christmas!

In informal English, you can use a positive question.

'How much?' – 'A hundred million.' – 'Are you crazy?'
Have you no shame!

Wh-questions, especially ones containing modals, are also used.

How on earth should I know?
Why must she be so nasty to me?
Why bother?

See Chapter 5 for more information about **questions**.

Addressing people

9.95 When you are talking to people, you can address them using their first name or, more formally, by using a title followed by their surname like *Mr Jones* or *Mrs Matthews*. Sometimes, the way you address people shows your feelings towards them or your relationship to them. For example, you might address them using a word like *darling* or *idiot*. Words used like this are called **vocatives**.

position

9.96 The names you use for addressing people are often placed at the end of a sentence or clause. In writing, they are usually preceded by a comma.

Where are you staying, Mr Swallow?
That's lovely, darling.

You can put them at the beginning of a sentence in order to attract someone's attention before speaking to them.

John, how long have you been at the university?
Dad, why have you got that suit on?

titles

9.97 When you address someone in a fairly formal way, you use their **title** and surname. Information about titles is given in 1.55 to 1.57.

Goodbye, <u>Dr Kirk</u>.
Thank you, <u>Mr Jones</u>.
How old are you, <u>Miss Flewin</u>?

Titles indicating a special qualification, rank, or job can be used on their own.

What's wrong, <u>Doctor</u>?
Well, <u>professor</u>?

! **BE CAREFUL**

9.98   The titles *Mr, Mrs, Miss*, and *Ms* are generally used only with a surname. To address people formally without their surname, *sir* and *madam* (usually contracted to *ma'am* in American English) are used, especially by employees to customers or clients, and, in American English, to address a person whose name you do not know and who appears to be older than you.

Good afternoon, <u>sir</u>. How can I help you?
Would you like to see the dessert menu, <u>madam</u>?
Can I help you with something, <u>ma'am</u>? (American)

other ways of addressing people

9.99 You can use noun phrases to show your opinion of someone. Those that show dislike or contempt are often used with *you* in front of them.

No, <u>you fool</u>, the other way.
Shut your big mouth, <u>you stupid idiot</u>.

Ways of addressing people that show affection are usually used by themselves, but *my* is sometimes used in more old-fashioned or humorous contexts.

Goodbye, <u>darling</u>.
We've got to go, <u>my dear</u>.

Nouns that refer to family or social relationships can be used for addressing people.

Someone's got to do it, <u>mum</u>.
Sorry, <u>Grandma</u>.
She'll be all right, <u>mate</u>.
Trust me, <u>kid</u>.

Forms of address are occasionally used in the plural.

Sit down, <u>children</u>.
Stop her, <u>you fools</u>!

Note that *ladies, gentlemen*, and *children* are only used in the plural.

<u>Ladies</u> and <u>gentlemen</u>, thank you for coming.

Chapter 10

Making a text hold together

10 Making a text hold together

10.1 When you speak or write, you very often want to make some connection with other things that you are saying or writing. There are several ways of using language to hold your whole message together and to give it meaning.

The most common way of doing this is by referring back to something that has already been mentioned. The different ways of **referring back** are explained in paragraphs 10.2 to 10.39.

There are also a few ways of **referring forward** to what you are about to say. These are explained in paragraphs 10.40 to 10.47.

Another way of making connections between what you have just said and what you are going to say is by using **sentence connectors**. These are explained in paragraphs 10.48 to 10.59.

People often avoid repeating words when they are referring back. This is explained in paragraphs 10.60 to 10.81.

Referring back

10.2 When you speak or write, you very often refer back to something that has already been mentioned or make a connection with it.

`pronouns`

10.3 One common way of referring back to something is to use a **personal pronoun** such as *she*, *it*, or *them*, or a **possessive pronoun** such as *mine* or *hers*.

Andrew found an old camera in a rubbish bin. He cleaned it up and used it to win several photography awards.
Tom and Jo are back from Australia. In fact I saw them in town the other day. They were buying clothes.
I held her very close. My cheek was against hers.

Personal pronouns are explained in paragraphs 1.95 to 1.106. **Possessive pronouns** are explained in paragraphs 1.107 to 1.110.

There are also other pronouns that can be used to refer back. These include pronouns such as *another* and *many* which have the same form as indefinite determiners. These are explained in paragraph 1.154.

...programs that tell the computer to do one thing rather than another.

You can also use a **quantity expression** or a **cardinal number**.

The women were asked to leave. Some of them refused.
These soldiers were ready for anything. Many of them had already been involved in fighting.
...the Guatemalan earthquake which killed 24,000 people and injured 77,000.

Quantity expressions are explained in paragraphs 2.175 to 2.207. **Numbers** are explained in paragraphs 2.208 to 2.231.

10.4 Another common way of referring back to something is to use a **definite determiner** such as *the* or *its* in front of a noun.

A man and a woman were walking up the hill. The man wore shorts, a t-shirt, and sandals. The woman wore a blue dress.
Thanks, said Brody. He hung up, turned out the light in his office, and walked out to his car.

Definite determiners are explained in paragraphs 1.162 to 1.212.

Some **indefinite determiners** can also be used to refer back to something.

A dog was running around in the yard. Soon another dog appeared.

Here is a list of indefinite determiners that are used to refer back to something:

another	each	every	other
both	either	neither	

These are explained fully in paragraphs 1.223 to 1.250.

10.5 As indicated above, pronouns and determiners used to refer back are explained in Chapter 1, where other pronouns and determiners are explained.

The **demonstratives** *this* and *that* are often used to refer back to whole sentences and sections of text. These uses are set out in the following section (paragraphs 10.7 to 10.17). The same section also explains other words that are used to refer back in a specific way.

10.6 There are also several other ways of referring back to something that has already been mentioned. These involve

▶ the use of various nouns to refer back to sections of text

These are explained in paragraphs 10.18 to 10.23.

▶ the use of *so* and *not* as substitutes for several types of word or structure that you want to avoid repeating

This use of *so* and *not* is explained in paragraphs 10.24 to 10.27.

▶ the use of *such*, adjectives, and adverbs to make comparisons with things that have already been mentioned.

This is explained in paragraphs 10.28 to 10.39.

Referring back in a specific way

10.7 *This* and *that*, and the plural forms *these* and *those*, are used to refer back clearly to a thing or fact that has just been mentioned.

They can be used both as pronouns and as determiners.

More and more money is being pumped into the educational system, and we assume this will continue.
I did a parachute jump a few months ago. This event was a lot more frightening than I had anticipated.

Note that *this* and *that* are not very often used as pronouns to refer to people. When they are used like this, they are only used in front of the verb *be*.

'A kind young man helped me to my seat.' – *'That was John.'*

10.8 When you use *this* or *these*, you are linking yourself with the thing you are referring to.

After you've decided on your goals, make a list. Anything that is worth doing should go on this list.
Only small trees are left. Many of these are twisted and stunted.
Over 2 million animals were destroyed. The vast majority of these animals did not need to die.

In contrast, when you use *that* or *those*, you are distancing yourself slightly from the thing you are referring to.

There's a lot of material there. You can use some of that.
There's one boss and that boss is in France.
There were only strangers around to observe him, and not many of those.

10.9 Although *this* and *that* are singular pronouns, you can use them to refer back to a number of things or facts that have just been mentioned, instead of using a plural pronoun.

He's got a terrible temper, but despite all this he's very popular.
He had played rugby at school, and had briefly been a professional footballer. That was to his favour when the job came up later.

demonstratives referring to sentences

10.10 Demonstratives can also be pronouns or determiners that refer back to a whole sentence or a number of sentences.

'You're the new doctor, aren't you?' – *'That's right.'*
'I'll think about it,' said Mum. That statement was the end of most of their discussions.
I accept neither of these arguments.

Note that when *these* and *those* are pronouns referring back to a whole statement they are only used in front of the verb *be*.

It was hard for me to believe these were his real reasons for wanting to get rid of me.
She put her arms around him. Thanks, Ollie. Those were her last words.

previous

10.11 You can also use the adjective *previous* before a noun to refer back to a section of text.

As explained in the previous paragraph, the bottle needs only to be washed in cold water.
I think we can now answer the question posed at the end of the previous chapter.

above

10.12 In written English you can also refer to what you have just mentioned by using *above*. You can put *above* before or after the noun.

I have not been able to validate the above statement.
...the figures discussed in the paragraph above.

You can also use *the above* without a noun phrase after it.

Keep supplies of rice and spaghetti. Also, to go with the above, Parmesan cheese and tins of tomatoes.

former and latter

10.13 When you have just referred separately to two things or groups of things, you can refer to the first one as *the former* and the second one as *the latter*. These expressions are used mainly in formal written English.

> *It used to be said that the oil exporting countries depended on the oil importing countries just as much as the latter depended on the former.*
> *I could do one of two things–obey him, or get my own protection. I chose the latter.*

Former and *latter* can also be adjectives. They always go before a noun.

> *You have the option of one or two bedrooms. The former choice allows room for a small bathroom.*
> *Guy had studied Greek and philosophy at Oxford and had continued to have an interest in the latter subject.*

i USAGE NOTE

10.14 When you want to refer generally to a whole class of things like the one that has been mentioned, you can say *things of this kind* or *things of that kind*. Alternatively you can say *this kind of thing* or *that kind of thing*.

> *We'll need a special new application to deal with payments, invoices, and things of that kind.*
> *Most of us would attach a great deal of importance to considerations of this kind.*
> *I don't see many advantages in that kind of education.*
> *All arts theatres have that type of problem.*

If you are referring to things of two or more kinds, you use *these* and *those* in front of *kinds*, *sorts*, or *types*, followed by *of* and a noun.

> *Both these countries want to reduce the production of these kinds of weapons.*
> *There are specific regulations governing these types of machines.*
> *Outsiders aren't supposed to make those kinds of jokes.*

You can also use *such* to refer back to things of a type that has just been mentioned. This is explained in paragraphs 10.28 to 10.32.

time

10.15 The adverb *then* is used to refer back to the time that has just been mentioned or discussed.

> *In ancient times poetry was a real force in the world. Of course the world was different then.*

place

10.16 The adverb *there* is used to refer back to the place that has just been mentioned.

> *I decided to try Newmarket. I soon found a job there.*
> *I hurried back into the kitchen. There was nothing there.*

manner

10.17 After describing a way of doing something or a way in which something happens, you can refer back to it using the adverb *thus*. *Thus* is a formal word.

> *Joanna was pouring the drinks. While she was thus engaged, Charles took the guests' coats.*
> *It not only pleased him to work with them, but the money thus earned gave him an enormous sense of importance.*

Note that *in this way* or *in that way* are commonly used instead.

Last week I received the Entrepreneur of the Year award. It's a privilege to be honoured <u>in this way</u>.

Referring back in a general way

10.18 There are various groups of nouns that are used to refer back in a general way to what has already been said. They refer to whole sections of spoken or written text.

referring to spoken or written texts

10.19 You can often refer back to what has already been said in a text by using a noun that classes it as a type of verbal action, for example an admission, suggestion, or question.

'Martin, what are you going to do?' – *'That's a good <u>question</u>, Larry.'*
'You claim to know this man's identity?' – *'I do.'* – *'Can you prove this <u>claim</u>?'*

The noun that you use to refer back like this not only refers to the text but also shows your feelings about it. For example, if you refer back to someone's reply to something using the noun *response*, this shows that your feelings about it are quite neutral, whereas if you use the noun *retort*, this shows that your feelings about the reply are much stronger.

Here is a list of nouns that refer back to texts, classing them as types of verbal action:

account	defence	prophecy
accusation	definition	proposal
acknowledgement	demand	proposition
admission	denial	protest
advice	denunciation	question
allegation	description	reference
announcement	digression	refusal
answer	disclosure	remark
apology	discussion	reminder
appeal	endorsement	reply
argument	excuse	report
assertion	explanation	request
assurance	exposition	response
boast	gossip	retort
charge	information	revelation
claim	judgement	rumour
comment	lie	statement
complaint	message	stipulation
compliment	narrative	story
concession	objection	suggestion
condemnation	observation	summary
confession	plea	tale
contention	point	threat
correction	prediction	verdict
criticism	promise	warning
declaration	pronouncement	

Note that many of these nouns are related to reporting verbs. **Reporting verbs** are explained in Chapter 7.

People will feel the need to be <u>informed</u> and they will go wherever they can to get this <u>information</u>.
'I don't know what we should do about that.' This <u>remark</u> was totally unexpected.
She <u>remarked</u> that she preferred funerals to weddings.

referring to ideas

10.20 In the same way, you can also refer back to ideas that you know or think someone has by using a noun that also indicates your feelings about the ideas. For example, if you refer to someone's idea using the noun *view*, this shows that your feelings about it are quite neutral, whereas if you use the noun *delusion*, this shows that your feelings are stronger.

His opinion of marriage is that it can destroy a relationship. Even previously unmarried people can hold <u>this view</u> if they experienced the break-up of their parents' marriage.
There is nothing to cry for. They cannot keep me there against my will. Secure in this <u>belief</u>, he hugged her reassuringly and went out.

Here is a list of nouns that refer to ideas and show your feelings about the ideas:

analysis	estimate	opinion
assessment	evaluation	picture
assumption	fear	plan
attitude	finding	position
belief	guess	reasoning
conclusion	hope	scheme
conjecture	idea	supposition
concept	illusion	theory
deduction	inference	thinking
delusion	insight	view
diagnosis	interpretation	viewpoint
doctrine	misinterpretation	vision
doubt	notion	wish

referring to what is mentioned

10.21 You can also refer back to actions and events using nouns that show your feelings about the action or event. For example, if you use the noun *incident* to refer to an accident at a nuclear power station, this simply describes the event, whereas if you use the noun *disaster*, this shows your reaction to the event.

Gwen was not the kind to make a fuss. In any event, she could handle the <u>situation</u>.
I believed the press would cooperate on this <u>issue</u>.
Parents may complain that their child does not eat a variety of healthy food. This <u>problem</u> doesn't arise because the parents have been lenient about food in the past.

Here is a list of nouns that refer to events and are usually neutral:

act	fact	process
action	factor	reason
affair	feature	respect
aspect	incident	result
case	issue	situation
circumstances	matter	state
context	method	state of affairs
development	move	subject
effect	phenomenon	system
episode	position	thing
event	possibility	topic
experience	practice	way

Here is a list of nouns that refer to events and show your feelings about them:

achievement	debacle	feat	predicament
advantage	difficulty	fiasco	problem
answer	disadvantage	gaffe	solution
catastrophe	disaster	nightmare	tragedy
crisis	exploit	plight	

⊗ **BE CREATIVE**

10.22 When you are referring back to something that has been said or mentioned, you can use almost any noun that refers to texts, ideas, events, and sometimes even to people. The noun you use allows you to express your exact reaction to the thing that is being referred to. For example, you can refer to a football defeat using nouns such as *tragedy* or *farce*, and you can refer to an argument using nouns such as *row* and *battle*.

referring to pieces of writing

10.23 You can refer in a neutral way to a previous piece of writing.

As explained in the previous paragraph, the bottle needs only to be washed clean.
We have seen in this chapter how the tax burden has increased fastest for households with children.

Here is a list of nouns used to refer to a piece of writing:

chapter	extract	phrase	sentence	table
example	paragraph	quotation	statement	text
excerpt	passage	section	summary	words

Substituting for something already mentioned: using *so* and *not*

so as a substitute for an adjective

10.24 *So* is sometimes used in formal English as a substitute for an adjective that has already been mentioned.

They are wildly inefficient and will remain so for some time to come.
They are just as isolated, if not more so, than before.

so and *not* after *if*

10.25 *So* is used to substitute for a clause after *if*, when the action or situation you are talking about has already been mentioned.

Will that be enough? If so, do not ask for more.

Not is used to substitute for a negative clause, to suggest the opposite situation to the one already mentioned.

You will probably have one of the two documents mentioned below. If not, you will have to buy one.

so and *not* with reporting verbs

10.26 *So* and *not* are also used to substitute for clauses after some common reporting verbs. They are also used after the expression *I'm afraid*, which is used to report an unwelcome fact.

'Are you all right?' – 'I think so.'
You're a sensible woman – I've always said so.
'You think he's failed, don't you?' – 'I'm afraid so.'
'It doesn't often happen.' – 'No, I suppose not.'
'You haven't lost the ticket, have you?' – 'I hope not.'

Here is a list of reporting verbs that can be followed by *so* and *not*:

believe	hope	say	tell
expect	imagine	suppose	think

Note that the use of *not* as a substitute with *think*, *expect*, and *believe* is rare or formal. When *not* is occasionally used with *say*, there is a modal in front of *say*.

'Is this a coincidence?' – 'I would say not.'

Occasionally *so* is put at the beginning of the clause. This often has the effect of casting doubt on the truth of the fact involved.

Everybody in the world, so they say, has a double.

So can also be used at the beginning of a clause for **emphasis**. This is explained in paragraph 9.62.

do so

10.27 *Do so* is used to mean *perform the action just mentioned*. The various forms of the verb *do* can be used. This structure is rather formal.

A signal which should have turned to red failed to do so.
Most of those who signed the letter did so under pressure from their bosses.

She asked him to wait while she considered. He did so.
Individuals are free to choose private insurance, and 10% of the population have done so.

Comparing with something already mentioned

10.28 The word *such* can be used in several ways to hold a text together. You use it when you want to indicate that something is of the same sort as something that has already been mentioned. The grammatical patterns of *such* are unique. It can behave as a **determiner**, a **predeterminer**, and an **adjective**.

such as a determiner

10.29 *Such* can be a determiner referring back to something that has already been mentioned.

Most of the state's electricity comes from burning imported oil, the highest use of such fuel in the country.
New business provides the majority of new jobs. By their nature, such businesses take risks.

such as a predeterminer

10.30 *Such* can be a **predeterminer** (see paragraph 1.251) referring back to something that has already been mentioned. It comes in front of the determiner *a* or *an*.

They lasted for hundreds of years. On a human time scale, such a period seems an eternity.
On one occasion the school parliament discussed the dismissal of a teacher. But such an event is rare.

such as an adjective

10.31 *Such* can be an adjective referring back to something that has already been mentioned.

He can be very cruel. This was one such occasion.
'Did you call me a liar?' – 'I never said any such thing!'
Mr Bell's clubs were privately owned. Like most such clubs everywhere, they were organizations of people who shared a certain interest.
I hated the big formal dances and felt very out of place at the one or two such events I attended.

adjectives

10.32 Some adjectives are used to indicate a comparison, contrast, or connection with something that has already been mentioned.

same

10.33 The adjective *same* is used attributively to emphasize that you are referring back to something that has just been mentioned.

A man opened the door and said Next please. About ten minutes later, the same man returned.
He watched her climb into a compartment of the train, and he chose the same one so he could watch her more closely.

Note that when *same* is used before a noun or pronoun, it nearly always follows *the*, but it can occasionally follow other definite determiners.

These same smells may produce depression in others.

10.34 *Same* can also come after a linking verb when you want to show that something is similar in every way to something that has just been mentioned. When *same* is used after a linking verb it always follows *the*.

The Queen treated us very well. The Princess Royal was just the same.
My brothers and myself were very poor, but happy. I think other families were the same.

10.35 You can also use *the same* without a following noun as the subject or object of a clause, to refer back to something that has just been mentioned.

The conversion process is very inefficient. The same is true of nuclear power stations.
'I've never heard of him.' – 'I wish I could say the same.'

The same thing can be used exactly like *the same*, as a subject or object.

He was stopped and sent back to get a ticket. On the return journey the same thing happened.
I learnt how to cheat and win every time. And I'm not proud of the fact that I taught a number of other people to do the same thing.

opposite and reverse

10.36 The adjectives *opposite* and *reverse* are used to say that something is as different as possible from the thing that has already been mentioned. They usually follow *the*.

It was designed to impress, but it probably had the opposite effect.
In the past ten years I think we've seen the reverse process.

When *opposite* is used before a noun, it occasionally follows *an*.

Other studies draw an opposite conclusion.

You can sometimes use *the opposite* and *the reverse* without a following noun to refer back to something.

The police officer said that we would have to learn to live with crime. I think the opposite is true; we have to learn not to live with crime.
He is well known for saying one thing and doing the opposite.
Older males are often desirable to women but the reverse is not usually true.
It hasn't happened. The reverse has happened.

other adjectives

10.37 You can also use a variety of other adjectives to say that something is similar to, different from, or connected with something that has already been mentioned. Some of these adjectives are only used before a noun and others can also come after a linking verb.

She wore a red dress with a red matching hat.
West Germany, Denmark and Italy face declines in young people. We are confronted with a contrasting problem.
That's what I would say. But his attitude was different altogether.

Here is a list of adjectives that can only be used in front of a noun to refer back:

adjacent	contrasting	matching
conflicting	corresponding	opposing
contradictory	equal	parallel
contrary	equivalent	

Here is a list of adjectives that can be used both in front of a noun and after a linking verb to refer back:

analogous	different	separate
comparable	identical	similar
compatible	related	unrelated

adverbials

10.38 To say that an action or a way of doing something is similar to the one just mentioned, you can use *in the same way*, *in a similar way*, *similarly*, or *likewise*.

She spoke of Jim with pride. And presumably she spoke to him of me in the same way.
Sam was engaged in conversation; Richard and Patrick were similarly occupied.

10.39 To show that an action or a way of doing something is different from the one just described, you can use the adverbs *otherwise* and *differently*.

I thought life was simply splendid. I had no reason to think otherwise.
She was ashamed of her actions, but she had been totally incapable of doing otherwise.
My parents were very strict, but I'm going to do things differently with my kids.

Referring forward

10.40 There are various ways of referring forward to things that are about to be mentioned. These ways often involve the nouns listed in paragraphs 10.18 to 10.23, which are more commonly used when you are referring back to something.

this and these

10.41 The use of *this* to refer back to something was explained in paragraphs 10.7 to 10.10. You can also use *this* or *these* to refer forward to what you are about to say. They can be both pronouns and determiners. Note that *these* can only be a pronoun when it is the subject.

Well, you might not believe this but I don't drink very much.
Perhaps I shouldn't say this, but I did on one occasion break the law.
This chapter will follow the same pattern as the previous one.
These were the facts: on a warm February afternoon, Gregory Clark and a friend were cruising down Washington Boulevard in a Mustang.
On the blackboard these words were written: Reading. Writing. Arithmetic.

10.42 When *this* and *these* are used as determiners to refer forward to something, they are most commonly used with nouns that refer to a piece of writing (see paragraph 10.23). Sometimes they are used with nouns that refer to what is said (see paragraph 10.19) and with nouns that refer to ideas (see paragraph 10.20). They occasionally occur with nouns that refer to actions or events (see paragraph 10.21).

following

10.43 You can also refer to what you are about to mention using the adjective *following* before a noun. When *following* is used like this, it is used with nouns that refer to texts, ideas, and pieces of writing (see paragraphs 10.19, 10.20, and 10.23.). Very occasionally, it is used with nouns that refer to actions and events (see paragraph 10.21.).

After a while he received the following letter: Dear Sir, The Secretary of State regrets that he is unable to reconsider your case.

The following account is based on notes from that period.
They arrived at the following conclusion: children with disabilities are better off in normal classes.

You can also used *the following* without a noun phrase after it.

...a box containing the following: a packet of tissues, two handkerchiefs, and a clothes brush.

next

10.44 The adjective *next* is often used to refer forward with nouns that refer to pieces of writing.

In the next chapter, we will examine this theory in detail.

below

10.45 You can also use *below* to refer forward to something you are about to mention. You use *below* like this after nouns that refer to texts and pieces of writing (see paragraphs 10.19 and 10.23).

For full details, see the report below.
The figures can be seen in the table below.

Below can occasionally be used to refer forward with nouns that refer to actions and things. When it is used with them, it comes after a word like *given*, *shown*, or *set out*.

The report given below appeared in the Daily Mail on 8 August 1985.

such

10.46 *Such* is sometimes used as a predeterminer to refer to a kind of thing that is specified immediately afterwards in a phrase or clause beginning with *as*.

You might think that in such a book as this, there is no need to deal with these matters.

Such is also sometimes used to qualify a noun, followed by a specifying phrase or clause beginning with *as*.

...a general rise in prices such as occurred in the late 1960s.
Try putting the items under headings such as I've suggested.

other ways

10.47 There are also other ways of referring forward to things that also involve focusing on the thing referred to. These involve **split sentences**, which are explained in paragraphs 9.25 to 9.30 and sentences beginning with *there*, which are explained in paragraphs 9.46 to 9.55.

Showing connections between sentences

10.48 The following section explains the functions of different groups of linking expressions, or **sentence connectors**. Sentence connectors are used to show what sort of connection there is between one sentence and another.

indicating an addition

10.49 In the course of speaking or writing, you can introduce a related comment or an extra reinforcing piece of information using one of the following adverbials:

also	besides	on top of that
as well	furthermore	too
at the same time	moreover	

I cannot apologize for his comments. Besides, I agree with them.
Moreover, new reserves continue to be discovered.
His first book was published in 1932, and it was followed by a series of novels. He also wrote a book on British pubs.
The demands of work can cause gaps in regular attendance. On top of that, many students are offered no extra lessons during the vacations.

Note that too is not usually placed at the beginning of a sentence.

He was hard-working, and honest, too.

indicating a similar point

10.50 You can show that you are adding a fact that illustrates the same point as the one you have just made, or a suggestion that has the same basis, by using one of the following adverbials:

again	equally	likewise
by the same token	in the same way	similarly

Every baby's face is different from every other's. In the same way, every baby's pattern of development is different.
Being a good player doesn't guarantee you will be a good manager, but, by the same token, neither does having all the coaching badges.
Never feed your rabbit raw potatoes that have gone green–they contain a poison. Similarly, never feed it rhubarb leaves.

contrasts and alternatives

10.51 When you want to add a sentence that contrasts with the previous one or gives another point of view, you can use one of the following adverbials:

all the same	instead	still
alternatively	nevertheless	then again
by contrast	nonetheless	though
conversely	on the contrary	yet
even so	on the other hand	
however	rather	

He had forgotten that there was a rainy season in the winter months. It was, however, a fine, soft rain and the air was warm.
Her aim is to punish the criminal. Nevertheless, she is not convinced that imprisonment is always the answer.
Her children are hard work. She never loses her temper with them though.

If you are mentioning an alternative, you can use instead, alternatively, or conversely.

People who normally consulted her began to ask other people's advice instead.
The company is now considering an appeal. Alternatively, they may submit a new application.

causes

10.52 When you want to say that the fact you are mentioning exists because of the fact or facts previously given, you link your statements using one of the following adverbs:

accordingly	consequently	so	therefore
as a result	hence	thereby	thus

Oxford and Cambridge have a large income of their own. So they are not in quite the same position as other universities.
It isn't giving any detailed information. Therefore it isn't necessary.
We want a diverse press and we haven't got it. I think as a result a lot of options are closed to us.

showing sequence in time

10.53 Some time adverbials are used to indicate that something takes place after or before an event that you have already mentioned or at the same time as that event:

afterwards	last	soon
at the same time	later	soon after
beforehand	meanwhile	subsequently
earlier	next	suddenly
ever since	presently	then
finally	previously	throughout
first	simultaneously	
in the meantime	since	

Go and see Terry Brown about it. Come back to me afterwards.
Published in 1983, the book has since gone through six reprints.
Never set out on a journey without telling someone beforehand.
We look forward to the Commission studying this agreement. In the meantime we are pressing ahead with our plans.

putting points in order

10.54 In formal writing and speech, people often want to say what stage they have reached in writing or speaking. They do this using the following sentence connectors:

first	secondly	finally	then
firstly	third	in conclusion	to sum up
second	thirdly	lastly	

What are the advantages of geothermal energy? Firstly, there's no fuel required, the energy already exists. Secondly, there's plenty of it.
Finally, I want to say something about the heat pump.

conjunctions

10.55 When people are speaking or writing informally, they often add an extra piece of information using one of the conjunctions *and*, *but*, *yet*, *or*, and *nor* to begin a new sentence.

He's a very good teacher. And he's good-looking.
I think it's motor cycling. But I'm not sure.
It's not improving their character. Nor their home life.

10.56 Sentence connectors are often put after the conjunctions *and* or *but* at the beginning of a clause or sentence.

That will take a long time and besides you'd get it wrong.
They were familiar and therefore all right.
Her accent is not perfect. But still, it's a marvellous performance.

If you are linking two negative sentences or clauses, you can put *either* at the end of the second one.

I can't use it, but I can't bear not to use it either.

Linking parts of a conversation together

10.57 Sometimes people want to avoid abruptness when changing the topic of conversation, or when starting to talk about a different aspect of it. They do this by using a particular group of sentence connectors.

The following adverbials are commonly used in this way:

actually	incidentally	okay	well
anyhow	look	right	well now
anyway	now	so	well then
by the way	now then	then	you know

They usually occur at the beginning of a clause. However, a few of them can be used in other places in the clause, when you want to pause or want to draw attention to the fact that you are introducing a new topic.

Actually, anyhow, anyway, by the way, incidentally, and *you know* can be used at the end of a clause. *By the way, incidentally,* and *you know* can be used after the subject or after the first word in a verb phrase.

Here are some examples showing sentence connectors being used to change the topic of a conversation:

Actually, Dan, before I forget, she asked me to tell you about my new job.
Well now, we've got a very big task ahead of us.

Here are some examples showing sentence connectors being used to start talking about a different aspect of the same topic:

What do you sell there anyway?
This approach, incidentally, also has the advantage of being cheap.

Then by itself is not used at the beginning of a clause, only at the end.

That's all right then.
Are you fond of her, then?

10.58 Some sentence connectors are used at the beginning of a clause to introduce a fact, often one that corrects the statement just made. They can also be used at the end of a clause, and elsewhere, to emphasize the fact.

actually	as it happens	indeed
as a matter of fact	I mean	in fact

Note that *actually* is used here to add information on the same topic, whereas in the previous paragraph it indicated a change of topic.

Actually, I do know why he wrote that letter.
He rather envies you actually.
I'm sure you're right. In fact, I know you're right.
There's no reason to be disappointed. As a matter of fact, this could be rather amusing.
They cannot hop or jump. Indeed, they can barely manage even to run.

You see is used to introduce or point to an explanation.

'Are you surprised?' – 'No. You see, I've known about it for a long time.'
He didn't have anyone to talk to, you see.

After all is used to introduce or point to a reason or justification of what you have just said.

She did not regret accepting his offer. He was, after all, about the right age.

USAGE NOTE

10.59 Prepositional phrases are sometimes used to introduce a new topic or a different aspect of the same topic. *As to* or *as for* can be used at the beginning of a sentence to introduce a slightly different topic.

As to what actually transpired at the headquarters, there are many differing accounts.
We will continue to expand our business. As for our competitors, they may well struggle.

With and *in the case of* are sometimes used to mention another thing that is involved in a type of situation that was previously mentioned.

With children, you have to plan a bit more carefully.
When the death was expected, the period of grief is usually shorter than in the case of an unexpected death.

Leaving words out

10.60 In English, people often leave words out rather than repeating them. Leaving words out is called **ellipsis**. This sometimes occurs in clauses that are linked by words like *and*, *but* or *or*, and coordinated groups of words. These are explained in paragraphs 8.152 to 8.176.

This section deals with how words can be left out in subordinate clauses and separate sentences as well as in coordinate clauses. The second clause or sentence could be said or written by the same person, or it could be part of a reply or comment by someone else. Omission of certain words in conversation is explained in paragraphs 10.74 to 10.81.

contrasting subjects

10.61 If you have just described an action or state and you want to introduce a new subject only, you do not need to repeat the rest of the sentence. Instead, you can just use an **auxiliary**.

There were 19- and 20-year-olds who were earning more than I was.
They can hear higher sounds than we can.

contrasting the verb form or the modal verb

10.62 If you want to change only the verb form or the modal, you use a new auxiliary, with a subject referring to the same person or thing.

> *They would stop it if they <u>could</u>.*
> *Very few of us have that sort of enthusiasm, although we know we <u>ought to</u>.*
> *I never went to Stratford, although I probably <u>should have</u>.*
> *This topic should have attracted far more attention from the press than it <u>has</u>.*

do

10.63 If you choose no other auxiliary verb, you usually use *do*, *does*, or *did*.

> *You look just as bad as he <u>does</u>.*
> *I think we want it more than they <u>do</u>.*

be as a main verb

10.64 However, the linking verb *be* is repeated, in an appropriate form. For example, *I was scared and the children were too.*

> *'I think you're right.' – 'I'm sure I <u>am</u>.'*

If the second verb phrase contains a modal, you usually put *be* after the modal.

> *'I'm from Glasgow.' – 'I thought you <u>might be</u>.'*
> *'He thought that it was hereditary in his case.' – 'Well, it <u>might be</u>.'*

However, this is not necessary if the first verb phrase also contains a modal.

> *I'll be back as soon as I <u>can</u>.*

Be is sometimes used after a modal in the second clause to contrast with another linking verb such as *seem*, *look*, or *sound*.

> *'It <u>looks</u> like tea to me.' – 'Yes, it <u>could be</u>.'*

have as a main verb

10.65 If the first verb is the main verb *have*, a form of *have* is sometimes used instead of a form of *do*.

> *She probably has a temperature–she certainly looks as if she <u>has</u>.*

leaving words out with *not*

10.66 You can make the second verb phrase negative by adding *not* to the auxiliary. These combinations are contracted in informal speech and writing to *don't*, *hasn't*, *isn't*, *mustn't*, and so on (see paragraph 5.61 for a list of these **contractions**). You use the same forms for a negative response to a question.

> *Some managed to vote but most of them <u>didn't</u>.*
> *'You're staying here!' – 'But Gertrude, I <u>can't</u>, I <u>mustn't</u>!'*
> *'And did it work?' – 'No, I'm afraid it <u>didn't</u>.'*
> *Widows receive state benefit; widowers <u>do not</u>.*
> *He could have listened to the radio. He <u>did not</u>.*

USAGE NOTE

10.67 With passives, *be* is often, but not always, kept after a modal.

He argued that if tissues could be marketed, then anything <u>could be</u>.

However, with perfect passives, you can just use the auxiliary *have* or *has*. For example, you could say, *Have you been interviewed yet? I have.*

Note that when a modal with *have* is used for a passive or progressive verb phrase, *been* cannot be omitted.

I'm sure it was repeated in the media. It <u>must have been</u>.
She was not doing her homework as she <u>should have been</u>.

10.68 If the second verb phrase contains the auxiliary *have* in any form, speakers of British English sometimes add *done* to the group. For example, instead of saying *He says he didn't see it but he must have*, they sometimes say *He says he didn't see it but he must have done*.

He hadn't kept a backup, but he <u>should have done</u>.

 American speakers repeat only the auxiliary verb *have*.

He hadn't kept a backup, but he <u>should have</u>.
It would have been nice to have won, and I <u>might have done</u> if I had tried harder.

Similarly, British speakers sometimes use *do* after modals.

He responded almost as a student <u>might do</u>.

 American speakers do not use *do* after modals.

Note that when the verb used in the first mention of an action or state is the main verb *have*, instead of using *do* after a modal in the second mention, you often use *have* instead.

'Do you think that academics <u>have</u> an understanding of the real world?' – 'No, and I don't think they <u>should have</u>.'

10.69 Usually, the clause with words omitted comes after a clause in which the action or state has been mentioned in full with a main verb. Occasionally, however, for a deliberate effect, it comes before the clause that mentions the action or state in full.

The problems in the economy are now being reflected, as they <u>should be</u>, in the housing market

repeating the main verb

10.70 If you want to be emphatic, you repeat the main verb, instead of leaving it out.

It was the largest swarm of wasps that had ever been seen or that ever would be <u>seen</u>.

contrasting objects and adverbials

10.71 Note that if you want to contrast two different things affected by an action, or two different factors or circumstances, you can put a new object or adverbial in the second clause, with an auxiliary or form of *be*.

Cook <u>nettles</u> exactly as you <u>would spinach</u>.
You don't get as much bickering <u>on a farm</u> as you <u>do in most jobs</u>.
Survival rates for cancer are twice as high <u>in America</u> as they <u>are in Britain</u>.
No one liked being young <u>then</u> as they <u>do now</u>.

However, the main verb is sometimes repeated.

Can't you at least <u>treat me</u> the way you <u>treat regular clients</u>?

USAGE NOTE

10.72 You can omit a verb after the semi-modals *dare* and *need*, but only when they are used in the negative.

'I don't mind telling you what I know.' – 'You <u>needn't</u>. I'm not asking you for it.'
'You must tell her the truth.' – 'But, Neill, I <u>daren't</u>.'

Similarly, the verb is only omitted after the modal expressions *had rather* and *would rather* when they are used in the negative. However, the verb is sometimes omitted after *had better* even when it is used affirmatively.

'Will she be happy there?' – 'She<u>'d better</u>.'
It's just that I<u>'d rather</u> not.

10.73 You can also leave words out of *to*-infinitive clauses. Instead of using a full *to*-infinitive clause after a verb, you can just use *to*, if the action or state has already been mentioned.

Don't tell me if you don't want <u>to</u>.
At last he agreed to do what I asked him <u>to</u>.

You can also do this in conversation.

'Do you ever visit a doctor?' I asked her. – 'No. We can't afford <u>to</u>.'

Note that there are some verbs, such as *try* and *ask*, that are also often used on their own, without *to*.

They couldn't help each other, and it was ridiculous to <u>try</u>.
I'm sure she'll help you, if you <u>ask</u>.

In conversation

10.74 People often leave words out in conversation in replies and questions. When this happens, it can involve leaving out the main verb in the ways that have been explained above (see paragraphs 10.60 to 10.73). This is common with questions that show that you find what someone has said interesting or surprising, or that you do not agree with them. These questions always have a pronoun as their subject.

'He gets free meals.' – '<u>Does he?</u>'
'They're starting up a new arts centre there.' – '<u>Are they?</u>'
'I've checked everyone.' – '<u>Have you now?</u>'

leaving words out in questions

10.75 You can often leave words out in questions when the context makes it clear what is meant. The question can consist of just a *wh*-word.

'Someone's in the house.' – '<u>Who?</u>' – 'I think it might be Gary.'
'But I'm afraid there's more.' – '<u>What?</u>'
'Can I speak to you?' I asked, undaunted. – '<u>Why?</u>' – 'It's important.'
'We're going on holiday tomorrow.' – '<u>Where?</u>' – 'To Majorca.'

Note that you can also use *why not*.

'Maria! We won't discuss that here.' – '<u>Why not?</u>'

Note also that you can use a *wh*-word after a reporting verb, especially *why*.

I asked <u>why</u>.
They enquired <u>how</u>.

10.76 Other questions can also consist of only a very few words when the context makes it clear what is meant. Short questions of this kind are often used to express surprise or to offer something to someone.

'Could you please come to Ira's right away and help me out?' – '<u>Now?</u>'
'<u>Tonight?</u>' – 'It's incredibly important.'
'He's going to die, you see.' – '<u>Die?</u>'
'<u>Cup of coffee?</u>' Lionel asked, kindly.
He drank the water and handed me the glass. '<u>More?</u>' 'No, that's just fine, thank you.'

leaving words out in replies

10.77 When you reply to *wh*-questions, you can often use one word or a group of words rather than a full sentence. You do this to avoid repeating words used in the question. For example, if someone asks *What is your favourite colour?*, the normal reply is a single word, for example *Blue*, rather than a sentence such as *My favourite colour is blue*.

'What's your name?' – 'Pete.'
'How do you feel?' – '<u>Strange.</u>'
'Where do you come from?' – '<u>Cardiff.</u>'
'Where are we going? – '<u>Up the coast.</u>'
'How long have you been out of this country?' – '<u>About three months.</u>'
'How much money is there in that case?' – '<u>Six hundred pounds.</u>'
'Why should they want me to know?' – '<u>To scare you</u>, perhaps. Who can tell?'

Wh-questions are explained in paragraphs 5.23 to 5.36.

10.78 You can often use a **sentence adverbial** or an **adverb of degree** rather than a sentence in answer to a *yes/no*-question.

'Do you think you could keep your mouth shut if I was to tell you something?' – '<u>Definitely.</u>'
'Do you think they're very important?' – '<u>Maybe.</u>'
'Do you enjoy life at the university?' – 'Oh yes, <u>very much</u>.'
'Are you interested?' – '<u>Very.</u>'
'Are you ready, Matthew?' – '<u>Not quite.</u>'
'Is she sick?' – '<u>Not exactly.</u>'

10.79 You can also answer a *yes/no*-question with a pronoun and a verb phrase that reflects the original question. The absence of *not* in your reply indicates *yes*. The presence of *not* indicates *no*.

'Does Lydia Walker live here?' – '<u>She does.</u>'
'Have you taken advantage of any of our offers in the past?' – '<u>I haven't.</u>'

Yes/no-questions are explained in paragraphs 5.12 to 5.14. **Sentence adverbials** are listed in Chapter 9 (9.56 to 9.68). **Adverbs of degree** are listed in Chapter 2 (2.140 to 2.156) and Chapter 6 (6.45 to 6.52).

leaving words out when you are agreeing

10.80 You often leave words out when you want to show that you agree with something that has just been said, or to say that it also applies to someone or something else. One way of doing this is by using *too* after an auxiliary or form of *be*.

'I like baked beans.' – 'Yes, I do <u>too</u>.'
'I failed the exam.' – 'I did <u>too</u>.'

The other way of doing this is to use *so* followed by the auxiliary or form of *be*, followed by the subject.

'I find that amazing.' – *'So do I.'*

Note that you can also use this form within a sentence to say that someone or something is the same.

He does half the cooking and so do I.

10.81 You can also leave out words when you want to show that you agree with something negative that has just been said, or to say that it also applies to someone or something else. One way of doing this is by using an auxiliary or form of *be* followed by *not* and *either*.

'I don't know.' – *'I don't either.'*
'I can't see how she does it.' – *'I can't either.'*

The other way is to use *nor* or *neither* followed by an auxiliary or form of *be*, followed by the subject.

'I don't like him.' – *'Nor do I.'*
'I'm not going to change my mind.' – *'Nor should you.'*
'I'm not joking, Philip.' – *'Neither am I.'*

Note that you can also do this within a sentence.

I don't know what you're talking about, Miss Haynes, and I'm pretty sure you don't either.
I will never know what was in his head at the time, nor will anyone else.
I can't do anything about this and neither can you.

Reference section

Reference section

Pronunciation guide

R1 Here is a list of the phonetic symbols for English:

British English vowel sounds	American English vowel sounds
ɑː heart, start, calm.	ɑ calm, drop, fall.
æ act, mass, lap.	ɑː draw, saw.
aɪ dive, cry, mine.	æ act, mass, lap.
aɪə fire, tyre, buyer.	ai drive, cry, lie.
aʊ out, down, loud.	aiər fire, tire, buyer.
aʊə flour, tower, sour.	au out, down, loud.
e met, lend, pen.	auər flour, tower, sour.
eɪ say, main, weight.	e met, lend, pen.
eə fair, care, wear.	ei say, main, weight.
ɪ fit, win, list.	eər fair, care, wear.
iː feed, me, beat.	ɪ fit, win, list.
ɪə near, beard, clear.	i feed, me, beat.
ɒ lot, lost, spot.	ɪər cheer, hear, clear.
əʊ note, phone, coat.	ou note, phone, coat.
ɔː more, cord, claw.	ɔ more, cord, sort.
ɔɪ boy, coin, joint.	ɔi boy, coin, joint.
ʊ could, stood, hood.	ʊ could, stood, hood.
uː you, use, choose.	u you, use, choose.
ʊə sure, pure, cure.	jʊər sure, pure, cure.
ɜː turn, third, word.	ɜr turn, third, word.
ʌ but, fund, must.	ʌ but, fund, must.
ə (the weak vowel in) butter, about, forgotten.	ə (the weak vowel in) about, account, cancel.

consonant sounds

b bed	l lip	v van	tʃ cheap
d done	m mat	w win	θ thin
f fit	n nine	x loch	ð then
g good	p pay	z zoo	dʒ joy
h hat	r run	ʃ ship	
j yellow	s soon	ʒ measure	
k king	t talk	ŋ sing	

Here is a list of the vowel letters:

a e i o u

Here is a list of the consonant letters:

b c d f g h j k l m n p q r s t v w x y z

The consonant y, when it falls in the middle or at the end of a syllable, has the status of a vowel and has a range of pronunciations similar to i.

Forming plurals of countable nouns

R2   Information on which nouns have plurals is given in Chapter 1 (1.14 to 1.193).

R3   In most cases, the plural is written s.

hat	→	hats
tree	→	trees

R4   The plural is written es after sh, ss, x, or s, and it is pronounced /ɪz/.

bush	→	bushes
glass	→	glasses
box	→	boxes
bus	→	buses

The plural is also written es and pronounced /ɪz/ after ch, when the ch is pronounced /tʃ/.

church	→	churches
match	→	matches
speech	→	speeches

R5   When the s follows one of the sounds /f/, /k/, /p/, /t/, or /θ/, it is pronounced /s/.

belief	→	beliefs
week	→	weeks
cap	→	caps
pet	→	pets
moth	→	moths

R6   When the s follows one of the sounds /s/, /z/, or /dʒ/, it is pronounced /ɪz/.

service	→	services
prize	→	prizes
age	→	ages

R7   Some nouns that end with the sound /θ/, for example mouth, have their plural forms pronounced as ending in /ðz/. With others, such as bath and path, the pronunciation can be either /θs/ or /ðz/. You may need to check the pronunciations of words like these in a Cobuild dictionary.

R8   In most other cases the s is pronounced /z/.

bottle	→	bottles
degree	→	degrees
doctor	→	doctors
idea	→	ideas

leg	→	legs
system	→	systems
tab	→	tabs

R9 With nouns that end in a consonant letter followed by y, you substitute *ies* for y to form the plural.

country	→	countries
lady	→	ladies
opportunity	→	opportunities

With nouns that end in a vowel letter followed by y, you just add s to form the plural.

boy	→	boys
day	→	days
valley	→	valleys

R10 There are a few nouns ending in f or fe where you form the plural by substituting *ves* for f or fe.

calf	→	calves
elf	→	elves
half	→	halves
knife	→	knives
leaf	→	leaves
life	→	lives
loaf	→	loaves
scarf	→	scarves
sheaf	→	sheaves
shelf	→	shelves
thief	→	thieves
wife	→	wives
wolf	→	wolves

R11 With many nouns that end in o, you just add s to form the plural.

photo	→	photos
radio	→	radios

However, the following nouns ending in o have plurals ending in *oes* :

domino	embargo	negro	tomato
echo	hero	potato	veto

The following nouns ending in o have plurals that can end in either s or es:

buffalo	ghetto	memento	stiletto
cargo	innuendo	mosquito	tornado
flamingo	mango	motto	torpedo
fresco	manifesto	salvo	volcano

R12 The following nouns in English have special plural forms, usually with different vowel sounds from their singular forms:

child	→	children
foot	→	feet
goose	→	geese
louse	→	lice
man	→	men
mouse	→	mice
ox	→	oxen
tooth	→	teeth
woman	→	women

R13 Most nouns that refer to people and that end with *man*, *woman*, or *child* have plural forms ending with *men*, *women*, or *children*.

postman	→	postmen
Englishwoman	→	Englishwomen
grandchild	→	grandchildren

R14 In addition to the nouns mentioned above, there are words that are borrowed from other languages, especially Latin, and that still form their plurals according to the rules of those languages. Many of them are technical or formal, and some of those that are given below are also used with a regular *s* or *es* plural ending in non-technical or informal contexts. You may need to check these in a Cobuild dictionary.

R15 Some nouns ending in *us* have plurals ending in *i*.

cactus	→	cacti
focus	→	foci
nucleus	→	nuclei
radius	→	radi
stimulus	→	stimuli

R16 Some nouns ending in *um* have plurals ending in *a*.

aquarium	→	aquaria
memorandum	→	memoranda
referendum	→	referenda
spectrum	→	spectra
stratum	→	strata

R17 Most nouns ending in *is* have plurals in which the *is* is replaced by *es*.

analysis	→	analyses
axis	→	axes
basis	→	bases
crisis	→	crises
diagnosis	→	diagnoses
hypothesis	→	hypotheses

neurosis	→	neuroses
parenthesis	→	parentheses

R18 With some nouns ending in *a*, the plurals are formed by adding *e*.

larva	→	larvae
vertebra	→	vertebrae

Some, such as *antenna*, *formula*, *amoeba*, and *nebula*, also have less formal plurals ending in *s*.

R19 Other nouns form their plurals in other ways. Some of these have two plural forms, one formed with *s* and one formed in a different way. Usually the form with *s* is used in less formal English.

appendix	→	appendices *or* appendixes
automaton	→	automata *or* automatons
corpus	→	corpora *or* corpuses
criterion	→	criteria
genus	→	genera
index	→	indices *or* indexes
matrix	→	matrices
phenomenon	→	phenomena
tempo	→	tempi *or* tempos
virtuoso	→	virtuosi *or* virtuosos
vortex	→	vortices

Forming comparative and superlative adjectives

R20 Information on how to use the **comparatives** and **superlatives** of adjectives is given in Chapter 2 (2.103 to 2.122).

R21 The comparative of an adjective is formed either by adding *er* to the end of the normal form of the adjective, or by putting *more* in front of it. The superlative is formed by adding *est* to the end of the adjective, or by putting *most* in front of it.

The choice between adding *er* and *est* or using *more* and *most* usually depends on the number of syllables in the adjective.

Superlatives are usually preceded by *the*.

R22 With one-syllable adjectives, you usually add *er* and *est* to the end of the normal form of the adjective.

tall	→	taller	→	the tallest
quick	→	quicker	→	the quickest

Here is a list of common one-syllable adjectives that form their comparatives and superlatives usually, or always, by adding *er* and *est*:

big	clean	cool	dry	fat
bright	clear	cross	dull	fine
broad	close	dark	fair	firm
cheap	cold	deep	fast	flat

fresh	long	poor	short	thin
full	loose	proud	sick	tight
great	loud	quick	slow	tough
hard	low	rare	small	warm
high	new	rich	soft	weak
hot	nice	rough	strong	wet
large	old	sad	sweet	wide
late	pale	safe	tall	wild
light	plain	sharp	thick	young

Note that when *er* and *est* are added to some adjectives, a spelling change needs to be made.

The patterns of spelling change in forming comparatives and superlatives from adjectives are explained in paragraph R27.

R23 You usually add *er* and *est* to two-syllable adjectives ending in *y*, such as *funny*, *dirty*, and *silly*.

happy	→	happier	→	the happiest
easy	→	easier	→	the easiest

Note that there is a spelling change here, which is explained in paragraph R27.

Some other two-syllable adjectives, not ending in *y*, also have comparatives and superlatives that are usually formed with *er* and *est*.

Here is a list of common two-syllable adjectives whose comparatives and superlatives are usually formed like this:

busy	easy	heavy	pretty	simple
dirty	funny	lovely	quiet	steady
clever	happy	lucky	silly	tiny

R24 Some other two-syllable adjectives usually have comparatives and superlatives formed with *more* and *most*.

careful	→	more careful	→	the most careful
famous	→	more famous	→	the most famous

Here is a list of common adjectives whose comparative and superlative forms are usually formed with *more* and *most*:

careful	handsome	obscure	sudden
common	likely	pleasant	
famous	mature	polite	

R25 Many two-syllable adjectives can have comparatives and superlatives with either the endings *er* and *est*, or *more* and *most*. In many cases, the *er* and *est* forms are more commonly found directly before the noun (in **attributive** position), and the *more* and *most* forms more commonly follow a linking verb such as *be* or *become* (in **predicative** position), particularly when a modifier such as *a bit*, *significantly*, *considerably*, *far*, *much* and *a little* is used. For more information about **attributive** and **predicative adjectives**, see paragraphs 2.42 to 2.52.

...*major hurricanes such as Katrina, the* <u>costliest</u> *disaster in U.S. history.*
Energy is becoming <u>much more costly</u> *and supplies are drying up.*

Less space seemed to make for a <u>friendlier</u> *neighborhood feeling.*
We are encouraging employers to be <u>a bit more friendly</u> *to the local environment.*

Here is a list of common adjectives that can have either type of comparative and superlative:

angry	friendly	remote	stupid
costly	gentle	risky	subtle
cruel	narrow	shallow	

R26 Adjectives that have three or more syllables usually have comparatives and superlatives with *more* and *most*.

dangerous → more dangerous → the most dangerous

ridiculous → more ridiculous → the most ridiculous

However, some three-syllable adjectives are formed by adding *un* to the beginning of other adjectives. For example, *unhappy* is related to *happy* and *unlucky* to *lucky*. These three-syllable adjectives have comparatives and superlatives formed either by adding *er* and *est* or by using *more* and *most*.

He felt crosser and <u>unhappier</u> *than ever.*

R27 When you add *er* or *est* to an adjective, you sometimes need to make another change to the end of the adjective as well.

If a one-syllable adjective ends in a single vowel letter followed by a single consonant letter, you double the consonant letter when adding *er* or *est*.

big → bigger → the biggest

hot → hotter → the hottest

However, you do not do this with two-syllable adjectives.

clever → cleverer → the cleverest

stupid → stupider → the stupidest

If an adjective ends in *e*, you remove the *e* when adding *er* or *est*.

wide → wider → the widest

simple → simpler → the simplest

Note that with adjectives ending in *le*, the comparative and superlative have two syllables, not three. For example, *simpler* (from *simple* /'sɪmpəl/) is pronounced /'sɪmplə/.

If an adjective ends in a consonant letter followed by *y*, you replace the *y* with *i* when adding *er* or *est*.

dry → drier → the driest

angry → angrier → the angriest

unhappy → unhappier → the unhappiest

Note that with *shy, sly,* and *spry*, you add *er* and *est* in the ordinary way.

R28 *Good* and *bad* have special comparatives and superlatives, which are not formed by adding *er* and *est* or by using *more* and *most*.

Good has the comparative *better* and the superlative *the best*.

There might be <u>better</u> ways of doing it.
This is the <u>best</u> museum we've visited yet.

Bad has the comparative *worse* and the superlative *the worst*.

Things are <u>worse</u> than they used to be.
The airport there was the <u>worst</u> place in the world.

Note that *ill* does not have a comparative form and so *worse* is used instead.

Each day Kunta felt a little <u>worse</u>.

R29   The adjective *old* has regular comparative and superlative forms but, in addition, it has the forms *elder* and *the eldest*. These forms are used only to talk about people, usually relatives.

...the death of his two <u>elder</u> brothers in the First World War.
Bill's <u>eldest</u> daughter is a doctor.

Note that unlike *older*, *elder* never has *than* after it.

R30   There is no comparative or superlative of *little* in Standard English, although children sometimes say *littler* and *the littlest*. When you want to make a comparison, you use *smaller* and *the smallest*.

R31   The comparatives and superlatives of compound adjectives are usually formed by putting *more* and *most* in front of the adjective.

| self-effacing | → | more self-effacing | → | the most self-effacing |
| nerve-racking | → | more nerve-racking | → | the most nerve-racking |

Some compound adjectives have adjectives as their first part. Comparatives and superlatives of these compounds are sometimes formed using the comparative and superlative of the adjective.

| good-looking | → | better-looking | → | the best-looking |

Similarly, some compound adjectives have adverbs as their first part. Their comparatives and superlatives are sometimes formed using the comparative and superlative of the adverb.

| well-paid | → | better-paid | → | the best-paid |
| badly-planned | → | worse-planned | → | the worst-planned |

The **comparatives and superlatives of adverbs** are explained in paragraphs R150 to R154.

The spelling and pronunciation of possessives

R32   The use of the possessive form of names and other nouns is explained in Chapter 1 (1.211 to 1.221).

R33   The possessive form of a name or other noun is usually formed by adding apostrophe s ('s) to the end.

<u>Ginny's</u> mother didn't answer.
Howard came into the <u>editor's</u> office.

R34   If you are using a plural noun ending in s to refer to the possessor, you just add an apostrophe (').

I heard the <u>girls'</u> steps on the stairs.
We often go to <u>publishers'</u> parties in Bloomsbury.

However, if you are using an irregular plural noun that does not end in s, you add apostrophe s ('s) to the end of it.

It would cost at least three policemen's salaries per year.
The Equal Pay Act has failed to bring women's earnings up to the same level.

...children's birthday parties.

R35 If something belongs to more than one person or thing whose names are linked by *and*, the apostrophe s ('s) is put after the second name.

...Martin and Tim's apartment.
...Colin and Mary's wedding.

R36 If you want to say that two people or things each possess part of a group of things, both their names have apostrophe s ('s).

The puppy was a superb blend of his father's and mother's best qualities.

R37 When you are using a name that already ends in s, you can simply add an apostrophe, for example *St James' Palace*, or you can add apostrophe s ('s), for example *St James's Palace*. These spellings are pronounced differently. If you simply add an apostrophe, the pronunciation remains unaltered, whereas if you add apostrophe s ('s), the possessive is pronounced /ɪz/.

R38 Apostrophe s ('s) is pronounced differently in different words. It is pronounced

▶ /s/ after the sound /f/, /k/, /p/, /t/, or /θ/.

▶ /ɪz/ after the sound /s/, /z/, /ʃ/, /ʒ/, /tʃ/, or /dʒ/.

▶ /z/ after all other sounds.

R39 If you are using a compound noun, you add apostrophe s ('s) to the last item in the compound.

He went to his mother-in-law's house.
The parade assembled in the Detective Constable's room.

R40 Apostrophe s ('s) can be added to abbreviations and acronyms in the same way as to other words.

He will get a majority of MPs' votes in both rounds.
He found the BBC's output, on balance, superior to that of ITV.
The majority of NATO's members agreed.

Numbers

R41 The uses of **cardinal numbers**, **ordinal numbers**, and **fractions** have been explained in Chapter 2 (2.208 to 2.249). The use of ordinals to express dates is explained in paragraph 4.88. Lists of numbers and details about how to say and write numbers and fractions are given below.

Cardinal numbers

R42 Here is a list of cardinal numbers. The list shows the patterns of forming numbers greater than 20.

0	zero, nought, nothing, oh	5	five
1	one	6	six
2	two	7	seven
3	three	8	eight
4	four	9	nine

10	ten	60	sixty
11	eleven	70	seventy
12	twelve	80	eighty
13	thirteen	90	ninety
14	fourteen	100	a hundred
15	fifteen	101	a hundred and one
16	sixteen	110	a hundred and ten
17	seventeen	120	a hundred and twenty
18	eighteen	200	two hundred
19	nineteen	1000	a thousand
20	twenty	1001	a thousand and one
21	twenty-one	1010	a thousand and ten
22	twenty-two	2000	two thousand
23	twenty-three	10,000	ten thousand
24	twenty-four	100,000	a hundred thousand
25	twenty-five	1,000,000	a million
40	forty	2,000,000	two million
50	fifty	1,000,000,000	a billion

R43 When you say or write in words a number over 100, you put *and* before the number expressed by the last two figures. For example, 203 is said or written *two hundred and three* and 2840 is said or written *two thousand, eight hundred and forty*.

Four hundred and eighteen men were killed and a hundred and seventeen wounded.

 And is often omitted in American English.

...one hundred fifty dollars.

R44 If you want to say or write in words a number between 1000 and 1,000,000, there are various ways of doing it. For example, the number 1872 can be said or written in words as

▶ eighteen hundred and seventy-two

▶ one thousand eight hundred and seventy-two

▶ one eight seven two

▶ eighteen seventy-two

Note that you cannot use *a* instead of *one* for the second way.

The third way is often used to identify something such as a room number. With telephone numbers, you always say each figure separately like this.

The last way is used if the number is a date.

R45 Unlike some other languages, in English when numbers over 9999 are written in figures, a comma is usually put after the fourth figure from the end, the seventh figure from the end, and so on, dividing the figures into groups of three. For example, 15,500 or 1,982,000. With numbers between 1000 and 9999, a comma is sometimes put after the first figure. For example 1,526.

When a number contains a full stop, the number or numbers after the full stop indicate a fraction. For example, 2.5 is the same as two and a half.

Ordinal numbers

R46 Here is a list of ordinal numbers. The list shows the patterns of forming ordinal numbers greater than 20.

1st	first	26th	twenty-sixth
2nd	second	27th	twenty-seventh
3rd	third	28th	twenty-eighth
4th	fourth	29th	twenty-nineth
5th	fifth	30th	thirtieth
6th	sixth	31st	thirty-first
7th	seventh	40th	fortieth
8th	eighth	41st	forty-first
9th	nineth	50th	fiftieth
10th	tenth	51st	fifty-first
11th	eleventh	60th	sixtieth
12th	twelfth	61st	sixty-first
13th	thirteenth	70th	seventieth
14th	fourteenth	71st	seventy-first
15th	fifteenth	80th	eightieth
16th	sixteenth	81st	eighty-first
17th	seventeenth	90th	ninetieth
18th	eighteenth	91st	ninty-first
19th	nineteenth	100th	hundredth
20th	twentieth	101st	hundred and first
21st	twenty-first	200th	two hundredth
22nd	twenty-second	1000th	thousandth
23rd	twenty-third	1,000,000th	millionth
24th	twenty-fourth	1,000,000,000th	billionth
25th	twenty-fifth		

R47   As shown in the above list, ordinals can be written in abbreviated form, for example in dates or headings, or in informal writing. You write the last two letters of the ordinal after the number expressed in figures. For example, *first* can be written as *1st*, *twenty-second* as *22nd*, *hundred and third* as *103rd*, and *fourteenth* as *14th*.

...on August 2nd.
...the 1st Division of the Sovereign's Escort.

Fractions and percentages

R48   You can write a fraction in figures, for example ½, ¼, ¾, and ⅔. These correspond to *a half*, *a quarter*, *three-quarters*, and *two-thirds* respectively.

R49   Fractions are often given in a special form as a number of hundredths. This type of fraction is called a **percentage**. For example, *three-hundredths*, expressed as a percentage, is *three per cent*. It can also be written as *three percent* or *3%*. A *half* can be expressed as *fifty per cent*, *fifty percent*, or *50%*.

About 60 per cent of our students are women.
Ninety percent of most food is water.

Before 1960 45% of British trade was with the Commonwealth.

You can use percentages on their own as noun phrases when it is clear what they refer to.

Ninety per cent were self employed.
...interest at 10% per annum.

Verb forms and the formation of verb phrases

R50   Verbs have several forms. These forms can be used on their own or combined with special verbs called **auxiliaries**. When a verb or a combination of a verb and an auxiliary is used in a clause, it is called a **verb phrase**. Verb phrases can be **finite** or **non-finite**. If a verb phrase is finite, it has a **tense**. A **non-finite** verb phrase contains a verb in the form of an **infinitive** or an **-ed** or **-ing participle**.

Verb phrases are used to refer to actions, states, and processes. The use of verb phrases in clauses to make statements is explained in Chapter 3.

R51   Verb phrases can be **active** or **passive**. You use an active verb phrase if you are concentrating on the performer of an action, and you use a passive verb phrase if you are concentrating on someone or something that is affected by an action. Further information on the use of passive verb phrases is given in Chapter 9 (9.8 to 9.24).

R52   Regular verbs have the following forms:

▶ a base form e.g. *walk*

▶ an s form e.g. *walks*

▶ an -*ing* participle e.g. *walking*

▶ a past form e.g. *walked*

The base form of a verb is the form that is used in the infinitive. It is the form that is given first in a dictionary where a verb is explained, and that is given in the lists in this grammar.

The s form of a verb consists of the base form with s on the end.

The -*ing* participle usually consists of the base form with *ing* on the end. It is sometimes called the **present participle**.

The past form of a verb usually consists of the base form with *ed* on the end.

In the case of regular verbs, the past form is used for the past tense and is also used as the *-ed* participle. It is sometimes called the past participle.

However, with many irregular verbs (see paragraph R72) there are two different forms:

▶ a past tense form e.g. *stole*

▶ an *-ed* participle form e.g. *stolen*

There are rules about the spelling of the different forms of verbs, depending on their endings. These are explained in paragraphs R54 to R70.

Certain verbs, especially common ones, have irregular forms. These are listed in paragraphs R72 to R75.

The forms of the auxiliaries *be*, *have*, and *do* are given in paragraph R80.

R53 Each verb form has various uses.

The base form is used for the present tense, the imperative, and the infinitive, and is used after modals.

The *s* form is used for the third person singular of the present tense.

The *-ing* participle is used for progressive forms, *-ing* adjectives, *-ing* nouns, and some clauses.

The past form is used for the past simple, and for the *-ed* participle of regular verbs.

The *-ed* participle is used for perfect forms, passives, *-ed* adjectives, and some clauses.

R54 The basic verb forms have been described in paragraph R52. The following paragraphs explain how the various forms of verbs are spelled. They also give details of verbs that have irregular forms. The forms of the auxiliaries *be*, *have*, and *do* are dealt with separately in paragraphs R80 to R88.

R55 The *s* form of most verbs consists of the base form of the verb with *s* added to the end.

| sing | → | sings |
| write | → | writes |

When the *s* follows one of the sounds /f/, /k/, /p/, /t/, or /θ/, it is pronounced /s/.

| break | → | breaks |
| keep | → | keeps |

When the *s* follows one of the sounds /s/, /z/, or /dʒ/, it is pronounced /ɪz/.

| dance | → | dances |
| manage | → | manages |

In most other cases the *s* is pronounced /z/.

| leave | → | leaves |
| refer | → | refers |

R56 With verbs whose base form ends in a consonant letter followed by *y*, you substitute *ies* for *y* to form the *s* form.

| try | → | tries |
| cry | → | cries |

R57 With verbs which end in *sh, ch, ss, x, zz,* or *o, es* rather than *s* is added to the base form of the verb. The *es* is pronounced /ɪz/ when it is added to a consonant sound, and pronounced /z/ when it is added to a vowel sound.

diminish → diminishes

reach → reaches

pass → passes

mix → mixes

buzz → buzzes

echo → echoes

R58 With one-syllable verbs that end in a single *s*, you usually add *ses*. Forms with a single *s* are more common in American English.

bus → busses → buses

gas → gasses → gases

R59 Most verbs have *-ing* participles formed by adding *ing* to the base form, and past forms formed by adding *ed* to the base form.

paint → painting → painted

rest → resting → rested

With all *-ing* participles, the *ing* is pronounced as a separate syllable: /ɪŋ/.

With verbs whose base form ends with one of the sounds /f/, /k/, /p/, /s/, /ʃ/, or /tʃ/, the *ed* of the past form is pronounced /t/. For example, *pressed* is pronounced /prest/ and *watched* is pronounced /wɒtʃt/.

With verbs whose base forms ends with the sound /d/ or /t/, the *ed* of the past form is pronounced /ɪd/. For example, *patted* is pronounced /pætɪd/ and *faded* is pronounced /feɪdɪd/.

With all other verbs, the *ed* of the past form is pronounced /d/. For example, *joined* is pronounced /dʒɔɪnd/ and *lived* is pronounced /lɪvd/.

R60 With most verbs that end in *e*, the *-ing* participle is formed by substituting *ing* for the final *e*. Similarly, you substitute *ed* for the final *e* to form the past form.

dance → dancing → danced

smile → smiling → smiled

fade → fading → faded

R61 In the case of a few verbs ending in *e*, you just add *ing* in the normal way to form the *-ing* participle. You still substitute *ed* for *e* to form the past.

singe → singeing → singed

agree → agreeing → agreed

Here is a list of these verbs:

age	dye	knee	tiptoe
agree	eye	queue	whinge
binge	flee	referee	
canoe	free	see	
disagree	glue	singe	

R62 To form the -*ing* participle of a verb that ends in *ie*, you substitute *ying* for *ie*.

tie   →   tying

Note that the past form of such verbs is regular, following the pattern in R60.

R63 To form the past form of a verb that ends in a consonant letter followed by *y*, you substitute *ied* for *y*.

cry   →   cried

Note that the -*ing* participle of such verbs is regular, following the pattern in R59.

R64 If the base form of a verb has one syllable and ends with a single vowel letter followed by a consonant letter, you double the final consonant letter before adding *ing* to form the -*ing* participle or *ed* to form the past form.

dip	→	dipping	→	dipped
trot	→	trotting	→	trotted

Note that this does not apply if the final consonant letter is *w*, *x*, or *y*.

row	→	rowing	→	rowed
box	→	boxing	→	boxed
play	→	playing	→	played

R65 The final consonant letter of some two-syllable verbs is also doubled. This happens when the second syllable ends in a single vowel letter followed by a consonant letter, and is stressed.

refer	→	referring	→	referred
equip	→	equipping	→	equipped

R66 In British English, when a two syllable verb ends in a single vowel letter followed by a single *l*, the *l* is doubled before *ing* or *ed* is added to it, even if there is no stress on the last syllable.

travel	→	travelling	→	travelled
quarrel	→	quarrelling	→	quarrelled

A few other verbs also have their final consonant letter doubled.

program	→	programming	→	programmed
worship	→	worshipping	→	worshipped
hiccup	→	hiccupping	→	hiccupped
kidnap	→	kidnapping	→	kidnapped
handicap	→	handicapping	→	handicapped

R67 All the verbs described in R66, except *handicap*, can have their -*ing* participle and past form spelled with a single consonant letter in American English.

travel	→	traveling	→	traveled
worship	→	worshiping	→	worshiped

R68 Here is a list of the verbs whose final consonant letter is doubled before *ing* and *ed* in both British and American English:

ban	blot	brim	chip	clot	cup
bar	blur	bug	chop	cram	dab
bat	bob	cap	clap	crib	dam
beg	brag	chat	clog	crop	dim

din	hum	plod	slim	tag	emit
dip	jam	plug	slip	tan	enrol
dot	jet	pop	slop	tap	enthral
drag	jig	prod	slot	thin	equip
drop	jog	prop	slum	throb	excel
drug	jot	rib	slur	tip	expel
drum	knit	rig	snag	top	incur
dub	knot	rip	snap	trap	instil
fan	lag	rob	snip	trek	occur
fit	lap	rot	snub	trim	omit
flag	log	rub	sob	trip	outwit
flap	lop	sag	spot	trot	patrol
flip	man	scan	squat	vet	propel
flop	mar	scar	stab	wag	rebel
fog	mob	scrap	star	wrap	rebut
fret	mop	scrub	stem	~	recap
gas	mug	ship	step	abet	recur
gel	nag	shop	stir	abhor	refer
glut	net	shred	stop	acquit	regret
grab	nip	shrug	strap	admit	remit
grin	nod	shun	strip	allot	repel
grip	pad	sin	strut	commit	submit
grit	pat	sip	stun	compel	transfer
grub	peg	skid	sun	confer	transmit
gun	pen	skim	swab	control	~
gut	pet	skin	swap	defer	handicap
hem	pin	skip	swat	deter	
hop	pit	slam	swig	distil	
hug	plan	slap	swot	embed	

Note that verbs such as *re-equip* and *unclog*, which consist of a prefix and one of the above verbs, also have their final consonant letter doubled.

R69 Here is a list of verbs whose final consonant letter is doubled before *ing* and *ed* in British English but not always in American English:

bedevil	equal	level	pummel	stencil
cancel	fuel	libel	quarrel	swivel
channel	funnel	marshal	refuel	total
chisel	gambol	marvel	revel	travel
dial	grovel	model	rival	tunnel
duel	hiccup	panel	shovel	unravel
enamel	initial	pedal	shrivel	worship
enrol	kidnap	pencil	snivel	yodel
enthral	label	program	spiral	

R70 With verbs ending in *c*, *king* and *ked* are usually added instead of *ing* and *ed*.

mimic → mimicking → mimicked

panic → panicking → panicked

R71 A large number of verbs have irregular forms, which are not formed by adding *ed* to the base form.

With regular verbs, the -*ed* participle is the same as the past form. However, with some irregular verbs, the two forms are different.

R72 The table opposite gives a list of irregular verbs and their forms.

Note that the past form and -*ed* participle of *read* appear the same as the base form but are pronounced differently. The base form is pronounced /riːd/ and the past form and -*ed* participle /red/. See a Cobuild dictionary for the pronunciation of irregular forms of verbs.

R73 Some verbs have more than one past form or -*ed* participle form. For example, the past form and -*ed* participle of *spell* can be either *spelled* or *spelt*, and the -*ed* participle of *prove* can be either *proved* or *proven*.

He burned several letters.
He burnt all his papers.

His foot had swelled to three times normal size.
His wrist had swollen up and become huge.

R74 Some verbs have two forms that can be used as the past form and the -*ed* participle. Here is a list of these verbs. The regular form is given first, although it may not be the more common one.

All of the irregular forms ending in *t* are far more common in British English than in American English, which generally uses the regular form for these verbs.

burn → burned, burnt

bust → busted, bust

dream → dreamed, dreamt

dwell → dwelled, dwelt

fit → fitted, fit

hang → hanged, hung

kneel → kneeled, knelt

lean → leaned, leant

leap → leaped, leapt

light → lighted, lit

smell → smelled, smelt

speed → speeded, sped

spell → spelled, spelt

spill → spilled, spilt

spoil → spoiled, spoilt

wet → wetted, wet

R75 Here is a list of verbs with two past forms:

bid → bid, bade

| wake | → | waked, woke |
| weave | → | weaved, wove |

Here is a list of verbs with two *-ed* participle forms:

bid	→	bid, bidden
mow	→	mowed, mown
prove	→	proved, proven
swell	→	swelled, swollen
wake	→	waked, woken
weave	→	weaved, woven

 In American English, *gotten* is usually used instead of *got* as the *-ed* participle of *get*. However, American English always uses *got* rather than *gotten* in two common constructions: *have got* (meaning *own* or *possess*), and *have got to* meaning *must*).

Have you got change for the parking meter?
You have got to start paying more attention to deadlines.

The past forms of these constructions in American English are never *had got*. Instead, they use the past form of *have*.

Did you have change for the parking meter?
She said I had to start paying more attention to deadlines.

Note that some verbs appear in both the above lists as they have a different past form and *-ed* participle form, each of which has more than one form.

base form	past form	-ed participle	base form	past form	-ed participle
arise	arose	arisen	catch	caught	caught
awake	awoke	awoken	choose	chose	chosen
bear	bore	borne	cling	clung	clung
beat	beat	beaten	come	came	come
become	became	become	cost	cost	cost
begin	began	begun	creep	crept	crept
bend	bent	bent	cut	cut	cut
bet	bet	bet	deal	dealt	dealt
bind	bound	bound	dig	dug	dug
bite	bit	bitten	dive	dove (Am)	dived
bleed	bled	bled	draw	drew	drawn
blow	blew	blown	drink	drank	drunk
break	broke	broken	drive	drove	driven
breed	bred	bred	eat	ate	eaten
bring	brought	brought	fall	fell	fallen
build	built	built	feed	fed	fed
burst	burst	burst	feel	felt	felt
buy	bought	bought	fight	fought	fought
cast	cast	cast	find	found	found

base form	past form	-ed participle	base form	past form	-ed participle
fit	fit (Am)	fit (Am)	ride	rode	ridden
flee	fled	fled	ring	rang	rung
fling	flung	flung	rise	rose	risen
fly	flew	flown	run	ran	run
forbear	forbore	forborne	saw	sawed	sawn
forbid	forbade	forbidden	say	said	said
forget	forgot	forgotten	see	saw	seen
forgive	forgave	forgiven	seek	sought	sought
forsake	forsook	forsaken	sell	sold	sold
forswear	forswore	forsworn	send	sent	sent
freeze	froze	frozen	set	set	set
get	got	got	sew	sewed	sewn
give	gave	given	shake	shook	shaken
go	went	gone	shed	shed	shed
grind	ground	ground	shine	shone	shone
grow	grew	grown	shoe	shod	shod
hear	heard	heard	shoot	shot	shot
hide	hid	hidden	show	showed	shown
hit	hit	hit	shrink	shrank	shrunk
hold	held	held	shut	shut	shut
hurt	hurt	hurt	sing	sang	sung
keep	kept	kept	sink	sank	sunk
know	knew	known	sit	sat	sat
lay	laid	laid	slay	slew	slain
lead	led	led	sleep	slept	slept
leave	left	left	slide	slid	slid
lend	lent	lent	sling	slung	slung
let	let	let	slink	slunk	slunk
lose	lost	lost	sow	sowed	sown
make	made	made	speak	spoke	spoken
mean	meant	meant	spend	spent	spent
meet	met	met	spin	spun	spun
pay	paid	paid	spread	spread	spread
put	put	put	spring	sprang	sprung
quit	quit	quit	stand	stood	stood
read	read	read	steal	stole	stolen
rend	rent	rent	stick	stuck	stuck

base form	past form	-ed participle	base form	past form	-ed participle
sting	stung	stung	tear	tore	torn
stink	stank	stunk	tell	told	told
strew	strewed	strewn	think	thought	thought
stride	strode	stridden	throw	threw	thrown
strike	struck	struck	thrust	thrust	thrust
string	strung	strung	tread	trod	trodden
strive	strove	striven	understand	understood	understood
swear	swore	sworn	wear	wore	worn
sweep	swept	swept	weep	wept	wept
swim	swam	swum	win	won	won
swing	swung	swung	wind	wound	wound
take	took	taken	wring	wrung	wrung
teach	taught	taught	write	wrote	written

R76 In some cases, different past forms or -ed participle forms relate to different meanings or uses of the verb. For example, the past form and the -ed participle of the verb *hang* is normally *hung*. However, *hanged* can also be used but with a different meaning. Check the different meanings in a Cobuild dictionary.

An Iron Cross hung from a ribbon around the man's neck.
He had been found guilty of murder hanged.

They had bid down the chemical company's stock.
He had bidden her to buy the best.

R77 Some verbs consist of more than one word, for example *browbeat* and *typeset*, and some consist of a prefix plus a verb, for example *undo* and *disconnect*.

His teachers underestimate his ability.
We are always trying to outdo our competitors.
The figures show that the government has mismanaged the economy.

R78 Verbs that consist of more than one word or of a prefix plus a verb usually inflect in the same way as the verbs that form their final part. For example, the past form of *foresee* is *foresaw* and the -ed participle is *foreseen*, and the past form and past -ed of *misunderstand* is *misunderstood*.

I underestimated him.
He had outdone himself.

I had misunderstood and mismanaged everything.
She had disappeared into the kitchen and reappeared with a flashlight.

R79 With many verbs of this type, the fact that they consist of two parts does not make any difference to their forms. They follow the normal spelling rules.

Here is a list of verbs whose second part is an irregular verb:

browbeat	miscast	overcome	overdo
broadcast	recast	undercut	undo
forecast	typecast	outdo	withdraw

overeat	mislead	beset	undertake
befall	remake	reset	foretell
forego	repay	typeset	retell
undergo	misread	outshine	rethink
outgrow	override	overshoot	overthrow
overheat	outrun	oversleep	misunderstand
mishear	overrun	misspell	rewind
behold	re-run	withstand	unwind
uphold	foresee	hamstring	rewrite
withhold	oversee	mistake	underwrite
mislay	outsell	overtake	
waylay	resell	retake	

Note the past forms and -ed participle of the verbs shown below, whose second part is a verb with alternative past forms and -ed participle.

refit	→	refitted	→	refitted
overhang	→	overhung	→	overhung
floodlight	→	floodlit	→	floodlit

Here is a list of compound verbs whose second part is an irregular verb:

bottle-feed	force-feed	baby-sit	proof-read	ghost-write
breast-feed	spoon-feed	lip-read	sight-read	

R80 The different forms of the auxiliaries *be*, *have*, and *do* are summarized in the table below.

	be		have		do
present simple: **with *I***	am	'm	have	've	do
with *you*, *we*, *they*, & plural noun groups	are	're			
with *he*, *she*, *it*, & singular noun groups	is	's	has	's	does
past simple: **with *I*, *he*, *she*, *it*, & singular noun groups**	was		had	'd	did
with *you*, *we*, *they*, & plural noun groups	were				
Participles: **present participle** **-ed participle**	being been		having had		doing done

R81 The present forms of *be* can usually be contracted and added to the end of the subject of the verb, whether it is a noun or a pronoun. This is often done in spoken English or in informal written English.

I'm interested in the role of women all over the world.
You're late.

We're making some progress.
It's a delightful country.

My car's just across the street.

The contracted forms of *be* are shown in the table above.

R82 Contracted forms of *be* are not used at the end of affirmative statements. The full form must be used instead. For example, you say *Richard's not very happy but Andrew is.* You cannot say *Richard's not very happy but Andrew's.*

However, you can use a contracted form of *be* at the end of a negative statement if it is followed by *not.* For example, *Mary's quite happy, but her mother's not'*

R83 When *be* is used in negative clauses, either the verb or *not* can be contracted. For more information on contractions in negative clauses, see paragraphs 5.61 to 5.62.

R84 The present and past forms of *have* can also be contracted. This is usually only done when *have* is being used as an auxiliary.

I've changed my mind.
This is the first party we've been to in months.

She's become a very interesting young woman.
I do wish you'd met Guy.

She's managed to keep it quiet.
We'd done a good job.

The contracted forms of *have* are shown in the table at paragraph R80.

R85 *'s* can be short for either *is* or *has.* You can tell what *'s* represents by looking at the next word. If *'s* represents *is*, it is followed by an *-ing* participle, complement, or adverbial. If it represents *has*, it is usually followed by an *-ed* participle.

She's going to be all right.
She's a lovely person.

She's gone to see some social work people.

R86 A noun ending in *'s* could also be a **possessive**. It is followed by another noun when this is the case. For more information on possessives see paragraphs 1.211 to 1.221.

R87 *Is* and *has* are written in full after nouns ending in *x, ch, sh, s,* or *z*, although in speech *has* is sometimes pronounced as /əz/ after these nouns.

R88 *'d* can be short for either *had* or *would.* You can tell what *'d* represents by looking at the next word. If *'d* represents *would*, it is followed by the base form of a verb. If it represents *had*, it is usually followed by an *-ed* participle.

We'd have to try to escape.
'It'd be cheaper to go by train,' Alan said.

At least we'd had the courage to admit it.
She'd bought new sunglasses with tinted lenses.

The formation of tenses

R89 A **finite verb phrase** is the type of verb phrase that goes with a subject. It contains a form of the **main verb** (the one that you are using to convey your meaning), and often one or more **auxiliaries**.

A finite verb phrase has the following structure:

(modal)(have)(be)(be) main verb.

You choose the elements in brackets according to, for example, whether you are talking about the past or the present, or whether you are concentrating on the performer of an action or the thing affected by it. They are called **auxiliaries**.

If you want to indicate possibility, or to show your attitude to your hearer or to what you are saying, you use a type of auxiliary called a **modal**. Modals must be followed by a base form (an infinitive without *to*). The use of modals is explained in Chapter 5 (5.94 to 5.258).

She might see us.
She could have seen us.

If you want to use a perfect form, you use a form of *have*. This must be followed by an *-ed* participle.

She has seen us.
She had been watching us for some time.

If you want to use a progressive form, you use a form of *be*. This must be followed by an *-ing* participle.

She was watching us.
We were being watched.

If you want to use the passive, you use a form of *be*. This must be followed by an *-ed* participle.

We were seen.
We were being watched.

If there is an auxiliary in front of the main verb, you use an appropriate form of the main verb, as mentioned above. If there is no auxiliary, you use an appropriate simple form.

The verb *do* is also used as an auxiliary, with simple forms, but only in questions, negative statements, and negative imperative clauses, or when you want to be very emphatic. It is followed by the base form of the main verb. Detailed information on the uses of *do* is given in Chapter 5.

Do you want me to do something about it?
I do not remember her.
I do enjoy being with you.

R90 A finite verb phrase always has a **tense**, unless it begins with a modal. **Tense** is the relationship between the form of a verb and the time to which it refers.

This section deals with the ways in which main verbs and auxiliaries can be used to construct different forms. The way in which particular forms are used to indicate particular times in relation to the time of speaking or to the time of an event is covered in paragraphs 4.7 to 4.69.

R91 When a verb is being used in a **simple form**, that is, the **present simple** or the **past simple**, it consists of just one word, a form of the main verb.

I feel tired.
Mary lived there for five years.

For **progressive** and **perfect** forms, one or more auxiliaries are used in combination with the main verb.

I am feeling reckless tonight.
I have lived here all my life.

R92   The first word of a finite verb phrase must agree with the subject of the clause. This affects the present simple, and all forms that begin with the present or past tense of *be* or the present tense of *have*.

For example, if the form is the present perfect and the subject is *John*, then the form of the auxiliary *have* must be *has*.

John has seemed worried lately.
She likes me.

Your lunch is getting cold.

R93   In this section the examples given are declarative clauses. The order of words in questions is different from the order in declarative clauses. See paragraphs 5.10 to 5.36 for information about this.

R94   **Progressive forms** are constructed using an appropriate tense of the auxiliary *be* and the *-ing* participle. Detailed information on how to construct these forms is included below. The uses of progressive forms are explained in detail in paragraphs 4.7 to 4.69.

R95   The formation of active sentences is explained below. The formation of the passive is explained in paragraphs R109 to R118.

R96   The **present simple** form of a verb is the same as the base form with all subjects except the third person singular.

I want a breath of air.
We advise everyone to call half an hour before they arrive.
They give you a certificate and then tell you to get a job.

The third person singular form is the s form.

Flora puts her head back, and laughs again.
Money decides everything, she thought.
Mr Paterson plays Phil Hoskins in the TV drama.

R97   The **present progressive** is formed by using the present tense of *be* and the *-ing* participle of the main verb.

People who have no faith in art are running the art schools.
The garden industry is booming.
Things are changing.

R98   The **past simple** form of a regular verb is formed by adding *ed* to the base form of regular verbs.

The moment he entered the classroom all eyes turned on him.
He walked out of the kitchen and climbed the stairs.
It was dark by the time I reached East London.

R99   The **past progressive** is formed by using the past tense of *be* and the *-ing* participle of the main verb.

Their questions were beginning to drive me crazy.
We believed we were fighting for a good cause.
At the time, I was dreading the exam.

R100   The **present perfect** is formed by using the present tense of *have* and the *-ed* participle of the main verb.

Advances have continued, but productivity has fallen.
Football has become international.
I have seen this before.

R101 The **present perfect progressive** is formed by using the present perfect of *be* and the *-ing* participle of the main verb.

Howard has been working hard over the recess.
What we have been describing is very simple.
Their shares have been going up.

R102 The **past perfect** is formed by using *had* and the *-ed* participle of the main verb.

The Indian summer had returned for a day.
Everyone had liked her.
Murray had resented the changes I had made.

R103 The **past perfect progressive** is formed by using *had been* and the *-ing* participle of the main verb.

She did not know how long she had been lying there.
For ten years of her life, teachers had been making up her mind for her.
I had been showing a woman around with her little boy.

R104 There are several ways of referring to the future in English. The simple future involves using the modal *will* or *shall* and the base form of the verb.

It is exactly the sort of scheme he will like.
My receptionist will help you choose the frames.
Don't drop crumbs or we shall have mice.

In spoken English, the contracted form *'ll* is usually used instead of *will* or *shall*, unless you want to be emphatic.

Send him into the Army; he'll learn a bit of discipline there.
As soon as we get the tickets they'll be sent out to you.
Next week we'll be looking at the history of dance.

R105 If the full forms are used, *will* is generally used if the subject of the verb is not *I* or *we*. *Shall* is sometimes used if the subject is *I* or *we*, otherwise *will* is used.

Inflation is rising and will continue to rise.
I shall be away tomorrow.

R106 The **future progressive** is formed by using *will* or *shall*, followed by *be* and the *-ing* participle of the main verb.

Indeed, we will be opposing that policy.
Ford manual workers will be claiming a ten per cent pay rise.
I shall be leaving soon.

R107 The **future perfect** is formed by using *will* or *shall*, followed by *have* and the *-ed* participle of the main verb.

Long before you return, they will have forgotten you.
By next week will have reached the end of the book.
By that time, I shall have retired.

R108 The **future perfect progressive** is formed by using *will* or *shall*, followed by *have been* and the *-ing* participle of the main verb.

By March, I will have been doing this job for six years.
Saturday week, I will have been going out with Susan for three months.

R109 Passive forms are constructed using an appropriate tense of *be* and the *-ed* participle of the main verb. Detailed information on forming the passive is given below.

R110 The **present simple passive** is formed by using the present simple of *be* and the -*ed* participle of the main verb.

> *The earth is baked by the sun into a hard, brittle layer.*
> *If you are on a full-time course you are treated as your parents' dependent.*
> *Specific subjects are discussed.*

R111 The **present progressive passive** is formed by using the present progressive of *be* and the -*ed* participle of the main verb.

> *The buffet counter is being arranged by the attendant.*
> *It is something quite irrelevant to what is being discussed.*
> *Jobs are still being lost.*

R112 The **past simple passive** is formed by using the past simple of *be* and the -*ed* participle of the main verb.

> *No date was announced for the talks.*
> *The walls were covered with pictures of actors.*
> *Several new cottages were built on the land.*

R113 The **past progressive passive** is formed by using the past progressive of *be* and the -*ed* participle of the main verb.

> *The stage was being set for future profits.*
> *Before long, machines were being used to create codes.*
> *Strenuous efforts were being made last night to end the dispute.*

R114 The **present perfect passive** is formed by using the present perfect of *be* and the -*ed* participle of the main verb.

> *The guest-room window has been mended.*
> *I think real progress has been made.*
> *The dirty plates have been stacked in a pile on the table.*

R115 The **past perfect passive** is formed by using *had been* and the -*ed* participle of the main verb.

> *They had been taught to be critical.*
> *They had been driven home in the station wagon.*

R116 The **future passive** is formed by using *will* or *shall*, followed by *be* and the -*ed* participle of the main verb.

> *His own authority will be undermined.*
> *Congress will be asked to approve an increase of 47.5 per cent.*

R117 The **future perfect passive** is formed by using *will* or *shall*, followed by *have been* and the -*ed* participle of the main verb.

> *Another goal will have been achieved.*
> *The figures will have been distorted by the effects of the strike.*

R118 The future progressive passive and the perfect progressive passive are rarely used.

R119 The table below gives a summary of the active and passive forms. The passive forms marked with a star are very rarely used.

	active	passive
present simple	He eats it.	It is eaten.
present progressive	He is eating it.	It is being eaten.
present perfect	He has eaten it.	It has been eaten.
present perfect progressive	He has been eating it.	It has been being eaten.*
past simple	He ate it.	It was eaten.
past progressive	He was eating it.	It was being eaten.
past perfect	He had eaten it.	It had been eaten.
past perfect progressive	He had been eating it.	It had been being eaten.*
future	He will eat it.	It will be eaten.
future progressive	He will be eating it.	It will be being eaten.*
future perfect	He will have eaten it.	It will have been eaten.
future perfect progressive	He will have been eating it.	It will have been being eaten.*

R120   There are some verbs that are not usually used in the progressive, and some that are not used in the progressive in one or more of their main meanings.

Here is a list of verbs that are not usually used in the progressive:

astonish	consist	have	own	suppose
be	contain	know	possess	suspect
believe	deserve	last	resemble	understand
belong	envy	matter	satisfy	
concern	exist	owe	seem	

Verbs of this type are sometimes called **stative verbs**. Verbs that can be used in the progressive are sometimes called **dynamic verbs**. For more information about **stative verbs**, see paragraph 4.69.

There are other verbs that are traditionally described as stative, but that are sometimes used in the progressive, particularly in less formal texts. For more information about these verbs, see 4.69.

R121   *Be* is not generally used as a main verb in the progressive with adjectives that indicate permanent characteristics, or with attributes that do not relate to behaviour. However, *be* is used in the progressive to indicate someone's behaviour at a particular time.

He is extremely nice.
He was an American.

You 're being very silly.

Have is not used as a main verb in the progressive when it indicates possession, but it is sometimes used in the progressive when it indicates that someone is doing something.

I have two dinghies.
We were just having a philosophical discussion.

R122 Some verbs have very specific senses in which they are not used in the progressive. For example, *smell* is often used in the progressive when it means *to smell something*, but rarely when it means *to smell of something*. Compare the sentences *I was just smelling your flowers*, and *Your flowers smell lovely*.

Here is a list of verbs that are not usually used in the progressive when they have the meanings indicated:

appear (seem)	measure (have length)
depend (be related to)	recognize (identify a person)
feel (have an opinion)	smell (of something)
fit (be suitable/be the right size)	taste (of something)
hear (be aware of a sound)	weigh (have weight)
mean (have a particular meaning)	

R123 The **imperative** form of a verb is regarded as finite, because it can stand as the verb of a main clause. However, it does not show tense in the same way as other finite verb phrases. It is always in the base form. See paragraphs 5.37 to 5.41 for the uses of the **imperative**.

Stop being silly.
Come here.

Infinitives and participles

R124 Infinitives and -*ing* participles are used after certain verbs such as *stop*, *like*, and *want* (see paragraphs 3.182 to 3.212) and -*ing* and -*ed* participles also used in certain **subordinate clauses** (see the section on subordinate clauses in Chapter 8). Infinitives and -*ing* participles are also used in some structures with **impersonal *it*** (see paragraphs 9.31 to 9.45).

To-infinitives are also used after some nouns and adjectives (see paragraphs 2.293 to 2.302, and 2.51 to 2.62). You can also use -*ing* participles as the objects of prepositions.

Participles and infinitives can have objects, complements, or adverbials after them, just like verbs that have a tense. A clause beginning with a *to*-infinitive is called a *to*-infinitive clause, a clause beginning with an -*ing* participle is called an -*ing* participle clause, and a clause beginning with an -*ed* participle is called an -*ed* participle clause.

R125 The order of auxiliaries is the same as for verbs that have a tense (see paragraph R89).

R126 The active **to-infinitive** consists of *to* and the base form of the verb. This is sometimes simply called the **infinitive**.

I want to escape from here.
I asked David to go with me.

R127 The active **infinitive without to** consists of the base form of the verb. It is sometimes called the **bare infinitive**.

They helped me get settled here.

R128 Other active infinitive forms are occasionally used.

The **present progressive infinitive** consists of *to be* or *be*, followed by the -*ing* participle.

It is much better for young children to be living at home.

The **perfect** or **past infinitive** consists of *to have* or *have*, followed by the -*ed* participle.

Only two are known to have defected.
She must have drowned.

The **perfect** or **past progressive infinitive** consists of *to have been* or *have been*, followed by the *-ing* participle.

I seem to have been eating all evening.

R129 There are also **passive infinitives**. The ordinary **passive infinitive** consists of *to be* or *be*, followed by the *-ed* participle.

I didn't want to be caught off guard.
He let it be known that he would be home all evening.

The **perfect** or **past passive infinitive** consists of *to have been* or *have been*, followed by the *-ed* participle.

He seems to have been completely forgotten.

R130 The table below gives a summary of infinitives. The passive infinitives marked with a star are very rarely used.

	active	passive
present progressive **perfect** **perfect progressive**	(to) eat (to) be eating (to) have eaten (to) have been eating	(to) be eaten (to) be being eaten* (to) have been eaten (to) have been being eaten*

R131 The **-ing participle** is used as a verb phrase, usually with an active meaning.

You could play me a tune, said Simon, sitting down.
He could keep in touch with me by writing letters.

R132 Combinations beginning with *having* are occasionally used.

The **perfect** or **past-*ing* form** consists of *having* and the *-ed* participle.

Ash, having forgotten his fear, had become bored and restless.

R133 There are also combinations beginning with *being* and *having*, which have a passive meaning.

The ordinary **passive -*ing* form** consists of *being* and the *-ed* participle.

...fears that patients would resent being interviewed by a computer.

The **perfect** or **past -*ing* form** consists of *having been* and the *-ed* participle.

Having been declared insane, he was confined in a prison hospital.
They were taken to hospital after having been wounded by gunshot.

R134 The table below gives a summary of *-ing* forms. The *-ing* form marked with a star is very rarely used.

	active	passive
perfect **perfect progressive**	eating having eaten having been eating	being eaten having been eaten having been being eating*

R135 The **-ed participle** is also used as a verb phrase, with a passive meaning.

Stunned by the attack, the enemy were overwhelmed.
When challenged, she seemed quite surprised.

Forming adverbs

R136 The uses of adverbs are explained in Chapters 2, 4, 6, and 10.

R137 Most adverbs are related to adjectives in form, and often in meaning. They are formed by adding *ly* to the adjective. For information on which adjectives you can add *ly* to, see paragraphs 6.17 to 6.27.

sad	→	sadly
cheerful	→	cheerfully
private	→	privately
accidental	→	accidentally
surprising	→	surprisingly

R138 Sometimes the formation is slightly different.

With adjectives ending in *le*, you replace the *le* with *ly*.

suitable	→	suitably
terrible	→	terribly
gentle	→	gently

Note that *whole* has the related adverb *wholly*.

R139 With adjectives ending in *y*, you replace the *y* with *ily*.

easy	→	easily
satisfactory	→	satisfactorily

Note that one-syllable adjectives ending in *y* usually have *ly* added, in the normal way.

wry	→	wryly
shy	→	shyly

Note that the adverb related to *dry* can be spelled *drily* or *dryly*.

R140 With adjectives ending in *ic*, you add *ally*.

automatic	→	automatically
tragic	→	tragically

Note that *public* has the related adverb *publicly*.

R141 With a few adjectives ending in *e* (not *le*), you replace the *e* with *ly*.

due	→	duly
true	→	truly
undue	→	unduly
eerie	→	eerily

R142 With *full* and *dull*, you just add *y*.

full	→	fully
dull	→	dully

R143 Note that *ly* is not generally added to adjectives ending in *ed* to form adverbs. However, here is a list of adverbs that are formed in this way:

absent-mindedly	delightedly	half-heartedly	single-handedly
admittedly	deservedly	heatedly	supposedly
allegedly	determinedly	hurriedly	undoubtedly
assuredly	distractedly	light-heartedly	unexpectedly
belatedly	doggedly	markedly	unhurriedly
blessedly	exaggeratedly	pointedly	wholeheartedly
contentedly	excitedly	repeatedly	wickedly
crookedly	fixedly	reportedly	
decidedly	frenziedly	reputedly	
dejectedly	guardedly	resignedly	

R144 A few adverbs that end in *ly* are related to nouns.

These include some time adverbs.

day	→	daily
fortnight	→	fortnightly
hour	→	hourly
month	→	monthly
quarter	→	quarterly
week	→	weekly
year	→	yearly

Note the spelling of *daily*. These words are also themselves used as adjectives. Other adverbs related to nouns are shown below.

name	→	namely
part	→	partly
purpose	→	purposely
body	→	bodily

R145 A few adverbs ending in *ly* are not related to any adjective or noun.

accordingly	jokingly	manfully
exceedingly	longingly	presumably

R146 Here is a list of adverbs that have the same form as adjectives:

alike	far	further	long
all right	fast	hard	loud
alone	fine	high	low
clean	first	just	next
deep	free	kindly	non-stop
direct	freelance	last	off-hand
even	full	late	only
extra	full-time	little	outright

overall	pretty	slow	straight	wide
part-time	quick	solo	tight	wrong
past	right	still	well	

Note that the adverb is sometimes not related in meaning to the adjective whose form it shares. Check the meanings in a Cobuild dictionary.

With some of these words, there are also related forms ending in *ly*.

cleanly	finely	hardly	lately	slowly
directly	firstly	highly	loudly	tightly
deeply	freely	justly	quickly	widely
evenly	fully	lastly	rightly	wrongly

Note that these *ly* forms sometimes have the same meaning as the other adverb form, and sometimes not.

The time adverbials ending in *ly*, which are mentioned in paragraph R144, also have the same form as adjectives.

R147   Note that **ordinal numbers** are used both as modifiers and as adverbs. They also have related adverbs ending in *ly*.

R148   Here is a list of adverbs that are not related to any adjective:

afresh	besides	indeed	otherwise	though
alas	doubtless	instead	perhaps	thus
alike	either	likewise	quite	together
almost	enough	maybe	rather	too
aloud	forthwith	meanwhile	regardless	very
also	furthermore	more	so	whatsoever
altogether	half	moreover	somehow	
anyhow	hence	much	somewhat	
anyway	hereby	nevertheless	therefore	
apart	however	nonetheless	thereupon	

R149   Time adverbials and many adverbs of place are also not related to adjectives. See Chapters 4 and 6 for lists of these adverbs.

Forming comparative and superlative adverbs

R150   Information on how to use **comparatives** and **superlatives** of adverbs, and which adverbs have them, is given in Chapter 6 (6.30 to 6.35).

R151   The comparative of an adverb usually consists of the normal form of the adverb preceded by *more*.

freely	→	more freely
appropriately	→	more appropriately

R152 The superlative of an adverb usually consists of the normal form of the adverb preceded by *most*.

commonly	→	most commonly
eagerly	→	most eagerly

R153 A few very common adverbs have comparatives and superlatives that are single words and not formed using *more* and *most*.

Well has the comparative *better* and the superlative *best*.

She would ask him later, when she knew him <u>better</u>.

I have to find out what I can do <u>best</u>.

Badly has the comparative *worse* and the superlative *worst*.

She was treated far <u>worse</u> than any animal.

The manufacturing industries were hit <u>worst</u>.

Adverbs that have the same form as adjectives have the same comparatives and superlatives as the adjectives. For example, the comparative and superlative of the adverb *fast* are *faster* and *fastest*, and the comparative and superlative of the adverb *hard* are *harder* and *hardest*.

Prices have been rising <u>faster</u> than incomes.

You probably learn <u>quicker</u> by having lessons.

The older people work <u>the hardest</u>.

The ones with the shortest legs run <u>the slowest</u>.

R154 Here is a list of time adverbials and adverbs of place that have comparative and superlative forms. See Chapter 4 (4.70, 4.114, and 4.123) and Chapter 6 (6.60). Note that a few have irregular comparatives and superlatives.

early	→	earlier	→	earliest
late	→	later (no superlative)		
soon	→	sooner (no superlative)		
long	→	longer	→	longest
deep	→	deeper	→	deepest
far	→	farther, further	→	farthest, furthest
near	→	nearer	→	nearest
close	→	closer	→	closest

Grammar section

The grammar of business English

The grammar of academic English

The grammar of business English

Introduction

There are certain areas of life and activity where particular features of language are found more frequently than in other areas. For example, doctors and engineers commonly use very specific vocabulary in their work-related communication.

Apart from specialized vocabulary, there are also grammatical patterns that occur more frequently in particular contexts. This section looks at forms that are common in the field of business and commerce. Examples of how language is used are organized into four areas:

▶ Networking
▶ Negotiating
▶ Presenting
▶ Meetings

In many cases, of course, the language that is described can be used in more than one of these topic areas.

Networking

Making social and business arrangements

The dialogue below is an example of the type of conversation that might take place between two people who want to make an arrangement to meet at a later time.

A Do you want to meet up for lunch sometime next week?

B Yes. That would be nice. We can talk about the FCL deal. I'm not in on Monday. I'm going to work from home. How about next Tuesday?

A Let's see. No, I can't. I'm taking some clients to the riverside development. What about Wednesday?

B I'm going to Germany on Wednesday. My flight leaves around five so I don't need to get away until after lunch. Is that okay?

A Fine. Let's meet at one.

use of verb forms with future meaning

You can use the **present progressive** (see 4.60) to talk about future arrangements that you would put in a diary. Normally these arrangements involve other people.

We're having a meeting to discuss the proposal next Tuesday.

The people from ILC are coming for lunch at two.

When future arrangements are not firm plans, but it is your intention that they will happen, you use *be going to* followed by an infinitive (see 4.58).

I'm going to have an early night because I'm tired.

We'll have some time after the meeting so we're going to explore the old part of the city.

You use the **present simple** to talk about events in schedules such as transport timetables or conference programmes (see 4.60).

Our flight leaves at six and gets in at eight.

The morning plenary session starts at nine thirty.

expressions for making suggestions

There are several ways in which you can make suggestions about what you and someone else should do.

You can use *Let* followed by *us* shortened to *Let's* (see 5.41).

Let's have a break and go for a coffee.

Let's stay in contact.

You can use a question beginning with *Shall we* (see 5.188).

Shall we meet outside the restaurant?

Shall we reward ourselves with a little lunch?

You can use a question beginning with *Why don't we* (see 5.48).

Why don't we have a working breakfast in the hotel?

Why don't we stay an extra day?

You can use a question beginning with *What about* or *How about* in front of a noun phrase (see 5.48).

How about a drink after the meeting?

How about next Sunday?

What about the twentieth of March?

Asking for and confirming information

To form the different type of commonly used questions in English you can use a variety of structures, where the word order and the use of auxiliaries can be confusing. The dialogue below is a phone call which might take place between two people where details of an order are discussed.

A   Hello. I'm phoning about an order. The ID number is 28443AB.

B   *When did you place the order* please?

A   Last week.

B   Sorry. *What was the order number again?*

A   28443AB.

B   Oh yes, it was for some switcher units, *wasn't it?*

A   That's right. Can you tell me if it's been processed yet?

B   Yes. They were out of stock but we got some in yesterday. *Didn't you get an email?*

A   Er, no. *Haven't they been sent off yet?*

B   They went off this morning.

A   So *do you have any idea when we can expect delivery?*

B   They should be with you tomorrow.

A   Okay. Thanks.

yes/no questions

When you are using the present simple or past simple form of *be* you simply put the verb at the beginning of the clause, followed by the subject (see 5.14).

Are you with me so far?

Is Simon up to the job?

Were they at the meeting?

When the verb is not *be* you need to use an auxiliary verb (or *do*, *does*, or *did*), followed by the subject and then the main verb (see 5.12 and 5.13).

Is he staying here tonight?

Do you work in a team?

Did they want to talk to me?

Will they accept that?

Have you got the figures with you?

If there is more than one auxiliary verb, the first auxiliary comes at beginning of the clause, followed by the subject and then other auxiliaries and the main verb.

Has the problem been reported?

Have they been waiting long?

wh-questions

If you are using the present simple or past simple form of *be*, the verb goes after the wh-word and in front of the subject (see 5.26).

How was your meeting?

Where is the customer?

So where were your auditors during all of this?

If you are using the present simple or the past simple of any verb except *be*, you put *do*, *does*, or *did* in front of the subject (see 5.26).

Which department did you want?

Who do you work for?

How did she make the decision?

What does he really think about the deal?

When a wh-word is the **subject** of a verb, or when it forms part of the subject, the word order is the same as in an **affirmative clause** (see 5.25).

Who invited you?

What happened earlier on?

Which bid won?

other types of question

You can use indirect questions like *Can you tell me*, *Could you tell me*, *Do you know* and *Have you any idea* in order to be more polite (see 5.15).

For yes/no questions, you use *if* or *whether* followed by a clause with affirmative word order.

Can you tell me if he got my message?

Do you know whether the units have arrived?

For wh-questions, you use a wh-word followed by a clause with affirmative word order.

Could you tell me what you've got on today?

Have you any idea what it would cost?

You can ask for confirmation that something is true by making a statement, and then adding a **question tag** such as *isn't it?* or *doesn't she?* (see 5.16 to 5.22).

They work on Saturdays, <u>don't they</u>?

You can park there, <u>can't you</u>?

You can use a **negative question** to express surprise at a situation.

<u>Didn't you arrange</u> to meet them at the airport?

<u>Wasn't</u> the meeting at nine?

<u>Haven't you finished</u> yet?

Talking about experience

talking about the present

You use the **present simple** to talk about permanent facts and routines (see 4.9 to 4.11).

We <u>offer</u> a wide range of services for the bio industry.

Every week, Susan <u>drives</u> to Edmonton for a meeting with the factory manager.

The first thing we <u>do</u> is a site survey.

You use the **present progressive** to talk about current situations when you want to emphasize that they are temporary or in progress at the time of speaking (see 4.17 to 4.19).

We <u>are updating</u> our flight rules to adapt to the new scenario.

Users <u>are looking</u> at other ways of financing IT projects.

He<u>'s staying</u> there as the guest of our Taiwan-based supplier.

talking about finished past situations

If you want to talk about a situation or an event that happened at a particular time in the past which is finished, you use the **past simple**. Time expressions like *last week* and *a year ago*, which refer to finished time periods in the past, can be used to make the time reference clear (see 4.27 to 4.29).

Ballmer <u>flew</u> to California last week and proposed the merger.

After Harvard, he <u>studied</u> at Oxford University.

Ms. Caridi previously <u>worked</u> in the legal department at Lehman Brothers.

You use the **past progressive** to emphasize an action in progress or to give the background context for events (see 4.31 and 4.32).

▶ The company <u>was losing</u> money, so he decided to sell.

The plant <u>was making</u> a profit of $250,000 a year and the market <u>was growing</u> steadily.

talking about past situations in relation to the present

The **present perfect simple** can be used to talk about:

▶ experiences, without stating a specific time

▶ events and situations that started in the past and continue up to the present

▶ events and situations that have an immediate effect on the present.

You cannot use time expressions like *yesterday*, *last year*, or *at Christmas* with the present perfect simple (see 4.33 to 4.35).

Yes, I've bumped into him a number of times.
We've met with all the major shareholders.
Spending has risen steadily since the beginning of the year.
Have you brought the report with you?

You use the **present perfect progressive**:

▶ when you want to talk about situations that started in the past, that may or may not be completed, but that you see as temporary

▶ when you want to emphasize duration (see 4.36).

We have been looking for a European partner for some time.
The company has been working hard to reduce its overhead.

talking about a particular time in the past

If you want to show that one event happened before another in the past you can use the **past perfect** (see 4.37).

When people left the meeting, they were more enthusiastic than when they had arrived.
Before the negotiations started, they had decided to give employees a 4% pay rise.

Negotiating

Making and modifying proposals

softening the message

You can use **comparatives** to show that you are prepared to negotiate on a particular point (see 2.103 to 2.111).

We need a more flexible arrangement.
I'm looking for figure closer to three dollars sixty a unit.
Would you be happier with a fixed rate?

You can use the **modals** would, could, may and might to make your message less direct.

We might be able drop the price.
Could we look at that side of your proposal later?
Would you consider reducing discounts?

thinking about possible future events and exploring possibilities

The **modals** could, may and might are also used to say that a particular result or situation is possible (see 5.126).

There may be a slight delay.
Yes, that might be possible.
Yes, I can see that this could have great potential.

You can use **conditional sentences** to discuss options and explore possibilities in a hypothetical way (see 8.25 to 8.42).

If you could give us exclusivity, we can settle this now.
The discount could be bigger if you increased the quantity.
If I drop the price, have we got a deal?
Unless you can show a bit of flexibility, we might as well call it a day.

Rejecting ideas and proposals

distancing yourself from a situation

To distance yourself from an opinion, and therefore sound less direct, you can use the **passive** form of a **reporting verb** with *it* as the **impersonal subject** (see 7.69).

It was understood that if we were successful in securing the takeover, Sarong would become a part of International Latex.

It is assumed that share prices will rise as a result of the operation.

It was agreed that the details would remain confidential.

being diplomatic

You can use a **qualifier** such as *a little*, *a bit*, or *rather* to make a negative message seem less strong (see 2.162).

That sounds a little expensive.

They may be a bit late, I'm afraid.

Unfortunately, we were rather disappointed with the quality of the last delivery.

Expressions like *not very*, *not totally*, *not completely*, and *not entirely* followed by a positive adjective sound more diplomatic than using a negative adjective.

We aren't totally convinced by the idea of using road transport.

I wouldn't be very happy with that arrangement.

You don't seem absolutely certain about that.

The **past progressive** can be used to make a statement more indirect in order to be polite (see 4.31 and 4.32).

We were expecting to hear a new proposal today.

I was aiming to establish a framework for further discussion.

We were hoping to reach agreement about this before we go.

Presenting

Describing change

the past compared to the present

You can use the **present perfect simple** to talk about events or situations that are still important in the present (see 4.33).

The FTSE Index has strengthened further since this morning.

We have made changes based on your concerns and feedback.

the present moment

To talk about change that is still in progress at the present moment, you can use the **present progressive** (see 4.19).

The economy is growing, but if we look closer there are some worrying trends.

In the country's major cities, the quality of life is improving.

Making predictions

opinions about the future

You can use *will* when you are certain about a situation in the future (see 4.53).

The cuts will certainly have a negative effect on the economy.
I believe this attitude will soon become the norm.

You can also use *be going to* instead of *will* to make predictions (see 4.58).

She predicts that earnings are going to come down sharply.
We are trying to decide whether the economy is going to go into recession.

expressing a negative opinion about the future

If you want to make a negative prediction, it sounds more polite to introduce an affirmative clause with a phrase like *I don't think* than to use a negative clause.

I don't think this will go down well with the union.
I don't think it's going to be a great success.

degrees of certainty about the future

You can use *could*, *may*, or *might* to say that it is possible that something will happen (see 5.126).

These economic problems could cause huge problems for the rest of Europe.
New technology might be able to halve the amount of water we use.
The market may eventually accomplish what environmentalists want.

You use *be likely* followed by a *to*-infinitive to say something will probably happen.

Emerging economies are likely to face continuing problems.

You use *be bound* followed by a *to*-infinitive to say strongly that something is certain to happen in the future (see 5.234).

The pressure on margins is bound to make success difficult.

Contrasts and comparisons

concessive clauses

You use conjunctions like *while*, *although*, *in spite of*, and *despite* to contrast one idea with another (see 8.66).

Until now, only 8,000 people have registered with the site, although the company said the number is still increasing.
In spite of the crisis, sales are actually up on last year.
Retail sales are plummeting, while consumer prices are rising.

Whilst and *whereas* are more formal.

In France there was a small improvement, whereas there was no change in Germany.
Micro's online store is almost empty, whilst Azar's has nearly 50,000 products.

making comparisons

You can use an adjective with either -er added to the end (*cheaper*, *older*) or *more* placed in front of the adjective (*more expensive,more interesting*), followed by *than* (see 2.103 to 2.111).

The chip is <u>more economical than</u> a dedicated system.

Kondex is <u>bigger than</u> Gartex in terms of sales.

You can also use *not as … as* or *not so … as* to compare things (see 2.128).

Our factories are still <u>not as efficient as</u> the car plants in Japan.
Traditional forms of advertising are <u>not as effective as</u> they used to be.

emphasizing degrees of difference

You can use *much*, *a lot* or *far* in front of comparative adjective forms to emphasize a big difference.

Manufacturers are <u>much more cautious</u> than before about investment plans.
The job provides her with a <u>far greater</u> challenge than ordinary office work would.

You can use *slightly*, *a bit* or *a little* to emphasize small differences.

The first-quarter increase was <u>slightly higher</u> at 1.2 %.
If anything, European and Pacific Rim executives are <u>a little more aggressive</u> than the Japanese.

To emphasize small differences with the *not as … as* structure you can add *quite*.

But by other measures, oil is <u>not quite as expensive as</u> it seems.

Linking ideas

You can show what sort of connection there is between one sentence and another by using sentence connectors. In a presentation, these connectors prepare the listener for what is coming next.

adding strength to your argument

Connectors such as *on top of that* and *at the same time* can be used to add strength to your argument. In writing, or in more formal situations, you can use *moreover* or *furthermore* (see 10.49).

The financial crisis continues. <u>On top of that</u>, exceptional weather has devastated crops.
Unemployment has grown rapidly. <u>At the same time</u>, there is low demand for existing skills.
Experts predict that the downturn will be less severe than expected. <u>Furthermore</u>, banks plan to lend more freely in the next three months.

contrast

You use connectors like *however*, *on the other hand*, or *nevertheless* when you want to give another point of view (see 10.51).

If you want job security, this is not the post for you. <u>On the other hand</u>, the salary is good.
There was a fall in sales last month. <u>However</u>, revenue from digital products rose by nearly 20% in the first half.
It is necessary for foreign currency traders to think quickly and accurately. <u>Nevertheless</u>, mistakes do occasionally occur.

cause and effect

When you want to show that the fact or situation you are mentioning is a result

BUSINESS ENGLISH

of what you have just referred to, you can begin your statement using a connector like *so* or *as a result*. If you want to sound more formal you can use *consequently* or *therefore* (see 10.52).

Another 3,100 jobs were lost last year. <u>So</u> people no longer trust the company.

We lost sight of what our customers wanted. <u>As a result</u>, sales slumped.

Confidence is still low. <u>Consequently</u>, firms are not willing to make new investments.

Distancing yourself

the passive

You use the passive when you want to focus on actions, views and decisions, rather than on the people responsible for them (see 9.8 to 9.24). It is frequently used in reports, and it is more common in written English.

In 2006, 18.3 % of the world's electricity <u>was produced</u> using renewable sources.

When materials <u>were coated</u> in the substance, the plating remained stable at room temperature.

The passive is often used to describe processes with adjuncts like *first*, *second*, *then*, and *finally* to indicate order (see 10.54).

<u>First</u>, the raw data <u>is collated</u> in tables, It <u>is then prepared</u> for processing. <u>Finally</u>, the data model <u>is produced</u>.

Meetings

Interrupting

can, could

When you are participating in a meeting you can use *can I* and *could I* to interrupt politely. *Could* is more polite than *can*.

<u>Can I</u> ask a question here?

<u>Could I</u> just interrupt here for a minute?

Making suggestions

Can and *could* are also used for making suggestions.

<u>Could we</u> maybe develop a new payment system?

<u>Can we</u> ask Network Solutions to help?

To sound more persuasive you can use a negative question.

<u>Couldn't we</u> ask them to come in for a demonstration?

<u>Can't we</u> do this later?

Let's ..., Why don't we ...

You can also use *Let's ...* and *Why don't we ...* to make suggestions.

<u>Let's</u> call it a day.

<u>Why don't we</u> move on to the next point on the agenda.

Making requests

Can you ...?, Could you ...?

You can use *Can you ...* or *Could you ...* to ask someone to do something. *Could* is more polite than *can*.

Can you summarize the main points, please?
Could you explain that again?

Would you mind ...

The phrase *Would you mind* following by the *-ing* form is also used to make polite requests.

Would you mind going back to the previous graphic?
Would you mind just waiting a minute while I answer that?

conditional sentences

Various conditional sentences can also be used in questions to direct a meeting in a polite way.

Would it be all right if we go over that again?
Is it okay if we leave this till later?
Do you mind if we start with a few introductions, please?
Would you mind if I investigate this a little further?

Disagreeing politely

Yes, but ...

If you want to disagree with someone without offending them, you can use an expression of agreement followed by *but*.

Well, I agree but I see it slightly differently.
I see what you mean but I still don't think it's possible.
I take your point about the costs but we could still do it.

think, believe

If you want to contradict somebody, or say something that other people may disagree with, you can avoid sounding rude by using a reporting verb such as *I think...* (or *I don't think...*) or *I believe...* (or *I don't believe...*).

I think it's time we stopped.
I don't think that's actually the case.
I don't believe we committed ourselves to maintaining the price.

seem, appear

You can avoid sounding absolutely certain of your information by using the verbs *seem* or *appear*.

This seems to be the only possible solution to the problem.
It appears that the cost of the new system would be minimal.

The grammar of academic English

Introduction

When you write or speak in academic contexts, it is important to:

▶ be clear about what you want to say

▶ connect and sequence your message

▶ establish your relationship with the reader appropriately.

The language you choose is related to the purpose of your text. This will vary according to (i) the form in which your message will be presented and (ii) your audience.

A **lecture** or **seminar** presents information and points out areas of disagreement. A lecture is often certain in tone, but it raises questions that can be explored. A seminar is an occasion where views are presented and discussed. The speaker often uses *you* and *we*.

An **essay** or **assignment** brings together and discusses information. A **dissertation** or a **journal article** investigates a topic. These texts are formal, and the tone is generally impersonal.

A **textbook** presents information for teaching and reference: it tells the reader what is known, and its tone suggests certainty.

Being clear about what you want to say: noun and verb phrases

The aim of academic speech and writing is to communicate a message precisely, and without using too many words. In order to achieve this, speakers and writers concentrate information mainly in noun and verb phrases.

Research involves investigating or analysing a subject. This means that nouns and verbs used in academic texts often relate to processes and concepts.

Nominalization

Verbs are often nominalized (= made into nouns) in order to focus the reader on a concept or idea instead of the action. For example:

verb	noun
demonstrate	demonstration
discover	discovery
measure	measurement
assess	assessment
assist	assistance
maintain	maintenance

The *demonstration* of brain mechanisms at work is not proof that rehabilitation has been achieved.

In 1898 Marie and Pierre Curie announced their *discovery* of a new element.

After an initial *measurement* of the patient's blood glucose, they are given 50g of soluble lactose to drink.

They base their *assessment* of risk on available scientific evidence.

The *maintenance* of blood pressure is achieved less rapidly as we age.

Laboratory technicians can provide *assistance* when required.

The noun phrase (1): Premodifying noun phrases

Premodification allows you to concentrate a lot of information in the noun phrase. You can build the noun phrase in the following ways:

▶ noun + noun (+ noun)

...a *food preservation process*.

▶ adverb + *-ed* participle + noun + noun (+ noun)

...a *recently developed food preservation process*.

...*strongly motivated history students*.

...a *well-organized advertising campaign*.

▶ *-ed* adjectives

Some *-ed* adjectives (see 2.77 to 2.93) carry the meaning of something that has already been completed.

...*finalized* plans. (= plans that have been agreed)

...a previously *exhibited* work of art. (= a work of art that has been shown previously)

...a *closed* case. (= a case belonging to the group of cases that have been solved)

...a recently *completed* project. (= a project that has recently been finished)

▶ adverb + *-ed* participle + adjective + noun + noun (+ noun)

...a *recently developed cost effective food preservation process*.

...a *newly discovered major oil field*.

▶ *-ing* adjectives

-ing adjectives (see 2.63) are used for describing an effect or a process, or a state that continues over a period of time.

Further changes may well bring *diminishing* returns.

...measures to control the *rising* cost of living.

Using more than four premodifiers makes the noun phrase difficult to understand, especially when this consists only of nouns. For example:

...the *school team game playing area*.

In this case, it would be better to use a prepositional phrase (see **prepositional phrases** below).

...playing areas *for school team games*.

The noun phrase (2): Postmodifying noun phrases

When you need to be more precise about the noun phrase, or to give the reader more information, you can use a relative clause, a participle or infinitive clause, or a prepositional phrase.

To identify a subject clearly, you use a **defining relative clause** introduced by a relative pronoun (see 1.146 to 1.150). The most common relative pronoun in academic English is *which*:

A magnet is a device which strongly attracts certain metals.

reducing the relative clause

The relative clause is often reduced in academic writing. You can reduce the relative clause in the following ways.

▶ leaving out the relative pronoun (when the defining relative clause refers to the object of the sentence).

The hard drive was erased because of the confidential information (~~which~~) it contained.

▶ using a participle clause

Participle clauses reduce the relative clause to either an **-ing participle** or an **-ed participle**.

…one of the hundreds of Internet entrepreneurs (~~who are~~) launching startups in Palo Alto.
They recommend four to twelve doses (~~which are~~) given a few days apart.

Other common verbs that are used to reduce the relative clause are *use*, *base*, *cause*, *make* and *concern*.

▶ using an infinitive clause

Infinitive clauses are less frequent than participle clauses. An infinitive clause often suggests that it is important to do something.

A problem to watch for is loosening of the joints at the top of the legs.
(…instead of *A problem which you should watch for is…*)
There are some basic psychological principles to bear in mind.
(…instead of *There are some basic psychological principles which you should bear in mind.*)

▶ replacing the relative clause with a prepositional phrase.

When a relative clause contains *have*, you can reduce it to a prepositional phrase using *with*:

Parliament is a national governing body with the highest level of legislative power.
(…instead of *…a national governing body which has the highest level…*)

When a relative clause contains *is* + preposition, you can reduce it to a simple prepositional phrase:

A second central concept (~~which is~~) at the core of much developmental research is…

▶ adding an identifying noun phrase

You can give further information about a person or thing by using a noun phrase that describes or identifies them or it (see 2.302).

The Marianas Trench, 11,034 m at its deepest point, is deeper than the height of Mount Everest.
A quicker alternative, a simple search program, makes it easier to search the corpus.

This is common when you are introducing or defining acronyms, abbreviations or technical terms.

The Scientific Advisory Committee on Nutrition (SACN) has issued a draft report.

non-defining relative clauses

A **non-defining relative clause** is not needed to identify the person, thing or group you are talking about; instead, it gives the reader more information about the subject, or it evaluates or comments on the subject (see 8.85).

Dark matter, which may be invisible for many reasons, has become increasingly important.

The verb phrase

In general, academic English is less concerned with events, and more concerned with what has been learnt from the event. Therefore, the focus of the sentence moves away from the verb phrase to the noun phrase. Verbs are often nominalized (= made into nouns) – see **Nominalization**.

The range of tenses used in academic English is more restricted than in everyday English: simple forms of verbs are used more frequently; progressive forms, the past perfect, and the future perfect are used less often.

The tense you use shows your attitude and other people's attitude to the subject. For example, it shows whether a piece of research or an idea is still generally accepted or not.

the present simple

The **present simple** is commonly used in the following ways.

▶ to refer to something that you believe is still valid

The two theories are known as 'ridge push' versus 'slab pull' respectively.

▶ to state continuing objectives

The aim is to direct the energy of the radiation to kill the cancerous cells.

▶ to describe general principles or laws

When water freezes, it expands.

▶ to explain or discuss data or results.

The results show that only a portion of world trade is affected.

▶ to make reference to or relate events in literary works, films, etc.

Shakespeare, in King Lear, emphasizes the social causes of madness.

the present perfect

The **present perfect** is commonly used in the following ways.

▶ to review research

There is a vast literature looking at development issues, the main elements of which have been reviewed here.

▶ to make a general statement about the state of research activity in a given area

Little research has been done on microscopic plastics.

▶ to summarize a text

In light of the evidence that has been reviewed thus far in this book...

the past simple

The **past simple** is commonly used in the following ways:

▶ to indicate that something happened or was true at a particular time in the past, and that it may be less valid today

The almost universal view was that the liver was the main organ in the blood system.

▶ to describe samples and procedures

A full study was conducted with a sample of managers from the UK head office.

▶ to report findings

Their research showed that over half of all cancer cases could be prevented.

 will

Will is used to state your intention.

This study will examine the effects of depression.

Will often occurs with an adverb such as *often* or *probably*, because academic writers must avoid suggesting that their personal ideas and theories are facts.

The desert regions will probably become more extensive.
Changes in practice will often be the result of a long political process.

linking verbs

Linking verbs are used for describing a situation or a quality, and so they occur frequently in academic English. Linking verbs that are commonly used in academic English are *be, become, look, remain, seem, appear, prove,* and *represent* (see 3.126 to 3.181).

At first glance, the system seems overwhelmingly complex.
Scientists fear that some viruses may prove challenging to deal with.
The source of the information must remain anonymous.

Common complements include:

▶ nouns

The results of this experiment remain a secret.
Their decision represents a turnaround.

▶ adjectives

The patients appeared to be immune to the HIV virus.
Predictions for next year look increasingly uncertain.

▶ object complements

You can put a noun or adjective complement after the object of some transitive verbs. This complement describes the object, and is called an **object complement**.

They cannot keep the options of both politics and terrorism open.
Television scored significantly higher amongst those who found politics interesting.
Some analysts do not consider it a virus.

Ordering and connecting your message

There are several ways of using language to hold your whole message together and to give it meaning. The first step is to arrange content into a recognizable pattern. When you are planning a piece of work or a talk, you can use the following pattern to sequence your ideas:

describe a situation → outline any problems → suggest a solution → provide an evaluation.

The following sections describe techniques for ensuring that your writing or speech holds together well, and that both your intention and your message are clear:

- ▶ using grammatical structures and vocabulary to *signpost* your intention
- ▶ referring back and referring forward
- ▶ providing connectors to hold sections together.

Using grammatical structures and vocabulary to 'signpost' your intention

There are several ways in which you can use grammatical structures and vocabulary within a section of text to express the following ideas:

- ▶ the arrangement of events in time
- ▶ procedure (= how something is done)
- ▶ cause and effect
- ▶ comparisons and contrast
- ▶ advantages and disadvantages.

arrangement of events in time

If you want to show that one thing happened soon after the other, you can use a finite verb in the main clause, and an *-ing* participle in the subordinate clause:

They <u>headed</u> rapidly for the Channel ports, <u>showing</u> their passports at the barriers.

You can also indicate the order in which things happened using ordinals and adverbs such as *first, then, later,* etc.

<u>Later</u>, in December 1985, the committee decided …

procedure

You can use the same structure – a finite verb in the main clause, and an *-ing* participle in the subordinate clause – to show how something is done.

Researchers <u>determined</u> the size of each machine, <u>taking</u> into account the properties of the material.

cause/effect

The same structure can be used to show that one thing happened as a result of another.

Many of the men <u>returned</u> home, <u>causing</u> local unemployment.

Note that you can also indicate cause and effect in a main clause using a verb such as *cause, lead to,* or *result in,* or a noun such as *effect, result,* or *outcome.*

The consumption of an excessive number of sweets can <u>cause</u> obesity.

The <u>effect</u> of the famine in 1921–22 was devastating.

comparison and contrast

You can compare and contrast information in the following ways.

- ▶ using a sentence connector

Conversely, the effect of intravenous administration of the drug is immediate.
By contrast, the more recent publication is more straightforward.

▶ using a comparative adverb

Owner-controlled companies performed *better* than those subject to management control.

▶ using a verb

The aim of this report is to *compare* and *contrast* these two business structures.
We will *compare* our own findings with those of Mortimore et al. (1988).
These findings *contrast* strongly with those from other tests.

for and against

You can provide an evaluation leading to a conclusion in the following ways.

▶ using an adjective

This method of production is *preferable*.

▶ using a verb

Consumers *prefer* our products for their quality and finish.

▶ using a noun

This type of surgery has the *advantage* that no abdominal incision is needed.

▶ using an adverbial clause of reason or purpose

This type of organization should be much smaller, *since it will not need personnel concerned
with line management*.
You must take as much care as possible, *in order to avoid accidents*.

Referring back and referring forward

The most common way of making a text hold together is to refer back to something
that you have mentioned earlier, by using pronouns, demonstratives, determiners,
and adjectives (see 10.2 to 10.39). It is also common to refer forward, particularly in
longer texts (see 10.40 to 10.47).

referring back

This and *those* are common in academic contexts:

...they had commissioned a specific piece of research. *This* came somewhat late.
There were, however, wide differences of opinion about party chances. Some of *those*
differences...

Note that the demonstrative is often linked with a noun referring to:

▶ spoken events

That's a good question.

▶ ideas

This view is also held by Rey and Stiglitz (1988).

▶ actions and events

During *this* process, cracks appeared in the limestone.
This situation continued for almost two decades.

▶ pieces of writing

As *this* research has shown, customer brand loyalty is very hard to achieve.

You use *such* as a determiner and predeterminer to refer back (10.29 and 10.30).

They generally agree on which aspects of police work they like and dislike. Such a consensus was originally explained as...

The report highlights the high level of overcrowding in some prisons. In such circumstances...

Other words and expressions used for referring back are *previous*, *above*, and *the former ... the latter*.

The previous arguments have pointed to two ways in which the system might be improved.

What is said above gives the background to what follows.

The French have two words for citizenship: 'citoyenté' and 'civisme', the former describing the status, the latter, attitude and behaviour.

referring forward

To refer forward to sections of the text, you can use:

▶ *following* as an adjective, or *the following*, to refer to texts, ideas, and pieces of writing (see 10.43)

Symptoms of the condition may include any of the following: chest pains, headache, difficulty breathing, and joint pain.

The following passage summarizes Schmidt's views:...

▶ the adverb *below*, normally after nouns referring to texts and pieces of writing (see 10.45)

The trade blockade with India, described below, resulted in severe energy shortages.

sentence connectors

Sentence connectors show the relationship between two sentences, clauses, or sections of text. The following are particularly common in academic speech and writing:

function	sentence connectors
indicating a further argument	additionally, in addition, also, furthermore, moreover
indicating a similar situation	again, equally, likewise, similarly
indicating contrast	alternatively, in contrast, conversely, even so, however, nevertheless, nonetheless, on the contrary, on the other hand, although
indicating cause	accordingly, as a result, as a consequence, consequently, hence, thereby, therefore, thus
indicating purpose	in order to, so that, lest

The style of your message

Once you have decided on your message, you need to formulate it so that you can achieve the effect you are aiming for. Common ways of presenting information are described below.

ACADEMIC ENGLISH

Distancing

Present your text using an impersonal voice. This allows you to focus on the issues rather than on the people involved. The structures below are especially useful for avoiding *I*.

impersonal *it*

You can remove focus from people by using impersonal *it* (see 9.31 to 9.45).

It is almost an occupational hazard accepted by virologists.

Use impersonal *it* and a passive form of a reporting verb if your message is an opinion held by an unspecified group of people (see 7.69 to 7.73).

It is widely believed that this substance is harmful.
It is acknowledged that resources are unevenly distributed.

Note that you can also use a reporting verb in the passive, followed by a *to*-infinitive (see 7.69).

This substance is believed to be harmful.
UVB and UVA are both reported to cause skin cancer.

there is, there are

When you want to say that something exists, or you want to introduce something new, use *there* as a subject (see 9.46 to 9.55).

There are several claims to be considered in relation to this perspective.
There are no fewer than thirteen different species of otter.

research or text in subject position

In a conclusion or an example, do not write *I have discovered....* Instead, put a word such as *findings* or *results* in subject position.

These findings suggest that there are two different processing methods.
The results show that this problem is widespread.

the passive

You can use the passive without *by* to describe procedures when the performer of the action does not need to be specified.

The tissue sample was removed, analysed and stored.
The engine was re-tested after the malfunction.

Note that it is important not to over-use the passive, as it can make your writing difficult to read.

verbs that indicate a change of state

Use verbs such as *continue*, *decrease*, and *increase* to describe events that involve a change of state (see 3.59 to 3.67).

The situation continues to be a cause for concern.
The rate of change slowed in the second half of the year.

The result of a change of state can be shown in a subordinate clause beginning with an *-ing* form (see 8.141).

Prices rose, <u>leading to</u> a fall in demand.
Appetite is lessened, <u>resulting in</u> weight loss and dietary problems.

Reporting

An important aspect of academic speaking and writing involves reporting (or *citing*) the work of other academics.

Citations can be used to explain the basis of your work, to support and illustrate your arguments, or to contrast your ideas with other writers' theories.

Citations sometimes take the form of direct quotes; however, the reported information is usually summarized in your own words.

The following reporting verbs are commonly used in academic English to introduce cited material (see 7.5 to 7.11).

Theses verbs indicate the type of activity reported:

If the activity is:	research-related	mental	verbal
use:	measure	think	state
	calculate	believe	write
	estimate	consider	define
	find	focus on	challenge
	obtain		

Nuttall and Gipps (1982) <u>estimate</u> that the direct cost of the APU was £800,000 per year.
Collins and Ellis (2001) also <u>challenge</u> the traditional concept of the individual.

Note that the verbs that you use will depend on your academic discipline. Research-related verbs are more common in technical and scientific writing; mental and verbal activity verbs are more common in the humanities and social sciences.

These verbs indicate your attitude to the reported material:

If you think it is:	valid	not valid	neutral
use:	show	fail to	discuss
	establish	overlook	respond
	demonstrate	ignore	comment
			suggest

Wenger's data <u>show</u> that 43 percent of elderly people named as a confidant someone they had known for at least 50 years.
This evidence <u>fails to</u> acknowledge the importance of the children's diet.

These verbs indicate the cited author's attitude to the material:

If the author is:	positive	negative	neutral	tentative
	argue	refute	state	suggest
use:	maintain	object	write	believe
	see	challenge	discuss	imply
	hold		comment	allude to

Both Smith and Goodman (2000) maintain that skilled adult reading is far from error-free.
Bly argues that the process of initiation into adulthood is easier for women than for men.

Note that verbs that indicate attitude are more commonly used in the humanities and the social sciences.

Expressing degrees of certainty

When you are formulating your message, you need to consider how strongly you want to make your claim. Different structures express different degrees of certainty, and allow you to establish a position that you can defend if you are criticized.

For example, it is possible to defend the following statement:

Certain researchers have attempted to show that some underprivileged children cannot engage in play.

The following would be less easy to defend:

Researchers have shown that underprivileged children cannot engage in play.

not being precise

You can use the following adverbs when the available information is not precise.

quantity	frequency	degree	limitation
roughly	often	rather	predominantly
approximately	frequently	quite	mostly
around	occasionally	somewhat	partly
	seldom		
	rarely		partially

Increased risk of infection is predominantly linked to poor sanitation.

cautious language

You can use more cautious language when you think that other people may disagree with your statement, or when you want to express uncertainty about whether or not a proposition is true. This may be because you really are uncertain, or because you want to create opportunities for readers to decide for themselves.

The following lists show distancing structures that are commonly used for making stements sound more cautious.

modal verbs	semi-auxiliary verbs	adverbs	prepositional phrases	adjectives
could	seem	possibly	in some respects	uncertain
might	appear	seemingly	in a sense	possible
may		arguably	in most cases	
can		likely	in general	
		apparently	in principle	
		evidently		
		generally		
		normally		
		typically		

There is, <u>arguably</u>, a common thread in all these positions.

As will be seen later, current models are inadequate <u>in some respects</u>.

Note that if you express too much uncertainty, or if you repeatedly show that you are not sure if something is true, your message will have less worth, and it will be difficult to interpret.

Emphasizing

In general English, you can use strong words to emphasize a point. In academic English, you often show emphasis by changing the normal word order of a statement.

subordinate clause in first position

Subordinate clauses normally occur in first position in academic texts. The main clause carries the new or most important information.

You can use the following structures to show that something important is going to be announced at the end of the sentence.

▶ nominal relative clauses (see 8.112 to 8.116)

<u>What is now required</u> is a systematic investigation of the data.

▶ prefacing structures (see 9.73 to 9.78)

<u>The question we now need to consider is</u> whether the dosage should be reduced.

▶ split sentences (see 9.25 to 9.30)

<u>It was this declaration</u> which triggered the events that followed.

Index

Note: entries in **bold** are grammatical terms; entries in *italics* are lexical terms. At certain entries (for example, **nouns** and **verbs**), there is a list of terms with the • symbol; these lists will help you to quickly find all the main categories in a long section of the book. A number preceded by R refers to a paragraph in the Reference Section.

U

V